H. Dillon

2.40

CONSTRUCTIVE THEME WRITING

FOR COLLEGE FRESHMEN

By

MARY ELLEN CHASE

ASSOCIATE PROFESSOR OF ENGLISH LANGUAGE AND LITERATURE
SMITH COLLEGE

HENRY HOLT AND COMPANY
NEW YORK

PRINTED IN THE
UNITED STATES OF AMERICA

ACKNOWLEDGMENTS

Acknowledgment to various publishers and to editors for permission to reprint material is given throughout this volume. In addition, I wish especially to thank the following persons who have been most generous in their willingness that essays and sketches, written or controlled by them, should be quoted here: Mr. Frederick Allen of *Harper's Magazine*, Mr. Robert P. Tristram Coffin, Mrs. Frank Moore Colby, Mr. John Corbin, Mr. Herbert Croly of *The New Republic*, Mr. Wilbur Cross of *The Yale Review*, Mr. Philip Curtiss, Mr. Walter Prichard Eaton, Miss Imogen Foster, Mr. Willis Fletcher Johnson of *The North American Review*, Mr. Robert M. Gay, Miss Grace Guiney, Mr. Theodore Maynard, Mr. William B. Munro, Mr. Ellery Sedgwick of *The Atlantic Monthly*, Mr. Robert Palfrey Utter, Mr. G. Van Santvoord, Miss Caroline E. Vose, the late Mr. Thomas Walsh, and Mr. Stark Young.

There are many acknowledgments aside from these and less tangible than they. The associates and associations of fifteen years, spent largely in the teaching of English composition to college students, have all contributed to the making of this book and to whatever in it may prove of value. And yet I want to single out for special gratitude Mr. Joseph M. Thomas of the University of Minnesota, who has for many years designed and conducted an unusually fine course in Freshman Composition and with whom I had the privilege of working for eight years; the members of the English staff of the College of St. Catherine in St. Paul, who so gladly have shared experiences in teaching and lent helpful suggestions; Miss Marjorie Nicolson, my colleague at Smith College, whose commonsense, wide experience, and splendid teaching have proved invaluable; Miss Anne Hart and Miss Margaret Macgregor, the former and the present Director of the Freshman English Course at Smith, whose interest and

iii

advice have been constantly drawn upon; and Miss Sophie Hart, the Head of the Department of English Composition at Wellesley College, who during the formation of this book so generously assisted with her confidence and assurance.

M. E. C.

A PREFACE TO TEACHERS

Each year I examine too many text-books and books of selections designed for college freshmen not to be well aware of the various receptions which will be accorded this volume. Many instructors will think it incomplete; others, too full. Some will find it overly suggestive; others, lacking in certain exercises which, they feel, every student should employ. Many who teach both theory and practice will miss the theory and become convinced that no sort of practice can take its place. Those who believe above all else in the inception and promulgation of ideas will hold much of the material too simple and unprovocative.

No book can be all things to all instructors of freshman composition; but surely each can make its claim and then be used or set aside as various temperaments and circumstances must dictate. This book is the result of many years spent in teaching composition to both university and college freshmen, to both men and women, to students, poor, mediocre, and excellent. It is the result of a conviction that the study and appreciation of good writing is more fruitful and infinitely more interesting than the study of the principles of composition, that practice from the start is better than theory. Its plan, that is, its threefold division into the various types and kinds of themes, has arisen from long experimenting with theme subjects from fall to spring. Every one of its models has been tried out on classes and not found wanting in suggestions both practical and esthetic.

It is true that much is lacking to which many instructors are accustomed. There is no practice in sentence correction; there are no rules for diction; there is no review of grammar. The terms, Unity, Coherence, and Emphasis, are conspicuous by their absence. All these I have omitted because I believe from experience that rules may be learned and applied more readily through one of the good handbooks easily available and that the principles may be assimilated with much less pain and much more interest through the recognition of them in good writing rather than through the reading about them as principles. Suggestions and exercises for paragraph development are given, briefly but, I think, adequately, as are models for outlining and for the making of a bibliography and the use of footnotes.

Nor does the book lay any claim to completeness in the types of themes chosen for discussion and presentation. For instance, in Part II, Chapter III, "The Analysis," I have purposely included for explanation and example only three kinds of analysis. I have chosen these three because I believe they are at once more suitable and more interesting for the average freshman to experiment with than are the other more difficult forms which are best presented, it seems to me, in courses devoted to more advanced composition. Argumentation as a type of writing is not given here at all. That, too, I must think, is best handled in a more specialized course for more advanced students.

Again, the instructor who teaches by types of composition, who gives the first quarter to exposition, the second to narration, and the third to description, will be perhaps dissatisfied and even confused by what seems to be, on my part, a total disregard for forms and types. My own experience has been such as to make me doubt the advisability of teaching distinct types of composition to freshmen. What we all want, I am sure, is to get the student *to write* with interest and accuracy; and I have found that he does it better if he is unimpaired by warnings lest he stray from exposition. Wide and, perhaps, general experience has proved that exposition is the best type for him; and yet surely exposition may well take the form of narrative if narrative is best suited to the purpose of the theme under construction. Practically all the themes suggested and the models given in this book are expository in nature and in aim, and yet the methods of treatment are various. I must think the variety an advantage.

The division into parts, which deal respectively with themes of experience, of information, and of thought, is not in any sense intended to be arbitrary. One instructor may prefer to begin with themes of experience; another has long begun with expositions of processes and sees no good reason for change; a third is convinced that ideas should be immediately lodged in the student's mind and opinions extricated. There is surely no valid reason why the year's themes may not begin with those suggested under Part II or under Part III rather than with those in Part I.

As for the models, which make up the greater part of the book, I should like to say that they have been chosen for all kinds and degrees of freshmen. Some of the more difficult, more "literary" selections will doubtless lack interest and meaning for many students; but the knowledge that they will appeal to the finer minds, the richer imaginations, surely justifies their presence. Others are obviously here because they will prove of interest and of help to the majority.

There are many instructors who will, and quite rightly, regard the *Exercises* at the close of each chapter as unnecessary and, perhaps, even as presumptuous. May I say simply that they are a direct result of my own confused and anxious hours as a young instructor? In those days I should have been grateful for any assistance, for any suggestion which would have helped me to fill profitably those first endless class periods or to make more constructive assignments. If any new instructor finds them helpful, surely their inclusion is worthwhile.

The *Suggested Reading Lists* need no explanation and, it seems to me, call for no justification. They are the result of months of search and of careful reading. I cannot but feel that they must prove of value both to instructors and to students.

This book has been written and compiled with constant recourse to experience and to commonsense. I can only hope that it may justify its entrance into a field, already overcrowded. If it can interest any number of students, however small, so that they will want to learn to write creditably and even well, so that they will appreciate good and lively expression on the part of others, and so that their minds may be clarified, sharpened, and enriched, it will have served its purpose.

MARY ELLEN CHASE.

Smith College,
February, 1929.

CONTENTS

PART I

THEMES OF EXPERIENCE

PART II

THEMES OF FACT AND INFORMATION

PART III

THEMES OF THOUGHT AND REFLECTION

LIST OF SELECTIONS

PART I

PART II

LIST OF SELECTIONS

PART I

THEMES OF EXPERIENCE

There are three main sources from which an author, be he good or bad, draws his material. Before writing was, these three existed; indeed, they motivated and made the oral compositions of prehistoric man as he described in detail the great beast who evaded his pitfall, or taught his son how best to shape an arrow-head, or, during an eclipse of the moon, confided his beliefs and convictions to men of lesser mind. They are experience, information, and thought. The first is inescapable and inevitable, although its acceptance is too often passive instead of active; the second is, in a greater or a lesser degree, the common possession of all normal human beings beyond the stage of infancy; the third in its best and highest sense is, as Emerson declared in his essay on Shakespeare, "the property of him who can entertain it, and of him who can adequately place it."

It is quite safe to say that for the average freshman the best source of these three is that of experience. The new instructor, fresh from the graduate school, makes a safer bet on the success of his first assignment if he asks for five hundred words on "How I Spent My Summer Vacation" than on "My Philosophy of Life." Outworn and invariably unwelcome as is such a subject, it is at least fundamentally not absurd; and it or its popular twin sister, "My First Impressions of College Life," will leave less anguish in their wake after a night of reading and correction than "My Philosophy of Life" or "My Personal Idea of God."

But it is well, before further attempt to present experience as a reasonable and abundant source of initial theme material, to define the term as used in this connection. Just as all kinds of wood will not weather in the same way, so many persons of wide experience are still inexperienced. Those who have read Cardinal Newman's essay on *Knowledge and Learning* will recall his seafaring men who "range from one end of the earth to the other; but the multiplicity of external objects, which they have en-

3

countered, forms no symmetrical and consistent picture upon their imagination; they see the tapestry of human life, as it were on the wrong side, and it tells no story. They sleep, and they rise up, and they find themselves, now in Europe, now in Asia; they see visions of great cities and wild regions; they are in the marts of commerce, or amid the islands of the south; they gaze on Pompey's Pillar, or on the Andes; and nothing which meets them carries them forward or backward to any idea beyond itself. Nothing has a drift or relation; nothing has a history or a promise. Everything stands by itself and comes and goes in its turn, like the shifting scenes of a show, which leave the spectator where he was."

Yet Ulysses, the prince of seafaring men, was of a different sort. Tennyson makes him say:

> "I am a part of all that I have met;
> Yet all experience is an arch wherethro'
> Gleams that untravelled world whose margin fades
> Forever and forever when I move."

It is his "experience" which may be the unfathomable source of material, the experience which, viewed in relation to the unseen and unknown, takes on a new value in the mind and imagination of its owner.

A homelier analogy, a better definition, presents itself. In a certain Maine coast village a quarter of a century ago the winter hog-killing was invariably succeeded by a process known as "trying-out." Into huge iron vats, beneath which hardwood fires were kept burning, were thrown substantial portions of the more worthless flesh, which was well encased with fat. The early sizzling and snapping gave place as time went on to the crackling of boiling lard out of which the now useless pieces of meat were dipped. The lard was then strained and poured into small wooden kegs or earthenware crocks where, after a few hours, it became white and hard, and ready to be borne into butteries and cellars.

Now to "try out," one recalls, is the exact meaning of "experience." The word, indeed, suggests in its very derivation some such process as the one just described. The student who can best use his own experience as a basis and source for writing is the one who can separate what is pertinent and valuable from what is merely accessory, and who, holding close to that better part, can relate it in turn to the larger issues and graver realities of life,—to

"that untravelled world whose margin fades
Forever and forever when I move."

For after all it is not human experience but rather the evaluation of it which has made the great books and great personalities of our own and of every other age. It is Fielding's evaluation of the manifold experiences of his hero which makes *Tom Jones* so incomparably greater than most other English novels. In precisely the same way it will be largely to the young writer's ability at appraisal and relation that his early themes will owe their success or their failure.

Two excellent examples of the evaluation of experience are quoted in Chapter III of Part I: one, W. H. Hudson's "The Death of an Old Dog" and the other, Kenneth Grahame's "The Secret Drawer." In the first, the death of the dog, painful as it is to the boy concerned, is as nothing compared to the terrible import of the words of the schoolmaster, words which made the author, fifty years later, characterize the event as the most important of his childhood. Thus the experience itself finds its value only in the larger, common experience of mankind. In the second, the boy's search for the secret drawer, his dreams of needed wealth, and even his delighted discovery lose their own significance in a larger as he stands in that silent room and seems to touch the hand of another boy, long since dead.

"Not the fruit of experience but experience itself is the end," writes Pater in the beautiful "Conclusion" of *The Renaissance;* and Marius as a schoolboy in Pisa [1] reiterates the dictum as his own hard-won philosophy. Well, such a shadowy distinction is doubtless delicate nourishment for the poetic or the philosophic mind; but there are, sad to say, few Mariuses among undergraduates, and inevitably it *is* the fruit of experience which must figure large as the best source of supply for the first term of

[1] *Marius the Epicurean,* Chapter VIII.

Freshman English. Not in moral or in precept let us use it, but in the ever heightening ability to separate the pertinent from the useless, to evaluate what is worth keeping, and finally to relate it to that larger experience from which it draws alike its own sustenance and worth.

CHAPTER I

The Autobiography

The autobiography at once presents itself as one of the earliest and most fundamental themes of experience. It may prove as well one of the most interesting if those who are to write it are intelligently alive to its possibilities.

There are three inescapable problems before the student who is to write an autobiography: (1) that of incident and detail; (2) that of evaluation and choice; (3) that of plan and organization.

A conversation, not imaginary, and only recently held with a college freshman, may serve to illustrate this first problem:

"I wish I could write a different theme, Miss C——. This one is bound to be stupid. There isn't a thing in my life worth telling."

"That's too bad. Why such a dull life?"

"Oh, I've lived in the country and in Nebraska—of all places!"

"What's the matter with Nebraska? Miss Cather seems to have found something interesting."

"Well,—yes. But *I* can't. She's different."

"When were you born?"

"Oh, eighteen years ago—in the winter."

"On just an ordinary day?"

"No, not exactly. They say there was a blizzard."

"That's not a bad start for any one. Remember the blizzard in *My Antonia?*"

"Yes, but—well, anyway, I guess it was a bad blizzard. The doctor couldn't get through the snow."

"Better still. What about your childhood?"

"Oh, just going to a country school on the prairie."

"Well, the prairie. What about that? Weren't there flowers

7

or storms or cold days? How did you get to school—walk or ride? Were there animals about? What were the teachers like? Were your neighbors foreign or American born? What did you raise on your farm? Did you ever have a scourge of locusts or a hail-storm or a cyclone?"

In half an hour by means of somewhat impatient labor, for it is irritating to find a person so blind to the drama of environment, I discovered that this girl, who had had nothing in her life worth telling, had been born in a blizzard, had learned to ride when she was four years old, for seven years had ridden three miles morning and afternoon in all weathers to and from school, had made a collection of prairie wild-flowers, which had won first prize at the State Fair, had herself earned five hundred dollars toward her college expenses by growing a plot of wheat, and had lived through a cyclone which tore the roof from the school-house and killed three children! And yet her theme was bound to be stupid! I recommended more of Willa Cather and Anna Howard Shaw's *The Story of a Pioneer* and with a long sigh sent her to the library.

Obviously the first thing for the amateur writer of autobiography to do is to search his life for interesting incident and detail. Huxley takes time and space for the swarming of bees on the window-sill and for his early preaching to the maids, his pinafore "wrong side forwards in order to represent a surplice." Such material is the light of all such writing. Nor is incident, dramatic though it may be, necessarily more valuable or interesting than well-chosen detail. The "odor of wood-smoke" in Huxley; the "hateful, off-standing ears and small greenish eyes" of the bully whom Ludwig Lewisohn describes; Benjamin Franklin's pockets stuffed out with shirts and stockings, and the two "great puffy rolls" under his arms—details such as these add untold vividness and charm to the writing of autobiography.

Nor must they of necessity occur in connection with incident. Many lives which seem bare of drama are yet rich in detail. Had the freshman under consideration missed both blizzard and cyclone, she would still have had the morning and evening rides over the prairie with its sunlight and rain, its stretches of snow, its spring awakenings. Indeed, she might well have written her theme about her interest in Nebraskan wild-flowers since they clearly had greatly influenced her life. The gathering of flowers may or may not be a dramatic incident—that will depend upon the viewpoint of the gatherer—but at least it may afford an abundance of bright detail.

The Nebraskan freshman was not unusual in her point of view. She could not feel that her life on the prairie, interesting to her in spite of her insistence upon its worthlessness as theme material, could possibly interest others. Now that attitude is a great mistake which must be corrected at the outset. No one but yourself can evaluate the happenings and the emotions of your life; and it is safe to say that, given genuine interest on your part, your theme, no matter what its other and lesser defects, cannot be dull. Remember Pater's fine contention "that to know when oneself is interested is the first condition of interesting other people." [1]

This matter of evaluation and of choice of material is a very important one. It is foolish to spend two paragraphs in relating a week's visit to New York at fourteen, which you think *ought* to have influenced you, and to neglect the discovery that bank-swallows invariably face the sun, which really *did* interest you profoundly at ten years of age. Listen again to Pater as he recounts the young Flavian's decision as to his own literary work: "To be forcibly interested in the first place; and in the next, to find the means of making visible to others that which was vividly apparent, delightful, of lively interest to *himself*, to the exclusion of all that was but middling, tame, or only half-true even to *him*. [2]

The decision is as good to-day as in the second century A.D. Try honestly to evaluate the incidents and the details you have already gleaned from your eighteen years of life and list those which most forcibly impress *you*, not those which may conceivably interest your instructor. Exclude those of "middling" interest even though you feel they *should* have impressed you.

[1] *Marius the Epicurean*, Chapter VI.
[2] *Ibid.*, Chapter VI.

And finally, having made your choice of material, strive by much careful reading of other autobiography, by thought and visualization, by attention to words and to sentences "to find the means of making visible to others" those things which have really meant something in your life.

There are almost as many ways of presenting autobiographical material as there are kinds of material to present. The story of your life need not begin with your birth and close with your entrance into college. You may well choose to concentrate your attention upon a given period, to write in fuller detail a chapter of your autobiography in place of the complete sketch. Ludwig Lewisohn does this in the selection which follows. In his case it is his high school experience which he narrates, the influences therein which were of startling importance to him. W. H. Hudson does the same thing in a chapter called "My First Visit to Buenos Ayres" from *Far Away and Long Ago*, a book so rich in fascinating autobiographical material that no freshman can afford to be ignorant of it. Or, deciding against any well-defined period, you may prefer to write about an influence in your life like that of books or of nature or of people. Read carefully the chapter from John Stuart Mill. In this, after the briefest statement of his birth and two paragraphs concerning his father, who was inseparably connected with his early reading, he devotes himself to the story of that reading under his father's guidance. Again, you may wish to try to give your readers something of the novelty and excitement you felt when, like Franklin, you first started "on your own" to seek adventure and fortune.

Each of the model autobiographies which follow has been included here because it exemplifies a certain plan of treatment. A careful reading and study of every one will repay you. It is suggested, moreover, that the exercises at the close of the section may call attention to certain matters which might otherwise pass unobserved.

AUTOBIOGRAPHY [1]

By Thomas Henry Huxley

And when I consider, in one view, the many things . . . which I have upon my hands, I feel the burlesque of being employed in this manner at my time of life. But, in another view, and taking in all circumstances, these things, as trifling as they may appear, no less than things of greater importance, seem to be put upon me to do.

—BISHOP BUTLER to the DUCHESS OF SOMERSET.

The "many things" to which the Duchess's correspondent here refers are the repairs and improvements of the episcopal seat at Auckland. I doubt if the great apologist, greater in nothing than in the simple dignity of his character, would have considered the writing an account of himself as a thing which could be put upon him to do whatever circumstances might be taken in. But the good bishop lived in an age when a man might write books and yet be permitted to keep his private existence to himself; in the pre-Boswellian epoch, when the germ of the photographer lay concealed in the distant future, and the interviewer who pervades our age was an unforeseen, indeed unimaginable, birth of time.

At present, the most convinced believer in the aphorism "Bene qui latuit, bene vixit," [2] is not always able to act up to it. An importunate person informs him that his portrait is about to be published and will be accompanied by a biography which the importunate person proposes to write. The sufferer knows what that means; either he undertakes to revise the "biography" or he does not. In the former case, he makes himself responsible; in the latter, he allows the publication of a mass of more or less fulsome inaccuracies for which he will be held responsible by those who are familiar with the prevalent art of self-advertisement. On the whole, it may be better to get over the "burlesque of being employed in this manner" and do the thing himself.

It was by reflections of this kind that, some years ago, I was led to write and permit the publication of the subjoined sketch.

[1] From *Collected Essays.*
[2] "He who has well concealed himself has well lived."

I was born about eight o'clock in the morning on the 4th of May, 1825, at Ealing, which was, at that time, as quiet a little country village as could be found within half-a-dozen miles of Hyde Park Corner. Now it is a suburb of London with, I believe, 30,000 inhabitants. My father was one of the masters in a large semi-public school which at one time had a high reputation. I am not aware that any portents preceded my arrival in this world, but, in my childhood, I remember hearing a traditional account of the manner in which I lost the chance of an endowment of great practical value. The windows of my mother's room were open, in consequence of the unusual warmth of the weather. For the same reason, probably, a neighbouring beehive had swarmed, and the new colony, pitching on the window-sill, was making its way into the room when the horrified nurse shut down the sash. If that well-meaning woman had only abstained from her ill-timed interference, the swarm might have settled on my lips, and I should have been endowed with that mellifluous eloquence which, in this country, leads far more surely than worth, capacity, or honest work, to the highest places in Church and State. But the opportunity was lost, and I have been obliged to content myself through life with saying what I mean in the plainest of plain language, than which, I suppose, there is no habit more ruinous to a man's prospects of advancement.

Why I was christened Thomas Henry I do not know; but it is a curious chance that my parents should have fixed for my usual denomination upon the name of that particular Apostle with whom I have always felt most sympathy.[1] Physically and mentally I am the son of my mother so completely—even down to peculiar movements of the hands, which made their appearance in me as I reached the age she had when I noticed them—that I can hardly find any trace of my father in myself, except an inborn faculty for drawing, which unfortunately, in my case, has never been cultivated, a hot temper, and that amount of tenacity of purpose which unfriendly observers sometimes call obstinacy.

My mother was a slender brunette, of an emotional and energetic temperament, and possessed of the most piercing black eyes

[1] See *John* 20:24-25.

I ever saw in a woman's head. With no more education than other women of the middle classes in her day, she had an excellent mental capacity. Her most distinguishing characteristic, however, was rapidity of thought. If one ventured to suggest she had not taken much time to arrive at any conclusion, she would say, "I cannot help it, things flash across me." That peculiarity has been passed on to me in full strength; it has often stood me in good stead; it has sometimes played me sad tricks, and it has always been a danger. But, after all, if my time were to come over again, there is nothing I would less willingly part with than my inheritance of mother wit.

I have next to nothing to say about my childhood. In later years my mother, looking at me almost reproachfully, would sometimes say, "Ah! you were such a pretty boy!" whence I had no difficulty in concluding that I had not fulfilled my early promise in the matter of looks. In fact, I have a distinct recollection of certain curls of which I was vain, and of a conviction that I closely resembled that handsome, courtly gentleman, Sir Herbert Oakley, who was vicar of our parish, and who was as a god to us country folk, because he was occasionally visited by the then Prince George of Cambridge. I remember turning my pinafore wrong side forwards in order to represent a surplice, and preaching to my mother's maids in the kitchen as nearly as possible in Sir Herbert's manner, one Sunday morning when the rest of the family were at church. That is the earliest indication I can call to mind of the strong clerical affinities which my friend Mr. Herbert Spencer has always ascribed to me, though I fancy they have for the most part remained in a latent state.

My regular school training was of the briefest, perhaps fortunately, for though my way of life has made me acquainted with all sorts and conditions of men, from the highest to the lowest, I deliberately affirm that the society I fell into at school was the worst I have ever known. We boys were average lads, with much the same inherent capacity for good and evil as any others; but the people who were set over us cared about as much for our intellectual and moral welfare as if they were baby-farmers. We were left to the operation of the struggle for existence among ourselves, and bullying was the least of the ill practices current among us. Almost the only cheerful reminiscence in connection with the place which arises in my mind is that of a battle I had with one of my classmates who had bullied me until I could stand it no longer. I was a very slight lad, but there was a wild-cat element in me which, when roused, made up for lack of weight, and I licked my adversary effectually. However, one of my first experiences of the extremely rough-and-ready nature of justice, as exhibited by the course of things in general, arose out of the fact that I—the victor—had a black eye, while he—the vanquished—had none, so that I got into disgrace and he did not. We made it up, and thereafter I was unmolested. One of the greatest shocks I ever received in my life was to be told a dozen years afterwards by the groom who brought me my horse in a stable-yard in Sydney that he was my quondam antagonist. He had a long story of family misfortune to account for his position, but at that time it was necessary to deal very cautiously with mysterious strangers in New South Wales, and on inquiry I found that the unfortunate young man had not only been "sent out," [1] but had undergone more than one colonial conviction.

As I grew older, my great desire was to be a mechanical engineer, but the fates were against this and, while very young, I commenced the study of medicine under a medical brother-in-law. But, though the Institute of Mechanical Engineers would certainly not own me, I am not sure that I have not all along been a sort of mechanical engineer *in partibus infidelium*.[2] I am now occasionally horrified to think how very little I ever knew or cared about medicine as the art of healing. The only part of my professional course which really and deeply interested me was physiology, which is the mechanical engineering of living machines; and, notwithstanding that natural science has been my proper business, I am afraid there is very little of the genuine naturalist in me. I never collected anything, and species work was always a burden to me; what I cared for was the architectural and engineering part of the business, the working out of the

---

[1] Exiled (under criminal sentence).
[2] In the land of the heathen.

wonderful unity of plan in the thousands and thousands of diverse living constructions, and the modifications of similar apparatuses to serve diverse ends. The extraordinary attraction I felt towards the study of the intricacies of living structure nearly proved fatal to me at the outset. I was a mere boy—I think between thirteen and fourteen years of age—when I was taken by some older student friends of mine to the first *post-mortem* examination I ever attended. All my life I have been most unfortunately sensitive to the disagreeables which attend anatomical pursuits, but on this occasion my curiosity overpowered all other feelings, and I spent two or three hours in gratifying it. I did not cut myself, and none of the ordinary symptoms of dissection-poison supervened, but poisoned I was somehow, and I remember sinking into a strange state of apathy. By way of a last chance, I was sent to the care of some good, kind people, friends of my father's, who lived in a farmhouse in the heart of Warwickshire. I remember staggering from my bed to the window on the bright spring morning after my arrival, and throwing open the casement. Life seemed to come back on the wings of the breeze, and to this day the faint odor of wood-smoke, like that which floated across the farm-yard in the early morning, is as good to me as the "sweet south upon a bed of violets." I soon recovered, but for years I suffered from occasional paroxysms of internal pain, and from that time my constant friend, hypochondriacal dyspepsia, commenced his half century of co-tenancy of my fleshly tabernacle.

Looking back on my "Lehrjahre," [1] I am sorry to say that I do not think that any account of my doings as a student would tend to edification. In fact, I should distinctly warn ingenuous youth to avoid imitating my example. I worked extremely hard when it pleased me, and when it did not—which was a very frequent case—I was extremely idle (unless making caricatures of one's pastors and masters is to be called a branch of industry)— or else wasted my energies in wrong directions. I read everything I could lay hands upon, including novels, and took up all sorts of pursuits to drop them again quite as speedily. No doubt

[1] Student-years; apprenticeship.

it was very largely my own fault, but the only instruction from which I ever obtained the proper effect of education was that which I received from Mr. Wharton Jones, who was the lecturer on physiology at the Charing Cross School of Medicine. The extent and precision of his knowledge impressed me greatly, and the severe exactness of his method of lecturing was quite to my taste. I do not know that I have ever felt so much respect for anybody as a teacher before or since. I worked hard to obtain his approbation, and he was extremely kind and helpful to the youngster who, I am afraid, took up more of his time than he had any right to do. It was he who suggested the publication of my first scientific paper—a very little one—in the *Medical Gazette* of 1845, and most kindly corrected the literary faults which abounded in it, short as it was; for at that time, and for many years afterwards, I detested the trouble of writing, and would take no pains over it.

It was in the early spring of 1846 that, having finished my obligatory medical studies and passed the first M.D. examination at the London University,—though I was still too young to qualify at the College of Surgeons,—I was talking to a fellow-student (the present eminent physician, Sir Joseph Fayrer), and wondering what I should do to meet the imperative necessity for earning my own bread, when my friend suggested that I should write to Sir William Burnett, at that time Director-General for the Medical Service of the Navy, for an appointment. I thought this rather a strong thing to do, as Sir William was personally unknown to me, but my cheery friend would not listen to my scruples, so I went to my lodgings and wrote the best letter I could devise. A few days afterwards I received the usual official circular acknowledgment, but at the bottom there was written an instruction to call at Somerset House on such a day. I thought that looked like business, so at the appointed time I called and sent in my card, while I waited in Sir William's ante-room. He was a tall, shrewd-looking old gentleman, with a broad Scotch accent—and I think I see him now as he entered with my card in his hand. The first thing he did was to return it, with the frugal reminder that I should probably find it useful on some other occasion. The second was to ask whether I was an Irishman. I suppose the air of modesty about my appeal must have struck him. I satisfied the Director-General that I was English to the backbone, and he made some inquiries as to my student career, finally desiring me to hold myself ready for examination. Having passed this, I was in Her Majesty's Service, and entered on the books of Nelson's old ship, the *Victory*, for duty at Haslar Hospital, about a couple of months after I made my application.

My official chief at Haslar was a very remarkable person, the late Sir John Richardson, an excellent naturalist, and far-famed as an indomitable Arctic traveller. He was a silent, reserved man, outside the circle of his family and intimates; and, having a full share of youthful vanity, I was extremely disgusted to find that "Old John," as we irreverent youngsters called him, took not the slightest notice of my worshipful self either the first time I attended him, as it was my duty to do, or for some weeks afterwards. I am afraid to think of the lengths to which my tongue may have run on the subject of the churlishness of the chief, who was, in truth, one of the kindest-hearted and most considerate of men. But one day, as I was crossing the hospital square, Sir John stopped me, and heaped coals of fire on my head by telling me that he had tried to get me one of the resident appointments, much coveted by the assistant surgeons, but that the Admiralty had put in another man. "However," said he, "I mean to keep you here till I can get you something you will like," and turned upon his heel without waiting for the thanks I stammered out. That explained how it was I had not been packed off to the West Coast of Africa, like some of my juniors, and why, eventually, I remained altogether seven months at Haslar.

After a long interval, during which "Old John" ignored my existence almost as completely as before, he stopped me again as we met in a casual way, and, describing the service on which the *Rattlesnake* was likely to be employed, said that Captain Owen Stanley, who was to command the ship, had asked him to recommend an assistant surgeon who knew something of science; would I like that? Of course I jumped at the offer. "Very well, I give you leave; go to London at once and see Captain

Stanley." I went, saw my future commander, who was very civil to me, and promised to ask that I should be appointed to his ship, as in due time I was. It is a singular thing that, during the few months of my stay at Haslar, I had among my messmates two future Directors-General of the Medical Service of the Navy (Sir Alexander Armstrong and Sir John Watt-Reid), with the present President of the College of Physicians and my kindest of doctors, Sir Andrew Clark.

Life on board Her Majesty's ship in those days was a very different affair from what it is now, and ours was exceptionally rough, as we were often many months without receiving letters or seeing any civilized people but ourselves. In exchange, we had the interest of being about the last voyagers, I suppose, to whom it could be possible to meet with people who knew nothing of fire-arms—as we did on the south coast of New Guinea—and of making acquaintance with a variety of interesting savage and semi-civilized people. But, apart from experience of this kind and the opportunities offered for scientific work, to me, personally, the cruise was extremely valuable. It was good for me to live under sharp discipline; to be down on the realities of existence by living on bare necessaries; to find out how extremely well worth living life seemed to be when one woke up from a night's rest on a soft plank, with the sky for canopy and cocoa and weevilly biscuit the sole prospect for breakfast; and, more especially, to learn to work for the sake of what I got for myself out of it, even if it all went to the bottom and I along with it. My brother officers were as good fellows as sailors ought to be and generally are, but, naturally, they neither knew nor cared anything about my pursuits, nor understood why I should be so zealous in pursuit of the objects which my friends, the middies, christened "Buffons," after the title conspicuous on a volume of the *Suites à Buffon*,[1] which stood on my shelf in the chart room.

During the four years of our absence, I sent home communication after communication to the "Linnean Society," with the same result as that obtained by Noah when he sent the raven out of his ark. Tired at last of hearing nothing about them, I

[1] Supplements to Buffon (the naturalist).

determined to do or die, and in 1849 I drew up a more elaborate paper and forwarded it to the Royal Society. This was my dove, if I had only known it. But owing to the movements of the ship, I heard nothing of that either until my return to England in the latter end of the year 1850, when I found that it was printed and published, and that a huge packet of separate copies awaited me. When I hear some of my young friends complain of want of sympathy and encouragement, I am inclined to think that my naval life was not the least valuable part of my education.

Three years after my return were occupied by a battle between my scientific friends on the one hand and the Admiralty on the other, as to whether the latter ought, or ought not, to act up to the spirit of a pledge they had given to encourage officers who had done scientific work by contributing to the expense of publishing mine. At last the Admiralty, getting tired, I suppose, cut short the discussion by ordering me to join a ship, which thing I declined to do, and as Rastignac, in the *Père Goriot,* says to Paris, I said to London *"à nous deux."* [1] I desired to obtain a Professorship of either Physiology or Comparative Anatomy, and as vacancies occurred I applied, but in vain. My friend, Professor Tyndall, and I were candidates at the same time, he for the Chair of Physics, and I for that of Natural History in the University of Toronto, which, fortunately, as it turned out, would not look at either of us. I say fortunately, not from any lack of respect for Toronto, but because I soon made up my mind that London was the place for me, and hence I have steadily declined the inducements to leave it, which have at various times been offered. At last, in 1854, on the translation of my warm friend Edward Forbes, to Edinburgh, Sir Henry de la Beche, the Director-General of the Geological Survey, offered me the post Forbes vacated of Paleontologist and Lecturer on Natural History. I refused the former point blank, and accepted the latter only provisionally, telling Sir Henry that I did not care for fossils, and that I should give up Natural History as soon as I could get a physiological post. But I held the office for thirty-one years, and a large part of my work has been paleontological.

[1] "We have a score to settle."

At that time I disliked public speaking, and had a firm conviction that I should break down every time I opened my mouth. I believe I had every fault a speaker could have (except talking at random or indulging in rhetoric), when I spoke to the first important audience I ever addressed, on a Friday evening at the Royal Institution, in 1852. Yet, I must confess to having been guilty, *malgré moi*,[1] of as much public speaking as most of my contemporaries, and for the last ten years it ceased to be so much of a bugbear to me. I used to pity myself for having to go through this training, but I am now more disposed to compassionate the unfortunate audiences, especially my ever friendly hearers at the Royal Institution, who were the subjects of my oratorical experiments.

The last thing that it would be proper for me to do would be to speak of the work of my life, or to say at the end of the day whether I think I have earned my wages or not. Men are said to be partial judges of themselves. Young men may be, I doubt if old men are. Life seems terribly foreshortened as they look back, and the mountain they set themselves to climb in youth turns out to be a mere spur of immeasurably higher ranges when, by failing breath, they reach the top. But if I may speak of the objects I have had more or less definitely in view since I began the ascent of my hillock, they are briefly these: To promote the increase of natural knowledge and to forward the application of scientific methods of investigation to all the problems of life to the best of my ability, in the conviction which has grown with my growth and strengthened with my strength, that there is no alleviation for the sufferings of mankind except veracity of thought and of action, and the resolute facing of the world as it is when the garment of make-believe by which pious hands have hidden its uglier features is stripped off.

It is with this intent that I have subordinated any reasonable, or unreasonable, ambition for scientific fame which I may have permitted myself to entertain to other ends; to the popularization of science; to the development and organization of scientific education; to the endless series of battles and skirmishes over

[1] In spite of myself.

evolution; and to untiring opposition to that ecclesiastical spirit, that clericalism, which in England, as everywhere else, and to whatever denomination it may belong, is the deadly enemy of science.

In striving for the attainment of these objects, I have been but one among many, and I shall be well content to be remembered, or even not remembered, as such. Circumstances, among which I am proud to reckon the devoted kindness of many friends, have led to my occupation of various prominent positions, among which the Presidency of the Royal Society is the highest. It would be mock modesty on my part, with these and other scientific honours which have been bestowed upon me, to pretend that I have not succeeded in the career which I have followed, rather because I was driven into it than of my own free will; but I am afraid I should not count even these things as marks of success if I could not hope that I had somewhat helped that movement of opinion which has been called the New Reformation.

CHILDHOOD AND EARLY EDUCATION [1]

By John Stuart Mill

It seems proper that I should prefix to the following biographical sketch, some mention of the reasons which have made me think it desirable that I should leave behind me such a memorial of so uneventful a life as mine. I do not for a moment imagine that any part of what I have to relate can be interesting to the public as a narrative, or as being connected with myself. But I have thought that in an age in which education and its improvement are the subject of more, if not of profounder, study than at any former period of English history, it may be useful that there should be some record of an education which was unusual and remarkable, and which, whatever else it may have done, has proved how much more than is commonly supposed may be taught, and well taught, in those early years which, in the common modes of what is called instruction, are little better

[1] From *Autobiography.*

than wasted. It has also seemed to me that in an age of transition in opinions, there may be somewhat both of interest and of benefit in noting the successive phases of any mind which was always pressing forward, equally ready to learn and to unlearn either from its own thoughts or from those of others. But a motive which weighs more with me than either of these, is a desire to make acknowledgment of the debts which my intellectual and moral development owes to other persons; some of them of recognized eminence, others less known than they deserve to be, and the one to whom most of all is due, one whom the world had no opportunity of knowing. The reader whom these things do not interest, has only himself to blame if he reads farther, and I do not desire any other indulgence from him than that of bearing in mind that for him these pages were not written.

I was born in London, on the 20th of May, 1806, and was the eldest son of James Mill, the author of the *History of British India*. My father, the son of a petty tradesman and (I believe) small farmer, at Northwater Bridge, in the county of Angus, was, when a boy, recommended by his abilities to the notice of Sir John Stuart, of Fettercairn, one of the Barons of the Exchequer in Scotland, and was, in consequence, sent to the University of Edinburgh, at the expense of a fund established by Lady Jane Stuart (the wife of Sir John Stuart) and some other ladies for educating young men for the Scottish Church. He there went through the usual course of study, and was licensed as a preacher, but never followed the profession; having satisfied himself that he could not believe the doctrines of that or any other church. For a few years he was a private tutor in various families in Scotland, among others that of the Marquis of Tweeddale, but ended by taking up his residence in London and devoting himself to authorship. Nor had he any other means of support until 1819, when he obtained an appointment in the India House.

In this period of my father's life there are two things which it is impossible not to be struck with: one of them unfortunately a very common circumstance, the other a most uncommon one. The first is, that in his position, with no resource but the precarious one of writing in periodicals, he married and had a large family; conduct than which nothing could be more opposed, both as a matter of good sense and of duty, to the opinions which, at least at a later period of life, he strenuously upheld. The other circumstance, is the extraordinary energy which was required to lead the life he led, with the disadvantages under which he labored from the first, and with those which he brought upon himself by his marriage. It would have been no small thing, had he done no more than to support himself and his family during so many years by writing, without ever being in debt, or in any pecuniary difficulty; holding, as he did, opinions, both in politics and in religion, which were more odious to all persons of influence, and to the common run of prosperous Englishmen in that generation than either before or since: and being not only a man whom nothing would have induced to write against his convictions, but one who invariably threw into everything he wrote, as much of his convictions as he thought the circumstances would in any way permit: being, it must also be said, one who never did anything negligently; never undertook any task, literary or other, on which he did not conscientiously bestow all the labor necessary for performing it adequately. But he, with these burdens on him, planned, commenced, and completed, the *History of India;* and this in the course of about ten years, a shorter time than has been occupied (even by writers who had no other employment) in the production of almost any other historical work of equal bulk, and of anything approaching to the same amount of reading and research. And to this is to be added, that during the whole period, a considerable part of almost every day was employed in the instruction of his children, in the case of one of whom, myself, he exerted an amount of labor, care, and perseverance rarely, if ever, employed for a similar purpose, in endeavoring to give, according to his own conception, the highest order of intellectual education.

A man who, in his own practice, so vigorously acted up to the principle of losing no time, was likely to adhere to the same rule in the instruction of his pupil. I have no remembrance of the time when I began to learn Greek, I have been told that it was when I was three years old. My earliest recollection on the subject, is that of committing to memory what my father termed vocables, being lists of common Greek words, with their signification in English, which he wrote out for me on cards. Of grammar, until some years later, I learned no more than the inflexions of the nouns and verbs, but, after a course of vocables, proceeded at once to translation; and I faintly remember going through *Æsop's Fables*, the first Greek book which I read. The *Anabasis*, which I remember better, was the second. I learned no Latin until my eighth year. At that time I had read, under my father's tuition, a number of Greek prose authors, among whom I remember the whole of Herodotus, and of Xenophon's *Cyropædia* and *Memorials* of Socrates; some of the lives of the philosophers by Diogenes Laertius; part of Lucian, and *Isocrates ad Demonicum* and *Ad Nicoclem*. I also read, in 1813, the first six dialogues (in the common arrangement) of Plato, from the *Euthyphron* to the *Theoctetus* inclusive: which last dialogue, I venture to think, would have been better omitted, as it was totally impossible I should understand it. But my father, in all his teaching, demanded of me not only the utmost that I could do, but much that I could by no possibility have done. What he was himself willing to undergo for the sake of my instruction, may be judged from the fact that I went through the whole process of preparing my Greek lessons in the same room and at the same table at which he was writing: and as in those days Greek and English lexicons were not, and I could make no more use of a Greek and Latin lexicon than could be made without having yet begun to learn Latin, I was forced to have recourse to him for the meaning of every word which I did not know. This incessant interruption, he, one of the most impatient of men, submitted to, and wrote under that interruption several volumes of his *History* and all else that he had to write during those years.

The only thing besides Greek, that I learned as a lesson in this part of my childhood, was arithmetic: this also my father taught me: it was the task of the evenings, and I well remember its disagreeableness. But the lessons were only a part of the daily instruction I received. Much of it consisted in the books

I read by myself, and my father's discourses to me, chiefly during our walks. From 1810 to the end of 1813 we were living in Newington Green, then an almost rustic neighborhood. My father's health required considerable and constant exercise, and he walked habitually before breakfast, generally in the green lanes toward Hornsey. In these walks I always accompanied him, and with my earliest recollections of green fields and wild flowers, is mingled that of the account I gave him daily of what I had read the day before. To the best of my remembrance, this was a voluntary rather than a prescribed exercise. I made notes on slips of paper while reading, and from these in the morning walks, I told the story to him; for the books were chiefly histories, of which I read in this manner a great number: Robertson's histories, Hume, Gibbon; but my greatest delight, then and for long afterward, was Watson's *Philip the Second and Third*. The heroic defence of the Knights of Malta against the Turks, and of the revolted provinces of the Netherlands against Spain, excited in me an intense and lasting interest. Next to Watson, my favorite historical reading was Hooke's *History of Rome*. Of Greece I had seen at that time no regular history, except school abridgements and the last two or three volumes of a translation of Rollin's *Ancient History*, beginning with Philip of Macedon. But I read with great delight Langhorne's translation of *Plutarch*. In English history, beyond the time at which Hume leaves off, I remember reading Burnet's history of his own time, though I cared little for anything in it except the wars and battles; and the historical part of the *Annual Register*, from the beginning to about 1788, where the volumes my father borrowed for me from Mr. Bentham left off. I felt a lively interest in Frederic of Prussia during his difficulties, and in Paoli, the Corsican patriot; but when I came to the American war, I took my part, like a child as I was (until set right by my father), on the wrong side, because it was called the English side. In these frequent talks about the books I read, he used, as opportunity offered, to give me explanations and ideas respecting civilization, government, morality, mental cultivation, which he required me afterward to restate to him in my own words. He also made me read, and give him a verbal account of, many books which would not have interested me sufficiently to induce me to read them of myself: among others, Millar's *Historical View of the English Government,* a book of great merit for its time, and one which he highly valued, Mosheim's *Ecclesiastical History,* McCrie's *Life of John Knox,* and even Sewell and Rutty's histories of the Quakers. He was fond of putting into my hands books which exhibited men of energy and resource in unusual circumstances, struggling against difficulties and overcoming them: of which works I remember Beaver's *African Memoranda,* and Collin's *Account of the First Settlement of New South Wales.* Two books which I never wearied of reading were *Anson's Voyages,* so delightful to most young persons, and a collection (Hawkesworth's I believe) of voyages round the world, in four volumes beginning with Drake and ending with Cook and Bougainville. Of children's books, any more than of playthings, I had scarcely any, except an occasional gift from a relation or acquaintance: among those I had, *Robinson Crusoe* was preeminent, and continued to delight me throughout all my boyhood. It was no part, however, of my father's system to exclude books of amusement, though he allowed them very sparingly. Of such books he possessed at that time next to none, but he borrowed several for me; those which I remember are the *Arabian Nights,* Cazotte's *Arabian Tales, Don Quixote,* Miss Edgeworth's *Popular Tales,* and a book of some reputation in its day, Brooke's *Fool of Quality.*

In my eighth year I commenced learning Latin, in conjunction with a younger sister, to whom I taught it as I went on, and who afterward repeated the lessons to my father: and from this time, other sisters and brothers being successively added as pupils, a considerable part of my day's work consisted of this preparatory teaching. It was a part which I greatly disliked; the more so, as I was held responsible for the lessons of my pupils, in almost as full a sense as for my own. I, however, derived from this discipline the great advantage of learning more thoroughly and retaining more lastingly the things which I was set to teach: perhaps, too, the practice it afforded in explaining difficulties to others may even at that age have been useful. In other respects, the experience of my boyhood is not favorable to the plan of teaching children by means of one another. The teaching, I am sure, is very inefficient as teaching, and I well know that the relation between teacher and taught is not a good moral discipline to either. I went in this manner through the Latin grammar, and a considerable part of *Cornelius Nepos* and *Cæsar's Commentaries*, but afterward added to the superintendence of these lessons, much longer ones of my own.

In the same year in which I began Latin, I made my first commencement in the Greek poets with the *Iliad*. After I had made some progress in this, my father put Pope's translation into my hands. It was the first English verse I had cared to read, and it became one of the books in which for many years I most delighted: I think I must have read it from twenty to thirty times through. I should not have thought it worth while to mention a taste apparently so natural to boyhood, if I had not, as I think, observed that the keen enjoyment of this brilliant specimen of narrative and versification is not so universal with boys, as I should have expected both *à priori* and from my individual experience. Soon after this time I commenced *Euclid*, and somewhat later, algebra, still under my father's tuition.

From my eighth to my twelfth year, the Latin books which I remember reading were, the *Bucolics* of Virgil, and the first six books of the *Æneid;* all Horace, except the *Epodes;* the *Fables* of Phædrus; the first five books of Livy (to which from my love of the subject I voluntarily added, in my hours of leisure, the remainder of the first decade); all Sallust; a considerable part of Ovid's *Metamorphoses;* some plays of Terence; two or three books of Lucretius; several of the *Orations* of Cicero, and of his writings on oratory; also his letters to Atticus, my father taking the trouble to translate to me from the French the historical explanations in Mingault's notes. In Greek I read the *Iliad* and *Odyssey* through; one or two plays of Sophocles, Euripides, and Aristophanes, though by these I profited little; all Thucydides; the *Hellenics* of Xenophon; a great part of Demosthenes, Æschines, and Lysias; Theocritus, Anacreon; part of the

Anthology; a little of Dionysius; several books of Polybius; and lastly Aristotle's *Rhetoric,* which, as the first expressly scientific treatise on any moral or psychological subject which I had read, and containing many of the best observations of the ancients on human nature and life, my father made me study with peculiar care, and throw the matter of it into synoptic tables. During the same years I learned elementary geometry and algebra thoroughly, the differential calculus, and other portions of the higher mathematics far from thoroughly; for my father, not having kept up this part of his early acquired knowledge, could not spare time to qualify himself for removing my difficulties, and left me to deal with them, with little other aid than that of books, while I was continually incurring his displeasure by my inability to solve difficult problems for which he did not see that I had not the necessary previous knowledge.

As to my private reading, I can only speak of what I remember. History continued to be my strongest predilection, and most of all ancient history. Mitford's *Greece* I read continually; my father had put me on my guard against the Tory prejudices of this writer, and his perversions of facts for the whitewashing of despots, and blackening of popular institutions. These points he discoursed on, exemplifying them from the Greek orators and historians, with such effect that in reading Mitford my sympathies were always on the contrary side to those of the author, and I could, to some extent, have argued the point against him: yet this did not diminish the ever new pleasure with which I read the book. Roman history, both in my old favorite, Hooke, and in Ferguson, continued to delight me. A book which, in spite of what is called the dryness of its style, I took great pleasure in, was the *Ancient Universal History,* through the incessant reading of which, I had my head full of historical details concerning the obscurest ancient people, while about modern history, except detached passages, such as the Dutch War of Independence, I knew and cared comparatively little. A voluntary exercise, to which throughout my boyhood I was much addicted, was what I called writing histories. I successively composed a Roman History, picked out of Hooke; an Abridgment of the Ancient Universal History; a History of Holland, from my favorite Watson and from an anonymous compilation; and in my eleventh and twelfth year I occupied myself with writing what I flattered myself was something serious. This was no less than a History of the Roman Government, compiled (with the assistance of Hooke) from Livy and Dionysius: of which I wrote as much as would have made an octavo volume, extending to the epoch of the Licinian Laws. It was, in fact, an account of the struggles between the patricians and plebeians, which now engrossed all the interest in my mind which I had previously felt in the mere wars and conquests of the Romans. I discussed all the constitutional points as they arose: though quite ignorant of Niebuhr's researches, I, by such lights as my father had given me, vindicated the Agrarian Laws on the evidence of Livy, and upheld, to the best of my ability, the Roman Democratic party. A few years later, in my contempt of my childish efforts, I destroyed all these papers, not then anticipating that I could ever feel any curiosity about my first attempts at writing and reasoning. My father encouraged me in this useful amusement, though, as I think judiciously, he never asked to see what I wrote; so that I did not feel that in writing it I was accountable to any one, nor had the chilling sensation of being under a critical eye.

But though these exercises in history were never a compulsory lesson, there was another kind of composition which was so, namely, writing verses, and it was one of the most disagreeable of my tasks. Greek and Latin verses I did not write, nor learned the prosody of these languages. My father, thinking this not worth the time it required, contented himself with making me read aloud to him, and correcting false quantities. I never composed at all in Greek, even in prose, and but little in Latin. Not that my father could be indifferent to the value of this practice, in giving a thorough knowledge of these languages, but because there really was not time for it. The verses I was required to write were English. When I first read Pope's *Homer*, I ambitiously attempted to compose something of the same kind, and achieved as much as one book of a continuation of the *Iliad*. There, probably, the spontaneous promptings of my poetical ambition would have stopped; but the exercise, begun from choice, was continued by command. Conformably to my father's usual practice of explaining to me, as far as possible, the reasons for what he required me to do, he gave me, for this, as I well remember, two reasons highly characteristic of him: one was, that some things could be expressed better and more forcibly in verse than in prose: this, he said, was a real advantage. The other was, that people in general attached more value to verse than it deserved, and the power of writing it, was, on this account, worth acquiring. He generally left me to choose my own subjects, which, as far as I remember, were mostly addresses to some mythological personage or allegorical abstraction; but he made me translate into English verse many of Horace's shorter poems: I also remember his giving me Thomson's *Winter* to read, and afterward making me attempt (without book) to write something myself on the same subject. The verses I wrote were, of course, the merest rubbish, nor did I ever attain any facility of versification, but the practice may have been useful in making it easier for me, at a later period, to acquire readiness of expression. I had read, up to this time, very little English poetry. Shakespeare my father had put into my hands, chiefly for the sake of the historical plays, from which, however, I went on to the others. My father never was a great admirer of Shakespeare, the English idolatry of whom he used to attack with some severity. He cared little for any English poetry except Milton (for whom he had the highest admiration), Goldsmith, Burns, and Gray's *Bard,* which he preferred to his *Elegy;* perhaps I may add Cowper and Beattie. He had some value for Spenser, and I remember his reading to me (unlike his usual practice of making me read to him), the first book of the *Faërie Queene;* but I took little pleasure in it. The poetry of the present century he saw scarcely any merit in, and I hardly became acquainted with any of it till I was grown up to manhood, except the metrical romances of Walter Scott, which I read at his recommendation and was intensely delighted with; as I always was with animated narrative. Dryden's poems were among my father's books, and many of these he made me read, but I never cared for any of them except "Alexander's Feast," which, as well as many of the songs of Walter Scott, I used to sing internally, to a music of my own: to some of the latter, indeed, I went so far as to compose airs, which I still remember. Cowper's short poems I read with some pleasure, but never got far into the longer ones; and nothing in the two volumes interested me like the prose account of his three hares. In my thirteenth year I met with Campbell's poems, among which *Lochiel, Hohenlinden, The Exile of Erin,* and some others, gave me sensations I had never before experienced from poetry. Here, too, I made nothing of the longer poems, except the striking opening of *Gertrude of Wyoming,* which long kept its place in my feelings as the perfection of pathos.

During this part of my childhood, one of my greatest amusements was experimental science; in the theoretical, however, not the practical sense of the word; not trying experiments—a kind of discipline which I have often regretted not having had—nor even seeing, but merely reading about them. I never remember being so wrapped up in any book, as I was in Joyce's *Scientific Dialogues;* and I was rather recalcitrant to my father's criticisms of the bad reasoning respecting the first principles of physics, which abounds in the early part of that work. I devoured treatises on chemistry, especially that of my father's early friend and schoolfellow, Dr. Thomson, for years before I attended a lecture or saw an experiment.

From about the age of twelve, I entered into another and more advanced stage in my course of instruction; in which the main object was no longer the aids and appliances of thought, but the thoughts themselves.

During this time, the Latin and Greek books which I continued to read with my father were chiefly such as were worth studying, not for the language merely, but also for the thoughts. This included much of the orators, and especially Demosthenes, some of whose principal orations I read several times over, and wrote out by way of exercise, a full analysis of them. My father's comments on these orations when I read them to him were very instructive to me. He not only drew my attention to the insight they afforded into Athenian institutions, and the principles of legislation and government which they often illustrated, but pointed out the skill and art of the orator—how everything important to his purpose was said at the exact moment when he had brought the minds of his audience into the state most fitted to receive it; how he made steal into their minds, gradually and by insinuation, thoughts which, if expressed in a more direct manner would have roused their opposition. Most of these reflections were beyond my capacity of full comprehension at the time; but they left seed behind, which germinated in due season. At this time I also read the whole of Tacitus, Juvenal, and Quintilian. The latter, owing to his obscure style and to the scholastic details of which many parts of his treatise are made up, is little read, and seldom sufficiently appreciated. His book is a kind of encyclopedia of the thoughts of the ancients on the whole field of education and culture; and I have retained through life many valuable ideas which I can distinctly trace to my reading of him, even at that early age. It was at this period that I read, for the first time, some of the most important dialogues of Plato, in particular the *Gorgias*, the *Protagoras* and the *Republic*. There is no author to whom my father thought himself more indebted for his own mental culture, than Plato, or whom he more frequently recommended to young students.

*　　*　　*　　*　　*　　*　　*

At this point concluded what can properly be called my lessons: when I was about fourteen I left England for more than a year; and after my return, though my studies went on under my father's general direction, he was no longer my schoolmaster. I shall therefore pause here, and turn back to matters of a more general nature connected with the part of my life and education included in the preceding reminiscences.

My Fate [1]

By Ludwig Lewisohn

In October, 1893, after an oral examination which, thanks to my mother's instruction, I passed with ease, I was admitted to

[1] From *Upstream*. By permission of Boni and Liveright.

the High School of Queenshaven. The school building is plain
and dignified, somewhat after the fashion of an English mansion
of the eighteenth century. What the school has become in recent
years I do not know. I have heard rumours of courses in book-
keeping and shorthand and other dexterities that have nothing
to do with the education of youth. In my time it was a good
school. The pupils were all boys and they were taught by men.
They were young enough to be grounded in the necessities of a
liberal education without having their callow judgment consulted,
and to be caned when they were lazy or rowdy. The school
had one grave fault: Greek was an elective study. Through this
fault my life sustained an irreparable loss. Yet when I consider
what might have happened to my mind if the school had been
like the High Schools of 1921, I am filled with a sense of gratitude. For I was enabled to lay the foundations of a sound and
permanent knowledge of Latin and French; I was taught to
study with thoroughness and accuracy under pain of tangible
and very wholesome penalties, and it was not the fault of the
school that my mind was and is all but impervious to any form
of mathematical reasoning.

I passed into the rough and tumble of school life with a distinct shudder. There was no direct hazing but there was a good
deal of rather cruel horse-play. You were apt to be tripped up
and thrown on your back, to have pins and needles stuck
viciously into you, to be held under the pump until you nearly
choked. Also, during the first year, I was taunted with being
a foreigner and a Jew. One boy especially tormented me—a
tallish fellow with huge mouth always distorted by idiotic
laughter, hateful, offstanding ears and small, greenish eyes. I
was no match for him in strength and he persisted in cuffing and
thumping and taunting me. I tried to avoid him, for I shrank
from the thought of touching him as shudderingly as I did from
his touch. Then, one day he clapped me brutally on the back
and yelled with laughter. Two scarlet lights danced before my
eyes and I leapt at his throat. Boys hurried from all sides of the
playground and formed a ring around us. Cries arose: "Fight
fair!" I remembered how the contemptuous thoughts raced

through my brain. Fight fair! Oh yes, give the over-grown lout a chance to trounce me as a reward for months of bruises and insults. I didn't want to fight him and suffer more undeserved pain and humiliation. I wanted to hurt him, to hurt him so effectively that he would never again dare lay his red, bony claws on me. I did. A teacher had to come into the yard and order me to be torn from my gasping and bloody victim. I had no trouble after that. . . .

Gradually, too, I fell in with a group of boys that belonged to the gentler families of Queenshaven. I shall have more to say of them later, for these classmates passed together through school and college with me and so lived on terms of daily intimacy with me for eight years. Through their companionship, at all events, I soon felt at home in the school, an equal among equals in play and study.

I have said that our teachers were men. Real men, I hasten to add, not the spiritual starvelings who are content nowadays with the wage-slavery of the High School. The salaries of these Queenshaven teachers were rather better than such salaries are to-day and the purchasing power of money was of course far greater. The principal was the only man I have ever known who truly embodied the peculiar ideal of the Christian gentleman. He had both sweetness and strength, profound piety and wide charity. I can still see the beautiful benevolence in his searching blue eyes and hear his clear, bell-like voice. I do not know whether he consciously thought of the methods of Arnold of Rugby; it is certain that he practiced them. The better natured of my schoolmates and I never resented his punishments; we knew he was incapable of inflicting them until in his kind and manly judgment forgiveness would have been morally harmful to the offender. His influence and example drew me back to the Methodist church. . . . It is a sad reflection that this good man's end was pitiful. A trusted brother in the church absconded with all our principal's modest savings. They were small enough, for he was liberal in his charities beyond the bounds of discretion. But this blow both in its moral and in its physical aspect overwhelmed him. He fell into a state of melancholia and I remem-

ber him, in later years, a mild, vague-eyed, broken figure on the
Queenshaven streets.

I shall not linger over the burly and severe but sound pedagogue
who taught us history and physics nor over the graceful youth—
still young and vivid in his middle age—who taught French
and German with a stringent accuracy and sternness that added
virility to his Greek profile and his curving locks. It is on our
teacher of Latin that I must dwell. I cannot estimate his influence over me. To this day I find myself using locutions and
mannerisms that are ultimately traceable to him. He was—I
beg his pardon for writing of him as in the past, but to me he
lives only in the past, though admirably and fruitfully to others
in the present—he was the son of an Italian gentleman, obviously
of gentle lineage and exquisite breeding. His face and head and
hands and form had in them something indescribably Roman.
Roman of the empire. But for his severer modern morals he
might have been a friend of Petronius and, like him, an *arbiter
elegantiarum*. Or, from another point of view, a gentleman of
the age of Queen Anne—a friend of Addison. Of course this
does not render the whole man. But he was singularly free from
all the modern maladies of the soul—a devout Catholic with a
frugal and pagan delight in the good things of the world, a lover
of the arts without morbid intensity or perverting ambitions, a
believer in that golden mean which he interpreted so well. I
need hardly say that the particular objects of his tireless and
exquisite zeal were Vergil and Horace and, among English writers,
Milton and Tennyson and Thackeray.

As a teacher he was strict, though always with a light touch—
stinging the lazy and loutish by some ironic turn of speech. He
taught us to appreciate a fine and mellow Latinity as well as the
human warmth and living power of the literature we read. But
he was tireless, too, in the humbler portions of his task. I find
I know my Latin accidence and syntax better to-day than graduate students who "major" in Latin at our universities. And I
can still hear his voice as, repeating some line of Vergil, he first
awakened me to the magic of a great and perfect style:

"... et jam nox umida coelo
praecipitat suadentque cadentia sidera somnos."

It was in the third year of High School. He was teaching us
to scan Vergil. We were repeating a passage in unison. Suddenly he swung on his heels and pointed his finger straight at me:
"That is the only boy who has a natural ear for verse!" he cried.
A keen, strange quiver went through me. I realized the meaning suddenly of that constant scribbling which I had been impelled to during the preceding months. I had a gift for literature!
I knew it now; I never doubted it again. My fate had found me.

SEEKING MY FORTUNE [1]

By Benjamin Franklin

My inclinations for the sea were by this time worn out, or
I might now have gratified them. But, having a trade, and sup-
posing myself a pretty good workman, I offered my services to
the printer in the place, old Mr. William Bradford, who had
been the first printer in Pennsylvania, but removed from thence
upon the quarrel of George Keith. He could give me no employment, having little to do, and help enough already; but says he,
"My son at Philadelphia has lately lost his principal hand,
Aquila Rose, by death; if you go thither, I believe he may employ you." Philadelphia was a hundred miles further; I set
out, however, in a boat for Amboy, leaving my chest and things
to follow me round by sea.

In crossing the bay, we met with a squall that tore our rotten
sails to pieces, prevented our getting into the Kill, and drove
us upon Long Island. On our way, a drunken Dutchman, who
was a passenger too, fell overboard; when he was sinking, I
reached through the water to his shock pate, and drew him up,
so that we got him in again. His ducking sobered him a little,
and he went to sleep, taking first out of his pocket a book, which
he desired I would dry for him. It proved to be my old favorite
author, Bunyan's *Pilgrim's Progress,* in Dutch, finely printed on

[1] From *The Autobiography of Benjamin Franklin.* Chapter II.

good paper, with copper cuts, a dress better than I had ever seen it wear in its own language. I have since found that it has been translated into most of the languages of Europe, and suppose it has been more generally read than any other book, except perhaps the Bible. Honest John was the first that I know of who mixed narration and dialogue; a method of writing very engaging to the reader, who in the most interesting parts finds himself, as it were, brought into the company and present at the discourse. De Foe in his *Crusoe*, his *Moll Flanders, Religious Courtship, Family Instructor,* and other pieces, has imitated it with success, and Richardson has done the same in his *Pamela,* etc.

When we drew near the island, we found it was at a place where there could be no landing, there being a great surf on the stony beach. So we dropped anchor, and swung round towards the shore. Some people came down to the water edge and hallooed to us, as we did to them; but the wind was so high, and the surf so loud, that we could not hear so as to understand each other. There were canoes on the shore, and we made signs, and hallooed that they should fetch us; but they either did not understand us, or thought it impracticable, so they went away, and night coming on, we had no remedy but to wait till the wind should abate; and, in the meantime, the boatman and I concluded to sleep, if we could; and so crowded into the scuttle, with the Dutchman, who was still wet; and the spray beating over the head of our boat, leaked through to us, so that we were soon almost as wet as he. In this manner we lay all night, with very little rest; but the wind abating the next day, we made a shift to reach Amboy before night, having been thirty hours on the water, without victuals, or any drink but a bottle of filthy rum, the water we sailed on being salt.

In the evening I found myself very feverish, and went in to bed; but having read somewhere that cold water drank plentifully was good for a fever, I followed the prescription, sweat plentifully most of the night, my fever left me, and in the morning, crossing the ferry, I proceeded on my journey on foot, having fifty miles to Burlington,[1] where I was told I should find boats that would carry me the rest of the way to Philadelphia.

It rained very hard all the day; I was thoroughly soaked, and by noon a good deal tired; so I stopped at a poor inn, where I stayed all night, beginning now to wish that I had never left home. I cut so miserable a figure, too, that I found, by the questions asked me, I was suspected to be some runaway servant, and in danger of being taken up on that suspicion. However, I proceeded the next day, and got in the evening to an inn, within eight or ten miles of Burlington, kept by one Dr. Brown. He entered into conversation with me while I took some refreshment, and, finding I had read a little, became very sociable and friendly. Our acquaintance continued as long as he lived. He had been, I imagine, an itinerant doctor, for there was no town in England, or country in Europe, of which he could not give a very particular account. He had some letters, and was ingenious, but much of an unbeliever, and wickedly undertook, some years after, to travesty the Bible in doggerel verse, as Cotton had done Virgil. By this means he set many of the facts in a very ridiculous light, and might have hurt weak minds if his work had been published; but it never was.

At his house I lay that night, and the next morning reached Burlington, but had the mortification to find that the regular boats were gone a little before my coming, and no other expected to go before Tuesday, this being Saturday; wherefore I returned to an old woman in the town, of whom I had bought gingerbread to eat on the water, and asked her advice. She invited me to lodge at her house till a passage by water should offer; and being tired with my foot traveling, I accepted the invitation. She, understanding I was a printer, would have had me stay at that town and follow my business, being ignorant of the stock necessary to begin with. She was very hospitable, gave me a dinner of ox-cheek with great good will, accepting only of a pot of ale in return; and I thought myself fixed till Tuesday should come. However, walking in the evening by the side of the river, a boat came by, which I found was going towards

[1] In New Jersey.

Philadelphia, with several people in her. They took me in, and, as there was no wind, we rowed all the way; and about midnight, not having yet seen the city, some of the company were confident we must have passed it, and would row no farther; the others knew not where we were; so we put toward the shore, got into a creek, landed near an old fence, with the rails of which we made a fire, the night being cold, in October, and there we remained till daylight. Then one of the company knew the place to be Cooper's Creek, a little above Philadelphia, which we saw as soon as we got out of the creek, and arrived there about eight or nine o'clock on the Sunday morning, and landed at the Market Street wharf.

I have been the more particular in this description of my journey, and shall be so of my first entry into that city, that you may in your mind compare such unlikely beginnings with the figure I have since made there. I was in my working-dress, my best clothes being to come round by sea. I was dirty from my journey; my pockets were stuffed out with shirts and stockings, and I knew no soul nor where to look for lodging. I was fatigued with traveling, rowing, and want of rest, I was very hungry; and my whole stock of cash consisted of a Dutch dollar,[1] and about a shilling in copper. The latter I gave the people of the boat for my passage, who at first refused it on account of my rowing; but I insisted on their taking it, a man being sometimes more generous when he has but a little money than when he has plenty, perhaps through fear of being thought to have but little.

Then I walked up the street, gazing about till near the market-house I met a boy with bread. I had made many a meal on bread, and inquiring where he got it, I went immediately to the baker's he directed me to, in Second Street, and asked for biscuit, intending such as we had in Boston; but they, it seems, were not made in Philadelphia. Then I asked for a three-penny loaf, and was told they had none such. So not considering or knowing the difference of money, and the greater cheapness nor the names of his bread, I bade him give me three-penny worth

[1] The metal currency at that time was of foreign coinage.

of any sort. He gave me, accordingly, three great puffy rolls. I was surprised at the quantity, but took it, and having no room in my pockets, walked off with a roll under each arm, and eating the other. Thus I went up Market Street as far as Fourth Street, passing by the door of Mr. Read, my future wife's father; when she, standing at the door, saw me, and thought I made, as I certainly did, a most awkward, ridiculous appearance. Then I turned and went down Chestnut Street and part of Walnut Street, eating my roll all the way, and coming round, found myself again at Market Street wharf, near the boat I came in, to which I went for a draught of the river water; and being filled with one of my rolls, gave the other two to a woman and her child that came down the river in the boat with us, and were waiting to go farther.

Thus refreshed, I walked again up the street, which by this time had many clean-dressed people in it, who were all walking the same way. I joined them, and thereby was led into the great meeting-house of the Quakers near the market. I sat down among them, and after looking round a while and hearing nothing said, being very drowsy through labor and want of rest the preceding night, I fell fast asleep, and continued so till the meeting broke up, when one was kind enough to rouse me. This was, therefore, the first house I was in or slept in, in Philadelphia.

EXERCISES

1. Huxley's *Autobiography* is an example of the type which relies upon careful choice of incident and of detail to get within comparatively narrow limits the outstanding events and influences of a relatively long life. In length it hardly exceeds a long term or semester theme, and yet it covers sixty-four years. Outline the selection in some way that will show Huxley's fine observance of the principle of proportion. If you have decided to sketch your own life instead of concentrating on a portion of it, outline your own theme in an attempt to secure the same excellence of proportion.

2. For one who for many years "detested the trouble of writing," Huxley surely learned how to express his thoughts in a clear

and direct style. Select from his sketch those ten sentences which seem to you most emphatic because of the clearness of their construction and their diction. Of course, your selection will include the fine sentence of the last paragraph but one. Why "of course"? What right has that sentence had for many years to be regarded as one of the finest in English prose?

3. Are there in Huxley's *Autobiography* examples of characterization by anecdote? By detail?

4. John Stuart Mill's "Childhood and Early Education" seems to some readers little else than a catalog of erudite books; and yet others have called it one of the most vivid chapters in his *Autobiography*. Can you make out any case for the latter contention? This is a good subject for a ten-minute debate.

5. Ludwig Lewisohn's sketch, which depicts an education eighty years later than that of John Stuart Mill, is to most readers far more dramatic than Mill's account. What qualities make for drama? Is drama dependent upon the inclusion of exciting episodes? Is there such a thing as drama in single words apart from their context? List Lewisohn's adjectives and study them from the point of view of dramatic effectiveness.

6. Prepare a report for the class on the similarity between Franklin's style and that of the *New Testament,* particularly of the *Gospels* and of the *Acts of the Apostles,* in the King James Version. What traits are common to both? Chapters 27 and 28 of the *Acts* will form a good basis for this comparative study.

7. The descriptive adjective is very much in vogue to-day. It is indispensable and invaluable and yet has its dangers. Study Franklin's use of it.

8. Read the brief autobiography of Margaret Cavendish, Duchess of Newcastle, the full title of which is given in the list of suggested readings. Remember that this autobiography was written in 1667. Lamb was a great admirer of the Duchess and of her work. Can you yourself find grounds for his enthusiasm and for the adjectives "fantastical" and "original-brained" which he uses in describing her? If you can, and your own enthusiasm mounts high, ask your instructor if you cannot give an oral theme before the class on "The Duchess of Newcastle and Her Autobiography," that is, of course, in place of a written one. He, recalling the fact that your request means one less theme for him to read, may be most gracious in his permission!

9. One of the most delightful autobiographies on the list of suggested readings is Percy Lubbock's *Earlham*. Objection has been made to it by certain critics on the ground that it is "too idealized." Is that your opinion?

SUGGESTED READINGS

Adams, Henry, *The Education of Henry Adams,* Chapters I and II, Houghton Mifflin, Boston.

Anderson, Sherwood, *A Story Teller's Story,* Book I, B. W. Huebsch, New York.

Antin, Mary, *The Promised Land,* Houghton Mifflin, Boston.

Cavendish, Margaret, *A True Relation of the Birth, Breeding, and Life of Margaret Cavendish, Duchess of Newcastle,* 1667.

Cellini, Benvenuto, *Autobiography.*

Clifford, Lady Anne, Her Diary, 1603-1619, Doubleday, Doran, New York.

Davies, William H., *The Autobiography of a Super-Tramp,* Alfred A. Knopf, New York.

Garland, Hamlin, *A Son of the Middle Border,* Macmillan, New York.

Gosse, Edmund, *Father and Son,* Scribner's, New York.

Hamilton, Lord Frederick, *The Days Before Yesterday,* Doubleday, Doran, New York.

Hudson, W. H., *Far Away and Long Ago,* E. P. Dutton, New York.

Jensen, Carl Christian, *An American Saga,* the early chapters, Little, Brown, Boston.

Lagerlof, Selma, *Mårbacka,* Doubleday, Doran, New York.

Lawrence, T. E., *Revolt in the Desert,* Doubleday, Doran, New York.

Lewisohn, Ludwig, *Upstream,* Boni and Liveright, New York.

Loti, Pierre, *The Story of a Child,* Frederick A Stokes, New York.

Lubbock, Percy, *Earlham,* Scribner's, New York.

Lynn, Margaret, *A Stepdaughter of the Prairie,* Macmillan, New York.

Mallet, Captain Thierry, "A Frozen Diary," *The Atlantic Monthly,* March 1927.

Muir, John, *The Story of My Boyhood and Youth,* Houghton Mifflin, Boston.

Pupin, Michael, *From Immigrant to Inventor,* Scribner's, New York.

Riis, Jacob, "Going into Business," from *The Making of an American,* Macmillan, New York.

Shaw, Anna Howard, *The Story of a Pioneer,* Harper's, New York.

Soskice, Juliet, *Chapters from Childhood,* Harcourt, Brace, New York.

Stevens, James, "A Boy in Idaho" from *Brawnyman,* Alfred A. Knopf, New York.

Twain, Mark, "A Boy in Missouri" from *Autobiography,* Harper's, New York.

Yeats, William Butler, *Reveries over Childhood and Youth,* Macmillan, New York.

CHAPTER II

The Reminiscence

No normal child ever lived who did not like to hear his elders talk about their childhood, their games and adventures, their misdeeds and punishments, their haunts and their hobbies. Part of this perennial charm lies without doubt in the discovery of the sameness of human experience and behavior; part of it, in the tales themselves; but much, yes, even most of it, springs from the fact that the past is never without a strange and quite illogical glamour merely because it *is* the past. To children no phrases are so beloved as "Once upon a time" and "Long, long ago." As one begins to possess a train of experiences and emotions of his own, the pleasure in recollection increases; and although it may not be so strong at eighteen as at eighty, it is yet strong enough to ensure at least a relative welcome to the assignment of a theme based on reminiscence.

The welcome ought rightly to claim another reason besides the fact that memories, cherished or hateful, are the common possession of mankind; for, although many students may not be aware of them, there are literally scores of reminiscent narratives, essays, and sketches, at once absorbing, suggestive, and easily procurable in any averagely good library. It is in the hope that you will become acquainted with the best of such writing that a reading list has been added to this as to every section. Choose from it [1] on the basis of previous acquaintance with authors, on the advice of your instructor or even at random, and browse at will, not forgetting Stevenson's contention in *A College Magazine* that the way to learn to write is *to read and then to imitate.*

[1] The reading list for the "Reminiscent Incident" may be considered supplementary to the one for the "Reminiscence."

After you have read, in addition to the three models given in this book, certain selections from, let us say, W. H. Hudson, Kenneth Grahame, and Henry W. Nevinson, who are among our best writers of reminiscence, you will begin to see, that is, if you have read thoughtfully, that good reminiscence does not "run on" without rhyme or reason like the talk of the nurse in *Romeo and Juliet*. Instead it is unified by some centralizing object, place, or purpose which is employed to give a sense of form or of completion to the finished work. To illustrate: In the first sketch reprinted here, a portion of *The Lantern Bearers* by Robert Louis Stevenson, "a certain easterly fishing village" is the unifying force. The mind of the reader is never allowed to stray from it. It is described in the first paragraph with precision and detail; the pleasures which it afforded the boys follow the description; then come the dismal memories which throng any recollection of its streets and houses; and at last the sport "peculiar to the place," that of lantern-bearing, is presented. It is hardly necessary to comment on the effectiveness of such a method in contrast to the rambling and formless sketch of a less careful writer.

Miss Tynan's *An Irish Garden* is by no means so carefully unified, and yet it is not without its centralizing feature. Here it is "the great summer," "the golden summer" of 1868 or 1869 which serves as a background for the varied and various activities of the children, and her reiteration of the season recurs like a colored thread through all parts of a tapestry.

The centralizing object of *District Thirteen* is not the district nor yet the red school-house, but the bumper "crop" of boys and girls, into whose backbones New England granite was bred. It is they who hold Mr. Coffin's essay together; the ledges, the games, and the books are only complementary to them.

One more illustration may not come amiss. In each of the three selections already considered, the unifying influence has been a concrete one—a place, a time, a group of persons. Sometimes, however, it is an idea or an emotion. In Mr. Nevinson's reminiscent narrative, which he calls "Sabrina Fair" [1] and which

---

[1] From *Between the Acts* by Henry W. Nevinson.

is an account of his life at Shrewsbury School, he uses as a controlling purpose the idea of the boys that Greek was quite the most important thing in the world. They were, in fact, so permeated with the idea that they tacitly believed the very epics, orations, and plays which they read to have been written by the Greeks expressly for Shrewsbury School; and not even in their plays and games did they escape the influence of Greek. If you will read this charming reminiscence, you will see how Mr. Nevinson manages to use this idea of the boys as a means of giving unity to his work.

This attention to form, to the means of bringing symmetry and unity into your own writing, is one of the first lessons which you should learn. It is just as easy as not to decide upon some strengthening and unifying element which will hold your reminiscence together and increase its effectiveness a hundredfold. A place may be your choice—a hayloft, an old swimming-hole, a vacant city lot, an apple tree with a convenient crotch for reading; or, instead of a place, a person who was indissolubly connected with certain pastimes of your childhood; or, instead of a place or a person, an ideal, a wish, a fear, a dream, an ambition, a strange fancy. There are thousands of possibilities!

If you will for ten minutes try the experiment of closing your eyes to all external objects and of consciously summoning before your inward vision a place, a period, or an incident of your past life, I think you will become convinced that you see in sharp and concrete detail and that your other senses are called into instant service. For instance, suppose you recall the doorway of your home. You do not see it merely as a means of entrance into your house; but you see rather the color of the door, the brass knocker upon it, the cracked panel you effected in a moment of impatience. You see it, perhaps, in a given season, framed in blossoming lilacs or banked with snow or untidy with autumn leaves. With your sense of touch you feel the coldness of the snow; you smell the lilacs; you hear the swirling patter of the leaves. Again, remembering your mother's kitchen on baking days, you actually smell hot gingerbread, or taste the sparse ingredients of the discarded frosting-bowl, or see clearly the identical pattern of a certain apron she used to wear.

Now all this sharpening of your senses is of incalculable value in the writing of reminiscence. The use of sense impressions, of color, of sound, smell, even of taste and of touch, the searching for the lively and suggestive word, the good use of detail—all these will lend tone and atmosphere to your theme. The danger will lie in overdoing any or all of them, and this your own taste and judgment must guard against. Stevenson in one of his letters doubts the possibility of aesthetic appeal in prose which is unlighted by sense impressions. We have no space here to refute or to corroborate his opinion. Suffice it is to say that he ably followed his own precept!

A couplet from Pope's *Essay on Man* comes to mind as an excellent maxim for writers of reminiscence:

> Remembrance and reflection how allied!
> What thin partitions sense from thought divide!

Perhaps Pope would have been less sanguine could he have taught Freshman English! For too often, alas! the partitions which separate thought and reflection from sense, aye from sentiment, seem far from thin! A good reminiscent theme, remember, cannot be written unless form and plan, which result in unity of effect, have been the fruit of careful thought and reflection. The very fact that you feel deeply about your subject matter may be the worst of stumbling-blocks. You must *think* also, so hard and so clearly that the light from your thought, gleaming through Pope's "thin partition," will temper and refine your remembrance.

The Lantern Bearers [1]

By Robert Louis Stevenson

These boys congregated every autumn about a certain easterly fisher-village, where they tasted in a high degree the glory of

---

[1] From *The Lantern Bearers*. By permission of Charles Scribner's Sons, the authorized publishers.

existence. The place was created seemingly on purpose for the diversion of young gentlemen. A street or two of houses, mostly red and many of them tiled; a number of fine trees clustered about the manse and the kirkyard, and turning the chief street into a shady alley; many little gardens more than usually bright with flowers; nets a-drying, and fisher-wives scolding in the backward parts; a smell of fish, a genial smell of seaweed; whiffs of blowing sand at the street-corners; shops with golf-balls and bottled lollipops; another shop with penny pickwicks (that remarkable cigar) and the *London Journal,* dear to me for its startling pictures, and a few novels, dear for their suggestive names: such, as well as memory serves me, were the ingredients of the town. These, you are to conceive posted on a spit between two sandy bays, and sparsely flanked with villas—enough for the boys to lodge in with their subsidiary parents, not enough (not yet enough) to cocknify the scene: a haven in the rocks in front: in front of that, a file of gray islets: to the left, endless links and sand-wreaths, a wilderness of hiding-holes, alive with popping rabbits and soaring gulls: to the right, a range of sea-weed crags, one rugged brow beyond another; the ruins of a mighty and ancient fortress on the brink of one; coves between —now charmed into sunshine quiet, now whistling with wind and clamorous with bursting surges; the dens and sheltered hollows redolent of thyme and southernwood, the air at the cliff's edge brisk and clean and pungent of the sea—in front of all, the Bass Rock, tilted seaward like a doubtful bather, the surf ringing it with white, the solan-geese hanging round its summit like a great and glittering smoke. This choice piece of seaboard was sacred, besides, to the wrecker; and the Bass, in the eye of fancy, still flew the colors of King James; and in the ear of fancy the arches of Tantallon still rang with horseshoe iron, and echoed to the commands of Bell-the-Cat.

There was nothing to mar your days, if you were a boy summering in that part, but the embarrassment of pleasure. You might golf if you wanted; but I seem to have been better employed. You might secrete yourself in the Lady's Walk, a certain sunless dingle of elders, all mossed over by the damp as green as grass, and dotted here and there by the stream-side with roofless walls, the cold homes of anchorites. To fit themselves for life, and with a special eye to acquire the art of smoking, it was even common for the boys to harbor there; and you might have seen a single penny pickwick, honestly shared in lengths with a blunt knife, bestrew the glen with these apprentices. Again, you might join our fishing-parties, where we sat perched as thick as solan-geese, a covey of little anglers, boy and girl, angling over each other's heads, to the much entanglement of lines and loss of podleys and consequent shrill recrimination—shrill as the geese themselves. Indeed, had that been all, you might have done this often; but though fishing be a fine pastime, the podley is scarce to be regarded as a dainty for the table; and it was a point of honor that a boy should eat all that he had taken. Or again, you might climb the Law, where the whale's jawbone stood landmark in the buzzing wind, and behold the face of many counties, and the smokes and spires of many towns, and the sails of distant ships. You might bathe, now in the flaws of fine weather, that we pathetically call our summer, now in a gale of wind, with the sand scouring your bare hide, your clothes thrashing abroad from underneath their guardian stone, the froth of the great breakers casting you headlong ere it had drowned your knees. Or you might explore the tidal rocks, above all in the ebb of springs, when the very roots of the hills were for the nonce discovered; following my leader from one group to another; groping in slippery tangle for the wreck of ships, wading in pools after the abominable creatures of the sea, and ever with an eye cast backward on the march of the tide and the menaced line of your retreat. And then you might go Crusoeing, a word that covers all extempore eating in the open air; digging perhaps a house under the margin of the links, kindling a fire of the seaware, and cooking apples there—if they were truly apples, for I sometimes suppose the merchant must have played us off with some inferior and quite local fruit, capable of resolving, in the neighborhood of fire, into mere sand and smoke and iodine; or perhaps pushing to Tantallon, you might lunch on sandwiches and visions in the grassy court, while the wind hummed in the crumbling turrets; or clambering along the coast, eat geans (the worst, I must suppose, in Christendom) from an adventurous gean-tree that had taken root under a cliff, where it was shaken with an ague of east wind, and silvered after gales with salt, and grew so foreign among its bleak surroundings that to eat of its produce was an adventure in itself.

There are mingled some dismal memories with so many that were joyous. Of the fisher-wife, for instance, who had cut her throat at Canty Bay; and of how I ran with the other children to the top of the Quadrant, and beheld a posse of silent people escorting a cart, and on the cart, bound in a chair, her throat bandaged, and the bandage all bloody—horror!—the fisher-wife herself, who continued thenceforth to hagride my thoughts, and even to-day (as I recall the scene) darkens daylight. She was lodged in the little old jail in the chief street; but whether or no she died there, with a wise terror of the worst, I never inquired. She had been tippling; it was but a dingy tragedy, and it seems strange and hard that, after all these years, the poor crazy sinner should be still pilloried on her cart in the scrap-book of my memory. Nor shall I readily forget a certain house in the Quadrant where a visitor died, and a dark old woman continued to dwell alone with the dead body; nor how this old woman conceived a hatred to myself and one of my cousins, and in the dread hour of the dusk, as we were clambering on the garden-walls, opened a window in that house of mortality and cursed us in a shrill voice and with a marrowy choice of language. It was a pair of very colorless urchins that fled down the lane from this remarkable experience! But I recall with a more doubtful sentiment, compounded out of fear and exultation, the coil of equinoctial tempests; trumpeting squalls, scouring flaws of rain; the boats with their reefed lugsails scudding for the harbor mouth, where danger lay, for it was hard to make when the wind had any east in it; the wives clustered with blowing shawls at the pier-head, where (if fate was against them) they might see boat and husbands and sons—their whole wealth and their whole family—engulfed under their eyes; and (what I saw but once) a troop of neighbors forcing such an unfortunate homeward, and she squalling and battling in their midst, a figure scarcely human, a tragic Mænad.

These are things that I recall with interest; but what my memory dwells upon the most, I have been all this while withholding. It was a sport peculiar to the place, and indeed to a week or so of our two months' holiday there. Maybe it still flourishes in its native spot; for boys and their pastimes are swayed by periodic forces inscrutable to man; so that tops and marbles reappear in their due season, regular like the sun and moon; and the harmless art of knucklebones has seen the fall of the Roman empire and the rise of the United States. It may still flourish in its native spot, but nowhere else, I am persuaded; for I tried myself to introduce it on Tweedside, and was defeated lamentably; its charm being quite local, like a country wine that cannot be exported.

The idle manner of it was this:—

Toward the end of September, when school-time was drawing near and the nights were already black, we would begin to sally from our respective villas, each equipped with a tin bull's-eye lantern. The thing was so well known that it had worn a rut in the commerce of Great Britain; and the grocers, about the due time, began to garnish their windows with our particular brand of luminary. We wore them buckled to the waist upon a cricket belt, and over them, such was the rigor of the game, a buttoned top-coat. They smelled noisomely of blistered tin; they never burned aright, though they would always burn our fingers; their use was naught; the pleasure of them merely fanciful; and yet a boy with a bull's-eye under his top-coat asked for nothing more. The fishermen used lanterns about their boats, and it was from them, I suppose, that we had got the hint; but theirs were not bull's-eyes, nor did we ever play at being fishermen. The police carried them at their belts, and we had plainly copied them in that; yet we did not pretend to be policemen. Burglars, indeed, we may have had some haunting thoughts of; and we had certainly an eye to past ages when lanterns were more common, and to certain story-books in which we had found them to figure very largely. But take it for all in all, the pleasure of the thing was substantive; and to be a boy with a bull's-eye under his top-coat was good enough for us.

When two of these asses met, there would be an anxious "Have you got your lantern?" and a gratified "Yes!" That was the shibboleth, and very needful too; for, as it was the rule to keep our glory contained, none could recognize a lantern-bearer, unless (like the pole-cat) by the smell. Four or five would sometimes climb into the belly of a ten-man lugger, with nothing but the thwarts above them—for the cabin was usually locked, or choose out some hollow of the links where the wind might whistle overhead. There the coats would be unbuttoned and the bull's-eye discovered, and in the checkering glimmer, under the huge windy hall of the night, and cheered by a rich steam of toasting tinware, these fortunate gentlemen would crouch together in the cold sand of the links or on the scaly bilges of the fishing-boat, and delight themselves with inappropriate talk. Woe is me that I may not give some specimens—some of their foresights of life, or deep inquiries into the rudiments of man and nature, these were so fiery and so innocent, they were so richly silly, so romantically young. But the talk, at any rate, was but a condiment; and these gatherings themselves only accidents in the career of the lantern-bearer. The essence of this bliss was to walk by yourself in the black night; the slide shut, the top-coat buttoned; not a ray escaping, whether to conduct your footsteps or to make your glory public: a mere pillar of darkness in the dark; and all the while, deep down in the privacy of your fool's heart, to know you had a bull's-eye at your belt, and to exult and sing over the knowledge.

An Irish Garden [1]

By Katharine Tynan

Somewhere about 1868 my father acquired the lands and house of Whitehall, Clondalkin, where my later childhood and youth were to be spent. The house had once belonged to Curran,

[1] By permission of Devin-Adair Company, the authorized publishers.

the great Irish lawyer and patriot, whose daughter, Sarah, should have married Robert Emmet. It was a small cottage building with little windows under immense overhanging eaves of thatch and a hall door within a porch of green trellis. There was a very quaint little lawn in front in which grew an immense tree-peony, a fuschia as big, and a great many Portugal laurels and laurestinus. The cottage was flanked by a building of two stories. The lower story was the kitchen of the cottage. Its green door opened on a long strip of courtyard. There was a stone bench by the door, useful for many things.

Our first summer there was 1869, when we three children were there in charge of a nurse. The house had not yet been altered to accommodate a family. Of the two-story edifice only one-fourth belonged to us. My father's steward and his wife lived in half the lower story and the upper floor. What had been a door of communication was boarded up and filled in with a row of shelves.

Our kitchen was a true toy-kitchen. It was whitewashed and floored with red tiles. One little window with a deep sill looked down the strip of courtyard: another, exactly alike, looked into an orchard which, I think now, must have been a fairyland. There was a settle under one window on which a child could stand and read by the hour, her book laid open on the deep sill which propped her elbows when she would lean with her hands in her curls.

My mother had pantries full of china, beautiful old china for the most part, and that sent down for our use was a delicate embossed china with a pattern in grayish brown of all manner of seashells. The pieces stood on the little rows of shelves and they seem to me a part of the enchantment of the place. From the kitchen a door opened into the dining-room. Beyond that was a hall, from which three little bedrooms opened: beyond that a drawing-room, with a glass door leading into an old walled garden full of flowers and fruit. Close by the end gable of the house, a green paling atop of a low white wall overlooked the orchard, and there was a wicket gate to the orchard round the corner just out of sight.

It must have been one of the few great summers that come to Ireland. The cottage was wrapped up in monthly roses and woodbine—honeysuckle is the clover blossom in Ireland—fuschias, jessamine, and the hardy yellow Scotch rose. These put out tendrils and climbed the thatch. In one room a tendril had come through the window and boldly climbed a wall and spread, and no one had detached it.

In the orchard and the garden the low fruit-trees stood thick. They were mainly apple-trees. Three sorts I keep in my memory. One was the Irish peach, of which there were several. A little low, gnarled one which had planted itself among the flower-beds at some prehistoric period is in my mind as though it had life. Its fruit ripened first and it bore well. The apples, though they were small, were of a delicious flavor. Long after the peach-apples were done there was a tree hanging over our summer-house, the fruit of which yellowed with the autumn leaves and were so many honey morsels. There was a third tree with apples of a pale green, the sides broadly ribbed and mottled with spots. I have no name for these delights, and a tragedy befell—for in the autumn following that summer the trees were thinned, and the most beautiful were cut down. No one thought of consulting the children, who had the best knowledge of good and bad fruit after all.

Fortunately the little tree in the flower-beds survived and, so far as I know, still survives. Spanish iris clustered about its feet, with forget-me-nots and wall-flowers and narcissi, with masses of pansies. The beds with their box borders made a most intricate pattern, all the tiny walks leading towards the summer-house. There was a deal of greenery, as there always is in an Irish garden: and when the lilies sprang up every July they looked like rows of young angels.

Was it in '68 or was it in '69? Whatever year it was it was the great summer. Think of a pack of children who had lived in the town and only had the country by snatches turned loose a whole summer in this place packed with old-fashioned delights.

The little rooms were very flowery. Because we were on the ground floor perhaps, with only a nurse in charge, we had our windows shuttered of nights. A long slit of light used to come between the shutters in the golden mornings, suffusing the room with a green and golden light.

For a time we had a perilous delight, for a bull grazed in the orchard and would sometimes lift his head to roar quite at the window-pane. You can imagine the delighted terror of the child who lay a-bed, the formidable beast only separated from her by a thin sheet of glass: and what a joy it was to peep through the slit in the shutters at the immense head with its splendid curls, knowing one's self unseen, but not unapprehended, for the bull would occasionally paw the earth as though scenting an enemy, and utter a roar like thunder.

That summer we learned all the country delights, having only known them before by snatches. There was a big farm-yard and a hay-yard or rick-yard. The rick-yard is always associated in my mind with Hans Andersen's *Ugly Duckling*, which I must have read at the time. I always imagined the Ugly Duckling's mother sitting hatching her eggs under the great docks in the rick-yard. Side by side with it ran the very pond where the Ugly Duckling met with one of his most terrifying adventures. The pond was much overgrown and deep enough to make it an adventure to reach the islet in the midst, on which a water-hen lived and reared her brood. On a summer day when all was still you would see the little ones taking to the water, just emerged from the egg, their brothers and sisters yet perhaps in the eggs only chipping beneath the mother's breast.

There too was a well, clear and cool, which had the reputation of never drying up even in the hottest summer. It was cool and dark under its hood of stone over which wet lichens and water-weeds had grown. It smelt of streams and freshness, a mirage for London in the hot days. We used to dip in a jug or pail and bring up little silvery minnows—"pinkeens" we called them—swimming round and round in the cool pure water. The well was fed from the mountains and the water chattered over beds of jewels in all the ditches. It was always summer there in my thoughts of it. The snail in his shell hanging on the thorn had a most wonderful house of opal iridescence. There were little blue moths, which I have never seen in England, flying about among the flowers, and black or brown butterflies with blotches of crimson on their wings. There must have been autumn though, for I remember the crab-apples in the hedgerows, a fairy fruit for beauty, and the quickes-berries hanging like drops of blood. I remember the loneliness of autumnal fields after the reaping was over, the gathering of blackberries and mushrooms, the pleasant terror of the Moat, which was a fairy rath, in the heart of it a dry quarry where the biggest and juiciest black-berries grew. Gathering them one never liked to be far from one's companions, lest harm befell. In the evening when it was dark it was pleasant to steal out and see the darkness of the Moat at a distance: and when the misted harvest moon rose above it we thought it was a fairy fire and it afforded us a marvel for many days to come. Then there were the ripe apples, so to be sure it must have been autumn sometime.

Every Sunday morning our excellent nurse trailed the whole family off to Mass. We used to take a short cut, being always rather pressed for time, across a field in which grazed the bull— his name was Young Leviathan, and he deserved it—that bellowed at our ears. There must have been seven or eight children for the intrepid woman to convey unhurt. We were happy when the bull grazed in a remote corner from the pathway. What a scurry it used to be! There was a gate leading from the field on the road, which was padlocked: and the gap by which we emerged had a steep descent. The bull usually discovered us before we were clear. I have a vivid memory of his charge as I tumbled down the steep ditch. That was the occasion, I think, on which another child lost her shoe, leaving it to the tender mercies of the bull. We used to return by a safe detour, which was slower and less exciting. I have often wondered since at the hardihood of that nurse.

The village "innocent" used sometimes to put in his foolish head terrifying us at our games. He looked like Smike in the Hablot K. Browne illustrations to *Nicholas Nickleby* and he had a mordant wit. He made remarks about your personal appear-ance unless you were very civil. He and his kind have for the greater part disappeared or been gathered into asylums. Not all. Back again in Ireland I meet a God's fool from time to time as I walk the country lanes, a ruddy-faced, weather-beaten man who talks incessantly with a running laugh between the speech. Sometimes his talk is unintelligible—but again it is of the immortality of the soul. "The Kingdom of Heaven's within you. The soul's its own place and can make Heaven or Hell. The soul or the mind: it's all the same. But where does the soul go when it's out of the body—tell me that."

He sums up Irish intolerance of disagreement in a pregnant phrase. "Over there," he says, waving his hand across the Irish Sea, "you can say what you like. But here they'd knock the gob off you."

That autumn after the golden summer I had my first intimate experience of death. We had gone back to town and then hurriedly returned to the country because of the illness of the elder sister just home from the convent school and only awaiting impatiently the time when she might return to its novitiate. It was October then and the country was in ruins—only a few late apples on the trees and the wind and the rain bringing down the last leaves. That eldest sister was my first love. I thought her the most wonderful creature. Something of the innocency and fragrance of the convent hung about her, making her elusive, saint-like. She had brought home her sheaves, among them a glass-topped table painted with flowers behind which silver foil gave depths of light to the colors. I hung over that table entranced. She had her drawings—and I was not critical. Various triumphs of needlework in the shape of cushions, anti-macassars, tea-cosies, and the like, dazzled me. She sang "The Bridge," words by Longfellow, and my heart wept tears as I listened. I am not sure that it does not weep now. I had to hide behind window curtains to conceal my agitation when she sang.

She was just a brief, lovely vision. I have no memory of her at all before that vacation. She knew I adored her and she petted me. She let me see just a glimpse of her supernatural secret. It made me determined to be a nun, and the determination lasted for a good dozen years afterwards. There was something

Heavenly in the vision, something of long convent corridors, dazzlingly clean, flooded with light and air, sweet with the smell of lilies and a thought of incense, of little convent cells naked and pure, of convent gardens, places where

> "The Brides of Christ
> Lie hid, emparadised."

I was allowed to wait on her the first day of her illness, and she must have been a little delirious, for she talked of strange things and then apologized gently. How I loved to be her servant, her slave!

Then we were back in the country again and it was sad. I lived with my nose in a book. Sometimes my father came with a disturbed face. There was a talk of a crisis. "Next Tuesday about will be the crisis. Till after that we cannot hope for good tidings."

I read and read incessantly. The nurse, who was a somewhat harassing person, let me be. I suppose that she was glad that one of us should be off her hands. I was reading *Picciola, the Prison Flower,* in my favorite place for reading now that the wet autumn had come, kneeling on a table in front of one of the deep-set little windows of the cottage, on the sill of which rested my open book and my elbows. Below the window was the stone bench upon which the beggars used to take a seat, or the tinker when he mended our pots and pans. There I had sat and shelled peas for a summer's day dinner, and had eaten the peas as I shelled them, giving up only a basket of empty pods to my justly enraged nurse.

There came a father, with a more disturbed face than ever, working as we looked at him, his voice tangled in his throat. "Mary is dead," he said, and rushed away into the rain. Desolation swept my soul for a space. I do not know how long. Presently, with a sensation of guilt, I returned to the reading of *Picciola, the Prison Flower.* Even for death a book did not fail of comfortable distraction in those days when Heaven was a vision of story-books to be read incessantly without any troublesome elder intervening.

DISTRICT THIRTEEN [1]

By Robert P. Tristram Coffin

The plains of Troy may lie hidden under a very dull name.
Hissarlik and District Thirteen. I suppose there must be some
tens of thousands of buildings as like the country schoolhouse
where I first met the Muses as peas in a pod. With the rows
of sculptured children for Elizabethan tombs, they were turned
out all alike. Red, square, two windows to a side, one room, with
an airtight so placed that no single radiation of heat should be
wasted in the smoke as it traversed the length of the room
through the pipe to the back, a single door, a dark corridor
across the front with cordwood and pegs for hats and coats.
The first principles of architecture and the last—lintel, walls,
and a roof as innocent of flourishes as New England charity.
Yet I and others, in this schoolhouse and its companion pieces,
found it a place like a temple, a house of awe; and years afterward we knew that Beauty had sat there knee to our knees and
had bent over a desk so carved and notched that the pen stumbled in the epigraphy of forgotten grandsires.

Our forbears, who made it their hearty life work to raise boys
by the baker's dozen so that there should be hands enough to
fence in all their acres with stonewalls, ran against the Gospel
teaching and the Sermon on the Mount. For they scattered the
seedlings of their loins on hard places among the stones. They
cut off a scant acre of ledges and junipers and said in their
saving hearts, "There's the place for the schoolhouse." Their
potatoes had to have dark soil to grow in; but their sons and
their daughters could do with rocks that the crows used to crack
their cockle shells and clams upon. And the miracle was that
the boys with the skim-milk eyes and the girls with the thin and
wistful hair sent their roots down into these waste places and
brought forth yields a thousand fold. This crop turned out
the bumper one. New England's chief export became, not ice,

[1] From *The North American Review,* May 1928. By the kind permission of the author and of the editor.

not hay, not potatoes, but men. Most of the younger States of the Union can testify to the fact that the New England seed is the seed that loves rock best. It thrives on adversity. It is a good thing to have granite bred into the backbone.

The granite around my own schoolhouse was as fine a place for glory as any walls of Troy. It heaved itself aloft into galleons of the Caribbees with a scrub pine or two for masts to rig and man. It was convenient to crack boiled eggs on in the luncheon hour. The taste of boiled eggs to this day makes me taste granite. I should like a physicist to explain to me why eggs that had awaited one through a long forenoon of Spencerian flourishes and incipient fractions should get to resemble nuggets of granite when one came to open and eat. We climbed our ledges with Montcalm in white silk breeches and all the grenadiers of great France drawn up to expect us. It didn't matter to us that Montcalm had freckles so thick that you couldn't put a pin down, and knickers that were stayed at the seat with twine. I doubt if Wolfe's heart ever came so up into his throat as ours when we scaled the cliff to win another continent for the race of the blue-eyed.

The ledge taught us, too, to keep our feet in wrestling. It was no easy mat for the falling. I have seen my yellow hair— worn in hateful ringlets which my mother was loath to see go —scattered about the fissures of rock like the armor of the Achæans when Hector was in flower. But my adversary learned to his regret, after the handholds on my head had given way at their roots, that ears are a more stable grip than hair. His ears were longer than mine, and they served well as handles to a head that saw stars before I was through. Homer can sing of fighters who longed to eat out the hearts of foemen, and Cooper can cry of Redskins who bit the dust; but no man of letters ancient or new has ever put into words the venom we had rankling in our muscles and the hate that glowed like pine coals in us when we stood up big toes to big toes with boys whom we liked and walked home with and fought over again some battle resurrected from the pages of books. War is in us from the cradle. And there are worse things than war. The Feudal

System, Chivalric Love, Thermopylæ, and the race called Marathon, have come out of battle and the taste of blood. It is not all widows weeping!

Nor did we subsist entirely upon the rocks that humped their spines through the world around our schoolhouse. We held all the country for miles around in fee. It was mostly run-out farms with houses that had grown back into nature, through whose paneless sashes the blue-brown swallows wheeled. The swallows reared their young on mantels which had the classic grace of Adam and the spaciousness of Anne's day three thousand miles from England. Lilacs bivouacked by green cellars where houses had gone the way of last year's leaves. Elder hedges ran through fields full of Queen Anne's lace and black-eyed Susans. In the tangles of birch and maple, stonewalls everywhere. The arbutus, the flower that brings back Christ among the lingering northern snows, trailed the land with miles of fragrance. Lady-slippers and bird-on-the-wing. Nature had taken back this old cradle of men; she rocked her shyer children here. In the heat of our games we came upon fawns whose wide round eyes mooned upon us, and bucks with many points on their antlers marched across our meadows with their heads held high and their does behind them.

Our games were cut to the country. They led us afar through swamps and over and under walls. "Wolf" was the king of games. Two hunters bore brooms for guns, and the rest of us scattered into all manner of woods before them. When a wolf was touched by the broom, he must stand dead until a comrade freed him with another touch. I have stood thus with many a long sunny afternoon washing around me and the knowledge that history, which I loved best of all books, was on the dock back at the schoolhouse. Partridges grew bold and eyed me, and squirrels worked themselves into a lather of curiosity above me; but I kept my honor bright and moved not. It took a deal of time to school new teachers in the tenets of honor. Often they used the rod upon boys who were patterns of loyalty and sportsmen extraordinary. "Hare and hounds" is a fine game, I know, but it lacks the charm of our "wolf." We travelled with our hearts in our temples, each for himself and all of us to the twenty-four corners of the sky. It took a Daniel Boone in knee breeches to run us all down separately. I am glad to say that there was no coddling of the weaker sex among us. Our sisters were Amazons that outfooted the best that warmed breeches with flying legs. They climbed as tall trees and barked their shins on walls as high. And our best teachers, even though they went in skirts, ran their way home to our hearts and carried cards of safety pins for binding up our wounds and theirs.

Some of our games we made up for ourselves out of whole cloth. "Tolly over the schoolhouse" was such a one. We chose sides and distributed ourselves along the two sides of the building. Back and forth between us over the ridgepole went an erratic ball that one had to catch before it hit the ground. Such ballistic madness as lay in that ball's flight is hard to conceive. You were on your bruised knees, and the ball was elsewhere. Parents miles away could hear the school when the sphere put in an appearance on the rim of the Andes. The best players knew how to score surely with a volley so high that the ball did not touch the roof on its downward swoop until it was a foot from the eaves. As you can well imagine, the most important player in this game was the umpire. He stood at the schoolhouse's end so that he could see both sides and give his decisions. He needed to be a cross between a Solomon and a John L. Sullivan, for quite the hardest bruises often came his way when his judgment slipped. The teachers, once they were trained, were the wisest choice here.

Then there was "plunder," another game of sides in which each tried to capture a handkerchief behind the line of combat without being seized and "frozen" until freed by his own men. This was, next to "wolf," the hardest on our mothers. One sometimes got the handkerchief at the loss of his corduroy breeches. All the ninety and nine vintages of "tag" we had, and "blind man's buff," in which we once brought down the whole length of the overhead stovepipe, for rainy days. Another favorite was again an invention of our own. Some of us had seen in town a game of baseball played without catching on any too well to the basic principles. Baseball was not a game for widely separated farmers' children with uncertain fields to disport themselves upon. So our sport of bat-and-ball was a queer combination of cricket and baseball, with mayhem thrown in as a spice. We had a pitcher and bases; but the bat was a paddle, and the striker who tipped the ball even slightly was greeted with the cry, "Tick, two more!" Any sort of pitch, grounded or overhead, was legal tender, provided one could reach it by three steps to either side or a moderately high jump into the air. An expert at leaping and plunging could stay at bat for the afternoon. If he ever did hit the ball any distance whatever, backwards or forwards, he had to run out to a base and back and take his chances of mortality by acting as a target for the lucky boy who retrieved the ball and did his level best to "bore" him in transit. A "boring" meant an out, and often it was more literal than that; water might have to be applied to a spouting nose. The crippled cared for, each man in the field moved up one place. There was only one batter at a time. I was an expert at the game, in all modesty I say it; for my father made me a bat that was light as goose down and wide enough to comb everything out of the earth or air. It was my pride until the dismal day when Albert, the school featherbrain, got hold of it to assault an innocent toad that we had put into his jaws when he was silly enough to open his mouth and close his eyes to get something—which he so sorely needed—to make him wise.

Games, though, were not the making of our school. The scholars were that. I do not believe there has ever been brought together under one roof more boys with the Devil in them all bigger than a woodchuck, as our parents would say. Albert comes first easily. In intellect he was "small potatoes and few in a hill." That New England adage hits the nail exactly. But Albert was the prince of our school. Shakespeare knew him. He called him now Falstaff, now Touchstone, now Feste. Shakespeare knew that clownishness is one of the necessary things that make the world wag on its merry way between rather dubious and forbidding stars. Fools may be cruel jests of nature; but life, with its hawks and boys, has a splendor in its cruelty. And

Albert had a royal good time with his light head. He was proud of his distinction of being the one who would be forced to try the skim ice of the roadside pool first. He would rather pluck out his heart than take a dare. So he immersed himself up to the elbows in the evil morass of a barnyard when we dared him to trust himself upon the crust of chaff that coated it. No windows that the teacher could open that afternoon could purge away the memory of his folly. He was such a one as could make even a Monday morning rosy. He it was who must ride to the top of the flagpole in a bottomless basket; and it took the visiting school superintendent, whom I met years after man to man in the dewy *Odyssey*, to shin up, Jovian beard and all, and unlash the rope we had secured on high, and let our school clown down.

Indoors everybody egged Albert on till the daily patience of the teacher was broken and the command rang out, "Albert, pass into the corridor!" The rest was rawhide. The darkness of the antechamber was a fit usher for retribution. Albert would clench his fists, but he got only welted knuckles for his pains. Once, though, he turned the tables on us. Alone in the hall he gorged himself upon all the sweeter tidbits in our lunchboxes there, and, sated, ran off home. At whipping times he could command great gushes of tears. It was a physical charm he had along with an ability to make his ears move independently and in unison, like those of a donkey, until the room shook with mirth. A licking over, the sun came out again behind his homely face, and he looked about for new folly to kick his heels at. Such brains as he had ran down into his heels mostly, and it took a smart horse to outstrip him when, lunchbox in hand, he flew each morning schoolwards to the inevitable whippings that awaited him. The Lord has given few of His children such capacity for running thus cheerfully to the daily disasters that life turns out to be. And in these darkly enlightened days society has taken to segregating such children as Albert from their more regular and drabber brethren; and so some of the ancient sunshine has gone from the world.

The school had its villain, too. He was the son, as it so often runs, of a pillar and deacon of the country church and the warden of the school. He felt his father's position so heavily that he cut the birch rods for our corduroys. He stood in strongly with those teachers who came to the school with the preconception that they were lion tamers. He it was who told the wielder of authority how we had come two hours early and thrown stones with painstaking labor into the chimney top until we had clogged the flue above the stovepipe vent. He it was who proposed the plan for a half hour "nooning" in place of our hour recess, which was all too short as it was for the games we had to play. But it turned out that his own tail wore out the rods he had cut for ours. There were such things as after hours when teachers were gone home to their week's boarding place, and justice came into her own. His father could not always be coming to fetch him safe home behind his team of bays. Some days it rained.

One boy, who stood at the opposite pole of the universe from our tattletale, was all whipcord and blue steel. He could whip any two of us together, and he did so. And he could stand by one and keep the faith in the hour when the arch of heaven tottered. For all his strength, strange shynesses and reticences were in him when he stood apart from us on the windy skylines of our days, like the king that he was. So Hector must have walked on the Trojan walls. His nature was as square and as full of possibilities of comfort as a Maine farmhouse. No meanness of bullying ever went unpunished by him. Perhaps he was the finest teacher we were ever to have.

There were girls as well as boys to build up our glory. One had a nose that made me, for some unknown reason, think of morning-glories. But I kept that thought carefully to myself. She once put her arm across my shoulders as we walked the ruts to school. I liked it at the time; but some prying eyes were open, and it took me a year to live down that blunder of hers. Another girl was plump and fresh as a pan of new biscuits. Her lunchbox showed the reason. It must have snowed meat and drink in her home as it did in the house of Chaucer's Franklin. Another girl was as wild as a thistle and as hard to handle; she led the boys into building a fire in May that, transported by the teacher into our Gargantuan stove, we had to sit close over until our very souls perspired.

All of us were full of a wiry clannishness that has stood the older stock of America in good stead, a temper old as Anglo-Saxon England and alive in the town meetings of New England to this day. Independence and democracy were in us, too, I think. It was dangerous for one of us to come to school too conscious of new clothes or special possessions. I was unwise enough once to strut like a young rooster in the striped sweater which my father, like Joseph's, had put upon me in his love. My garment came to great grief. Full of exuberance, we were full of a grim reserve and silent loyalties. Barring Albert, the boys could take the bitterest punishment without flinching and with the mask of a smile.

We could act like young Vandals; yet when it came right down to the business of books, I think we loved them as most of us have not loved them since. We had to work hard at home, most of us; we had to walk miles for our learning; we worked at the desks as we worked at the sawhorse. And in that little house on the hungry half acre we met Jason and Arthur, Hercules and Thor, the granite-faced men of Hawthorne's tales and the hard-headed builders of our own country; and the narrow fields we lived in stretched out to meet a bigger world that some of us were going to walk some day, and a world that only poets and dreamers have ever set foot upon. The two miles of pine-woods and the bay I had to cross each night were peopled for me with folk long dust on the other side of the earth, with folk who had never lived in these fields where men are so quick to grow old and roses to fall. Demigods and men who have made the history books seemed close enough then to come upon in the next thicket. I know that the teaching we had was home-spun. Our morning's music might often be only a camp-meeting hymn of redemption and bare grace. But we sang it like the Hallelujah Chorus from Handel.

Looking back, I can see as clear as if set in crystal the gentians that came out with blue lace in the September fields to call us back to the cracked doorstep and the battered pail of water for our refreshment and the one long-handled dipper for us all. And I know now that the dogeared books that smelled like learning to us *were* learning. It has been my good fortune to read in famous houses of learning since; but I have never known, even in Duke Humfrey's room in the Bodleian, such an edge on my appetite for books as in that one-room schoolhouse where boys sat on patches and read so hard that they broke the backs of their books. The last flowers of the year, the wistful, faded asters, half buried the door. Hungry flowers. . . . Perhaps we were like them. Hunger can be a thing precious beyond all other things.

EXERCISES

1. Study carefully the third sentence in "The Lantern Bearers," its construction and its diction. By what means does Stevenson make his "easterly fisher village" stand out? This sentence makes a splendid model for a sentence theme. Choose some place which you know and like and describe it in one sentence, modelled carefully on this one. This is a good class-room exercise, twenty minutes for writing, the rest of the time for comparison and criticism.

2. The first two paragraphs in "The Lantern Bearers" contain some of the best diction in Stevenson. List the most effective adjectives. How many of them are distinct sense impressions? How many suggested' or implied sense impressions? Compare these adjectives with those in the paragraphs from "A Gossip on Romance" on pages 500 ff.

3. Stevenson is famous for his descriptions of wind. Study all references to wind in this selection. Then read his fine essay, written while he was yet but a boy and called "On the Enjoyment of Unpleasant Places," and compare the wind descriptions in both essays.

4. Do you think Stevenson's style in "The Lantern Bearers" especially well suited to reminiscence? Criticize it, *pro* and *con.*

5. Study Miss Tynan's essay for color, for other detail.

6. What services do the classical allusions in "District Thirteen" perform? You ought to be able to find at least three distinct contributions. Do the references to American history perform the same?

7. What sentences in "District Thirteen" deal more with the evaluation of experience than with experience itself?

8. Read "Sabrina Fair" from Henry W. Nevinson's *Between the Acts*. Then read it a second time to trace through it the sentences and phrases which give it unity of effect.

9. Read Stevenson's "Memoirs of an Islet" from *Memories and Portraits*. How does the reminiscent style here differ from that of "The Lantern Bearers"? Does it enable you to visualize more clearly. If so, why?

SUGGESTED READINGS

Anonymous, "The Passing of Emily Ruggles's," Tanner, *Essays and Essay Writing,* Little, Brown, Boston.

Grahame, Kenneth, *The Golden Age,* Dodd, Mead, New York. *Dream Days,* Dodd, Mead, New York.

Hudson, W. H., "My New Home," Chapter II, and "My Visit to Buenos Ayres," Chapter VII from *Far Away and Long Ago,* E. P. Dutton, New York. "Wind, Wave, and Spirit," Chapter V, from *Afoot in England,* E. P. Dutton, New York.

Lynahan, Margaret, "Antiques," *The Commonweal,* September 12, 1928.

McFee, William, *Harbours of Memory,* Doubleday, Doran, New York.

Middleton, Richard, "On Going to Bed" from *The Day Before Yesterday,* T. Fisher Unwin, Ltd., London.

Nevinson, Henry W., "Sabrina Fair" from *Between the Acts,* E. P. Dutton, New York.

Price, Lucien, "Olympians in Homespun," *The Atlantic Monthly,* April, 1926. "Hardscrabble Hellas," *The Atlantic Monthly,* February, 1927.

Repplier, Agnes, *In Convent Days,* Houghton Mifflin, Boston.

Riesenberg, Felix, *Vignettes of the Sea,* Harcourt, Brace, New York.

Russell, George W. (A.E.), "Retrospect" from *The Candle of Vision,* Macmillan, New York.

Stevenson, Robert Louis, "Memoirs of an Islet," "The Manse," and "Some College Memories" from *Memories and Portraits,* Scribner's, New York.

Wiggin, Kate Douglas, *My Garden of Memory,* Houghton Mifflin, Boston.

CHAPTER III

The Reminiscent Incident

Although reminiscence is often narrative in form, one, perhaps oddly, seldom thinks of it as narration. The reason for this is not easy to spot. It may lie in the fact that, since the happenings of the reminiscence are so toned and shadowed by the memory and the sentiment of the writer, their dramatic qualities are diminished, at least as drama. Or it may be that in a reminiscence the emphasis is usually placed on the customary occurrences of a given place or period rather than on any one single occurrence which took place at a specific time. At all events, it is true that rarely in a reminiscence is any one happening, no matter how interesting it may be, accorded the space or the treatment it may well deserve.

In every life there are some incidents too memorable to be neglected and yet too significant to share curtailed space with a score of lesser matters. These, springing as it were from the quiet background of reminiscence, stand out against that background by the very strength of their own value in our experience. By them and through them we became aware of things we had not known before; or we were seized with new and sudden fears; or we were made conscious of a swift and painful change in mood or in viewpoint. They taught us, all unconscious, how to evaluate our own experience in terms of the larger and perennial experiences of life. They were the generous providers of "growing pains" for our minds and our emotions.

It is interesting to try to relate such incidents as these, and we are especially fortunate in the three models which we are privileged to reprint. There are no better examples of reminiscent incident to be found. The first step, before you begin to search your past for significant occurrences, is to read, and read carefully, all three.

Once having done this, you will have arrived at certain suggestive conclusions:

1. Each incident is highly centralized by the very force of its own material; that is, there is no need for any unifying device as in the reminiscence.

2. Introductions are avoided. The author begins as directly as possible with the incident itself.

3. There is no possible place here for matter which does not bear on the incident at hand. The attention and interest of the reader must be kept, as it were, in motion.

4. Although detail and impression are by no means neglected (witness particularly "The Secret Drawer") they exist not for their own sake so much as for the *single effect* which the author wishes to achieve. Thus in Kenneth Grahame's incident the "twist of tarry string," appealing as it is in its concreteness of detail and impression, is more appealing in its contribution to the final effect.

5. Such incidents as these are really *expository* in result even although they are largely narrative in method. One might not go far wrong, in fact, in insisting that they are essays. Certainly each of them attempts, or *essays,* to get across to the reader by means of narrative a far larger thing than just an incident. The incident, indeed, is only a key. The boy, standing by the secret drawer, was suddenly faced by the mystery of time, before which tiny worldly possessions became all at once of no account. Surely to show this sudden and stupendous discovery by a child is Mr. Grahame's aim in writing the incident. The narrative is but a means to an end. The same thing is true of W. H. Hudson's "The Death of an Old Dog." The paroxysm of terror which seized the little boy at Mr. Trigg's words, the hours of anxiety that followed, and at last the release from a prison of torture— these are what the author wants us to feel. Old Cæsar's death is again but the means to an end. "Bibles at Hell Gate" would seem upon first reading to be an exception, but it is really not one at all. Humorous and light as is the incident, we lose the whole

point if we read it only *as* an incident. It is first and foremost a study of contrasts, as its very title indicates. Imagine the pious and rather stupid ladies who donated the Bibles; visualize their consternation at the thought of such a gift lying twenty years below the water line; get the absurdity of expecting such a parcel of boys, "tough as hell," to read the Bible during their hours off; and finally glimpse the inimitable picture of the fleet "drifting in single column towards Hell Gate"! The narrative is delightful enough; but the effect which it produces lingers far longer in the mind as an appreciative and whimsical commentary on two widely divergent types of human nature.

The source for the reminiscent incident best lies in your own experience. There are few children who have not been touched by the great realities of death, of time, of change in some such way as were Kenneth Grahame and W. H. Hudson when they were young; there are fewer who have not experienced some occasion or some happening which opened their eyes and sharpened their perceptions in regard to lesser but more imminent matters of everyday concern. Nor must the child necessarily have felt the real significance of the occurrence or glimpsed its import. Years may be needed for that. As librarian on the old *St. Mary's*, Mr. Riesenberg doubtless did not realize the full character of the incident he was later to relate. What struck him then as rather an ironic joke from which he was saved only by luck developed as years went by its complete stature of absurdity and humor. Such may well have been the case with you.

THE DEATH OF AN OLD DOG [1]

By W. H. Hudson

When recalling the impressions and experiences of that most eventful sixth year, the one incident which looks biggest in memory, at all events in the last half of that year, is the death of Cæsar. There is nothing in the past I can remember so well:

[1] From *Far Away and Long Ago*. By the kind permission of E. P. Dutton & Company.

it was indeed the most important event of my childhood—the first thing in a young life which brought the eternal note of sadness in.

It was in the early spring, about the middle of August, and I can even remember that it was windy weather and bitterly cold for the time of year, when the old dog was approaching his end.

Cæsar was an old valued dog, although of no superior breed: he was just an ordinary dog of the country, short-haired, with long legs and a blunt muzzle. The ordinary dog or native cur was about the size of a Scotch collie; Cæsar was quite a third larger, and it was said of him that he was as much above all other dogs of the house, numbering about twelve or fourteen, in intelligence and courage as in size. Naturally, he was the leader and master of the whole pack, and when he got up with an awful growl, baring his big teeth, and hurled himself on the others to chastise them for quarrelling or any other infringement of dog law, they took it lying down. He was a black dog, now in his old age sprinkled with white hairs all over his body, the face and legs having gone quite grey. Cæsar in a rage, or on guard at night, or when driving cattle in from the plains, was a terrible being; with us children he was mild-tempered and patient, allowing us to ride on his back, just like old Pechicho the sheep-dog, described in the first chapter. Now, in his decline, he grew irritable and surly, and ceased to be our playmate. The last two or three months of his life were very sad, and when it troubled us to see him so gaunt, with his big ribs protruding from his sides, to watch his twitchings when he dozed, groaning and wheezing the while, and marked, too, how painfully he struggled to get up on his feet, we wanted to know why it was so —why we could not give him something to make him well? For answer they would open his great mouth to show us his teeth— the big blunt canines and old molars worn down to stumps. Old age was what ailed him—he was thirteen years old, and that did verily seem to me a great age, for I was not half that, yet it seemed to me that I had been a very, very long time in the world.

No one dreamed of such a thing as putting an end to him—

no hint of such a thing was ever spoken. It was not the custom in that country to shoot an old dog because he was past work. I remember his last day, and how often we came to look at him and tried to comfort him with warm rugs and the offer of food and drink where he was lying in a sheltered place, no longer able to stand up. And that night he died: we knew it as soon as we were up in the morning. Then, after breakfast, during which we had been very solemn and quiet, our schoolmaster said: "We must bury him to-day—at twelve o'clock, when I am free, will be the best time; the boys can come with me, and old John can bring his spade." This announcement greatly excited us, for we had never seen a dog buried, and had never even heard of such a thing having ever been done.

About noon that day old Cæsar, dead and stiff, was taken by one of the workmen to a green open spot among the old peach trees, where his grave had already been dug. We followed our schoolmaster and watched while the body was lowered and the red earth shovelled in. The grave was deep, and Mr. Trigg assisted in filling it, puffing very much over the task and stopping at intervals to mop his face with his coloured cotton handkerchief.

Then, when all was done, while we were still standing silently around, it came into Mr. Trigg's mind to improve the occasion. Assuming his schoolroom expression he looked round at us and said solemnly: "That's the end. Every dog has his day and so has every man; and the end is the same for both. We die like old Cæsar, and are put into the ground and have the earth shovelled over us."

Now these simple, common words affected me more than any other words I have heard in my life. They pierced me to the heart. I had heard something terrible—too terrible to think of, incredible—and yet—and yet if it was not so, why had he said it? Was it because he hated us, just because we were children and he had to teach us our lessons, and wanted to torture us? Alas! no, I could not believe that! Was this, then, the horrible fate that awaited us all? I had heard of death—I knew there was such a thing; I knew that all animals had to die, also that some men died. For how could any one, even a child in its sixth year, overlook such a fact, especially in the country of my birth—a land of battle, murder, and sudden death? I had not forgotten the young man tied to the post in the barn who had killed some one, and would perhaps, I had been told, be killed himself as a punishment. I knew, in fact, that there was good and evil in the world, good and bad men, and the bad men—murderers, thieves, and liars—would all have to die, just like animals; but that there was any life after death I did not know. All the others, myself and my own people included, were good and would never taste death. How it came about that I had got no further in my system or philosophy of life I cannot say; I can only suppose that my mother had not yet begun to give me instruction in such matters on account of my tender years, or else that she had done so and that I had understood it in my own way. Yet, as I discovered later, she was a religious woman, and from infancy I had been taught to kneel and say a little prayer each evening: "Now I lay me down to sleep, I pray the Lord my soul to keep"; but who the Lord was or what my soul was I had no idea. It was just a pretty little way of saying in rhyme that I was going to bed. My world was a purely material one, and a most wonderful world it was, but how I came to be in it I didn't know; I only knew (or imagined) that I would be in it always, seeing new and strange things every day, and never, never get tired of it. In literature it is only in Vaughan, Traherne, and other mystics, that I find any adequate expression of that perpetual rapturous delight in nature and my own existence which I experienced at that period.

And now these never-to-be-forgotten words spoken over the grave of our old dog had come to awaken me from that beautiful dream of perpetual joy!

When I recall this event I am less astonished at my ignorance than at the intensity of the feeling I experienced, the terrible darkness it brought on so young a mind. The child's mind we think, and in fact know, is like that of the lower animals; or if higher than the animal mind, it is not so high as that of the simplest savage. He cannot concentrate his thought—he cannot think at all; his consciousness is in its dawn; he revels in colours, in odours, is thrilled by touch and taste and sound, and is like a well-nourished pup or kitten at play on a green turf in the sunshine. This being so, one would have thought that the pain of the revelation I had received would have quickly vanished—that the vivid impressions of external things would have blotted it out and restored the harmony. But it was not so; the pain continued and increased until it was no longer to be borne; then I sought my mother, first watching until she was alone in her room. Yet when with her I feared to speak lest with a word she should confirm the dreadful tidings. Looking down, she all at once became alarmed at the sight of my face, and began to question me. Then, struggling against my tears, I told her of the words which had been spoken at the old dog's burial, and asked her if it was true, if I—if she—if all of us had to die and be buried in the ground? She replied that it was not wholly true; it was only true in a way, since our bodies had to die and be buried in the earth, but we had an immortal part which could not die. It was true that old Cæsar had been a good, faithful dog, and felt and understood things almost like a human being, and most persons believed that when a dog died he died wholly and had no after-life. We could not know that; some very great, good men had thought differently; they believed that the animals, like us, would live again. That was also her belief— her strong hope; but we could not know for certain, because it had been hidden from us. For ourselves, we knew that we could not really die, because God Himself, who made us and all things, had told us so, and His promise of eternal life had been handed down to us in His Book—in the Bible.

To all this and much more I listened trembling, with a fearful interest, and when I had once grasped the idea that death when it came to me, as it must, would leave me alive after all—that, as she explained, the part of me that really mattered, the myself, the I am I, which knew and considered things, would never perish, I experienced a sudden immense relief. When I went out from her side again I wanted to run and jump for joy and cleave the air like a bird. For I had been in prison and had suffered torture, and was now free again—death would not destroy me!

BIBLES AT HELL GATE [1]

By Felix Riesenberg

Schoolships (and what finer place for a school than on board a ship?) have had a rather bad name in days past on this little island of Manhattan. Very old citizens may remember the *Mercury,* filled with really bad boys. This old hulk for many years cast a shadow of reproach over the schoolship *St. Mary's,* on which the New York Nautical School began its great career in 1875. People, even as far along as 1896, referred to the old *St. Mary's* as a reform school.

But any school worthy of the name must be somewhat of a reform school, of character and perhaps also of ideas. The *St. Mary's,* a wooden sloop of war, ship rigged, built at Washington in 1844, of live oak framing and white oak planking, fastened with mighty bolts and spikes of red copper, had wrought into her ribs and keel a strength and durability unknown to the steel ships of to-day. This old craft housed a hundred boys, more or less bad, many from the crowded slums, and a large proportion from the respectable comfort of plain homes. She even held a few wild spirits cast off, or run away, from luxurious moorings. Let us admit that the old ship was a tough packet.

Built as a slave chaser, her underbody had the sharp lines of a yacht. Her copper sheathing, her tall spars, her great spread of sail, filled the youth upon her clean white decks with a spirit of romantic abandon that obtuse persons often interpreted as vicious. Of course there were a great many fights on board, conducted regularly forward of the mast. Loose talk always led to blows. There was very little disturbance in the way of vocal bickering under this system. But the stern rule on board gave the hard-fisted youth an exaggerated air of piratical importance. They were tough as hell and liked to show it.

Something must be done to save these boys. It was the duty

[1] From *Vignettes of the Sea.* By permission of Harcourt, Brace and Company, and of the author.

of certain good persons to care for their souls. A consignment of fifty Bibles was sent on board, the idea being that the Bibles would work watch and watch, as the youngsters did, four on and four off, when at sea. A spirit of commendable economy divided the good books on this system and also caused them to be stamped in a dozen different places with the name of the society, to prevent loss by theft.

These Bibles had reposed under a large locker in the little cubbyhole of the ship's library, down on the berth deck, for many years. The writer's literary career began as librarian on the old *St. Mary's*. Being librarian carried with it many great privileges. Not the least of these was the discreet use of the snug cabin itself. A small round port light pierced the thick oak sides of the hull, not more than two feet above the water line, and on the inside of the ship's skin a huge "dagger knee," a broad diagonal brace of oak, was providentially set below the light. The librarian often reclined on this wide hook of oak, the light over his left shoulder, a book in hand, enjoying such ease and comfort as even the captain might have envied. Of course this secret pleasure was unknown to the executive officer and first lieutenant.

The cabin also had other secret advantages. It was small, lined with shelves, and might be used for the modest stowage of private provisions behind the upper rows of books. Just previous to the starting of the foreign cruise, while anchored in the East River off Twenty-third Street, a large box of groceries was received on board, a consignment from the mother of the librarian. This contraband had to be hidden from the searching eye of the executive. Deposited in the library, after a great deal of maneuvering, a problem presented itself. Where might the dozens of jars and cans of potted chicken, marmalade, pickles, and so forth, be stowed?

The one locker, under the dagger knee, was filled with the fifty Bibles—musty, soggy, unread Bibles, Bibles marred by great red stamps of an admirable society. These Bibles were below the water line of the hull. They had been there in dank confinement for nearly twenty years.

On the deck, on top of the locker, and all about, were cans and bottles and jars filled with seductive jellies, sparkling, enticing juices, and mouth-watering condiments. Outside was the entrance to the wardroom country, the sacred habitat of officers. On deck one of these lordly beings walked back and forth between the gangway and the horse block. It was late forenoon of a Saturday. The washdown was over. Liberty would be granted after dinner, and at Sunday morning inspection the library door would be opened and the librarian, cap in hand, would stand by while the captain, the executive, and the surgeon peered into the ordered neatness of the den of books.

The huge consignment (only a mother can do these things largely) must be hidden. A great resolve, a huge wrench, half conscience lifting from its moorings, half relief, and the port light was unscrewed. The locker was quickly opened, and Bibles began to drop through the open port.

Suddenly there was a rap at the door. The last Bible had been pushed out into the waters.

"What in the name of blankety blank are you doing?" a voice called through the lattice. I opened cautiously. It was my chum, Dick Rush.

"Come up on deck, quick!"

We gained the spar deck and stepped to the port gangway. A few feet from the ship and drifting up the East River with the flood tide was a fleet of fifty floating Bibles, stretching a quarter mile and drifting in single column towards Hell Gate.

"My God, Dick! I thought they would sink," I exclaimed.

For a half hour we stood breathless, lest the officer of the deck walk to port and sight the slowly departing flotilla of the Gospel.

Then we went below and stowed the empty locker with the delights of the flesh and ate unwholesome quantities of jam and pickles.

The Secret Drawer [1]

By Kenneth Grahame

It must surely have served as a boudoir for the ladies of old time, this little-used, rarely-entered chamber where the neglected old bureau stood. There was something very feminine in the faint hues of its faded brocades, in the rose and blue of such bits of china as yet remained, and in the delicate, old-world fragrance of potpourri from the great bowl—blue and white, with funny holes in its cover—that stood on the bureau's flat top. Modern aunts disdained this out-of-the-way, backwater, upstairs room, preferring to do their accounts and grapple with their correspondence in some central position more in the whirl of things, whence one eye could be kept on the carriage-drive, while the other was alert for malingering servants and marauding children. Those aunts of a former generation—I sometimes felt—would have suited our habits better. But even by us children, to whom few places were private or reserved, the room was visited but rarely. To be sure, there was nothing in particular in it that we coveted or required—only a few spindle-legged, gilt-backed chairs; an old harp on which, so the legend ran, Aunt Eliza herself used once to play in years remote, unchronicled; a corner cupboard with a few pieces of china; and the old bureau. But one other thing the room possessed peculiar to itself: a certain sense of privacy—a power of making the intruder feel that he *was* intruding—perhaps even a faculty of hinting that some one might have been sitting on those chairs, writing at the bureau, or fingering the china just a second before one entered. No such violent word as "haunted" could possibly apply to this pleasant old-fashioned chamber, which indeed we all rather liked; but there was no doubt it was reserved and stand-offish, keeping itself to itself.

Uncle Thomas was the first to draw my attention to the possibilities of the old bureau. He was pottering about the house one afternoon, having ordered me to keep at his heels for

[1] From *The Golden Age*. By permission of Dodd, Mead & Company.

company—he was a man who hated to be left one minute alone —when his eye fell on it. "H'm! Sheraton!" he remarked. (He had a smattering of most things, this uncle, especially the vocabularies.) Then he let down the flap, and examined the empty pigeonholes and dusty panelling. "Fine bit of inlay," he went on; "good work, all of it. I know the sort. There's a secret drawer in there somewhere." Then, as I breathlessly drew near, he suddenly exclaimed, "By Jove, I do want to smoke!" And wheeling round, he abruptly fled for the garden, leaving me with the cup dashed from my lips. What a strange thing, I mused, was this smoking, that takes a man suddenly—be he in the court, the camp, or the grove—grips him like an Afreet, and whirls him off to do its imperious behests! Would it be even so with myself, I wondered, in those unknown grown-up years to come?

But I had no time to waste in vain speculations. My whole being was still vibrating to those magic syllables "secret drawer"; and that particular chord had been touched that never fails to thrill responsive to such words as *cave, trap-door, sliding-panel, bullion, ingots,* or *Spanish dollars.* For, besides its own special bliss, who ever heard of a secret drawer with nothing in it? And oh, I did want money so badly! I mentally ran over the list of demands which were pressing me the most imperiously.

First, there was a pipe I wanted to give George Jannaway. George, who was Martha's young man, was a shepherd, and a great ally of mine; and the last fair he was at, when he bought his sweetheart fairings, as a right-minded shepherd should, he had purchased a lovely snake expressly for me—one of the wooden sort, with joints, waggling deliciously in the hand; with yellow spots on a green ground, sticky and strong-smelling, as a fresh-painted snake ought to be; and with a red-flannel tongue pasted cunningly into its jaws. I loved it much, and took it to bed with me every night till what time its spinal cord was loosed and it fell apart, and went the way of all mortal joys. I thought it very nice of George to think of me at the fair, and that's why I wanted to give him a pipe. When the young year was chill and lambing-time was on, George inhabited a little wooden house on wheels,

far out on the wintry downs, and saw no faces but such as were
sheepish and woolly and mute; and when he and Martha were
married, she was going to carry his dinner out to him every day,
two miles; and after it, perhaps he would smoke my pipe. It
seemed an idyllic sort of existence for both the parties concerned;
but a pipe of quality, a pipe fitted to be part of such a life as
this, could not be procured (so Martha informed me) for a
smaller sum than eighteenpence. And meantime—

Then there was the fourpence I owed Edward; not that he was
bothering me for it, but I knew he was in need of it himself to
pay back Selina, who wanted it to make up a sum of two shillings
to buy Harold an ironclad for his approaching birthday—
H.M.S. *Majestic,* now lying uselessly careened in the toy-shop
window, just when her country had such sore need of her.

And then there was that boy in the village who had caught
a young squirrel, and I had never possessed one; and he wanted
a shilling for it, but I knew that for ninepence in cash— But
what was the good of these sorry, threadbare reflections? I had
wants enough to exhaust any possible find of bullion, even if it
amount to half a sovereign. My only hope now lay in the magic
drawer; and here I was, standing and letting the precious minutes
slip by! Whether "findings" of this sort could, morally speaking,
be considered "keepings" was a point that did not occur to me.

The room was very still as I approached the bureau; possessed,
it seemed to be, by a sort of hush of expectation. The faint odor
of orris root that floated forth as I let down the flap seemed to
identify itself with the yellows and browns of the old wood, till
hue and scent were of one quality and interchangeable. Even
so, ere this, the potpourri had mixed itself with the tints of the
old brocade, and brocade and potpourri had long been one. With
expectant fingers I explored the empty pigeonholes and sounded
the depths of the softly-sliding drawers. No books that I knew
of gave any general recipe for a request like this; but the glory,
should I succeed unaided, would be all the greater.

To him who is destined to arrive, the fates never fail to afford
on the way their small encouragements. In less than two minutes I had come across a rusty buttonhook. This was truly

magnificent. In the nursery there existed, indeed, a general buttonhook, common to either sex; but none of us possessed a private and special buttonhook, to lend or to refuse, as suited the high humour of the moment. I pocketed the treasure carefully, and proceeded. At the back of another drawer three old foreign stamps told me I was surely on the highroad to fortune.

Following on these bracing incentives came a dull, blank period of unrewarded search. In vain I removed all the drawers and felt over every inch of the smooth surfaces from front to back. Never a knob, spring, or projection met the thrilling finger-tips; unyielding the old bureau stood, stoutly guarding its secret, if secret it really had. I began to grow weary and disheartened. This was not the first time that Uncle Thomas had proved shallow, uninformed—a guide into blind alleys where the echoes mocked you. Was it any good persisting longer? Was anything any good whatever? In my mind I began to review past disappointments, and life seemed one long record of failure and of non-arrival. Disillusioned and depressed I left my work and went to the window. The light was ebbing from the room, and seemed outside to be collecting itself on the horizon for its concentrated effort of sunset. Far down in the garden, Uncle Thomas was holding Edward in the air reversed, and smacking him. Edward, gurgling hysterically, was striking blind fists in the direction where he judged his uncle's stomach should rightly be; the contents of his pockets—a motley show—were strewing the lawn. Somehow, though I had been put through a similar performance myself an hour or two ago, it all seemed very far away and cut off from me.

Westward, the clouds were massing themselves in a low violet bank; below them, to north and south, as far round as eye could reach, a narrow streak of gold ran out and stretched away, straight along the horizon. Somewhere very far off a horn was blowing, clear and thin; it sounded like the golden streak grown audible, while the gold seemed the visible sound. It pricked my ebbing courage, this blended strain of music and color. I turned for a last effort; and Fortune thereupon, as if half ashamed of the unworthy game she had been playing with me, relented, opening her clenched fist. Hardly had I put my hand once more to the obdurate wood, when with a sort of small sigh, almost a sob— as it were—of relief, the secret drawer sprang open.

I drew it out and carried it to the window, to examine it in the failing light. Too hopeless had I gradually grown in my dispiriting search to expect very much and yet at a glance I saw that my basket of glass lay in shivers at my feet. No ingots or dollars were here, to crown me the little Monte Cristo of a week. Outside, the distant horn had ceased its gnat song, the gold was paling to primrose, and everything was lonely and still. Within, my confident little castles were tumbling down like so many card houses, leaving me stripped of estate, both real and personal, and dominated by the depressing reaction.

And yet, as I looked again at the small collection that lay within that drawer of disillusions, some warmth crept back to my heart as I recognized that a kindred spirit to my own had been at the making of it. Two tarnished gilt buttons—naval, apparently; a portrait of a monarch unknown to me, cut from some antique print and deftly colored by hand in just my own bold style of brushwork; some foreign copper coins, thicker and clumsier of make than those I hoarded myself; and a list of birds' eggs, with names of the places where they had been found. Also a ferret's muzzle, and a twist of tarry string, still faintly aromatic! It was a real boy's hoard, then, that I had happened upon. He, too, had found out the secret drawer, this happy-starred young person; and here he had stowed away his treasures, one by one, and had cherished them secretly awhile; and then— what? Well, one would never know now the reason why these priceless possessions lay still here unreclaimed; but across the void stretch of years I seemed to touch hands a moment with my little comrade of seasons—how many seasons?—long since dead.

I restored the drawer, with its contents, to the trusty bureau, and heard the spring click with a certain satisfaction. Some other boy, perhaps, would some day release that spring again. I trusted he would be equally appreciative. As I opened the door to go, I could hear, from the nursery at the end of the passage, shouts and yells, telling that the hunt was up. Bears, apparently, or bandits, were on the evening bill of fare, judging by the character of the noises. In another minute I would be in the thick of it, in all the warmth and light and laughter. And yet—what a long way off it all seemed, both in space and time, to me yet lingering on the threshold of that old-world chamber!

EXERCISES

1. Recalling the suggestion of conclusion 4 that concrete detail and impression in the reminiscent incident are used less for their own sake than to enhance the single effect which the author wishes to make, study the lavish use of both on pages 79-81. In what ways do the impressions and details contribute to the final effect and effectiveness?

2. Would "The Death of an Old Dog" gain in appeal and in literary worth if its author had been more generous in detail and impression? Consider this question carefully and give definite reasons for your decision.

3. Read "My First Play" from Lamb's *Essays of Elia*. Why is it an excellent model for a freshman theme? In what ways does it as a reminiscent incident differ from the three already considered?

4. Do you think that the characters in the reminiscent incidents you have read are subordinated to the main happening itself? Illustrate your point of view.

5. James Norman Hall's "Sing: A Song of Sixpence," suggested on the reading list, is a chain of incidents, one linked within another, and all too good to miss. If your instructor doesn't indulge himself and you by reading it aloud in class, don't miss it!

6. *The Golden Age* by Kenneth Grahame is filled with reminiscent incidents. Is any other better than "The Secret Drawer"?

SUGGESTED READINGS

Beerbohm, Max, "A Relic" from *And Even Now,* E. P. Dutton, New York.

Cather, Willa, "The Legend of Fray Baltazar" from *Death Comes for the Archbishop,* Alfred A. Knopf, New York.

de la Mare, Walter, *Memoirs of a Midget,* Alfred A. Knopf, New York.

Gardiner, Alfred G. (Alpha of the Plough) "On a Map of the Oberland" from *Leaves in the Wind,* E. P. Dutton, New York.

Garland, Hamlin, "Getting the Doctor" from *A Son of the Middle Border,* Macmillan, New York.

Grahame, Kenneth, *The Golden Age,* Dodd, Mead, New York. *Dream Days,* Dodd, Mead, New York.

Hall, James Norman, "Sing: A Song of Sixpence," *The Atlantic Monthly,* December 1925. "Some Reminiscences of a Middle Western School," *The Atlantic Monthly,* June 1923.

Hudson, W. H., "A Serpent Mystery," Chapter XVI, from *Far Away and Long Ago,* E. P. Dutton, New York.

Lamb, Charles, "My First Play" from *Essays of Elia.*

Muir, John, "The Ploughboy," Chapter VI, and "The World and the University," Chapter VIII, from *The Story of My Boyhood and Youth,* Houghton Mifflin, Boston.

Rihbany, Abraham Mitrie, "In New York with Nine Cents," Chapter VIII, from *A Far Journey,* Houghton Mifflin, Boston.

Stewart, Elinor Rupert, *Letters on an Elk Hunt,* Houghton Mifflin, Boston.

Twain, Mark, "Jim Wolf and the Cats" from *Autobiography,* Harper's, New York.

Van Dyke, John C., "Misadventures with a Canoe" from *The Open Sea,* Scribner's, New York.

CHAPTER IV

THEMES ABOUT PEOPLE AND ANIMALS

I. PORTRAITS AND OBSERVATIONS

This division of *Themes of Experience* is, naturally enough, the longest of the chapters; for when we come to consider people as a source of experience, our thoughts and impressions instantly begin to divide and to subdivide in a limitless fashion. There are people beautiful and ugly, alluring and repelling, startling and stupid; there are people whom we ticket at once as belonging to a type or within a group, and there are others who defy any such labelling. There are amusing, and absurd, and eccentric people, whom we dub as "characters." There are people whom we, in common with many others, admire or despise because of well-defined and inescapable traits; and there are in every life some few persons who, in a peculiar and often intangible sense, are of invaluable consequence and concern. Such a catalog can have no conclusion.

Lovers of animals will insist that the same is true of them. There are typical cows and individual cows, cows that infuriate and cows that charm. There are cats that howl all night along the back fence and cats with the dignity, grace, and mystery of Miss Repplier's Agrippina or with the reckless spirit of Horace Walpole's "fair Selina," drowned in a bowl of gold-fish and commemorated by no less a poet than Thomas Gray. That "teeming hen" of Robert Herrick's who laid "her egg each day" must have stood apart from the others of her flock; and surely poets from Homer to the present have not eulogized dogs, generic and specific, merely for want of other pastime.

It is because of this great variety and wealth of material for themes on people and animals that I have thought best to suggest some method of organizing and handling it. The simplest and most reasonable first assignment would seem to be that of a portrait or, in the case of an animal, perhaps an observation such as Gilbert White makes in his study of the swallow. The very words "portrait" and "observation" give the key-note to the position of the author in such a theme. He stays in the background, his business being first and foremost to present his subject, not himself.

Each of the models chosen to illustrate portraiture has many interesting and helpful suggestions; but before studying them one might well recall some good counsel given by Charles Lamb on this matter of the presentation of a person. The advice occurs in a fine essay by Hazlitt called *Of Persons One Would Wish to Have Seen*, an essay which should be known by every college freshman. Certain literary men of the day are discussing the question of whom among those dead and gone they would wish to see if they but had their choice. Lamb objects to John Locke and Sir Isaac Newton on the ground that they were not *persons,* that is, that beyond the contents of their books, there was nothing personally interesting in the men. He says, "But what we want to see any one *bodily* for is when there is something peculiar, striking in the individuals."

This is good advice for the writer of portraiture. Indeed, it has dictated the choice of the models that follow. The person you select to present or portray must, first of all, be a person of "peculiar" and "striking" appearance or individuality, and you must make the most of those characteristics which insure the right to the two adjectives. Detail must be uppermost in your mind, details of dress, face, bearing, manner, speech, especially those details which belong *uniquely* to the person, which make him so irrevocably himself. After the choice of details, which may be considered the coloring of your portrait, will come the arrangement of them in sentences and paragraphs, which you may call its perspective. Finally, when your colors are chosen and your perspective arranged for, you must consider the lighting of your portrait by diction which will bring out its full effect.

It is also with especial view to these matters of arrangement and of diction that the following selections have been chosen. Note how Thackeray in his picture of Beatrix Esmond as she descends the stairs—a picture which, although it may seem quaint and old-fashioned to you, is yet known to every one even relatively well-acquainted with English literature—has planned his work. Far more effective even than Beatrix herself is Thackeray's placing of her on the stairs, his illumination of her with her lighted candle.

Hardy's portrait of Eustacia Vye shows the same careful preparation for effect. His first sentence is in itself halting and compelling by its daring comparison, which never once is allowed to leave the memory. See the clever way in which he manages to keep it in the consciousness of the reader. His paragraph arrangement also is worth careful study. Note how each most striking feature is given space by itself. Here, too, is splendid use of detail. Do not let any of it escape you.

Beatrix on the stairs, Eustacia on Egdon Heath, and Mrs. Battle at her card-table to which she inseparably belongs. And yet with Mrs. Battle there is a difference. You will see that Lamb is interested, not primarily in her physical appearance, but in the effect of her personality upon those who knew her. Here are no details at all, but instead terse, balanced constructions with their semicolons, and short, direct sentences to suggest her upright, rigid posture, the tenseness of her eager face and figure. And in what an inimitable way does the diction of the second paragraph suggest her pent-up energy. If you know Lamb at all in his other essays, you will perceive that this one is unique in its suggestive diction surely chosen to harmonize with and to complement the character of old Sarah Battle.

"Queequeg" differs from the three portraits already briefly considered, first, because it is definitely narrative in method, and, second, because we see the terrifying harpooner not so much through the eyes of the author as through those of the frightened bedfellow. In this way we catch as a supplementary picture to Queequeg that of the frightened boy cowering in bed in the shadows of the candle and dreading the moment when his strange

and terrible roommate must join him. Our own excitement is
quickened by our sympathy for the poor lad through whose impressions we get our own.

But if Mr. Melville's style is in the direct manner of a boy
who excitedly recounts his quickly succeeding impressions of a
monster—and of a monster with whom he must soon sleep!—
Miss Soskice's manner is that of a very original child writing a
diary or a letter. Indeed, the way these paragraphs are written
is quite as interesting as the material within them. They hurry
on in the inconsequential talk of a child, the person or idea in
the concluding sentence of one giving rise to the person or idea
in the opening sentence of the next. It might not be wise to
suggest this naïve, informal style as a model, and yet the selection
has much to teach one in simplicity, directness, and use of detail, not to mention the delightful reading it affords.

If you do not know your English history at least fairly well,
read John Richard Green on the Tudor period [1] before beginning
Princess Mary and Princess Elizabeth; otherwise the two girls
so fascinatingly presented here will escape you. This imaginary
conversation by Walter Savage Landor is included in the hope
that this method of portraiture by dialogue may appeal to some
students. It affords numberless possibilities for sharpened and
acute character drawing; and for writers interested in contrasts
of personality and especially in certain intriguing personalities
of history or literature, it should offer some hours of real enjoyment concluded with a pleasurable sense of accomplishment and
profit.

On the two animal portraits given here, the observation of the
swallow by Gilbert White and Dr. John Brown's picture of his
dog Toby, it seems hardly necessary to comment. And yet it
would be a pity if you should miss in the first the delicate and
rhythmic style which makes poetic the accuracy of the simple
description, and in the second the fine use of detail and incident
from the advent to the exit of Toby. If you are country-bred
and, unlike many rural products, know something of animal life

[1] *A Short History of the English People,* by John Richard Green,
pp. 353-374.

from your own discoveries, it would be interesting to attempt an observation after the manner of Gilbert White, who, you may not know, was an English curate in a tiny Surrey parish between the years 1755 and 1793. Probably your own life in the twentieth century will make impossible the natural cadences of his style, so like the Surrey hills and slopes and so suggestive of his hours of contemplation in wandering through the country. But at all events you can aim at least for his care and accuracy. A theme suggested by or modelled on "Toby" would probably mean an easier job. If you try it, do not fail first to study those features which make its worth and its appeal; *the straightforward and un-adorned style, the use of incident, the value of the few literary allusions, the skillful way in which the author characterizes persons as well as Toby, the picturesque and dramatic use of verbs and adjectives.*

Beatrix Descending the Stairs [1]

By William Makepeace Thackeray

This laughing colloquy took place in the hall of Walcote House: in the midst of which is a staircase that leads from an open gallery, where are the doors of the sleeping chambers; and from one of these, a wax candle in her hand, and illuminating her, came Mistress Beatrix—the light falling indeed upon the scarlet riband which she wore, and upon the most brilliant white neck in the world.

Esmond had left a child and found a woman, grown beyond the common height; and arrived at such a dazzling completeness of beauty, that his eyes might well show surprise and delight at beholding her. In hers there was a brightness so lustrous and melting, that I have seen a whole assembly follow her as if by an attraction irresistible; and that night the great Duke was at the playhouse after Ramillies, every soul turned and looked (she chanced to enter at the opposite side of the theatre at the same moment) at her, and not at him. She was a brown beauty: that is, her eyes, hair, and eyebrows and eyelashes were dark; her

[1] From *Henry Esmond.*

hair curling with rich undulations and waving over her shoulders; but her complexion was as dazzling white as snow in sunshine; except her cheeks, which were a bright red, and her lips which were of a still deeper crimson. Her mouth and chin, they said, were too large and full, and so they might be for a goddess in marble, but not for a woman whose eyes were fire, whose look was love, whose voice was the sweetest low song, whose shape was perfect symmetry, health, decision, activity, whose foot as it planted itself on the ground, was firm but flexible, and whose motion, whether rapid or slow, was always perfect grace—agile as a nymph, lofty as a queen—now melting, now imperious, now sarcastic—there was no single movement of hers but was beautiful. As he thinks of her, he who writes feels young again, and remembers a paragon.

So she came holding her dress with one fair rounded arm, and her taper before her, tripping down the stair to greet Esmond.

EUSTACIA VYE [1]

By Thomas Hardy

Eustacia Vye was the raw material of a divinity. On Olympus she would have done well with a little preparation. She had the passions and instincts which make a model goddess, that is, those which make not quite a model woman. Had it been possible for the earth and mankind to be entirely in her grasp for awhile, had she handled the distaff, the spindle, and the shears at her own free will, few in the world would have noticed the change of government. There would have been the same inequality of lot, the same heaping up of favours here, of contumely there, the same generosity before justice, the same perpetual dilemmas, the same captious alternation of caresses and blows that we endure now.

She was in person full-limbed, and somewhat heavy; without ruddiness, as without pallor; and soft to the touch as a cloud. To see her hair was to fancy that a whole winter did not contain

[1] From *The Return of the Native.*

darkness enough to form its shadow: it closed over her forehead like nightfall extinguishing the western glow.

Her nerves extended into those tresses, and her temper could always be softened by stroking them down. When her hair was brushed she would instantly sink into stillness and look like the Sphinx. If in passing under one of the Egdon banks, any of the thick skeins were caught, as they sometimes were, by a prickly tuft of the large *ulex Europoeus*—which will act as a sort of hairbrush—she would go back a few steps, and pass against it a second time.

She had Pagan eyes, full of nocturnal mysteries. Their light, as it came and went, and came again, was partially hampered by their oppressive lids and lashes; and of these the under lid was much fuller than it usually is with English women. This enabled her to indulge in reverie without seeming to do so: she might have been believed capable of sleeping without closing them up. Assuming that the souls of men and women were visible essences, you could fancy the colour of Eustacia's soul to be flame-like. The sparks from it that rose into her dark pupils gave the same impression.

The mouth seemed formed less to speak than to quiver, less to quiver than to kiss. Some might have added, less to kiss than to curl. Viewed sideways, the closing line of her lips formed, with almost geometric precision, the curve so well known in the arts of design as the cimarecta, or ogee. The sight of such a flexible bend as that on grim Egdon was quite an apparition. It was felt at once that that mouth did not come over from Sleswig with a band of Saxon pirates whose lips met like the two halves of a muffin. One had fancied that such lip-curves were mostly lurking underground in the South as fragments of forgotten marbles. So fine were the lines of her lips, that, though full, each corner of her mouth was as clearly cut as the point of a spear. This keenness of corner was only blunted when she was given over to sudden fits of gloom, one of the phases of the night-side of sentiment which she knew too well for her years.

Her presence brought memories of such things as Bourbon roses, rubies, and tropical midnights; her moods recalled lotus-eaters and the march in "Athalie"; her motions, the ebb and flow of the sea; her voice, the viola. In a dim light, and with a slight rearrangement of her hair, her general figure might have stood for that of either of the higher female deities. The new moon behind her head, an old helmet upon it, a diadem of accidental dew-drops round her brow, would have been adjuncts sufficient to strike the note of Artemis, Athena, or Hera respectively, with as close an approximation to the antique as that which passes muster on many respected canvases.

But celestial imperiousness, love, wrath, and fervour had proved to be somewhat thrown away on netherward Egdon. Her power was limited, and the consciousness of this limitation had biassed her development. Egdon was her Hades, and since coming there she had imbibed much of what was dark in its tone, though inwardly and eternally unreconciled thereto. Her appearance accorded well with this smouldering rebelliousness, and the shady splendour of her beauty was the real surface of the sad and stifled warmth within her. A true Tartarean dignity set upon her brow, and not factitiously or with marks of constraint, for it had grown in her with years.

Across the upper part of her head she wore a thin fillet of black velvet, restraining the luxuriance of her shady hair, in a way which added much to this class of majesty by irregularly clouding her forehead. "Nothing can embellish a beautiful face more than a narrow band drawn over the brow," said Richter. Some of the neighbouring girls wore coloured ribbons for the same purpose, and sported metallic ornaments elsewhere; but if any one suggested coloured ribbon and metallic ornaments to Eustacia Vye, she laughed and went on.

MRS. BATTLE [1]
(IN PART)

By Charles Lamb

"A clear fire, a clean hearth, and a rigor of the game." This was the celebrated *wish* of old Sarah Battle (now with God), who,

[1] From "Mrs. Battle's Opinions on Whist," in *Essays of Elia.*

next to her devotions, loved a good game of whist. She was none of your lukewarm gamesters, your half-and-half players who have no objection to take a hand, if you want one to make up a rubber, who affirm that they have no pleasure in winning; that they like to win one game and lose another; that they can while away an hour very agreeably at a card-table, but are indifferent whether they play or no; and will desire an adversary, who has slipped a wrong card, to take it up and play another. These insufferable triflers are the curse of a table. One of these flies will spoil a whole pot. Of such it may be said that they do not play at cards, but only play at playing at them.

Sarah Battle was none of that breed. She detested them as I do, from her heart and soul, and would not, save upon a striking emergency, willingly seat herself at the same table with them. She loved a thorough-paced partner, a determined enemy. She took and gave no concessions. She hated favors. She never made a revoke, nor ever passed it over in her adversary without exacting the utmost forfeiture. She fought a good fight: cut and thrust. She held not her good sword (her cards) "like a dancer." She sat bolt upright; and neither showed you her cards, nor desired to see yours. All people have their blind side—their superstitions; and I have heard her declare, under the rose, that hearts was her favorite suit.

I never in my life—and I knew Sarah Battle many of the best years of it—saw her take out her snuff-box when it was her turn to play; or snuff a candle in the middle of a game; or ring for a servant, till it was fairly over. She never introduced, or connived at miscellaneous conversation during its process. As she emphatically observed, cards were cards; and if I ever saw unmingled distaste in her fine last-century countenance, it was at the airs of a young gentleman of a literary turn, who had been with difficulty persuaded to take a hand; and who, in his excess of candor, declared that he thought there was no harm in unbending the mind now and then, after serious studies in recreations of that kind! She could not bear to have her noble occupation, to which she wound up her faculties, considered in that light.

It was her business, her duty, the thing she came into the world to do, and she did it. She unbent her mind afterward—over a book.

Pope was her favorite author: his *Rape of the Lock* her favorite work. She once did me the favor to play over with me (with the cards) his celebrated game of Ombre in that poem; and to explain to me how far it agreed with, and in what points it would be found to differ from tradrille. Her illustrations were apposite and poignant; and I had the pleasure of sending the substance of them to Mr. Bowles; but I suppose they came too late to be inserted among his ingenious notes upon that author.

Quadrille, she has often told me, was her first love; but whist had engaged her maturer esteem. The former, she said, was showy and specious, and likely to allure young persons. The uncertainty and quick shifting of partners—a thing which the constancy of whist abhors; the dazzling supremacy and regal investiture of Spadille—absurd, as she justly observed, in the pure aristocracy of whist, where his crown and garter give him no proper power above his brother-nobility of the aces; the giddy vanity, so taking to the inexperienced, of playing alone; above all, the overpowering attractions of a *Sans Prendre Vole*, to the triumph of which there is certainly nothing parallel or approaching, in the contingencies of whist; all these, she would say, make quadrille a game of captivation to the young and enthusiastic. But whist was the *solider* game: that was her word. It was a long meal; not like quadrille, a feast of snatches. One or two rubbers might co-extend in duration with an evening. They gave time to form rooted friendships, to cultivate steady enmities. She despised the chance-started, capricious, and ever-fluctuating alliances of the other. The skirmishes of quadrille, she would say, reminded her of the petty ephemeral embroilments of the little Italian states, depicted by Machiavel: perpetually changing postures and connections; bitter foes to-day, sugared darlings to-morrow; kissing and scratching in a breath; but the wars of whist were comparable to the long, steady, deep-rooted, rational antipathies of the great French and English nations.

*   *   *   *   *   *   *

Queequeg [1]

By Herman Melville

Whether that mattress was stuffed with corn-cobs or broken crockery, there is no telling, but I rolled about a good deal, and could not sleep for a long time. At last I slid off into a light doze, and had pretty nearly made a good offing towards the land of Nod, when I heard a heavy footfall in the passage, and saw a glimmer of light come into the room from under the door.

Lord save me, thinks I, this must be the harpooner, the infernal head-pedlar. But I lay perfectly still, and resolved not to say a word till spoken to. Holding a light in one hand, and that identical New Zealand head in the other, the stranger entered the room, and without looking towards the bed, placed his candle a good way off from me on the floor in one corner, and then began working away at the knotted cords of the large bag before spoken of as being in the room. I was all eagerness to see his face, but he kept it averted for some time while employed in unlacing the bag's mouth. This accomplished, however, he turned round— when, good heavens! what a sight! Such a face! It was of a dark, purplish, yellow colour, here and there stuck over with large, blackish looking squares. Yes, it's just as I thought, he's a terrible bedfellow; he's been in a fight, got dreadfully cut, and here he is, just from the surgeon. But at that moment he chanced to turn his face so towards the light that I plainly saw they could not be sticking-plasters at all, those black squares on his cheeks. They were stains of some sort or other. At first I knew not what to make of this; but soon an inkling of the truth occurred to me. I remembered a story of a white man—a whaleman, too—who, falling among the cannibals, had been tattooed by them. I concluded that this harpooner, in the course of his distant voyages, must have met with a similar adventure. And what is it, thought I, after all! It's only his outside; a man can be honest in any sort of skin. But then, what to make of his unearthly complexion, that part of it, I mean, lying round

<hr>

[1] From *Moby Dick*.

about, and completely independent of the squares of tattooing. To be sure, it might be nothing but a good coat of tropical tanning; but I never heard of a hot sun's tanning a white man into a purplish yellow one. However, I had never been in the South Seas; and perhaps the sun there produced these extraordinary effects upon the skin. Now, while all these ideas were passing through me like lightning, this harpooner never noticed me at all. But, after some difficulty having opened his bag, he commenced fumbling in it, and presently pulled out a sort of tomahawk, and a sealskin wallet with the hair on. Placing these on the old chest in the middle of the room, he then took the New Zealand head—a ghastly thing enough—and crammed it down into the bag. He now took off his hat—a new beaver hat—when I came nigh singing out with fresh surprise. There was no hair on his head—none to speak of at least—nothing but a small scalp-knot twisted up on his forehead. His bald purplish head now looked for all the world like a mildewed skull. Had not the stranger stood between me and the door, I would have bolted out of it quicker than ever I bolted a dinner. . . .

Meanwhile, he continued the business of undressing, and at last showed his chest and arms. As I live, these covered parts of him were checkered with the same dark squares as his face; his back, too, was all over the same dark squares; he seemed to have been in a Thirty Years' War, and just escaped from it with a sticking-plaster shirt. Still more, his very legs were marked, as if a parcel of dark green frogs were running up the trunks of young palms. It was now quite plain that he must be some abominable savage or other shipped aboard of a whaleman in the South Seas, and so landed in this Christian country. I quaked to think of it. A pedlar of heads, too—perhaps the heads of his own brothers. He might take a fancy to mine— heavens! look at that tomahawk!

But there was no time for shuddering, for now the savage went about something that completely fascinated my attention and convinced me that he must indeed be a heathen. Going to his heavy grego, or wrapall, or dreadnaught, which he had previously hung on a chair, he fumbled in the pockets, and produced at length a curious little deformed image with a hunch on its back, and exactly the colour of a three days' old Congo baby. Remembering the embalmed head, at first I almost thought that this black mannikin was a real baby preserved in some similar manner. But seeing that it was not at all limber, and that it glistened a good deal like polished ebony, I concluded that it must be nothing but a wooden idol, which indeed it proved to be. For now the savage goes up to the empty fireplace, and removing the papered fireboard, sets up this little hunchbacked image, like a tenpin, between the andirons. The chimney jambs and all the bricks inside were very sooty, so that I thought this fireplace made a very appropriate little shrine or chapel for this Congo idol.

I now screwed my eyes hard towards this half-hidden image, feeling but ill at ease meantime—to see what was next to follow. First he takes about a double handful of shavings out of his grego pocket, and places them carefully before the idol; then laying a bit of ship biscuit on top and applying the flame from the lamp, he kindled the shavings into a sacrificial blaze. Presently, after many hasty snatches into the fire, and still hastier withdrawal of his fingers (whereby he seemed to be scorching them badly), he at last succeeded in drawing out the biscuit; then blowing off the heat and ashes a little, he made a polite offer of it to the little negro. But the little devil did not seem to fancy such dry sort of fare at all; he never moved his lips. All these strange antics were accompanied by still stranger guttural noises from the devotee, who seemed to be praying in a sing-song or else singing some pagan psalmody or other, during which his face twitched about in the most unnatural manner. At last extinguishing the fire, he took the idol up very unceremoniously, and bagged it again in his grego pocket as carelessly as if he were a sportsman bagging a dead woodcock. . . .

The interval I spent in deliberating what to say was a fatal one. Taking up his tomahawk from the table, he examined the head on it for an instant, and then holding it to the light, with his mouth at the handle, he puffed out great clouds of tobacco smoke. The next moment the light was extinguished, and this wild cannibal, tomahawk between his teeth, sprang into bed with me. I sang out, I could not help it now; and giving a sudden grunt of astonishment, he began feeling me.

KITCHEN PORTRAITS [1]

By Juliet Soskice

The kitchen was at the end of a stone passage at the foot of a flight of stone steps. I liked to go there, but I was not really allowed to. I liked it best of all in the evening when the servants had finished supper, and sometimes the cook would let me sit on a chair in the corner near the stove. She was rather an ill-tempered cook, though she often used to laugh. She had been in the family ever since my mother was quite a little girl. She had a dark yellow face and brown eyes and black hair. It was quite straight like tape, and she scraped it back from her forehead and did it in a funny knob behind. It wasn't black really, but she used an excellent hair dye, and said, what did it matter if it came off on the pillow cases? She said nobody need look their age if only they would take the trouble to look young. But she didn't look young herself, because she was so bony and her face so dreadfully wrinkled. She looked very nice though when she laughed and showed her false white teeth. They looked whiter than other people's false teeth, because her face was so yellow and her eyes so dark. Occasionally she flew into an awful temper and swore so dreadfully that it shocked every one who heard her. But at other times she was quite cheerful and told very funny stories.

She had a treacherous friend who was a hunch-backed lady. They both loved the same gentleman, but he couldn't marry them because he had a wife already. The hunch-backed lady used to come in the evening and sit down in the kitchen and say how ill the wife was, and that she couldn't last much longer; but she did. The hunch-backed lady said that as soon as she was dead the gentleman they loved would want to marry the cook, and

[1] From *Chapters from Childhood*. By permission of Harcourt, Brace and Company.

that he really loved her much better than his wife. The cook believed it, and she said if he had only known his mind when they were young together all the bother would have been saved.

The hunch-backed lady wore a woolly black cloak, and a big fur on her shoulders to hide the hunch, a black velvet bonnet with strings and sparkling jet ornaments, and an expensive gold watch-chain. She had a very heavy face with her chin right on her chest, and light blue eyes and a handsome curly fringe. She used to drink quantities of tea out of a saucer, very hot, but the cook said she really liked whisky much better when she could get it.

Once she ceased coming and the cook went to look for her, and she found out that the wife had really been dead all the while, and the hunch-backed lady had got married to the gentleman they loved. He didn't want to be married, but she made him. She was afraid that if the cook had known his wife was dead she would have made him first.

There was a page-boy in this house too, but not an anarchist. He wore no buttons, and he had to stop down in the kitchen and help the cook because of her "poor leg."

She got it through going out to buy three pounds of fish at the fishmonger's and slipping on a piece of orange-peel outside the door. It used to give way just at the most awkward moments, and she said she almost believed it knew and did it on purpose. If she had a saucepan in her hand, or a piece of toast, or a leg of mutton it was all the same—she had to put it down on the floor and clutch herself round the knee to pull her leg straight again. Everybody knew about it, and the first thing they said when they came into the kitchen was, "Good morning, cook, and how's your poor leg?" and then she told them about it. When she sat down the boy used to arrange a chair in front of her for her to rest it on.

He had a fat, red face, and he was always smiling. The cook said she wouldn't have believed that any living mouth could stretch so far. It used to make people angry, because whenever they looked at him he smiled, even when there was nothing at all to smile at. My grandfather said he was like the man in Shake-

speare who smiled and was a villain. He liked eating apples
and a sweet-stuff called stick-jaw that glued his teeth together.
The cook said he was the biggest liar that ever walked the earth.
He always pretended he had a serious illness and he must go and
see the doctor. But instead he went and played in Regent's Park.
Once he tied his face up in a bandage for two days and said
he was going to the dentist to have a double tooth out. And he
borrowed a huge cart-horse from one of the stables in the mews
and went for a ride on it, without a saddle, and with an old
piece of rope instead of reins; and that was how he got found out.
The horse insisted on going past the house when it wanted to
return to its stable. He tugged at it as hard as he could to
make it go home round the back way, but it refused, and the
cook was on the area steps and saw him. She said she wouldn't
have been so certain if he hadn't had an enormous apple in one
hand. When he came next day, he said it was the dentist's horse,
and he had sent him for a ride on it to get rid of the effects of
laughing gas. But we knew the very stable where it lived, and
so he was dismissed.

The housemaid was Irish, and she couldn't read or write, but
she believed in ghosts. She had been a long time in the family
too, and she was very fat, with a big pink face and little beady
eyes. She was the kindest person I ever knew. Whenever we
liked anything she had she always wanted to give it to us, and
it really grieved her if we wouldn't have it. She gave away all
her money to the beggars at the garden gate and if she heard of
any of us being ill or punished it made her cry, just as if she
herself were in trouble. She used to fall about a great deal.
If there was any place she could fall into she always did. She
said she had measured her length upon every free space of ground
in the house, and bumped her head on every stair, and caught
her foot in every rug and carpet. But she didn't let it worry
her. One night, when she was standing on the slippery little
knob at the end of the bannisters to light the gas outside the
studio door, she fell off and lay quite still with her leg doubled
under her until the family had finished dinner, because she didn't
want to disturb them by calling out. Once she fell into the

drawing-room with a great big tea-tray when there was a tea-party and alarmed the guests exceedingly. But my grandmother was not angry. She said nothing at all, but helped her to get up and pick the tea-things up again.

She believed in ghosts most firmly. She said that her mother had seen so many in Ireland that she simply took no notice of them. They were in every room in the house and up and down the stairs. They used to ring the bells when nothing was wanted and knock people about when they got in their way, and whenever anybody died or anything was going to happen they made a horrible noise outside the windows in the night. Once, she said, she passed a woman nursing her own head on a stone by the roadside, and they just looked at one another, but neither of them spoke.

A gentleman in a nightshirt had hanged himself from a hook in the middle of the ceiling in the servants' bedroom, before my grandfather came to the house, and the housemaid said his spirit haunted the top storey. She woke up one night and saw a figure standing in the middle of the room and looking at her. She knew it was the same gentleman, because he still wore his night-shirt and had the rope round his neck, and he was standing just underneath the place where the hook would have been had it not been taken down when the ceiling was whitewashed. He was looking at her fixedly. If he had looked the other way he might have noticed the cook in the other bed as well, and that would have been some relief. But he didn't. He gazed and gazed as though his heart was going to break. She was so frightened that she shook the bed with trembling; and she shut her eyes and put her hand under the pillow and got out her rosary, and said five "Hail Mary's." And when she opened them again he was still there, only not quite so solid. After another five he got so misty that she could see the furniture through him, and after the third five he had disappeared. But she was so terrified, she said, that she didn't get a wink of sleep that night, and when she woke in the morning her nightdress and sheets were quite damp with terror.

The cook didn't believe it. She said it was pure popery. She

was sure no ghost could possibly come in in the night like that
without her noticing it, because she was such a light sleeper.
But as a matter of fact, she snored so dreadfully that my grandfather once asked a builder for an estimate for padding the walls
of the servants' room all round so that she couldn't be heard on
the floor underneath, but she was so offended that it wasn't
padded.

They sometimes used to laugh at the housemaid in the kitchen
for being a Catholic. But she didn't care. She stuck to her
religion. She was so certain that the Virgin Mary was taking
care of her, or she would have been worse hurt in the dreadful
accidents she used to have. She said no living being could have
stood it without divine protection. When she was doing something that she thought really might be dangerous, she just said,
"Jesus, Mary, Joseph, help!" and took more care, and nothing
happened.

The cook said why she didn't like Catholics was because she
thought they were wicked for burning the Protestants alive on
posts in the streets in the olden days when there were no police.
I said that the Protestants burnt the Catholics first, but she
was offended. She said that no Protestant would ever have
thought of such a thing if it hadn't been put into their heads
by bad example. They argued so angrily about which burnt
the other first that the housemaid put her apron over her head
and sat down on a chair and began to cry aloud like the Irish do
at funerals. But then she left off and went upstairs to do her
work, and she tumbled about so badly in the bedroom over the
studio that my grandfather got down from his painting chair to
go upstairs and see what the matter was, and when he found out
why she was crying he was very angry. He stumped right downstairs to the top of the kitchen flight and with his spectacles on
top of his head, his palette in one hand and his paint-brush in
the other. It was difficult for him to get downstairs because of
his gout. But he did, and put his head over the bannisters and
forbade the subject ever again to be mentioned in the kitchen.
And it was not, and they were quite good friends again after that.

The person who most hated Catholics was Mrs. Hall, the wife

of the most pious cabman in the mews at the corner. She was the beautiful woman who sat in the barge and nursed the healthy baby that had been painted as twins. She was so beautiful that it was quite remarkable. Her hair was jet black, and when one day she sat down in a chair in the kitchen and let it down for us to see, it trailed upon the floor. Her eyes were dark blue and extremely big and bright, but the doctor said that the brightness was unnatural, and that later she might go blind. She was very tall, and whenever she stood she used to look strong and composed and like the statues that stand round on pedestals in museums. Her husband used to say God punished her for her sins by not giving her a baby.

The husband went to a chapel where any one who liked could get up and preach, and the others were obliged to listen. He preached every time he got a chance, and he said he never felt inclined to stop. He loved his fellow creatures so much that he felt compelled to save their souls. He always carried a bundle of tracts about in his pocket, and when any one paid him his fare he gave them some free of charge in exchange. My grandfather used to say to him, "It's no good, Hall, I'm past all redemption," because he didn't want the tracts, but Mr. Hall stuffed a bundle into the pocket of his overcoat while he was helping him to get out of the cab. Mrs. Hall said that he wrestled with God for his soul in private. They were allowed to do that at his chapel.

He was so religious that he thought both Catholics and Protestants were wicked. He said the mistake that everybody made was to think there was more than one door open into Heaven. He said, "Is there more than one door open into Heaven? No! And why is there not more than one door open into Heaven? Because if there was more than one door open into Heaven there would be a draught in Heaven. And would the Lord tolerate a draught in Heaven? No!" That was part of one of his sermons. It really meant that it was only the door of his chapel that led into Heaven, and that other people hadn't got a chance.

Some people said he was a handsome man, but I didn't think

so. He was small and his hair was such a bright yellow that it looked as if it had been painted. He had strawberry-coloured cheeks and his nose was deadly white. Whenever he met a very nice young girl he used to take her to prayer-meeting, because he loved her soul. He knew a great many. His wife was angry because he took so much trouble about their souls, and the more he loved them the more she hated them. She used to cry and tell the cook which particular one he was saving then, and the cook used to say "The saucy hussy! I'd save 'er, and 'im too!"

*   *   *   *   *   *   *

The kitchen was really pleasantest of all in the evening when they were resting after supper. Sometimes there were quite a lot of people there. The charwoman used to unscrew her wooden leg and lean it up against her chair. She said you couldn't think what a relief it gave her. But, of course, if she'd had to get up suddenly for anything before she'd had time to screw it on again she would certainly have fallen. The cook had her leg up on the chair in front of her and talked about them. But the charwoman talked most. She was a middle-sized woman with greasy greeny-greyish hair, and there always seemed to be perspiration on her face. She talked whatever she was doing. She talked so much that people could never understand how she got through all the work she did. At first it was disturbing, like rain pattering on a roof, but after a time you wouldn't notice it.

She said that her husband and her husband's mother and her husband's father had all got wooden legs. She said that it was fate, and when the doctor in the hospital had told her that her right must go it was hardly any shock to her. She had a little girl called Sarah, and whenever she had anything the matter with her the first thing she always did with her was to test her legs at once. Even if it was only a cold or something wrong at quite another end of her body she always did. The housemaid said that it was tempting Providence to talk like that, but she didn't care.

She talked most of all with Mrs. Catlin, the woman who did fine needlework and used to make my grandfather's shirts. She was a caretaker in one of the great big houses in Ormonde Terrace, and she used to look so young and innocent that everybody called her the "little woman," when she wasn't there. When she had finished some work she used to bring it round in the evening after her babies were in bed, and then she'd stand near the dresser and talk, but she never sat down round the table with the others. She was rather plump and she always looked pink and clean as though she'd come straight out of a bath. She had nice fluffy hair and blue eyes, and her nose turned up just a little at the end, but gently and not suddenly like Tommy Haughty's mother's. She talked a good deal too, but she had a pretty tinkling voice. She said when you'd been shut up in a great big barracks of a place the whole day long you simply must let loose or burst. Sometimes she and the charwoman talked both at once for a long time. They seemed not to hear at all what the others said, but it made no difference. Cook said it was like pandemonium in a hailstorm when those two got together.

PRINCESS MARY AND PRINCESS ELIZABETH [1]

effective word

By Walter Savage Landor

Mary. My dear dear sister! it is long, very long, since we met.

Elizabeth. Methinks it was about the time they chopped off our uncle Seymour's head for him. Not that he was *our* uncle though . . . he was only Edward's.

Mary. The Lord Protector, if not your uncle, was always doatingly fond of you; and he often declared to me, even within your hearing, he thought you very beautiful.

Elizabeth. He said as much of you, if that is all; and he told me why . . . "*not to vex me*" . . . as if, instead of vexing me, it would not charm me. I beseech your Highness, is there anything remarkable or singular in thinking me . . . what he thought me?

Mary. No, indeed; for so you are. But why call me *High-*

[1] From *The Pentameron and Other Imaginary Conversations.*

ness? drawing back and losing half your stature in the circumference of the curtsey.

Elizabeth. Because you are now, at this blessed hour, my lawful queen.

Mary. Hush, prythee hush! The parliament has voted otherwise.

Elizabeth. They would chouse you.

Mary. What would they do with me?

Elizabeth. Trump you.

Mary. I am still at a loss.

Elizabeth. Bamboozle you.

Mary. Really, my dear sister, you have been so courted by the gallants, that you condescend to adopt their language, in place of graver.

Elizabeth. Cheat you then . . . will that do?

Mary. Comprehensibly.

Elizabeth. I always speak as the thing spoken of requires. To the point. Would our father have minded the caitiffs?

Mary. Naming our father, I should have said, *our father now in bliss;* for surely he must be; having been a rock of defence against the torrent of irreligion.

Elizabeth. Well; in bliss or out, there, here, or anywhere, would he, royal soul! have minded parliament? No such fool he. There were laws before there were parliaments; and there were kings before there were laws. Were I in your Majesty's place (God forbid the thought should ever enter my poor weak head, even in a dream!) I would try the mettle of my subjects: I would mount my horse, and head them.

Mary. Elizabeth! you were always a better horsewoman than I am: I should be ashamed to get a fall among the soldiers.

Elizabeth. Pish! Pish! it would be among knights and nobles . . . the worst come to the worst. Lord o' mercy! do you think they never saw such a thing before?

Mary. I must hear of no resistance to the powers that be. Besides, I am but a weak woman.

Elizabeth. I do not see why women should be weak, unless they like.

Mary. Not only the Commons, but likewise the peers, have sworn allegiance.

Elizabeth. Did you ever in your lifetime, in any chronicle or commentary, read of any parliament that was not as ready to be forsworn as to swear?

Mary. Alas!

Elizabeth. If ever you did, the book is a rare one, kept in an out-of-the-way library, in a cedar chest all to itself, with golden locks and amber seals thereto.

Mary. I would not willingly think so ill of men.

Elizabeth. For my part, I can't abide 'em. All that can be said, is, some are not so bad as others. You smile, and deem the speech a silly and superfluous one. We may live, sister Mary, to see and acknowledge that it is not quite so sure and flat a verity as it now appears to us. I never come near a primrose but I suspect an adder under it; and the sunnier the day the more misgivings.

Mary. But we are now, by the settlement of the monarchy, farther out of harm's way than ever.

Elizabeth. If the wench has children to-morrow, as she may have, they will inherit.

Mary. No doubt they would.

Elizabeth. No doubt? I will doubt: and others shall doubt too. The heirs of my body . . . yours first . . . God prosper them! Parliament may be constrained to retrace its steps. One half sees no harm in taking bribes, the other no guilt in taking fright. Corruption is odious and costly: but, when people have yielded to compulsion, conscience is fain to acquiesce. Men say they were forced, and what is done under force is invalid.

Mary. There was nothing like compulsion.

Elizabeth. Then let there be. Let the few yield to the many, and all to the throne. Now is your time to stir. The furnace is mere smut, and no bellows to blow the embers. Parliament is without a leader. Three or four turnspits are crouching to leap upon the wheel; but, while they are snarling and snapping one at another, what becomes of the roast? Take them by the scruff, and out with 'em. The people will applaud you. They want bread within doors, and honesty without. They have seen enough of partisans and parliaments.

Mary. We can not do without one.

Elizabeth. Convoke it then: but call it with sound of trumpet. Such a body is unlikely to find a head. There is little encouragement for an honest knight or gentleman to take the station. The Commons slink away with lowered shoulders, and bear hateful compunction against the very names and memory of those braver men, who, in dangerous times and before stern authoritative warlike sovrans, supported their pretensions. Kings, who peradventure would have strangled such ringleaders, well remember and well respect them: their fellows would disown their benefactors and maintainers. Kings abominate their example; clowns would efface the images on their sepulchres. What forbearance on our part can such knaves expect, or what succour from the people?

Mary. What is done is done.

Elizabeth. Oftentimes it is easier to undo than to do. I should rather be glad than mortified at what has been done yonder. In addition to those churls and chapmen in the lower house, there are also among the peers no few who voted most audaciously.

Mary. The majority of them was of opinion that the Lady Jane should be invested with royal state and dignity.

Elizabeth. The majority! So much the better . . . so much the better, say I. I would find certain folk who should make sharp inquest into their title-deeds, and spell the indentures syllable by syllable. Certain lands were granted for certain services; which services have been neglected. I would not in such wise neglect the lands in question, but annex them to my royal domains.

Mary. Sister! sister! you forget that the Lady Jane Gray (as was) is now queen of the realm.

Elizabeth. Forget it indeed! The vile woman! I am minded to call her as such vile women are called out of doors.

Mary. Pray abstain; not only forasmuch as it would be unseemly in those sweet, slender, delicate lips of yours, but also by reason that she is adorned with every grace and virtue, bating (which indeed outvalues them all) the true religion. Sister! I hope and believe I in this my speech have given you no offence: for your own eyes, I know, are opened. Indeed, who that is not wilfully blind can err in so straight a road, even if so gentle and so sure a guidance were wanting? The mind, sister, the mind itself must be crooked which deviates a hair's breadth. Ay, that intelligent nod would alone suffice to set my bosom quite at rest thereupon. Should it not?

Elizabeth. It were impudent in me to declare my real opinion at this juncture. We must step warily when we walk among cockatrices. I am barely a saint; indeed far from it; and I am much too young to be a martyr. But that odious monster, who pretends an affection for reformation, and a reverence for learning, is counting the jewels in the crown, while you fancy she is repeating her prayers, or conning her Greek.

Sister Mary! as God is in heaven, I hold nothing so detestable in a woman as hypocrisy. Add thereunto, as you fairly may, avarice, man-hunting, lasciviousness. The least atom of the least among these vices is heavy enough to weight down the soul to the bottomless pit.

Mary. Unless divine grace—

Elizabeth. Don't talk to me. Don't spread the filth fine.

Now could not that empty fool, Dudley, have found some other young person of equal rank with Mistress Jane, and of higher beauty? Not that any other such, pretty as the boy is, would listen to his idle discourse.

And, pray, who are these Dudleys? The first of them was made a man of by our grandfather. And what was the man after all? Nothing better than a huge smelting-pot, with a commodious screw at the colder end of the ladle.

I have no patience with the bold harlotry.

Mary. I see you have not, sister!

Elizabeth. No, nor have the people. They are on tip-toe for rising in all parts of the kingdom.

Mary. What can they do? God help them!

Elizabeth. Sister Mary! good sister Mary! did you say *God help them?* I am trembling into a heap. It is well you have uttered such words to safe and kindred ears. If they should ever come whispered at the Privy Council, it might end badly.

I believe my visit hath been of as long continuance as may seem befitting. I must be gone.

Mary. Before your departure, let me correct a few of your opinions in regard to our gentle kinswoman and most gracious queen. She hath nobly enlarged my poor alimony. Look here! to begin.

Elizabeth. What! all golden pieces? I have not ten groats in the world.

Mary. Be sure she will grant unto you plenteously. She hath condescended to advise me of her intent. Meanwhile I do entreat you will take home with you the purse you are stroking down, thinking about other things.

Elizabeth. Not I, not I, if it comes from such a creature.

Mary. You accept it from me.

Elizabeth. Then indeed unreservedly. Passing through your hands the soil has been wiped away. However, as I live, I will carefully wash every piece in it with soap and water. Do you believe they can lose anything of their weight thereby?

Mary. Nothing material.

Elizabeth. I may reflect and cogitate upon it. I would not fain offer anybody light money.

Troth! I fear the purse, although of chamois and double stitched, is insufficient to sustain the weight of the gold, which must be shaken violently on the road as I return. Dear sister Mary! as you probably are not about to wear that head-tire, could you, commodiously to yourself, lend it me awhile, just to deposit a certain part of the moneys therein? for the velvet is stout, and the Venetian netting close and stiff: I can hardly bend the threads. I shall have more leisure to admire its workmanship at home.

Mary. Elizabeth! I see you are grown forgiving. In the commencement of our discourse I suggested a slight alteration of manner in speaking of our father. Do you pray for the repose of his soul morning and night?

Elizabeth. The doubt is injurious.

Mary. Pardon me! I feel it. But the voices of children, O Elizabeth! come to the ear of God above all other voices. The best want intercession. Pray for him, Elizabeth! pray for him.

Elizabeth. Why not? He did indeed, but he was in a passion, order my mother up the three black stairs, and he left her pretty head on the landing: but I bear him no malice for it.

Mary. Malice! The baneful word hath shot up from hell in many places, but never between child and parent. In the space of that one span, on that single sod from Paradise, the serpent never trailed. Husband and wife were severed by him, then again clashed together: brother slew brother: but parent and child stand where their Creator first placed them, and drink at the only source of pure untroubled love.

Elizabeth. Beside, you know, being king, he had clearly a right to do it, plea or no plea.

Mary. We will converse no longer on so dolorous a subject.

Elizabeth. I will converse on it as long as such is my pleasure.

Mary. Being my visitor, you command here.

Elizabeth. I command nowhere. I am blown about like a leaf: I am yielding as a feather in a cushion, only one among a million. But I tell you, honestly and plainly, I do not approve of it anyhow! It may have grown into a trick and habit with him: no matter for that: in my view of the business, it is not what a husband ought to do with a wife. And, if she did . . . but she did not . . . and I say it.

Mary. It seems indeed severe.

Elizabeth. Yea, afore God, methinks it smacks a trifle of the tart.

Mary. Our father was God's vicegerent. Probably it is for the good of her soul, poor lady! Better suffer here than hereafter. We ought to kiss the rod, and be thankful.

Elizabeth. Kiss the rod, forsooth. I have been constrained erewhile even unto that; and no such a child neither. But I would rather have kissed it fresh and fair, with all its buds and knots upon it, than after it had bestowed on me, in such a roundabout way, such a deal of its embroidery and lace-work. I thank my father for all that. I hope his soul lies easier than my skin did.

Mary. The wish is kind; but prayers would much help it. Our father of blessed memory, now (let us hope) among the saints, was somewhat sore in his visitations; but they tended heavenward.

Elizabeth. Yea, when he cursed and cuffed and kicked us.

Mary. He did kick, poor man!

Elizabeth. Kick! Fifty folks, young and old, have seen the marks his kicking left behind.

Mary. We should conceal all such his infirmities. They arose from an irritation in the foot, whereof he died.

Elizabeth. I only know I could hardly dance or ride for them; chiefly caught, as I was, fleeing from his wrath. He seldom vouchsafed to visit me: when he did, he pinched my ear so bitterly, I was fain to squeal. And then he said, I should turn out like my mother, calling me by such a name moreover as is heard but about the kennel; and even there it is never given to the young.

Mary. There was choler in him at certain times and seasons. Those who have much will, have their choler excited when opposite breath blows against it.

Elizabeth. Let them have will; let them have choler too, in God's name; but it is none the better, as gout is, for flying to hand or foot.

Mary. I have seen . . . now do, pray forgive me . . .

Elizabeth. Well, what have you seen?

Mary. My sweet little sister lift up the most delicate of all delicate white hands, and with their tiny narrow pink nails tear off ruffs and caps, and take sundry unerring aims at eyes and noses.

Elizabeth. Was that any impediment or hindrance to riding and dancing? I would always make people do their duty, and always will. Remember (for your memory seems accurate enough) that, whenever I scratched anybody's face, I permitted my hand to be kist by the offender within a day or two.

Mary. Undeniable.

Elizabeth. I may, peradventure, have been hasty in my childhood: but all great hearts are warm; all good ones are relenting. If, in combing my hair, the hussy lugged it, I obeyed God's command, and referred to the *lex talionis.* I have not too much of it; and every soul on earth sees its beauty. A single one would be a public loss. Uncle Seymour . . . but what boots it? there are others who can see perhaps as far as uncle Seymour.

Mary. I do remember his saying that he watched its growth as he would a melon's. And how fondly did those little sharp grey eyes of his look and wink when you blushed and chided his flattery.

Elizabeth. Never let any man dare to flatter me: I am above it. Only the weak and ugly want the refreshment of that perfumed fan. I take but my own; and touch it who dares.

Really it is pleasant to see in what a pear-form fashion both purse and cowl are hanging. Faith! they are heavy: I could hardly lift them from the back of the chair.

Mary. Let me call an attendant to carry them for you.

Elizabeth. Are you mad? They are unsealed, and ill-tied: any one could slip his hand in.

And so that . . . the word was well nigh out of my mouth . . . gave you all this gold.

Mary. For shame! O for shame!

Elizabeth. I feel shame only for her. It turns my cheeks red . . . together with some anger upon it. But I can not keep my eyes off that book, if book it may be, on which the purse was lying.

Mary. Somewhat irreverently, God forgive me! But it was sent at the same time by the same fair creature, with many kind words. It had always been kept in our father's bedroom closet, and was removed from Edward's by those unhappy men who superintended his education.

Elizabeth. She must have thought all those stones are garnets: to me they look like rubies, one and all. Yet, over so large a cover, they cannot all be rubies.

Mary. I believe they are, excepting the glory in the centre, which is composed of chrysolites. Our father was an excellent judge in jewellery, as in every thing else, and he spared no expenditure in objects of devotion.

Elizabeth. What creature could fail in devotion with an object such as that before the eyes? Let me kiss it . . . partly for my Saviour's and partly for my father's sake.

Mary. How it comforts me, O Elizabeth, to see you thus press it to your bosom! Its spirit, I am confident, has entered there. Disregard the pebbles: take it home: cherish it evermore. May there be virtue, as some think there is, even in the stones about it! God bless you, strengthen you, lead you aright, and finally bring you to everlasting glory.

Elizabeth (*going*). The Popish puss!

THE SWALLOW [1]

By Gilbert White

LETTER XVIII

TO THE HONOURABLE DAINES BARRINGTON

Selborne, Jan. 29, 1774.

Dear Sir:

The house-swallow, or chimney-swallow, is undoubtedly the first comer of all the British *hirundines;* and appears in general on or about the thirteenth of April, as I have remarked from many years' observation. Not but now and then a straggler is seen much earlier: and, in particular, when I was a boy I observed a swallow for a whole day together on a sunny, warm Shrove Tuesday; which day could not fall out later than the middle of March, and often happened early in February.

It is worth remarking that these birds are seen first about lakes and mill-ponds; and it is also very particular, that if these early visitors happen to find frost and snow, as was the case of the two dreadful springs of 1770 and 1771, they immediately withdraw for a time. A circumstance this much more in favor of hiding than migration; since it is much more probable that a

[1] From *The Natural History of Selborne.*

bird should retire to its hybernaculum just at hand, than return for a week or two only to warmer latitudes.

The swallow, though called the chimney-swallow, by no means builds altogether in chimneys, but often within barns and out-houses against the rafters; and so she did in Virgil's time:

. . . "Antè
Garrula quàm tignis nidos suspendat hirundo."

In Sweden she builds in barns, and is called *ladu swala*, the barn-swallow. Besides, in the warmer parts of Europe, there are no chimneys to houses, except they are English-built: in these countries she constructs her nest in porches, and gateways, and galleries, and open halls.

Here and there a bird may affect some odd, peculiar place; as we have known a swallow build down the shaft of an old well, through which chalk had been formerly drawn up for the purpose of manure: but in general with us this *hirundo* breeds in chimneys; and loves to haunt those stacks where there is a constant fire, no doubt for the sake of warmth. Not that it can subsist in the immediate shaft where there is a fire; but prefers one adjoining to that of the kitchen, and disregards the per-petual smoke of that funnel, as I have often observed with some degree of wonder.

Five or six or more feet down the chimney does this little bird begin to form her nest about the middle of May, which consists, like that of the house-martin, of a crust or shell composed of dirt or mud, mixed with short pieces of straw to render it tough and permanent; with this difference, that whereas the shell of the martin is nearly hemispheric, that of the swallow is open at the top, and like half a deep dish: this nest is lined with fine grasses, and feathers which are often collected as they float in the air.

Wonderful is the address which this adroit bird shows all day long in ascending and descending with security through so narrow a pass. When hovering over the mouth of the funnel, the vibra-tions of her wings acting on the confined air occasion a rumbling like thunder. It is not improbable that the dam submits to this inconvenient situation so low in the shaft, in order to secure her broods from rapacious birds, and particularly from owls, which frequently fall down chimneys, perhaps in attempting to get at these nestlings.

The swallow lays from four to six white eggs, dotted with red specks; and brings out her first brood about the last week in June, or the first week in July. The progressive method by which the young are introduced into life is very amusing: first, they emerge from the shaft with difficulty enough, and often fall down into the rooms below: for a day or so they are fed on the chimney-top, and then are conducted to the dead leafless bough of some tree, where, sitting in a row, they are attended with great assiduity, and may then be called perchers. In a day or two more they become flyers, but are still unable to take their own food; therefore they play about near the place where the dams are hawking for flies; and when a mouthful is collected, at a certain signal given, the dam and the nestling advance, rising toward each other, and meeting at an angle; the young one all the while uttering such a little quick note of gratitude and complacency, that a person must have paid very little regard to the wonders of nature that has not often remarked this feat.

The dam betakes herself immediately to the business of a second brood as soon as she is disengaged from her first; which at once associates with the first broods of house-martins; and with them congregates, clustering on sunny roofs, towers, and trees. This *hirundo* brings out her second brood toward the middle and end of August.

All the summer long is the swallow a most instructive pattern of unwearied industry and affection; for, from morning to night, while there is a family to be supported, she spends the whole day in skimming close to the ground, and exerting the most sudden turns and quick evolutions. Avenues, and long walks under hedges, and pasture-fields, and mown meadows where cattle graze, are her delight, especially if there are trees interspersed; because in such spots insects most abound. When a fly is taken a smart snap from her bill is heard, resembling the noise at the shutting of a watch-case; but the motion of the mandibles is too quick for the eye.

The swallow, probably the male birl, is the *excubitor* to house-martins, and other little birds, announcing the approach of birds of prey. For as soon as an hawk appears, with a shrill alarming note he calls all the swallows and martins about him; who pursue in a body, and buffet and strike their enemy till they have driven him from the village, darting down from above on his back, and rising in a perpendicular line in perfect security. This bird also will sound the alarm, and strike at cats when they climb on the roofs of houses, or otherwise approach the nests. Each species of *hirundo* drinks as it flies along, sipping the surface of the water; but the swallow alone, in general, washes on the wing, by dropping into a pool for many times together: in very hot weather house-martins and bank-martins dip and wash a little.

The swallow is a delicate songster, and in soft sunny weather sings both perching and flying; on trees in a kind of concert, and on chimney-tops: is also a bold flyer, ranging to distant downs and commons even in windy weather, which the other species seem much to dislike; nay, even frequenting exposed sea-port towns, and making little excursions over the salt water. Horsemen on wide downs are often closely attended by a little party of swallows for miles together, which plays before and behind them, sweeping around, and collecting all the skulking insects that are roused by the trampling of the horses' feet: when the wind blows hard, without this expedient, they are often forced to settle to pick up their lurking prey.

This species feeds much on little *coleoptera*, as well as on gnats and flies: and often settles on dug ground, or paths for gravels to grind and digest its food. Before they depart for some weeks, to a bird, they forsake houses and chimneys, and roost in trees; and usually withdraw about the beginning of October; though some few stragglers may appear on at times till the first week in November.

Some few pairs haunt the new and open streets of London next the fields, but do not enter, like the house-martin, the close and crowded parts of the city.

Both male and female are distinguished from their congeners by the length and forkedness of their tails. They are undoubtedly the most nimble of all the species: and when the male pursues the female in amorous chase, they then go beyond their usual speed, and exert a rapidity almost too quick for the eye to follow.

After this circumstantial detail of the life and discerning στοργὴ of the swallow, I shall add, for your farther amusement, an anecdote or two not much in favor of her sagacity:

A certain swallow built for two years together on the handles of a pair of garden-shears, that were stuck up against the boards in an out-house, and therefore must have her nest spoiled whenever that implement was wanted: and, what is stranger still, another bird of the same species built its nest on the wings and body of an owl that happened by accident to hang dead and dry from the rafter of a barn. This owl, with the nest on its wings, and with eggs in the nest, was brought as a curiosity worthy the most elegant private museum in Great Britain. The owner, struck with the oddity of the sight, furnished the bringer with a large shell, or conch, desiring him to fix it just where the owl hung: the person did as he was ordered, and the following year a pair, probably the same pair, built their nest in the conch, and laid their eggs.

The owl and the conch make a strange grotesque appearance, and are not the least curious specimens in that wonderful collection of art and nature.

Thus is instinct in animals, taken the least out of its way, an undistinguishing, limited faculty; and blind to every circumstance that does not immediately respect self-preservation, or lead at once to the propagation or support of their species.

I am,

With all respect, etc., etc.

TOBY [1]

By Dr. John Brown

Was the most utterly shabby, vulgar, mean-looking cur I ever beheld: in one word, *a tyke*. He had not one good feature except his teeth and eyes, and his bark, if that can be called a feature.

[1] From *Rab and His Friends*.

He was not ugly enough to be interesting; his color black and white, his shape leggy and clumsy; altogether what Sydney Smith would have called an extraordinarily ordinary dog; and, as I have said, not even greatly ugly, or, as the Aberdonians have it, *bonnie wi' ill-fauredness*. My brother William found him the centre of attraction to a multitude of small blackguards who were drowning him slowly in Lochend Loch, doing their best to lengthen out the process, and secure the greatest amount of fun with the nearest approach to death. Even then Toby showed his great intellect by pretending to be dead, and thus gaining time and an inspiration. William bought him for twopence, and as he had it not, the boys accompanied him to Pilrig Street, when I happened to meet him, and giving the twopence to the biggest boy, had the satisfaction of seeing a general engagement of much severity, during which the twopence disappeared; one penny going off with a very small and swift boy, and the other vanishing hopelessly into the grating of a drain.

Toby was for weeks in the house unbeknown to any one but ourselves two and the cook, and from my grandmother's love of tidiness and hatred of dogs and of dirt I believe she would have expelled "him whom we saved from drowning," had not he, in his straightforward way, walked into my father's bedroom one night when he was bathing his feet, and introduced himself with a wag of his tail, intimating a general willingness to be happy. My father laughed most heartily, and at last Toby, having got his way to his bare feet, and having begun to lick his soles and between his toes with his small rough tongue, my father gave such an unwonted shout of laughter that we—grandmother, sisters, and all of us—went in. Grandmother might argue with all her energy and skill, but as surely as the pressure of Tom Jones' infantile fist upon Mr. Allworthy's forefinger undid all the arguments of his sister, so did Toby's tongue and fun prove too many for grandmother's eloquence. I somehow think Toby must have been up to all this, for I think he had a peculiar love for my father ever after, and regarded grandmother from that hour with a careful and cool eye.

Toby, when full grown, was a strong, coarse dog; coarse in

shape, in countenance, in hair, and in manner. I used to think that, according to the Pythagorean doctrine, he must have been, or been going to be a Gilmerton carter. He was of the bull terrier variety, coarsened through much mongrelism and a dubious and varied ancestry. His teeth were good, and he had a large skull, and a rich bark as of a dog three times his size, and a tail which I never saw equaled—indeed it was a tail *per se;* it was of immense girth and not short, equal throughout like a policeman's baton; the machinery for working it was of great power, and acted in a way, as far as I have been able to discover, quite original. We called it his ruler.

When he wished to get into the house, he first whined gently, then growled, then gave a sharp bark, and then came a resounding, mighty stroke which shook the house; this, after much study and watching, we found was done by his bringing the entire length of his solid tail flat upon the door, with a sudden and vigorous stroke; it was quite a *tour de force* or a *coup de queue,* and he was perfect in it at once, his first *bang* authoritative, having been as masterly and telling as his last.

With all this inbred vulgar air, he was a dog of great moral excellence—affectionate, faithful, honest up to his light, with an odd humor as peculiar and as strong as his tail. My father, in his reserved way, was very fond of him, and there must have been very funny scenes with them, for we heard bursts of laughter issuing from his study when they two were by themselves; there was something in him that took that grave, beautiful, melancholy face. One can fancy him in the midst of his books, and sacred work and thoughts, pausing and looking at the secular Toby, who was looking out for a smile to begin his rough fun, and about to end by coursing and *gurrin'* round the room, upsetting my father's books, laid out on the floor for consultation, and himself nearly at times, as he stood watching him—and off his guard and shaking with laughter. Toby had always a great desire to accompany my father up to town; this my father's good taste and sense of dignity, besides his fear of losing his friend (a vain fear!), forbade, and as the decision of character of each was great and nearly equal, it was often a drawn game. Toby ultimately, by making it his entire object, triumphed. He usually was nowhere to be seen on my father leaving; he however saw him, and lay in wait at the head of the street, and up Leith Walk he kept him in view from the opposite side like a detective, and then, when he knew it was hopeless to hound him home, he crossed unblushingly over, and joined company, excessively rejoiced of course.

One Sunday he had gone with him to church, and left him at the vestry door. The second psalm was given out, and my father was sitting back in the pulpit, when the door at its back, up which he came from the vestry was seen to move, and gently open, then, after a long pause, a black shining snout pushed its way steadily into the congregation, and was followed by Toby's entire body. He looked somewhat abashed, but snuffing his friend, he advanced as if on thin ice, and not seeing him, put his forelegs on the pulpit, and behold there he was, his own familiar chum. I watched all this, and anything more beautiful than his look of happiness, of comfort, of entire ease when he beheld his friend,—the smoothing down of the anxious ears, the swing of gladness of that mighty tail,—I don't expect soon to see. My father quietly opened the door, and Toby was at his feet and invisible to all but himself; had he sent old George Peaston, the "minister's man," to put him out, Toby would probably have shown his teeth, and astonished George. He slunk home as soon as he could, and never repeated that exploit.

I never saw in any other dog the sudden transition from discretion, not to say abject cowardice, to blazing and permanent valor. From his earliest years he showed a general meanness of blood, inherited from many generations of starved, bekicked, and down-trodden forefathers and mothers, resulting in a condition of intense abjectness in all matters of personal fear; anybody, even a beggar, by a *gowl* and a threat of eye, could send him off howling by anticipation, with that mighty tail between his legs. But it was not always so to be, and I had the privilege of seeing courage, reasonable, absolute, and for life, spring up in Toby at once, as did Athené from the skull of Jove. It happened thus:—

Toby was in the way of hiding his culinary bones in the small gardens before his own and the neighboring doors. Mr. Scrymgeour, two doors off, a bulky, choleric, red-haired, red-faced man —*torvo vultu*—was, by the law of contrast, a great cultivator of flowers, and he had often scowled Toby into all but nonexistence by a stamp of his foot and a glare of his eye. One day his gate being open, in walks Toby with a huge bone, and making a hole where Scrymgeour had two minutes before been planting some precious slip, the name of which on paper and on a stick Toby made very light of, substituted his bone, and was engaged covering it, or thinking he was covering it up with his shoveling nose (a very odd relic of paradise in the dog), when S. spied him through the inner glass door, and was out upon him like the Assyrian, with a terrible *gowl*. I watched them. Instantly Toby made straight at him with a roar too, and an eye more torve than Scrymgeour's, who, retreating without reserve, fell prostrate, there is reason to believe, in his own lobby. Toby contented himself with proclaiming his victory at the door, and returning finished his bone-planting at his leisure; the enemy, who had scuttled behind the glass-door, glaring at him.

From this moment Toby was an altered dog. Pluck at first sight was lord of all; from that time dated his first tremendous deliverance of tail against the door which we called "come listen to my tail." That very evening he paid a visit to Leo, next door's dog, a big, tyrannical bully and coward, which its master thought a Newfoundland, but whose pedigree we knew better; this brute continued the same system of chronic extermination which was interrupted at Lochend,—having Toby down among his feet, and threatening him with instant death two or three times a day. To him Toby paid a visit that very evening, down into his den, and walked about, as much as to say "Come on, Macduff!" but Macduff did not come on, and henceforward there was an armed neutrality, and they merely stiffened up and made their backs rigid, pretended each not to see the other, walking solemnly round, as is the manner of dogs. Toby worked his new-found faculty thoroughly, but with discretion. He killed cats, astonished beggars, kept his own in his own garden against all comers,

and came off victorious in several well-fought battles; but he
was not quarrelsome or foolhardy. It was very odd how his
carriage changed, holding his head up, and how much pleasanter
he was at home. To my father, next to William, who was his
Humane Society man, he remained stanch. And what of his
end? for the misery of dogs is that they die so soon, or as Sir
Walter says, it is well they do; for if they lived as long as a
Christian, and we liked them in proportion, and they then died,
he said that was a thing he could not stand.

His exit was miserable, and had a strange poetic or tragic
relation to his entrance. My father was out of town; I was away
in England. Whether it was that the absence of my father had
relaxed his power of moral restraint, or whether through neglect
of the servant he had been desperately hungry, or most likely
both being true, Toby was discovered with the remains of a cold
leg of mutton, on which he had made an ample meal; this he was
in vain endeavoring to plant as of old, in the hope of its remaining undiscovered till to-morrow's hunger returned, the whole
shank bone sticking up unmistakably. This was seen by our
excellent and Rhadamanthine grandmother, who pronounced sentence on the instant; and next day, as William was leaving for
the High School, did he in the sour morning, through an easterly
haur, behold him "whom he saved from drowning," and whom,
with better results than in the case of Launce and Crab, he had
taught, as if one should say, "thus would I teach a dog," dangling by his own chain from his own lamp-post, one of his hind
feet just touching the pavement, and his body preternaturally
elongated.

William found him dead and warm, and falling in with the
milk-boy at the head of the street, questioned him, and discovered
that he was the executioner, and had got twopence, he—Toby's
every morning crony, who met him and accompanied him up
the street, and licked the outside of his can—had, with an eye
to speed and convenience, and a want of taste, not to say principle and affection, horrible still to think of, suspended Toby's
animation beyond all hope. William instantly fell upon him,
upsetting his milk and cream, and gave him a thorough licking,
to his own intense relief; and, being late, he got from Pyper, who

was a martinet, the customary palmies, which he bore with something approaching to pleasure. So died Toby; my father said little, but he missed and mourned his friend.

There is reason to believe that by one of those curious intertwistings of existence, the milk-boy was that one of the drowning party who got the penny of the twopence.

EXERCISES

1. List the topic sentences of "Eustacia Vye," noting that paragraph 1 is made up of comparison, that 2 has to do with her figure and hair, that 3 extends and develops the description of her hair, that 4 deals with her eyes, 5, her mouth, 6, the memories which her presence suggested, 7, her relation to her locality, and 8, the use of some distinguishing mark or detail in dress. This makes an excellent model arrangement for a portrait. Choose some outstanding personality whom you wish to present and model your work closely on "Eustacia Vye."

2. Study the use of consonants in paragraphs 1 and 2 of "Mrs. Battle." Which consonant sounds are predominant in the first? Which in the second? What is the effect of each? Try to construct a paragraph in your theme which will show the effectiveness of either consonant or vowel sounds to express personality.

3. Study the last sentence of this portion of "Mrs. Battle." What is the effect of the semicolons and of the units which they separate? What is the effect of the succession of adjectives and of the adjectives themselves in the last clause?

4. Are monosyllables pleasing or tiresome in "Kitchen Portraits"? What plots for stories are suggested here? When you have finished the selection, are the people blurred or distinct? Why?

5. Study the use of similes in "Queequeg." Why are they especially appropriate? Try to use at least two first-class similes in your next theme. What makes a simile first-class? (Here is food for thought!)

6. Write an imaginary conversation with the ideal of characterization in mind between

Joseph and his brother Benjamin
Gene Tunney and William Shakespeare
Henry D. Thoreau and a hunter in the Walden woods
H. L. Mencken and Edgar A. Guest

Calvin Coolidge and the postmistress of Plymouth, Vermont
Sir Roger de Coverley and Will Honeycomb
Charles Lindbergh and a college freshman
Emmeline Pankhurst and Carrie Nation
The President of the D. A. R. and a prominent Bolshevist
Queen Elizabeth and Amy Robsart
Falstaff and his pious mother
Henry Ford and Thomas A. Edison
John D. Rockefeller and his golf caddy
Queen Victoria and Disraeli
Thomas and Jane Carlyle
Joan of Arc and her father
Richard Coeur de Lion and Blondell
Odysseus and Penelope upon his return
Any two members of your faculty
Tennyson's Maud and the lily maid of "Astolat"
The Dean and the Janitor
King Arthur and George P. Babbitt
The Football Coach and the Dean of Women

SUGGESTED READINGS

Addison, Joseph, "Sir Roger at Church" from *Sir Roger de Coverley Papers.*

Anonymous, "Butterfly Psychology," in Tanner, *Essays and Essay Writing,* Little, Brown, Boston.

Austen, Jane, "Miss Bates at the Ball" from *Emma,* Vol. III, Chapter II, E. P. Dutton, New York.

Beerbohm, Max, "A Clergyman," in *Modern Essays,* First Series, Harcourt, Brace, New York.

Boswell, James, "Johnson at Oxford" from Boswell's *Life of Samuel Johnson, Year 1728.*

Bradford, Gamaliel, "Pepys and His Wife" from *The Soul of Samuel Pepys,* Houghton Mifflin, Boston.

Brooke, Tucker, "Shakespeare's Queen," *The Yale Review,* January 1927.

Brown, Dr. John, "Our Dogs" from *Rab and His Friends,* E. P. Dutton, New York.

Burghes, Charlotte, "Bee No. 599," *The Atlantic Monthly,* May 1926.

Davis, Elmer, "Portrait of a Cleric" from *Show Window*, John Day, New York.

Defosse, F. J., "Tiger, Tiger," *The Atlantic Monthly*, November 1926. "Elephants," *The Atlantic Monthly*, April 1928.

Galsworthy, John, "The Latest Thing" from *The Little Man and Other Satires*, Scribner's, New York. "Ultima Thule" and "A Portrait" from *Caravan*, Scribner's, New York.

Guedalla, Philip, "Mr. Bernard Shaw" and "M. Anatole France" from *A Gallery*, Putnam's, New York. "Jane Welsh Carlyle" and "Emily Tennyson" from *Bonnet and Shawl*, Putnam's, New York.

Hudson, W. H., "A Patriarch of the Pampas," Chapter XIII, from *Far Away and Long Ago*, E. P. Dutton, New York.

Lamb, Charles, "Captain Jackson" from *Last Essays of Elia*. "The Old Benchers of the Inner Temple" from *Essays of Elia*.

Landor, Walter Savage, "Henry VIII and Anne Boleyn," "Bossuet and the Duchess de Fontanges," both from *Imaginary Conversations*, E. P. Dutton, New York.

Lubbock, Percy, "Grandmother" from *Earlham*, Scribner's, New York.

Meredith, George, "Clara Middleton" from *The Egoist*, Chapter V, Scribner's, New York.

Meynell, Alice, "Mrs. Johnson" from *Essays*, Scribner's, New York.

Morley, Christopher, "An Oxford Landlady" from *Shandygaff*, Doubleday, Doran, New York.

Pater, Walter, "Denys L'Auxerrois" from *Imaginary Portraits*, Macmillan, New York.

Scoville, Samuel, Jr., "The Peregrine Falcon," *The Yale Review*, July 1927.

Williamson, Henry, "Muggy, The Rabbit Agent," *The Atlantic Monthly*, November 1927.

Young, Stark, "Portraits in Encaustic" from *Encaustics*, The New Republic, Inc., 1926.

II. TYPES OF PEOPLE

A second interesting way to portray people is to depict them as typical of a group or a class. Here again the method is objective, the author remaining in the background so that the full attention of the reader is focussed on the subject presented. True, the writer's presence may now and again be necessary as he relates for purposes of illustration some incident in which he himself may play a part; or, as in Lamb's "Poor Relations," he describes the effect of the poor relation on those whom he visits; or as he takes the part of an interlocutor as Mr. Stark Young does in "Citizen Tom." The effect of the theme, however, must leave no question in the reader's mind as to which is the central object.

Here as in portraiture detail is valuable. Could one find better use of it than in Macaulay's paragraphs on the Puritans? To be sure, there cannot be so much preparation for dramatic effect in the presentation of a type as of an individual, and yet well-chosen detail is seldom amiss. Moreover, there is always the chance to characterize or to depict the type *through* the individual, as Mr. Young portrays a certain sort of college president through his narrative about President C— or as John Galsworthy by means of Mr. Nilson and Mr. Tandram draws the English business man on a spring morning.

The models quoted are proof, as has already been suggested, of the various ways in which a theme on this subject may be written. Macaulay in a few paragraphs, which have been cited for years as examples of perfect construction, exposes the paradoxical character of the Puritans. You can not find better models than the third or the fourth of these paragraphs if you decide to handle your material by means of a paragraph theme. (See Exercise 1 at the close of the section.) Thackeray's method in "University Snobs" is far more informal and familiar than that of Macaulay, and yet it, too, is expository.

Lamb in "Poor Relations" indulges his unquenchable humor by the extravagant use of metaphors and of parody. An attempt to test one's own power of comparison in dealing with the type of his choice would be a wholesome, if disillusioning, mental and intellectual exercise. Lamb's metaphors in his first paragraph number twenty-seven culled from the Bible, folk and fairy lore, and mythology as well as from his own experience. The style and diction of his second paragraph is obviously a parody on those of the *Proverbs*. His third is somewhat nearer the earth.

One of Mr. Galsworthy's best qualifications as a novelist is his beautiful use of dialogue. The perfect naturalness of it in his sketch, "The Japanese Quince," is of indispensable value in the characterization. The same thing is true of the dialogue in "Citizen Tom." Although it is perhaps less polished than Galsworthy's, it admirably serves its purpose. Both of these depictions of types by the use of narrative are rich in mannerisms and detail—President C—'s favorite oath, the "foolish strength" of his features, his heavily padded shoulders, the identical features of Mr. Nilson and Mr. Tandram, their black frock coats, their morning papers clasped behind them. Both of them may well suggest to a student who sees things and people at once dramatically and concretely an interesting way to handle material for this sort of theme.

THE PURITANS [1]

By *Thomas Babington Macaulay*

We would speak first of the Puritans, the most remarkable body of men, perhaps, which the world has ever produced. The odious and ridiculous parts of their character lie on the surface. He that runs may read them; nor have there been wanting attentive and malicious observers to point them out. For many years after the Restoration, they were the theme of unmeasured invective and derision. They were exposed to the utmost licentiousness of the press and of the stage, at the time when the press and the stage were most licentious. They were not men of letters; they were, as a body, unpopular; they could not defend themselves; and the public would not take them under its protection. They were therefore abandoned, without reserve, to the tender mercies of the satirists and dramatists. The ostentatious simplicity of their dress, their sour aspect, their nasal twang, their stiff posture, their long graces, their Hebrew names, the Scriptural phrases which they introduced on every occasion, their contempt of human learning, their detestation of polite

[1] From *The Essay on Milton*.

amusements, were indeed fair game for the laughers. But it is not from the laughers alone that the philosophy of history is to be learnt. And he who approaches this subject should carefully guard against the influence of that potent ridicule which has already misled so many excellent writers.

*   *   *   *   *   *   *

Those who roused the people to resistance, who directed their measures through a long series of eventful years, who formed, out of the most unpromising materials, the finest army that Europe had ever seen, who trampled down King, Church, and Aristocracy, who, in the short intervals of domestic sedition and rebellion, made the name of England terrible to every nation on the face of the earth, were no vulgar fanatics. Most of their absurdities were mere external badges, like the signs of freemasonry, or the dresses of friars. We regret that these badges were not more attractive. We regret that a body to whose courage and talents mankind has owed inestimable obligations had not the lofty elegance which distinguished some of the adherents of Charles the First, or the easy good-breeding for which the court of Charles the Second was celebrated. But, if we must make our choice, we shall, like Bassanio in the play, turn from the specious caskets which contain only the Death's head and the Fool's head, and fix on the plain leaden chest which conceals the treasure.

The Puritans were men whose minds had derived a peculiar character from the daily contemplation of superior beings and eternal interests. Not content with acknowledging, in general terms, an overruling Providence, they habitually ascribed every event to the will of the Great Being, for whose power nothing was too vast, for whose inspection nothing was too minute. To know him, to serve him, to enjoy him, was with them the great end of existence. They rejected with contempt the ceremonious homage which other sects substituted for the pure worship of the soul. Instead of catching occasional glimpses of the Deity through an obscuring veil, they aspired to gaze full on his intolerable brightness, and to commune with him face to face.

Hence originated their contempt for terrestrial distinctions. The difference between the greatest and the meanest of mankind seemed to vanish, when compared with the boundless interval which separated the whole race from him on whom their own eyes were constantly fixed. They recognised no title to superiority but his favour; and, confident of that favour, they despised all the accomplishments and all the dignities of the world. If they were unacquainted with the works of philosophers and poets, they were deeply read in the oracles of God. If their names were not found in the registers of heralds, they were recorded in the Book of Life. If their steps were not accompanied by a splendid train of menials, legions of ministering angels had charge over them. Their palaces were houses not made with hands; their diadems crowns of glory which should never fade away. On the rich and the eloquent, on nobles and priests, they looked down with contempt: for they esteemed themselves rich in a more precious treasure, and eloquent in a more sublime language, nobles by the right of an earlier creation, and priests by the imposition of a mightier hand. The very meanest of them was a being to whose fate a mysterious and terrible importance belonged, on whose slightest action the spirits of light and darkness looked with anxious interest, who had been destined, before heaven and earth were created, to enjoy a felicity which should continue when heaven and earth should have passed away. Events which shortsighted politicians ascribed to earthly causes, had been ordained on his account. For his sake empires had risen, and flourished, and decayed. For his sake the Almighty had proclaimed his will by the pen of the evangelist, and the harp of the prophet. He had been wrested by no common deliverer from the grasp of no common foe. He had been ransomed by the sweat of no vulgar agony, by the blood of no earthly sacrifice. It was for him that the sun had been darkened, that the rocks had been rent, that the dead had risen, that all nature had shuddered at the sufferings of her expiring God.

Thus the Puritan was made up of two different men, the one all self-abasement, penitence, gratitude, passion; the other proud, calm, inflexible, sagacious. He prostrated himself in the dust before his Maker: but he set his foot on the neck of his king. In his devotional retirement, he prayed with convulsions, and groans, and tears. He was half-maddened by glorious or terrible illusions. He heard the lyres of angels or the tempting whispers of fiends. He caught a gleam of the Beatific Vision, or woke screaming from dreams of everlasting fire. Like Vane, he thought himself intrusted with the sceptre of the millennial year. Like Fleetwood, he cried in the bitterness of his soul that God had hid his face from him. But when he took his seat in the council, or girt on his sword for war, these tempestuous workings of the soul had left no perceptible trace behind them. People who saw nothing of the godly but their uncouth visages, and heard nothing from them but their groans and their whining hymns, might laugh at them. But those had little reason to laugh who encountered them in the hall of debate or in the field of battle. These fanatics brought to civil and military affairs a coolness of judgment and an immutability of purpose which some writers have thought inconsistent with their religious zeal, but which were in fact the necessary effects of it. The intensity of their feelings on one subject made them tranquil on every other. One overpowering sentiment had subjected to itself pity and hatred, ambition and fear. Death had lost its terrors and pleasure its charms. They had their smiles and their tears, their raptures and their sorrows, but not for the things of this world. Enthusiasm had made them Stoics, had cleared their minds from every vulgar passion and prejudice, and raised them above the influence of danger and of corruption. It sometimes might lead them to pursue unwise ends, but never to choose unwise means. They went through the world, like Sir Artegal's iron man Talus with his flail, crushing and trampling down oppressors, mingling with human beings, but having neither part nor lot in human infirmities, insensible to fatigue, to pleasure, and to pain, not to be pierced by any weapon, not to be withstood by any barrier.

Such we believe to have been the character of the Puritans. We perceive the absurdity of their manners. We dislike the sullen gloom of their domestic habits. We acknowledge that the tone of their minds was often injured by straining after things too high for mortal reach: and we know that, in spite of their hatred of Popery, they too often fell into the worst vices of that bad system, intolerance and extravagant austerity, that they had their anchorites and their crusades, their Dunstans and their De Montforts, their Dominics and their Escobars. Yet, when all circumstances are taken into consideration, we do not hesitate to pronounce them a brave, a wise, an honest, and an useful body.

POOR RELATIONS [1]

(IN PART)

By Charles Lamb

A Poor Relation is the most irrelevant thing in nature, a piece of impertinent correspondency, an odious approximation, a haunting conscience, a preposterous shadow, lengthening in the noontide of our prosperity; an unwelcome remembrancer, a perpetually recurring mortification, a drain on your purse, a more intolerable dun upon your pride, a drawback upon success, a rebuke to your rising, a stain in your blood, a blot on your 'scutcheon, a rent in your garment, a death's head at your banquet, Agathocles' pot, a Mordecai in your gate, a Lazarus at your door, a lion in your path, a frog in your chamber, a fly in your ointment, a mote in your eye, a triumph to your enemy, an apology to your friends, the one thing not needful, the hail in harvest, the ounce of sour in a pound of sweet.

He is known by his knock. Your heart telleth you "That is Mr. ———." A rap, between familiarity and respect, that demands, and at the same time seems to despair of, entertainment. He entereth smiling and embarrassed. He holdeth out his hand to you to shake, and draweth it back again. He casually looketh in about dinner-time—when the table is full. He offereth to go away, seeing you have company, but is induced to stay. He filleth a chair, and your visitor's two children are accommodated at a side-table. He never cometh upon open days, when your wife says, with some complacency, "My dear, perhaps Mr.

[1] From *Last Essays of Elia*.

—— will drop in to-day." He remembereth birthdays, and professeth he is fortunate to have stumbled upon one. He declareth against fish, the turbot being small, yet suffereth himself to be importuned into a slice against his first resolution. He sticketh by the port, yet he will be prevailed upon to empty the remainder glass of claret, if a stranger press it upon him. He is a puzzle to the servants, who are fearful of being too obsequious, or not civil enough, to him. The guests think "they have seen him before." Every one speculateth upon his condition; and the most part take him to be a tide-waiter. He calleth you by your Christian name to imply that his other is the same with your own. He is too familiar by half, yet you wish he had less diffidence. With half his familiarity he might pass for a casual dependent; with more boldness, he would be in no danger of being taken for what he is. He is too humble for a friend, yet taketh on him more state than befits a client. He is a worse guest than a country tenant, inasmuch as he bringeth up no rent, yet 'tis odds, from his garb and demeanor, that your guests take him for one. He is asked to make one at the whist table; refuseth on the score of poverty, and resents being left out. When the company breaks up, he proffereth to go for a coach, and lets the servant go. He recollects your grandfather, and will thrust in some mean and quite unimportant anecdote of the family. He knew it when it was not quite so flourishing as "he is blest in seeing it now." He reviveth past situations, to institute what he calleth favorable comparisons. With a reflecting sort of congratulation he will inquire the price of your furniture, and insults you with a special commendation of your window-curtains. He is of opinion that the urn is the more elegant shape; but, after all, there was something more comfortable about the old tea-kettle, which you must remember. He dare say you must find a great convenience in having a carriage of your own, and appealeth to your lady if it is not so. Inquireth if you have had your arms done on vellum yet; and did not know, till lately, that such-and-such had been the crest of the family. His memory is unseasonable; his compliments perverse; his talk a trouble; his stay pertinacious; and when he goeth away, you dismiss his chair into a corner as precipitately as possible, and feel fairly rid of two nuisances.

There is a worse evil under the sun, and that is a female poor relation. You may do something with the other; you may pass him off tolerably well; but your indigent she-relative is hopeless. "He is an old humourist," you may say, "and affects to go threadbare. His circumstances are better than folks would take them to be. You are fond of having a character at your table, and truly he is one." But in the indications of female poverty there can be no disguise. No woman dresses below herself from caprice. The truth must out without shuffling. "She is plainly related to the L——s; or what does she at their house?" She is, in all probability, your wife's cousin. Nine times out of ten, at least, this is the case. Her garb is something between a gentlewoman and a beggar, yet the former evidently predominates. She is most provokingly humble, and ostentatiously sensible to her inferiority. He may require to be repressed sometimes— *aliquando sufflaminandus erat*—but there is no raising her. You send her soup at dinner, and she begs to be helped—after the gentlemen. Mr. —— requests the honor of taking wine with her; she hesitates between Port and Madeira, and chooses the former because he does. She calls the servant *Sir;* and insists on not troubling him to hold her plate. The housekeeper patronizes her. The children's governess takes upon her to correct her, when she has mistaken the piano for a harpsichord.

*   *   *   *   *   *   *

CITIZEN TOM [1]

By Stark Young

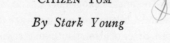

My first sight of President C— was in the telephone booth of a railway junction. "Hello, President C— speaking," he said. And then a moment later a tall, broad man in a blue serge suit with heavily padded shoulders, his hair red, his features large and decisive and full of a kind of foolish strength,

[1] From *Encaustics*. By the kind permission of the author.

emerged and stood looking up and down the station, large, firm, like a swelling piece of civic virtue. I knew the outlines of the president's career. He had been first a baseball player of renown, he had then entered the ministry, and now after several years of service had become the president of a New England college. In this state, I had been told, his athletic piety and direct manhood had made him adored. There were, as might be expected nowadays, some restless and Reddish students who rebelled at President C—'s quality and influence; the majority of the college body took him for their ideal.

President C— and I became acquainted not long after this first sight I had of him. We sat together on a government educational commission, a left-over from the war. He never talked easily or was able to flow into simple human connections with other men, but he frequently conducted a monologue or crashed into debate. And so, in the course of things, I had a chance to learn his theory of education.

I am not sure that I ever understood it quite, but the gist of it, as I gathered when I stripped it of its eloquence and vigor, was this: The purpose of education is making men. A man among men. It makes leaders of men, however, also. The ideal education develops both mind and body, *mens sana in corpore sano*. Men learn to mix by being at college. Nothing teaches them to mix with their fellow men so well as athletics, as clean contest. Let us never forget the noble exercise of the mind! President C— himself might never have been able to mingle with men if it had not been for baseball. It had saved him. College men learn to be men not so much through book learning as through their freshman experiences, the rough and tumble of the dormitories. College connections are valuable in after-life. The purpose of education is to make young men citizens.

These, as the world must know by now, for he has expanded them into many addresses, were President C—'s theories of education.

I have a friend, or rather a friend of the family, who sent her son last year to President C—'s college, partly because it is well known, partly to get him into the country and out of New

York. Tom, the son, by some maternal engineering, by caresses and spanks and bribes, had been got through preparatory schools, and rather miraculously past the test of college entrance requirements. That was last year.

A week or two ago I met President C— on the street; he is naturally on another commission and had run down to New York for the meeting. We talked as we walked along Park Avenue. Finally I asked:

"What about my friend Mrs. L—'s boy, President C—? He is at your college, isn't he?"

A look of disgust came over the president's face.

"L—," he said, "oh, that chap? I think I remember him; I make an effort to keep our men individually in mind. I was gravely disappointed in the course he pursued in college. You can see he is a shy boy, with some ability, the dean tells me, if he would apply himself. But he made a total failure of it. He neglected his grades. He did not know how to mix with the men. He took no part in athletics or the life of the college. No fraternity invited him to join. He wasted the year. In the spring he decided to leave. I urged him to remain. Buckle down, I said. Play the game. If he had stayed, a fraternity would have asked him to be a member undoubtedly, he was not a bad-looking youth. But he was unapproachable apparently. He disregarded my opinion and left college."

"But suppose," I ventured, "Tom never wanted to be one of the college men? • Why distort what he is to be like the others? There must be a man now and then who learns little from fraternity life, or from having freshmen rub molasses in his hair and keep him up all night, don't you think? For many men your college scheme may be quite right, but why not grant men who may be different their own kind of thing?"

"This college experience will teach them the life of the race," the president said—though here I can only quote his words without quite following his meaning: "L— never gave himself the chance."

"The chance for what, President C—?" I asked.

"A chance for learning to live among his fellow men."

"But what's the use of learning to live with men if you can't live with yourself?"

President C— looked at me patiently and powerfully like a big, fine, influential spirit. I could see him judging me as a man of little weight. I shifted the subject slightly. I asked what Tom was doing this year, if he had not returned to college.

"L—," the president replied, "so the dean tells me, wrote in answer to the questionnaire that the college sends out in August, that he had entered a theater school."

President C— was silent and I looked at him. Silent and swollen like that, he seemed to me like a platitude at prayer.

But I knew that what had happened was that Tom, timid, wrapped in his own world, dreaming, vague, useless if you like, had got under the president's skin. It hit the president's vanity to fail of even so negligible a worshiper.

"And how has he done?" I asked.

"Now that I can't tell you. We can probably imagine."

"Is it a good theater school, I wonder?" I said, tentatively.

President C— had no way of knowing that either. But he told me the exact name of the place— Tom, I reflected, had indeed impressed him.

"But that," I said, "is only around the corner more or less. What do you think, shall we run in and see what is going on?"

President C— looked at me a moment and decided.

"By the living God I will," he said. I knew of old that admirable oath of his, in which by putting in the living you take out the profanity. "I've never seen one of these places."

Neither had I and I said as much. And we started off to find Tom's school.

But I had seen art schools full of students. I began to think gleefully of those students coming on the run every morning and staying till the last light had faded and the janitors pulled down the blinds. And then the talk, talk, talk, looking at one another's work, criticizing, intense, happy with the head and hands working together, believing in art, in the future, delighting in the world. Many of these students were without talent, many lazy, many destined to clerkships; but for the time they moved in a happy, drifting, believing atmosphere. Then I thought of the colleges, with their muddled aims, their exhorting grades, their rules, degrees and prizes to keep the thing going. I thought of those bored groups of men around fraternity house fires, the victrola grinding, tobacco smoke rising—a scene sweetly remembered years afterward, but at the time rather flat—how little it connected with the life of the mind, with the life of human thought! Some of these college men study, some love learning, some find stimulation in a handful of professors who are hated by the faculty at large. But all are encouraged by the dean, the alumni, the fraternities and the class spirit, to hold college offices, to be leaders with buttons and pennants, to compete, to fill the time. The art school was busy, but had to get on with mere art and high hopes; it had no baseball, class honors, clubs, or letters for sweaters and caps. These sweet thoughts made me feel more gently toward President C—. I was relying on the tone of the theater school to take him down.

We entered the school to the sound of a tremendous hammering and talking. In the hallway there was a class in diction. In the auditorium itself there was a pantomime rehearsing; and on the stage some one was directing a scene from a play. Over in a far corner they were painting scenery, and two men lay sprawled on the floor around a drawing. We were presently introduced to the director. Was it always like this, we asked? Was every one always at it? From nine in the morning until eleven at night, said the director. There were lessons in literature, in diction, fencing, dancing, stage decoration. There were rehearsals, and every night there was a performance of one-act plays, for the students must get the theater endurance. Few of them would ever be distinguished artists, but every one worked, there was so much to be learned.

And how was Mr. Tom L— getting on? we asked.

The director beamed. Mr. L—, he said, was one of the lights of the school. He came early and stayed late. He was insatiable, he killed himself trying to learn everything. And his acting was very promising; he had in comedy a certain wistful quality that ought to go far. We might find Tom, the director said, in the basement somewhere; he was experimenting with stage lighting.

We came upon Tom on his knees with a reflecting apparatus. He was rather pale and a little thinner perhaps but his eyes were shining. He gesticulated, swept out a notebook with designs, he led us around to his machines, he chattered about his plans. "Believe me," he said, "it's a great life if you don't weaken."

Meanwhile I watched President C—. He was very reserved, very kind, in the few things he said he took a tone of national encouragement. What a big, manly spirit he represented there among the lighting machines and painted sets! And I could see that he still wanted to be the boy's ideal.

As for me I was shamelessly thrilled over seeing a man find what he wanted. I felt encouraged, set up, sentimental. On the street again a moment later I could still see that young face, a dreamer's, an artist's. He was like a blossoming tree, he was like a child listening to music.

I lost my sense of humor and began to say to President C— how splendid it was to see a chap discover like this his education and his happiness together.

The president said nothing.

I persisted. Did he not think so?

"Probably," he assented. "But still—"

"But still—?"

The president, knitting his brows together, measured his words, making me at the same moment how grateful that he should run so true to form!

"I question his judgment, nevertheless," he said. "What of his citizenship?"

On University Snobs [1]

By William Makepeace Thackeray

I should like to fill several volumes with accounts of various University Snobs; so fond are my reminiscences of them, and so numerous are they. I should like to speak, above all, of the

[1] From *The Book of Snobs*.

wives and daughters of some of the Professor-Snobs; their amusements, habits, jealousies; their innocent artifices to entrap young
men; their picnics, concerts, and evening parties. I wonder what
has become of Emily Blades, daughter of Blades the Professor
of the Mandingo language? I remember her shoulders to this
day, as she sat in the midst of a crowd of about seventy young
gentlemen, from Corpus and Catherine Hall, entertaining them
with ogles and French songs on the guitar. Are you married,
fair Emily of the shoulders? What beautiful ringlets those were
that used to dribble over them!—what a waist!—what a killing
sea-green shot-silk gown!—what a cameo, the size of a muffin!
There were thirty-six young men of the University in love at one
time with Emily Blades: and no words are sufficient to describe
the pity, the sorrow, the deep, deep commiseration—the rage,
fury, and uncharitableness, in other words—with which the Miss
Trumps (daughter of Trumps, the Professor of Phlebotomy)
regarded her, because she *didn't* squint, and because she *wasn't*
marked with the smallpox.

As for the young University Snobs, I am getting too old, now,
to speak of such very familiarly. My recollections of them lie
in the far, far past—almost as far back as Pelham's time.

We *then* used to consider Snobs, raw-looking lads, who never
missed chapel; who wore high-lows and no straps; who walked
two hours on the Trumpington road every day of their lives;
who carried off the college scholarships, and who overrated themselves in hall. We were premature in pronouncing our verdict of
youthful Snobbishness. The man without straps fulfilled his
destiny and duty. He eased his old Governor, the Curate in
Westmorland, or helped his sisters to set up the Lady's School.
He wrote a Dictionary, or a Treatise on Conic Sections, as his
nature and genius prompted. He got a fellowship: and then
took to himself a wife, and a living. He presides over a parish
now, and thinks it rather a dashing thing to belong to the Oxford
and Cambridge Club; and his parishioners love him, and snore
under his sermons. No, no, *he* is not a Snob. It is not straps
that make the gentleman, or high-lows that unmake him, be they
ever so thick. My son, it is you who are the Snob if you lightly

despise a man for doing his duty, and refuse to shake an honest man's hand because it wears a Berlin glove.

We then used to consider it not the least vulgar for a parcel of lads who had been whipped three months previous, and were not allowed more than three glasses of port at home, to sit down to pine-apples and ices at each other's rooms, and fuddle themselves with Champagne and Claret.

One looks back to what was called "a wine party" with a sort of wonder. Thirty lads round a table covered with bad sweetmeats, drinking bad wines, telling bad stories, singing bad songs over and over again. Milk punch—smoking—ghastly headache—frightful spectacle of dessert table next morning, and smell of tobacco—your guardian, the clergyman, dropping in in the midst of this—expecting to find you deep in Algebra, and discovering the Gyp administering soda-water.

There were young men who despised the lads who indulged in the coarse hospitalities of wine-parties, who prided themselves in giving *récherchés* little French dinners. Both wine-party-givers and dinner-givers were Snobs.

There were what used to be called "dressy" Snobs:—Jimmy, who might be seen at five o'clock elaborately rigged out, with a camellia in his button-hole, glazed boots, and fresh kid gloves twice a day:—Jessamy, who was conspicuous for his "jewellery,"—a young donkey,—glittering all over with chains, rings, and shirt-studs;—Jacky, who rode every day solemnly on the Blenheim Road, in pumps and white silk stockings, with his hair curled,—all three of whom flattered themselves they gave laws to the University about dress—all three most odious varieties of Snobs.

Sporting Snobs of course there were, and are always—those happy beings in whom Nature has implanted a love of slang: who loitered about the horsekeeper's stables, and drove the London coaches—a stage in and out, and might be seen swaggering through the courts in pink of early mornings, and indulged in dice and blind-hookey at nights, and never missed a race, or a boxing-match; and rode flat races, and kept bull-terriers. Worse Snobs even than these were poor miserable wretches, who did not like hunting at all, and could not afford it, and were in mortal fear at a two-foot ditch; but who hunted because Glenlivat and Cinqbars hunted. The Billiard Snob and the Boating Snob were varieties of these, and are to be found elsewhere than in Universities.

Then there were philosophical Snobs, who used to ape statesmen at the Spouting Clubs, and who believed as a fact, that Government always had an eye on the University where to select orators for the House of Commons. There were audacious Freethinkers, who adored nobody or nothing, except perhaps Robespierre and the Koran, and panted for the day when the pale name of priest should shrink and dwindle away before the indignation of an enlightened world.

But the worst of all University Snobs, are those unfortunates who go to rack and ruin from their desire to ape their betters. Smith becomes acquainted with great people at College, and is ashamed of his father the tradesman. Jones has fine acquaintances, and lives after their fashion like a gay, free-hearted fellow as he is, and ruins his father, and robs his sister's portion, and cripples his younger brother's outset in life, for the pleasure of entertaining my lord, and riding by the side of Sir John. And though it may be very good fun for Robinson to fuddle himself at home as he does at College, and to be brought home by the policeman he has just been trying to knock down—think what fun it is for the poor old soul, his mother!—the half-pay Captain's widow, who has been pinching herself all her life long, in order that that jolly young fellow might have a University Education.

THE JAPANESE QUINCE [1]

By John Galsworthy

As Mr. Nilson, well known in the City, opened the window of his dressing-room on Campden Hill, he experienced a peculiar sweetish sensation in the back of his throat, and a feeling of emptiness just under his fifth rib. Hooking the window back,

[1] From *Caravan*. By permission of Charles Scribner's Sons, the authorized publishers.

he noticed that a little tree in the Square Gardens had come out in blossom, and that the thermometer stood at sixty. "Perfect morning," he thought; "spring at last!" ·

Resuming some meditations on the price of Tintos, he took up an ivory-backed hand-glass and scrutinised his face. His firm, well-coloured cheeks, with their neat brown moustaches, and his round, well-opened, clear grey eyes, wore a reassuring appearance of good health. Putting on his black frock coat, he went downstairs.

In the dining-room his morning paper was laid out on the sideboard. Mr. Nilson had scarcely taken it in his hand when he again became aware of that queer feeling. Somewhat concerned, he went to the French window and descended the scrolled iron steps into the fresh air. A cuckoo clock struck eight.

"Half an hour to breakfast," he thought; "I'll take a turn in the Gardens."

He had them to himself, and proceeded to pace the circular path with his morning paper clasped behind him. He had scarcely made two revolutions, however, when it was borne in on him that, instead of going away in the fresh air, the feeling had increased. He drew several deep breaths, having heard deep breathing recommended by his wife's doctor; but they augmented rather than diminished the sensation—as if some sweetish liquor in course within him, together with a faint aching just above his heart. Running over what he had eaten the night before, he could recollect no unusual dish, and it occurred to him that it might possibly be some smell affecting him. But he could detect nothing except a faint sweet lemony scent, rather agreeable than otherwise, which evidently emanated from the bushes budding in the sunshine. He was on the point of resuming his promenade, when a blackbird close by burst into song, and, looking up, Mr. Nilson saw at a distance of perhaps five yards a little tree, in the heart of whose branches the bird was perched. He stood staring curiously at this tree, recognising it for that which he had noticed from his window. It was covered with young blossoms, pink and white, and little bright green leaves both round and spiky; and on all this blossom and these leaves the sunlight glistened. Mr. Nilson smiled; the little tree was so alive and pretty! And instead of passing on, he stayed there smiling at the tree.

"Morning like this!" he thought; "and here I am the only person in the Square who has the—to come out and—!" But he had no sooned conceived this thought than he saw quite near him a man with his hands behind him, who was also staring up and smiling at the little tree. Rather taken aback, Mr. Nilson ceased to smile, and looked furtively at the stranger. It was his next-door neighbour, Mr. Tandram, well known in the City, who had occupied the adjoining house for some five years. Mr. Nilson perceived at once the awkwardness of his position, for, being married, they had not yet had occasion to speak to one another. Doubtful as to his proper conduct, he decided at last to murmur: "Fine morning!" and was passing on, when Mr. Tandram answered: "Beautiful, for the time of year!" Detecting a slight nervousness in his neighbour's voice, Mr. Nilson was emboldened to regard him openly. He was of about Mr. Nilson's own height, with firm, well-coloured cheeks, neat brown moustaches, and round, well-opened, clear grey eyes; and he was wearing a black frock coat. Mr. Nilson noticed that he had his morning paper clasped behind him as he looked up at the little tree. And, visited somehow by the feeling that he had been caught out, he said abruptly:

"Er—can you give me the name of that tree?"

Mr. Tandram answered:

"I was about to ask you that," and stepped towards it. Mr. Nilson also approached the tree.

"Sure to have its name on, I should think," he said.

Mr. Tandram was the first to see the little label, close to where the blackbird had been sitting. He read it out.

"Japanese quince!"

"Ah!" said Mr. Nilson, "thought so. Early flowerers."

"Very," assented Mr. Tandram, and added: "Quite a feelin' in the air to-day."

Mr. Nilson nodded.

"It was a blackbird singin'," he said.

"Blackbirds," answered Mr. Tandram, "I prefer them to thrushes myself; more body in the note." And he looked at Mr. Nilson in an almost friendly way.

"Quite," murmured Mr. Nilson. "These exotics, they don't bear fruit. Pretty blossom!" and he again glanced up at the blossom, thinking: "Nice fellow, this, I rather like him."

Mr. Tandram also gazed at the blossom. And the little tree, as if appreciating their attention, quivered and glowed. From a distance the blackbird gave a loud, clear call. Mr. Nilson dropped his eyes. It struck him suddenly that Mr. Tandram looked a little foolish; and, as if he had seen himself, he said: "I must be going in. Good morning!"

A shade passed over Mr. Tandram's face, as if he, too, had suddenly noticed something about Mr. Nilson.

"Good morning," he replied, and clasping their journals to their backs they separated.

Mr. Nilson retraced his steps towards his garden window, walking slowly so as to avoid arriving at the same time as his neighbour. Having seen Mr. Tandram mount his scrolled iron steps, he ascended his own in turn. On the top step he paused.

With the slanting spring sunlight darting and quivering into it, the Japanese quince seemed more living than a tree. The blackbird had returned to it, and was chanting out his heart.

Mr. Nilson sighed; again he felt that queer sensation, that choky feeling in his throat.

The sound of a cough or sigh attracted his attention. There, in the shadow of his French window, stood Mr. Tandram, also looking forth across the Gardens at the little quince tree.

Unaccountably upset, Mr. Nilson turned abruptly into the house, and opened his morning paper.

EXERCISES

1. Macaulay's paragraphs have for nearly one hundred years been cited as models of construction. From the topic sentence, which with Macaulay as with most other good writers of exposi-

tory prose usually begins the paragraph, to the concluding one, there is not only perfect unity of idea and of effect, but there is also a conscious *development* of that idea and of that effect. It is this matter of development which makes the study of the paragraph, especially of paragraphs like Macaulay's, so interesting and so valuable to the student of composition.

Expository paragraphs are usually developed by rather definite means. Among those most often employed are (1) repetition, (2) particulars and details, (3) comparison and contrast, (4) illustration and example, (5) cause and effect. Not infrequently a single paragraph will show instances of the use of more than one of these processes.

To illustrate: In his first paragraph on the Puritans the topic sentence is obviously the second sentence, as in the first the author is merely introducing his subject. The key words of the topic sentence are "odious," "ridiculous," and "lie on the surface." The situation which these words assert is developed through the following sentences, first, by repetition in other words of the idea in the topic sentence, and secondly, by the fine use of details. Again in the third paragraph the topic sentence (here the first) is developed by repetition, by comparison and contrast, and by illustration. The fourth, which is perhaps the best paragraph of all from the points of view of clearness of style, of variety of sentence structure, and of dramatic and vivid diction, is developed largely by comparison and contrast although illustration and detail are also used.

For students who find it hard to stick irrevocably to a topic sentence or for those who have difficulty in thinking of a paragraph as a unit of thought, this careful construction of the idea in a given sentence into the larger and more complete idea of a paragraph is an excellent exercise. The following topic sentences as subjects for paragraph themes of one hundred and fifty words are suggested:

> The American Indian, whatever his shortcomings, was an heroic figure. (Try developing this sentence into a paragraph first by repetition and then by details. Then develop it into another paragraph wholly by comparison and contrast.)
>
> The common notion of success is fallacious.

The study of Latin may be for one student as practical as the study of engineering for another.

Books are sometimes better companions than persons.

Monopolies are seldom (are often) beneficial to the people.

Well-written books are sometimes extremely tedious.

Freedom is by no means an unmixed blessing.

A twelve-year-old boy is rarely himself.

Novels are more effective than sermons as teachers of morality.

2. Substituting in place of Mr. Nilson and Mr. Tandram two Irish workmen (gardeners, policemen, street-sweepers, etc.) re-write "The Japanese Quince."

3. Characterize Tom by having two of his college classmates discuss his attitude toward college life.

4. Characterize by means of a conversation between Tom and one of the students at the theatre school the group of fraternity men who asked him to join them. Or, abolishing the dialogue, characterize the men as a type from Tom's viewpoint.

5. After reading "The Positive Negatives of New Englanders" in *The Atlantic Monthly* for June 1927 use it as a suggestion for your own characterization of people in some other section of the country, or of some group of people with strong racial attributes.

6. Study Hazlitt's paragraphs in his essay called "Merry England" and note how he develops his main idea in each. Hazlitt's style has been called "intellectually honest." Do you think the term a good one? Why? Why not?

7. What instances do you find in "The Puritans" of Macaulay's repetition of construction for effect? Of his effective use of adjectives? Of his employment of dramatic imagery?

SUGGESTED READINGS

Anonymous, "The Positive Negatives of New Englanders," *The Atlantic Monthly*, June 1927.

Belloc, Hilaire, "The Normans" from *Hills and the Sea*, "Ely," Scribner's, New York.

Colby, Frank Moore, "The People Next Door" from *Imaginary Obligations*, Dodd, Mead, New York.

de Madariaga, Salvador, "Englishman, Frenchman, Spaniard," *The Atlantic Monthly*, April 1928.

Hazlitt, William, "On People with One Idea" from *Table Talk*.
"The Character of John Bull" and "Merry England" from
Essays, The Modern Readers' Series, Macmillan, New York.

Lamb, Charles, "The Old and the New Schoolmaster" from *Essays
of Elia*.

Macaulay, Thomas Babington, "The Country Gentleman of the
Seventeenth Century" from "England in 1685," Chapter III,
The History of England.

Repplier, Agnes, "The Urbane Intolerance of Americans," *The
Atlantic Monthly*, December 1926.

Smith, Alexander, "On Vagabonds" from *Dreamthorp*, Doubleday,
Doran, New York.

Stevenson, Robert Louis, "The English Admirals" from *Virginibus
Puerisque*, Scribner's, New York. "The Character of Dogs"
from *Memories and Portraits*, Scribner's, New York.

Strunsky, Simeon, "Real People" from *Post-Impressions*, Dodd,
Mead, New York.

West, Rebecca, "These American Women," *Harper's Magazine*,
November 1925.

Whitehead, Alfred North, "The Education of an Englishman,"
The Atlantic Monthly, August 1926.

Wordsworth, Dorothy, "The Beggars" from *The Journals of
Dorothy Wordsworth*, Tuesday, 10th June, 1800.

III. APPRECIATIONS

The appreciation of a person or of an animal is fundamentally
different from the presentation either of a person or of a type.
Here the approach is not only objective but distinctly subjective as well. In every theme of this sort two elements must be
clearly felt: the person written about and the writer. The possible excellence of such work as this depends first of all upon
the weighing and the balancing of both elements.

Clearly the more important of the two is the person appreciated. He is first and foremost in the author's mind; he it is
who has aroused interest, gratitude, admiration, and affection;
he it is who is worthy of recognition and praise. And yet the
very depth and intensity of the feeling he has awakened in the
author dictate the presence of the latter. The theme of appre-

ciation, then, is *subjective* in that it expresses with frankness and enthusiasm the feeling of the author, and *objective* in that the object of that feeling is always in the ascendancy.

In the accomplishment of a difficult task example is better than precept. The four essays which are given here illustrate perfectly not only the relative space but also the other means of emphasis given to the one who appreciates and the one who is appreciated. Christopher Morley is in every paragraph of his essay on his old teacher, Doctor Gummere, and yet he is there, first of all, as a means of making Doctor Gummere real and admirable to us. The same is true of Stevenson in "An Old Scotch Gardener," of Dr. John Brown in "Jeems the Door-keeper," and of Robert M. Gay in his delightful appreciation of his dog Peggy. If you will note the topic sentences of any of the paragraphs of these essays (with the exception of the purely intro-ductory paragraph in Stevenson) you will see that each and every one of them is concerned, not with the writer but with the object of the writer's appreciation, and the development of these sen-tences into paragraphs has just the result we should rightly expect. Thus, the main topics have to do with the subject of the theme; the sub-topics which develop the main may and often do include the writer. And yet the writer's appreciation creates an atmosphere in which the whole theme is bathed.

A few cautionary suggestions as to the writing of this theme may not come amiss:

1. Don't choose as a subject some one about whom you are only lukewarm.

2. Don't economize on time or space. This theme, to be good, will require hours for quiet thought and work. It might well be the "long theme" of the quarter or of the semester.

3. Don't try to work without some clear plan in mind. (See Exercise 1 for suggestions as to an outline.)

4. Note especially the beginnings of the models given and of others from the reading list. A good start is half the battle.

5. Read as widely as you can from the list before you start your theme.

6. Note the attention paid by other (and better) writers than

you to *mannerisms, tricks of speech, incidents, concrete detail, literary allusions, comparisons, sense impressions.*

7. *Cherish sentiment, but disown sentimentality.*

In Memoriam

Francis Barton Gummere [1]

By Christopher Morley

I often wonder what inward pangs of laughter or despair he may have felt as he sat behind the old desk in Chase Hall and watched us file in, year after year! Callow, juvenile, ignorant, and cocksure—grotesquely confident of our own manly fullness of worldly *savoir*—an absurd rabble of youths, miserable flint-heads indeed for such a steel! We were the most unpromising of all material for the scholar's eye; comfortable, untroubled middle-class lads most of us, to whom study was neither a privilege nor a passion, but only a sober and decent way of growing old enough to enter business.

We did not realize how accurately—and perhaps a trifle grimly —the strong, friendly face behind the desk was searching us and sizing us up. He knew us for what we were—a group of nice boys, too sleek, too cheerfully secure to show the ambition of the true student. There was among us no specimen of the lean and dogged crusader of learning that kindles the eye of the master: no fanatical Scot, such as rejoices the Oxford or Cambridge don; no liquid-orbed and hawk-faced Hebrew with flushed cheek bones, such as sets the pace in the classrooms of our large universities. No: we were a hopelessly mediocre, well-fed, satisfied, and characteristically Quakerish lot. As far as the battle for learning goes, we were pacifists—conscientious objectors.

It is doubtful whether any really great scholar ever gave the best years of his life to so meagerly equipped a succession of youngsters! I say this candidly, and it is well it should be said, for it makes apparent the true genius of Doctor Gummere's

[1] From *Plum Pudding.* By permission of Doubleday, Doran and Company.

great gift. He turned this following of humble plodders into lovers and zealots of the great regions of English letters. There was something knightly about him—he, the great scholar, who would never stoop to scoff at the humblest of us. It might have been thought that his shining gifts were wasted in a small country college, where not one in fifty of his pupils could follow him into the enchanted lands of the imagination where he was fancy free. But it was not so. One may meet man after man, old pupils of his, who have gone on into the homely drudging rounds of business, the law, journalism—men whose faces will light up with affection and remembrance when Doctor Gummere's name is mentioned. We may have forgotten much of our Chaucer, our Milton, our Ballads—though I am sure we have none of us forgotten the deep and thrilling vivacity of his voice reciting:

O where hae ye been, Lord Randal, my son?
O where hae ye been, my handsome young man?
I hae been to the wild wood; mither, make my bed soon,
For I'm weary wi' hunting and fain wad lie doun.

But what we learned from him lay in the very charm of his personality. It was a spell that no one in his classroom could escape. It shone from his sparkling eye; it spoke in his irresistible humor; it moved in every line of that well-loved face, in his characteristic gesture of leaning forward and tilting his head a little to one side as he listened, patiently, to whatever juvenile surmises we stammered to express. It was the true learning of which his favorite Sir Philip Sidney said:

This purifying of wit, this enriching of memory, enabling of judgment, and enlarging of conceit, which commonly we call learning, under what name soever it come forth or to what immediate end soever it be directed, the final end is to lead and draw us to as high a perfection as our degenerate souls, made worse by their clay lodgings, can be capable of.

Indeed, just to listen to him was a purifying of wit, an enriching of memory, an enabling of judgment, an enlarging of imagination. He gave us "so sweet a prospect into the way as will entice any man to enter into it."

He moved among all human contacts with unerring grace. He was never the teacher, always the comrade. It was his way to pretend that we knew far more than we did; so with perfect courtesy and gravity, he would ask our opinion on some matter of which we knew next to nothing; and we knew it was only his exquisiteness of good manners that impelled the habit; and we knew he knew the laughableness of it; yet we adored him for it. He always suited his strength to our weakness; would tell us things almost with an air of apology for seeming to know more than we; pretending that we doubtless had known it all along, but it had just slipped our memory. Marvelously he set us on our secret honor to do justice to this rare courtesy. To fail him in some task he had set became, in our boyish minds, the one thing most abhorrent in dealing with such a man—a discourtesy. He was a man of the rarest and most delicate breeding, the finest and truest gentleman we had known. Had he been nothing else, how much we would have learned from that alone.

What a range, what a grasp, there was in his glowing, various mind! How open it was on all sides, how it teemed with interests, how different from the scholar of silly traditional belief! We used to believe that he could have taught us history, science, economics, philosophy—almost anything; and so indeed he did. He taught us to go adventuring among masterpieces on our own account, which is the most any teacher can do. Luckiest of all were those who, on one pretext or another, found their way to his fireside of an evening. To sit entranced, smoking one of his cigars,[1] to hear him talk of Stevenson, Meredith, or Hardy—(his favorites among the moderns) to marvel anew at the infinite scope and vivacity of his learning—this was to live on the very doorsill of enchantment. Homeward we would go, crunching across the snow to where Barclay crowns the slope with her evening blaze of lights, one glimpse nearer some realization of

[1] It was characteristic of him that he usually smoked *Robin Hood,* that admirable five-cent cigar, because the name, and the picture of an outlaw on the band, reminded him of the fourteenth century ballads he knew by heart.

the magical colors and tissues of the human mind, the rich perplexity and many-sided glamour of life.

It is strange (as one reviews all the memories of that good friend and master) to think that there is now a new generation beginning at Haverford that will never know his spell. There is a heavy debt on his old pupils. He made life so much richer and more interesting for us. Even if we never explored for ourselves the fields of literature toward which he pointed, his radiant individuality remains in our hearts as a true exemplar of what scholarship can mean. We can never tell all that he meant to us.

Gropingly we turn to little pictures in memory. We see him crossing Cope Field in the green and gold of spring mornings, on his way to class. We see him sitting on the veranda steps of his home on sunny afternoons, full of gay and eager talk on a thousand diverse topics. He little knew, I think, how we hung upon his words. I can think of no more genuine tribute than this: that in my own class—which was a notoriously cynical and scoffish band of young sophisters—when any question of religious doubt or dogma arose for discussion among some midnight group, some one was sure to say, "I wish I knew what Doctor Gummere thought about it!" We felt instinctively that what he thought would have been convincing enough for us.

He was a truly great man. A greater man than we deserved, and there is a heavy burden upon us to justify the life that he gave to our little college. He has passed into the quiet and lovely tradition that surrounds and nourishes that place we all love so well. Little by little she grows, drawing strength and beauty from human lives around her, confirming herself in honor and remembrance. The teacher is justified by his scholars. Doctor Gummere might have gone elsewhere, surrounded by a greater and more ambitiously documented band of pupils. He whom we knew as the greatest man we had ever seen, moved little outside the world of learning. He gave himself to us, and we are the custodians of his memory.

Every man who loved our vanished friend must know with what realization of shamed incapacity one lays down the tributary

pen. He was so strong, so full of laughter and grace, so truly
a man, his long vacation still seems a dream, and we feel that
somewhere on the well-beloved campus we shall meet him and
feel that friendly hand. In thinking of him I am always reminded of that fine old poem of Sir Henry Wotton, a teacher
himself, the provost of Eton, whose life has been so charmingly
written by another Haverfordian—Logan Pearsall Smith.

THE CHARACTER OF A HAPPY LIFE

How happy is he born and taught
    That serveth not another's will;
Whose armor is his honest thought,
    And simple truth his utmost skill!

Whose passions not his masters are;
    Whose soul is still prepared for death
Not tied unto the world by care
    Of public fame or private breath;

Who envies none that chance doth raise,
    Nor vice; who never understood
How deepest wounds are given by praise;
    Nor rules of state, but rules of good;

Who hath his life from rumors freed;
    Whose conscience is his strong retreat;
Whose state can neither flatterers feed,
    Nor ruin make oppressors great;

Who God doth late and early pray
    More of His grace than gifts to lend;
And entertains the harmless day
    With a well-chosen book or friend;

This man is freed from servile bands
    Of hope to rise or fear to fall:
Lord of himself, though not of lands,
    And having nothing, yet hath all.

Such was the Happy Man as Sir Henry Wotton described him.
Such, I think, was the life of our friend. I think it must have
been a happy life, for he gave so much happiness to others.

An Old Scotch Gardener [1]

By Robert Louis Stevenson

From this defunct periodical [2] I am going to reprint one of my own papers. The poor little piece is all tail-foremost. I have done my best to straighten its array, I have pruned it fearlessly, and it remains invertebrate and wordy. No self-respecting magazine would print the thing; and here you behold it in a bound volume, not for any worth of its own, but for the sake of the man whom it purports dimly to represent and some of whose sayings it preserves; so that in this volume of Memories and Portraits, Robert Young, the Swanston gardener, may stand alongside of John Todd, the Swanston shepherd. Not that John and Robert drew very close together in their lives; for John was rough, he smelt of the windy brae; and Robert was gentle, and smacked of the garden in the hollow. Perhaps it is to my shame that I liked John the better of the two; he had grit and dash, and that salt of the Old Adam that pleases men with any savage inheritance of blood; and he was a wayfarer besides, and took my gipsy fancy. But however that may be, and however Robert's profile may be blurred in the boyish sketch that follows, he was a man of a most quaint and beautiful nature, whom, if it were possible to recast a piece of work so old, I should like well to draw again with a maturer touch. And as I think of him and of John, I wonder in what other country two such men would be found dwelling together, in a hamlet of some twenty cottages, in the woody fold of a green hill.

*   *   *   *   *   *   *

I think I might almost have said the last: somewhere, indeed, in the uttermost glens of the Lammermuir or among the southwestern hills there may yet linger a decrepit representative of this by-gone good fellowship; but as far as actual experience goes, I have only met one man in my life who might fitly be quoted in

[1] From *Memories and Portraits*. By permission of Charles Scribner's Sons, the authorized publishers.
[2] A college magazine.

the same breath with Andrew Fairservice,—though without his vices. He was a man whose very presence could impart a savour of quaint antiquity to the baldest and most modern flower-plots. There was a dignity about his tall stooping form, and an earnestness in his wrinkled face that recalled Don Quixote; but a Don Quixote who had come through the training of the Covenant, and been nourished in his youth on *Walker's Lives* and *The Hind let Loose.*

Now, as I could not bear to let such a man pass away with no sketch preserved of his old-fashioned virtues, I hope the reader will take this as an excuse for the present paper, and judge as kindly as he can the infirmities of my description. To me, who find it so difficult to tell the little that I know, he stands essentially as a *genius loci.* It is impossible to separate his spare form and old straw hat from the garden in the lap of the hill, with its rocks overgrown with clematis, its shadowy walks, and the splendid breadth of champaign that one saw from the north-west corner. The garden and gardener seem part and parcel of each other. When I take him from his right surroundings and try to make him appear for me on paper, he looks unreal and phantasmal: the best that I can say may convey some notion to those that never saw him, but to me it will be ever impotent.

The first time that I saw him, I fancy Robert was pretty old already: he had certainly begun to use his years as a stalking horse. Latterly he was beyond all the impudencies of logic, considering a reference to the parish register worth all the reasons in the world. *"I am old and well stricken in years,"* he was wont to say; and I never found any one bold enough to answer the argument. Apart from this vantage that he kept over all who were not yet octogenarian, he had some other drawbacks as a gardener. He shrank the very place he cultivated. The dignity and reduced gentility of his appearance made the small garden cut a sorry figure. He was full of tales of greater situations in his younger days. He spoke of castles and parks with a humbling familiarity. He told of places where under-gardeners had trembled at his looks, where there were meres and swanneries, labyrinths of walk and wildernesses of sad shrubbery in his control, till you could not help feeling that it was condescension on his part to dress your humbler garden plots. You were thrown at once into an invidious position. You felt that you were profiting by the needs of dignity, and that his poverty and not his will consented to your vulgar rule. Involuntarily you compared yourself with the swineherd that made Alfred watch his cakes, or some bloated citizen who may have given his sons and his condescension to the fallen Dionysius. Nor were the disagreeables purely fanciful and metaphysical, for the sway that he exercised over your feelings he extended to your garden, and, through the garden, to your diet. He would trim a hedge, throw away a favourite plant, or fill the most favoured and fertile section of the garden with a vegetable that none of us could eat, in supreme contempt for our opinion. If you asked him to send you in one of your own artichokes, *"That I wull, mem,"* he would say, *"with pleasure, for it is mair blessed to give than to receive."* Ay, and even when, by extra twisting of the screw, we prevailed on him to prefer our commands to his own inclination, and he went away, stately and sad, professing that *"our wull was his pleasure,"* but yet reminding us that he would do it *"with feelin's,"*—even then, I say, the triumphant master felt humbled in his triumph, felt that he ruled on sufferance only, that he was taking a mean advantage of the other's low estate, and that the whole scene had been one of those "slights that patient merit of the unworthy takes."

In flowers his taste was old-fashioned and catholic; affecting sunflowers and dahlias, wall-flowers and roses, and holding in supreme aversion whatsoever was fantastic, new-fashioned, or wild. There was one exception to this sweeping ban. Foxgloves, though undoubtedly guilty on the last count, he not only spared, but loved; and when the shrubbery was being thinned, he stayed his hand and dexterously manipulated his bill in order to save every stately stem. In boyhood, as he told me once, speaking in that tone that only actors and the old-fashioned common folk can use nowadays, his heart grew *"proud"* within him when he came on a burn-course among the braes of Manor that shone purple with their graceful trophies; and not all his apprenticeship

and practice for so many years of precise gardening had ban-
ished these boyish recollections from his heart. Indeed, he was
a man keenly alive to the beauty of all that was by-gone. He
abounded in old stories of his boyhood, and kept pious account
of all his former pleasures; and when he went (on a holiday)
to visit one of the fabled great places of the earth where he had
served before, he came back full of little pre-Raphaelite reminiscences that showed real passion for the past, such as might have
shaken hands with Hazlitt or Jean-Jacques.

But however his sympathy with his old feelings might affect
his liking for the foxgloves, the very truth was that he scorned
all flowers together. They were but garnishings, childish toys,
trifling ornaments for ladies' chimney-shelves. It was towards
his cauliflowers and peas and cabbage that his heart grew warm.
His preference for the more useful growths was such that cabbages were found invading the flower-plots, and an outpost of
savoys was once discovered in the centre of the lawn. He would
prelect over some thriving plant with wonderful enthusiasm, piling
reminiscence on reminiscence of former and perhaps yet finer
specimens. Yet even then he did not let the credit leave himself. He had, indeed, raised *"finer o' them"*; but it seemed that
no one else had been favoured with a like success. All other
gardeners, in fact, were mere foils to his own superior attain-
ments; and he would recount, with perfect soberness of voice
and visage, how so and so had wondered, and such another could
scarcely give credit to his eyes. Nor was it with his rivals only
that he parted praise and blame. If you remarked how well a
plant was looking, he would gravely touch his hat and thank
you with solemn unction; all credit in the matter falling to him.
If, on the other hand, you called his attention to some back-
going vegetable, he would quote Scripture: *"Paul may plant and
Apollos may water"*; all blame being left to Providence, on the
score of deficient rain or untimely frosts.

There was one thing in the garden that shared his preference
with his favourite cabbages and rhubarb, and that other was the
bee-hive. Their sound, their industry, perhaps their sweet product also had taken hold of his imagination and heart, whether

by way of memory of no I cannot say, although perhaps the
bees too were linked to him by some recollection of Manor braes
and his country childhood. Nevertheless, he was too chary of his
personal safety or (let me rather say) his personal dignity to
mingle in any active office towards them. But he could stand
by while one of the contemned rivals did the work for him, and
protest that it was quite safe in spite of his own considerate distance and the cries of the distressed assistant. In regard to bees,
he was rather a man of word than deed, and some of his most
striking sentences had the bees for text. *"They are indeed won-
derfu' creatures, mem,"* he said once. *"They just mind me o'
what the Queen of Sheba said to Solomon—and I think she said
it wi' a sigh—'The half of it hath not been told unto me.'"*

As far as the Bible goes he was deeply read. Like the old
Covenanters, of whom he was the worthy representative, his
mouth was full of sacred quotations; it was the book that he had
studied most and thought upon most deeply. To many people
in his station the Bible, and perhaps Burns, are the only books
of any vital literary merit that they read, feeding themselves,
for the rest, on the draff of country newspapers, and the very
instructive but not very palatable pabulum of some cheap educational series. This was Robert's position. All day long he
had dreamed of the Hebrew stories, and his head had been full
of Hebrew poetry and Gospel ethics; until they had struck deep
root into his heart, and the very expressions had become a part
of him; so that he rarely spoke without some antique idiom or
Scripture mannerism that gave a raciness to the merest triviali-
ties of talk. But the influence of the Bible did not stop here.
There was more in Robert than quaint phrase and ready store
of reference. He was imbued with a spirit of peace and love:
he interposed between man and wife: he threw himself between
the angry, touching his hat the while with all the ceremony of
an usher: he protected the birds from everybody but himself,
seeing, I suppose, a great difference between official execution
and wanton sport. His mistress telling him one day to put
some ferns into his master's particular corner, and adding,
"Though, indeed, Robert, he doesn't deserve them, for he

wouldn't help me to gather them," *"Eh, mem,"* replies Robert, *"but I wouldnae say that, for I think he's just a most deservin' gentleman."* Again, two of our friends, who were on intimate terms, and accustomed to use language to each other somewhat without the bounds of the parliamentary, happened to differ about the position of a seat in the garden. The discussion, as was usual when these two were at it, soon waxed tolerably insulting on both sides. Every one accustomed to such controversies several times a day was quietly enjoying this prize-fight of somewhat abusive wit—every one but Robert, to whom the perfect good faith of the whole quarrel seemed unquestionable, and who, after having waited till his conscience would suffer him to wait no more, and till he expected every moment that the disputants would fall to blows, cut suddenly in with tones of almost tearful entreaty: *"Eh, but, gentlemen, I wad hae nae mair words about it!"* One thing was noticeable about Robert's religion: it was neither dogmatic nor sectarian. He never expatiated (at least, in my hearing) on the doctrines of his creed, and he never condemned anybody else. I have no doubt that he held all Roman Catholics, Atheists, and Mahometans as considerably out of it; I don't believe he had any sympathy for Prelacy; and the natural feelings of man must have made him a little sore about Free-Churchism; but at least, he never talked about these views, never grew controversially noisy, and never openly aspersed the belief or practice of anybody. Now all this is not generally characteristic of Scotch piety; Scotch sects being churches militant with a vengeance, and Scotch believers perpetual crusaders the one against the other, and missionaries the one to the other. Perhaps Robert's originally tender heart was what made the difference; or, perhaps, his solitary and pleasant labour among fruits and flowers had taught him a more sunshiny creed than those whose work is among the tares of fallen humanity; and the soft influences of the garden had entered deep into his spirit,

> "Annihilating all that's made
> To a green thought in a green shade."

But I could go on for ever chronicling his golden sayings or telling of his innocent and living piety. I had meant to tell of his cottage, with the German pipe hung reverently above the fire, and the shell box that he had made for his son, and of which he would say pathetically: *"He was real pleased wi' it at first, but I think he's got a kind o' tired o' it now"*—the son being then a man of about forty. But I will let all these pass. " 'Tis more significant: he's dead." The earth, that he had digged so much in his life, was dug out by another for himself; and the flowers that he had tended drew their life still from him, but in a new and nearer way. A bird flew about the open grave, as if it too wished to honour the obsequies of one who had so often quoted Scripture in favour of its kind: "Are not two sparrows sold for one farthing? and yet not one of them falleth to the ground."

Yes, he is dead. But the kings did not rise in the place of death to greet him "with taunting proverbs" as they rose to greet the haughty Babylonian; for in his life he was lowly, and a peacemaker, and a servant of God.

JEEMS THE DOORKEEPER [1]

By Dr. John Brown

When my father was in Broughton Place Church, we had a doorkeeper called *Jeems,* and a formidable little man and doorkeeper he was; of unknown age and name, for he existed to us, and indeed still exists to me—though he has been in his grave these sixteen years—as *Jeems,* absolute and *per se,* no more needing a surname than did or do Abraham or Isaac, Samson or Nebuchadnezzar. We young people of the congregation believed that he was out in the '45, and had his drum shot through and quenched at Culloden; and as for any indication on his huge and grey visage of his ever having been young, he might safely have been *Bottom* the Weaver in "A Midsummer Night's Dream," or that excellent, ingenious, and "wise-hearted" Bezaleel, the son of Uri, whom *Jeems* regarded as one of the greatest of men and

[1] From *Rab and His Friends.*

of weavers, and whose "ten curtains of fine twined linen, and blue, and purple, and scarlet, each of them with fifty loops on the edge of the selvedge in the coupling, with their fifty taches of gold," he, in confidential moments, gave it to be understood were the sacred triumphs of his craft; for, as you may infer, my friend was a man of the treddles and the shuttle as well as the more renowned grandson of Hur.

Jeems's face was so extensive, and met you so formidably and at once, that it mainly composed his whole; and such a face! Sydney Smith used to say of a certain quarrelsome man, "His very face is a breach of the peace." Had he seen our friend's, he would have said he was the imperative mood on two (very small) legs, out on business in a blue greatcoat. It was in the nose and the keen small eye that his strength lay. Such a nose of power, so undeniable, I never saw, except in what was said to be a bust from the antique, of Rhadamanthus, the well-known Justice-Clerk of the Pagan Court of Session! Indeed, when I was in the Rector's class, and watched *Jeems* turning interlopers out of the church seats, by merely presenting before them this tremendous organ, it struck me that if Rhadamanthus had still been here, and out of employment, he would have taken kindly to *Jeems's* work,—and that possibly he was that potentate in a U. P. disguise.

Nature having fashioned the huge face, and laid out much material and idea upon it, had finished off the rest of *Jeems* somewhat scrimply, as if she had run out of means; his legs especially were of the shortest, and, as his usual dress was a very long blue greatcoat, made for a much taller man, its tails resting upon the ground, and its large hind buttons in a totally preposterous position, gave him the look of being planted, or rather after the manner of Milton's beasts at the creation, in the act of emerging painfully from his mother earth.

Now, you may think this was a very ludicrous old object. If you had seen him, you would not have said so; and not only was he a man of weight and authority,—he was likewise a genuine, indeed a deeply spiritual Christian, well read in his Bible, in his own heart, and in human nature and life, knowing both its warp and woof; more peremptory in making himself obey his Master, than in getting himself obeyed, and this is saying a good deal; and, like all complete men, he had a genuine love and gift of humour,[1] kindly and uncouth, lurking in those small, deep-set grey eyes, shrewd and keen, which, like two sharpest of shooters, enfiladed that massive and redoubtable bulwark, the nose.

One day two strangers made themselves over to *Jeems* to be furnished with seats. Motioning them to follow, he walked majestically to the farthest in the corner, where he had decreed they should sit. The couple found seats near the door, and stepped into them, leaving *Jeems* to march through the passages alone, the whole congregation watching him with some relish and alarm. He gets to his destination, opens the door, and stands aside; nobody appears. He looks sharply round, and then gives a look of general wrath "at lairge." No one doubted his victory. His nose and eye fell, or seemed to fall, on the two culprits, and pulled them out instantly, hurrying them to their appointed place; *Jeems* snibbed them slowly in, and gave them a parting look they were not likely to misunderstand or forget.

At that time the crowds and the imperfect ventilation made fainting a common occurrence in Broughton Place, especially among "*thae young hizzies,*" as *Jeems* called the servant girls. He generally came to me, "the young Doctor," on these occasions with a look of great relish. I had indoctrinated him in the philosophy of *syncopes*, especially as to the propriety of laying the "*hizzies*" quite flat on the floor of the lobby, with the head as low as the rest of the body; and as many of these cases were owing to what *Jeems* called "that bitter yerkin" of their boddices, he and I had much satisfaction in relieving them, and giving them a moral lesson, by cutting their stay-laces, which ran before the knife, and cracked "like a bowstring," as my coadjutor said. One day a young lady was our care. She was lying out, and

---

[1] On one occasion a descendant of Nabal having put a crown piece into "the plate" instead of a penny, and staring at its white and precious face, asked to have it back, and was refused—"In once, in for ever." "A weel, a weel," grunted he, "I'll get credit for it in heaven." "Na, na," said *Jeems*, "ye'll get credit only for the penny!"

slowly coming to. *Jeems,* with that huge terrific visage, came round to me with his open *gully* in his hand, whispering, "Wull oo ripp 'er up noo?" It happened not to be a case for ripping up. The gully was a great sanitary institution, and made a decided inroad upon the *yerking* system—*Jeems* having, thanks to this and Dr. Coombe, every year fewer opportunities of displaying and enjoying its powers.

He was sober in other things besides drink, could be generous on occasion, but was careful of his siller; sensitive to fierceness ("we're uncommon *zeelyous* the day," was a favourite phrase when any church matter was stirring) for the honour of his church and minister, and to his too often worthless neighbours a perpetual moral protest and lesson—a living epistle. He dwelt at the head of Big Lochend's Close in the Canongate, at the top of a long stair—ninety-six steps, as I well know—where he had dwelt, all by himself, for five-and-thirty years, and where, in the midst of all sorts of flittings and changes, not a day opened or closed without the well-known sound of *Jeems* at his prayers,—his "exercise,"—at "the Books." His clear, fearless, honest voice in psalm and chapter, and strong prayer, came sounding through that wide *"land,"* like that of one crying in the wilderness.

Jeems and I got great friends; he called me John as if he was my grandfather; and though as plain in speech as in feature, he was never rude. I owe him much in many ways. His absolute downrightness and *yaefauldness;* his energetic, unflinching fulfilment of his work; his rugged, sudden tenderness; his look of sturdy age, as the thick silver-white hair lay on his serious and weatherworn face, like moonlight on a stout old tower; his quaint Old Testament exegetics, his lonely and contented life, his simple godliness,—it was no small privilege to see much of all this.

But I must stop. I forget that you didn't know him; that he is not your *Jeems.* If it had been so, you would not soon have wearied of telling or of being told of the life and conversation of this "fell body." He was not communicative about his early life. He would sometimes speak to me about *"her,"* as if I knew who and where she was, and always with a gentleness and solemnity unlike his usual gruff ways. I found out that he had been married when young, and that "she" (he never named her) and their child died on the same day,—the day of its birth. The only indication of married life in his room, was an old and strong cradle, which he had cut down so as to rock no more, and which he made the depository of his books—a queer collection.

I have said that he had what he called, with a grave smile, *family* worship, morning and evening, never failing. He not only sang his psalm, but gave out or chanted *the line* in great style; and on seeing me one morning surprised at this, he said, "Ye see John, *oo*," meaning himself and his wife, "began that way." He had a firm, true voice, and a genuine though roughish gift of singing, and being methodical in all things, he did what I never heard of in any one else,—he had seven fixed tunes, one of which he sang on its own set day. Sabbath morning it was *French,* which he went through with great *birr.* Monday, *Scarborough,* which, he said, was like my father cantering. Tuesday, *Coleshill,* that soft exquisite air,—monotonous and melancholy, soothing and vague, like the sea. This day, Tuesday, was the day of the week on which his wife and child died, and he always sang more verses then than on any other. Wednesday was *Irish;* Thursday, *Old Hundred;* Friday, *Bangor;* and Saturday, *Blackburn,* that humdrummest of tunes, "as long, and lank, and lean, as is the ribbed sea-sand." He could not defend it, but had some secret reason for sticking to it. As to the evenings, they were just the same tunes in reversed order, only that on Tuesday night he sang *Coleshill* again, thus dropping *Blackburn* for evening work. The children could tell the day of the week by *Jeems's* tune, and would have been as much astonished at hearing *Bangor* on Monday, as at finding St. Giles's half-way down the Canongate.

I frequently breakfasted with him. He made capital porridge, and I wish I could get such buttermilk, or at least have such a relish for it, as in those days. *Jeems* is away—gone over to the majority; and I hope I may never forget to be grateful to the dear and queer old man. I think I see and hear him saying his grace over our bickers with their *brats* on, then taking his two books out of the cradle and reading, not without a certain homely majesty, the first verse of the 99th Psalm,

> "Th' eternal Lord doth reign as king,
>   Let all the people quake;
> He sits between the cherubims,
>   Let th' earth be mov'd and shake;"

then launching out into the noble depths of *Irish*. His chapters were long, and his prayers short, very scriptural, but by no means stereotyped, and wonderfully real, *immediate*, as if he was near Him whom he addressed. Any one hearing the sound and not the words, would say, "That man is speaking to some one who is with him—who is present,"—as he often said to me, "There's nae gude dune, John, till ye get to *close grups*."

PEGGY [1]

By Robert M. Gay

Peggy is the kind of dog of which friendly strangers on the street ask, "What kind of dog is that?" I always reply, "Oh, she's a kind of Irish terrier," and then I hasten to add, "She isn't my dog. She's my little girl's dog."

Examining my motives for such a reply, I think that I make it because of some subtle feeling I have that a grown man ought to apologize for being out for a walk with a dog like Peggy. I am sorry to feel so about a friend, but I cannot help it. The fact is that, though we enjoy a complete mutual understanding which leads her incessantly to look up at my face to see whether I am cheerful and contented, I cannot lead Peggy on a leash without feeling foolish. Try as I will to remember her sterling character, I cannot forget that she lacks the dignity a dog out walking with a man ought to have. When I go along the street with her, I find myself oddly remembering a tiny motor-boat in which I once went sailing. I felt foolish in that boat, because it was so

[1] From *The Atlantic Monthly*, June 1925 under the title "Stray Notes of a Somewhat Dogged Tendency." By the kind permission of the editor and of the author.

small that I seemed to bulge all round outside it, and the stout owner and his fat son and I looked, from the shore, like the three wise men of Gotham who went to sea in a bowl.

I often tell Peggy she has not only the appearance of a yellow dog but the manners of a flapper; and yet she does not appear chagrined. The trouble is that she does not look like anything in particular. She is not standardized at all. And she has no dignity whatever. To feel at ease on the street with a dog, one ought to have a dog of at least moderate size and dignity, and the dog ought to be one of which people sitting on porches will say, "That's an Airedale," or "That's a collie," and not, "What kind of dog is that?" I often tell myself that I will not go walking with Peggy any more; but she knows perfectly well how weak I am, and that if she goes to the head of the stairs and noses at her leash and whines I will go.

Now Peggy's father and mother were not only Irish terriers but conventional and standardized Irish terriers. They had heads and hair and legs and tails and other things of a certain so-to-speak predetermined shape and kind. Looking at them, one knew instantly what they were. They respected the conventions, both in appearance and in manners. I never saw them on the street, but I have no doubt that they walked along with poise and decorum, and never tried to look backward and walk forward simultaneously, with a resultant gait that can be compared only to that of a water spider; they never attempted to trot and to scratch their ears at the same time; and they never suddenly changed their minds about trotting at all, sat down, and slid a few yards along the sidewalk, before their owner became aware of their altered intentions. Peggy does all these things and several others. Besides, her head, legs, hair, and tail are no more conventional than her manners. If she only looked like what my friends call "a regular dog"—they are fond of asking me why I don't get a regular dog—one could overlook her other peculiarities. But she seems to take pride in looking ordinary.

Of course, I may be oversensitive; but let me give you an illustration of Peggy's plebeian tendencies. Last month we were crossing the automobile ferry that runs over the Sheepscot River between Bath and Woolwich, Maine, and our car, with Peggy sitting on the front seat, stopped alongside a limousine with an Airedale sitting on its front seat. It was a "regular" Airedale, too: there was no doubt about that. Instantly Peggy began to hop about and shiver and yawn, with shrill feminine squeals. I suspect that she was trying to flirt with him. But did he reciprocate? He did not. After giving her one supercilious stare, he turned and gazed across the river at the hills of Woolwich and continued to gaze, sitting up with all the hauteur of a footman or a butler—and there is nothing in the world more terrifying than that. We were all humiliated, except Peggy; and we agreed among ourselves that when we were buying a dog we might have picked out one with a little more style.

Of course, she is not really ordinary. I tell my friends constantly what a remarkable dog she is, and try to narrate to them examples of the unusually brilliant things she does. But they never listen, because they are thinking up something remarkable that some dog of theirs once did. They really do not consider Peggy remarkable, anyway. They judge her by her looks and these always make them laugh. But I never listen to their stories either, any more than I listen when they tell about their remarkable children. I merely assume a fixed expression of interest or astonishment and then, the moment I get a chance, tell them about my little girl or my little dog—my little girl's little dog, I mean. I shall not tell any of Peggy's remarkable doings here, however, because the reader would be thinking all the while that they were nothing to what he could tell about his dog.

When I go walking with Peggy—usually at night—I study her. There is a philosophical principle, for which a good deal can be said, that if one studies anything, however insignificant,—like Peggy, for instance,—if one studies this thing long enough and follows out to their conclusions all the thoughts suggested, one will end by knowing everything, not only about that thing, but about everything. I have never had time to apply the theory exhaustively, though perhaps sometime, when I am on a summer vacation, I shall; but I have experimented with it in a modest way and have found it very amusing. Now it is one thing and now another I use for the purpose, and just at this time it is Peggy. She is my "flower in the crannied wall," so to speak.

My studies do not take the laborious and pedestrian form known as experimental or laboratory psychology. My little girl and I did once experiment on Peggy for perhaps ten minutes, but she is not a good laboratory subject and I am naturally indolent. She has not the calm and poise that such a subject should have if one is to obtain the best results. Our experiment was a form of intelligence test, for I wished to satisfy myself whether what looked like intelligence in Peggy was really intelligence or only vivacity. I have often wondered the same thing about human beings. To this end, then, we laid two pieces of cake, a small one and a large one, on the floor, in order to determine whether, if she were permitted to choose freely between them, she would always choose the larger. Now such a test, to be significant, must be properly controlled, and Peggy refused to be controlled. We felt that scientific procedure required that the two objects should be placed at the same distance from the subject, since otherwise the closer proximity of one or the other piece to her would vitiate the experiment. But we had to give it up, because the subject took too great an interest in the objects and managed to gulp them indiscriminately before we could be quite certain whether she was using her brain at all. We became exhausted before she did, and I have since confined my studies to empirical observations.

As Peggy trots or gambols before, behind, or all round me, while we are taking our walks,—usually, as I have said, at night, —I ask myself questions about her and then look about in my mind for any stray items of information on the subject or any original ideas that may hitherto have lain there unnoticed. Last night, for example, I asked myself, "Has she a soul?" This question, though interesting, is a hard one, because to answer it one would have first to decide what a soul is, and then to determine whether Peggy carries anything like that about with her. I have decided that she certainly carries something about, but whether it fulfills the specifications of the theologians is another matter entirely.

The first time I ever saw Peggy—that is, when I went to buy her—I knelt on the ground and held out my hands, and she jumped into them and, planting her forepaws on my chest, looked steadfastly into my eyes. At that moment I detected—or thought I did—a certain something that looked at me and answered to a certain something in me understandingly. That something I feel free to call a soul if I wish to, whichever of the two somethings is indicated. It really seems conceited to call my "something" by one name and hers by another.

Anyway, there is something about Peggy—and you may call it whatever you please—that is simply Peggy and nobody else. I have watched it grow, too, and it seems to become more intrinsically Peggy all the time. I have known many fine dogs and have always been struck by the fact that they were so singularly themselves—much more so than most human beings. You are never quite sure about a human being, whether what you see is really himself or is his histrionic creation of a self that he keeps for show; but you are always sure about a dog. When I look at Peggy, for example, I know that I am seeing her and not her attempt to look and act like the dog around the corner. And it is the same way with the dog around the corner, whose name is Betty. She is even funnier-looking than Peggy, but is not at all humble on that account. She looks like a composite picture of a very large mole, a very small kangaroo, and a muskrat, while Peggy looks only like a dog that tried to look like an Irish terrier and then changed her mind. But Betty, in spite of her rococo appearance, is still every inch herself, and I always know exactly how to take her. I know, for instance, that she feels a profound scorn of Peggy and that she will try to bite her whenever she can. I think that she objects to Peggy's lack of dignity, though it may be that she remembers how Peggy used to wear, last winter, a green sweater that made her look like a cucumber. Betty does not believe in dogs wearing green sweaters. Peggy, however, far from cherishing any grudge, lives under the unalterable delusion that Betty wants to play with her.

Peggy's complete independence of mind, considering her size, is almost humiliating to a human being who sometimes knows his own mind and sometimes does not. She always knows hers. In fact, I often call her "Mr. F.'s Aunt," after the startling old lady in *Little Dorrit*, who I suspect, by the way, has been reincarnated in her. For just as Mr. F.'s Aunt had only one idea at a time but had that with all her might, so does Peggy; and just as Mr. F.'s Aunt shook her venerable fist under poor inoffensive Clennam's nose, so does Peggy object to our iceman. She even disapproves of icemen as a class, and flies into a rage the moment she hears the rumble of an ice-wagon on the block. She begins to rumble herself, making in her throat a terrifying noise which, by long practice, she is able to keep up unintermittently and without losing her breath, until the iceman has come upstairs and has gone down again. She also erects the hair along her spine, and draws back her lips in an expression that would chill the heart of the most frigid iceman; and when he has left the pantry and is well on his way downstairs she rushes to the door and breathes hard through the crack under it.

There seems to be no good reason why she should do this three or four times a week for months on end. No iceman has ever done anything to her, and our iceman has made many overtures of peace. The only reason I can think of is that she enjoys doing it; and that, I suspect, is her reason. I cannot help admiring her and even envying her a little, for it must be very amusing to fly into such a terrible rage for no reason whatever.

What I especially admire in her is the stability of her opinions. When she has once made up her mind on any subject, there is nothing more to be said. That is her opinion, whether it rests on any rational grounds or not. It must be very comfortable to feel like that. We human beings look before and after and pine for what is not; Peggy never does—at least, not for any length of time. We, as the poet says, fluctuate idly without term or scope and each of us strives, nor knows for what he strives, and each half-lives a hundred different lives; but that does not describe Peggy in the least. She is living only one life at a time, but she is living it for all she is worth and not worrying her small head about all the it-might-have-been's and if-there-were's that so commonly assail human beings. When she is sad, she is the complete and final epitome of sorrow, from the twitching black button that answers for a nose to the last quivering red hair at the tip of her somewhat too long tail. When she is glad, she is equally a compendium of all the denotations and connotations of joy. When she is hungry, she is just that; and when she eats, well— perhaps the less said about that the better.

Her soul is probably a simple little elementary soul, but it is crystal clear. It might not carry a man very far toward the skies, and yet he would be lucky if his were as honest and as staunch and as brave.

While I have been writing that last paragraph, Peggy has been making her bed. This is a serious matter, which occupies her for half an hour every night. She pulls her blankets up in little points with her teeth, then tramples them down with her feet, ploughs them up with her nose, tramples them down again, and sighs and snorts, while her basket creaks like a ship in heavy weather. At last she turns around half a dozen times, and flops with a thump and a final deep sigh. I sigh, too, thinking that her efforts are ended. But no! So long as there is a light in the house, she has to make the rounds of the rooms at intervals to be sure that all the family are safe. She has just been in to see me, laying her black nose on my knee and looking up at me with her brown eyes. I have pulled her ears, and scratched her back, and now I hear her toenails scratching on the oilcloth, as she goes to her basket in the kitchen once more. "Good night, Peg," I say, "you're a good dog."

EXERCISES

1. No theme of the length requisite for an appreciation was ever effective without a clearly defined plan either in the mind of the author or on paper. Ideally it might well be in both places! In fact, this assignment may effectually be the occasion for the intro- duction of an outline, which will prove not only in its own con- struction but in the later construction of this and future themes of inestimable value. The wise instructor, unless he is rushed for time, will do well to make the outline his assignment, instead of the theme, for the week before the theme is due. Then the student

will be more (or less) sure that he has planned well, and will be ready with a greater degree of confidence to proceed with the writing of his theme. The week intervening will, in addition, have given him time to think more about his subject. Would that the old poem were true and that we lived "in thoughts" as well as in words!

A model outline follows. It was written by a freshman student in preparation for her 1,500-word appreciation of *Angel,* a maid of all work in her family.

Angel

Introduction

(Our family has never risen to the dignity of keeping a real maid, one, I have always imagined, who would wear a black uniform and starched frills for her cap and apron. But we have always had Angel.)

I. Angel's arrival, it is safe to say, will never fade from my memory.
    A. I stood peering around the corner, amazed at her odd appearance.
    B. I called her Angel although her name was Mrs. Andel.

II. She was at once put to work about the house.
    A. She could not rid herself of my attentions.
    B. She made matters worse by being most indulgent to me.

III. On days when Mother was at home, I was never allowed to bother Angel, but when Mother was out, I left everything to watch her.
    A. I loved to see her wash.
    B. I was custodian of the clothespins when she hung the clothes to dry.
    C. I stood absorbed at the end of her board while she ironed.

IV. Sometimes she washed windows.
    A. I can still see her sitting on the sill so that only her feet were inside.
    B. She polished the glass like no one else in the world.

V. When she had leisure, she would produce her embroidery, most remarkable work.
  A. Shall I ever forget the table-cover with two fat kewpies under umbrella trees?
  B. I have to-day a bureau scarf with very blue blue-birds flying recklessly among purple daisies.
VI. She liked to talk as she sewed or worked.
  A. Her descriptions of the war in Europe were inimitable.
VII. Angel was easily sorrowful.
  A. She cried over my scratched knees and other small accidents and ailments.
  B. She was plunged into gloom over the sad stories I manufactured for her.
  C. She killed my goldfish by overfeeding, and then she suffered deepest melancholy from her act.
VIII. Many impressions of Angel come back to me as I write:
  A. I see her thick-fingered hands smoothing starched, white linen.
  B. I hear her quick, creaking steps.
  C. I see her squat figure trotting after a distant trolley car.

Conclusion

(I can think of no one in appearance less like the popular conception of an angel; yet as far as any human being approaches the angels—in kindness, in sympathy, in loyalty, in simplicity— Angel deserved her name.)

An extended analysis of the outline given hardly seems necessary. The Roman numerals suggest paragraphs, each with its topic sentence; the sub-topics, A B C etc., denote the material which develops the paragraphs. In some cases, however, the writer may decide that a sub-topic may well begin a paragraph by itself. For example, in the outline given, C under VII might better head a new paragraph, for, although in the outline it surely belongs under VII, it is yet obviously an incident important enough for its own paragraph. The student's own judgment must determine when an entry needs a paragraph by itself in the theme.

Then, too, in the matter of introduction and conclusion there is no rule except preference and judgment. Christopher Morley in his essay has a clearly defined conclusion but no introduction. Some writers will prefer to have no formal introduction but to incorporate whatever there may be of an introductory nature into the first paragraph of the theme. A conclusion is also a matter of choice.

2. Outline Christopher Morley's essay on Francis Barton Gummere in the manner given above.

3. Study the Biblical allusions in the first paragraph of "Jeems the Doorkeeper." Why are they so effective?

4. If you feel sufficiently strongly against some individual, write a *depreciation* instead of an appreciation, using the same general method.

5. Read "Noah's Wife" by Robert M. Gay in *The Atlantic Monthly* for July 1922. If it affords you an idea of some literary or Biblical character upon whom you might write, seize upon it! Whatever you do, never lose a *bona fide idea!*

6. *Margaret Ogilvy* by James Matthew Barrie is filled with various and unique methods of appreciation. Are all of them too difficult for the amateur? Give a class report on your findings and your opinions. Don't feel injured if you are asked to do this. To read *Margaret Ogilvy* is an experience!

SUGGESTED READINGS

Of People:

Abbott, Lyman, "Theodore Roosevelt," *The Outlook,* January 15, 1919.

Anonymous, "Ear-Trumpeting with Friar Juniper" and "The Passing of Emily Ruggles's" in Tanner, *Essays and Essay Writing,* Little, Brown, Boston. "Dody," *The Atlantic Monthly,* June 1927.

Barrie, James Matthew, "A Day in Her Life" from *Margaret Ogilvy,* Scribner's, New York.

Benson, Arthur Christopher, "The Old Family Nurse" from *Along the Road,* Putnam's, New York.

Brooks, Charles S., "The Tread of the Friendly Giants," from *Chimney-Pot Papers,* Yale University Press, New Haven.

Galsworthy, John, "Quality" from *Caravan,* Scribner's, New York.

Gay, Robert M., "Noah's Wife," *The Atlantic Monthly,* July 1922.

Hazlitt, William, the sketch of his father from "My First Acquaintance with Poets" in *Essays,* The Modern Readers' Series, Macmillan, New York.

Kellogg, Charlotte, "The Passing of the Great Cardinal," *The Atlantic Monthly,* May 1926.

Lucas, Edward Verrall, "A Funeral" from *A Little of Everything,* Macmillan, New York.

Mallett, Captain Thierry, "My Friend Kakoot," *The Atlantic Monthly,* September 1927.

Morley, Christopher, "Silas Orrin Howes" from *Pipefuls,* Doubleday, Doran, New York. "A Letter to a Sea Captain" from *Plumpudding,* Doubleday, Doran, New York.

Newton, A. Edward, "A Word in Memory" from *The Amenities of Book Collecting,* Little, Brown, Boston.

Slattery, Charles Lewis, "Josiah Royce," *The Outlook,* January 15, 1919.

Stevenson, Robert Louis, "Thomas Stevenson, Civil Engineer" from *Memories and Portraits,* Scribner's, New York. "The Manse" from the same.

Of Animals:

Anonymous, "Jonas and Matilda" and "Human Nature in Chickens" in Tanner, *Essays and Essay Writing,* Little, Brown, Boston.

Benson, Arthur Christopher, "Roddy" from *Along the Road,* Putnam's, New York.

Coffin, Robert P. Tristram, "Whom Poets Have Neglected," *The Yale Review,* July 1928.

Dounce, Harry Esty, "Some Nonsense about a Dog" in *Modern Essays,* Harcourt, Brace, New York.

Hudson, W. H., "Some Bird Adventures," Chapter VI, from *Far Away and Long Ago,* E. P. Dutton, New York.

Hunt, Leigh, "On the Graces and Anxieties of Pig Driving" from *Essays and Sketches.*

McDowall, Arthur, "Cows" from *Ruminations,* Houghton Mifflin, Boston.

Morrison, Theodore, "As the Swift Ships," *The Atlantic Monthly*, November 1925.

Repplier, Agnes, "Agrippina" from *Essays in Idleness*, Houghton Mifflin, Boston. "Old World Pets" from *Essays in Miniature*, Houghton Mifflin, Boston.

Richardson, Caroline Francis, "Story Animals," *The Yale Review*, January 1924.

Sharp, Dallas Lore, "The Edge of Night" from *The Face of the Fields*, Houghton Mifflin, Boston.

Thomas, Sir W. Beach, "A Letter to My Dog," *The Atlantic Monthly*, July 1927.

CHAPTER V

Themes About Places

If you have read Barrie's *Sentimental Tommy* (and if you have not, you are to be pitied!) you will remember how Jean Myles, the mother of Tommy and Elspeth, told her children about Thrums, its town-house, its west end, its Auld Licht Kirk. An exile from it, ill and lonely in the slums of London, Thrums became to her an ideal place, so ideal, in fact, that when, after her death, Tommy and Elspeth went there, they were sadly disillusioned. Their mother's Thrums was not Thrums at all!

This feeling for a place, which so tore the heart of poor Jean Myles, is one of the most common feelings in the world. Already you have associated your college acquaintances and friends with the localities they are always extolling. You laugh uproariously at one who is constantly talking of a small town in North Dakota, which you, born and reared in the hills, are willing to wager is flat and new and ugly. He, on his part, lends a grudging ear to the praises of Chicago as a summer resort or to the fascination of the sand dunes of northern Indiana. This love of a place, endeared by years of familiar association, seems as instinctive as filial devotion. "Everybody dreams of it," says Barrie in *Sentimental Tommy*, "though not all call it Thrums."

And yet love for the old and familiar has, at least in certain minds and imaginations, a formidable rival in the interest and curiosity which the new engenders. Like Willa Cather's young sculptor one may want to be buried in an ugly prairie town, but one wants just as intensely to spend his life in Boston or New York.

Sentiment for the old, curiosity and interest in the new, these are emotions known to every one of us, and these form the

179

main sources for theme material on the subject of places. But there is yet another. Places like persons have, or acquire through years of existence, personality and atmosphere, and it is essential that those who write about them be conscious of that atmosphere and able to suggest it to their readers. Remember how Stevenson in "A Gossip on Romance" describes this very possession when he says, "Some places speak distinctly. Certain dank gardens cry aloud for a murder; certain houses demand to be haunted; certain coasts are set apart for shipwreck."

It is obvious that the more intensely you feel about a place, the more sensitive you are to its atmosphere and the more able to present or to suggest that atmosphere to others. Love is not necessarily your feeling at all; indeed, you may hate the place as bitterly and revengefully as Eustacia Vye in *The Return of the Native* hated Egdon Heath, or you may fear it as the villagers in Victor Hugo's *Toilers of the Sea* feared the Bû de la Rue. The one essential thing is that you shall recognize its atmosphere, whether that lie only in the quiet charm of a country village or unaccountably darken that village with strange and sinister influence.

The choice of a subject for this theme about a place affords the broadest of fields, and the models have been selected in anticipation of a wide variety in choice. In spite of the inroads of a machine age, isolated villages and hamlets do and will remain, just as they do and will continue to seem idyllic to some people. Dreamthorp is such a village, and no one could have caught and held its quaint and quiet atmosphere better than Alexander Smith in his essay.

The atmosphere of Egdon Heath is a less intimate, but more basic and overwhelming thing. Hardy makes us feel the brooding age of the heath, its mysterious watchfulness, its waiting through many centuries for the "final overthrow." He endows it with the dark personality of some sleeping and breathing monster without physical form, yet with a nature all its own—a creature whose lovers and friends are storms and winds. Here, details, although they definitely contribute to the atmosphere, slip away from it; and as we close Hardy's paragraphs, we are possessed by a mood rather than conscious of what created it. Such a presentation as this is not easy of imitation, nor are subjects easily procured from the average experience of the average person. Still it is possible that some of you may have been impressed by a tract of country, a body of water, a house or even a room in a house, which in some mysterious way casts like Egdon its spell upon the beholder. And at all events, if few can emulate Hardy's example, all can appreciate his work.

The two selections which deal with houses will be far more suggestive of subjects. F. Hopkinson Smith in "The Doctor's Home" shows us how useful can be the device of contrast in making a place stand out. His is also a good example of the value of vivid detail; but contrast is the bigger lesson to be learned from his old house in Bedford Place. Detail is at its best in "Peggoty's House," the bright, clear-cut detail so characteristic of a child's story. From the smoking iron funnel for the chimney of the old boat to Abraham and Isaac, Daniel and the green lions, from the blue mug to the smell of lobster—all is told by means of the sense impressions of the little David Copperfield. This selection affords excellent hints for themes on play-houses of various kinds or on any building or room which seems quaint and strange to a child —better, which *did* seem quaint and strange to you when you were a child.

Ruskin's "St. Mark's" is given here, not so much because it is an excellent model for freshmen (indeed, there is grave question whether it is a good model or not!) but because it illustrates better perhaps than any other piece of English prose the skillful and wonderful employment of words and sounds to bring about desired effects. It should be studied, not for its style but for its consonant and vowel sounds, for its use of light and dark imagery, and for the extreme and beautiful suggestiveness of its single words. If it can bring you to a sense of the charm and influence in single words, if it can make you more scrupulous in regard to your own diction, then its inclusion will have been worthwhile.

Elsewhere in these paragraphs it has been suggested that affection for a place is not a necessary possession of the person who wishes to write a theme about it. Hatred, fear, curiosity, interest, amazement—these are all reputable emotions with which to begin one's work. Nor must the place appeal necessarily to the æsthetic sense. It need not be beautiful or charming or quaint or romantic; it may, on the contrary, be ugly and dirty, crude and repelling. City-bred students often complain that they know of no idyllic places to extol in themes, that they cannot "wax sentimental over the country." Why should they, since they have other material exactly as valuable and appealing in its own way? These students should take particular delight in Mr. Strunsky's sketch of Broadway at twilight. Here is a wealth of detail and sense impression; here is swift and clever portraiture; here is imagery, ugly but real and, therefore, satisfying. One of the best themes I ever read was on a vacant city lot behind some railway yards, a lot where the author played as a boy. It had been a paradise to him at thirteen; and something of his gratitude for the good times it had afforded cast a glamour over its burdocks and its tumbleweed, its tin cans and discarded barbed wire, its dreariness and its dirt. That dingy vacant lot under his hands and in his imagination had as much atmosphere as Dreamthorp, and doubtless had meant as much in his life as that idealized English hamlet meant to Alexander Smith.

The first job, therefore, before you if you have been told to write a theme about a place is to decide upon one which *has meant something to you,* either because it is old and familiar or new and exciting, because it contributed something to your childhood or because it has recently brought something of value or influence into your life. Remember you are not trying to charm an instructor who may prefer Sorrento when the almonds are in blossom to a city dump in a pelting rain. You are writing in an attempt to make this place of your choice and its atmosphere stand out by means of *detail,* or *contrast,* or *accuracy of observation,* or *sense impressions,* or *careful weighing of word values,* or by a *combination of any or of all these features.*

DREAMTHORP [1]

(IN PART)

By Alexander Smith

It matters not to relate how or when I became a denizen of
Dreamthorp; it will be sufficient to say that I am not a born
native, but that I came to reside in it a good while ago now. The
several towns and villages in which, in my time, I have pitched a
tent did not please, for one obscure reason or another: this one
was too large, t'other too small; but when, on a summer evening
about the hour of eight, I first beheld Dreamthorp, with its west-
ward-looking windows painted by sunset, its children playing in
the single straggling street, the mothers knitting at the open doors,
the fathers standing about in long white blouses, chatting or
smoking; the great tower of the ruined castle rising high into the
rosy air, with a whole troop of swallows—by distance made as
small as gnats—skimming about its rents and fissures,—when I
first beheld all this, I felt instinctively that my knapsack might
be taken off my shoulders, that my tired feet might wander no
more, that at last, on the planet, I had found a home. From
that evening I have dwelt here, and the only journey I am like
now to make, is the very inconsiderable one, so far at least as
distance is concerned, from the house in which I live to the grave-
yard beside the ruined castle. There, with the former inhabitants of the place, I trust to sleep quietly enough, and nature
will draw over our heads her coverlet of green sod, and tenderly
tuck us in, as a mother her sleeping ones, so that no sound from
the world shall ever reach us, and no sorrow trouble us any more.

The village stands far inland; and the streams that trot through
the soft green valleys all about have as little knowledge of the sea
as the three-years' child of the storms and passions of manhood.
The surrounding country is smooth and green, full of undulations;
and pleasant country roads strike through it in every direction,
bound for distant towns and villages, yet in no hurry to reach
them. On these roads the lark in summer is continually heard;

[1] From *Dreamthorp and Other Essays.*

nests are plentiful in the hedges and dry ditches; and on the grassy banks, and at the feet of the bowed dikes, the blue-eyed speedwell smiles its benison on the passing wayfarer. On these roads you may walk for a year and encounter nothing more remarkable than the country cart, troops of tawny children from the woods, laden with primroses, and at long intervals—for people in this district live to a ripe age—a black funeral creeping in from some remote hamlet; and to this last the people reverently doff their hats and stand aside. Death does not walk about here often, but when he does, he receives as much respect as the squire himself. Everything round one is unhurried, quiet, moss-grown, and orderly. Season follows in the track of season, and one year can hardly be distinguished from another. Time should be measured here by the silent dial, rather than by the ticking clock, or by the chimes of the church. Dreamthorp can boast of a respectable antiquity, and in it the trade of the builder is un-known. Ever since I remember, not a single stone has been laid on the top of another. The castle, inhabited now by jackdaws and starlings, is old; the chapel which adjoins it is older still; and the lake behind both, and in which their shadows sleep, is, I suppose, as old as Adam. A fountain in the market-place, all mouths and faces and curious arabesques—as dry, however, as the castle moat—has a tradition connected with it; and a great noble, riding through the street one day several hundred years ago, was shot from a window by a man whom he had injured. The death of this noble is the chief link which connects the place with authentic history. The houses are old, and remote dates may yet be deciphered on the stones above the doors; the apple-trees are mossed and ancient; countless generations of sparrows have bred in the thatched roofs, and thereon have chirped out their lives. In every room of the place men have been born, men have died. On Dreamthorp centuries have fallen, and have left no more trace than have last winter's snowflakes. This commonplace sequence and flowing on of life is immeasurably affecting. That winter morning when Charles lost his head in front of the banqueting-hall of his own palace, the icicles hung from the eaves of the houses here, and the clown kicked the snowballs from his clouted shoon, and thought but of his supper when, at three o'clock, the red sun set in the purple mist. On that Sunday in June while Waterloo was going on, the gossips, after morning service, stood on the country roads discussing agricultural prospects, without the slightest suspicion that the day passing over their heads would be a famous one in the calendar. Battles have been fought, kings have died, history has transacted itself; but, all unheeding and untouched, Dreamthorp has watched apple-trees redden and wheat ripen, and smoked its pipe, and quaffed its mug of beer, and rejoiced over its newborn children and with proper solemnity carried its dead to the churchyard. As I gaze on the village of my adoption, I think of many things very far removed, and seem to get closer to them. The last setting sun that Shakespeare saw reddened the windows here, and struck warmly on the faces of the hinds coming home from the fields. The mighty storm that raged while Cromwell lay a-dying made all the oak woods groan round about here, and tore the thatch from the very roofs I gaze upon. When I think of this, I can almost, so to speak, lay my hand on Shakespeare and on Cromwell. These poor walls were contemporaries of both, and I find something affecting in the thought. The mere soil is, of course, far older than either, but *it* does not touch one in the same way. A wall is the creation of a human hand, the soil is not.

This place suits my whim, and I like it better year after year. As with everything else, since I began to love it I find it gradually growing beautiful. Dreamthorp—a castle, a chapel, a lake, a straggling strip of gray houses, with a blue film of smoke over all —lies embosomed in emerald. Summer, with its daisies, runs up to every cottage door. From the little height where I am now sitting, I see it beneath me. Nothing could be more peaceful. The wind and the birds fly over it. A passing sunbeam makes brilliant a white gable-end, and brings out the colors of the blossomed apple-tree beyond, and disappears. I see figures in the street, but hear them not. The hands on the church clock seem always pointing to one hour. Time has fallen asleep in the afternoon sunshine. I make a frame of my fingers, and look at my picture. On the walls of the next Academy's Exhibition will hang nothing half so beautiful!

My village is, I think, a special favorite of summer's. Every window-sill in it she touches with color and fragrance; everywhere she wakens the drowsy murmurs of the hives; every place she scents with apple-blossom. Traces of her hand are to be seen on the weir beside the ruined mill; and even the canal, along which the barges come and go, has a great white water lily asleep on its olive-colored face. Never was velvet on a monarch's robe so gorgeous as the green mosses that beruff the roofs of farm and cottage, when the sunbeam slants on them and goes. The old road out towards the common, and the hoary dikes that might have been built in the reign of Alfred, have not been forgotten by the generous adorning season; for every fissure has its mossy cushion, and the old blocks themselves are washed by the loveliest gray-green lichens in the world, and the large loose stones lying on the ground have gathered to themselves the peacefulest mossy coverings. Some of these have not been disturbed for a century. Summer has adorned my village as gaily, and taken as much pleasure in the task, as the people of old, when Elizabeth was queen, took in the adornment of the Maypole against a summer festival. And, just think, not only Dreamthorp, but every English village she has made beautiful after one fashion or another —making vivid green the hill slope on which straggling white Welsh hamlets hang right opposite the sea; drowning in apple-blossom the red Sussex ones in the fat valley. And think, once more, every spear of grass in England she has touched with a livelier green; the crest of every bird she has burnished; every old wall between the four seas has received her mossy and licheny attentions; every nook in every forest she has sown with pale flowers, every marsh she has dashed with the fires of the marigold. And in the wonderful night the moon knows, she hangs —the planet on which so many millions of us fight, and sin, and agonize, and die—a sphere of glowworm light.

*　　　*　　　*　　　*　　　*　　　*　　　*

EGDON HEATH [1]

By Thomas Hardy

A Saturday afternoon in November was approaching the time of twilight, and the vast tract of unenclosed wild known as Egdon Heath embrowned itself moment by moment. Overhead the hollow stretch of whitish cloud shutting out the sky was as a tent which had the whole heath for its floor.

The heaven being spread with this pallid screen and the earth with the darkest vegetation, their meeting-line at the horizon was clearly marked. In such contrast the heath wore the appearance of an installment of night which had taken up its place before its astronomical hour was come; darkness had to a great extent arrived hereon, while day stood distinct in the sky. Looking upwards, a furze-cutter would have been inclined to continue work; looking down, he would have decided to finish his faggot and go home. The distant rims of the world and of the firmament seemed to be a division in time no less than a division in matter. The face of the heath by its mere complexion added half an hour to evening; it could in like manner retard the dawn, sadden noon, anticipate the frowning of storms scarcely generated, and intensify the opacity of a moonless midnight to a cause of shaking and dread.

In fact, precisely at this transitional point of its nightly roll into darkness the great and particular glory of the Egdon waste began, and nobody could be said to understand the heath who had not been there at such a time. It could best be felt when it could not clearly be seen, its complete effect and explanation lying in this and the succeeding hours before the next dawn: then, and only then, did it tell its true tale. The spot was, indeed, a near relation of night, and when night showed itself an apparent tendency to gravitate together could be perceived in its shades and the scene. The sombre stretch of woods and hollows seemed to rise and meet the evening gloom in pure sympathy, the heath exhaling darkness as rapidly as the heavens precipitated it. And

[1] From *The Return of the Native.*

so the obscurity in the air and the obscurity in the land closed together in a black fraternization towards which each advanced half-way.

The place became full of watchful intentness now; for when other things sank brooding to sleep the heath appeared slowly to awake and listen. Every night its Titanic form seemed to await something; but it had waited thus unmoved during so many centuries, through the crises of so many things, that it could only be imagined to wait one last crisis—the final overthrow. . . . Twilight combined with the scenery of Egdon Heath to evolve a thing majestic without severity, impressive without showiness, emphatic in its admonitions, grand in its simplicity. . . .

The most thorough-going ascetic could feel that he had a natural right to wander on Egdon: he was keeping within the line of legitimate indulgence when he laid himself open to influences such as these. Colours and beauties so far subdued were, at least, the birthright of all. Only in summer days of highest feather did its mood touch the level of gaiety. Intensity was more usually reached by way of the solemn than by way of the brilliant, and such a sort of intensity was often arrived at during winter darkness, tempests, and mists. Then Egdon was aroused to reciprocity; for the storm was its lover, and the wind its friend. Then it became the home of strange phantoms; and it was found to be the hitherto unrecognized original of those wild regions of obscurity which are vaguely felt to be compassing us about in midnight dreams of flight and disaster, and are never thought of after the dream till revived by scenes like these.

It was at present a place perfectly accordant with man's nature—neither ghastly, hateful, nor ugly; neither commonplace, unmeaning, nor tame; but, like man, slighted and enduring; and withal singularly colossal and mysterious in its swarthy monotony. As with some persons who have lived long apart, solitude seemed to look out of its countenance. It had a lonely face, suggesting tragical possibilities.

THE DOCTOR'S HOME [1]

By F. Hopkinson Smith

The Doctor is not one of your new-fashioned doctors quartered in a brownstone house off the Avenue, with a butler opening the door; a pair of bob-tailed grays; a coupé with a note-book tucked away in its pocket bearing the names of various millionaires; an office panelled in oak; a waiting-room lined with patients reading last month's magazines until he should send for them. He has no such abode nor belongings. He lives all alone by himself in an old-fashioned house on Bedford Place—oh, such a queer, hunched-up old house and such a quaint old neighborhood poked away behind Jefferson Market—and he opens the door himself and sees everybody who comes—there are not a great many of them nowadays, more's the pity.

There are only a few such houses left up the queer old-fashioned street where he lives. The others were pulled down long ago, or pushed out to the line of the sidewalk and three or four stories piled on top of them. Some of these modern ones have big, carved marble porticos, made of painted zinc and fastened to the new brickwork. Inside these portals are a row of bronze bells and a line of speaking tubes with cards below bearing the names of those who dwell above.

The Doctor's house is not like one of these. It would have been had it not belonged to his old mother, who died long ago and who begged him never to sell it while he lived. He was thirty years younger then, but he is still there and so is the old house. It looks a little ashamed of its shabbiness when you come upon it suddenly hiding behind its pushing neighbors. First comes an iron fence with a gate never shut, and then a flagged path dividing a grass-plot, and then an old-fashioned wooden stoop with two steps, guarded by a wooden railing (many a day since these were painted); and over these railings and up the supports which carry the roof of the portico, straggles a

---

[1] From "'Doc' Shipman's Fee," in *The Under Dog*. By permission of Charles Scribner's Sons, the authorized publishers.

honeysuckle that does its best to hide the shabbiness of the shingles and the old waterspout and sagging gutter, and fails miserably when it gets to the farther cornice, which has rotted away, showing under its dismal paint the black and brown rust of decaying wood.

Then way in under the portico comes the door with the name-plate, and next to it, level with the floor of the piazza or portico —either you please, for it is a combination of both—are two long French windows, always open in summer evenings and alight on winter nights with the reflection of the Doctor's soft-coal fire, telling of the warmth and cheer within.

For it is a cheery place. It doesn't look like a doctor's office. There are dingy haircloth sofas, it is true, and a row of shelves with bottles, and funny-looking boxes on the mantel—one an electric battery—and rows and rows of books on the walls. But there are no dreadful instruments about. If there are, you don't see them.

The big chair he sits in would swallow up a smaller man. It is covered with Turkey red and has a roll cushion for his head. There are two of these chairs—one for you, or me; this last has big arms that come out and catch you under the elbows, a mighty help to a man when he has just learned that his liver or lungs or heart or some other part of him has gone wrong and needs overhauling.

Then there is a canary that sings all the time, and a small dog —oh, such a low-down, ill-bred, tousled dog; kind of a dog that might have been raised around a lumber-yard—was, probably— one ear gone, half of his tail missing; and there are some pots of flowers, and on the wall near the window where everybody can see is a case of butterflies impaled on pins and covered by a glass. No, you wouldn't think the Doctor's office a gruesome place, and you certainly wouldn't think the Doctor was a gruesome person —not when you come to know him.

PEGGOTTY'S HOUSE [1]

By Charles Dickens

Ham carrying me on his back and a small box of ours under his arm, and Peggotty carrying another small box of ours, we turned down lanes bestrewn with bits of chips and little hillocks of sand, and went past gas-works, rope-walks, boat-builders' yards, ship-wrights' yards, ship-breakers' yards, caulkers' yards, riggers' lofts, smiths' forges, and a great litter of such places, until we came out upon the dull waste I had already seen at a distance; when Ham said:

"Yon's our house, Mas'r Davy!"

I looked in all directions, as far as I could stare over the wilderness, and away at the sea, and away at the river, but no house could *I* make out. There was a black barge, or some other kind of superannuated boat, not far off, high and dry on the ground, with an iron funnel sticking out of it for a chimney and smoking very cosily; but nothing else in the way of a habitation that was visible to *me*.

"That's not it?" said I. "That ship-looking thing?"

"That's it, Mas'r Davy," returned Ham.

If it had been Aladdin's palace, roc's egg and all, I suppose I could not have been more charmed with the romantic idea of living in it. There was a delightful door cut in the side, and it was roofed in, and there were little windows in it; but the wonderful charm of it was, that it was a real boat which had no doubt been upon the water hundreds of times, and which had never been intended to be lived in, on dry land. That was the captivation of it to me. If it had ever been meant to be lived in, I might have thought it small, or inconvenient, or lonely; but never having been designed for any such use, it became a perfect abode.

It was beautifully clean inside, and as tidy as possible. There was a table, and a Dutch clock, and a chest of drawers, and on the chest of drawers there was a tea-tray with a painting on it of a lady with a parasol, taking a walk with a military-looking child

[1] From *David Copperfield*.

who was trundling a hoop. The tray was kept from tumbling down by a Bible; and the tray, if it had tumbled down, would have smashed a quantity of cups and saucers and a teapot that were grouped around the book. On the walls there were some common coloured pictures, framed and glazed, of Scripture subjects; such as I have never seen since in the hands of pedlars, without seeing the whole interior of Peggotty's brother's house again, at one view. Abraham in red going to sacrifice Isaac in blue, and Daniel in yellow cast into a den of green lions, were the most prominent of these. Over the little mantel-shelf was a picture of the *Sarah Jane* lugger, built at Sunderland, with a real little wooden stern stuck on to it; a work of art, combining composition with carpentry, which I considered to be one of the most enviable possessions that the world could afford. There were some hooks in the beams of the ceiling, the use of which I did not divine then; and some lockers and boxes and conveniences of that sort, which served for seats and eked out the chairs.

All this, I saw in the first glance after I crossed the threshold —child-like, according to my theory—and then Peggotty opened a little door and showed me my bedroom. It was the completest and most desirable bedroom ever seen—in the stern of the vessel; with a little window, where the rudder used to go through; a little looking-glass, just the right height for me, nailed against the wall, and framed with oyster-shells; a little bed, which there was just room enough to get into; and a nosegay of seaweed in a blue mug on the table. The walls were whitewashed as white as milk, and the patchwork counterpane made my eyes quite ache with its brightness. One thing I particularly noticed in this delightful house was the smell of fish; which was so searching, that when I took out my pocket-handkerchief to wipe my nose, I found it smelt exactly as if it had wrapped up a lobster. On my imparting this discovery in confidence to Peggotty, she informed me that her brother dealt in lobsters, crabs, and crawfish; and I afterwards found that a heap of these creatures, in a state of wonderful conglomeration with one another, and never leaving off pinching whatever they laid hold of, were usually to be found in a little wooden outhouse where the pots and kettles were kept.

St. Mark's [1]

By John Ruskin

And now I wish that the reader, before I bring him into St. Mark's Place, would imagine himself for a little time in a quiet English cathedral town, and walk with me to the west front of its cathedral. Let us go together up the more retired street, at the end of which we can see the pinnacles of one of the towers, and then, through the low grey gateway, with its battlemented top and small latticed window in the centre, into the inner private-looking road or close, where nothing goes in but the carts of the trades-men who supply the bishop and the chapter, and where there are little shaven grass-plots, fenced in by neat rails, before old-fashioned groups of somewhat diminutive and excessively trim houses, with little oriel and bay windows jutting out here and there, and deep wooden cornices and eaves painted cream colour and white, and small porches to their doors in the shape of cockle-shells, or little, crooked, thick, indescribable wooden gables, warped a little on one side; and so forward till we come to larger houses, also old-fashioned, but of red brick, and with gardens be-hind them, and fruit walls, which show here and there, among the nectarines, the vestiges of an old cloister arch or shaft, and looking in front on the cathedral square itself, laid out in rigid divisions of smooth grass and gravel walk, yet not uncheerful, especially on the sunny side, where the canon's children are walk-ing with their nurserymaids. And so, taking care not to tread on the grass, we will go along the straight walk to the west front, and there stand for a time, looking up at its deep-pointed porches and the dark places between their pillars where there were statues once, and where the fragments, here and there, of a stately figure are still left, which has in it the likeness of a king, perhaps indeed a king on earth, perhaps a saintly king long ago in heaven; and so, higher and higher up to the great mouldering wall of rugged sculpture and confused arcades, shattered, and grey, and grisly with heads of dragons and mocking fiends, worn

[1] From *Stones of Venice*.

by the rain and swirling winds into yet unseemlier shape, and coloured on their stony scales by the deep russet-orange lichen, melancholy gold; and so, higher still, to the bleak towers, so far above that the eye loses itself among the bosses of their traceries, though they are rude and strong, and only sees like a drift of eddying black points, now closing, now scattering, and now settling suddenly into invisible places among the bosses and flowers, the crowd of restless birds that fill the whole square with that strange clangour of theirs, so harsh and yet so soothing, like the cries of birds on a solitary coast between the cliffs and sea.

Think for a little while of that scene, and the meaning of all its small formalisms, mixed with its serene sublimity. Estimate its secluded, continuous, drowsy felicities, and its evidence of the sense and steady performance of such kind of duties as can be regulated by the cathedral clock; and weigh the influence of those dark towers on all who have passed through the lonely square at their feet for centuries, and on all who have seen them rising far away over the wooded plain, or catching on their square masses the last rays of the sunset, when the city at their feet was indicated only by the mist at the bend of the river. And then let us quickly recollect that we are in Venice, and land at the extremity of the Calle Lunga San Moisè, which may be considered as there answering to the secluded street that led us to our English cathedral gateway.

We find ourselves in a paved alley, some seven feet wide where it is widest, full of people, and resonant with cries of itinerant salesmen,—a shriek in their beginning, and dying away into a kind of brazen ringing, all the worse for its confinement between the high houses of the passage along which we have to make our way. Overhead, an inextricable confusion of rugged shutters, and iron balconies and chimney flues, pushed out on brackets to save room, and arched windows with projecting sills of Istrian stone, and gleams of green leaves here and there where a fig-tree branch escapes over a lower wall from some inner cortile, leading the eye up to the narrow stream of blue sky high over all. On each side, a row of shops, as densely set as may be, occupying, in fact, intervals between the square stone shafts, about eight

feet high, which carry the first floors: . . . the light in all cases
entering at the front only, and fading away in a few feet from
the threshold into a gloom which the eye from without cannot
penetrate, but which is generally broken by a ray or two from
a feeble lamp at the back of the shop, suspended before a print of
the Virgin. The less pious shopkeeper sometimes leaves his lamp
unlighted, and is contented with a penny print; the more religious one has his print coloured and set in a little shrine with a
gilded or figured fringe, with perhaps a faded flower or two on
each side, and his lamp burning brilliantly. Here, at the
fruiterer's, where the dark-green water-melons are heaped upon
the counter like cannon-balls, the Madonna has a tabernacle of
fresh laurel leaves; but the pewterer next door has let his lamp
out, and there is nothing to be seen in his shop but the dull gleam
of the studded patterns on the copper pans, hanging from his
roof in the darkness. . . .

A yard or two farther, we pass the hostelry of the Black Eagle,
and, glancing as we pass through the square door of marble,
deeply moulded, in the outer wall, we see the shadows of its
pergola of vines resting on an ancient well, with a pointed shield
carved on its side; and so presently emerge on the bridge and
Campo San Moisè, whence to the entrance into St. Mark's Place,
called the Bocci di Piazza . . . the Venetian character is nearly
destroyed. . . . We will push fast through them into the shadow
of the pillars at the end of the Bocci di Piazza, and then we
forget them all; for between those pillars there opens a great
light, and in the midst of it, as we advance slowly, the vast
tower of St. Mark's seems to lift itself visibly forth from the level
field of chequered stones; and, on each side, the countless arches
prolong themselves into ranged symmetry, as if the rugged and
irregular houses that pressed together above us in the dark alley
had been struck back into sudden obedience and lovely order, and
all their rude casements and broken walls had been transformed
into arches charged with goodly sculpture, and fluted shafts of
delicate stone.

And well may they fall back, for beyond those troops of ordered
arches there rises a vision out of the earth, and all the great square

seems to have opened from it in a kind of awe, that we may see it far away—a multitude of pillars and white domes, clustered into a long low pyramid of coloured light; a treasure-heap, it seems, partly of gold, and partly of opal and mother-of-pearl, hollowed beneath into five great vaulted porches, ceiled with fair mosaic, and beset with sculpture of alabaster, clear as amber and delicate as ivory—sculpture fantastic and involved, of palm leaves and lilies, and grapes and pomegranates, and birds clinging and fluttering among the branches, all twined together into an endless network of buds and plumes; and, in the midst of it, the solemn forms of angels, sceptered, and robed to the feet, and leaning to each other across the gates, their figures indiscreet among the gleaming of the golden ground through the leaves beside them, interrupted and dim, like the morning light as it faded back among the branches of Eden, when first its gates were angel-guarded long ago. And round the walls of the porches there are set pillars of variegated stones, jasper and porphyry, and deep-green serpentine spotted with flakes of snow, and marbles, that half refuse and half yield to the sunshine, Cleopatra-like, "their bluest veins to kiss"—the shadow, as it steals back from them, revealing line after line of azure undulation, as a receding tide leaves the waved sand; their capitals rich with interwoven tracery, rooted knots of herbage, and drifting leaves of acanthus and vine, and mystical signs, all beginning and ending in the Cross; and above them in the broad archivolts, a continuous chain of language and of life—angels, and the signs of heaven, and the labours of men, each in its appointed season upon the earth; and above these, another range of glittering pinnacles, mixed with white arches edged with scarlet flowers—a confusion of delight, amidst which the breasts of the Greek horses are seen blazing in their breadth of golden strength, and the St. Mark's Lion, lifted on a blue field covered with stars, until at last, as if in ecstasy, the crests of the arches break into a marble foam, and toss themselves far into the blue sky in flashes and wreaths of sculptured spray, as if the breakers on the Lido shore had been frost-bound before they fell, and the sea-nymphs had inlaid them with coral and amethyst.

Between that grim cathedral of England and this, what an interval! There is a type of it in the very birds that haunt them; for, instead of the restless crowd, hoarse-voiced and sable-winged, drifting on the bleak upper air, the St. Mark's porches are full of doves, that nestle among the marble foliage, and mingle the soft iridescence of their living plumes, changing at every motion, with the tints, hardly less lovely, that have stood unchanged for seven hundred years.

THE STREET [1]

By Simeon Strunsky

A foretaste of the langour of June is in the air. The turnstile storm doors in our office-building, which have been put aside for brief periods during the first deceptive approaches of spring, only to come back triumphant from Elba, have been definitely removed. The steel workers pace their girders twenty floors high almost in mid-season form, and their pneumatic hammers scold and chatter through the sultry hours. The soda fountains are bright with new compounds whose names ingeniously reflect the world's progress from day to day in politics, science, and the arts. From my window I can see the long black steamships pushing down to the sea, and they raise vague speculations in my mind about the cost of living in the vicinity of Sorrento and Fontainebleu. On such a day I am reminded of my physician's orders, issued last December, to walk a mile every afternoon on leaving my office. So I stroll up Broadway with the intention of taking my train farther up-town, at Fourteenth Street.

. . . In the city, where I should swing along briskly, I lounge. What is there on Broadway to linger over? On Broadway Nature has used her biggest, fattest typeforms. Tall, flat, building fronts, brazen with many windows and ribbed with commercial gilt lettering six feet high; shrieking proclamations of auction sales written in letters of fire on vast canvases; railway posters in scarlet and blue and green; rotatory barber poles

[1] From *Belshazzar Court*. By the kind permission of Henry Holt and Company.

striving at the national colors and producing vertigo; banners, escutcheons, crests in all the primary colors—surely none of these things needs poring over. And I know them with my eyes closed. I know the windows where lithe youths in gymnasium dress demonstrate the virtue of home exercises; the windows where other young men do nothing but put on and take off patent reversible near-linen collars; where young women deftly roll cigarettes; where other young women whittle at sticks with miraculously stropped razors. I know these things by heart, yet I linger over them in flagrantly unhygienic attitudes, my shoulders bent forward, and my chest and diaphragm precisely the reverse of that prescribed by the doctor.

Perhaps the thing that makes me linger before these familiar sights is the odd circumstance that in Broadway's shop windows Nature is almost never herself, but is either supernatural or artificial. Nature, for instance, never intended that razors should cut wood and remain sharp; that linen collars should keep on getting cleaner the longer they are worn; that glass should not break; that ink should not stain; that gauze should not tear; that an object worth five dollars should sell for $1.39; but all these things happen in Broadway windows. Williams, whom I meet now and then, who sometimes turns and walks up with me to Fourteenth Street, pointed out to me the other day how strange a thing it was that the one street which has become a synonym for "real life" to all good suburban Americans, is not real at all, but is crowded either with miracles or with imitations.

The windows on Broadway glow with wax fruits and with flowers of muslin and taffeta drawn by bounteous Nature from her storehouses in Parisian garret workshops. Broadway's ostrich feathers have been plucked in East Side tenements. The huge cigars in the tobacconists' windows are of wood. The enormous bottles of champagne in the saloons are of cardboard, and empty. The tall scaffoldings of proprietary medicine bottles in the drug shops are of paper. "Why," said Williams, "even the jewelry sold in the Japanese auction stores is not genuine, and the sellers are not Japanese."

This bustling mart of commerce, as the generation after the

Civil War used to say, is only a world of illusion. Artificial flowers, artificial fruits, artificial limbs, tobacco, rubber, silks, woolens, straws, gold, silver. . . . The ladies who smile out of charming morning costumes are obviously of lining and plaster. Their smug Herculean husbands in pajamas preserve their equanimity in the severest weather only because of their wire-and-plaster constitutions. The baby reposing in its beribboned crib is china and excelsior. Illusion everywhere.

But the Broadway crowd is real. You only have to buffet it for five minutes to feel, in eyes and arms and shoulders, how real it is. When I was a boy and was taken to the circus, it was always an amazing thing to me that there should be so many people in the street moving in a direction away from the circus. . . . But on Broadway on a late summer afternoon . . . the natural thing is that the living tide as it presses south shall beat me back, halt me, eddy around me. I know that there are people moving north with me, but I am not acutely aware of them. This onrush of faces converges on me alone. It is I against half the world.

The crowd on lower Broadway is alert and well set up. . . . The men on the sidewalk are young, limber, sharp-faced, almost insolent young men. There are not very many old men in the crowd, though I see any number of gray-haired young men. Seldom do you detect the traditional signs of age, the sagging lines of the face, the relaxed abdominal contour, the tamed spirit. The young, the young-old, the old-young, but rarely quite the old.

I am speaking only of externals. Clean-cut eager faces are very frequently disappointing. A very ordinary mind may be working behind that clear sweep of brow and nose and chin. I have known the shock of young men who look like kings of Wall Street and speak like shoe clerks. They are shoe clerks. But the appearance is there, that athletic carriage which is helped out by our triumphant, ready-made clothing. I suppose I ought to detest the tailor's tricks which iron out all ages and all stations into a uniformity of padded shoulders and trim waistlines and hips. I imagine I ought to despise our habit of wearing elegant shoddy where the European chooses honest, clumsy woolens. But

I am concerned only with externals, and in outward appearances a Broadway crowd beats the world. . . .

I still have to speak of the women in the crowd. What an infinitely finer thing is a woman than a man of her class! To see this for yourself you have only to walk up Broadway until the southward-bearing stream breaks off and the tide begins to run from west to east. You have passed out of the commercial district into the region of factories. It is well on toward dark, and the barracks that go by the unlovely name of loft buildings are pouring out their battalions of needle-workers. The crowd has become a mass. The nervous pace of lower Broadway slackens to the steady, patient tramp of a host. It is an army of women, with here and there a flying detachment of the male. . . .

. . . I am now on a different Broadway. The crowd is no longer north and south, but flows in every direction. It is churned up at every corner and spreads itself across the squares and open places. Its appearance has changed. It is no longer a factory population. Women still predominate, but they are the women of the professions and trades which center about Madison Square—business women of independent standing, women from the magazine offices, the publishing houses, the insurance offices. You detect the bachelor girl in the current which sets in toward the home quarters of the undomesticated, the little Bohemias, the foreign eating places, whose fixed *table d'hôte* prices flash out in illumined signs from the side streets. Still farther north and the crowd becomes tinged with the current of that Broadway which the outside world knows best. The idlers begin to mingle with the workers, men appear in English clothes with canes, women desperately corseted with plumes and jeweled reticules. You catch the first heart-beat of Little Old New York.

The first stirrings of this gayer Broadway die down as quickly almost as they manifest themselves. The idlers and those who minister to them have heard the call of the dinner hour and have vanished, into hotel doors, into shabbier quarters by no means in keeping with the cut of their garments and their apparent indifference to useful employment. Soon the street is almost empty.

It is not a beautiful Broadway in this garish interval between the last of the matinée and shopping crowd and the vanguard of the night crowd. The monster electric sign boards have not begun to gleam and flash and revolve and confound the eye and the senses. At night the electric Niagara hides the squalid fronts of ugly brick, the dark doorways, the clutter of fire escapes, the rickety wooden hoardings. Not an imperial street this Broadway at 6.30 of a summer's afternoon. Cheap jewelry shops, cheap tobacconists' shops, cheap haberdasheries, cheap restaurants, grimy little newspaper agencies and ticket offices and "demonstration" stores for patent foods, patent waters, patent razors. . . .

O Gay White Way, you are far from gay in the fast-fading light, before the magic hand of Edison wipes the wrinkles from your face and galvanizes you into hectic vitality; far from alluring with your tinsel shop windows, with your puffy-faced, unshaven men leaning against doorposts and chewing pessimistic toothpicks, your sharp-eyed newsboys wise with the wisdom of the Tenderloin, and your itinerant women whose eyes flash from side to side. It is not in this guise that you draw the hearts of millions to yourself, O dingy Gay White Way, O Via Lobsteria Dolorosa!

Well, when a man begins to moralize, it is time to go home. I have walked farther than I intended, and I am soft from lack of exercise, and tired. The romance of the crowd has disappeared. Romance cannot survive that short passage of Longacre Square, where the art of the theater and the picture postcard flourish in an atmosphere impregnated with gasoline. As I glance into the windows of the automobile salesrooms and catch my own reflection in the enamel of Babylonian limousines, I find myself thinking all at once of the children at home. They expand and fill up the horizon. Broadway disappears. I smile into the face of a painted promenader, but how is she to know that it is not at her I smile, but at the sudden recollection of what the baby said at the breakfast table that morning? Like all good New Yorkers when they enter the subway, I proceed to choke up all my senses against contact with the external world, and thus resolving myself into a state of coma, I dip down into the bowels of the earth, whence in due time I am spewed out two short blocks from Belshazzar Court.

EXERCISES

1. Try to determine what features of the style in "Dreamthorp" make for the atmosphere of peace and contemplation which permeates it. Does the diction contribute? If so, how and where? The second paragraph will lend itself particularly well to this study.

2. What instances of repetition in construction or in diction do you find in "Dreamthorp"? Why are they effective?

3. Give a class-room report on the use of detail in "Dreamthorp."

4. "Egdon Heath" gives the effect of gloom and of darkness. List the words which are responsible for this. Has the style anything to do with it?

5. Find excuses, if you think it excusable, for the rather helter-skelter style of "The Doctor's Home."

6. List the adjectives in "St. Mark's" which you think are responsible for the difference in effect between the English and the Italian cathedrals. In pronouncing these aloud are you conscious of any continuity of sounds in either case? If so, what are they?

7. Why is Ruskin perhaps a dangerous model for young writers?

8. Do the verbs or the adjectives in Mr. Strunsky's essay add more to its general vitality? Make good your decision.

9. Get acquainted with Logan Pearsall Smith's *Trivia* and try some paragraphs modelled on those given in the reading list. Don't decide against this suggestion merely because no credit will probably be given for it! Besides, Mr. Smith might give you a brand new idea for your theme about a place. He has done it before!

SUGGESTED READINGS

Barrie, James Matthew, "The Painted Lady's House" from *Sentimental Tommy,* Chapter XVI, Scribner's, New York.

Belloc, Hilaire, "Delft" from *Hills and the Sea,* Scribner's, New York.

Benson, Arthur Christopher, "St. Anthony-in-the-Fells" from *Along the Road,* Putnam's, New York. "St. Govan's" from the same.

Brooke, Rupert, "Niagara Falls" from *Letters from America,* Scribner's, New York.

Brooks, Charles S., "Glorious Goodwood," *The Yale Review,* July 1926.

Burke, Thomas, "Rendezvous" from *Out and About London,* Henry Holt, New York.

Coffin, Robert P. Tristram, "Iffley the Unspoiled," *North American Review,* July 1923. "Backwaters of Berkshire," *North American Review,* October 1923. "Saints and Cream and Devon Things," *North American Review,* May 1924.

Dickens, Charles, "An Old-fashioned House" from *Bleak House,* Chapter X.

France, Anatole, "Saint Valery-sur-Somme" from *Pierre Noziere,* Dodd, Mead, New York.

Guedalla, Philip, "Fez" from *A Gallery,* Putnam's, New York.

Hemon, Louis, "The Chapdelaine Cottage" from *Maria Chapdelaine,* Chapter II, Macmillan, New York.

Hudson, W. H., "The Plantation," Chapter IV, from *Far Away and Long Ago,* E. P. Dutton, New York.

Lamb, Charles, "Blakesmoor in Herefordshire" from *Last Essays of Elia.*

Lewisohn, Ludwig, "The Berlin of the Eighties" from *Upstream,* Boni and Liveright, New York.

Mackenzie, Compton, "The Basket of Roses" from *The Passionate Elopement,* Chapter XXIX, Harper's, New York.

Morley, Christopher, *Travels in Philadelphia,* Doubleday, Doran, New York. "Pine Street" from *Pipefuls,* Doubleday, Doran, New York.

Polo, Marco, "Concerning the Palace of the Great Khan," Chapter X from Book II of *Travels,* Macmillan, Modern Readers' Series, New York.

Smith, Logan Pearsall, "Somewhere," "The Spring in London," "The Shrine of Mnemosyne" from *Trivia,* Doubleday, Doran, New York.

Stevenson, Robert Louis, "Edinburgh," "A Mountain Town in France," and "Davos in Winter" from *Essays of Travel,* Scribner's, New York.

CHAPTER VI

Themes About People Merged with Background

It is hard to separate certain persons from the backgrounds which seem inseparably their own. When we think of them, we think immediately of their surroundings. "What do you know about Goldsmith?" I once asked a student. "Not much," he said, "but I never see him except in a feather-bed." Such is the result in one mind at least of the story of Goldsmith's giving away his clothes and being obliged to seek refuge and shelter in a bed of feathers. Similarly it is not easy to think of the Ben Jonson circle away from *The Mermaid Tavern,* or of Horace except on his Sabine farm, or of John Burroughs on a city street instead of in the woods. The same is just as true of relatively unimportant persons. One belongs in a garden, you say; another at the wheel of an automobile; a third in a kitchen.

Themes which have this two-fold purpose of revealing such persons through their own backgrounds are interesting to plan and to write, and fortunately literature affords many interesting examples. The problem here is the determining of the position and the space to be accorded each element. In most examples as in the three which follow you will find that the background is given first place. Just as the stage is set for the characters of a play before they make their appearance, so the environment should be made ready for the person or persons you are presenting. How much space you will give to it will be decided (1) *by the nature of the background* and (2) *by the degree to which it is inseparable from the person within it.* To illustrate: In Barrie's sketch of "The Dovecot" from *Sentimental Tommy* Miss Ailie appears almost immediately, just as soon as the exterior and situation of the cottage are described. Her characterization begins delightfully with the sign in the garden, and she continues throughout the story of the Hanky School. But although Miss Ailie is charming and the Dovecot equally so, neither is a matter of great moment. We smile at both because they are so whimsical and so thoroughly original. No one, we say, but Barrie could have written such a thing.

But with the excerpt from *An Iceland Fisherman* by Pierre Loti we immediately see a great difference. Here, for six paragraphs before Yann and Sylvestre are introduced, Loti describes the fearful storm off Iceland and the *Marie* running before the wind, which ran, too, before some "mysterious and terrible power." No quiet cottage on a Scottish brae is this! We are dealing here with the mighty forces of Nature. What is more, Loti wants us to understand that Yann and Sylvestre are themselves a part of the confusion. Their songs are drowned in the uproar about them; they are swept by the sea until their beards are stiff with salt; they are lashed to the helm of their ship; they are drunk with "the excess of movement and noise." In short, they are inseparable from the elements in which they live. The sea is their life, and they cannot be separated from it.

The same is true of the paragraphs from Hardy's *Far from the Madding Crowd* although the setting here is the solemnity and grandeur of a clear night rather than storm and confusion. Hardy takes ample time to present Norcombe Hill at midnight, first of all because he wants his readers to get the beauty and the mystery of the scene. Here there is as much wonder in the sensation of the roll of the world eastward as there is in Loti's storm. Both backgrounds are gigantic and awful, and they cannot well be minimized by curtailing of space. But Hardy's larger reason is unquestionably that of Loti. Gabriel Oak is an integral part of the night on Norcombe Hill: he plays a flute like the shepherds of two thousand years and more ago; he lives in a hut which is a mere shadow under a hedge; he is Nature's assistant at the birth of lambs; he tells time by the constellations. He is a part of the hill and of the night just as Yann and Sylvestre are a part of their ship and of the wind and the waves.

Such a theme assignment as this is not easy; in fact, your instructor may pass it over as far too difficult. But if he gives you a try at it, there is no end to the interesting possibilities it may afford. And whether you try it or not, you will at least, if you read thoughtfully the selections given, have added to your knowledge of literature and of its "long effects."

THE DOVECOT [1]

By James Matthew Barrie

The Dovecot was a prim little cottage standing back from the steepest brae in Thrums and hidden by high garden walls, to the top of which another boy's shoulders were, for apple-lovers, but one step up. Jargonelle trees grew against the house, stretching their arms around it as if to measure its girth, and it was also remarkable for several "dumb" windows with the most artful blinds painted on them. Miss Ailie's fruit was famous, but she loved her flowers best, and for long a notice-board in her garden said, appealingly: "Persons who come to steal the fruit are requested not to walk on the flower-beds." It was that old bachelor, Dr. McQueen, who suggested this inscription to her, and she could never understand why he chuckled every time he read it.

There were seven rooms in the house, but only two were of public note, the school-room, which was downstairs, and the blue-and-white room above. The school-room was so long that it looked very low in the ceiling, and it had a carpet, and on the walls were texts as well as maps. Miss Ailie's desk was in the middle of the room, and there was another desk in the corner; a cloth had been hung over it, as one covers a cage to send the bird to sleep. Perhaps Miss Ailie thought that a bird had once sung there, for this had been the desk of her sister, Miss Kitty, who died years before Tommy came to Thrums. . . .

The pupils had to bring handkerchiefs to the Dovecot, which led to its being called the Hanky School, and in time these handkerchiefs may be said to have assumed a religious character,

[1] From *Sentimental Tommy.* By permission of Charles Scribner's Sons, the authorized publishers.

though their purpose was merely to protect Miss Ailie's carpet. She opened each scholastic day by reading fifteen verses from the Bible, and then said sternly, "Hankies!" whereupon her pupils whipped out their handkerchiefs, spread them on the floor and kneeled on them while Miss Ailie repeated the Lord's Prayer. School closed at four o'clock, again with hankies.

Only on great occasions were the boys and girls admitted to the blue-and-white room, when they were given shortbread, but had to eat it with their heads flung back so that no crumbs should fall. Nearly everything in this room was blue or white, or both. There were white blinds and blue curtains, a blue table-cover and a white crumb-cloth, a white sheepskin with a blue footstool on it, blue chairs dotted with white buttons. Only white flowers came into this room, where there were blue vases for them, not a book was to be seen without a blue alpaca cover. Here Miss Ailie received visitors in her white with the blue braid, and enrolled new pupils in blue ink with a white pen. Some laughed at her, others remembered that she must have something to love after Miss Kitty died.

Miss Ailie had her romance, as you may hear by and by, but you would not have thought it as she came forward to meet you in the blue-and-white room, trembling lest your feet had brought in mud, but too much a lady to ask you to stand on a newspaper, as she would have liked dearly to do. She was somewhat be-yond middle-age, and stoutly, even squarely, built, which gave her a masculine appearance; but she had grown so timid since Miss Kitty's death that when she spoke you felt that either her figure or her manner must have been intended for some one else. In conversation she had a way of ending a sentence in the middle which gave her a reputation of being "thro'ither," though an artificial tooth was the cause. It was slightly loose, and had she not at times shut her mouth suddenly, and then done some-thing with her tongue, an accident might have happened. This tooth fascinated Tommy, and once when she was talking he cried, excitedly, "Quick, it's coming!" whereupon her mouth snapped close, and she turned pink in the blue-and-white room.

Yann and Sylvestre [1]

By Pierre Loti

By midday, the *Marie* had assumed completely her foul-weather trim; with closed hatches and reefed sails, she bounded supple and light; amid the disorder that was commencing she had the air of playing as play the porpoises whom storms amuse. With only her fore-sail spread, she ran before the wind, according to the nautical expression which describes this particular trim.

Above, the heavens had become completely overcast, a closed, oppressive vault—with darker shadows spread over it in shapeless smudges; the impression was almost of an immobile dome, and it was necessary to look close to realise that on the contrary it was in a very whirl of movement: great grey sheets, hastening to pass, and replaced without ceasing by others which came from below the horizon; funereal tapestries unwinding as if from an inexhaustible roll. . . .

She ran before the wind, the *Marie,* ever more quickly—and the wind ran, too—before I know not what mysterious and terrible power. The wind, the sea, the *Marie,* the clouds, all were seized with the same madness of flight and speed in the same direction. That which ran ahead the fastest was the wind; then the great heavings of the water, more lumbering, slower, followed after it; then the *Marie,* dragged in the universal movement. The waves pursued her, with their pale crests, which rolled on in a perpetual crashing, and she—continually overtaken, continually outstripped—escaped them, none the less, thanks to a wake she skillfully left behind her, an eddy on which their fury broke.

And in this movement of flight, the chief sensation was an illusion of lightness; without any difficulty, without an effort, one felt oneself leap. When the *Marie* rose on the waves, she rose without a shock as if the wind had lifted her, and her descent afterwards was like a sliding, causing those internal qualms one

[1] From *An Iceland Fisherman.* By permission of Frederick A. Stokes Company.

has in the simulated fallings of the switchback or in the imaginary
descents of dreams. She slid backwards, as it were, the racing
mountains slipping away from under her to continue their course,
and then she was plunged again in one of those deep troughs
which raced in their turn; without taking hurt, she touched the
dreadful bottom of them, in a shower of spray which did not even
wet her, but which sped on like everything else; which sped on
and vanished ahead of her like smoke, like an intangible nothing. . . .

And so it went on continuously. But getting worse all the
time. The waves followed one another, becoming ever more
enormous, in long chains of mountains the valleys of which began
to cause fear. And all this madness of motion became faster,
under a sky that grew darker and darker, amid a noise that
swelled until it became a roar.

It was very heavy weather, indeed, and it was necessary to
keep watch. But, then, there was so much free space before
them, space in which to run! And it happened also, that this
year the *Marie* had spent the season in the most western part
of the Iceland fisheries; so that this headlong flight towards the
coast was so much way made in their voyage home.

Yann and Sylvestre were at the helm lashed by the waist.
They were singing the song of "Jean-François de Nantes"; drunk
with the movement and speed, they sang at the top of their
voices, laughing to find they could not hear each other amid
all this unloosing of noise, turning round in their high spirits, to
sing against the wind and losing breath for their pains. . . .

They were not afraid, having a very exact notion of what was
manageable, having confidence in the solidity of their boat, in
the strength of their arms. And also in the protection of the
faïence Virgin who, during forty years of voyages to Iceland,
had so often danced this same disagreeable dance, forever smiling
between her bouquets of artificial flowers. . . . Jean-François de
Nantes, Jean-François. Jean-François!

In general, they could see but a short distance around them:
some hundreds of yards away everything seemed to end in mon-
strous waves whose pale crests stood erect, shutting out the view.

One seemed always to be in the middle of a restricted scene, which, nevertheless, was perpetually changing; and, in addition, things were drowned in this kind of watery smoke, which scudded like a cloud, with an extreme swiftness, over all the surface of the sea.

But, from time to time, a rift appeared in the northwest from which a sudden shift of wind would come; then, a glancing light arrived from the horizon; a trailing reflection, making the dome of the sky seem darker, shed itself on the white agitated crests. And this rift was sad to see; these glimpsed distances, these vistas, oppressed the heart the more in that they made you realize only too well that there was the same chaos everywhere, the same fury—even beyond the great empty horizon, and infinitely beyond that again: the terror had no limits, and one was alone in the midst of it.

A gigantic clamor issued from things like an apocalyptic prelude sounding the alarm of the end of the world. And thousands of voices could be distinguished in it; from above came whistling voices and deep voices, which seemed almost distant because they were immense; that was the wind, the mighty soul of this disorder, the invisible power directing the whole commotion. It was terrifying enough; but there were other noises, closer, more material, carrying a more imminent menace of destruction, which the tormented water gave out, spluttering as if on burning coals.

And still the storm waxed fiercer.

And in spite of their close trim, the sea began to cover them, to "eat" them as they said: first, the spray lashing from behind, then water in masses, hurled with smashing force. The waves rose higher still, more madly high, and the higher they rose the more jagged they became; one saw large greenish tatters of them, rags of falling water which the wind scattered everywhere. Some of them fell in heavy masses on the deck, with a smacking sound, and then the *Marie* shook in her whole being as if in pain. Now one could distinguish nothing, on account of all this white scattering foam; when the blasts roared more fiercely one saw it rushing in thicker clouds—like the dust of the roads in summer. A heavy rain, which had begun, fell slantwise also, almost horizontally, and these things together whistled, whipped, hurt like blows of a lash.

They remained both at the helm, bound and holding firm, clothed in their oilskins, which were tough and glistening as the skins of sharks; they had tied them tight at the neck, by tarred laces, and tight at the wrists and ankles, so as to keep the water out; and everything streamed over them, who bowed their backs when it fell too thick, buttressing themselves well so as not to be borne completely over. The skin of their cheeks burnt, and at every minute they caught their breath. After each great mass of water had fallen, they looked at each other —and smiled to see the salt amassed in their beards.

In time, nevertheless, it became an extreme weariness, this fury which did not abate, which remained always at its same exasperated paroxysm. The rage of men, the rage of beasts, exhausts itself and quickly subsides; one has perforce to suffer long the rage of inanimate things which is without cause and without aim, mysterious as life and as death.

Jean-François de Nantes; Jean-François, Jean-François.

Through their lips, which had become white, the refrain of the old song passed still, but like an aphonous thing, continued from time to time unconsciously. The excess of movement and noise had made them drunk; it was in vain that they were young, their smiles grimaced on their teeth which chattered in their trembling from the cold; their eyes, half-closed under burning, flickering eyelids, remained fixed in a grim atony. Lashed to the helm like two marble buttresses, they made, with their cramped, blue fingers, the efforts that were necessary, almost without thinking, by simple habit of the muscles. With streaming hair, and contracted mouths, they had become strange, and in them reappeared a whole background of primitive savagery.

They could see no longer! They knew only that they were still there, side by side. At the moments of greatest danger, every time that behind them the new mountain of water rose up, overhanging, clamorous, horrible, dashing against their boat with a mighty thud, one of their hands moved involuntarily in the sign of the cross. They no longer thought of anything, not of Gaud, not of any woman, nor of any marriage. It was lasting too long and they were past all thinking; their intoxication of noise, of weariness, of cold, obscured everything in their heads. They were now only two pillars of stiff flesh who kept the helm; only two vigorous beasts clinging there by instinct so that they should not die.

GABRIEL OAK ON NORCOMBE HILL [1]

By Thomas Hardy

It was nearly midnight on the eve of St. Thomas's, the shortest day in the year. A desolating wind wandered from the north over the hill whereon Oak had watched the yellow waggon and its occupant in the sunshine of a few days earlier.

Norcombe Hill—forming part of Norcombe Ewelease—was one of the spots which suggest to a passer-by that he is in the presence of a shape approaching the indestructible as nearly as any to be found on earth. It was a featureless convexity of chalk and soil—an ordinary specimen of those smoothly-outlined protuberances of the globe which may remain undisturbed on some great day of confusion, when far grander heights and dizzy granite precipices topple down.

The hill was covered on its northern side by an ancient and decaying plantation of beeches, whose upper verge formed a line over the crest, fringing its arched curve against the sky, like a mane. To-night these trees sheltered the southern slope from the keenest blasts, which smote the wood and floundered through it with a sound as of grumbling, or gushed over its crowning boughs in a weakened moan. The dry leaves in the ditch simmered and boiled in the same breezes, a tongue of air occasionally ferreting out a few, and sending them spinning across the grass. A group or two of the latest in date amongst this dead multitude had remained till this very mid-winter time on the twigs which bore them, and in falling rattled against the trunks with smart taps.

[1] From *Far from the Madding Crowd*. By permission of Harper and Brothers.

Between this half-wooded, half-naked hill, and the vague, still horizon that its summit indistinctly commanded, was a mysterious sheet of fathomless shade—the sounds from which suggested that what it concealed bore some humble resemblance to features here. The thin grasses, more or less coating the hill, were touched by the wind in breezes of differing powers, and almost of differing natures—one rubbing the blades heavily, another raking them piercingly, another brushing them like a soft broom. The instinctive act of human-kind was to stand and listen, and learn how the trees on the right and the trees on the left wailed or chaunted to each other in the regular antiphonies of a cathedral choir; how hedges and other shapes to leeward then caught the note, lowering it to the tenderest sob; and how the hurrying gust then plunged into the south, to be heard no more.

The sky was clear—remarkably clear—and the twinkling of all the stars seemed to be but throbs of one body, timed by a common pulse. The North Star was directly in the wind's eye, and since evening the Bear had swung round it outwardly to the east, till he was now at a right angle with the meridian. A difference of colour in the stars—oftener read of than seen in England—was really perceptible here. The kingly brilliancy of Sirius pierced the eye with a steely glitter, the star called Capella was yellow, Aldebaran and Betelgueux shone with a fiery red.

To persons standing alone on a hill during a clear midnight such as this, the roll of the world eastward is almost a palpable movement. The sensation may be caused by the panoramic glide of the stars past earthly objects, which is perceptible in a few minutes of stillness, or by the better outlook upon space that a hill affords, or by the wind, or by the solitude; but whatever be its origin, the impression of riding along is vivid and abiding. The poetry of motion is a phrase much in use, and to enjoy the epic form of that gratification it is necessary to stand on a hill at a small hour of the night, and, having first expanded with a sense of difference from the mass of civilised mankind, who are horizontal and disregardful of all such proceedings at this time, long and quietly watch your stately progress through the stars. After such a nocturnal reconnoitre among these astral clusters, aloft from the customary haunts of thought and vision, some men may feel raised to a capability for eternity at once.

Suddenly an unexpected series of sounds began to be heard in this place up against the sky. They had a clearness which was to be found nowhere in the wind, and a sequence which was to be found nowhere in nature. They were the notes of Farmer Oak's flute.

The tune was not floating unhindered into the open air: it seemed muffled in some way, and was altogether too curtailed in power to spread high or wide. It came from the direction of a small dark object under the plantation hedge—a shepherd's hut—now presenting an outline to which an uninitiated person might have been puzzled to attach either meaning or use.

The image as a whole was that of a small Noah's Ark on a small Ararat, allowing the traditionary outlines and general form of the Ark which are followed by toy-makers—and by these means are established in men's imaginations among their firmest, because earliest impressions—to pass as an approximate pattern. The hut stood on small wheels, which raised its floor about a foot from the ground. Such shepherd's huts are dragged into the fields when the lambing season comes on, to shelter the shepherd in his enforced nightly attendance.

It was only latterly that people had begun to call Gabriel "Farmer" Oak. During the twelvemonth preceding this time he had been enabled by sustained efforts of industry and chronic good spirits to lease the small sheep farm of which Norcombe Hill was a portion, and stock it with two hundred sheep. Previously he had been a bailiff for a short time, and earlier still a shepherd only, having from his childhood assisted his father in tending the flocks of large proprietors, till old Gabriel sank to rest.

This venture, unaided and alone, into the paths of farming as master and not as man, with an advance of sheep not yet paid for, was a critical juncture with Gabriel Oak, and he recognised his position clearly. The first movement in his new progress was the lambing of his ewes, and sheep having been his specialty from his youth, he wisely refrained from deputing the task of tending them at this season to a hireling or a novice.

The wind continued to beat about the corners of the hut, but the flute-playing ceased. A rectangular space of light appeared in the side of the hut, and in the opening the outline of Farmer Oak's figure. He carried a lantern in his hand, and closing the door behind him, came forward and busied himself about this nook of the field for nearly twenty minutes, the lantern light appearing and disappearing here and there, and brightening him or darkening him as he stood before or behind it.

Oak's motions, though they had a quiet energy, were slow, and their deliberateness accorded well with his occupation. Fitness being the basis of all beauty, nobody could have denied that his steady swings and turns in and about the flock had elements of grace. Yet, although if occasion demanded he could do or think a thing with as mercurial a dash as can the men of towns who are more to the manner born, his special power, morally, physically, and mentally, was static, owing little or nothing to momentum as a rule.

A close examination of the ground hereabout, even by the wan starlight only, revealed how a portion of what would have been casually called a wild slope had been appropriated by Farmer Oak for his great purpose this winter. Detached hurdles thatched with straw were stuck into the ground at various scattered points, amid and under which the whitish forms of his meek ewes moved and rustled. The ring of the sheep-bell, which had been silent during his absence, recommenced, in tones that had more mellowness than clearness, owing to an increasing growth of surrounding wool. This continued till Oak withdrew again from the flock. He returned to the hut, bringing in his arms a new-born lamb, consisting of four legs large enough for a full-grown sheep, united by an unimportant membrane about half the substance of the legs collectively, which constituted the animal's entire body just at present.

The little speck of life he placed on a wisp of hay before the small stove, where a can of milk was simmering. Oak extinguished the lantern by blowing into it and then pinching out the snuff, the cot being lighted by a candle suspended by a twisted wire. A rather hard couch, formed of a few corn sacks thrown carelessly down, covered half the floor of this little habitation, and here the young man stretched himself along, loosened his woollen cravat, and closed his eyes. In about the time a person unaccustomed to bodily labour would have decided upon which side to lie, Farmer Oak was asleep.

The inside of the hut, as it now presented itself, was cosy and alluring, and the scarlet handful of fire in addition to the candle, reflecting its own genial colour upon whatever it could reach, flung associations of enjoyment even over utensils and tools. In the corner stood the sheep-crook, and along a shelf at one side were ranged bottles and canisters of the simple preparations pertaining to ovine surgery and physic; spirits of wine, turpentine, tar, magnesia, ginger, and castor-oil being the chief. On a triangular shelf across the corner stood bread, bacon, cheese, and a cup for ale or cider, which was supplied from a flagon beneath. Beside the provisions lay the flute, whose notes had lately been called forth by the lonely watcher to beguile a tedious hour. The house was ventilated by two round holes, like the lights of a cabin, with wood slides.

The lamb, revived by the warmth, began to bleat, and the sound entered Gabriel's ears and brain with an instant meaning, as expected sounds will. Passing from the profoundest sleep to the most alert wakefulness with the same ease that had accompanied the reverse operation, he looked at his watch, found that the hour-hand had shifted again, put on his hat, took the lamb in his arms, and carried it into the darkness. After placing the little creature with its mother, he stood and carefully examined the sky, to ascertain the time of night from the altitudes of the stars.

The Dog-star and Aldebaran, pointing to the restless Pleiades, were half way up the Southern sky, and between them hung Orion, which gorgeous constellation never burnt more vividly than now, as it swung itself forth above the rim of the landscape. Castor and Pollux with their quiet shine were almost on the meridian: the barren and gloomy Square of Pegasus was creeping round to the north-west; far away through the plantation, Vega sparkled like a lamp suspended amid the leafless trees, and

Cassiopeia's chair stood daintily poised on the uppermost boughs. "One o'clock," said Gabriel.

EXERCISES

1. Study the description of the wind in paragraphs 3 and 4 of the selection from Hardy. What use does he make of verbs here? Compare these paragraphs with the first paragraph from his *Under the Greenwood Tree*.

2. In Loti's description of the storm what elements of the style and the diction suggest *motion?* What suggest *commotion?* Make a careful study of this.

3. Does the refrain which Yann and Sylvestre sing contribute anything definite to the effectiveness of the whole?

4. There are several distinct types of humor in "The Dovecot." Find and analyze them.

5. If you know Hudson's *Green Mansions* (or if you don't and are looking for a book which you cannot lay down) you will find a beautiful illustration in Chapter V of a character merged with background. It may suggest yet another approach to and treatment of your theme.

SUGGESTED READINGS

Gerould, Katharine Fullerton, "Our Northwestern States," *Harper's Magazine,* March 1925.

Grogan, Elmira F., "Rose Hill: A Plantation Sketch," *The Yale Review,* October 1927.

Hall, James Norman, "An Autumn Sojourn in Iceland," *Harper's Magazine,* January 1924. "Snowbound," *The Atlantic Monthly,* April 1925.

Hardy, Thomas, "Tess of the D'Urbervilles," Chapter XX, *Harper's,* New York.

Hudson, W. H., "Our Nearest English Neighbor," Chapter X, from *Far Away and Long Ago,* E. P. Dutton, New York. "Rima in the Forest," Chapter V, *Green Mansions,* Modern Library, Boni and Liveright, New York.

Lamb, Charles, "The Old Benchers of the Inner Temple," *Essays of Elia.*

Stevenson, Robert Louis, "Our Lady of the Snows" from *Travels with a Donkey,* Scribner's, New York.

Whitehead, Alfred North, "England and the Narrow Seas," *The Atlantic Monthly,* June 1927.

Young, Stark, "Texas Lights" from *Encaustics,* The New Republic, Inc.

CHAPTER VII

THEMES ON FAVORITE OCCUPATIONS AND PREOCCUPATIONS

In a recent novel one of the characters, a little girl, is asked by her old uncle what is the best thing in all the world? Not understanding, of course, that the question must forever in its fullest sense be unanswerable, except perhaps now and then by some thrice fortunate individual, she mulls it over in her mind as it teases her for a reply. A great vine, growing over the old Southern house, seemed, she thought, the best thing to her aunt, who years before had brought its beginning from Virginia, planted and cherished it. Perhaps gifts were the best thing, she thought again, or caresses, or people singing in church, or compliments from others, or beautiful words like *asphodel* and *Mnemosyne,* words whose meaning she did not know but whose cadences lingered delightfully in her ears. But the question remained unanswered. She could not tell what was the best thing in the world.

If the question is put by the average person to himself, it is quite safe to predict that, setting aside all those intangible and baffling intellectual, esthetic, and spiritual claims which make the question unanswerable, and coming down to the "brass tacks" of everyday life and living, he will decide that the best thing in the world is the recreation he himself most enjoys, the occupation he indulges in when he is free to do so. One has little hesitation in prophesying that a large majority of successful business men will say at once golf or fishing in the Maine lakes. There are others, however, who tell us through the pages of our better magazines that their favorite preoccupation is browsing about old book-shops like George Gissing or attending book auctions, which Gissing was too poor to do, for rare and old editions. Collecting of all sorts—coins, books, stamps, shells, silver spoons (I know an old woman on a Maine island who has three hundred pitchers of every conceivable kind and shape!)— this is for some persons a preoccupation, at least during certain years. Games of various sorts, exercise of all kinds, motoring, cooking, berrying, travelling, reading, gardening, yes, even hating (for Hazlitt actually considered hating a pleasure and wrote an essay on the subject!)—the field is limited only by the various and numberless idiosyncrasies of the human mind.

It is perhaps best that no suggestions or cautions be given to one who writes about his favorite occupation or preoccupation, his hobby. He might well consider it an intrusion, a lack of good manners, for this theme is perhaps more subjective than any other he has yet been asked to write. That which he chooses to do as a recreation, that which re-creates him, is a personal matter, and he, it is hoped, will know best how he wishes to present it. The models given are themselves rich in suggestions. They will show one how he may start his theme, suggest careful and original organization of material, and, best of all, help in the difficult process of analyzing one's pet occupation in an attempt to discover whether the by-products are not fully as delightful and alluring as the products themselves. It is hoped, too, that the exercises at the close of the section may prove particularly illuminating.

On Going a Journey [1]

(in part)

By William Hazlitt

One of the pleasantest things in the world is going a journey; but I like to go by myself. I can enjoy society in a room; but out of doors, nature is company enough for me. I am then never less alone than when alone.

"The fields his study, nature was his book."

I cannot see the wit of walking and talking at the same time. When I am in the country, I wish to vegetate like the country.

[1] From *Table Talk*.

I am not for criticising hedge-rows and black cattle. I go out of town in order to forget the town and all that is in it. There are those who for this purpose go to watering-places, and carry the metropolis with them. I like more elbow-room, and fewer incumbrances. I like solitude, when I give myself up to it, for the sake of solitude; nor do I ask for

> "—— a friend in my retreat,
> Whom I may whisper solitude is sweet."

The soul of a journey is liberty, perfect liberty, to think, feel, do just as one pleases. We go a journey chiefly to be free of all impediments and of all inconveniences; to leave ourselves behind, much more to get rid of others. It is because I want a little breathing-space to muse on indifferent matters, where Contemplation

> "May plume her feathers and let grow her wings,
> That in the various bustle of resort
> Were all too ruffled, and sometimes impair'd,"

that I absent myself from the town for awhile, without feeling at a loss the moment I am left by myself. Instead of a friend in a postchaise or in a Tilbury, to exchange good things with, and vary the same stale topics over again, for once let me have a truce with impertinence. Give me the clear blue sky over my head, and the green turf beneath my feet, a winding road before me, and a three hours' march to dinner—and then to thinking! It is hard if I cannot start some game on these lone heaths. I laugh, I run, I leap, I sing for joy. From the point of yonder rolling cloud, I plunge into my past being, and revel there, as the sun-burnt Indian plunges headlong into the wave that wafts him to his native shore. Then long-forgotten things, like "sunken wrack and sumless treasuries," burst upon my eager sight, and I begin to feel, think, and be myself again. Instead of an awkward silence, broken by attempts at wit or dull commonplaces, mine is that undisturbed silence of the heart which alone is perfect eloquence. No one likes puns, alliterations, antitheses, argument, and analysis better than I do; but I sometimes had

rather be without them. "Leave, oh, leave me to my repose!"
I have just now other business in hand, which would seem idle
to you, but is with me "very stuff of the conscience." Is not
this wild rose sweet without a comment? Does not this daisy
leap to my heart set in its coat of emerald? Yet if I were to
explain to you the circumstance that has so endeared it to me,
you would only smile. Had I not better then keep it to myself,
and let it serve me to brood over, from here to yonder craggy
point, and from thence onward to the far-distant horizon? I
should be but bad company all that way, and therefore prefer
being alone. I have heard it said that you may, when the moody
fit comes on, walk or ride on by yourself, and indulge your
reveries. But this looks like a breach of manners, a neglect of
others, and you are thinking all the time that you ought to rejoin
your party. "Out upon such half-faced fellowship," says I. I
like to be either entirely to myself, or entirely at the disposal
of others; to talk or be silent, to walk or sit still, to be sociable
or solitary. I was pleased with an observation of Mr. Cobbett's,
that "he thought it a bad French custom to drink our wine with
our meals, and that an Englishman ought to do only one thing
at a time." So I cannot talk and think, or indulge in melancholy
musing and lively conversation by fits and starts. "Let me have
a companion of my way," says Sterne, "were it but to remark how
the shadows lengthen as the sun declines." It is beautifully
said: but in my opinion, this continual comparing of notes inter-
feres with the involuntary impression of things upon the mind,
and hurts the sentiment. If you only hint what you feel in a
kind of dumb show, it is insipid: if you have to explain it, it is
making a toil of a pleasure. You cannot read the book of
nature, without being perpetually put to the trouble of translat-
ing it for the benefit of others. I am for the synthetical method
on a journey, in preference to the analytical. I am content to lay
in a stock of ideas then, and to examine and anatomise them
afterwards. I want to see my vague notions float like the down
of the thistle before the breeze, and not to have them entangled
in the briars and thorns of controversy. For once, I like to
have it all my own way; and this is impossible unless you are

alone, or in such company as I do not covet. I have no objection to argue a point with any one for twenty miles of measured
road, but not for pleasure. If you remark the scent of a bean-
field crossing the road, perhaps your fellow-traveller has no
smell. If you point to a distant object, perhaps he is shortsighted, and has to take out his glass to look at it. There is a
feeling in the air, a tone in the colour of a cloud which hits your
fancy, but the effect of which you are unable to account for.
There is then no sympathy, but an uneasy craving after it, and
a dissatisfaction which pursues you on the way, and in the end
probably produces ill humour. Now I never quarrel with myself, and take all my own conclusions for granted till I find it
necessary to defend them against objections. It is not merely
that you may not be of accord on the objects and circumstances
that present themselves before you—these may recall a number
of objects, and lead to associations too delicate and refined to be
possibly communicated to others. Yet these I love to cherish,
and sometimes still fondly clutch them, when I can escape from
the throng to do so. To give way to our feelings, before company, seems extravagance or affectation; and on the other hand,
to have to unravel this mystery of our being at every turn, and
to make others take an equal interest in it (otherwise the end is
not answered) is a task to which few are competent. We must
"give it an understanding, but no tongue." My old friend
C——, however, could do both. He could go on in the most
delightful explanatory way over hill and dale, a summer's day,
and convert a landscape into a didactic poem or a Pindaric ode.
"He talked far above singing." If I could so clothe my ideas
in sounding and flowing words, I might perhaps wish to have
some one with me to admire the swelling theme; or I could be
more content, were it possible for me still to hear his echoing
voice in the woods of All-Foxden.

*   *   *   *   *   *   *

In general, a good thing spoils out-of-door prospects: it should
be reserved for Table-talk. L——[1] is for this reason, I take it,

[1] Lamb.

the worst company in the world out of doors; because he is the best within. I grant, there is one subject on which it is pleasant to talk on a journey; and that is, what one shall have for supper when we get to our inn at night. The open air improves this sort of conversation or friendly altercation, by setting a keener edge on appetite. Every mile of the road heightens the flavour of the viands we expect at the end of it. How fine it is to enter some old town, walled and turreted just at the approach of night-fall, or to come to some straggling village, with the lights streaming through the surrounding gloom; and then after inquiring for the best entertainment that the place affords, to "take one's ease at one's inn!" These eventful moments in our lives' history are too precious, too full of solid, heart-felt happiness to be frittered and dribbled away in imperfect sympathy. I would have them all to myself, and drain them to the last drop: they will do to talk of or to write about afterwards. What a delicate speculation it is, after drinking whole goblets of tea,

"The cups that cheer, but not inebriate,"

and letting the fumes ascend into the brain, to sit considering what we shall have for supper—eggs and a rasher, a rabbit smothered in onions, or an excellent veal-cutlet! Sancho in such a situation once fixed upon cow-heel; and his choice, though he could not help it, is not to be disparaged. Then in the intervals of pictured scenery and Shandean contemplation, to catch the preparation and the stir in the kitchen—*Procul, O procul este profani!* These hours are sacred to silence and to musing, to be treasured up in the memory, and to feed the source of smiling thoughts hereafter. I would not waste them in idle talk; or if I must have the integrity of fancy broken in upon, I would rather it were by a stranger than a friend. A stranger takes his hue and character from the time and place; he is a part of the furniture and costume of an inn. If he is a Quaker, or from the West Riding of Yorkshire, so much the better. I do not even try to sympathise with him, and he breaks no squares. I associate nothing with my travelling companion but present objects and passing events. In his ignorance of me and my affairs, I in a manner forget myself. But a friend reminds one of other things, rips up old grievances, and destroys the abstraction of the scene. He comes in ungraciously between us and our imaginary character. Something is dropped in the course of conversation that gives a hint of your profession and pursuits; or from having some one with you that knows the less sublime portions of your history, it seems that other people do. You are no longer a citizen of the world: but your "unhoused free condition is put into circumscription and confine." The *incognito* of an inn is one of its striking privileges—"lord of one's-self, uncumber'd with a name." . . . Oh, it is great to shake off the trammels of the world and of public opinion—to lose our importunate, tormenting, everlasting personal identity in the elements of nature, and become the creature of the moment, clear of all ties—to hold to the universe only by a dish of sweet-breads, and to owe nothing but the score of the evening—and no longer seeking for applause and meeting with contempt, to be known by no other title than *the Gentleman in the parlour!* One may take one's choice of all characters in this romantic state of uncertainty as to one's real pretensions, and become indefinitely respectable and negatively rightworshipful. We baffle prejudice and disappoint conjecture; and from being so to others, begin to be objects of curiosity and wonder even to ourselves. We are no more those hackneyed commonplaces that we appear in the world: an inn restores us to the level of nature, and quits scores with society! I have certainly spent some enviable hours at inns—sometimes when I have been left entirely to myself, and have tried to solve some metaphysical problem, as once at Witham-common, where I found out the proof that likeness is not a case of the association of ideas—at other times, when there have been pictures in the room, as at St. Neot's (I think it was), where I first met with Gribelin's engravings of the Cartoons, into which I entered at once, and at a little inn on the borders of Wales, where there happened to be hanging some of Westall's drawings, which I compared triumphantly (for a theory that I had, not for the admired artist) with the figure of a girl who had ferried me over the Severn, standing up in the boat between me and the twilight

—at other times I might mention luxuriating in books, with a peculiar interest in this way, as I remember sitting up half the night to read Paul and Virginia, which I picked up at an inn at Bridgewater, after being drenched in the rain all day; and at the same place I got through two volumes of Madame D'Arblay's Camilla. It was on the tenth of April, 1798, that I sat down to a volume of the New Eloise, at the inn at Llangollen, over a bottle of sherry and a cold chicken. The letter I chose was that in which St. Preux describes his feelings as he first caught a glimpse from the heights of the Jura of the Pays de Vaud, which I had brought with me as a *bon bouche* to crown the evening with. It was my birth-day, and I had for the first time come from a place in the neighbourhood to visit this delightful spot. The road to Llangollen turns off between Chirk and Wrexham; and on passing a certain point, you come all at once upon the valley, which opens like an amphitheatre, broad, barren hills rising in majestic state on either side, with "green upland swells that echo to the bleat of flocks" below, and the river Dee babbling over its stony bed in the midst of them. The valley at this time "glittered green with sunny showers," and a budding ash-tree dipped its tender branches in the chiding stream. How proud, how glad I was to walk along the high road that overlooks the delicious prospect, repeating the lines which I have just quoted from Mr. Coleridge's poems! But besides the prospect which opened beneath my feet, another also opened to my inward sight, a heavenly vision, on which were written, in letters large as Hope could make them, these four words, LIBERTY, GENIUS, LOVE, VIRTUE; which have since faded into the light of common day, or mock my idle gaze.

"The beautiful is vanished, and returns not."

Still I would return some time or other to this enchanted spot; but I would return to it alone. What other self could I find to share that influx of thoughts, of regret, and delight, the fragments of which I could hardly conjure up to myself, so much have they been broken and defaced! I could stand on some tall rock, and overlook the precipice of years that separates me from what I then was. I was at that time going shortly to visit the poet whom I have above named. Where is he now? Not only I myself have changed; the world, which was then new to me, has become old and incorrigible. Yet will I turn to thee in thought, O sylvan Dee, in joy, in youth and gladness as thou then wert; and thou shalt always be to me the river of Paradise, where I will drink of the waters of life freely!

*   *   *   *   *   *   *

My Books [1]

By George Gissing

As often as I survey my bookshelves I am reminded of Lamb's "ragged veterans." Not that all my volumes came from the second-hand stall; many of them were neat enough in new covers, some were even stately in fragrant bindings, when they passed into my hands. But so often have I removed, so rough has been the treatment of my little library at each change of place, and, to tell the truth, so little care have I given to its well-being at normal times (for in all practical matters I am idle and inept), that even the comeliest of my books show the results of unfair usage. More than one has been foully injured by a great nail driven into a packing-case—this but the extreme instance of the wrongs they have undergone. Now that I have leisure and peace of mind, I find myself growing more careful—an illustration of the great truth that virtue is made easy by circumstance. But I confess that, so long as a volume hold together, I am not much troubled as to its outer appearance.

I know men who say they had as lief read any book in a library copy as in one from their own shelf. To me that is unintelligible. For one thing, I know every book of mine by its *scent*, and I have but to put my nose between the pages to be reminded of all sorts of things. My Gibbon, for example, my well-bound eight-volume Milman edition, which I have read and read and read again for more than thirty years—never do I

[1] From *The Private Papers of Henry Ryecroft.*

open it but the scent of the noble page restores to me all the exultant happiness of that moment when I received it as a prize. Or my Shakespeare, the great Cambridge Shakespeare—it has an odor which carries me yet further back in life; for these volumes belonged to my father, and before I was old enough to read them with understanding it was often permitted me, as a treat, to take down one of them from the bookcase, and reverently to turn the leaves. The volumes smell exactly as they did in that old time, and what a strange tenderness comes upon me when I hold one of them in hand. For that reason I do not often read Shakespeare in this edition. My eyes being good as ever, I take the Globe volume, which I bought in days when such a purchase was something more than an extravagance; wherefore I regard the book with that peculiar affection which results from sacrifice.

Sacrifice—in no drawing-room sense of the word. Dozens of my books were purchased with money which ought to have been spent upon what are called the necessaries of life. Many a time I have stood before a stall, or a bookseller's window, torn by conflict of intellectual desire and bodily need. At the very hour of dinner, when my stomach clamored for food, I have been stopped by sight of a volume so long coveted, and marked at so advantageous a price, that I *could* not let it go; yet to buy it meant pangs of famine. My Heyne's *Tibullus* was grasped at such a moment. It lay on the stall of the old bookshop in Goodge Street—a stall where now and then one found an excellent thing among quantities of rubbish. Sixpence was the price—sixpence! At that time I used to eat my midday meal (of course, my dinner) at a coffee shop in Oxford Street, one of the real old coffee shops, such as now, I suppose, can hardly be found. Sixpence was all I had—yes, all I had in the world: it would purchase a plate of meat and vegetables. But I did not dare to hope that the *Tibullus* would wait until the morrow, when a certain small sum fell due to me. I paced the pavement, fingering the coppers in my pocket, eyeing the stall, two appetites at combat within me. The book was bought and I went home with it, and as I made a dinner of bread and butter I gloated over the pages.

In this *Tibullus* I found pencilled on the last page; "Perlegi,

Oct. 4, 1792." Who was that possessor of the book, nearly a
hundred years ago? There was no other inscription. I like to
imagine some poor scholar, poor and eager as I myself, who
bought the volume with drops of his blood, and enjoyed the
reading of it even as I did. How much *that* was I could not
easily say. Gentle-hearted Tibullus!—of whom there remains
to us a poet's portrait more delightful, I think, than anything
of the kind in Roman literature.

> *An tacitum silvas inter reptare salubres,*
> *Curantem quidquid dignum sapiente bonoque est?*

So with many another book on the thronged shelves. To take
them down is to recall, how vividly, a struggle and a triumph.
In those days money represented nothing to me, nothing I cared
to think about, but the acquisition of books. There were books
of which I had passionate need, books more necessary to me
than bodily nourishment. I could see them, of course, at the
British Museum, but that was not at all the same thing as having and holding them, my own property, on my own shelf. Now
and then I bought a volume of the raggedest and wretchedest
aspect, dishonored with foolish scribbling, torn, blotted—no
matter, I liked better to read out of that than out of a copy that
was not mine. But I was guilty at times of mere self-indulgence;
a book tempted me, a book which was not one of those for which
I really craved, a luxury which prudence might bid me forego.
As, for instance, my *Jung-Stilling*. It caught my eye in Holywell Street; the name was familiar to me in *Wahrheit und Dich-
tung,* and curiosity grew as I glanced over the pages. But that
day I resisted; in truth, I could not afford the eighteenpence,
which means that just then I was poor indeed. Twice again did
I pass, each time assuring myself that *Jung-Stilling* had found
no purchaser. There came a day when I was in funds. I see myself hastening to Holywell Street (in those days my habitual pace
was five miles an hour), I see the little gray old man with whom
I transacted my business—what was his name?—the bookseller
who had been, I believe, a Catholic priest, and still has a certain priestly dignity about him. He took the volume, opened it,

mused for a moment, then, with a glance at me, said, as if thinking aloud: "Yes, I wish I had time to read it."

Sometimes I added the labor of a porter to my fasting endured
for the sake of books. At the little shop near Portland Road
Station I came upon a first edition of Gibbon, the price an absurdity—I think it was a shilling a volume. To possess those
clean-paged quartos I would have sold my coat. As it happened, I had not money enough with me, but sufficient at home.
I was living at Islington. Having spoken with the bookseller,
I walked home, took the cash, walked back again, and—carried
the tomes from the west end of Euston Road to a street in Islington far beyond the *Angel*. I did it in two journeys—this being
the only time of my life when I thought of Gibbon in avoirdupois.
Twice—three times, reckoning the walk for the money—did I
descend Euston Road and climb Pentonville on that occasion.
Of the season and the weather I have no recollection; my joy
in the purchase I had made drove out every other thought.
Except, indeed, of the weight. I had infinite energy, but not
much muscular strength, and the end of the last journey saw
me upon a chair, perspiring, flaccid, aching—exultant!

The well-to-do person would hear this story with astonishment. Why did I not get the bookseller to send me the volumes?
Or, if I could not wait, was there no omnibus along that London
highway? How could I make the well-to-do person understand
that I did not feel able to afford, that day, one penny more than
I spent on the books? No, no, such labor-saving expenditure
did not come within my scope; whatever I enjoyed I earned it,
literally, by the sweat of my brow. In those days I hardly knew
what it was to travel by omnibus. I have walked London streets
for twelve and fifteen hours together without ever a thought of
saving my legs, or my time, by paying for waftage. Being poor
as poor can be, there were certain things I had to renounce, and
this was one of them.

Years after, I sold my first edition of Gibbon for even less
than it cost me; it went with a great many other fine books in
folio and quarto, which I could not drag about with me in my
constant removals; the man who bought them spoke of them as

"tombstones." Why has Gibbon no market value? Often has my heart ached with regret for those quartos. The joy of reading the *Decline and Fall* in that fine type! The page was appropriate to the dignity of the subject; the mere sight of it tuned one's mind. I suppose I could easily get another copy now; but it would not be to me what that other was, with its memory of dust and toil.

TRAVELING IN AMERICA [1]

By Rebecca West

I spent but four months of the seven that I was in America in travelling, and I regret it, for I have never been in any country where the mere act of journeying from place to place was more seductive. Willingly could I, who have always imagined that I loathed travelling by land, have done nothing but wander on from town to town up and down the length and breadth of the United States. This is partly due to the genius of the place, but it is also due to the extreme comfort of American trains. It is true that they are all of them equipped with instruments of torture in the form of an apparatus known as the air-brake, which works in such a way that every time the train starts there is a preliminary jar so severe that it feels as if not only every carriage but every individual had been struck a heavy blow with a club. The explanation is, I fancy, that the average American is so full of nervous energy that he can suffer this violent shock without the pain that we depleted and over-sensitive creatures feel; but it may be that some slight measure of discomfort has to be inserted into the railway system to deter people from spending their entire lives on the train. I found myself sometimes regretting that I need ever step out of the Pullman car save to have a bath.

It is, you see, so exquisitely irresponsible from the very beginning. One packs one's trunks, in no particular hurry; it will do if they are ready an hour before starting. One gives them

[1] Reprinted by permission of the author and of *The New Republic*.

to the hotel porter, who in return presents one with checks. Never does one think of them again till one gives the checks to the express company at the station where one ends one's journey, and it delivers them at one's hotel. This, you will allow, is different from England where one has to keep watch on one's luggage as on a sick child. Thus disembarrassed, one goes nonchalantly to the train which, should one be in New York, starts from a cathedral. Europeans to whom I have said that the Americans are geniuses in architecture would be angry with me for having understated the case if I could show them the Pennsylvania station in New York. We in Europe have tried to treat the railway station in the grand manner. England made its great comic efforts in the cruet-stand Gothic of St. Pancras and the monumental mason's nightmare of Euston, and then gave up the attempt and relapsed into the formless chaos of Victoria and Waterloo. Germany kept up the struggle longer, but to no good. Leipzig Hauptbahnhof, vast as it is, is only remarkable because it produces, as one could not have believed that masonry could, the effect of obesity. One longs to advise it to give up bread and potatoes. But here, in New York, is a marvel of noble stone arching over an infinity of pearly light, with a certain ultimate beauty in its proportions which gives a solemnity to all that happens beneath. The crowds hurrying between the booking offices and the platform look dwarfed, yet for all that, more and not less significant, as processions of worshipers do in great churches. For some things—and those great and admirable things—one must go to America.

The Pullman car is too hot, but then every interior in America is. That is why one acquires on arrival the art of continually slaking oneself with ice-water. It has however every other advantage except reasonable temperature. There is abundant space round one's arm-chair. One's suitcase and attaché case are not exiled to a rack but stand openable at one's knee. Newspapers and books—quite good books—are sold on the train. One is encouraged to carry on one's correspondence by telegram. In the dining-cars there are meals that the Americans esteem but lightly, but which nevertheless are better than most meals one gets in quite good hotels in provincial England. And one is adopted by a Negro porter. For no extravagant recompense in the way of tips he is prepared to act as one's father and mother for the duration of the journey. He brushes one's clothes, he polishes one's shoes, he will even very respectfully draw one's attention to the fact that one is nearing one's destination and that one's hat is not on at quite the proper angle, and he does one a service deeper than these by showing one what life might be if one kept the heart of a child, and laughed aloud at happiness, and drooped for not more than a minute when things went wrong. Sad he is fundamentally, for he is a strayed child, a lost child, who will never get back to his own nursery in Africa but must wander forever in this grown-up world of the United States, but he gets an exquisite infantile glee out of the simplest things. One morning, when I was traveling from Chicago to Omaha, I rose from my sleeping berth before the rest of the passengers had risen, and going along the aisle to wash in the dressing room, encountered two Pullman porters in the corridor. One was polishing the patent leather shoes of the other, and the polishee was standing with his arms outspread, beaming down on the proceedings and chanting with the extremest voluptuousness: "Ah doan care about ma hands—and Ah doan care about ma face—but—Ah—do—like—clean *shoes!*"

They have, too, moments of imagination by which the traveller benefits. Once, when I was travelling through the Rockies, from Salt Lake City to Pueblo, Colorado, the train halted at the highest point of our journey, and the Negro porter called me to the window and showed me a pool beside the railway track. Just a pool, just such a dark ditchful as one might see by an English railway line. But the darky's eyeballs rolled in his head, his glistening black hands waved impressively, his soft voice dipped and soared, as he laid before me the fact, which indeed thrilled me, that this pool was lying on the Great Divide. The trickle that ran from it at the one end became, in the long last, an arm of the Colorado river which winds away and away for fifteen hundred miles through the strangest country of cliffs cut by water and weather to shapes fine drawn as spires or fantastic as a dinosaur and are like a sunset sky, with splashes of scarlet and purple and emerald earths, till it reaches the warm Pacific. And the trickle that ran from the other end was the Arkansas river that tumbles down the boulders of the Rockies and becomes a slow silver stream that crawls over the green flat plains for a thousand miles and more till it joins the corpulent brown body of the Mississippi, and moves like a vast sliding lake on to the Gulf of Mexico. Here was a prodigious birth and beginning.

I was grateful to the Pullman porter for having the imagination to recognize the quality of that sight, for it was part of the pageant of rivers which to me is one of the most valid reasons why every one ought to visit America before he dies. Till one sees the Hudson river one cannot believe that for three hundred and fifty miles of New York state, as far as from London to Edinburgh—it runs through country as lovely as our Lake district. Hour after hour one travels past wooded mountains falling to quiet waters, as beautiful as the finest moments of Derwentwater or Ullswater. There is the Susquehanna, too, which is as lovely as its Indian name, broad and shining, with forests on each side that mount sugar-loaf hills and crown craggy heights. Its tributary, the Julietta, runs through woodland as sweet as our own Exmoor valley. But even better than these is the Connecticut river in its upper reaches, running deep blue under a cloudless winter sky, a tangle of red bramble and amber grasses jewelled with frost on its brink, and the bare silver birches standing by like shapely ghosts. All these woodland rivers have a special beauty in the autumn and the winter that cannot be foreseen by the English imagination, for in autumn the foliage passes through a range of colors that is infinitely more varied than anything ever seen in Europe, and we have no conception of the golden clarity of their winter sunshine. Though the rivers of the Middle West are apt to be as tame as our East Anglian rivers since they run on the flat prairies, they have their character. With the coppices on their banks, and the marshes where the bullrushes grow, they look like the kind of places where small boys love to play; one thinks of Tom Sawyer and Huckleberry Finn and their not unworthy descendant, Booth Tarkington's Penrod. And in the Middle West there comes the greatest thrill in all this pageant of rivers. Who could look on the Mississippi without emotions? It is a hero among rivers, a watery Hercules. I first saw it one sunset in Minnesota, where it runs between Minneapolis and St. Paul. At the bottom of a deep trench whose walls were hung with flaming autumn trees, it lay in the shadow, almost tenuous, shining whitely, with shadows ribbed with the velvety bars of sandbanks. One could imagine Red Indians. I saw it again later, a day's journey southward, down on the Iowa and Illinois border. On each bank was a steel-colored rectangular Middle West town; east, west, north and south stretched the sallow prairies. On a grassy island in the river stood a white wooden house, evidently some sort of a public building dating back to the early nineteenth century or so, a beautiful example of the colonial style of architecture, with its classical colonnade and pediment all wrought in wood; like all the houses of that type in this country which was but recently so painfully claimed from savagery, its delicacy had an air of pathos, like a noble lady enduring poverty. Past this flowed a river that had lost its looks, that was nearly featureless, that was just a river, but that had a look of power. I saw it a third time, again a day's journey south, down by St. Louis. Even flatter there than the Middle West, and oozier of earth; on the dark fields stood the withered maize plants, as tall as men, and looking with their limpness and outthrust leaves, like men in attitudes of desperation. At the bottom of a clay cutting ran the Mississippi, mud-yellow, quite featureless now, and to apply a word that until then one would not have thought applicable to a river, shapeless. Just water running between two banks. It is odd that it was there, where the Mississippi is just water, that I realized that I would never be content till I had come back and known this river, and had taken a journey on it by steamer, down between Missouri and Kentucky, between Arkansas and Tennessee, between Louisiana and Mississippi, all the way to the Gulf of Mexico. It is an absurd desire. Probably no such steamers run. But have you never been in love with somebody plain and probably unattainable? It is like that.

Really, it is just like that. America is a continent with which one can have innumerable love-affairs. I am not monogamous myself in my passion for the Mississippi. There are times when I think with as insistent a longing for a place named Bingham, which is in the state of Utah. It is a mining-camp. One drives in one's automobile on noble roads planted with poplars over a green and fertile plain (it was desert till the Mormons irrigated it) to a canyon that drives a wedge into the foothills of the snow-peaked mountains. There is one long winding street of wooden houses, paintless, dilapidated; some with verandas on which men in broad hats sit in rocking chairs, spitting slowly and with an infinity of sagacity; some with plate-glass windows, on which the washed-off word "saloon" still shows as a pathetic shadow, which are eating-houses of incredible bareness and dinginess, some others with plate-glass windows that show you men on high chairs with white sheets round them being shaved, and tin cans everywhere. Then at the end of the street one comes on a mountain of copper. Just that, a mountain of copper. Pyramid-shaped it is, and cut into regular terraces all the way from the apex to the base, where lies a pool of water emerald as Irish grass. It sounds the hardest thing in the world, and the terraces have as sharp an edge as a steel knife. Yet it seems a shape just taken for an instant by the ether. One feels as if one were standing in front of a breaking wave of a substance more like cloud-stuff than water, yet like the sea; for the whole hillside is luminously and transparently pale, and reticulated with mineral veins that are blue and green like sea water. I want to see that marvel again, that mountain that is made of metal, that looks as if you could put your hand through it. I want to go back, just as I want to go back to San Francisco, which is a day and a night further west from Bingham. For that is like the Bay of Naples, but it is all done in the delicate pastel shades and the gentle grey-ness of Edinburgh. Sailing ships lie in the harbor, with their lovely rigging. There is a dead volcano looking over the Bay at the city, whose musical name is Tamalpais; she is shaped like Fujiyama, and I am enough in love to swear she is as beautiful. Round her are daughterly green hills running down to the indenting waters, their slopes blue and white with wild lupins. I love these places.

It is real love. One has been fond of European places, but the affection has been mild and reasonable. I have imagined that I loved Rome and Granada, but there they are, both within two days and two nights of London, for no undue expenditure, and I have visited neither for the last two years. But I know that I am capable of getting up and going to have a look at San Francisco at a time when I ought not, though it means five days on the water and five days and five nights on the train, and many pounds and more dollars than I can afford to spend on merely going to have a look at anything.

This is the real unreasonable thing that is called love. And mind you, it is not only one that feels it. I am not telling you about myself; I am telling you about the American people. For this love that their Continent has the power to evoke is one of the most powerful factors in the moulding of their lives. It makes them wanderers. And that is the thing that marks them off from all other modern peoples. They are migrating. They are nomads. It makes their cities enchanting. For each of these marks an occasion when these wanderers have fallen so deeply in love with a place that for a time they abandoned their nomadism. This is a most romantic country.

It is at first hard for the stranger to realize how nomadic the Americans are, because one is apt to draw a false conclusion of stability from the facts that, in the towns at least, they have the best homes in the world, and that their women are incomparably the best housekeepers. But unlike the successful domestic women of other climes, the American housewife is not tethered to the cooking stove. She is astonishingly mobile. Of an evening, after dinner, should she and her husband be alone, the weather will have to be pretty bad before they will settle down before the fire. They are more likely to take the automobile out for a run of a length that would be considered a whole day's expedition in this country. If they live in Salt Lake City they will have a marvellous homecoming. Beautifully did the Mormons build on this perfect site that they found after their thousand mile

trek through the desert, a city of broad lawny streets with a
Capitol that stands out against the sunset on a ledge on a hill
as finely as any building raised by the old Romans; widely
stretches the plain that was desert till the Mormons came, that
is green and plenteous because of their tillage and irrigation, in
the East to the feet of the mountains whose arms are now blue
with nightfall, in the West to the great Salt Lake where the last
light lies rosy on the peaks of the unvisited islands where buffalo
still roam. There is romance for you. You would go out and
look at it if it were at your backdoor. Even if you lived on the
prairies of Nebraska, that are as flat as the mud at Southend,
you would still take that nocturnal ride. For here, as always
on the plains, what one loses on the swings one makes up on the
roundabouts. What the landscape lacks in interest, the cloud-
scape supplies. It is good to drive there by night, under bright
stars that look as if they were nailed onto the dark roof of some
not too elevated tent.

The mobility of the American housewife manifests itself of
course in much more startling ways than that. She will up at
any moment and start out at a few hours' notice on an automobile
trip of several days, up into the mountains or across the desert,
and serve her family with a succession of meals that the English
mind cannot conceive as being born of the casualness of a picnic.
Lovely it is to travel on the Ridge Route from Los Angeles
to San Francisco, high among the blue mountains with sharp
spiny ridges that lie up against each other like so many vast
lizards; or to cross the Nevadan desert and see the mirage
change a peak as big as Ben Nevis to an island floating on a
lake whose magic waters are drunk at their not-existing shore by
horses never to be bridled by tangible riders. These are love-
affairs with the American continent that are worth having; there
are other, more extensive ones, that she has. American summer
holidays are longer than ours and run, indeed, to a full three
months.

Then the American housewife takes up her house and lifts it
any distance up to a thousand or fifteen hundred miles. The
Salt Lake City woman will take her family up to the far North

West in Oregon. The Nebraska woman will find a summer home in the woods of Maine, in New England. There is a difference between these trancontinental leaps and our nervous August toddles to Newquay or Aldeburgh. And what is even more remarkable is the way that elderly people will leave the districts where they have lived all their lives and start over again in some strange place that has caught at their imagination. There is a town in southern California, Los Angeles, which is developing an enormous belt of suburbs that rather resemble one of our riverside towns like Maidenhead in their expanses of cheerful houses with flowery gardens. It is populated largely by retired farmers and their families from Iowa, which is in the Middle West. I cannot imagine a fashion springing up among Essex farmers for settling in the south of France or on the Italian Riviera; yet the distance is not more great.

They run up and down their continent, they run across it. They are wooing her beauty, they are seeking the adventures she gives them with both hands. It is in their blood. The history of their country is the history of that chase. Firstly there was the settlement of the East; then the more vigorous stocks pushed out for the Middle West. Then there was a double movement: of the gentler spirits who wanted to found an American culture, back to the East; of the bolder spirits, who wanted to extend the United States, out West. That adventurous spirit spills sometimes outside the cup; up to the gold-mines in the Klondike. It is a strong and beautiful thing, as lovely in its way as the English love of stability and a settled home.

I mean to go back to America again and again. I want to see more of these love-affairs between America and the American people.

THE AMATEUR CHESSMAN [1]

By Frances Lester Warner

I used to envy chess-players. Now I play. My method of learning the game was unprincipled. I learned the moves from

[1] By permission of and by arrangement with Houghton Mifflin Company, the authorized publishers.

the encyclopædia, the traditions from "Morphy, On Chess," and the practice from playing with another novice as audacious as I. Later, finding some people who could really play, I clove to them until they taught me all that I could grasp. My ultimate ambition is, I suppose, the masterly playing of the game. Its austere antiquity rebukes the mildest amateur into admiration. I therefore strive, and wistfully aspire. Meanwhile, however, I am enjoying the gay excitement of the unskilled player.

There is nobody like the hardy apprentice for getting pleasure out of chess. We find certain delights which no past-master can know; pleasures exclusively for the novice. Give me an opponent not too haughty for my unworthy steel, one who may perhaps forget to capture an exposed bishop of mine, an opponent who, like me, will know the early poetry of mad adventure and the quiet fatalism of unexpected defeat. With this opponent I will engage to enjoy three things which, to Mr. Morphy, immortality itself shall not restore—three things: a fresh delight in the whimsical personality of the various chessmen; the recklessness of uncertainty and of unforeseen adventure; the unprecedented thrill of checkmating my opponent by accident.

Mr. Morphy, I admit, may perhaps have retained through life a personal appreciation of the characters of the pieces: the conservative habits of the king; the politic, sidelong bishop; the stout little roundhead pawns. But since his forgotten apprenticeship he has not known their many-sided natures. To Mr. Morphy they long since became subject—invariably calculable. With a novice, the men and women of the chess-board regain their individuality and their Old World caprices, their mediæval greatness of heart. Like Aragon and the Plantagenets, they have magnificent leisure for the purposeless and aimless quest. The stiff, kind, circular eyes of my simple boxwood knight stare casually about him as he goes. Irresponsibly he twists among his enemies, now drawing rein in the cross-country path of an angry bishop, now blowing his horn at the very drawbridge of the king. And it is no cheap impunity that he faces in his errant hardihood. My opponent seldom lapses. My knights often die in harness, all unshriven. That risk lends unfailing zest. Most of all, I love my gentle horsemen.

My opponent, too, has her loyalties, quixotic and unshaken. Blindly, one evening, I imperiled my queen. Only the opposing bishop needed to be sacrificed to capture her. The spectators were breathless at her certain fate. But my opponent sets high value upon her stately bishop. Rather this man saved for defense than risked for such a captive, feminist though she be, and queen. With ecclesiastical dignity the bishop withdrew, and my queen went on her tranquil way.

Of all the men, the king reveals himself least readily. A noncommittal monarch at best. At times imperial and menacing, my king may conquer, with goodly backing from his yeomen and his chivalry. Sometimes, again, like Lear, he is no longer terrible in arms, his royal guard cut down. And at his death he loves always to send urgently for his bishop, who is solacing, though powerless to save.

All this is typical of our second pleasure, the exhilaration of incautious and unpremeditated moves. Inexplicable, for example, this pious return of the outbound bishop at the last battle-cry of the king. At times, however, a move may well be wasted to the end that all may happen decently and in order. My opponent shares with me this respect for ceremony. Together we lament the ruins when a lordly castle falls. Our atrocities are never heartless; we never recriminate.

My opening moves, in general, are characterized by no mean regard for consequences. Let my men rush forth to the edge of the hostile country. Once there, there will be time enough to peer about and reconnoitre and see what we shall see. Meanwhile, the enemy is battering gloriously at my postern-gate, but at least the fight is on! Part of our recklessness in these opening moves consists in our confidential revelations to each other of all our plans and disquieting problems.

"This needn't worry you at present," I remark, planting my castle on an irrational crag. "I'm only putting it there in *case*."

That saves much time. My opponent might otherwise have found it necessary to waste long minutes in trying to fathom the

unknowable of my scheme. Without this companionable interchange chess is the most lonely of human experiences. There you
sit, a being solitary and unsignaled—a point of thought, a mere
center of calculation. You have no partner. All the world is
canceled for the time, except, perched opposite you, another
hermit intellect implacably estranged and sinister. Oh, no! As
yet we discuss our plots.

Poor journeymen players of the royal game! Strange clues to
character appear around the friendly chess-board. There is the
supposedly neutral observer of the game, who must murmur
warnings or lament the ill-judged moves; without him, how would
life and chess be simplified? There is the stout-hearted player
who refuses to resign though his defeat is demonstrably certain,
but continues to jog about the board, eluding actual capture;
in life would he resign? There is the player who gives little
shrieks at unexpected attacks; the player who explains his mistakes and what he had intended to do instead; the player who
makes no sign whether of gloating or of despair. Most striking
of all is the behavior of all these when they face the necessity of
playing against the handicap of past mistakes; a wrong move may
never be retracted by the thoroughbred. No apology, no re-
tracting of the path; we must go on as if the consequences were
part of our plan. It lures to allegory, this checkered board, these
jousts and far crusades.

Then, on to checkmate, the most perfect type of utter finality,
clear-cut and absolute. Shah-mat! Checkmate! The king is
dead. In most conclusions there is something left ragged; something still in abeyance, in reserve. Here, however, is no shading,
no balancing of the scales. We win, not by majority, as in cards;
success or failure is unanimous. There was one ballot, and that
is cast. No matter how ragged the playing that went before,
the end of a game of chess is always perfect. It satisfies the
spirit. Always at last comes contentment of soul, though it be
our king that dies.

WINTER MIST [1]

By Robert Palfrey Utter

From a magazine with a rather cynical cover I learned very recently that for pond skating the proper costume is brown homespun with a fur collar on the jacket, whereas for private rinks one wears a gray herringbone suit and taupe-colored alpine. Oh, barren years that I have been a skater, and no one told me of this!   And here's another thing.   I was patiently trying to acquire a counterturn under the idle gaze of a hockey player who had no better business till the others arrived than to watch my efforts. "What I don't see about that game," he said at last, "is who wins?"   It had never occurred to me to ask.   He looked bored, and I remember that the pictures in the magazine showed the wearers of the careful costumes for rink and pond skating as having rather blank eyes that looked illimitably bored.   I have hopes of the "rocker" and the "mohawk"; I might acquire a proper costume for skating on a small river if I could learn what it is; but a bored look—why, even hockey does not bore me, unless I stop to watch it.   I don't wonder that those who play it look bored.   Even Alexander, who played a more imaginative game than hockey, was bored—poor fellow, he should have taken up fancy skating in his youth; I never heard of a human being who pretended to a complete conquest of it.

I like pond skating best by moonlight.   The hollow among the hills will always have a bit of mist about it, let the sky be clear as it may.   The moonlight, which seems so lucid and brilliant when you look up, is all pearl and smoke round the pond and the hills.   The shore that was like iron under your heel as you came down to the ice is vague, when you look back at it from the center of the pond, as the memory of a dream.   The motion is like flying in a dream; you float free and the world floats under you; your velocity is without effort and without accomplishment, for, speed as you may, you leave nothing behind and approach nothing.   You look upward.   The mist is overhead

[1] Reprinted by kind permission of the author and of *Harper's Magazine*.

now; you see the moon in a "hollow halo" at the bottom of an "icy crystal cup," and you yourself are in just such another. The mist, palely opalescent, drives past her out of nothing into nowhere. Like yourself, she is the center of a circle of vague limit and vaguer content, where passes a swift, ceaseless stream of impression through a faintly luminous halo of consciousness.

If by moonlight the mist plays upon the emotions like faint, bewitching music, in sunlight it is scarcely less. More often than not when I go for my skating to our cosy little river, a winding mile from the milldam to the railroad trestle, the hills are clothed in silver mist which frames them in vignettes with blurred edges. The tone is that of Japanese paintings on white silk, their color showing soft and dull through the frost-powder with which the air is filled. At the milldam the hockey players furiously rage together, but I heed them not, and in a moment am beyond the first bend, where their clamor comes softened on the air like that of a distant convention of politic crows. The silver powder has fallen on the ice, just enough to cover earlier tracings and leave me a fresh plate to etch with grapevines and arabesques. The stream winds ahead like an unbroken road, striped across with soft-edged shadows of violet, indigo, and lavender. On one side it is bordered with leaning birch, oak, maple, hickory, and occasional groups of hemlocks under which the very air seems tinged with green. On the other, rounded masses of scrub oak and alder roll back from the edge of the ice like clouds of reddish smoke. The river narrows and turns, then spreads into a swamp, where I weave my curves round the straw-colored tussocks. Here, new as the snow is, there are earlier tracks than mine. A crow has traced his parallel hieroglyph, alternate footprints with long dashes where he trailed his middle toe as he lifted his foot and his spur as he brought it down. Under a low shrub that has hospitably scattered its seed is a dainty, close-wrought embroidery of tiny bird feet in irregular curves woven into a circular pattern. A silent glide toward the bank, where among bare twigs little forms flit and swing with low conversational notes, brings me in company with a working crew of pine siskins, methodically rifling seed cones of birch and alder, chattering sotto voce the while.

Under a leaning hemlock the writing on the snow tells of a squirrel that dropped from the lowest branch, hopped aimlessly about for a few yards, then went up the bank. Farther on, where the river narrows again, a flutter-headed rabbit crossing at top speed has made a line seemingly as free from frivolous indirection as if it had been defined by all the ponderosities of mathematics. There is no pursuing track. Was it his own shadow he fled, or the shadow of a hawk?

The mist now lies along the base of the hills, leaving the upper ridges almost imperceptibly veiled and the rounded tops faintly softened. The snowy slopes are etched with brush and trees so fine and soft that they remind me of Dürer's engravings, the fur of Saint Jerome's lion, the cock's feathers in the coat of arms with the skull. From behind the veil of the southernmost hill comes a faint note as

> From undiscoverable lips that blow
> An immaterial horn.

It is the first far premonition of the noon train; I pause and watch long for the next sign. At last I hear its throbbing, which ceases as it pauses at the flag station under the hill. There the invisible locomotive shoots a column of silver vapor above the surface of the mist, breaking in rounded clouds at the top, look-ing like nothing so much as the photograph of the explosion of a submarine mine, a titanic outburst of force in static pose, a geyser of atomized water standing like a frosted elm tree. Then quick puffs of dusky smoke, the volley of which does not reach my ear till the train has stuck its black head out of fairyland and become a prosaic reminder of dinner. High on its narrow trestle it leaps across my little river and disappears between the sandbanks. Far behind it the mist is again spreading into its even layers. Silence is renewed, and I can hear the musical creaking of four starlings in an apple tree as they eviscerate a few rotten apples on the upper branches. I turn and spin down the curves and reaches of the river without delaying for embroideries or arabesques. At the milldam the hockey game still rages; the players take no heed of the noon train.

> Let Zal and Rustum bluster as they will,
> Or Hatim call to supper . . .

Their minds and eyes are intent on a battered disk of hard rubber. I begin to think I have misjudged them when I consider what effort of imagination must be involved in the concentration of the faculties on such an object, transcending the call of hunger and the lure of beauty. Is it to them as is to the mystic "the great syllable Om" whereby he attains Nirvana? I cannot attain it; I can but wonder what the hockey players win one-half so precious as the stuff they miss.

EXERCISES

1. Stevenson says that a tax should be levied on all persons who have not read Hazlitt's essay, "On Going a Journey." Why such enthusiasm, do you think? Is it because of the style which, as we have said earlier, one good critic has called the "most intellectually honest" style in English prose? Wherein does its honesty lie? And its "intellectual" honesty? Find examples elsewhere in this book of style that is honest, but not necessarily "intellectually" honest. Search Hazlitt for use of detail, for sense impressions. Under what circumstances does he use them? Why, do you suppose, does he use relatively few descriptive adjectives in this essay? Does this fact have anything to do with the "intellectual honesty" of his *style?* Think about this. Stevenson quotes in his own fine essay on "Walking Tours" (which, by the way, shows Hazlitt's influence) one of Hazlitt's sentences in "On Going a Journey" as an example of "amorous precision." Find the sentence.

2. Read the early chapters of Birrell's *William Hazlitt* in the English Men of Letters Series or those in P. P. Howe's biography, *The Life of William Hazlitt,* and see if you can discover anything in his personality that may account for his style.

3. What were some of the by-products in George Gissing's great love of books and of book-buying?

4. Is there anything of the rhythm of skating in Mr. Utter's sentences in "Winter Mist"? Search for those which may suggest it. How does he make exceedingly accurate observation poetic?

Try to see this essay in terms of color. What are the tones? In what ways do they lend harmony to the general effect?

5. Find examples in "The Amateur Chessman" of particularly effective diction and phrasing. In each case what makes for effectiveness? Why not use in your own theme Miss Warner's "strange clues to character"? Comment on the beginning of her essay.

6. In *The Yale Review* for October 1927 there is a little poem called "American Names." Read it and then apply its spirit and its enthusiasm to the proper names in Miss West's "Travelling in America." Study Miss West's use of color, her literary allusions, her mingling of the æsthetic with the prosaic.

7. Miss West enlivens her essay by clever character sketching. See if yours will lend itself to that inclusion.

8. Read widely from the reading list, not omitting more of Hazlitt and of Miss Warner.

SUGGESTED READINGS

Anonymous, "The Lure of the Berry," in Tanner, *Essays and Essay Writing,* Little, Brown, Boston.

Barbellion, W. N. P., "Enjoying Life" from *Enjoying Life and Other Literary Remains,* Doubleday, Doran, New York.

Chesterton, G. K., "On Lying in Bed" from *Tremendous Trifles,* Dodd, Mead, New York.

Eaton, Walter Pritchard, "Forgotten Roads" from *In Berkshire Fields,* W. A. Wilde, New York.

Hazlitt, William, "On the Pleasure of Hating" from *Essays,* Modern Readers' Series, Macmillan, New York.

Lucas, Edward Verrall, "Fires" from *Fireside and Sunshine,* E. P. Dutton, New York.

Lynd, Robert, "In Defense of Patent Medicines" from *The Peal of Bells,* D. Appleton, New York.

Marquis, Don, "Preface to a Book of Fish Hooks" from *Prefaces,* D. Appleton, New York.

Masson, Thomas L., "The Joy of Being an Invalid" in Tanner, *Modern Familiar Essays,* Little, Brown, Boston.

Milne, A. A., "A Man of Property" from *If I May,* E. P. Dutton, New York.

Morley, Christopher, "On Visiting Bookshops" and "Thoughts on Cider" from *Pipefuls,* Doubleday, Doran, New York.

Perry, Bliss, "Golf and Human Nature," in Tanner, *Modern Familiar Essays,* Little, Brown, Boston.

Scott, Dixon, "Motoring at Night" from *A Number of Things,* Peter Davies, Ltd., reprinted also in Tanner, *Modern Familiar Essays.*

Warner, Frances Lester, "Driftwood Fire" from *Endicott and I,* Houghton Mifflin, Boston. "Is There Any Mail?" "When Syrup Spins a Thread," and "A Study in Black Lacquer and Rust" from *Surprising the Family,* Houghton Mifflin, Boston.

Woolf, Virginia, "Street Haunting," *The Yale Review,* October 1927.

Young, Filson, "Going Away and Arriving" from *Letters from Solitude,* Chapman and Hall, Ltd., London.

CHAPTER VIII

THEMES ON LOCAL AND FAMILY CUSTOMS

If it had been possible, the first essay reprinted under this section would have been an inimitable sketch entitled "The Saturday Night Bath" and published anonymously a good many years ago in that treasure-house for theme-writers, the Contributors' Club of *The Atlantic Monthly.* Even the kindest of editors and publishers, however (and there is none kinder than he who first published the sketch in question),[1] sometimes for various reasons find it impossible to grant permission to reprint material. In such a case one can only hope that your instructor, who, if he is wise, will own a copy of Mr. William Tanner's *Essays and Essay Writing* for use in class, will read aloud the exigencies and the adventures accompanying that time-honored custom of the bath on Saturday night in rural homes and in those without "modern conveniences." The essay illustrates admirably what slender and perhaps despised material may form the subject matter for themes on local and family customs.

This type of theme is truly one of extremes. It may range from the homely New England custom of taking sulphur and molasses in March, which twenty-five years ago prevailed in nine out of ten rural families, to the beautiful and solemn religious processions of foreign countries, if you are so fortunate as to have witnessed them. Its appeal may be, on the one hand, prosaic and realistic, on the other, romantic and esthetic. Humor may, indeed, *should* in many cases play a great and important part—rampant humor as in "The Saturday Night Bath," quiet humor as in "Morning Prayers at Earlham," humor with a touch of irony as in "The Blessing of the Animals," the humor that lies in swift emotional changes as in "Córdoba en Fête."

[1] Mr. Ellery Sedgwick, the editor of *The Atlantic Monthly.*

The one thing especially to remember in planning your work is that the source of your theme is from experience. Moreover, it is first and foremost a subjective theme. Not the Christmas customs prevailing in the Virgin Islands does your instructor want unless you yourself know the Virgin Islands. Rather he will prefer that fatal day when the command for winter flannels was always made, or the weekly preparation of a large family for church, or the annual Fourth of July "fantastics" which your town enjoyed, or the hanging of May baskets. Nor is material for a theme of esthetic appeal necessarily impossible, even for one who has not seen the fêtes and the festivals of Spain and of Italy. What about family customs of reading aloud, of musical gatherings, of special holiday fires and feasts, of Sunday afternoon walks, of decorating the Christmas tree? You are especially fortunate if your people have clung to foreign customs and kept them in use and observance. And don't forget that the esthetic and the humorous may be made to walk hand in hand on most excellent terms. Each of the three models given here will prove that to you.

In all of the best work of this kind you will notice certain common features and attributes which lend charm and character:

1. The writer always assumes that his readers are deeply interested even in the least of things; in other words, he takes his readers in and makes them feel at home.

2. In practically all such writing the method is, at the outset at least, chronological, simply because, since the writer is presumably acquainting his readers with matters new to them, he wishes to give them every chance to follow step by step.

3. The writer again assumes that his readers wish to get acquainted with the persons concerned. One of the chief charms of "The Saturday Night Bath" lies in its introduction to the family, Frances with her abnormal desire for too much bathing, Tryphena who had inflammatory rheumatism, Arthur who founded the cult for outdoor bathing. Don't be afraid to be personal.

4. Incident is never overlooked nor is specific detail. Note in "Córdoba en Fête" the incident of the *padre* who upbraided the indecorous young men and handed them over to the high

officer. Note again in "Morning Prayers at Earlham" the care of
Mr. Lubbock in naming the hymns sung and in giving tiny details
so that we may see his grandfather, his grandmother, and the
sunny hall.

5. Remembering always that such customs endear themselves
to those participating quite as much through their vividness as
through any other quality, the wise writer will be generous with
those things that lend vividness, *sense impressions, the dramatic
in whatever guise it assumes, the suggestive word, the emphatic
construction.*

Morning Prayers at Earlham [1]

By Percy Lubbock

The slightest turn of memory takes me back at any time to
Earlham, to the big sunny hall where we used to assemble for
morning prayers. The shallow staircase descended on one side,
by the great front-door. Opposite to it another door opened to
the garden, and through two wide windows, tangled with roses and
vines, the sunshine welled into the house. The hall was broad
and square, rather bare of furniture; against the wall there were
seats, velveted and fringed, once of a strong old crimson, but now
faded away into rose-leaf colours under the suns of many summers; there was a round table, where our grandfather sat with
his large Bible. At prayer-time there were also benches, set out
in rows, for the servants who came filing in through a swing-door
in one corner. First the stout little bright-eyed cook, whose place
was next to the garden-door—she carefully shut it against the
dewy morning air if it happened to stand open; then the rest of
the household in due order. It struck us as an imposing procession; from our red seats under the windows we looked across and
watched it streaming and streaming through the swing-door, from
the back-region of the house.

Prayers began with an unaccompanied hymn. Our grandmother, standing before the wide chimney, struck into the first

[1] From *Earlham*. By permission of Charles Scribner's Sons, the
authorized publishers.

notes, with a little toss of her lace-capped head—lifted up her
singularly sweet and resonant voice, and the rest of us followed in
unison. She sang in her old age, with a voice as fresh as a girl's,
soaring and pealing with perfect ease; and her voice had a quality
that I never seem to have heard in another, clear and vivid and
plangent, like some kind of silver-wired harp. She soared into
the melody quite at random, with no thought of the pitch; and
sometimes it was a trying one for the congregation, and after
the first verse she would cry "A little lower," and start the second
verse in a more tenable key. She sang from the heart, and the
words of the hymn (soundly evangelical) floated upon the melody,
dominating it, *using* it, so that the tune became a real accompaniment to the words. Our repertory was not greatly varied; but
often and often as the same familiar song was repeated—"Hark
my soul," perhaps, or "Jesus stand among us,"—she would
utter the words of praise and thanksgiving with a thrill, a radiant
conviction, as though she made them her own for the first time.

Meanwhile our grandfather sat at his round table, one hand
propping the bald dome of his forehead, the other arm embracing
the big Bible that lay before him. He took no part in the hymn,
he waited; and when we were seated he read the chapter over
which he had been brooding. And then there was a pause, and
we settled ourselves anew, and a tract of time opened before us
that seemed very long indeed; it had no measurable length, like
a hymn or a chapter, for it depended on our grandfather alone.
There was first a commentary about the passage he had read;
he talked of it, I suppose he would explain and expound it; but
what do I know?—it was a time that passed for me in a methodical scrutiny of the assembly, our dear and well-known friends of
the household, ranged on their benches, our uncles and cousins on
the red settees. Presently the arm that embraced the Bible
began slowly, slowly to close it, and the exposition was at an
end, and we knelt; and then there was nothing to do but to wait,
helping oneself out with a little rhythmical fidgeting.

Our grandfather, fervently, appealingly, lyrically, delivered a
long improvisation of prayer. All of it is lost to me, save for an
occasional landmark that I could recognize and appreciate as it

passed; such were topical points, special invocations on behalf of members of the family, often ourselves, who had just arrived or were about to depart. Otherwise it is all vague; but I can hear the warm, mild old voice rising and falling with intonations like an autumn wind—or like the chant, as it strikes me now, of a minstrel of the family roof-tree, a voice soaring and sinking in slightly melancholy cadences, while it lingers over a half-extemporized, half-traditional lay. It was always a wonder to us—we had no other reflection upon the matter—that our grandfather could uplift his eloquence afresh on every morning of the year, with never a lapse or a hesitation; but it ran on lines long established, I imagine, as the eloquence of a bard over the glories of the past. It was certainly in its manner the voice of poetry. The minutes lengthened; and at last the voice rose in a familiar climax and fell on the words (always the same) "We ask it—in the name of—" and presently we were all joining in the Lord's Prayer, a goodly volume of sound, with the fervour of tension relieved. A last blessing, a pause, and the stir of life began again.

THE BLESSING OF THE ANIMALS [1]

By Stark Young

For this seventeenth of January, along toward four in the afternoon, there is a commotion at the little church of San Felipe de Jesus. From all over San Antonio, from out by Zazamora Street and the district of the Corpus Christi road, people have brought their favorite animals, parrots, dogs, cats, hens, birds, in their arms, in cages and baskets or on leash, to be blessed. This is the ceremony of the blessing of the animals, the feast of San Antonio de Abad.

On the steps of the church stand three little boys with puppies and a solemn flutter of little girls with puppies and birds and cats. There are men and women, mostly poor people, with parrots and dogs and chickens. The men have off their hats, the women wear bright skirts and have black ribosos over their heads.

[1] From *Encaustics*. Reprinted by kind permission of the author.

One woman with a dark blunt face under her riboso has three animals to be blessed; from her right hand hangs a large rush cage with a green parrot in it; on her left arm rests a small cage of canaries, and from it swings a long barrel-like cage of Spanish doves, who huddle together in the midst of such a concourse of men and beasts and before the shine, no doubt, of those white forms that emerge from the church and down the steps to the people under the trees—the Spanish father with his book and the acolytes with the cross and swinging censer.

In the road just outside there is a doubting Thomas in the form of a lady who sits in her motorcar, her dog on her lap. She has chanced by at the moment very likely and has stopped; the regard that she bends on the crowd is cool; you can see that she finds these Mexicans a poor lot. She and her dog enjoy the advantages of a superior civilization; these animals about to be blessed eat anything they can get hold of; she has dog-biscuit. The priest lifts his hand, the service begins. From the silver censer the smoke rises past the bare boughs toward the clear bright sky.

San Antonio de Abad, in whose memory this day opens its loving heart to the dumb creatures here, was an African saint of the fourth or fifth century. I am somewhat unfamiliar with this San Antonio, but my neighbor in the crowd, a little old señor, brown and dried up and kind, tells me something of him. In Egypt he lived, and for many years only in desert places, where he consorted with all animals, gentle and ferocious, taming lions and wild bears and living in brotherhood with all that has wings. Through the long stretch of sixty years he was fed by a raven who brought him every day half a loaf of bread; we know it because this raven on one occasion when St. Paul the Hermit paid Saint Anthony a visit, brought them a whole loaf. If Saint Anthony of Padua preached to the fishes after Saint Francis of Assisi had preached to the birds; Saint Jerome drew the thorn from the lion's foot; Saint Isidore tamed wild beasts; San Antonio de Abad was a greater lover still of wild creatures. His constant companion was a pig, even when he was—quite as you can see him sometimes in the pictures—carrying fire in his hands, which showed that he could cure the Sacred Fire, meaning erysipelas, you see. Sometimes when the devil wished to tempt San Antonio he appeared in the form of an animal, but the sign of the cross soon settled that.

The señor gives his terrier a smack for wanting to bark at the smoking incense. Little old women are scattered here and there hugging their cages of pets to them like bright bits of life. The señor points out one of them with a golden brown hen in one hand; she holds by the other a nanny goat's halter. Getting blessed can do the goat no harm, and if you left her at home the neighbors would steal in and milk her. The priest is raising his hand again and the gentle blessing descends on all creatures there.

Córdoba en Fête [1]

By Thomas Walsh

Among the many beautiful customs falling into decay, none perhaps shows more utter decline than the old institution of walking in procession. Indeed, most of us have so lost this processional sense that anything not savoring of a military parade strikes us as false to our modern conditions and theatric in character. How much our lives have been affected by hyper-consciousness is apparent from a glimpse at the serio-comic *cortege* of the Lord Mayor in London, or the uncomfortable gathering of caps-and-gowns at an American university. If it be to religious ceremonial that we must look for a remnant of the old procession, how often shall we not find, instead of the decorous, simple, and naïve advance of clergy and choristers, only the wooden attitudes and stony faces that suggest the regimental armory rather than the house of prayer!

But in speaking of the decay of processions, it is principally to the outdoor celebrations that we refer. Practically considered, there are not, with exception of a few coronations, and Mardi Gras survivals, any real processions left in the world outside of Spain. Even there the great ceremonials of Holy Week and

[1] Reprinted by kind permission of the author.

Corpus Christi begin to take on the municipal and military character that has gradually overcome the public celebrations of the Church at Munich and Vienna; it is only by chance, and in out-of-the-way corners of the Peninsula that we come upon the true "progress" or ceremonial outing of other days.

If we could take one of our old-time May Day processions, add perhaps some hundreds to it, including the clergy and village elders, and inspire them all with Andalusian leisure and Castilian dignity, we should then have something like the gathering that wound across our way one balmy February in the narrow streets of Córdoba. No holy calendar seems willing to enlighten us as to the purport of the celebration, which, as far as we know, may have been of merely local character and as much a civic, as a religious, feast.

Except during the annual fair the average traveler in Córdoba tarries long enough to run across the Roman-Moorish Bridge of Calahorra which spans the flats of the Guadalquiver, and to rush through the mosque of Abderrahman where the canons are chanting their Office to the Virgin of the Assumption as calmly as, across the seas, the *muezzin* is crying *"Allah Akbar"* from the minarets of the Christian shrine of Santa Sophia in Constantinople. Of the labyrinth of alleys with their whitewashed walls, their hidden gardens, lovely *patios*, churches, convents, and hospices, he rarely sees anything. We, however, were happy to find ourselves in a little plaza of rough cobble-stones, framed by a few dingy little shops, except where at one end spread a church façade elaborately decorated in the plateresque manner. We formed part of a group of some fifty or sixty men and youngsters—soldiers and bourgeois—in cloaks and shawls and ulsters notwithstanding the mildness of the afternoon. They seemed typical specimens of the male gentry of these shrunken cities, who, with very rare exceptions, know nothing and care nothing about the history of the ruins they inhabit; whose endless leisure in the ill-kempt *cafés* and *circolos* is taken up with interminable political and financial discussions, relieved only by the microscopic dissection of their neighbors' affairs. How these languid folk manage to subsist remains one of the great un-

solved problems in finance. As to the real social condition of
the majority, the romantic-minded need make no mistake; for
the historic families in almost every case have died out or deserted the smaller cities, and now congregate (sometimes pitifully
enough) in the social capitals. The gilded youths of these little
plazas and *campos* are almost invariably the sons of the mer-
cantile classes, who on their return from military and church
academies, devote themselves to the career of "fine gentlemen"
—which in such places amounts to swinging tinseled walking-
sticks, introducing strange habiliments supposed to originate in
Paris, reading the newspapers, and inditing long epistles over a
cup of coffee in the most crowded *café* of the town.

We had hardly arrived when the plaza began to be filled with
private equipages, and out of the church streamed several hundred
women and children as a military band was heard approaching.
Suddenly the bells from scores of churches began to jangle so
wildly as to send little "goose waves" running down the back.
Here at last was something we had despaired of ever beholding
—a real procession of the old time such as used to walk the streets
of every town and city of Europe when men's hearts were younger
and lighter.

The long line of coaches made the narrow *calle* almost im-
passable for the crowds that began to surge through it. Certainly
in no other country are carriage appointments more elegant, or
so much admired, as in even the small centers of Spain; nowhere
are the *mayoral* and grooms more handsome and dignified than
those who sat along this alleyway, their top-hats respectfully
held upon their knees. The noise from the belfries grew almost
painful in volume; although individually the bells were very
melodious when properly rung by hand; but from where we stood
we could see two or three urchins in every bell-loft doing their
very best with large mallets.

Down the *calle* came a detachment of the local cavalry whose
mounts recalled the barbs of romance only by way of contrast;
then a goodly number of laymen—ancient bedesmen perhaps—
escorting a large image of the King, Saint Ferdinand, with a
trailing velvet cloak, a tinsel crown, and a string of gory heads

in token of his efforts in delivering Córdoba from the Moors as far back as the year 1236. The next detachment consisted of a large body of boys of all ages, wearing the semi-military uniform that seems to be essential to the educational ideas of the Mediterranean mind. These were followed by tiny children many of whom were exquisitely beautiful, and then came the ladies of the city, all of them in the severest of black, with veils and mantillas. Everybody—man, woman, and child—carried a lighted candle; there was breeze enough to make this feature of the procession as exciting as it was beautiful, for the wax flew far and wide.

There now appeared a superb shrine of gold and silver holding a delicate image of the Madonna; it was borne on the shoulders of four elderly gentlemen evidently of great distinction; they were in court or evening dress, wore gorgeous decorations, and were escorted by mace-bearers in velvet robes, and followed by the municipal dignitaries. The brass band discoursed some rather irrelevant *opéra-bouffe* marches and waltzes while the procession moved along at a languid pace, pausing every now and then either to enable the bearers of the images to rest, or to do honor to certain shrines, or households where there were invalids, or families of great distinction who had prescriptive rights to such a *station*. Reverence and light-hearted curiosity made the throng delightful to observe. Wits are nowhere quicker than in Andalusia, but the processionists while they seemed quite aware that they were facing a critical gathering of their townsfolk, were able nevertheless through lifelong familiarity with the customs to preserve a natural ease and correctness of deportment which otherwise might have been difficult.

This was particularly interesting as regarded the young girls and women; they seemed to be representatives of all the respectable classes, from the splendid matron with the profile of a Grecian coin, and the jaunty *garba* whom Zarbaran would take as model for his saints, to the simple Gracias, Lolitas, and Paquitas of Murillo, and the *sandungas* and *saladas* whose allurements would rouse the enthusiasm of Goya. Let it not startle anybody to hear that some of these ladies had expended their rice-powder too freely, even in the cause of religion, for we are now in a land where even tiny infants are sometimes beautified in this manner. Standing near us were three or four young army officers of the unshaven, provincial variety; as some of the young ladies in the procession happened to arouse their interest, they now and then expressed opinions, evidently not on questions of faith, before the fair objects of their devotion were quite out of hearing. Most of the ladies took no notice; but once in a while there passed along a true daughter of Andalusia who under her breath gave back banter for banter in a fashion that evidently caused the young warriors some difficulty.

Single file, in two long parallel lines they went leisurely through the narrow tortuous *calles,* over the cobble-stones more or less neat, of the lost little town that was once the center of the arts and sciences of the European world. The uproar of the bells never ceased for a moment; rockets began to hiss into the blue sky of evening, and bombs exploded as though in a royal salute; one of the confraternities started a hymn, bold and daring at first, but it died away into plaintive confusion; the bells were too much for them.

Peace seemed to be spreading over the world—in spite of the bells; the distinguished señores who had carried the silver shrine were resigning their posts of honor to their servants, and stepping into their coaches where the *calle* took a sharp ascent, when suddenly down the line rushed a *padre,* who must have been master of ceremonies or in some high authority. He had just caught sight of our young friends of the army, and hurling himself among them, let forth a flood of pure Andalusian apostrophe and *pimenton* regarding their indecorum "especially in the presence of Englishmen," an infelicitous reference to ourselves. Not content with the rout and ignominy into which he left them helpless, he handed the culprits over to the high officer, evidently their chief, who was taking part in the procession. There was a moment of suspense in Cordovan military circles; a sphinx-like look that might be severity or just a dignified sort of satisfaction at seeing them publicly trounced, shot from under the commandant's shaggy eyebrows. The jollity of the officers was at an end; in view of all of us they limply disappeared down a dismal *calle* to take refuge on the lounges of the clubhouse, no doubt greatly aggrieved at this clerical outrage to their uniform.

We then observed that we had all the while been standing opposite a convent school—not the kind of convent that governments confiscate—all turrets and stone bric-à-brac—but a plain little house of plaster with screened balconies where the nuns and school-children can hang out their blue and white draperies, and peep down at the processions on beautiful evenings such as those we spent at Córdoba. When we came away a group of youngsters was looking down at us in undisguised curiosity and over the roof there was shining a brilliant evening star.

EXERCISES

1. Do not fail to read "The Baptizing of the Baby" from the list of suggested readings. This is one of the best of sketches, intriguing in its story as well as in its description of the various Faroe customs besides baptism.

2. See how easy it is to draw a diagram of the hall at Earlham from Mr. Lubbock's description of it. What does this teach you about the selection of detail?

3. Why, do you think, did Mr. Stark Young choose such simple style for his sketch? There is a good reason. Find it. Try to make a list of adjectives describing the atmosphere of "The Blessing of the Animals."

4. By means of what two words does Mr. Walsh suggest the mingling of emotions in his essay? Is "Córdoba en Fête" more rich in "human interest" than "The Blessing of the Animals"? Define the term "human interest."

5. For purely esthetic appeal read "The Religion of Numa" from *Marius the Epicurean,* Chapter I. What use does Pater in his description of the procession make of sense impressions? Can you detect the means by which he secures rhythm in his sentences? It *can* be detected.

SUGGESTED READINGS

Anonymous, "The Saturday Night Bath" and "Endicott and I Conduct an Orchestra" in Tanner, *Essays and Essay Writing,* Little, Brown, Boston.

Bacon, Lord Francis, "The Feast of the Family" from *The New Atlantis*.

Brooks, Charles S., "On Hanging a Stocking at Christmas" from *Chimney-Pot Papers,* The Yale University Press, New Haven.

Bryne, Donn, "The Procession of the Trade Guilds" from *Messer Marco Polo,* Century, New York.

Conrad, Joseph, "Christmas Day at Sea" from *Last Essays,* Doubleday, Doran, New York.

Frazer, Lady, "The Yule Log in Servia," "The Carnival of Viza," and "The Feast of Lanterns" from *Leaves from the Golden Bough,* Macmillan, New York.

Gulick, Charles Burton, "A Greek Wedding" from *The Life of the Ancient Greeks,* Chapter IX, D. Appleton, New York.

Lamb, Charles, "Grace before Meat" from *The Essays of Elia.*

Mansfield, Katherine, "Bank Holiday" from *The Garden Party,* Alfred A. Knopf, New York.

Pater, Walter, "The Religion of Numa," Chapter I, from *Marius the Epicurean,* Macmillan, New York. "The Launching of the Ship of Isis," Chapter VI, from the same.

Polo, Marco, "Concerning the Customs of the Cathayans," Chapter XXXIV, Book II, from *Travels,* Macmillan, New York. "Concerning the Tartar Customs of War," Chapter LIV, Book I, from the same.

Taylor, Elizabeth, "The Baptizing of the Baby," *The Atlantic Monthly,* February 1912, also in *Atlantic Classics,* Second Series, Little, Brown, Boston.

Thackeray, William Makepeace, "Founder's Day" from *The Newcomes,* Chapter LXXV, E. P. Dutton, New York.

Timmermans, Felix, "Kermis Morning" from *Pallieter,* Harper's, New York.

PART II

THEMES OF FACT AND INFORMATION

To one reared on Dickens the word *fact* instantly recalls the terrifying Mr. Thomas Gradgrind in *Hard Times* and his insistence alike in his school and in his home that nothing but *Facts* should be taught. Mr. Gradgrind's hard philosophy, one remembers, had a dire effect upon those trained under its tenets; for the brightest product of his school, young Bitzer, became a "soulless, heartless, calculating machine," too mean to merit even contempt, and his only son, Thomas, Jr., a sneak thief.

This is a sad picture surely. The dictionary affords a brighter one. Here we find that the word *fact* in its original meaning signifies something done, that is, a deed or an act. Christopher Marlowe proves to us that the word once held even the connotation of bravery, for in his *Tamburlaine* his hero is described as rattling "forth his facts of war and blood"; [1] and Jane Austen three hundred years later speaks in her novel *Emma* of one "gracious in fact if not in word." [2]

There was nothing of this original, dramatic sense in the facts which Mr. Gradgrind extolled and which Mr. M'Choakumchild taught, facts of watersheds and histories, of rivers and mountains, of manners and customs, of boundaries and productions; and yet there might well have been had not the two gentlemen in question exorcised, as it were, all the spirit from them before presenting them as dull and lifeless things to the school-children. Lifeless they are not, as their very name declares; and this is the first idea that must be lodged in the minds of those who are to use them as theme material.

But before considering their possible dramatic qualities, let us first sum up the rather obvious differences in material and in treatment between a theme based on the more personal sort of experience and one based on fact and information. The first is

[1] *Tamburlaine*, Part II, Act III, Sc. 2, l. 45.
[2] *Emma*, Vol. II, p. 12.

clearly *subjective;* the second, just as clearly *objective.* Even themes like the portrait, which, as has been shown, require a certain objectivity on the part of the writer, are yet subjective when compared with the purely informational theme. The first is motivated by sentiment which naturally matures into a desire to make the reader share, at least to some extent, the feelings of the writer toward certain influences and experiences in his life; the second is motivated by interest in or knowledge of some subject outside himself, an interest and a knowledge which has been born of observation, reading, and study, and by means of which the writer hopes to interest and to instruct his reader. The appeal of the first is largely emotional; that of the second, largely mental or intellectual, although emotional appeal is by no means necessarily absent. The method of treatment of the two types of themes differs as does the material. Since in the first the writer aims to appeal to the imagination and the sympathy of the reader, he will employ all the means in his power to present his experiences vividly and personally. Since in the second his aim is to explain something unfamiliar to the reader, to excite his curiosity, to interest and to instruct, he will employ every means to present his information clearly, accurately, enthusiastically, but, for the most part, impersonally. In the first, since his purpose is to attract and to appeal, he may with perfectly good taste exploit himself, within reason; in the second, since his purpose is to interest and to instruct, he is exploiting, not himself, but his information.

This two-fold aim, to interest and to instruct, should be kept constantly before the writer of themes dealing with fact and information. There is no valid reason for the assumption that a dispenser of facts must be dull; indeed, the original meaning of the word, which we have already described, disputes any such notion. Having chosen a subject interesting to him, the writer must study his material with the purpose of discovering those features within it which are in themselves interesting, unusual, lively, vivid, curious, exciting, suggestive, dramatic. He must be insured against boring his reader, for the stimulation of interest is the first step toward explanation or instruction.

And yet although the capture of the reader's interest must not be underestimated, nevertheless the outstanding purpose of writers of informative articles and books is to explain and to instruct. This purpose, then, dictates the handling and the presentation of material under consideration. Above all else that presentation must be *clear*—clear in plan and clear in execution. It must be orderly and accurate, precise and plain, and it must be these even at the sacrifice of features which are interesting but which do not contribute to the business at hand. There is something distinctly satisfying, even beautiful, in the perfect clearness of a mathematical explanation, or of a formula, devoid of imagination as it may seem to many of us; and there is a grievous lack in both writer and reader who cannot glimpse the satisfaction and the beauty in a clear and accurate piece of exposition even though it may have little imaginative appeal.

To discover how to preserve the interesting attributes of a given subject and how at the same time to subordinate them to the main purpose, that of explanation and instruction; to learn how to make the spectacular serve rather than dominate; and finally to convince oneself and one's readers of the literary value of clear, simple, and accurate expression is the difficult task before the writer of themes based on fact and information.

CHAPTER I

THE THEME OF EXPLANATION

I. OF A MECHANISM

Any first attempt to explain a mechanism, whether it be an egg-beater or the *Graf-Zeppelin,* is usually attended by revelations none too reassuring. The disillusioned writer too often is forced to admit that his task is more difficult than he ever imagined. To begin with, he unwisely assumes that his reader is at least partially acquainted with the mechanism in question, and, there-fore, that he does not have to go into minute detail. Moreover, he does not cut his pattern to fit his cloth, or, in other words, he does not order the plan of his theme and his manner of writing to suit his material. Finally, he is prone to forget that his own place in a theme of this sort is behind the scenes. After two hours of chaotic work he is apt to rise from his desk with a few incoherent pages which explain little except the muddle-headed-ness of himself.

Now the first step you must take if you are faced with the necessity of describing a mechanism is *to assume that your reader is completely, nay colossally ignorant of the mechanism you are about to describe or explain.* This step is absolutely indis-pensable. You must pretend, if need be, that he is foreign to all our devices, that he is blind, or only that he is stupid. His par-ticular brand of insufficiency matters little, but that he is totally insufficient in understanding your subject is absolutely necessary for you to assume.

Having convinced yourself of his utter ignorance as to every detail, your next move is *to begin at the very beginning.* You may even ask yourself with much profit, What is the beginning? In Mr. Alder's description of the incandescent lamp, for instance, his explanation proper starts on page 271 with the sentence, "The filament in the present-day incandescent lamp is made of a slender tungsten wire"; and yet he has seen fit to preface his explanation of the electric light bulb with four paragraphs which deal with the development of the lamp through experimentation. In the same way Robert B. Peck's spectacular explanation of our safety in the subway rush is prefaced by an appreciation of the reliability of the mind of man. Similarly Captain Lehmann in his enumeration and description of the characteristics of the *Graf-Zeppelin* begins by a delineation of the characteristics common to the Zeppelin type of rigid airship. From these he proceeds to the manifest improvements of this specific airship. Only Ruskin, in fact, plunges directly into the business at hand to tell us how a gondola is rowed. There is, then, or at least may well be, some question as to what one means by beginning at the beginning.

Once having answered the question, at least to your own satisfaction, your next problem is *to proceed step by step in your explanation.* Everything depends upon the clarity of your order of procedure, which in its turn depends upon your good judgment and common sense. The models quoted will give excellent suggestions. The author of "The Characteristics of the *Graf-Zeppelin*" enumerates in the order of their importance the improvements of this airship over others; Mr. Alder proceeds from the most important centralizing feature of the lamp, that is the filament, to the complete encasing of it in the glass bulb; Mr. Peck pictures, first, the towerman at his signal map, next, the subway motorman in his reception of the towerman's signals, and, finally, the new plans and inventions constantly being suggested; Ruskin, once he has explained the fórcola, follows minutely the movements of the gondolier from his simple to his more complex manipulations of the oar.

And from beginning to end your fourth problem is *to choose the simplest and the clearest style together with the simplest and the clearest diction possible,* for in this work it is especially essential that the style and the diction do not obscure the sense, that the manner does not dim the matter. Here again you cannot afford not to consult carefully your models. Note particularly the direct and accurate beginnings of the sentences, their reasonable length and uninvolved construction, the careful use of transitional words and phrases by which each sentence moves smoothly into its neighbor, the absence of unnecessary descriptive words once the writer is engrossed in explanation.

With these suggestions and others which you will discover for yourself the explanation of a mechanism ought to be a valuable exercise. If it can give you a heightened sense of the literary merit in clear and concise English, even without the vivid coloring of more subjective writing, it will have more than justified its inclusion in this book; and if it, perhaps, can reveal your own mind to you as a rather disorderly container much in need of being set to rights, it will have performed an inestimable service.

The Incandescent Lamp [1]

By George W. Alder

Light from electricity in the form of lightning has been visible to man since his creation. But the production by man of light from electricity is a comparatively recent accomplishment. In 1809 Sir Humphry Davy produced a spark through the agency of a voltaic battery which, incidentally, was at that time an experimental apparatus in the hands of the scientist. Davy's experiment was the forerunner of many by a number of scientists, some of whom made valuable contributions to scientific knowledge, but their work is frequently lost sight of in the brilliancy of the many accomplishments in a period nearer our own time.

On October 21, 1879, Thomas A. Edison, after a long series of experiments, made an electric lamp in which the light was produced by passing a current through a filament consisting of a piece of carbonized cotton thread supported in a glass bottle or bulb from which a high percentage of the air had been exhausted. This lamp Mr. Edison considered successful, because it burned continuously for forty-five hours before failing. This

[1] From *Good Housekeeping.* By permission of the editor.

performance was much better than anything he had previously been able to obtain. After this demonstration, which proved the feasibility of the filament type incandescent lamp, the problem arose of finding a substance better suited for practical use as a filament than the cotton thread. Finally, bamboo strips or fibers were adopted as the best material, and were used for many years.

Contemporaries of Edison had also reached the point of practical development of the incandescent lamp both abroad and in the United States. Two Americans, in particular, stand out in this period, namely: William Edward Sawyer and Albon Man. Legal controversies over patents took place between these two men, who worked together, and Mr. Edison, and not only scientists but many others took sides. Much of the controversy was regarding the use of carbon as the filament. Critics of Mr. Edison alleged that his work had been done mainly with the metal, platinum, and alloys, and that Sawyer and Man originated the idea of the carbon filament which at that time was considered to be the one satisfactory material for the filament. Strangely enough, the present-day lamp which, incidentally, is far superior in efficiency to the old carbon lamp, has a metal filament.

From the time the incandescent lamp was first brought to the practical stage, there have been constant efforts to improve it. As a result of these efforts, the metal filament lamp of to-day is about nine times as efficient as the first carbon lamps, and about three times as efficient as the carbon lamp at its highest state of development. This improvement has involved a tremendous amount of work on the part of many experimenters in the fields of chemistry, physics and electricity.

The filament in the present-day incandescent lamp is made of a slender tungsten wire. This is supported on small metal hooks secured in a glass stem, and the ends of it are connected to wires, called "leading-in wires," that extend through a hollow portion of the stem to the outside of the lamp. It is through these wires that the current flows to the filament. The filament and its support, which complete is called the "mount," is inserted in a glass bulb, and the mount and the bulb are fused together to make an air-tight joint. The air is then exhausted from the bulb, and in some cases a gas which will not support combustion is let into the bulb. A threaded metal base is cemented to the bulb, and the leading-in wires are soldered to it. In the modern lamp factory practically the whole assembly of the lamp is made in machines, manual labor being used only for feeding the various parts of the lamp into the different sections of the machine. About the only exception is in the placing of the filament on its support. This work is done by skilful women operators.

There are many different styles and sizes of incandescent lamps, suitable for use in the home. The type to select should be governed by the use to which the lamp is to be put. For example, there are so-called "clear" lamps with which everybody is familiar, these being the lamps that have a transparent glass bulb through which the filament may be seen. Clear bulb lamps should be used in the home only in fixtures with diffusing shades which will prevent the glare from the filament reaching the eyes. Again, there are the frosted, white, and bowl-enameled lamps in which the bulb itself is designed to diffuse the light from the filament. Small frosted lights of low wattage may be used in candelabra or similar fixtures without shades or other diffusing media. Of course it is also possible to obtain lamps with colored bulbs to be used in decorative lighting to produce color effects, but generally illumination from these lamps is secondary to the decorative function.

As many people know, the ordinary incandescent lamp has more yellow in its spectrum in proportion to the blue than has daylight. For this reason, it is sometimes difficult to judge colors accurately by the light of the ordinary incandescent lamp. To overcome this, the so-called "daylight lamp" has been developed. The bulb of this lamp is made of blue glass. In the home the ordinary lamp or, in fact, a lamp tinted to give the effect of firelight, produces a color that is more pleasing to the average person than the daylight bulb, so the latter has not replaced the ordinary lamp for general illumination. But the daylight lamp finds a definite place in the laundry, for under its light stains and discolorations and colors appear more nearly as they would in daylight and are therefore easier to detect.

Incandescent lamps are made to be used on circuits of a certain voltage. If the circuit voltage is lower than the lamp rating, the light from the lamp will be less than it should. If the circuit voltage is higher than the lamp rating, the filament will be heated excessively, and the life of the lamp will be correspondingly shortened. For example, if a lamp rated at 120 volts is used on a circuit where the voltage has dropped to 105, it will be noticeably dim. On the other hand, if a lamp rated at 120 volts is connected to a 220 volt circuit, it will probably flash bright for an instant and burn out. The voltage rating of the lamp, as well as the wattage rating, is in most cases etched on the bulb, and in purchasing lamps attention should be given as to whether or not the voltage rating is correct for your electric service, and further, whether the wattage rating is what you require for the fixture in which the lamp is to be used.

What Keeps You Safe in the Subway Rush [1]

By Robert B. Peck

The encroachment of mechanical devices upon man power in a rapid transit era, which sees ten-car trains operated by two men and the linked, fiery-eyed monsters of the underground taking turn-off switches apparently of their own volition, has not yet driven the towerman from his battery of switches.

He survives by reason of his brain and faithfulness, as does the lighthouse keeper in an age of automatic lighting and extinguishing devices, which may keep an untended beacon light in the hours of darkness for months on end.

No engine of human invention has been contrived which can be relied upon, month in and month out, to sort out trains at the rate of fifty-six a minute, as does the B.-M. T. towerman at the Essex Street station at the Manhattan end of the Williamsburg Bridge.

[1] From *The New York Herald-Tribune.* By permission of the editor.

No automotion has been invented upon which the B.-M. T. will rely to play the intricate chess game, with populous trains as pieces, which three nonchalant young men play in the tower at East New York, where three rapid transit lines converge, their tracks depressed or elevated in great arcs like the tracks of a roller coaster, so that no track crosses another at the same level.

There the trains of the Lexington Avenue, the Fulton Street and the Broadway lines hump themselves and leap or swoop in leisurely dignity like so many inch worms playing leapfrog, as they pick their way to Jamaica, Richmond Hill or Canarsie.

High above the tracks, where Jamaica Bay lies spread out below on one side and all of Brooklyn on the other, is the signal tower in the topmost room of which, glassed in like the light chamber of a lighthouse, is the battery of 168 signals, which controls the movement of the trains.

The handles project in a long, narrow row and are shaped much like those of a compass saw, though made of steel and far heavier. When one is pulled out the mechanism of a distant switch begins to move, but the movement of the handle cannot be completed nor the switch signal set to go ahead until a sharp click like a cocked pistol, informs the towerman the switch is locked.

Once the train has started forward to take the switch in obedience to the signal, the switch cannot be unlocked. This guard, which is automatic, is to prevent such accidents as the one which occurred recently in the Sunnyside yards of the Long Island Railroad, where a switch was thrown while a train was passing over it.

Although the inception of every train movement is of human origin, every such movement is hedged about with automatic safety devices, designed to eliminate so far as possible the factor of human fallibility. Only human brains and faithfulness are utilized.

The entire signal system operated from the tower is interlocked so that conflicting signals cannot be shown. The signal levers must be operated in a predetermined order.

"They're on roller skates up there during the rush hour," is the way an official of the signal department described the haste which the growing burden of trains imposed upon the three men

on duty at such times in the tower. But it is a haste which
cannot be misdirected. Swift as are the movements of the men,
they are restrained by an invisible barrier of automatic safeguards on every side which guide them in precisely the right
direction at all times.

The towermen do not have to glance aside from their work to
note the approach of a train. Before each of them is a map of the
tracks in the section governed by the signals under his hand and
a light flashes at the proper spot on it when a train is approaching.

Dusk of a fall evening is the time to see the towerman at work.
Glowing trainloads of homeward bound humanity stream
smoothly below him, converging, diverging, weaving above and
below each other, like the pattern in some gayly crocheted shawl.
For a moment they pause and goggle at the tower with eyes of
red or green or orange and then, in obedience to the slurring click
of the signal lever, slide smoothly on their way.

The towerman has small time to marvel at the brilliant sequence
of looping glow-worms that passes his eyrie. His eyes are upon
the map before him on the wall, where bulbs suddenly burn white
to show a train is waiting for the signal. With a dead cigarette
pendant and forgotten on his lower lip, the towerman hastens
from lever to lever, the slave of the vast mechanism, of which
he also is master.

Everywhere throughout the rapid transit system the human
element operates within certain safety zones, established by
mechanical devices. It is a balanced system of operation.

The subway motorman, approaching a block signal that shows
red, might possibly be suddenly stricken with some mental
affliction, causing him to ignore it. But his train would not pass
the danger signal. Regardless of the human element in the
driver's cab, the power would be shut off, the brakes applied and
the train would come to a stop.

This miracle is accomplished by a tripping device similar to
that in use in the Interborough subways. When the block signal,
which is set automatically by the last train to pass it, shows red,
a track current sets in operation a small but powerful motor
buried in a steel case at the tie level.

The motor raises from the roadbed beside the rail a steel arm, tipped with a head like that of a heavy hammer. The head comes to rest in the air at exactly the level of a pipe connected with the airbrakes which protrudes from the side of the subway car. If the train starts to enter the closed block, the hammer head comes in contact with the brake pipe, setting the brakes, and at the same time shutting off the power.

Only with full knowledge of where he is going can a motorman enter a block on which the signal shows red. There is a button on the side of the signal which he can reach out and press after bringing his train to a stop. Pressure on the button releases the upthrust hammer beside the track, and his train passes into the block unhindered, the hammer rising behind it to bring the next train to a stop. Such a counter device is necessary in order to prevent tie-ups which might be caused by faulty signals.

The signal system, however, is seldom at fault. Modifications of the trip-stop motor have been made recently, and some of those of the new design have remained sealed for almost a year without being touched by a repair man. The B.-M. T. has about a thousand such motors, which cost it $500 apiece.

There is another device which is installed on stretches of track where the speed is limited, which prevents the train from exceeding that limit.

As on the Interborough lines, the B.-M. T. subway trains are protected by the "dead man's button," which will cut off the power and apply the brakes the moment the motorman relinquishes his grip upon the controller. Only the pressure of his fingers keeps the button flush with the handle of the controller. The moment it springs out from its socket the brakes are applied and the power cut off.

Even the passengers themselves come directly under the sway of the automatic rulers of the subways. By means of a device in use on no other subway in the world, the force with which the brakes are applied on B.-M. T. trains is regulated by the weight of the load carried by the cars.

The heavier the load, the more pressure is exerted upon the brakes automatically. The momentum gathered by a heavily laden train is thus counterbalanced, and it may be brought to a stop with the same facility as a lighter train.

The automatically adjusted brakes are of especial value in the subway, where the steel cars are of comparatively light construction. The huge cars used by the B.-M. T. weigh 85,000 pounds apiece and have a capacity of 38,000 pounds of humanity. When crowded, therefore, they weigh about 45 per cent more than when empty.

A nice adjustment of the brake to the load is most necessary, the airbrake being the most powerful adjunct of a train. It has been figured that the airbrake on a passenger train is capable of more work in twenty seconds than the locomotive can accomplish in seven minutes.

Swift, smooth, accurate stops are necessary to the comfort of passengers in the subway and to the maintenance of the headway of trains. A constant braking power might lock the brake shoes on a light train so tight as to cause the wheels to slide, and, when the train was heavily loaded, might not be sufficient to bring it to a neat stop.

The efficacy of the combination of man and machine in the subways is testified to by the rarity of fatal accidents on the subway lines. It is far safer to ride in the subway than to cross the street. In the first six months of this year 448 persons were killed by automobiles in this city, while vehicular accidents of all other kinds, including subway accidents, resulted in only eighteen deaths.

Numerous as are the mechanisms governing the operation of the subways, there are numerous ambitious inventors with schemes to increase them. Frequent suggestions are received by officers of the B.-M. T. as to methods of operating their trains without either guards or motorman.

A typical plan was one submitted recently by a man who suggested a break in the third rail ahead of each station. As the power was thus shut off the brakes would be applied automatically with exactly the right force to bring the train to a stop at the station. The stopping of the train would bring into action another circuit which would open the doors of the cars for a certain specified time and the closing of the doors would complete another circuit which would release the brakes and gradually apply the power.

Scores of persons have written in to suggest the use of phonographs to announce the stations.

The B.-M. T., like other transit corporations, continually is experimenting along such lines. Not long ago it had the representative of the manufacturers who supply the London underground with its automatic station announcer experimenting with his device in B.-M. T. trains. It worked well in London, but conditions here were against it. The device consists of a list of stations, posted in each car, the name of the next station being illuminated as soon as the train pulls out of a station.

The London underground system consists of a central belt line from which radiate other lines to various parts of the city. Each line is operated independently as far as equipment goes. Cars used on a spoke are never transferred to the hub, or to any other spoke. Consequently, the roll of stations to be posted in each car is comparatively short, consisting only of the stations on that particular line.

Owing to the plan of the New York subway system, to the storage facilities for cars and to the demands of traffic, not only are cars transferred from one line to another with great frequency, but at certain hours, on the B.-M. T. system, trains skip certain stations at which, at other hours, they stop.

The London scheme was tried on the Bay Ridge line and, under the conditions existing here, was far from satisfactory. The list of stations was so long as to be confusing. It was impossible to adapt the illuminating device to the practice of skipping certain stations at certain hours.

The plan was abandoned, as many inventions, which seemed promising at first, have been. Nevertheless, the advances made in automatic equipment since the first subway was opened in this city twenty years ago are tremendous and rapid transit officials are not prepared to deny that the future may see subway trains as devoid of human control as the escalator in a department store.

Even the towerman may go. Already a tower here and there at turn-off switches on the Brooklyn elevated system has been abandoned, the switches being operated automatically, in much the same way that trolley switches are.

THE CHARACTERISTICS OF THE GRAF-ZEPPELIN [1]

By Capt. Ernst A. Lehmann

The principal characteristics of the Zeppelin type of rigid airship are already more or less generally known. The hull consists primarily of a rigid framework made up of longitudinal and transverse girders, which, by the way, if placed end to end on the ground would cover a length of about ten miles. This framework, which as a whole has the well-known cigar shape, is completely covered on its outside and protected from the weather by the so-called outer cover, made of an especially strong and lightweight cotton fabric as a base, to which several layers of dope or lacquer and of metal-powder have been applied, so that the finished outer cover is a combination of these three materials, incorporating the advantages of all three. The entire outer cover has been sandpapered all over after the final doping to obtain the smoothest possible surface and the minimum of resistance from friction in the air.

The silver-like, glittering color of the outer cover gives the appearance of a metal-sheeted airship, and the suggestion is frequently made that the cover should really be made of sheet-metal, insteal of fabric, which is commonly believed an inferior material. In fact, there is hardly a better one to be found for the specific airship purposes than the combination of fabric, dope and metal described above and practically nothing to be gained by the use of metal-sheet, which could, of course, be introduced, but would, even with the very thinnest of sheets, be so much heavier that several other far more important features of the present system would have to be sacrificed. The principal advantage of a metallic exterior is protection from the actinic rays

[1] Reprinted from *The New York Times* for October 13, 1928. By permission of the editor.

of the sun and from the radiant heat of the sun, both of which would have undesirable effects in the interior of the airship, and this advantage is being secured most effectively with the fabric-metal combination and with a minimum expenditure of weight.

The metal girders of the framework are made of a light alloy called duralumin, which has the strength of mild steel at a weight of only about one-third of steel and which is essentially a composition of aluminum and copper. The material of which the *Graf-Zeppelin* has been built has been substantially improved beyond previous standards; it is approximately 20 per cent. stronger for the same weight as the former metal, which was, for instance, used in the construction of the *ZR-3*, now the *Los Angeles*, which was built and delivered to the United States by the Zeppelin Company in 1924. This is the first of the special improvements in this airship. To gain a more concrete idea of the accomplishment of the designer one should imagine this huge metallic and perfectly rigid structure as being of the size of a large ocean liner but weighing altogether not more than a small-sized harbor tugboat.

The interior of this enormous hull is subdivided into seventeen compartments, each of which contains a separate gasbag or gascell for the lifting gas. The effect of this subdivision on the safety of the airship is, of course, the same as that of the water-tight bulkhead system in oceangoing vessels. It is almost impossible for the airship to lose so much of her buoyancy in any kind of an accident, that she would be forced to come down to the surface in an undesirable place, like, for instance, the middle of the Atlantic Ocean.

All along the lower keel inside of the hull, from the foremost tip of the ship's bow to the very tail end in the rear, she has a corridor, the so-called main service corridor, which affords lengthwise communication between all parts of the ship and along which also the various service rooms have been arranged, carefully distributed over the entire length. There are spaces for fuel tanks, oil tanks, ballast tanks, engine stores, general provisions and further various rooms for the airship crew—messrooms, sleeping accommodations. At a great many places there are rooms for freight so that it will be possible to stow or, if necessary, shift the loads according to the requirements of the longitudinal balance of the ship. From this main corridor other gangways branch off at right angles in certain places, which give access to the engine cars at the flanks of the big hull.

Besides all these corridors the *Graf-Zeppelin* has another one, which runs also in the fore and aft direction through the entire length of the airship. It is located high above the main corridor, just below the central axis of the ship and is therefore called the axial corridor. Its main purpose is to serve as a gangway, from which all the various gas cells can be kept under constant supervision and can be reached for repair if necessary. This is a new feature in airships and such an axial corridor has been incorporated for the first time in the *Graf-Zeppelin*. Besides it acts as a support for all the sixteen transverse bulkheads, thus greatly contributing to the strength and safety of the ship, in case that one or more of the gas cells should become damaged and partly or wholly deflated. This is the second improvement in the new airship.

The arrangement of the gas cells is different from all foregoing ships, because a most radical departure has been made in this ship with regard to the type of fuel used to drive the engines. Instead of gasoline, which has up to now been in general use, the engines of the *Graf-Zeppelin* burn a fuel gas; that is, the engine fuel is carried aboard in gaseous form. This gas is essentially not very different from the coal gas, which is in daily use in most any household, only it is heavier and is much more efficient as an engine fuel than coal gas would be. To make room in the interior of the airship for the storage of that fuel gas, the lifting gas cells in the twelve largest of the seventeen compartments instead of filling the whole space of their respective compartments as they did in all previous ships are made smaller so as to take up only about two-thirds of the space, thus leaving room for altogether twelve other gas cells, which hold the fuel gas and which are really best compared to twelve large and flexible gasometers inside the airship, within which the fuel gas is carried aboard under normal atmospheric pressure.

The introduction of this gaseous fuel is indeed a most novel departure from previous practice and it insures quite a number of advantages which can be listed as further improvements of the *Graf-Zeppelin* over former ships. The most important of them result from the fact that the fuel gas has approximately the same weight as air. Formerly when an airship was ready to land after an extended flight, she had naturally a surplus of lift due to the consumption of so and so many tons of gasoline during the flight. Before she could be brought to the ground that excess of lift had to be annihilated either by releasing great quantities of the lifting gas through the valves or by taking on ballast during the flight, for instance, from the surface of the water, or by manufacturing ballast from the exhaust gases of the engine.

All these methods have been and are being worked with fairly satisfactory results, but there still remain some positive disadvantages; for instance, the waste of lifting gas or the loss in air speed due to the ballast-recovery apparatus and several more. All these disadvantages are practically entirely eliminated with fuel gas. Since it has the same weight as air, it makes no difference to the lifting force of the airship whether the fuel is on board or not, whether the gasometers inside the airship are full or empty, whether the ship is just starting for flight or returning from half a week's cruise.

That is the third improvement in the *Graf-Zeppelin*. It is easy to see the importance it may have for airships operating with helium for lifting gas.

The next and fourth improvement is the great reduction of stresses in the structure of the airship due to the absence of the heavy loads of fuel. The *Los Angeles*, for instance, when she came from Germany across the Atlantic had thirty tons of gasoline tanks—that is the weight of a small locomotive—slung inside her keel. Imagine that weight trying to tear loose from the airship when both are being tossed about in squalls or storms and you will readily understand the increase in safety of the airship, which is due to the entire absence of all such mass-forces. For the fuel gas, having the same weight as air—that means in this connection practically no weight at all—cannot produce any such stresses.

The fifth improvement, also due to the gas fuel, is a material reduction of the danger of fire in the airship in comparison to gasoline. For the range of inflammability of gasoline fumes is much higher than that of mixtures of the fuel gas with air.

The sixth and most important improvement, however, of the *Graf-Zeppelin* over other ships results from the fact that for airships the use of gaseous fuel for the engines makes it possible to carry along on a voyage a much greater amount of energy than is possible with liquid fuels and than was hitherto the case with gasoline. An example will make that fact quite easy to understand.

Imagine an airship inflated with just so much lifting gas that she will lift her own weight and all other loads except the fuel. In that condition the lifting gas cells will have to be somewhere between half and two-thirds full. If she was now to take a full load of fuel in the form of gasoline, we would have to inflate her gas cells with additional lifting gas until all the remaining space of her interior body was filled up in order to make her lift and carry the maximum weight of gasoline. If we wanted to use the gaseous fuel, we would not need any more lifting force, because the fuel gas has only the weight of air—that is, popularly speaking, no weight. Instead we would use the empty space in her interior to insert some more gas cells and inflate them with fuel gas until the entire inside space was filled. Now we have in both cases a ship with a full load of fuel.

But there is one very great difference. The ship with fuel gas can go a much greater distance than the ship with gasoline. Why? Imagine one unit of volume of the empty part of the interior of the airship—it does not make any difference what unit we choose—say, one cubic meter. Now assume this cubic meter to be filled with lifting gas—for instance, hydrogen. This cubic meter of hydrogen will lift one kilogram of gasoline under average atmospheric conditions. One kilogram of gasoline contains about 11,000 heat units, which we can feed to the engines. Now let us put aside all this and take another cubic meter of empty space of the airship and fill it directly with fuel gas. This amount of fuel gas will then contain about 14,000 to 15,000 heat units; that is, the fuel gas airship will have about one-third more potential power on board than the gasoline airship. How much of this theoretical advantage will be actually realized will have to be shown by the practical experience of a greater series of flights of the new ship.

The fuel gas in itself is not a new thing or a special invention. In fact, there is a great variety of gases or mixtures of gases which can either be obtained from natural sources or manufactured quite cheaply. The common characteristic of all such fuel gases is this, that they are all medium-weight hydro-carbon gases and that for airship use they should, within certain limits, have the same weight as atmospheric air. The gas which is being used in the *Graf-Zeppelin* is made from crude oil and has been commercially known for many years by the name of Blau gas, because the manufacturing process was first invented and perfected by a certain Dr. Blau. It has nothing to do with a certain poison gas, which was called "blaukreuz" (blue-cross) and used during the World War, neither is there any such gas as "ethanogen," as the papers have reported at times.

Even the idea of using gas as a fuel for airships is not new. One of the first airships existing, that of the German inventor Paul Haenlein, built in 1872, incorporated already the idea of using the lifting gas, which was coal gas in that ship, at the same time as fuel for the engines. Later on it was proposed to use the hydrogen, which is the more modern lifting gas, for that same purpose, but it has proved hitherto a much too difficult problem to construct a satisfactory hydrogen engine.

Only the idea of using a gas for fuel which has about the same weight as air is new, but this limitation contains the whole secret.

There remains something to be said about the machinery of the airship.

The engines—five in number—are arranged exactly in the same way as on the *Los Angeles,* that is, two pairs at the sides of the hull and one engine under the rear end of the ship in the centre line. The motors are of the same type as in the *Los Angeles,* special airship motors designed and built by the May-bach Motor Company, a Zeppelin subsidiary at Friedrichshafen. They are materially improved, however, over the first model in power as well as in durability and reliability. Each of them de-velops 550 horsepower and they have stood tests of up to 300 hours at top speed. They are reversible and they are adapted to run on either fuel gasoline or fuel gas. The speed which they give to the airship is eighty miles an hour at full power and seventy to seventy-five miles an hour at cruising speed.

The arrangements for controlling and piloting or navigating the airship are essentially the same as in the *Los Angeles,* only the control-rooms are subdivided into two rooms, one of which might be called the bridge or the wheelhouse, the other corresponding to the charthouse in an ocean liner.

The passenger accommodations are in the front end of the airship, more exactly in the middle and rear of the great cabin, close to the control and navigating rooms. They comprise a roomy lounge and dining room and ten most comfortable sleeping chambers for twenty passengers. Of course, there is a well-equipped electric kitchen and all the passenger quarters are not only very beautifully decorated but also very practical and comfortable.

How a Gondola Is Rowed [1]

By John Ruskin

A gondola is in general rowed only by one man, standing at the stern, those of the upper classes having two or more boat-men, for greater speed and magnificence. In order to raise the oar sufficiently, it rests, not on the side of the boat, but on a piece of crooked timber like the branch of a tree, rising about a foot from the boat's side, and called a *"fórcola."* The *fórcola* is of different forms, according to the size and uses of the boat, and it is always somewhat complicated in its parts and curvature, allowing the oar various kinds of rests and catches on both its

[1] From *Stones of Venice.*

sides, but perfectly free play in all cases; as the management of the boat depends on the gondolier's being able in an instant to place his oar in any position. The *fórcola* is set on the right-hand side of the boat, some six feet from the stern: the gondolier stands on a little flat platform or deck behind it, and throws nearly the entire weight of his body upon the forward stroke. The effect of the stroke would be naturally to turn the boat's head round to the left, as well as to send it forward; but this tendency is corrected by keeping the blade of the oar under the water on the return stroke, and raising it gradually, as a full spoon is raised out of any liquid, so that the blade emerges from the water only an instant before it again plunges. A downward and lateral pressure upon the *fórcola* is thus obtained, which entirely counteracts the tendency given by the forward stroke; and the effort, after a little practice, becomes hardly conscious, though, as it adds some labor to the back stroke, rowing a gondola at speed is hard and breathless work, though it appears easy and graceful to the looker-on.

If then the gondola is to be turned to the left, the forward impulse is given without the return stroke; if it is to be turned to the right, the plunged oar is brought forcibly up to the surface, in either case a single stroke being enough to turn the light and flat-bottomed boat. But as it has no keel, when the turn is made sharply, as out of one canal into another very narrow one, the impetus of the boat in its former direction gives it an enormous leeway, and it drifts laterally up against the wall of the canal, and that so forcibly, that if it has turned at speed, no gondolier can arrest the motion merely by strength or rapidity of stroke of oar; but it is checked by a strong thrust of the foot against the wall itself, the head of the boat being of course turned for the moment almost completely round to the opposite wall, and greater exertion made to give it, as quickly as possible, impulse in the new direction.

EXERCISES

1. As a competitive fifteen minute class-room exercise explain one of the following familiar mechanisms: a Ford engine, a can-

opener, a corkscrew, a padlock, a coffee percolator, an egg-beater, a thermos bottle, a fountain pen, a table pencil sharpener, a lawn-mower, a bicycle.

2. Read Joseph Husband's *America at Work*. Why has this book been called "clear and artistic exposition"? Why not model a theme on one of these chapters, trying to earn both adjectives for your own work.

3. Study the sentence beginning in "The Incandescent Lamp." What do they teach you about this sort of exposition?

4. Why has Mr. Peck chosen to use so many short paragraphs? Comment on his similes in this article. Where are they placed in reference to the purely expository material? Why?

5. From what you may learn of Ruskin in this book alone, why are you justified in calling him a versatile man?

6. "The Characteristics of the *Graf-Zeppelin*" might be termed "newspaper English." Does it differ in any way or ways from the other material in this section?

II. OF A PROCESS

The successful explanation of a process requires careful attention to the very rules which govern the successful explanation of a mechanism. Here, too, you must assume ignorance on the part of your reader, must discover the best beginning and proceed point by point, must employ the clearest style and diction. Here, too, you must sacrifice interest to accuracy if a question of choice arises.

In at least two ways, however, the process theme affords greater possibilities: In the first place, the ideal of clearness is more easily realized as the plan of the theme is, by its very nature, chronological. In the second place, the range of subject matter is far wider since the word *process* is capable of a larger interpretation than is the word *mechanism*. To illustrate: Mary Antin in one chapter of *The Promised Land* called "The Making of an American" describes a process when she relates the various influences which made her, a little immigrant girl in school, into an American. Her process is mental and emotional, but none the less a process. A student writes a theme which he quite rightly insists belongs in this category and which he entitles "Selling a Man What He Doesn't Want"; another who is planning to be a physician writes on "The Making of a Modern Doctor"; a third, on "A Sure Way to Make Enemies." The very fact that such an interpretation of the word *process* is not only allowable but also often advisable means that the sacrifice of interest and appeal to accuracy is less likely to be demanded. Surely with this range of choice a student must be sadly lacking in imagination if he cannot find something to interest not only him but his reader.

Miss Vose in her charming explanation of how students in colonial days were "placed" again illustrates this wider interpretation. Her essay is, nevertheless, broadly speaking chronological, and she clearly explains the old and intriguing custom of social rating. No one would for a moment deny that her article belongs among the explanations of a process; and yet how delightfully it proves the originality and interest possible both in treatment and in the choice of material.

Stewart Edward White's advice to Dick and Edwin Stiger's description of the making of books are both nearer the narrower interpretation of the process; and yet they by no means sacrifice interest to accuracy. It would, indeed, be difficult to find clearer and better exposition than they both contain or more interesting material. Mr. White's early use of contrast is excellent as is Mr. Stiger's attention to the most minute detail of book-making. Each is a most valuable model for any student.

ON MAKING CAMP [1]

By Stewart Edward White

To those who tread the Long Trail the making of camp resolves itself into an algebraical formula. After a man has travelled all day through the Northern wilderness he wants to rest, and anything that stands between himself and his repose he must get rid of in as few motions as is consistent with reasonable

[1] From *The Forest*. By permission of Doubleday, Doran and Company.

thoroughness. The end in view is a hot meal and a comfortable dry place to sleep. The straighter he can draw the line to those two points the happier he is.

Early in his woods experience Dick became possessed with the desire to do everything for himself. As this was a laudable striving for self-sufficiency, I called a halt at about three o'clock one afternoon in order to give him plenty of time.

Now Dick is a good, active, able-bodied boy, possessed of average intelligence and rather more than average zeal. He even had theory of a sort, for he had read various *Boy Campers, or the Trapper's Guide, How to Camp Out, The Science of Wood-craft,* and other able works. He certainly had ideas enough, and confidence enough. I sat down on a log.

At the end of three hours' flustration, heat, worry, and good hard work, he had accomplished the following results: A tent, very saggy, very askew, covered a four-sided area—it was not a rectangle—of very bumpy ground. A hodge-podge bonfire, in the centre of which an inaccessible coffee-pot toppled menacingly, alternately threatened to ignite the entire surrounding forest or to go out altogether through lack of fuel. Personal belongings strewed the ground near the fire, and provisions cumbered the entrance to the tent. Dick was anxiously mixing batter for the cakes, attempting to stir a pot of rice often enough to prevent it from burning, and trying to rustle sufficient dry wood to keep the fire going. This diversity of interests certainly made him sit up and pay attention. At each instant he had to desert his flour sack to rescue the coffee-pot, or to shift the kettle, or to dab hastily at the rice, or to stamp out the small brush, or to pile on more dry twigs. His movements were not graceful. They raised a scurry of dry bark, ashes, wood dust, twigs, leaves, and pine needles, a certain proportion of which found their way into the coffee, the rice, and the sticky batter, while the smaller articles of personal belonging, hastily dumped from the duffle bag, gradually disappeared from view in the manner of Pompeii and ancient Vesuvius. Dick burned his fingers and stumbled about and swore, and looked so comically pathetically red-faced through the smoke that I, seated on the log, at the same time laughed and pitied. And in the end, when he needed a continuous steady fire to fry his cakes, he suddenly discovered that dry twigs do not make coals, and that his previous operations had used up all the fuel within easy circle of the camp.

So he had to drop everything for the purpose of rustling wood, while the coffee chilled, the rice cooled, the bacon congealed, and all the provisions, cooked and uncooked, gathered entomological specimens. At the last, the poor bedeviled theorist made a hasty meal of scorched food, brazenly postponed the washing of dishes until the morrow, and coiled about his hummocky couch to dream the nightmares of complete exhaustion.

Poor Dick! I knew exactly how he felt, how the low afternoon sun scorched, how the fire darted out at unexpected places, how the smoke followed him around, no matter on which side of the fire he placed himself, how the flies all took to biting when both hands were occupied, and how they all miraculously disappeared when he had set down the frying pan and knife to fight them. I could sympathize, too, with the lonely, forlorn, lost-dog feeling that clutched him after it was all over. I could remember how big and forbidding and unfriendly the forest had once looked to me in like circumstances, so that I had felt suddenly thrust outside into empty spaces. Almost was I tempted to intervene; but I liked Dick, and I wanted to do him good. This experience was harrowing but it prepared his mind for the seeds of wisdom. By the following morning he had chastened his spirit, forgotten the assurance breathed from the windy pages of the Boy Trapper Library, and was ready to learn.

Have you ever watched a competent portraitist at work? The infinite pains a skilled man spends on the preliminaries before he takes one step towards a likeness nearly always wears down the patience of the sitter. He measures with his eye, he plumbs, he sketches tentatively, he places in here a dab, there a blotch, he puts behind him apparently unproductive hours—and then all at once he is ready to begin something that will not have to be done over again. An amateur, however, is carried away by his desire for results. He dashes in a hit-or-miss early effect, which grows into an approximate likeness almost immediately, but which will require infinite labor, alteration, and anxiety to beat into finished shape.

The case of the artist in making camps is exactly similar, and the philosophical reasons for his failure are exactly the same. To the superficial mind a camp is a shelter, a bright fire, and a smell of cooking. So when a man is very tired he cuts across lots to those three results. He pitches his tent, lights his fire, puts over his food—and finds himself drowned in detail, like my friend Dick.

The following is, in brief, what during the next six weeks I told that youth, by precept, by homily, and by making the solution so obvious that he could work it out for himself.

When five or six o'clock draws near, begin to look about you for a good level dry place, elevated some few feet above the surroundings. Drop your pack or beach your canoe. Examine the location carefully. You will want two trees about ten feet apart, from which to suspend your tent, and a bit of flat ground underneath them. Of course the flat ground need not be particularly unencumbered by brush or saplings, so the combination ought not to be hard to discover. Now return to your canoe. Do not unpack the tent.

With the little axe clear the ground thoroughly. By bending a sapling over strongly with the left hand, clipping sharply at the strained fibres, and then bending it as strongly the other way to repeat the axe stroke on the other side, you will find that treelets of even two or three inches diameter can be felled by two blows. In a very few moments you will have accomplished a hole in the forest, and your two supporting trees will stand sentinel at either end of a most respectable-looking clearing. Do not unpack the tent.

Now, although the ground seems free of all but unimportant growths, go over it thoroughly for little shrubs and leaves. They look soft and yielding, but are often possessed of unexpectedly abrasive roots. Besides, they mask the face of the ground. When you have finished pulling them up by the roots, you will find that your supposedly level plot is knobby with hummocks. Stand directly over each little mound; swing the back of your axe vigorously against it, adze-wise, between your legs. Nine times out of ten it will crumble, and the tenth time means merely a root to cut or a stone to pry out. At length you are possessed of a plot of clean, fresh earth, level and soft, free from projections. But do not unpack your tent.

Lay a young birch or maple an inch or so in diameter across a log. Two clips will produce you a tent-peg. If you are inexperienced, and cherish memories of striped lawn markees, you will cut them about six inches long. If you are wise and old and gray in woods experience, you will multiply that length by four. Then your loops will not slip off, and you will have a real grip on mother earth, than which nothing can be more desirable in the event of a heavy rain and wind squall about midnight. If your axe is as sharp as it ought to be, you can point them more neatly by holding them suspended in front of you while you snip at their ends with the axe, rather than by resting them against a solid base. Pile them together at the edge of the clearing. Cut a crotched sapling eight or ten feet long. Now unpack your tent.

In a wooded country you will not take the time to fool with tent poles. A stout line run through the eyelets and along the apex will string it successfully between your two trees. Draw the line as tight as possible, but do not be too unhappy if, after your best efforts, it still sags a little. That is what your long crotched stick is for. Stake out your four corners. If you get them in a good rectangle and in such relation to the apex as to form two isosceles triangles of the ends, your tent will stand smoothly. Therefore, be an artist and do it right. Once the four corners are well placed, the rest follows naturally. Occasionally in the North Country it will be found that the soil is too thin, over the rocks, to grip the tent-pegs. In that case drive them at a sharp angle as deep as they will go, and then lay a large flat stone across the slant of them. Thus anchored, you will ride out a gale. Finally, wedge your long sapling crotch under the line— outside the tent, of course—to tighten it. Your shelter is up. If you are a woodsman, ten or fifteen minutes has sufficed to accomplish all this.

There remains the question of a bed, and you'd better attend to it now, while your mind is still occupied with the shelter problem. Fell a good thrifty young balsam and set to work pulling off the fans. Those you cannot strip off easily with your hands are too tough for your purpose. Lay them carelessly crisscross against the blade of your axe and up the handle. They will not drop off, and when you shoulder that axe you will resemble a walking haystack, and will probably experience a genuine emotion of surprise at the amount of balsam that can be thus transported. In the tent lay smoothly one layer of fans, convex side up, butts toward the foot. Now thatch the rest on top of this, thrusting the butt ends underneath the layer already placed in such a manner as to leave the fan ends curving up and down towards the foot of your bed. Your second emotion of surprise will assail you as you realize how much spring inheres in but two or three layers thus arranged. When you have spread your rubber blanket, you will be possessed of a bed as soft as and a great deal more aromatic and luxurious than any you would be able to buy in town.

The next care is to clear a living space in front of the tent. This will take you about twenty seconds, for you need not be particular as to stumps, hummocks, or small brush. All you want is room for cooking, and suitable space for spreading out your provisions. But do not unpack anything yet.

Your fireplace you will build of two green logs laid side by side. The fire is to be made between them. They should converge slightly, in order that the utensils to be rested across them may be of various sizes. If your vicinity yields flat stones, they build up even better than the logs—unless they happen to be of granite. Granite explodes most disconcertingly. Poles sharpened, driven upright into the ground, and then pressed down to slant over the fireplace, will hold your kettles a suitable height above the blaze.

Fuel should be your next thought. A roll of birch bark first of all. Then some of the small, dry, resinous branches that stick out from the trunks of medium-sized pines, living or dead. Finally, the wood itself. If you are merely cooking supper, and have no thought for a warmth fire or a friendship fire, I should advise you to stick to the dry pine branches, helped out, in the interest of coals for frying, by a little dry maple or birch. If you need more of a blaze, you will have to search out, fell, and split a standing dead tree. This is not at all necessary. I have travelled many weeks in the woods without using a more formidable implement than a one-pound hatchet. Pile your fuel—a complete supply, all you are going to need—by the side of your already improvised fireplace. But, as you value your peace of mind, do not fool with matches.

It will be a little difficult to turn your mind from the concept of fire, to which all these preparations have compellingly led it, —especially as a fire is the one cheerful thing your weariness needs the most at this time of day,—but you must do so. Leave everything just as it is, and unpack your provisions.

First of all, rinse your utensils. Hang your tea pail, with the proper quantity of water, from one slanting pole, and your kettle from the other. Salt the water in the latter receptacle. Peel your potatoes, if you have any; open your little provision sacks; puncture your tin cans, if you have any; slice your bacon; clean your fish; pluck your birds; mix your dough or batter; spread your table tinware on your tarpaulin or a sheet of birch bark; cut a kettle-lifter; see that everything you are going to need is within reach of your hand as you squat on your heels before the fireplace. Now light your fire.

The civilized method is to build a fire and then to touch a match to the completed structure. If well done and in a grate or stove, this works beautifully. Only in the woods you have no grate. The only sure way is as follows: Hold a piece of birch bark in your hand. Shelter your match all you know how. When the bark is caught, lay it in your fireplace, assist it with more bark, and gradually build up, twig by twig, stick by stick, from the first pin-point of flame, all the fire you are going to need. It will not be much. The little hot blaze rising between the parallel logs directly against the aluminum of your utensils will do the business in very short order. In fifteen minutes at most your meal is ready. And you have been able to attain to hot food thus quickly because you were prepared.

In case of very wet weather the affair is altered somewhat. If the rain has just commenced, do not stop to clear out very thoroughly, but get your tent up as quickly as possible, in order to preserve an area of comparatively dry ground. But if the earth is already soaked, you had best build a bonfire to dry out by, while you cook over a smaller fire a little distance removed, leaving the tent until later. Or it may be well not to pitch the tent at all, but to lay it across slanting supports at an angle to reflect the heat against the ground.

It is no joke to light a fire in the rain. An Indian can do it more easily than a white man, but even an Indian has more trouble than the story-books acknowledge. You will need a greater quantity of birch bark, a bigger pile of resinous dead limbs from the pine trees, and perhaps the heart of a dead pine stub or stump. Then, with infinite patience, you may be able to tease the flame. Sometimes a small dead birch contains in the waterproof envelope of its bark a species of powdery, dry touchwood that takes the flame readily. Still, it is easy enough to start a blaze—a very fine-looking, cheerful, healthy blaze; the difficulty is to prevent its petering out the moment your back is turned.

But the depths of woe are sounded and the limit of patience reached when you are forced to get breakfast in the dripping forest. After the chill of early dawn you are always reluctant in the best of circumstances to leave your blankets, to fumble with numbed fingers for matches, to handle cold steel and slippery fish. But when every leaf, twig, sapling, and tree contains a douche of cold water; when the wetness oozes about your moccasins from the soggy earth with every step you take; when you look about you and realize that somehow, before you can get a mouthful to banish that before-breakfast ill-humour, you must brave cold water in an attempt to find enough fuel to cook with, then your philosophy and early religious training avail you little. The first ninety-nine times you are forced to do this you will probably squirm circumspectly through the brush in a vain attempt to avoid shaking water down on yourself; you will resent each failure to do so, and at the end of your rage will personify the wilderness for the purpose of one sweeping anathema. The hundredth time will bring you wisdom. You will do the anathema —rueful rather than enraged—from the tent opening. Then you will plunge bodily in and get wet. It is not pleasant, but it has to be done, and you will save much temper, not to speak of time.

Dick and I earned our diplomas at this sort of work. It rained twelve of the first fourteen days we were out. Toward the end of that two weeks I doubt if even an Indian could have discovered a dry stick of wood in the entire country. The land was of Laurentian rock formation, running in parallel ridges of bare stone separated by hollows carpeted with a thin layer of earth. The ridges were naturally ill adapted to camping, and the cup hollows speedily filled with water until they became most creditable little marshes. Often we hunted for an hour or so before we could find any sort of a spot to pitch our tent. As for a fire, it was a matter of chopping down dead trees large enough to have remained dry inside, of armfuls of birch bark, and of the patient drying out, by repeated ignition, of enough fuel to cook very simple meals. Of course we could have kept a big fire going easily enough, but we were travelling steadily and had not time enough for that. In these trying circumstances Dick showed that, no matter how much of a tenderfoot he might be, he was game enough under stress.

But to return to our pleasant afternoon. While you are consuming the supper you will hang over some water to heat for the dish-washing, and the dish-washing you will attend to the moment you have finished eating. Do not commit the fallacy of sitting down for a little rest. Better finish the job completely while you are about it. You will appreciate leisure so much more later. In lack of a wash-rag you will find that a bunch of tall grass bent double makes an ideal swab.

Now brush the flies from your tent, drop the mosquito-proof lining, and enjoy yourself. The whole task, from first to last, has consumed but a little over an hour. And you are through for the day. In the woods, as nowhere else, you will earn your leisure only by forethought. Make no move until you know it follows the line of greatest economy. To putter is to wallow in endless desolation. If you cannot move directly and swiftly and certainly along the line of least resistance in everything you do, take a guide with you; you are not of the woods people. You will never enjoy doing for yourself, for your days will be crammed with unending labor.

It is but a little after seven. The long crimson shadows of the North Country are lifting across the aisles of the forest. You sit on a log, or lie on your back, and blow contented clouds straight up into the air. Nothing can disturb you now. The wilderness is yours, for you have taken from it the essentials of primitive civilization,—shelter, warmth, and food. An hour ago a rainstorm would have been a minor catastrophe. Now you do not care. Blow high, blow low, you have made for yourself an abiding place, so that the signs of the sky are less important to you than to the city dweller who wonders if he should take an umbrella. From your doorstep you can look placidly out on the great unknown. The noises of the forest draw close about you their circle of mystery, but the circle cannot break upon you, for here you have conjured the homely sounds of kettle and crackling flame to keep ward. Thronging down through the twilight steal the jealous woodland shadows, awful in the sublimity of the Silent Places, but at the sentry outposts of your fire-lit trees they pause like wild animals, hesitating to advance. The wilderness, untamed, dreadful at night, is all about; but this one little spot you have reclaimed. Here is something before unknown to the eerie spirits of the woods. As you sleepily knock the ashes from the pipe, you look about on the familiar scene with accustomed satisfaction. You are at home.

How Books Are Made [1]

By Edwin T. Stiger

Each year the American publishers place on the market something over 8,000 new publications, the editions of which range from the aristocratic few of the expensive limited editions to the hundreds of thousands of the "best sellers." Each one of

[1] From *The Independent*. By permission of the editor.

these new books represents an individual effort on the part of the author and the publisher to place something new in a new way before the public, to turn out a book which some appreciable portion of the millions of book buying inhabitants of this country can be made to think that it wants.

Did it ever occur to you as a reader of a portion of this great output that the laying out and manufacture of this mass of reading matter calls for the employment of an immense force of professionally trained minds outside of the thousands who labor in the carrying out of the details arranged for them; that every new book which appears means the study and application of ideas stored away in the brain of some one man or some little group of men who are spending their lives in the work of producing books attractive to the purchaser, and that each of these men must have a general knowledge, at least, of all branches of work that enter into the making of a book, not only of the idiosyncrasies of the English language, with its shading of punctuation, of types and typographical eccentricities, of the technicalities of electrotyping, paper-making, photo-engraving, printing and bookbinding, but of every one of these and its related branches?

Here, then, is the story of the making of a book.

When a publisher receives a manuscript from an author he gives it out to one of his readers, one of a force upon which he relies for opinions as to the advisability of publishing or probable salability after publishing. These readers are generally persons who have been well trained in the merits or demerits of popularity or authority, and, in spite of occasional errors of judgment inseparable from work of this nature, have developed exceptional ability in this line. If the manuscript appears hopeless for this particular publisher's use it will probably pass through the hands of but one or two readers. If, however, it shows prospects of success, it will be placed before several of these experts, each of whom will deliver an opinion, and it will go for final consideration to the head of the publishing firm. Let us consider that the manuscript has been accepted and the contract drawn up and signed by the author and the publisher. The next step is the sending of the manuscript to the head of the manufacturing department of the publishing house. This gentleman generally tries to talk the book over with the author, in an effort to include as many of his ideas in the production as may be possible considering the limits and the cost of manufacture. He is then ready to begin the building of the book.

Of course, if a new volume is to be added to a series which has already been begun, or if it is to be patterned after some book which has already been made, the plan of procedure is simple, the work to a great extent merely mechanical. If the book, however, must be constructed on lines of its own, the first thing to be done is to obtain a count of the number of words the manuscript contains. This is necessary as giving a gauge from which to determine the size of type and of the type page and to arrive approximately at the number of pages the book will make. This counting is not as easy as it sounds, and it is quite an art to do it accurately, since manuscript will vary considerably in different parts, and often the "copy," as the manuscript now becomes called, is made up of writing by different hands, or of magazine or newspaper extracts of varying sizes pasted or laid in. Then, too, the different sizes of types to be used must be considered, for long quotations or correspondence must be set in a different size from the text, and the estimator will also find that portions of the same manuscript will vary materially, according to the nature of the subject. For instance, in a novel a part given up to broken or short conversation will carry more words to a page than a similar amount of longer worded description. The words having been counted, the next proceeding is to decide on the type and type page.

While in the selection of type there are many fonts from which to choose, most of them, except for the more ornamental styles often used for booklets and special gift books, narrow themselves down to adaptations of three or four faces, their variations being due to peculiarities in the cut of the letters belonging to one or the other of these few standard styles. Some of these adaptations will get more letters on a line of a given length, and some less, than others set in the same size of type. In addition to the changes of types the manufacturing man is allowed some leeway by the "leading" or blanks, between the lines of type. Having decided whether the book is to be of approximately the size known by the book-buying public as "octavo" or "12mo," or some such designation, it is his work to settle upon a type and type page which will not run the book to such a length as to make its publishing too expensive, or, on the other hand, to make a book so small that the buyer will feel that he is not getting the worth of his money. In all of this he is bound down by the fact that his type page, whatever it is, must not be laid out contrary to certain proportions which the good taste of the past has made definite. After getting these matters worked out he sends the manuscript to the printer with instructions for a sample page to be set to confirm him in his decision, and often with a request to the printer to count the words and verify his estimate of the number of pages. Very often this sample page must be juggled, a line added, a fraction of an inch taken off, a page number put at the foot, a running head changed in style, or even an entirely new start made on an entirely different basis before an O. K. can be given. It might be said here that unless a manuscript offers unusual features a publisher does not necessarily ask the printer for an estimate of cost, for the manufacturing man has a schedule of the printer's prices and can figure this out for himself as closely as the printer himself could do it.

The sample page having finally been approved, the order is given to begin the work, the printer is told how many proofs will be required and where they are to be sent, and the last details about any irregularities to be met in the work are put in his hands. The printer starts his compositors to work, or, if the book is to be set by machine, arranges for the machines and operators who are to begin the composition, and the kind of progress that can be seen commences. Then follows the period of proofs and proofreading. The first proof, which is a galley proof, or one "pulled" (printed) on long slips of paper without any division into pages, is read and corrected several times before it leaves the printer's hands and is then read and marked for correction by the author and by some of the publisher's editorial force before its return to the printer. If the corrections required are many, it is customary to have further galley proofs, or "galley revises," sent out, so that the changes may be reduced to a minimum before the matter is made up into pages, when all corrections are apt to be more expensive to the publisher or author than if made in the galleys. Then, all the palpable errors having been corrected, and all the additions and excisions made which have up to that time been discovered by the author, the type is put into page form, the running heads and the page numbers added, and the proper sinkage allowed for the beginnings of chapters. More proofs follow, and perhaps page revises, before the final word is given that everything is correct and that electrotypes of the pages may now be made. Even then a plate proof is often required, and oftentimes late corrections are sent to be made in the plates themselves—an expensive proceeding, and one avoided whenever possible.

A word should here be said about this matter of corrections, for there is probably no one thing which causes as much friction between the author and the publisher, and the publisher and printer, as alterations from copy. The author, when he sees his work in type, naturally sees many things which escaped his notice in manuscript form. Moreover, there are often new developments of his subject or suggestions from friends brought to his notice, all of which he is anxious to include in his first edition. He cannot understand why just a few words added here or a line taken out there should, when repeated now and then, make such a seemingly excessive bill of errors. Such changes, however, which appear to him to be very slight, and which are so judging by their length, may require the changing of words and spaces throughout several lines, or, after paging, the readjustment of a number of pages. All of this takes a compositor's time; the printer has to pay the compositor for this time, and at the end of the work a considerable bill is rendered. If the author or editor will only remember that where a word or a sentence is lacking, one as near the same length as possible should be inserted whenever it can be done, or if he can cut out enough old matter to allow space for new he may wish to add, much wear and tear of feelings might be saved.

The making of the electrotype plates, although an intensely interesting process, need not be taken up in this article. It is enough to say of it that the type is pressed in page form into a waxen mold, that the mold is placed in a bath having copper in solution, that this copper is deposited on the mold by an electric current and chemical action, taking an exact impression of it, and that this copper shell, when backed with metal and trimmed to the required size, is ready for the printing press.

All this time, while the proofs are going back and forth, while the corrections are being made, and while the electrotypes are being produced, the manufacturing man is busily arranging the later details of the book. He is ordering the paper, seeing that it is delivered in time, arranging with the artist for illustrations if the book is to be embellished in that way, deciding upon the cover decoration and the binding, and perhaps even getting out partially finished books showing the binding and a few pages of printed matter from which the salesmen can take orders.

As soon as enough of the book is in type to insure accuracy as to the number of pages, or often merely taking the original estimate as a basis for the order, steps must be taken to have the paper on hand as soon as the electrotyping has been finished. When the size of the edition will permit it, the paper is generally made to order, a process requiring from two weeks up, according to the amount of business the paper mills are handling at the time. If the edition is small, or if such a paper is to be used as may readily be found in the stock regularly carried by a paper dealer, the paper is ordered from this stock, cutting it down to the proper size if the sheet required is smaller than the sizes ordinarily sold. The manufacturing man must decide upon the quality of the paper to be used, its size, weight, and finish, where it is to be obtained, how much is to be paid for it, and how large a quantity is to be used. He must obtain samples from different mills, consider these in relation to the price asked, make his decision and place his order, and then, often the hardest work of all, follow up the paper man incessantly to make sure that it is on the spot when it is wanted. The type page being fixed, he allows for the proper margins, considers whether he will print eight, sixteen, thirty-two, or sixty-four pages at one impression, and then figures the quantity by a scale which allows enough extra sheets for spoilage in the printing and binding. While all of this work may sound as a simple proposition, it is often far from that, for the paper must be chosen with some regard for the face of type which is to be used upon it, and it must very often be selected with a view toward making a too fat book thin and easy to hold, or toward padding out a small, insignificant book into something worth while to a prospective purchaser.

While the proofs are shuttling back and forth and while the paper is being made, it is also time for this supervisor of the work to be closing in any of the illustrative and decorative portions of the book. If cuts are to print with the text, the drawings and the cuts must be made in advance, in order not to hold back the paging; if, however, the cuts are to print separately and are to be pasted in by the binder, the work may be carried on while the composition is being done, the manuscript having been given the artist to read in advance of its being sent to the printer, or an early set of proofs sent him, that he may choose the situations that appeal to him for illustration. In a general way it may be said that the illustrative processes are two in number, although these branch out into infinity in their variations, and although there are more than these two and their variations required in special work. The two in question, used in the general run of books sold at retail, are the line cut, or zinc etching, made from line drawings, and drawings with solid blacks and whites, and the half tone, made from photographs and wash drawings. Both of these cuts, or engravings, are made by photography and chemical action, both may be reduced, or even enlarged to a certain degree, to any size proportional to the original subject, and both may be printed at the same time as the text pages, except for the fact that the finish of the paper must be adapted to the cuts. The line cut may be used on any paper whose surface is smooth enough to print without breaking the printed line, but the half tone, on account of its delicacy of line, may be used only on a coated paper or a paper of high finish. The printing of colored illustrations is simply the adaptation of one or the other of these two processes, breaking up the colors of a picture in such a way as to produce practically any of the colors of the spectrum—a complete art in itself and often carried out by printers who do no other kind of work, or else the arbitrary division of a picture into two or three colors and the printing of portions in each color, without regard to the fact that the combination of two certain colors will produce a third. Unless a book is so filled with cuts as to require a highly finished or a coated paper throughout, it is customary to print the cuts separately from the text.

Another of the artistic features to be looked after before the presswork has been completed is the designing of the cover and the making of the brass dies from which the binder stamps the design of the outside of the book. The artist to whom is delegated the work of making the cover design submits a scheme in its colors, usually painted on cloth or paper of the color suggested for use, so that an idea may be had of the general effect and a tentative estimate made of the cost. In general, the artist is held down to as few colors as possible, and is restricted in the use of gold and silver, on account of the extra cost of dies and stamping in the former case, and of precious gold and silver leaf in the latter. When the design is finally accepted it is given into the hands of the manufacturing man, who, determining the size of the cover and the thickness of the book, passes it along to the die cutter in order that the design or lettering may be cut in hard brass, from which any quantity of covers may be stamped or printed without showing any evidence of wear on the part of the die itself. Of late the cover inset has come into much vogue, this inset being generally an illustration printed on paper in one or more colors and pasted on the cover in relation to some part of the stamped design, thus giving an added attraction to the cover and making it more in keeping with the book, while at the same time holding down the cost.

Let us consider, then, that the electrotype plates are now ready for the press and that the paper is in the printer's hands. The book is ready to be printed. The publisher therefore tells the printer how large an edition he requires, and the signal is given to begin the printing. Any one unacquainted with the work going into a press room for the first time must be struck by the large number of presses seemingly lying idle when he has been given to understand that a press room is always a scene of whirring activity. This seeming quiet is on account of what is known as the "make ready"—the principal cause for expense in printing and the work which brings out the pressman's art and skill. This is the labor required to get the eight, or sixteen, or thirty-two, or sixty-four pages ready to be printed. The pressman lays out his form on the bed of his press, using a large block upon which the electrotypes may be placed and fastened, or else a number of small blocks, one to a page, arranged in their proper positions by wooden or metal strips laid between the blocks—"furniture," as these are called. As type matter or plates can never be absolutely even on the top, it is necessary for the pressman to build up the low spots and cut down the impression where it is too black. After placing the form on press, therefore, he runs a trial sheet of paper through the press, from which he is able to know where in the form his work of evening the impression is required. Then he starts this work, which is known as the "make ready," a labor which may require an hour or even two or three days, according to the character of the form or the quality of the work desired. Pieces of thin paper are pasted on the cylinder of the press in such positions as to touch certain spots in the form at the point where the cylinder carrying the sheet of paper is to be printed meets the plates, thus increasing the strength of the impression at that point, while other pieces are cut in the right size and shape and pasted under the plate, between it and the block, to gain a similar end. The former method is known as "overlaying" and the latter as "underlaying." This same process is carried out in printing the illustrations, only to a greater degree and generally with more care. When the "make ready" has been finished, the sheets of blank paper are lifted up on the press and fed one by one onto the cylinder, which carries them in its revolution against the plates, after which they are deposited in a pile to be removed, printed again on the other side, counted and packed for shipment to the binder. Similar work to this is carried out for every form of the book until it is all printed, when the scene is shifted to the bindery.

The first step in the binding is the folding of the sheets. While this was generally done in the past by hand by girls working with a flat piece of smooth ivory or similar substance, it is now almost universally executed by ingenious machines which take the sheet of paper, cut it, fold it accurately, insert one folded sheet within another if necessary, and deliver the folded signatures, as each single folded sheet is called, ready for the next process. These signatures are next "gathered," either by hand or by machinery, in the order in which they are to appear in the finished book, and they are then "collated," that is, verified, the collator making sure that all signatures are arranged in proper order and that none is missing. They are then sent to the sewing machines, which stitch the signatures together in one continuous row, making no division between the volumes, which have to be cut apart by hand. If the books are to have gilt tops it is here that this work comes in, the gilder placing a number of books in his press, squeezing them up very tightly with the edge to be gilded uppermost, scraping this edge very smooth, painting on it a thin albumen size, and then laying on the thin gold leaf, which is burnished down to smooth brilliancy by a tool worked by the hand of the gilder. The sewed and gilded book then moves along to be rounded and backed; that is, to be given the circular effect shown on the back of the book and to have the edge of the back, where the sewing is, forced out by pressure to make a groove in which the covers may have play. A piece of coarse, tough cloth, reinforced by a pasted strip of paper, is glued on the back, the edges of the cloth overhanging the edges by an inch or so on each side, a flexible glue is smeared on the back to strengthen it and to hold the signatures more closely together, and the book is ready for the cover, which in all probability has been made while this other work was going on in order to save time at the end.

Although machines are now generally used for the making of the cover itself, or "case," as it is called in the trade, they have simply adopted the method of the hand worker with more uniformity and speed. The plan of this work begins with the cutting of the stiff pasteboard into pieces of the proper size for each side, a similar cutting of the book cloth for the entire cover, the gluing of the inner surface of the cloth, the placing of the pieces of board in their proper positions, and of a strip of paper down the back, and the turning over of the edges of the cloth upon the board to give a finished edge and strengthen the case. The case then goes to the stamper, who places the brass dies the publisher has supplied for the lettering and the design on a metal block, inks them with colored ink, or, if gold or some other foil is to be used, has this foil stuck on with a size to the cover, and prints the design or lettering on it with his stamping press. If foil is used and the dies are not stamped against the foil, the waste foil which has not received the impression is rubbed off, collected and remelted. The book is then fitted into the case or cover, the blank pages at each end of the book which have been pasted on for this purpose are pasted back on the cover, and the book is finished. These pasted leaves, together with the reinforcing cloth, are all that hold the book to the cover in ordinary "edition work," as this style of binding is called, but that they are sufficient for all customary use is shown by the amount of hard usage one of these volumes will stand.

The books are now placed in a press and subjected to heavy pressure for a day or a night or more in order to set the mold, as one might say, and give them a proper chance to dry, after which they are packed in cases and shipped away to the market. In the selling of the product another department of the publishing house begins its work, while the manufacturing man gives a sigh of relief, comments perhaps to himself, perhaps to the printer or binder, on some details which had not worked out in just the way he had intended, and devotes his attention to the finishing of the next book on the publication list.

"PLACING" STUDENTS IN COLONIAL DAYS [1]

By Caroline E. Vose

Present-day university and college presidents, confronted with innumerable, ofttimes seemingly insuperable, difficulties, must occasionally think with envy of the light duties of their predecessors who served when American colleges were young. It is customary to sigh for the simplicity of earlier times, and to lament the complexity of our own. But just because times were earlier, were they of necessity simpler?

The college problems of the Colonies may have been different from ours, but they were none the less bothersome and perplexing. Surely nothing could be more delicate than the task of "placing" each student according to social position at recitation, at Commons, and in the chapel—a duty which had to be performed at Harvard and Yale until about the time of the Revolutionary War. What man to-day with that dire responsibility facing him would ever accept the presidency of a college? To determine a student's academic standing is hard enough, but to pass upon his social status is far more exacting. This custom of "placing" students—in force at Harvard from the beginning, and later adopted by Yale at its foundation in 1700—apparently originated at the former college, for foreign universities did not make use of this system, although Ebenezer Baldwin says the Yale statutes were chiefly modeled upon "those of European Universities, where the footsteps of monarchial regulation were discerned. . . . So difficult was it to divest the minds of wise men of the influence of venerable follies, that the printed catalogues of students [at Yale], until the year 1768, were arranged according to respectability of parentage." As a matter of fact the Yale statutes were modeled mostly upon those of Harvard.

It is odd that the two earliest colleges in the New England Colonies, where social distinctions might be least expected, should be the ones—and the only ones—in which they were rigidly

[1] From *The North American Review*. By permission of the author and the editor.

observed. Our New England forefathers were not entirely concerned, as we are often led to believe, with saving their own
souls, or even with the more congenial occupation of saving other
people's, but were spending some time and thought upon their
social position in the community. Theodore Woolsey, President
of Yale, in an historical address to the graduates in 1850, declared: "We at this day can hardly conceive to what extent the
social distinctions were then acknowledged and cherished. In
the manuscript laws of the infant college [Yale] we find the
following regulation which was borrowed from an early ordinance
of Harvard under President Dunster: 'Every student shall be
called by his sirname except he be the son of a nobleman, or a
knight's eldest son.' I know not whether such a *rara avis in terris*
ever received the honours of the college; but a kind of colonial
untitled aristocracy grew up composed of the families of chief
magistrates, and of other civilians and ministers. In the second
year of college life, precedency according to the aristocratic
scale was determined, and the arrangement of names on the
class roll was in accordance."

General John Winslow, whose son Pelham was in the class of
1753 at Harvard, was so impressed with his own and his son's
superiority that in October, 1749, he wrote a long letter to President Holyoke in which he stated that "as. . . . Rank in Our way
is Lookᵈ upon as a Sacred Thing and it is Generaly allowed That
the Sons of the New England Cambridge are Placed according
to the Degrees of their ancestors, I have therefore put in My
Pretentions for my Son;" after which he went on to give many
genealogical details, as well as a full account of his public offices.
As his son's name is second in a list of seventeen, General Winslow's "Pretentions" were evidently satisfactory.

At Harvard the "placing" was done by the President and
Fellows, and at Yale by the Rector—later called the President—
and the resident Fellows or Tutors. The lives of these individuals can have been none too happy immediately after the "placing" announcement. They were doubtless deluged with pro-
tests, and were aware of the ill feelings directed against them, to
say nothing of the Puritan conscience which tortured by in-

quiring, "Are you sure you did right? Were you fair? Were you just?" Any one who has wrestled with academic grades, who after tossing sleeplessly on his bed has finally risen to change a student's $C+$ to a B — can sympathize with these seventeenth and eighteenth century educators. To start in on an endowment campaign for millions is an immense undertaking, but to rank your contemporaries socially is in some ways equally stupendous.

It was virtually the parents who were "placed," for the son's ranking depended upon the father's position. At first, according to the late Franklin B. Dexter, family pedigree was very important, but later there was a gradual change in this respect. Wealth, too, was a consideration, while the father's business or profession and his public offices were vital factors. John Pickett, Yale 1705, was first in a class of six, his position being due to the prominence of his maternal grandfather, Captain Daniel Wetherell—entrusted with John's education—as a citizen of New London. Captain Joseph Wakeman was "a prominent civilian" in recognition of whose standing his son was put at the head of the 1720 class of ten at Yale. Clergymen's sons were often placed high, as one might expect, but so were the sons of laymen. Lawyers' sons could also lay claim to high ranking. President Woolsey of Yale, in 1850, told a delightful story that long was in circulation, of a shoemaker's son who upon being questioned as to his father's occupation answered that "he was upon the bench," which gave him, of course, a high place. Doctors' sons had little social standing unless they had reasons other than their fathers' profession for distinction, while the sons of teachers, curiously enough, were shown little consideration socially.

My own investigations lead me to agree with Mr. Dexter who, after careful study of the records, concluded that no definite system for "placing" students can be formulated. Such anomalies as the following are often found. The son of Governor Thomas Dudley was second in the class of 1665 at Harvard, while Benjamin Eliot, son of the apostle Eliot, was first. One might naturally expect a Governor's son to have precedence. Samuel

Ruggles was number twelve in the class of 1702 at Harvard out of a group of thirteen, while his brother Timothy was eighth on the list of seventeen students in the Harvard 1707 class, and another brother, Benjamin, was first in a class of fourteen at Yale in 1721. Such differences in the same family are hard to account for unless they are due to the father's possible rise in the social scale from 1698 to the year 1717.

Once a student was "placed," his ranking was almost never altered—unless he were expelled or "degraded" by way of punishment—and even great distinction in later life effected no change in the position of his name in the college catalogues. Chief Justice Benjamin Prat, for instance, Harvard 1737, who attained almost unprecedented eminence, always stood last in a class of thirty-four.

"Degradation," which was the next highest punishment to expulsion, consisted in lowering a student's name on the class list. The Harvard and Yale records show various offenses for which this was the penalty. Henry Flynt, in his *Commonplace Book* for November 4, 1717, notes the "degrading" of a Harvard student "below five in his class, because he had been before publicly admonished for card-playing." At a Yale Trustees' meeting on November 21, 1722, it was "agreed that if any Student shall go into a Tavern Victualling House or Inn to eat or drink except he be called by his parents or Guardians or some such Person as the Rector or Tutor shall accept of or spend his time there and be convicted thereof he shall . . . for the Second Offence of that Kind . . . be degraded." The firing of guns in 1731 was punishable at Yale by "degradation." In 1740 the Yale Trustees, in order to enforce the entering of freshmen earlier in the college year, decreed "that if any of them shal not attend before the End of the first Quarter, without being detained by Sickness or some extraordinary Reason, he shal be placed the lowest in the class." The case of Isaac Burr, Yale 1753, a clergyman's son, offers a chance for interesting speculation. He was six in a class of seventeen until his junior year when, alas, he was moved down three places "as part of his punishment for repeatedly kicking a senior, for what provocation is not given." Why did Isaac feel impelled to kick this senior? Was he merely prompted by a naturally pugnacious disposition, or did the senior deserve the chastisement? Was the punishment compensated for by the satisfaction of having delivered the kicks? One longs to have these questions answered. Knowing none of the facts, my own sympathies are with Isaac.

In many cases, if he repented of and confessed his fault, the "degraded" student was after a certain period reinstated. For instance, on July 20, 1776, it was voted at Harvard "that Trumbal, a Middle Bachelor, who was degraded to the bottom of his class for his misdemeanors when an undergraduate, having presented an humble confession of his faults, with a petition to be restored to his place in the class in the Catalogue now printing, be restored agreeable to his request."

Sometimes, however, the offender was less fortunate than Trumbal, as is evidenced by Samuel Melyen's sad experience. Melyen, originally fifth in a group of eight in the class of 1696 at Harvard, was dropped in his second year four places to the end of the list. The following letter written two years after his graduation shows how seriously college "placing" was regarded. On May 19, 1698, Melyen thus addressed Cotton Mather:

One favo^r, Worthy S^r! I should be exceedingly rejoyced to obtain at yor benign hands, if it may not engage yor self in a too great a trouble, which I will manifest after I have p^{r}mised, y^t towards ye End of o^r Sophymoreship by my audaciously calling freshmen at ye door of ye Worthy Mr Brattle in a way of contempt, ye Venerable & Reverend President with my Tutor, ye well deserving Mr Leverett saw it convenient to place me ye Lowest in ye class, whereas before I was placed between Sr Remington & Sr Whitman.

Now, S^r my humble request is . . . that you would be pleas'd to motion to ye Reverend President, that I may be reduced into my former station—Nothing S^r can be more gratefull to my Father & Mother nor anything more encouraging to me—I am very Sorry (& desire to be very penitent) that in that as well as in many other things I have displeased so worthy a Gentleman as ye President, & so kind a Tutor as Mr Leverett wth ye Revd Mr Brattle, hoping that ye remainder of my days may be so manidg'd that glory may redown to God, & thereby some satisfaction may be made for ye wrong I offer'd them—I . . . humbly beg their Pardon . . . hoping they will . . . grant me this favour, which will much encourage me in my labour & lay me und^r fresh obligations to serve them & yor noble self . . . —Had I, S^r! been placed at first Inferio^r to ye rest, I should have been contented & thought it my place, . . . but it being after such a nature as it was, makes me very desirous of reducem^t —Sr All our class y^t were placed at first beneath me, have voluntarily manifested unto me y^t they were very willing I should Enjoy my Antient standing. . . .

One can imagine the writer—as he anxiously awaited the outcome—hoping and praying that his plea might be heeded, feeling somehow that with his stain wiped out he could start again with fresh courage and vigour. Alas, it was not to be! He was never reinstated, but was even more humiliated by having the name of Cotton Mather's cousin, Roland Cotton—who had left college on account of ill health before taking his degree—inserted second on the class list. Thus in all the late catalogues Melyen is number nine instead of being eight as at first. His whole career was unsuccessful and unhappy. He died when he was young, his sensitive nature crushed perhaps by the severity of his punishment for a boyish indiscretion. One hesitates to comment upon Cotton Mather's action in this case.

As time went on the custom of grading students socially occasioned more and more dissatisfaction, so much so that in about 1762 a new college in Western Massachusetts was planned, all because—so rumour whispered—of the "placing" of Colonel Israel Williams's son. A little gossip of the times is available in a letter from Oxenbridge Thacher to Chief Justice Prat in 1762, in which the writer ironically says, ". . . what occasions ye most gaping of late, (we are not awake enough to speak,) is a charter for a new college in ye county of Hampshire. The Monarch of ye county [Col. Williams] . . . took great offence at his son's being placed some years ago something lower in a class at our college [Harvard] than befitted ye son of a king. He therefore, & his privy council came down ye last Sessions prepared with a petition to incorporate a college in y^t county which they modestly said was all they desired." The proposed college, however, was never established, and it is not known whether Col. Williams's feelings were ever assuaged.

Beginning with the class of 1768, Yale students' names were printed alphabetically. No definite reasons for this arrangement are assigned except the general trend of the times toward democracy. Harvard did not adopt the alphabetical order of names until a few years later, the class of 1773 being the first to be so arranged. While here too the growth of republican sentiments was probably the real cause, the immediate one seems to have been the case of Samuel Phillips, Jr., Harvard 1771, who later became Lieutenant-Governor of the Commonwealth of Massachusetts, and founder of Phillips Andover Academy. At a Trustees' meeting of Harvard College in August, 1769, the complaint of Samuel Phillips, Sr., about the ranking of his son was brought up. He had not been ranked with the sons of the Justices of the Quorum, and was placed below John Murray's son, although Samuel Phillips had been put in the Commission of Peace, and been made Justice of the Quorum before John Murray. The authorities after looking into the matter ordered that in future Samuel Phillips, Jr., should take his place above young Murray.

Mr. Phillip's shrewd letter to his son, just the kind a father might write to-day, makes the Phillipses delightfully real and human. Dated August 29, 1769, it reads:

You are now in the most difficult situation, & the eyes of all, above and below you, will be upon you, & I wish it might be that you could be at home till the talk about the change was a little over. Every word, action, and even your countenance, will be watched, particularly by those who envy you, and perhaps by those who do not. Therefore keep as much retired as possible, waive all conversation upon it, don't let it appear that you are in the least degree affected with the change. If any difficulties should arise with any of your classmates that now fall below you, treat them with all possible tenderness. If you want advice how to conduct consult Mr. Eliot & Mr. Hillyard, but let it be

in the most private manner, & keep the advice to yourself. If
Murray is uneasy and manifests it to you, say nothing to irritate him. What if you should ask him, whether it would be
any ease to his mind if you should continue to stand below him
in reciting? But by no means give the most distant hint of
yielding your place. But don't begin with him upon it. On the
whole say as little as possible.

The father had made too great an effort to secure this coveted
place to be willing to have it resigned again, and the son probably had no intention of suggesting its surrender, for according to
Timothy Dwight, who knew him well, he was no advocate of
democratic ideals. "The modern doctrine of liberty and equality he considered as a senseless and at the same time a most
mischievous absurdity." Give in to Daniel Murray? Never!
Unfortunately no records of the feelings of that superseded
lad remain. His side of the affair would doubtless be as interesting as the Phillipses'. What a pity it is lost!

Josiah Quincy in his *History of Harvard University* discusses
the abolishing of the custom of "placing" students. "This," he
says, ". . . was the frequent cause of discontent among the
students and their families; and, as the population of the Province increased, and republican principles began to prevail, the
principles of discrimination became more difficult and exciting."
Then after alluding to Mr. Phillips's protest he continues: "This
complaint exhibits one of the principles on which this offensive
discrimination was made, and the feelings it naturally excited.
On the recommendation of their visiting committee, the Over-
seers passed a vote, that, 'for the future, the practice should be
laid aside, and that the names of the scholars, in each class,
should be placed in alphabetical order,' " a ruling which, as
before mentioned, went into effect with the class of 1773. Thus
was abandoned a time-honoured college custom, just when the
American Colonies ceasing to be Colonies, were becoming the
United States, and were promulgating the doctrine of the equality of all men, a doctrine which, to-day, our colleges and universities claim—rightly or wrongly—to be upholding.

EXERCISES

1. Study style and diction, not forgetting sentence beginnings and sentence length, in the 4th, 5th, and 6th paragraphs of the essay, "On Making Camp." Then contrast all these features with the same in the 10th and following paragraphs. Has Mr. White purposely used means to suggest *confusion* in the first paragraphs and *order* in the others?

2. Where is most of Mr. White's esthetic appeal? Why? Is there any esthetic appeal in the most straightforward, orderly paragraphs? Think about this.

3. Study the use of descriptive adjectives in "How Books Are Made." What conclusion do you reach concerning their use in this article?

4. Does Miss Vose's essay have a charm apart from its great interest for us? If so, wherein does it lie?

5. Write a process theme on "How I Start the Winter Furnace," which shall be *clear, informal,* and *amusing.*

6. Consider the following as subjects for process themes. Condense them into titles.

> How the high school football star learned that other men could outplay him.
>
> How the small college man was initiated into a great university.
>
> How the jazz fiend learned that classical music is interesting.
>
> How the college graduate learned to fit into town circles after four years away.
>
> How the 100 per cent. American learned that his country does not hold a copyright on the amenities of life.

III. OF AN OCCASION OR A SITUATION

Something of the perennial interest of the reminiscent theme lurks in the explanation of an occasion or a situation. To be sure, the method here is objective rather than subjective; the one who explains or describes is lost in his description or his explanation; and yet the opportunity of portraying bygone customs and the chance such a theme presents for detail and incident afford much of the same glamour that clings about the reminiscence.

This is the sort of expository writing with which the good social historian delights us. His business is to catch the atmosphere as well as the accuracy of an age or of a period or of a place, and give it in his turn back to his readers. Although accuracy is his aim, if he is a good historian, atmosphere, too, is his safe investment if he wants to appeal to the majority of his readers.

Themes on occasions or situations presuppose rather wide information on at least some one subject. This information may well come from experience as John Corbin's unquestionably does in his explanation of a typical day in the life of an Oxford student, or as does Robert Dean Frisbie's knowledge of the social customs of Puka-Puka, which he sets forth so clearly and interestingly in an *Atlantic* article (see the list of suggested readings). More often, however, it comes from reading and study. Information thus gleaned is ideally portrayed in such books as William Stearns Davis's *Life on a Medieval Barony* and Eileen Power's *Medieval People*.

This theme, then, advises and urges you, especially if your experience has been relatively limited, to browse among bookshops and libraries for material on any subject which particularly interests you. There are no boundaries to your researches. You may decide you want to investigate a Puritan Christmas in colonial days, or to discover the methods of selling wares at a medieval fair, or to ascertain the daily life of a Vestal Virgin, or to find out the kinds of food consumed at a Greek banquet in the Age of Pericles.

Once you have collected your material from any, or all, available sources and made yourself familiar with it, several methods of handling it are before you, the most natural and straightforward of which are the following:

1. You may write a purely expository theme in which your aim is, above all else, to explain in the clearest and simplest English the occasion or the situation which you have chosen to

set forth. Your desire is, first of all, to instruct, and you prefer
not to appeal especially to the reader's imagination. This sort
of straightforward, expository theme has its merits particularly
if the occasion or situation to be explained is either unusually
unfamiliar or unusually difficult of portrayal. The third person,
either singular or plural, is used throughout, and the development is that of simple chronology.

2. You may choose, as John Corbin does in "A Day in an
Oxford College," some person whose experiences may be cited as
typical. He thus takes on an individuality such as the simple
third person cannot supply. And you may continue to profit by
Mr. Corbin's good example and sketch a typical day, say, a day
in a medieval university, a day at St. Bartholomew's Fair, a
day in an elementary school of the Augustan Age, or, forsaking
the past and coming down to the present, a day in a coal mine
or a day on a U. S. cruiser. The value of Mr. Corbin's work
lies particularly in the sense of activity he has been able to give
through his attention to *every* happening in *every* period of the
day. No detail or incident as you will see has been allowed
escape.

3. You may decide to make actual and specific a typical
occasion and situation. This William Stearns Davis has beautifully done in "A Medieval Wedding." He has chosen names for
his hero and heroine, Oliver and Alienor; he has placed them
in specific localities, Perseigne and St. Aliquis; he has made
their wedding with all its accessories and accoutrements from
Oliver's silk stockings to Alienor's vermillion shoes seem a single
and specific occasion when in reality it occurred daily throughout
the Middle Ages. In other words he has created persons and
personalities for the express purpose of making more real to us
the occasion of a medieval wedding. This is the same method
used so ably by Miss Eileen Power in her fascinating *Medieval
People* already mentioned (see the list of suggested readings) and
has many advantages as well as pleasures for both the writer
and the reader. It presupposes, however, a real sense of the
dramatic, a vast accumulation of detail (possible only through
wide reading or experience) and an accurate knowledge of the

subject one is attempting to handle. Here, if anywhere, *facts* certainly are made to assume their early meaning of *acts* and *deeds!*

Since this theme is very likely to be based on library reading (it may well be the "long theme" of the semester or quarter), some suggestions as to the proper compilation of a bibliography and as to the use of foot-notes will probably not come amiss. This information will be found immediately preceding the Exercises at the close of this section.

A Medieval Wedding [1]

By William Stearns Davis

* * * * * * *

Conon has negotiated a most satisfactory marriage. He will give his sister to Sire Olivier, the eldest son of the Count of Perseigne. The Perseignes are a great Burgundian family with many castles, and counts think themselves a little higher in the social scale than do barons, but St. Aliquis is also a powerful fief, and its alliance will be useful to Perseigne when he has his expected war with the Vidame of Dijon. Conon will give the young couple his outlying Burgundian Castle (not of great value to himself) and the alliance will enable him to talk roundly to his uncivil neighbors. A most excellent match; another sign that St. Aliquis has an extremely sage seigneur!

Alienor is now nearly seventeen and has been thinking about a wedding since before she was fifteen. Her nurses have long since reviewed all the eligible cavaliers for her. Her great dread has been lest she have to wed some old and very stupid man—as befell her cousin Mabila, who had been sent away tearful and pouting to Picardy, the bride of a three-times widower. Who can measure her relief when Conon declared he would not give her to old St. Saturnin? It was all very well for the jongleurs to sing, "An old man who loves a young maiden is not merely old, but a fool!" The thing has happened so often!

[1] From *Life on a Medieval Barony*. By kind permission of the author and of Harper & Brothers.

Her ideal is to have a "damoiseau (squire or young knight) just with his first beard"—one who is brave, valiant, and is, of course, courteous and handsome. She had once hoped that Conon would give a great tourney and award her to the conqueror; but this desire faded when she learned that the victor in the last tourney was ugly and brutal. She has been on very brotherly terms with William, Conon's first squire, but William is still too young, and it is not always honorable for a squire to push intrigues in the house of his lord. Thus she is in a very open state of mind when her brother says to her one day: "Fair sister, I have arranged your marriage with Olivier of Perseigne. He is a gallant cavalier. Any maiden might rejoice to have him. Consider well what I say because (here he adds a phrase which he hopes will not be taken too literally) I would not have you wed him against your wish."

If Alienor has anything against Olivier, if her antipathy were violent and based on reason, Conon, as a genuinely affectionate brother, might give it weight; but in fact, though she has met Olivier only a few times at a tourney, at the Christmas fête at the Duke of Quelqueparte's court, and once when he stopped at the castle, she has not the least objection. He has certainly large blue eyes, blonde hair, a large nose, and a merry laugh. He is reported to be kind to his servants, generous to a fault, and not overgiven to drinking or brawling. At the tourney he broke three lances fairly against a more experienced knight. His family is excellent and her brother's desires are obvious. She will not have to live too far from St. Aliquis. What more could be said? After a few hours of decent reflection she informs Adela that she will comply with Conon's wishes. After that the castle takes on a joyous activity.

Before the wedding had come the betrothal. It was a solemn ceremony, blessed by the Church. Sire Olivier visited the castle with a great following of relatives and met the shy and blushing Alienor. In the chapel, after suitable prayers by Father Gregoire, the pair had awkwardly enough exchanged their promises! "I will take you for my wife." "And I for my husband." After this there would have been great scandal had either side turned back. The Church affirms energetically, however, that betrothal is *not* marriage. Otherwise the affianced pair might have considered themselves somewhat wedded on trial, only to repudiate their obligations later. Also, not merely the young couple, but their parents or guardians, had to be present and add their consent; and, of course, all the pledges were sworn to over the holiest relics available.

Olivier, during all this happy time, has lodged at the castle of a friendly vassal of St. Aliquis, and he rides over frequently to visit his betrothed. He is excellently bred and knows everything expected of a prospective bridegroom of good family. The alliance has been largely negotiated by his parents, but he has been consulted, understands that Alienor is witty and beautiful, and he is wholly aware of the worldly advantages of being Conon's brother-in-law. At meals he and his beloved are allowed to sit together and above all to eat out of the same porringer, when he delicately leaves to his intended all the best morsels. He consults a competent jongleur, and with his aid produces suitable verses praising his fiancée's beauty. He gives her a gold ring with both his own name and hers engraved thereon. In return, besides a sleeve and a stocking to hang on his lances (gifts which she has already sent in mere friendship to other cavaliers), she bestows a lock of her hair set around a gold ring; likewise a larger lock which he may twine around his helmet. The happy pair are permitted to take long walks together, and to promenade up and down the garden, with Olivier holding his lady in the politest manner by one finger—the accepted method of showing intimacy.

We have said that Conon is resolved to knight his brother at the same time he gives his sister in marriage. This involves holding a tourney and many other proceedings really unnecessary for a wedding; but, of course, it will attract a much greater number of guests and advertise the prosperity of the baron of St. Aliquis to all northwestern France. The knighting and tourney will come after the bridal, however, and it is easier to explain the two things separately. We omit the gathering of the wedding guests—the coming of distant counts, barons, and sires; the erection around St. Aliquis of a real village of brilliant tents and pavilions; the ceremonious greetings; the frenzied efforts of the castle folk to make all ready; the inevitable despair, not once, but many times, of Adela, who directs everything.   At last it is the morning of *the* day, in midsummer.   No rain and, blessed be St. Martin, not too much heat.   Alienor is surrounded by a dozen women, old and young, arraying her for her wedding.

There is no regular bridal costume.   Alienor does not dress much differently from what she does on Easter or at some other major festival.   Her two great braids of hair are weighted down over her breasts with an extra intertwining with gold thread. Her pelisson is completely fringed with magnificent ermine, the gift of the Countess of Perseigne, and the garment itself is made of two cloths sewed together, the inner of fine wool, the outer of beautiful bendal of reddish violet.   The whole is laced tightly until Alienor can hardly breathe.   Above this garment floats the elegant bliaut, of green silk with long sleeves, many folds, and a long train.   There is more silk embroidery and elaborate flouncing.   Fairest of all is the girdle, made of many pieces of gold and each set with a good-luck stone—agate to guard against fever, sardonyx to protect against malaria, and many similar.   In the clasp are great sapphires which Baron Garnier originally "acquired" from a town merchant shortly before he hanged him. Finally, there is the mantle—again of silk intricately embroidered and dyed with a royal purple.

Alienor's pointed shoes are of vermillion leather from Cordova, with still more of gold-thread embroidery.   While one female minister is clasping these, her chief pucelle is putting on a small saffron-colored veil, circular, and held down by a golden circlet— a genuine crown; beautifully engraved and set with emeralds. Inevitably the whole process of dressing is prolonged.   Alienor is too excited to feel hot or pinched, but her attendants find her very exacting.   They bless the Virgin, however, that she is not as some noble brides, who fly into a passion if every hair in their eyebrows is not separately adjusted.

Meantime, in a secluded part of the castle, the groom has been wrestling with a similar problem, assisted by his two squires, although requiring less of time and agony. His legs are covered with fine brown silk stockings from Bruges; but it is effeminate to wear a silk shirt—one of fine white linen will answer. His pelisson is like his bride's, although less tightly laced—of cloth and silk, trimmed with rich fur; and the outer color is pale red, inevitably with much gold embroidery around the neck and sleeves. His bliaut does not come below his knees, but it is of blue sendal silk; his mantle is also edged with fur and of the same color as his pelisson. Simple as it is, it must hang exactly right. Everybody will ask, "Did the groom wear his mantle like a great baron?" The squires take a long time adjusting it. Olivier's shoes are of very fine leather. On his crisply curled hair they set a golden chaplet set with flashing gems—very much like that worn by his bride.

Hardly are the happy twain ready before the wedding procession forms in the bailey. So large a company could never crowd into the castle chapel. It will go across the bridge over the Claire to the parish church by the village—a Gothic structure sufficiently pretentious to suit the occasion. The Perseignes reckon a bishop among their cousins, and he is on hand to officiate.

So the procession forms. Ahead go a whole platoon of jongleurs puffing their cheeks for their flutes, twanging their harps, or rasping their viols. The Feudal Age delights in music, and does not mind if sometimes melody is exchanged merely for a joyous noise. Alienor comes next. She is on a black mule with extra long ears and a finely curried shining coat. His harness is of gold and his trappings of scarlet samite. She has been swung into the saddle by her eldest brother ("Alas! that her father, who should do this, is dead!" murmur all the women), and he as her guardian leads the mule. Olivier rides a tall white palfrey with a saddle of blue leather. His mother, Adela, and all the St. Aliquis and Perseignes female relatives follow on other mules, led by gayly dressed squires. Then come all the noble guests, the Duke of Quelqueparte at their head. No wonder there is no work being done in all the villages for miles around, and that all the villeins are lining the road, doffing caps, and cheering as the dazzling cortege sweeps past.

The details at the church we pass over. Among other features to be noted is the fact that the bride is swung down from her mule upon a great truss of straw, that the bishop meets them at the sacred portal, and that outside the actual building Olivier and Alienor exchange those vows which form the essential part of the marriage ceremony. After that Conon's chief provost recites in loud voice all the estates, horses, fine garments, and servitors which the bride brings as her dowry. This customary publication may avert bitter disputes later. Next the happy pair scatter newly coined silver deniers among the swarm of ill-favored mendicants permitted to elbow and scramble among the more pretentious guests.

Finally, the church is thrown open. The great nave opens mysterious and dark, but galaxies of candles are burning and the lofty stained-glass windows gleam like jewels. Olivier and Alienor occupy seats of honor in the choir, while the bishop says the very solemn mass of the Trinity and pronounces a special blessing over them. "Let this woman," intones the prelate, "be amiable as Rachel, wise as Rebecca, faithful as Sarah. Let her be sober through truth, venerable through modesty, and wise through the teaching of Heaven."

So at last the mass ends. The "Agnus Dei" is chanted. The bridegroom advances to the altar and receives from the bishop the kiss of peace. Then he turns, and right at the foot of the great crucifix embraces his wife and transmits the kiss to her. This act completes the ceremony. Away the whole company go from the church. They have been condemned to silence for nearly two hours, and are glad now to chatter like magpies. When back at St. Aliquis they find the great hall has been swept, garnished, and decorated as never before. The walls of the hall are hung with the pictured tapestries of beautiful pieces of red and green silk. Your feet crush fresh roses and lilies scattered on the floor. Alienor almost bursts with delight at the number of high-born cavaliers and dames who press up to kiss and congratulate. All the remainder of her life she will match weddings with her friends: "I had so many counts and barons at my wedding." "But I had so many!"

All these guests, however, expect to receive presents—bliauts, mantles, goblets, and other things, each suitable to the recipient. It is well that Conon has saved many livres in his strong box. The presenting of the gifts by the host is quite a ceremony; each article has to be accompanied by a well-turned speech. By the time this reception to the bride and groom is over, the trumpets sound furiously. They tell that the feast is ready in the fragrant garden under the trees. There is a fine tent of blue silk for the bridal party and the more exalted guests. All the others must sit on long tables open to the glad sunshine.

What Messire Conon's guests have to eat and drink is so serious a topic that we must tell thereof separately. We speak here merely concerning the festivities of the wedding. Olivier and Alienor are served by two barons as squires of state. The groom drinks from a great goblet, then sends it to his wife, who ceremoniously finishes the draught. In the bridal tent there is a reasonable amount of decorum, but elsewhere (Blessed martyrs!) what noise and tumult! All the villeins appear to be there, and burghers have even wandered up from Pontdebois. It will never do to have men say, "The bride was charming, but her brother stinted his hospitality." Enough food and drink is gorged and guzzled to stave off a famine next winter. The jongleurs keep quiet during the first part of the feast; later they earn their dinner by singing of the loves of Jourdain and Orabel or of Berte, who was the faithful wife of Girard of Roussillon through all of her lord's adversity. At many of the tables the jesting and horseplay become unspeakably ribald. After the wine circulates two petty nobles quarrel; one strikes the other with a drinking cup, but the sergeants pull them apart before they can whip out swords.

After three hours of this some guests are sleeping stertorously under the trees; but those nobles who have kept their wits go to another large tent, and, despite their heavy meal, dance with vigor. The bride and groom are expected to dance together, and everybody is prepared to admire the beauty of one and the grace and strength of the other. As evening advances a priest appears. He solemnly blesses the nuptial couch strewn with roses, while the new couple piously kneel. The couch is then "censed" like an altar, and the women guests join in the bizarre usages of "putting the bride to bed."

The morning after the marriage the newly wedded pair attend mass in the castle chapel. Here they are expected to make privately all kinds of vows of good conduct, and Alienor especially promises always to obey her husband, and call him dutifully, "mon sire" and "mon baron."

The festivities will last two weeks longer, and conclude with the dubbing of knights and the tournament, whereof more presently. After that Olivier and his wife will depart for their Burgundian castle without anything like a honeymoon to strange parts. . . .

A DAY IN AN OXFORD COLLEGE [1]

By John Corbin

When a freshman is once established in college, his life falls into a pleasantly varied routine. The day is ushered in by the scout, who bustles into the bedroom, throws aside the curtain, pours out the bath, and shouts, "Half past seven, sir," in a tone that makes it impossible to forget that chapel—or if one chooses, roll-call—comes at eight. Unless one keeps his six chapels or "rollers" a week, he is promptly "hauled" before the dean, who perhaps "gates" him. To be gated is to be forbidden to pass the college gate after dark, and fined a shilling for each night of confinement. To an American all this brings recollections of the paternal roof, where tardiness at breakfast meant, perhaps, the loss of dessert, and bedtime an hour earlier. I remember once, when out of training, deliberately cutting chapel to see with what mien the good dean performed his nursery duties. His calm was unruffled, his dignity unsullied. I soon came to find that the rules about rising were bowed to and indeed respected by all concerned even while they were broken. They are dis-

[1] From *An American at Oxford.* By kind permission of the author.

tinctly more lax than those the fellows have been accustomed to in the public schools, and they are conceded to be for the best welfare of the college.

Breakfast comes soon after chapel, or roll-call. If a man has "kept a dirty roller," that is, has reported in pyjamas, ulster, and boots, and has turned in again, the scout puts the breakfast before the fire on a trestle built of shovel, poker, and tongs, where it remains edible until noon. If a man has a breakfast party on, the scout makes sure that he is stirring in season, and, hurrying through the other rooms on the staircase, is presently on hand for as long as he may be wanted. The usual Oxford breakfast is a single course, which not infrequently consists of some one of the excellent English pork products, with an egg or kidneys. There may be two courses, in which case the first is of the no less excellent fresh fish. There are no vegetables. The breakfast is ended with toast and jam or marmalade. When one has fellows in to breakfast—and the Oxford custom of rooming alone instead of chumming makes such hospitality frequent— his usual meal is increased by a course, say, of chicken. In any case it leads to a morning cigarette, for tobacco aids digestion, and helps fill the hour or so after meals which an Englishman gives to relaxation.

At ten o'clock the breakfast may be interrupted for a moment by the exit of some one bent on attending a lecture, though one apologizes for such an act as if it were scarcely good form. An appointment with one's tutor is a more legitimate excuse for leaving; but even this is always an occasion for an apology, in behalf of the tutor of course, for one is certainly not himself responsible. If a quorum is left, they manage to sit comfortably by the fire, smoking and chatting in spite of lectures and tutors, until by mutual consent they scatter to glance at the *Times* and the *Sportsman* in the common-room, or even to get in a bit of reading.

Luncheon often consists of bread and cheese and jam from the buttery, with perhaps a half pint of bitter beer; but it may, like the breakfast, come from the college kitchen. In any case it is very light, for almost immediately after it everybody scatters to field and track and river for the exercise that the English climate makes necessary and the sport that the English temperament demands.

By four o'clock every one is back in college tubbed and dressed for tea, which a man serves himself in his rooms to as many fellows as he has been able to gather in on field or river. If he is eager to hear of the games he has not been able to witness, he goes to the junior common-room or to his club, where he is sure to find a dozen or so of kindred spirits representing every sport of importance. In this way he hears the minutest details of the games of the day from the players themselves; and before nightfall—such is the influence of tea—those bits of gossip which in America are known chiefly among members of a team have ramified the college. Thus the function of the "bleachers" on an American field is performed with a vengeance by the easy-chairs before a common-room fire; and a man had better be kicked off the team by an American captain than have his shortcomings served up with common-room tea.

The two hours between tea and dinner may be, and usually are, spent in reading.

At seven o'clock the college bell rings, and in two minutes the fellows have thrown on their gowns and are seated at table, where the scouts are in readiness to serve them. As a rule a man may sit wherever he chooses; this is one of the admirable arrangements for breaking up such cliques as inevitably form in a college. But in point of fact a man usually ends by sitting in some certain quarter of the hall, where from day to day he finds much the same set of fellows. Thus all the advantages of friendly inter-course are attained without any real exclusiveness. This may seem a small point; but an hour a day becomes an item in four years, especially if it is the hour when men are most disposed to be companionable.

In the evening, when the season permits, the fellows sit out of doors after dinner, smoking and playing bowls. There is no place in which Spring comes more sweetly than in an Oxford garden. The high walls are at once a trap for the first warm rays of the sun and a barrier against the winds of March. The daffodils and crocuses spring up with joy as the gardener bids; and the apple and cherry trees coddle against the warm north walls, spreading out their early buds gratefully to the mild English sun. For long, quiet hours after dinner they flaunt their beauty to the fellows smoking, and breathe their sweetness to the fellows playing bowls. "No man," exclaims the American visitor, "could live four years in those gardens of delight and not be made gentler and nobler!" Perhaps! though not altogether in the way the visitor imagines. When the flush of summer is on, the loiterers loll on the lawn full length; and as they watch the insects crawl among the grass they make bets on them, just as the gravest and most reverend seniors have been known to do in America.

In the windows overlooking the quadrangle are boxes of brilliant flowers, above which the smoke of a pipe comes curling out. At Harvard some fellows have geraniums in their windows, but only the very rich; and when they began the custom an ancient graduate wrote one of those communications to the *Crimson,* saying that if men put unmanly boxes of flowers in the window, how can they expect to beat Yale? Flower boxes, no sand. At Oxford they manage things so that anybody may have flower boxes; and their associations are by no means unmanly. This is the way they do it. In the early summer a gardener's wagon from the country draws up by the college gate, and the driver cries, "Flowers! Flowers for a pair of old bags, sir." *Bags* is of course the fitting term for English trousers—which don't fit; and I should like to inform that ancient graduate that the window boxes of Oxford suggest the very badge of manhood.

As long as the English twilight lingers, the men will sit and talk and sing to the mandolin; and I have heard of fellows sitting and talking all night, not turning in until the porter appeared to take their names at roll-call. On the eve of May day it is quite the custom to sit out, for at dawn one may go to see the pretty ceremony of heralding the May on Magdalen Tower. The Magdalen choir boys—the sweetest songsters in all Oxford —mount to the top of that most beautiful of Gothic towers, and, standing among the pinnacles—pinnacles afire with the spirituality of the Middle Ages, that warms all the senses with purity and beauty—those boys, I say, on that tower and among those pinnacles, open their mouths and sing a Latin song to greet the May. Meantime, the fellows who have come out to listen in the street below make catcalls and blow fish horns. The song above is the survival of a Romish, perhaps a Druidical, custom; the racket below is the survival of a Puritan protest. That is Oxford in symbol! Its dignity and mellowness are not so much a matter of flowering gardens and crumbling walls as of the traditions of the centuries in which the whole life of the place has deep sources; and the noblest of its institutions are fringed with survivals that run riot in the grotesque.

If a man intends to spend the evening out of college, he has to make a dash before nine o'clock; for love or for money the porter may not let an inmate out after nine. One man I knew was able to escape by guile. He had a brother in Trinity whom he very much resembled, and whenever he wanted to go out, he would tilt his mortarboard forward, wrap his gown high about his neck, as it is usually worn of an evening, and bidding the porter a polite good-night, say, "Charge me to my brother, Hancock, if you please." The charge is the inconsiderable sum of one penny, and is the penalty of having a late guest. Having profited by my experience with the similar charge for keeping my name on the college books, I never asked its why and wherefore. Both are no doubt survivals of some medieval custom, the authority of which no college employee—or don, for the matter of that —would question. Such matters interest the Oxford man quite as little as the question how he comes by a tonsil or a vermiform appendix. They are there, and he makes the best of them.

If a fellow leaves college for an evening, it is for a foregathering at some other college, or to go to the theatre. As a rule he wears a cloth cap. A "billy-cock" or "bowler," as the pot hat is called, is as thoroughly frowned on now in English colleges as it was with us a dozen years ago. As for the mortarboard and gown, undergraduate opinion rather requires that they be left behind. This is largely, no doubt, because they are required by law to be worn. So far as the undergraduates are concerned, every operative statute of the university, with the exception of those relating to matriculation and graduation, refers to conduct in the streets after nightfall, and almost without exception they are honored in the breach. This is out of disregard for the Vice-Chancellor of the university, who is familiarly called the Vice, because he serves as a warning to others for the practice of virtue. The Vice makes his power felt in characteristically dark and tortuous ways. His factors are two proctors, college dons in daytime but skulkers after nightfall, each of whom has his bull-dogs, that is, scouts, employed literally to spy upon the students. If these catch you without cap or gown, they cause you to be proctorized or "progged," as it is called, which involves a matter of five shillings or so. As a rule there is little danger of progging, but my first term fell in evil days. For some reason or other the chest of the university showed a deficit of sundry pounds, shillings and pence; and as it had long ceased to need or receive regular bequests—the finance of the institution being in the hands of the colleges—a crisis was at hand. A more serious problem had doubtless never arisen since the great question was solved of keeping undergraduates' names on the books. The expedient of the Vice-Chancellor was to summon the proctors, and bid them charge their bulldogs to prog all freshmen caught at night without cap and gown. The deficit in the university chest was made up at five shillings a head.

One of the Vice-Chancellor's rules is that no undergraduate shall enter an Oxford "pub." Now the only restaurant in town, Queen's, is run in conjunction with a pub, and was once the favorite resort of all who were bent on breaking the monotony of an English Sunday. The Vice-Chancellor resolved to destroy this den of Sabbath breaking, and the undergraduates resolved no less firmly to defend their stronghold. The result was a hand-to-hand fight with the bulldogs, which ended so triumphantly for the undergraduates that a dozen or more of them were sent down. In the articles of the peace that followed, it was stipulated, I was told, that so long as the restaurant was closed Sunday afternoons and nights, it should never suffer from the visit of proctor or bulldog. As a result, Queen's is a great scene of undergraduate foregatherings. The dinners are good enough and reasonably cheap; and as most excellent champagne is to be had at twelve shillings the bottle, the diners are not unlikely to get back to college a trifle buffy, in the Oxford phrase.

By an interesting survival of medieval custom, the Vice-Chancellor has supreme power over the morals of the town, and any citizen who transgresses his laws is visited with summary punishment. For a tradesman or publican to assist in breaking university rules means outlawry and ruin, and for certain offenses a citizen may be punished by imprisonment. Over the Oxford theatre the Vice-Chancellor's power is absolute. In my time he was much more solicitous that the undergraduate be kept from knowledge of the omnipresent woman with a past than that dramatic art should flourish, and forbade the town to more than one excellent play of the modern school of comedy that had been seen and discussed in London by the younger sisters of the undergraduates. The woman with a present is virtually absent.

Time was when no Oxford play was quite successful unless the undergraduates assisted at its first night, though in a way very different from that which the term denotes in France. The assistance was of the kind so generously rendered in New York and Boston on the evening of an athletic contest. Even to-day, just for tradition's sake, the undergraduates sometimes make a row. A lot of B. N. C. men, as the clanny sons of Brazenose College call themselves, may insist that an opera stop while the troupe listen to one of their own excellent vocal performances; and I once saw a great sprinter, not unknown to Yale men, rise from his seat, face the audience, and, pointing with his thumb over his shoulder at the soubrette, announce impressively, "Do you know, I rather *like* that girl!" The show is usually over just before eleven, and then occurs an amusing, if unseemly, scramble to get back to college before the hour strikes. A man who stays out after ten is fined threepence, after eleven the fine is sixpence. When all is said, why shouldn't one sprint for threepence?

If you stay out of college after midnight, the dean makes a star chamber offense of it, fines you a "quid" or two, and like as not sends you down. This sounds a trifle worse than it is; for if you must be away, your absence can usually be arranged for. If you find yourself in the streets after twelve, you may rap on some friend's bedroom window and tell him of your plight through the iron grating. He will then spend the first half of the night in your bed and wash his hands in your bowl. With such evidence as this to support him, the scout is not apt, if sufficiently retained, to report a suspected absence. I have even known fellows to make their arrangements in advance and spend the night in town; but the ruse has its dangers, and the penalty is to be sent down for good and all.

It is owing to such regulations as these that life in the English college has the name of being cloistral. Just how cloistral it is in spirit no one can know who has not taken part in a rag in the quad; and this is impossible to an outsider, for at midnight all visitors are required to leave, under a heavy penalty to their host.

The Making of a Bibliography

Whenever you find a book or an article which you think will be of help to you in the writing of a theme on an occasion or situation (or, as a matter of fact, any other theme) you should at once make a note of it. The ideal way to do this is to write each title on a card of its own. When you have completed your theme, copy your bibliography thus collected on sheets of paper and place it at the end of your manuscript. The following suggestions and examples will be of indispensable help to you:[1]

A. Arrangement of entries in the bibliography should always be alphabetically by the name of the author: surname, followed by given name. For proper forms for anonymous authors, for authors working in collaboration, and for editors, see examples below.

B. Where the books fall into distinct classes, there should be additional main divisions of the bibliography, each a complete, alphabetical bibliography, which should comprise the books of a single class. Thus, in a bibliography of a theme on Peter the Great, there might profitably be two divisions, the first to contain general histories of Russia, the second to contain biographies of Peter the Great himself.

C. Entries should include:

1. Name of author (see under A above), title of book, place of publication, name of publisher (the name of the publisher may be omitted), date of publication.

2. When the book is a general reference work, like the *Cambridge Modern History* or the *Encyclopedia Britan-*

---

[1] These suggestions and examples are taken from *Instructions to Students in Freshman English*, compiled by the English Department of the University of Minnesota and reprinted by permission of that Department.

nica, the title of the separate article and the name of the writer of that article, volume and page number.

3. When the entry concerns a magazine article, the name of the author, the title, the name of the magazine, the day and month of publication (optional), the year of publication, the volume number, the page number.

Examples for Bibliography

1. Separate books:

    Burr, Anna Robeson, *The Autobiography.* Boston, Houghton Mifflin Company (The name of the publisher may be omitted), 1909.

2. Works of general reference:

    Watts-Dunton, Theodore, *Poetry.* In *Encyclopedia Britannica* (Eleventh edition), 21: 877-890.

3. Essays. Single author:

    Emerson, Ralph Waldo, *The American Scholar.* In Emerson, R. W., *Nature Addresses and Lectures.* Boston, Houghton Mifflin Company, 1884, pp. 8-115.

4. Essays. Composite collections:

    De Quincey, Thomas, *Style.* In Brewster, William T., *Representative Essays on the Theory of Style.* New York, Macmillan, 1905, pp. 27-166.

5. Collaboration. When the work is one of collaboration between two authors, enter thus:

    Barnes, H. E., and Milner, B. A., *Selected Cases in Constitutional Law.* Philadelphia, Lyon and Armor, 1915.

    If by more than two authors, thus:

    Besant, A., *Industry under Socialism.* In Shaw, G. B. and others, *Fabian Essays in Socialism.* New York, Humbold Publishing Company, 1891, pp. 150-169.

6. United States documents:

    In referring to United States government documents give subject, Congress number, session number, House or Senate document, with number and volume, e.g.

    Desertion, Navy. 60 Congress, 2 Session. Senate Document 708, vol. 21.

7. In entering a book, the author of which is anonymous, form
   1 may be followed exactly with the exception, of course, that
   no author's name will be given, e.g.

   > *The Book of Peace;* A collection of essays on war and
   > peace. Boston, G. Beckwith, 1845.

8. Magazine articles:

   > Kipling, Rudyard, "Swept and Garnished." In *The Cen-*
   > *tury,* 89: 363-369. January, 1915.

The Use of Footnotes

Footnotes should be placed at the bottom of the page and not
at the conclusion of the theme. They should be numbered 1, 2,
3, 4, etc., and not indicated by Roman numerals or by asterisks.
They should be placed at the right of and a little above the text
of the passages to which they refer. They should be numbered
consecutively on each page, but not consecutively throughout the
theme, so that additional footnotes may be inserted on a given
page if necessary without renumbering. The first reference to a
work should contain full information in the footnote, i.e., author's
surname with initials, title of work underscored, place of publication or name of publisher, volume and page numbers. For
example:

> Lucas, E. V., *The Life of Charles Lamb,* G. P. Putnam's Sons,
> Vol. I, pp. 11-13.

If two references to the same work occur consecutively on the
same page the abbreviation *ibid.* may be used for author and title.
For example:

> *Ibid.,* Vol. II, p. 130.

If the author and book are very well known, it is sufficient to
give only the author's surname. For example:

> Shakespeare's *Julius Cæsar,* Act II, Sc. 1.

The student will find examples of footnotes on various pages of
this book.

EXERCISES

1. Can you think of any centralizing device for use in a theme on an occasion or situation which would prove as clear as the chronological method and more interesting?

2. Find specific instances in "A Day in an Oxford College" of the adaptation of the style to the mood of the writer.

3. Develop a theme on "A Day in (your own) University (or College)" following as nearly as possible Mr. Corbin's plan. Since your effect will probably be humorous anyway, you might try through contrast to heighten the humor.

4. What stories are suggested by Mr. Davis's brief references to Alienor's cousin Mabila, to "old St. Saturnin," to the squire William, to the town merchant who was hanged, to Alienor's dead father? Do these detract from or add to the business at hand?

5. Is detail overdone, do you think, in "A Medieval Wedding"? Does the author expect it to stand out minutely or does he use it for a general effect? What *is* the "general effect" of his sketch?

6. Read Steele's *A Day in London*. Using his plan and style as nearly as possible, write a sketch on "A Day on ———— Campus."

7. Read Leland Hall's "Salt Comes to Timbuctoo" in *Harper's Magazine* for February 1927. What means does he use for clearness in exposition? What for artistic effect?

SUGGESTED READINGS

Of a Mechanism:

"The Electric Burglar-Alarm," *Popular Science Monthly*, Vol. 18.

Eberle, Louise, "On the Making of Bronzes," *Scribner's Magazine*, February 1922. "The Sculptor at His Work," *Scribner's Magazine*, April 1923.

Husband, Joseph, "America at Work," Houghton Mifflin, Boston. "The Making of Mine Helmets" from *A Year in a Coal Mine*, Houghton Mifflin, Boston.

Pound, Arthur, *The Iron Man*, Little, Brown, Boston.

Thorndike, Ashley H., *The Physical Stage from Shakespeare's Theatre*, Chapter X, Macmillan, New York.

Of a Process:

Davis, William Stearns, "Dubbing a Knight," Chapter XII, from *Life on a Medieval Barony*, Harper's, New York.

Flandrau, C. M., "The Preparation of Coffee" from *Viva Mexico*, D. Appleton, New York.

Jordan, David Starr, "The Story of a Salmon" from *Science Sketches*, A. C. McClurg, Chicago.

Mills, Enos, "The Story of a Thousand Year Old Pine," Houghton Mifflin, Boston.

Moffett, Cleveland, "How to Make a Scientific Kite," *McClure's Magazine*, Vol. 6.

Peattie, Roderick, "Hunting Oil in Oklahoma," *The Atlantic Monthly*, May 1922.

Power, Eileen, "The Education of the Nuns," Chapter VI, from *Medieval English Nunneries*, Cambridge University Press, Cambridge, England.

Ward, Henshaw, "The Ways of the Weevil," *Harper's Magazine*, November 1925.

White, Stewart Edward, "Open-Water Canoeing" from *The Forest*, Doubleday, Doran, New York. "Lumbering in the Early '80's" from *The Blazed Trail*, Doubleday, Doran, New York.

Of an Occasion or a Situation:

Boswell, James, "The Shakespeare Jubilee at Stratford-on-Avon, 1719," from *The London Magazine*, 1769. Also reprinted in George, M.D., *England in Johnson's Day*, Harcourt, Brace, New York.

Botsford, G. W., "The Private and Social Life of the Romans," Chapter XV, from *The History of Rome*, Macmillan, New York.

Corbin, John, "The Oxford Freshman" from *An American at Oxford*, Houghton Mifflin, Boston.

Davis, William Stearns, "The Life of the Women," Chapter V, from *Life on a Medieval Barony*, Harper's, New York.

Frisbie, Robert Dean, "At Home in Puka-Puka," *The Atlantic Monthly*, July 1928.

Hall, Leland, "Salt Comes to Timbuctoo," *Harper's Magazine*, February 1927.

Jusserand, J. J., "Minstrels," pp. 194-217, from *Wayfaring Life in the Middle Ages*, T. Fisher Unwin, Ltd., London.

Polo, Marco, "How the Emperor Goes on a Hunting Expedition," Chapter XX, from *Travels*, Book II, Macmillan, New York.

Power, Eileen, "The Great Fair of St. Denys," pp. 21-23, from *Medieval People*, Methuen, London.

Sedgwick, Henry Dwight, "Manners and Customs," Chapter XI, from *Italy in the Thirteenth Century*, Vol. II, Houghton Mifflin, Boston.

Shaler, N. S., "Life at Harvard University in the Early Sixties," Houghton Mifflin, Boston.

Steele, Richard, "A Day in London" from *The Spectator*, No. 454. Also reprinted in George, M.D., *England in Johnson's Day*, Harcourt, Brace, New York.

CHAPTER II

THE DEFINITION

Years ago, when elementary and grammar schools were more rigid and less social organizations, we used to recite our geography lessons by the aid of a wall map and the teacher's pointer. "Bound Indiana," she would say, and we would bound it. That is, we would *shut it in* within Lake Michigan and Michigan on the north, Ohio on the east, the Ohio river on the south, and Illinois on the west. These boundaries set a definite limit to the extent of Indiana, in other words they *defined* it.

Now the definition of anything, from crop rotation to a Unitarian, consists in exactly the same process as the bounding of Indiana. The thing the writer really does is to set bounds to the subject or the object in question, that is, to limit it, to shut it off, to show its extent. How does he do this? In the first place, he discovers and states the class or the group to which the object of his definition belongs. In the second place, he tries to discover and to state the distinguishing features, attributes, and qualities which make that object *different* from the other members of the same class. In this way he limits and bounds his object from others similar and yet distinct and different, just as in school we used to limit and bound Indiana by setting it apart from Ohio and Illinois.

To illustrate: In Mr. Whipple's definition of wit and humor he begins by suggesting the class to which both wit and humor belong. Both are intellectual powers. But wit, he contends, has to do with the marrying of widely separated ideas "by a sudden jerk of the understanding" whereas humor "is the very juice of the mind—encircling and fertilizing wherever it falls." Once having established the large difference between the two, he proceeds with his definition by an analysis of each arranged by juxtaposition and dealt with by contrast. His closing sentence brings the two together in a suggestion of the result of their commingling in especially fortunate human nature.

Nor is Charles S. Brooks's delightfully informal way of considering the difference between the two really a departure from the definition. If you will compare the two selections carefully, you will discover that both authors have said virtually the same things, have suggested the identical differences between wit and humor. One has written objectively; the other has chatted informally and personally. But the result is the same, and both have been included here so that both methods may have equal chance as suggestions to the student who wants to know how to go about it.

In the same way John Dewey in the first paragraph of "What is Thought" defines his term, *thought*, by restricting and limiting it to four kinds of mental processes. After having done this, that is, having established by restriction and exclusion the class or group to which the term belongs, he proceeds to define in turn each of the four kinds in its relation to true reflective thought, the only kind "truly educative in value." The careful reader will note that in each of the four definitions the method is the same; that is, he defines by limiting and restricting his term in comparison with reflective thought.

Again, in a fourth example, Brander Matthews first defines *Americanism* as a word among many words in common circulation. Then he continues and amplifies his definition by the familiar method of restriction and limitation. Americanism, he says, is not simply another word for patriotism; it is something more than that. Nor is it "Jingoism" or "Spread-Eagleism." Those are too small words to be confused with real Americanism. Thus by comparison and contrast with other words belonging to the same general class he makes clear to us what his high conception of Americanism is.

The writing of good definition is as interesting as it is difficult. Its range, you will readily perceive, is very wide, extending from an attempt to define a purely concrete thing like the Statue of

Liberty to a purely abstract quality like *patriotism* or like *honor*. But the process remains the same whether the object or term to be defined is concrete or abstract. The Statue of Liberty is a monument, but it differs from others of its class in many ways; patriotism is a quality or attribute of the human mind and soul, but it is distinct from other similar qualities or attributes by virtue of certain characteristics of its own. Nor does the fact that the subject for definition is concrete rather than abstract remove difficulties of any moment from the writer; in fact, the identical cautions remain the same for both kinds of subjects:

First, *you must be sure you are defining and not merely "talking about" the subject.* Interesting comment is not definition. Second, *you must use the simplest and most familiar diction possible, especially if your definition is of the more formal sort.* Third, *by careful study of the various methods of definition,* you must try to select the best one for the defining of your own subject.

Of these various methods the clearest and most helpful for the writer new at definition are: *elimination, division, comparison and contrast,* and *illustration.*

The first, *elimination,* means simply the method of defining a thing by telling *what it is not,* by eliminating all things with which it might be confused. For example, suppose you were attempting to define *charm,* an abstract quality, by this method. You would begin by summoning in your mind all those qualities which are in some especial way, let us say, in their power to attract, often confused with charm. Charm is not *fascination.* Why? It is not *infatuation.* Why? It is not *hypnotism.* Why? Finally, having eliminated with good reasons these and all other erroneous interpretations of charm, you finally lead your reader to an understanding of what charm, at least in your opinion, really is.

The second, *division,* means simply dividing the subject into its features or qualities. One attempting this method must guard against incompleteness. The subject and its attributes must be exhausted before the definition may be considered complete.

Division is Mr. Matthews' method in "Americanism," and a study of his use of it is better than further precept.

The third, *comparison and contrast,* is especially valuable in the attempt to define two closely related terms. It is an enthusiastic and a lively method because of the balanced sentences which it often so well employs. Mr. Whipple's "Wit and Humor" is a perfect example of it at its best.

The fourth, *illustration,* is an easy and a natural method. It consists simply in giving examples or illustrations of the thing being defined. The concreteness of the example often makes the definition stand out clearly by affording vivid details. The only danger in using it is that one is likely to fall back on it as the easiest method of definition. For example, if one is defining *tenacity,* he is literally besieged by illustrations from Demosthenes to Robert Bruce and from Francis Parkman to Alfred E. Smith. There is danger not only in using so many illustrations that the writer defeats his own ends, but also in shirking the more difficult task of explaining the subject without such easy help.

Another serious problem in the definition theme is that of length. It may be a full length theme in which the subject defined is amplified by various methods or by one method stretched to its utmost. Or it may be a paragraph theme, like Mr. Whipple's "Wit and Humor," developed by concentrating on the main features of the subject defined and relying for greater effect upon its wise selection and presentation. The selections that follow give ample suggestions for the theme of full length. It may not come amiss to include here within the text another especially good paragraph of definition for those who are interested in the paragraph theme:

The quack novel is a thing which looks like a book, and which is compounded, advertised, and marketed in precisely the same fashion as Castoria, Wine of Cardui, Alcola, Mrs. Summer's free-to-you-my-sister Harmless Headache Remedy, Viavi Tablets, and other patent medicines, harmful and harmless. As the patent medicine is made of perfectly well-known drugs, so the quack novel of course contains perfectly familiar elements, and like the medicine, it comes wrapped in superlative testimonials from those who say they have swallowed it to their advantage. Instead of "After twenty years of bed-ridden agony, one bottle of your Fosforo cured every ache and completely restored my manhood," we have "The secret of his powers is the same God-given secret that inspired Shakespeare and upheld Dickens." This, from the Philadelphia *Sunday Dispatch,* accompanies a quack novel by Mr. Harold Bell Wright, of whom the Portland, Oregon, *Journal* remarks, "It is this almost clairvoyant power of reading the human soul that has made Mr. Wright's books among the most remarkable works of the present age." Similar to that aroma of piety and charity which accompanies the quack medicines, an equally perceptible odor of sanctity is wafted to us with Mr. Wright; and just as imitators will make their boxes and bottles to resemble those of an already successful trade article, so are Mr. Wright's volumes given that red cloth and gold lettering which we have come to associate with the bindings of Mr. Winston Churchill's very popular and agreeable novels. Lastly—like the quack medicines—the quack novel is (mostly) harmful; not always because it is poisonous (though this occurs), but because it pretends to be literature and is taken for literature by the millions who swallow it year after year as their chief mental nourishment, and whose brains it saps and dilutes. In short, both these shams—the book and the medicine—win and bamboozle their public through methods almost identical.[1]

WIT AND HUMOR [2]

By E. P. Whipple

Wit was originally a general name for all the intellectual powers, meaning the faculty which kens, perceives, knows, understands; it was gradually narrowed in its significance to express merely the resemblance between ideas; and lastly to note that resemblance when it occasioned ludicrous surprise. It marries ideas, lying wide apart, by a sudden jerk of the understanding. Humor originally meant moisture, a signification it metaphorically re-

[1] From *Quack Novels and Democracy* by Owen Wister. By permission of The Atlantic Monthly Company.
[2] From *Literature and Life.* By permission of and by arrangement with Houghton Mifflin Company, the authorized publishers.

tains, for it is the very juice of the mind, oozing from the brain, and enriching and fertilizing wherever it falls. Wit exists by antipathy; Humor by sympathy. Wit laughs *at* things; Humor laughs *with* them. Wit lashes external appearances, or cunningly exaggerates single foibles into character; Humor glides into the heart of its object, looks lovingly on the infirmities it detects, and represents the whole man. Wit is abrupt, darting, scornful, and tosses its analogies in your face; Humor is slow and shy, insinuating its fun into your heart. Wit is negative, analytical, destructive; Humor is creative. The couplets of Pope are witty, but Sancho Panza is a humorous creation. Wit, when earnest, has the earnestness of passion, seeking to destroy; Humor has the earnestness of affection, and would lift up what is seemingly low into our charity and love. Wit, bright, rapid, and blasting as the lightning, flashes, strikes, and vanishes, in an instant; Humor, warm and all-embracing as the sunshine, bathes its objects in a genial and abiding light. Wit implies hatred or contempt of folly and crime, produces its effects by brisk shocks of surprise, uses the whip of scorpions, and the branding-iron, stabs, stings, pinches, tortures, goads, teases, corrodes, undermines; Humor implies a sure conception of the beautiful, the majestic, and the true, by whose light it surveys and shapes their opposites. It is an humane influence, softening with mirth the ragged inequalities of existence, promoting tolerant views of life, bridging over the spaces which separate the lofty from the lowly, the great from the humble. Old Dr. Fuller's remark, that a negro is "the image of God cut in ebony," is humorous; Horace Smith's inversion of it, that the task-master is "the image of the devil cut in ivory," is witty. Wit can co-exist with fierce and malignant passions; but Humor demands good feeling and fellow-feeling, feeling not merely for what is above us, but for what is around and beneath us. When Wit and Humor are commingled, the result is a genial sharpness, dealing with its objects somewhat as old Izaak Walton dealt with the frog he used for bait,—running the hook neatly through his mouth and out at his gills, and in so doing "using him as though he loved him!" Sidney Smith and Shakespeare's Touchstone are examples.

On the Difference Between Wit and Humor [1]

By Charles S. Brooks

I am not sure that I can draw an exact line between wit and humor. Perhaps the distinction is so subtle that only those persons can decide who have long white beards. But even an ignorant man, so long as he is clear of Bedlam, may have an opinion.

I am quite positive that of the two, humor is the more comfortable and more livable quality. Humorous persons, if their gift is genuine and not a mere shine upon the surface, are always agreeable companions and they sit through the evening best. They have pleasant mouths turned up at the corners. To these corners the great Master of marionettes has fixed the strings and he holds them in his nimblest fingers to twitch them at the slightest jest. But the mouth of a merely witty man is hard and sour until the moment of its discharge. Nor is the flash from a witty man always comforting, whereas a humorous man radiates a general pleasure and is like another candle in the room.

I admire wit, but I have no real liking for it. It has been too often employed against me, whereas humor is always an ally. It never points an impertinent finger into my defects. Humorous persons do not sit like explosives on a fuse. They are safe and easy comrades. But a wit's tongue is as sharp as a donkey driver's stick. I may gallop the faster for its prodding, yet the touch behind is too persuasive for any comfort.

Wit is a lean creature with sharp inquiring nose, whereas humor has a kindly eye and comfortable girth. Wit, if it be necessary, uses malice to score a point—like a cat it is quick to jump—but humor keeps the peace in an easy chair. Wit has a better voice in a solo, but humor comes into the chorus best. Wit is as sharp as a stroke of lightning, whereas humor is diffuse like sunlight. Wit keeps the season's fashions and is precise in the phrases and judgments of the day, but humor is concerned

[1] From *Chimney-Pot Papers*. By permission of the Yale University Press.

with homely eternal things. Wit wears silk, but humor in home-
spun endures the wind. Wit sets a snare, whereas humor goes off
whistling without a victim in its mind. Wit is sharper company
at table, but humor serves better in mischance and in the rain.
When it tumbles wit is sour, but humor goes uncomplaining without its dinner. Humor laughs at another's jest and holds its
sides, while wit sits wrapped in study for a lively answer. But
it is a workaday world in which we live, where we get mud upon
our boots and come weary to the twilight—it is a world that
grieves and suffers from many wounds in these years of war: and
therefore as I think of my acquaintance, it is those who are
humorous in its best and truest meaning rather than those who
are witty who give the more profitable companionship.

And then, also, there is wit that is not wit. As some one has
written:

> Nor ever noise for wit on me could pass,
> When thro' the braying I discern'd the ass.

I sat lately at dinner with a notoriously witty person (a really
witty man) whom our hostess had introduced to provide the
entertainment. I had read many of his reviews of books and
plays, and while I confess their wit and brilliancy, I had thought
them to be hard and intellectual and lacking in all that broader
base of humor which aims at truth. His writing—catching the
bad habit of the time—is too ready to proclaim a paradox and
to assert the unusual, to throw aside in contempt the valuable
haystack in a fine search for a paltry needle. His reviews are
seldom right—as most of us see the right—but they sparkle and
hold one's interest for their perversity and unexpected turns.

In conversation I found him much as I had found him in his
writing—although, strictly speaking, it was not a conversation,
which requires an interchange of word and idea and is turn
about. A conversation should not be a market where one sells
and another buys. Rather, it should be a bargaining back and
forth, and each person should be both merchant and buyer. My
rubber plant for your victrola, each offering what he has and

seeking his deficiency. It was my friend B—— who fairly put the case when he said that he liked so much to talk that he was willing to pay for his audience by listening in his turn.

But this was a speech and a lecture. He loosed on us from the cold spigot of his intellect a steady flow of literary allusion —a practice which he professes to hold in scorn—and wit and epigram. He seemed torn from the page of Meredith. He talked like ink. I had believed before that only people in books could talk as he did, and then only when their author had blotted and scratched their performance for a seventh time before he sent it to the printer. To me it was an entirely new experience, for my usual acquaintances are good common honest daytime woollen folk and they seldom average better than one bright thing in an evening.

At first I feared that there might be a break in his flow of speech which I should be obliged to fill. Once, when there was a slight pause—a truffle was engaging him—I launched a frail remark; but it was swept off at once in the renewed torrent. And seriously it does not seem fair. If one speaker insists—to change the figure—on laying all the cobbles of a conversation, he should at least allow another to carry the tarpot and fill in the chinks. When the evening was over, although I recalled two or three clever stories, which I shall botch in the telling, I came away tired and dissatisfied, my tongue dry with disuse.

Now I would not seek that kind of man as a companion with whom to be becalmed in a sailboat, and I would not wish to go to the country with him, least of all to the North Woods or any place outside of civilization. I am sure that he would sulk if he were deprived of an audience. He would be crotchety at breakfast across his bacon. Certainly for the woods a humorous man is better company, for his humor in mischance comforts both him and you. A humorous man—and here lies the heart of the matter—a humorous man has the high gift of regarding an annoyance in the very stroke of it as another man shall regard it when the annoyance is long past. If a humorous person falls out of a canoe he knows the exquisite jest while his head is still bobbing in the cold water. A witty man, on the contrary, is sour until he is changed and dry: but in a week's time when company is about, he will make a comic story of it.

My friend A—— with whom I went once into the Canadian woods has genuine humor, and no one can be a more satisfactory comrade. I do not recall that he said many comic things, and at bottom he was serious as the best humorists are. But in him there was a kind of joy and exaltation that lasted throughout the day. If the duffle were piled too high and fell about his ears, if the dinner was burned or the tent blew down in a driving storm at night, he met these mishaps as though they were the very things he had come north to get, as though without them the trip would have lacked its spice. This is an easy philosophy in retrospect but hard when the wet canvas falls across you and the rain beats in. A—— laughed at the very moment of disaster as another man will laugh later in an easy chair. I see him now swinging his axe for firewood to dry ourselves when we were spilled in a rapids; and again, while pitching our tent on a sandy beach when another storm had drowned us. And there is a certain cry of his (dully, *Wow!* on paper) expressive to the initiated of all things gay, which could never issue from the mouth of a merely witty man.

Real humor is primarily human—or divine, to be exact—and after that the fun may follow naturally in its order. Not long ago I saw Louis Jouvet of the French Company play Sir Andrew Ague-Cheek. It was a most humorous performance of the part, and the reason is that the actor made no primary effort to be funny. It was the humanity of his playing, making his audience love him first of all, that provoked the comedy. His long thin legs were comical and so was his drawling talk, but the very heart and essence was this love he started in his audience. Poor fellow! how delightfully he smoothed the feathers in his hat! How he feared to fight the duel! It was easy to love such a dear silly human fellow. A merely witty player might have drawn as many laughs, but there would not have been the catching at the heart.

As for books and the wit or humor of their pages, it appears that wit fades, whereas humor lasts. Humor uses permanent nutgalls. But is there anything more melancholy than the wit of another generation? In the first place, this wit is intertwined with forgotten circumstance. It hangs on a fashion—on the style of a coat. It arose from a forgotten bit of gossip. In the play of words the sources of the pun are lost. It is like a local jest in a narrow coterie, barren to an outsider. Sydney Smith was the most celebrated wit of his day, but he is dull reading now. Blackwood's at its first issue was a witty daring sheet, but for us the pages are stagnant. I suppose that no one now laughs at the witticisms of Thomas Hood. Where are the wits of yesteryear? Yet the humor of Falstaff and Lamb and Fielding remains and is a reminder to us that humor, to be real, must be founded on humanity and on truth.

WHAT IS THOUGHT? [1]

By John Dewey

No words are oftener on our lips than *thinking* and *thought*. So profuse and varied, indeed, is our use of these words that it is not easy to define just what we mean by them. The aim of this chapter is to find a single consistent meaning. Assistance may be had by considering some typical ways in which the terms are employed. In the first place *thought* is used broadly, not to say loosely. Everything that comes to mind, that "goes through our heads," is called a thought. To think of a thing is just to be conscious of it in any way whatsoever. Second, the term is restricted by excluding whatever is directly presented; we think (or think of) only such things as we do not directly see, hear, smell, or taste. Then, third, the meaning is further limited to beliefs that rest upon some kind of evidence or testimony. Of this third type, two kinds—or, rather, two degrees—must be discriminated. In some cases, a belief is accepted with slight or almost no attempt to state the grounds that support it. In other cases, the ground or basis for a belief is deliberately sought and its adequacy to support the belief examined. This process

[1] From *How We Think.* By permission of D. C. Heath and Company.

is called reflective thought; it alone is truly educative in value, and it forms, accordingly, the principal subject of this volume. We shall now briefly describe each of the four senses.

I. In its loosest sense, thinking signifies everything that, as we say, is "in our heads" or that "goes through our minds." He who offers "a penny for your thoughts" does not expect to drive any great bargain. In calling the object of his demand *thoughts*, he does not intend to ascribe to them dignity, consecutiveness, or truth. Any idle fancy, trivial recollection, or flitting impression will satisfy his demand. Daydreaming, building of castles in the air, that loose flux of casual and disconnected material that floats through our minds in relaxed moments are, in this random sense, *thinking*. More of our waking life than we should care to admit, even to ourselves, is likely to be whiled away in this inconsequential trifling with idle fancy and unsubstantial hope.

In this sense, silly folk and dullards *think*. The story is told of a man in slight repute for intelligence, who, desiring to be chosen selectman in his New England town, addressed a knot of neighbors in this wise: "I hear you don't believe I know enough to hold office. I wish you to understand that I am thinking about something or other most of the time." Now reflective thought is like this random coursing of things through the mind in that it consists of a succession of things thought of; but it is unlike, in that the mere chance occurrence of any chance "something or other" in an irregular sequence does not suffice. Reflection involves not simply a sequence of ideas, but a *con*sequence—a consecutive ordering in such a way that each determines the next as its proper outcome, while each in turn leans back on its predecessors. The successive portions of the reflective thought grow out of one another and support one another; they do not come and go in a medley. Each phase is a step from something to something—technically speaking, it is a term of thought. Each term leaves a deposit which is utilized in the next term. The stream or flow becomes a train, chain, or thread.

II. Even when thinking is used in a broad sense, it is usually restricted to matters not directly perceived: to what we do not see, smell, hear, or touch. We ask the man telling a story if he saw a certain incident happen, and his reply may be, "No, I only thought of it." A note of invention, as distinct from faithful record of observation, is present. Most important in this class are successions of imaginative incidents and episodes which, having a certain coherence, hanging together on a continuous thread, lie between kaleidoscopic flights of fancy and considerations deliberately employed to establish a conclusion. The imaginative stories poured forth by children possess all degrees of internal congruity; some are disjointed, some are articulated. When connected, they simulate reflective thought; indeed, they usually occur in minds of logical capacity. These imaginative enterprises often precede thinking of the close-knit type and prepare the way for it. But *they do not aim at knowledge, at belief about facts or in truths;* and thereby they are marked off from reflective thought even when they most resemble it. Those who express such thoughts do not expect credence, but rather credit for a well-constructed plot or a well-arranged climax. They produce good stories, not—unless by chance—knowledge. Such thoughts are an efflorescence of feeling; the enhancement of a mood or sentiment is their aim; congruity of emotion, their binding tie.

III. In its next sense, thought denotes belief resting upon some basis; that is, real or supposed knowledge going beyond what is directly present. It is marked by *acceptance or rejection of something as reasonably probable or improbable.* This phase of thought, however, includes two such distinct types of belief that, even though their difference is strictly one of degree, not of kind, it becomes practically important to consider them separately. Some beliefs are accepted when their grounds have not themselves been considered, others are accepted because their grounds have been examined.

When we say, "Men used to think the world was flat," or "I thought you went to the house," we express belief: something is accepted, held to, acquiesced in, or affirmed. But such thoughts may mean a supposition accepted without reference to its real grounds. These may be adequate, they may not; but their value with reference to the support they afford the belief has not been considered.

Such thoughts grow up unconsciously and without reference to the attainment of correct belief. They are picked up—we know not how. From obscure sources and by unnoticed channels they insinuate themselves into acceptance and become unconsciously a part of our mental furniture. Tradition, instruction, imitation—all of which depend upon authority in some form, or appeal to our own advantage, or fall in with a strong passion—are responsible for them. Such thoughts are prejudices, that is, prejudgments, not judgments proper that rest upon a survey of evidence.

IV. Thoughts that result in belief have an importance attached to them which leads to reflective thought, to conscious inquiry into the nature, conditions, and bearings of the belief. To *think* of whales and camels in the clouds is to entertain ourselves with fancies, terminable at our pleasure, which do not lead to any belief in particular. But to think of the world as flat is to ascribe a quality to a real thing as its real property. This conclusion denotes a connection among things and hence is not, like imaginative thought, plastic to our mood. Belief in the world's flatness commits him who holds it to thinking in certain specific ways of other objects, such as the heavenly bodies, antipodes, the possibility of navigation. It prescribes to him actions in accordance with his conception of these objects.

The consequences of a belief upon other beliefs and upon behavior may be so important, then, that men are forced to consider the grounds or reasons of their belief and its logical consequences. This means reflective thought—thought in its eulogistic and emphatic sense.

Men *thought* the world was flat until Columbus *thought* it to be round. The earlier thought was a belief held because men had not the energy or the courage to question what those about them accepted and taught, especially as it was suggested and seemingly confirmed by obvious and sensible facts. The thought of Columbus was a *reasoned conclusion*. It marked the close of study into facts, of scrutiny and revision of evidence, of working out the implications of various hypotheses, and of comparing these theoretical results with one another and with known facts. Because Columbus did not accept unhesitatingly the current traditional theory, because he doubted and inquired, he arrived at his thought. Skeptical of what, from long habit, seemed most certain, and credulous of what seemed impossible, he went on thinking until he could produce evidence for both his confidence and his disbelief. Even if his conclusion had finally turned out wrong, it would have been a different sort of belief from those it antagonized, because it was reached by a different method. *Active, persistent, and careful consideration of any belief or supposed form of knowledge in the light of the grounds that support it, and the further conclusions to which it tends,* constitutes reflective thought. Any one of the first three kinds of thought may elicit this type; but once begun, it is a conscious and voluntary effort to establish belief upon a firm basis of reasons.

AMERICANISM—AN ATTEMPT AT A DEFINITION [1]

By Brander Matthews

There are many words in circulation among us which we understand fairly well, which we use ourselves, and which we should, however, find it difficult to define. I think that *Americanism* is one of these words; and I think also it is well for us to inquire into the exact meaning of this word, which is often most carelessly employed. More than once of late we have heard a public man praised for his "aggressive Americanism," and occasionally we have seen a man of letters denounced for his "lack of Americanism." Now what does the word really mean when it is thus used?

It means, first of all, a love for this country of ours, an appreciation of the institutions of this nation, a pride in the history of this people to which we belong. And to this extent *Americanism* is simply another word for *patriotism*. But it means, also, I

[1] From *Parts of Speech: Essays on English.* By permission of Charles Scribner's Sons, the authorized publishers.

think, more than this: it means a frank acceptance of the principles which underlie our government here in the United States. It means, therefore, a faith in our fellowman, a belief in liberty and in equality. It implies, further, so it seems to me, a confidence in the future of this country, a confidence in its destiny, a buoyant hopefulness that the right will surely prevail.

In so far as Americanism is merely patriotism, it is a very good thing. The man who does not think his own country the finest in the world is either a pretty poor sort of a man or else he has a pretty poor sort of a country. If any people have not patriotism enough to make them willing to die that the nation may live, then that people will soon be pushed aside in the struggle of life, and that nation will be trampled upon and crushed; probably it will be conquered and absorbed by some race of a stronger fiber and of a sterner stock. Perhaps it is difficult to declare precisely which is the more pernicious citizen of a republic when there is danger of war with another nation—the man who wants to fight, right or wrong, or the man who does not want to fight, right or wrong; the hot-headed fellow who would plunge the country into a deadly struggle without first exhausting every possible chance to obtain an honorable peace, or the cold-blooded person who would willingly give up anything and everything, including honor itself, sooner than risk the loss of money which every war surely entails. "My country, right or wrong," is a good motto only when we add to it, "and if she is in the wrong, I'll help to put her in the right." To shrink absolutely from a fight where honor is really at stake, this is the act of a coward. To rush violently into a quarrel when war can be avoided without the sacrifice of things dearer than life, this is the act of a fool.

True patriotism is quiet, simple, dignified; it is not blatant, verbose, vociferous. The noisy shriekers who go about with a chip on their shoulders and cry aloud for war upon the slightest provocation belong to the class contemptuously known as "Jingoes." They may be patriotic,—and as a fact they often are,—but their patriotism is too frothy, too hysteric, too unintelligent, to inspire confidence. True patriotism is not swift to resent an insult; on the contrary, it is slow to take offense, slow to believe that an insult could have been intended. True patriotism, believing fully in the honesty of its own acts, assumes also that others are acting with the same honesty. True patriotism, having a solid pride in the power and resources of our country, doubts always the likelihood of any other nation being willing carelessly to arouse our enmity.

In so far, therefore, as Americanism is merely patriotism it is a very good thing, as I have tried to point out. But Americanism is something more than patriotism. It calls not only for love of our common country, but also for respect for our fellow-man. It implies an actual acceptance of equality as a fact. It means a willingness always to act on the theory, not that "I'm as good as the other man," but that "the other man is as good as I am." It means leveling up rather than leveling down. It means a regard for law, and a desire to gain our wishes and to advance our ideas always decently and in order, and with deference to the wishes and ideas of others. It leads a man always to acknowledge the good faith of those with whom he is contending, whether the contest is one of sport or of politics. It prevents a man from declaring, or even from thinking, that all the right is on his side, and that all the honest people in the country are necessarily of his opinion.

And, further, it seems to me that true Americanism has faith and hope. It believes that the world is getting better, if not year by year, at least century by century; and it believes also that in this steady improvement of the condition of mankind these United States are destined to do their full share. It holds that, bad as many things may seem to be to-day, they were worse yesterday, and they will be better to-morrow. However dark the outlook for any given cause may be at any moment the man imbued with the true spirit of Americanism never abandons hope and never relaxes effort; he feels sure that everything comes to him who waits. He knows that all reforms are inevitable in the long run; and that if they do not finally establish themselves it is because they are not really reforms, though for a time they may have seemed to be.

And a knowledge of the history of the American people will

supply ample reason for this faith in the future. The sin of negro-slavery never seemed to be more secure from overthrow than it did in the ten years before it was finally abolished. A study of the political methods of the past will show that there has been immense improvement in many respects; and it is perhaps in our political methods that we Americans are most open to censure. That there was no deterioration of the moral stamina of the whole people during the first century of the American republic any student can make sure of by comparing the spirit which animated the inhabitants of the thirteen Colonies during the Revolution with the spirit which animated the population of the Northern States (and of the Southern no less) during the Civil War. We are accustomed to sing the praises of our grandfathers who won our independence, and very properly; but our grandchildren will have also to sing the praises of our fathers who stood up against one another for four years of the hardest fighting the world has ever seen, bearing the burdens of a protracted struggle with an uncomplaining cheerfulness which was not a characteristic of the earlier war.

True Americanism is sturdy but modest. It is as far removed from "Jingoism" in times of trouble as it is from "Spread-Eagleism" in times of peace. It is neither vainglorious nor boastful. It knows that the world was not created in 1492, and that July 4, 1776, is not the most important date in the whole history of mankind. It does not overestimate the contribution which America has made to the rest of the world, nor does it underestimate this contribution. True Americanism, as I have said, has a pride in the past of this great country of ours, and a faith in the future; but none the less it is not so foolish as to think that all is perfection on this side of the Atlantic, and that all is imperfection on the other side.

It knows that some things are better here than anywhere else in the world, that some things are no better, and that some things are not so good in America as they are in Europe. For example, probably the institutions of the nation fit the needs of the population with less friction here in the United States than in any other country in the world. But probably, also, there is no other one of the great nations of the world in which the government of the large cities is so wasteful and so negligent.

True Americanism recognizes the fact that America is the heir of the ages, and that it is for us to profit as best we can by the experience of Europe, not copying servilely what has been successful in the old world, but modifying what we borrow in accord with our own needs and our own conditions. It knows, and it has no hesitation in declaring, that we must always be the judges ourselves as to whether or not we shall follow the example of Europe. Many times we have refused to walk in the path of European precedent, preferring very properly to blaze out a track for ourselves. More often than not this independence was wise, but now and again it was unwise.

Finally, one more quality of true Americanism must be pointed out. It is not sectional. It does not dislike an idea, a man, or a political party because that idea, that man, or that party comes from a certain part of the country. It permits a man to have a healthy pride in being a son of Virginia, a citizen of New York, a native of Massachusetts, but only on condition that he has a pride still stronger that he is an American, a citizen of the United States. True Americanism is never sectional. It knows no North and no South, no East and no West. And as it has no sectional likes and dislikes, so it has no international likes and dislikes. It never puts itself in the attitude of the Englishman who said, "I've no prejudices, thank Heaven, but I do hate a Frenchman!" It frowns upon all appeals to the former allegiance of naturalized citizens of this country; and it thinks that it ought to be enough for any man to be an American without the aid of the hyphen which makes him a British-American, an Irish-American, or a German-American.

True Americanism, to conclude, feels that a land which bred Washington and Franklin in the last century, and Emerson and Lincoln in this century, and which opens its schools wide to give every boy the chance to model himself on these great men, is a land deserving of Lowell's praise as "a good country to live in, a good country to live for, and a good country to die for."

EXERCISES

1. Try to detect in Charles S. Brooks's essay the various methods of defining,—elimination, division, comparison and contrast, and illustration.

2. Write a theme of definition on one of the following subjects, trying to model it after John Dewey's "What is Thought?"

What is a Social Climber?   What is Good Breeding?
What is a Statesman?   What is Urbanity?
What is Courage?

3. Define New England as a place. Then define it as a state of mind. In like manner define the South, the Scottish Highlands, the South Sea Islands, Boston, Philadelphia, Chicago.

4. Define by comparison and contrast, writing a paragraph theme if your instructor approves:

Fame and Notoriety   Realist and Romanticist
Knowledge and Wisdom   Rationalist and Idealist
Religion and Theology   Common and "Horse" Sense
Enough and Sufficient   Prominence and Popularity
Behavior and Character   Talent and Genius
Browsing and Reading   Diplomacy and Lying

5. Write a paragraph theme on one of the following, developing it by one of the four methods suggested. Then write on the same subject, developing the new paragraph by another method.

highbrow   the unpardonable college crime
cad   tea hound
coca-cola   rushing
poor fish   college spirit
uplift   sundæ
rotter   Phi Beta Kappa
prize nut   sheepskin

6. Read as an outside assignment "What is a Religious Man?" from *The Atlantic Monthly* for May 1926. Do you consider it a good definition from the points of view of form and of methods of defining?

7. Compare Miss Repplier's essay on "Wit and Humor" from *Essays in Idleness* with Mr. Brooks's essay on the same subject.

SUGGESTED READINGS

Bradley, Henry, "Slang, A Definition," from the *Encyclopedia Brittanica.*

Canby, Henry Seidel, "The American Tradition" from *Definitions, First Series,* Harcourt, Brace, New York.

Crevecoeur, Saint John de, "What is an American?" from *Letters from an American Farmer,* 1782. See *Harper's Literary Museum,* edited by Ola E. Winslow, Harper's, New York.

Deming, W. C., "What is Dry Farming?" *The Independent,* Vol. 62.

Dickinson, G. Lowes, "Red Bloods and Mollycoddles" from *Appearances,* Doubleday, Doran, New York.

Eastman, Max, "Humour and Truth" from *The Sense of Humour,* Scribner's, New York. "Poetic People" from *The Enjoyment of Poetry, Scribner's,* New York.

Hart, Albert Bushnell, "The Machine and the Boss" from *Actual Government,* Longmans, Green, New York.

Hazlitt, William, "Familiar Style," paragraph 1, from *Table Talk.*

Newman, John Henry, "Definition of a Gentleman" from *The Idea of a University.*

Newton, Joseph Fort, "What is a Religious Man?" *The Atlantic Monthly,* May 1926.

Repplier, Agnes, "Wit and Humor" from *Essays in Idleness,* Houghton Mifflin, Boston.

Schauffler, Robert Haven, "What is Sportsmanship?" *The Outlook,* November 11, 1911.

Shelley, Percy Bysshe, "The Definition of Poetry" from *A Defense of Poetry.*

Wendell, Barrett, "The Meaning of Literature" from *The Literary History of America,* Scribner's, New York.

CHAPTER III

THE ANALYSIS

The word *analysis* comes from two Greek words which mean to loosen or to separate. When one writes an analysis, therefore, he breaks up or separates a subject into its component parts in order to see of what it is composed. There are two kinds of analysis which we may call for purposes of contrast, *logical* and *literary*. Sometimes they are called *formal* and *informal*, but these terms are less indicative of the character of each. Logical analysis always aims at being complete; literary analysis pretends only to make the subject under presentation clear and interesting to the average reader. The first is used often in formal writing such as in the report of a tariff commission, which obviously must be complete in every detail if it is to be of any real value; the second is used in the attempt to interpret or to illumine a given subject, and it makes no pretense of being complete. For instance, many of the articles in weeklies such as *The New Republic, The Outlook,* and *The Nation* are in this second sense analytical in character. They aim at giving the gist of the subject with sufficient facts of importance to supply background and development. But space determines that only the most vital things may be said. Thus a recent article on the reasons of a certain prominent citizen for favoring Mr. Hoover for President does not attempt to set forth every conceivable reason but only to enumerate and to develop the more significant.

The most important element in the writing of literary, or informal, analysis, the only kind which concerns us here, is the finding and the using of a *controlling and definite purpose*. Since, as has already been said, the writer cannot aim at com-

361

pleteness in the treatment of his subject, he must choose some
one basis or means of interpretation and try to be as lucid and
as interesting as possible in its handling.   In writing his appreciation and explanation of Lincoln, for example, Mr. Croly chose
as his definite and controlling purpose the idea that in certain
traits Lincoln was not only the finest type of American but that
he was *more* than that.   Suppose, for another example, that a
student wishes to write a five-hundred-word analysis on the superiority of his college over a neighboring institution.   Obviously
he can not possibly handle completely or even capably such a
subject in five hundred or even in five thousand words.   He must
then choose some controlling purpose, find some basis, for his
comparison, which shall at once limit his treatment of the two
colleges.   That basis may be the educational resources of each
institution, or the athletic record and prowess of each, or the
relative personnel of the student bodies, or the natural beauty
of each location.   A still better example is shown by the experience of a college student who wrote a two-thousand word paper
on "The Various Types of Humor in Lamb's Essays."   Instead
of choosing at once some definite purpose which should govern
her work, she began in a slapdash way to list the dozens of essays
and to point out in a most disorderly fashion the various types
of humor shown in each.   The result was a hodge-podge of confusing information.   How much easier her work and how much
clearer the result had she begun by listing the most important
types of humor used by Lamb, and proceeded by illustrating each
briefly and by showing in which essays each was found.   She
had, you see, entirely misinterpreted her subject.   She was
trying blindly to write on "Lamb's Essays and Their Humor"
when in reality her subject was "The Various Types of Humor
in Lamb's Essays."   Her controlling purpose was *types of humor*
and not *Lamb's essays*.

The writing of analysis is made still easier by choosing a form
or a mold for one's theme.   Three such forms are suggested and
illustrated here.   There are several others, but these have been
selected because of their practicality and of their frequent employment by our journalists and essayists:

The first is *analysis by enumeration*. This consists in making salient points in some reasonable order and is exemplified beautifully by Mr. Croly's delineation of those qualities of Lincoln, intellectuality, humanness, magnanimity, and humility which, united in one man, made him more than an American.

The second is *analysis by comparison and contrast*. In this kind of analysis one tries first of all to find a basis for comparison or contrast. Mr. Corbin in his "English and American Sportsmanship" finds this basis in the differences in the climates of the two countries. He does not start off hit or miss to contrast football and cricket or to compare the English graduate's attitude toward Oxford with the Harvard alumnus's attitude toward his college. He sees back of all differences the big fact of climate, and he uses this as his controlling purpose, moving on from it to other differences many of which really arise from this first and most important one and upon which he continues to compare the two kinds of sportsmanship.

The third is *analysis by classification*. This should have been the mold for the student who wrote on "The Various Types of Humor in Lamb's Essays." It is, most naturally, employed for subjects which lend themselves to the method of classification, which by their very nature divide themselves into classes, there to be handled and discussed. For example, such subjects as "Commercial Fertilizers," "The Forms of Democratic Government," "Minnesota Oaks," "Modern Cure-alls," and "Farming in Montana" are obviously subjects for analysis by classification. James Harvey Robinson's "On Various Kinds of Thinking" is given here as a splendid example of this type of analysis.

It may be well in closing to summarize the points already made: (1) that literary analysis makes no pretense of being complete; (2) that for the sake of clearness some controlling purpose or principle should be chosen which shall govern the choice, limitation, and arrangement of material; (3) that certain molds or forms of analysis are often used by writers and may well be studied for suggestions and help.

Lincoln as More Than an American [1]

By Herbert Croly

Lincoln's services to his country have been rewarded with such abundant appreciation that it may seem superfluous to insist upon them once again; but I believe that from the point of view of this book an even higher value may be placed, if not upon his patriotic service, at least upon his personal worth. The Union might well have been saved and slavery extinguished without his assistance; but the life of no other American has revealed with anything like the same completeness the peculiar moral promise of genuine democracy. He shows us by the full but unconscious integrity of his example the kind of human excellence which a political and social democracy may and should fashion; and its most grateful and hopeful aspect is, not merely that there is something partially American about the manner of his excellence, but that it can be fairly compared with the classic types of consummate personal distinction.

To all appearance nobody could have been more than Abraham Lincoln a man of his own time and place. Until 1858 his outer life ran much in the same groove as that of hundreds of other Western politicians and lawyers. Beginning as a poor and ignorant boy, even less provided with props and stepping stones than were his associates, he had worked his way to a position of ordinary professional and political distinction. He was not, like Douglas, a brilliant success. He was not, like Grant, an apparently hopeless failure. He had achieved as much and as little as hundreds of others had achieved. He was respected by his neighbors as an honest man and as a competent lawyer. They credited him with ability, but not to any extraordinary extent. No one would have pointed him out as a remarkable and distinguished man. He had shown himself to be desirous of recognition and influence; but ambition had not been the compelling motive in his life. In most respects his ideas, interests, and

---

[1] From *The Promise of American Life*. By the kind permission of the author.

standards were precisely the same as those of his associates. He accepted with them the fabric of traditional American political thought and the ordinary standards of contemporary political morality. He had none of the moral strenuousness of the reformer, none of the exclusiveness of a man whose purposes and ideas were consciously perched higher than those of his neighbors. Probably the majority of his more successful associates classed him as a good and able man who was somewhat lacking in ambition and had too much of a disposition to loaf. He was most at home, not in his own house, but in the corner grocery store, where he could sit with his feet on the stove swapping stories with his friends; and if an English traveller of 1850 had happened in on the group, he would most assuredly have discovered another instance of the distressing vulgarity to which the absence of an hereditary aristocracy and an established church condemned the American democracy. Thus no man could apparently have been more the average product of his day and generation. Nevertheless, at bottom Abraham Lincoln differed as essentially from the ordinary Western American of the Middle Period as St. Francis of Assisi differed from the ordinary Benedictine monk of the thirteenth century.

The average Western American of Lincoln's generation was fundamentally a man who subordinated his intelligence to certain dominant practical interests and purposes. He was far from being a stupid or slow-witted man. On the contrary, his wits had been sharpened by the traffic of American politics and business, and his mind was shrewd, flexible, and alert. But he was wholly incapable either of disinterested or of concentrated intellectual exertion. His energies were bent in the conquest of certain stubborn external forces, and he used his intelligence almost exclusively to this end. The struggles, the hardships, and the necessary self-denial of pioneer life constituted an admirable training of the will. It developed a body of men with great resolution of purpose and with great ingenuity and fertility in adapting their insufficient means to the realization of their important business affairs. But their almost exclusive preoccupation with practical tasks and their failure to grant their intelligence any room for independent exercise bent them into exceedingly warped and one-sided human beings.

Lincoln, on the contrary, much as he was a man of his own time and people, was precisely an example of high and disinterested intellectual culture. During all the formative years in which his life did not superficially differ from that of his associates, he was in point of fact using every chance which the material of Western life afforded to discipline and inform his mind. These materials were not very abundant; and in the use which he proceeded to make of them Lincoln had no assistance, either from a sound tradition or from a better educated master. On the contrary, as the history of the times shows, there was every temptation for a man with a strong intellectual bent to be betrayed into mere extravagance and aberration. But with the sound instinct of a well-balanced intelligence Lincoln seized upon the three available books, the earnest study of which might best help to develop harmoniously a strong and many-sided intelligence. He seized, that is, upon the Bible, Shakespeare, and Euclid. To his contemporaries the Bible was for the most part a fountain of fanatic revivalism, and Shakespeare, if anything, a mine of quotations. But in the case of Lincoln, Shakespeare and the Bible served, not merely to awaken his taste and fashion his style, but also to liberate his literary and moral imagination. At the same time he was training his powers of thought by an assiduous study of algebra and geometry. The absorbing hours he spent over his Euclid were apparently of no use to him in his profession; but Lincoln was in his way an intellectual gymnast and enjoyed the exertion for its own sake. Such a use of his leisure must have seemed a sheer waste of time to his more practical friends, and they might well have accounted for his comparative lack of success by his indulgence in such secret and useless pastimes. Neither would this criticism have been beside the mark, for if Lincoln's great energy and powers of work had been devoted exclusively to practical ends, he might well have become in the early days a more prominent lawyer and politician than he actually was. But he preferred the satisfaction of his own intellectual and social instincts, and so qualified himself for achievements beyond the power of a Douglas.

In addition, however, to these private gymnastics Lincoln shared with his neighbors a public and popular source of intellectual and human insight. The Western pioneers, for all their exclusive devotion to practical purposes, wasted a good deal of time on apparently useless social intercourse. In the Middle Western towns of that day there was, as we have seen, an extraordinary amount of good-fellowship, which was quite the most wholesome and humanizing thing which entered into the lives of these hard-working and hard-featured men. The whole male countryside was in its way a club; and when the presence of women did not make them awkward and sentimental, the men let themselves loose in an amount of rough pleasantry and free conversation, which added the one genial and liberating touch to their lives. This club life of his own people Lincoln enjoyed and shared much more than did his average neighbor. He passed the greater part of what he would have called his leisure time in swapping with his friends stories, in which the genial and humorous side of Western life was embodied. Doubtless his domestic unhappiness had much to do with his vagrancy; but his native instinct for the wholesome and illuminating aspect of the life around him brought him more frequently than any other cause to the club of loafers in the general store. And whatever the promiscuous conversation and the racy yarns meant to his associates, they meant vastly more to Lincoln. His hours of social vagrancy really completed the process of his intellectual training. It relieved his culture from the taint of bookishness. It gave substance to his humor. It humanized his wisdom and enabled him to express it in a familiar and dramatic form. It placed at his disposal, that is, the great classic vehicle of popular expression, which is the parable and the spoken word.

Of course, it was just because he shared so completely the amusements and the occupations of his neighbors that his private personal culture had no embarrassing effects. Neither he nor his neighbors were in the least aware that he had been placed thereby in a different intellectual class. No doubt the loneliness and sadness of his personal life may be partly explained by a dumb sense of difference from his fellows; and no doubt this very loneliness and sadness intensified the mental preoccupation which was both the sign and the result of his personal culture. But his unconsciousness of his own distinction, as well as his regular participation in political and professional practice, kept his will as firm and vigorous as if he were really no more than a man of action. His natural steadiness of purpose had been toughened in the beginning by the hardships and struggles which he shared with his neighbors; and his self-imposed intellectual discipline in no way impaired the stability of his character, because his personal culture never alienated him from his neighbors and threw him into a consciously critical frame of mind. The time which he spent in intellectual diversion may have diminished to some extent his practical efficiency previous to the gathering crisis. It certainly made him less inclined to the aggressive self-assertion which a successful political career demanded. But when the crisis came, when the minds of Northern patriots were stirred by the ugly alternative offered to them by the South, and when Lincoln was by the course of events restored to active participation in politics, he soon showed that he had reached the highest of all objects of personal culture. While still remaining one of a body of men who, all unconsciously, impoverished their minds in order to increase the momentum of their practical energy, he none the less achieved for himself a mutually helpful relation between a firm will and a luminous intelligence. The training of his mind, the awakening of his imagination, the formation of his taste and style, the humorous dramatizing of his experience,—all this discipline had failed to pervert his character, narrow his sympathies, or undermine his purposes. His intelligence served to enlighten his will, and his will, to establish the mature decisions of his intelligence. Late in life the two faculties became in their exercise almost indistinguishable. His judgments, in so far as they were decisive, were charged with momentum, and his actions were instinct with sympathy and understanding.

Just because his actions were instinct with sympathy and understanding, Lincoln was certainly the most humane statesman who ever guided a nation through a great crisis. He always regarded other men and acted towards them, not merely as the embodiment of an erroneous or harmful idea, but as human beings, capable of better things; and consequently all of his thoughts and actions looked in the direction of a higher level of human association. It is this characteristic which makes him a better and, be it hoped, a more prophetic democrat than any other national American leader. His peculiar distinction does not consist in the fact that he was a "Man of the People" who passed from the condition of splitting rails to the condition of being President. No doubt he was in this respect as good a democrat as you please, and no doubt it was desirable that he should be this kind of a democrat. But many other Americans could be named who were also men of the people, and who passed from the most insignificant to the most honored positions in American life. Lincoln's peculiar and permanent distinction as a democrat will depend rather upon the fact that his thoughts and his actions looked towards the realization of the highest and most edifying democratic ideal. Whatever his theories were, he showed by his general outlook and behavior that democracy meant to him more than anything else the spirit and principle of brotherhood. He was the foremost to deny liberty to the South, and he had his sensible doubts about the equality between the negro and the white man; but he actually treated everybody— the Southern rebel, the negro slave, the Northern deserter, the personal enemy—in a just and kindly spirit. Neither was this kindliness merely an instance of ordinary American amiability and good nature. It was the result, not of superficial feeling which could be easily ruffled, but of his personal, moral, and intellectual discipline. He had made for himself a second nature, compact of insight and loving-kindness.

It must be remembered, also, that this higher humanity resided in a man who was the human instrument partly responsible for an awful amount of slaughter and human anguish. He was not only the commander-in-chief of a great army which fought a long and bloody war, but he was the statesman who had insisted that, if necessary, the war should be fought. His mental attitude was dictated by a mixture of practical common sense with genuine human insight, and it is just this mixture which makes him so rare a man and, be it hoped, so prophetic a democrat. He could at one and the same moment order his countrymen to be killed for seeking to destroy the American nation and forgive them for their error. His kindliness and his brotherly feeling did not lead him, after the manner of Jefferson, to shirk the necessity and duty of national defence. Neither did it lead him, after the manner of William Lloyd Garrison, to advocate non-resistance, while at the same time arousing in his fellow-countrymen a spirit of fratricidal warfare. In the midst of that hideous civil contest which was provoked, perhaps unnecessarily, by hatred, irresponsibility, passion, and disloyalty, and which has been the fruitful cause of national disloyalty down to the present day, Lincoln did not for a moment cherish a bitter or unjust feeling against the national enemies. The Southerners, filled as they were with a passionate democratic devotion to their own interests and liberties, abused Lincoln until they really came to believe that he was a military tyrant, yet he never failed to treat them in a fair and forgiving spirit. When he was assassinated, it was the South, as well as the American nation, which had lost its best friend, because he alone among the Republican leaders had the wisdom to see that the divided House could only be restored by justice and kindness; and if there are any defects in its restoration to-day, they are chiefly due to the baleful spirit of injustice and hatred which the Republicans took over from the Abolitionists.

His superiority to his political associates in constructive statesmanship is measured by his superiority in personal character. There are many men who are able to forgive the enemies of their country, but there are few who can forgive their personal enemies. I need not rehearse the well-known instances of Lincoln's magnanimity. He not only cherished no resentment against men who had intentionally and even maliciously injured him, but he seems at times to have gone out of his way to do them a service. This is, perhaps, his greatest distinction. Lincoln's magnanimity is the final proof of the completeness of his self-discipline. The quality of being magnanimous is both the consummate virtue and the one which is least natural. It was certainly far from being natural among Lincoln's own people. Americans of his time were generally of the opinion that it was dishonorable to overlook a personal injury. They considered it weak and unmanly not to quarrel with another man a little harder than he quarreled with you. The pioneer was good-natured and kindly; but he was aggressive, quick-tempered, unreasonable, and utterly devoid of personal discipline. A slight or an insult to his personality became in his eyes a moral wrong which must be cherished and avenged, and which relieved him of any obligation to be just or kind to his enemy. Many conspicuous illustrations of this quarrelsome spirit are to be found in the political life of the middle period, which, indeed, cannot be understood without constantly falling back upon the influence of lively personal resentments. Every prominent politician cordially disliked or hated a certain number of his political adversaries and associates; and his public actions were often dictated by a purpose either to injure these men or to get ahead of them. After the retirement of Jackson these enmities and resentments came to have a smaller influence; but a man's right and duty to quarrel with anybody who, in his opinion, had done him an injury was unchallenged, and was generally considered to be the necessary accompaniment of American democratic virility.

As I have intimated above, Andrew Jackson was the most conspicuous example of this quarrelsome spirit, and for this reason he is wholly inferior to Lincoln as a type of democratic manhood. Jackson had many admirable qualities and on the whole he served his country well. He also was a "Man of the People" who understood and represented the mass of his fellow-countrymen, and who played the part, according to his lights, of a courageous and independent political leader. He also loved and defended the Union. But with all his excellence he should never be held up as a model to American youth. The world was divided into his personal friends and followers and his personal enemies, and he was as eager to do the latter an injury as he was to do the former a service. His quarrels were not petty, because Jackson was, on the whole, a big rather than a little man, but they were fierce and they were for the most part irreconcilable. They bulk so large in his life that they cannot be overlooked. They stamp him a type of the vindictive man without personal discipline, just as Lincoln's behavior towards Stanton, Chase, and others stamps him a type of the man who has achieved magnanimity. He is the kind of national hero the admiring imitation of whom can do nothing but good.

Lincoln had abandoned the illusion of his own peculiar personal importance. He had become profoundly and sincerely humble, and his humility was as far as possible from being either a conventional pose or a matter of nervous self-distrust. It did not impair the firmness of his will. It did not betray him into shirking responsibilities. Although only a country lawyer without executive experience, he did not flinch from assuming the leadership of a great nation in one of the gravest crises of its national history, from becoming commander-in-chief of an army of a million men, and from spending $3,000,000,000 in the prosecution of a war. His humility, that is, was precisely an example of moral vitality and insight rather than of moral awkwardness and enfeeblement. It was the fruit of reflection on his own personal experience—the supreme instance of his ability to attain moral truth both in discipline and in idea; and in its aspect of a moral truth it obtained a more explicit expression than did some other of his finer personal attributes. His practice of cherishing and repeating the plaintive little verses which inquire monotonously whether the spirit of mortal has any right to be proud indicates the depth and the highly conscious character of this fundamental moral conviction. He is not only humble himself, but he feels and declares that men have no right to be anything but humble; and he thereby enters into possession of the most fruitful and the most universal of all religious ideas.

Lincoln's humility, no less than his liberal intelligence and his magnanimous disposition, is more democratic than it is American; but in this as in so many other cases, his personal moral dignity and his peculiar moral insight did not separate him from his associates. Like them, he wanted professional success, public office, and the ordinary rewards of American life; and like them, he bears no trace of political or moral purism. But unlike them, he was not the intellectual and moral victim of his own purposes and ambitions; and unlike them, his life is a tribute to the sincerity and depth of his moral insight. He could never have become a national leader by the ordinary road of insistent and clamorous self-assertion. Had he not been restored to public life by the crisis, he would have remained in all probability a comparatively obscure and a wholly undervalued man. But the political ferment of 1856 and the threat of ruin overhanging the American Union pushed him again on to the political highway; and once there, his years of intellectual discipline enabled him to play a leading and a decisive part. His personality obtained momentum, direction, and increasing dignity from its identification with great issues and events. He became the individual instrument whereby an essential and salutary national purpose was fulfilled; and the instrument was admirably effective, precisely because it had been silently and unconsciously tempered and formed for high achievement. Issue as he was of a society in which the cheap tool, whether mechanical or personal, was the immediately successful tool, he had none the less labored long in the making of a consummate individual instrument.

Some of my readers may protest that I have over-emphasized the difference between Lincoln and his contemporary fellow-countrymen. In order to exalt the leader have I not too much disparaged the followers? Well, a comparison of this kind always involves the risk of unfairness; but if there is much truth in the foregoing estimate of Lincoln, the lessons of the comparison are worth its inevitable risks. The ordinary interpretation of Lincoln as a consummate democrat and a "man of the people" has implied that he was, like Jackson, simply a bigger and a better version of the plain American citizen; and it is just this interpretation which I have sought to deny and to expose. In many respects he was, of course, very much like his neighbors and associates. He accepted everything wholesome and useful in their life and behavior. He shared their good-fellowship, their strength of will, their excellent faith, and above all their innocence; and he could never have served his country so well, or reached as high a level of personal dignity, in case he had not been good-natured and strong and innocent. But, as all commentators have noted, he was not only good-natured, strong, and innocent; he had made himself intellectually candid, concentrated, and disinterested, and morally humane, magnanimous, and humble. All these qualities, which were the very flower of his personal life, were not possessed either by the average or the exceptional American of his day; and not only were they not possessed, but they were either wholly ignored or consciously undervalued. Yet these very qualities of high intelligence, humanity, magnanimity, and humility are precisely the qualities which Americans, in order to become better democrats, should add to their strength, their homogeneity, and their innocence; while at the same time they are just the qualities which Americans are prevented by their individualistic practice and tradition from attaining or properly valuing. Their deepest convictions make the average unintelligent man the representative democrat, and the aggressive successful individual the admirable national type; and in conformity with these convictions their uppermost ideas in respect to Lincoln are that he was a "Man of the People" and an example of strong will. He was both of these things, but his great distinction is that he was also something vastly more and better. He cannot be fully understood and properly valued as a national hero without an implicit criticism of these traditional convictions. Such a criticism he himself did not and could not make. In case he had made it, he could never have achieved his great political task and his great personal triumph. But other times bring other needs. It is as desirable to-day that the criticism should be made explicit as it was that Lincoln himself in his day should preserve the innocence and integrity of a unique unconscious example.

ENGLISH AND AMERICAN SPORTSMANSHIP [1]

By John Corbin

The prevalence of out-of-door sports in England, and the amenity of the English sporting spirit, may be laid, I think, primarily, to the influence of climate. Through the long, temperate summer, all nature conspires to entice a man out-of-doors, while in America sunstroke is imminent. All day long the village greens in England are thronged with boys playing cricket in many-colored blazers, while every stream is dotted with boats of all sorts and descriptions; and in the evenings, long after the quick American twilight has shut down on the heated earth, the English horizon gives light for the recreations of those who have labored all day. In the winter the result is the same, though the cause is very different. Stupefying exhalations rise from the damp earth, and the livelong twilight that does for day forces a man back for good cheer upon mere animal spirits. In the English summer no normal man could resist the beckoning of the fields and the river. In the winter it is sweat, man, or die. . . .

In a sportsman it would be most ungracious to inveigh against English weather. The very qualities one instinctively curses make possible the full and varied development of out-door games, which Americans admire without stint. Our football teams do day labor to get fit, and then, after a game or so, the sport is nipped in the bud. To teach our oarsmen the rudiments of the stroke we resort to months of the galley-slavery of tank-rowing. Our track athletes begin their season in the dead of winter with the dreary monotony of wooden dumb-bells and pulley-weights, while the baseball men are learning to slide for base in the cage. In England the gymnasium is happily unknown. Winter and summer alike the sportsman lives beneath the skies, and the sports are so diverse and so widely cultivated that any man, whatever his mental or physical capacity, finds suitable exercise that is also recreation.

It is because of this universality of athletic sports that Eng-

[1] From *An American at Oxford*. By kind permission of the author.

lish training is briefer and less severe. The American makes, and is forced to make, a long and tedious business of getting fit, whereas an Englishman has merely to exercise and sleep a trifle more than usual, and this only for a brief period. Our oarsmen work daily from January to July, about six months, or did so before Mr. Lehmann brought English ideas among us; the English 'varsity crews row together nine or ten weeks. Our football players slog daily for six or seven weeks; English teams seldom or never "practice," and play at most two matches a week. Our track athletes are in training at frequent intervals throughout the college year, and are often at the training-table six weeks; in England six weeks is the maximum period of training, and the men as a rule are given only three days a week of exercise on the cinder-track. To an American training is an abnormal condition; to an Englishman it is the consummation of the normal.

The moderation of English training is powerfully abetted by a peculiarity of the climate. The very dulness and depression that make exercise imperative also make it impossible to sustain much of it. The clear, bright American sky—the sky that renders it difficult for us to take the same delight in Italy as an Englishman takes, and leads us to prefer Ruskin's descriptions to the reality—cheers the American athlete; and the crispness of the atmosphere and its extreme variability keep his nerves alert. An English athlete would go hopelessly stale on work that would scarcely keep an American up to his highest pitch.

The effect of these differences on the temperament of the athlete is marked. The crispness and variety of our climate foster nervous vitality at the expense of physical vitality, while the equability of the English climate has the opposite effect. In all contests that require sustained effort—distance running and cross-country running, for example—we are in general far behind; while during the comparatively few years in which we have practiced athletic sports we have shown, on the whole, vastly superior form in all contests depending upon nervous energy—sprinting, hurdling, jumping, and weight-throwing.

Because of these differences of climate and of temperament,

no rigid comparison can be made between English and American training; but it is probably true that English athletes tend to train too little. Mr. Horan, the president of the Cambridge team that ran against Yale at New Haven, said as much after a very careful study of American methods; but he was not convinced that our thoroughness is quite worth while. The law of diminishing returns, he said, applies to training as to other things, so that, after a certain point, very little is gained even for a great sacrifice of convenience and pleasantness. Our American athletes are twice as rigid in denying the spirit—for an advantage, Mr. Horan admitted, of enough to win by.

The remark is worth recording; it strikes the note of difference between English and American sportsmanship. After making all allowances for the conditions here and abroad that are merely accidental, one vital difference remains. For better or for worse, a sport is a sport to an Englishman, and whatever tends to make it anything else is not encouraged; as far as possible it is made pleasant, socially and physically. Contests are arranged without what American undergraduates call diplomacy; and they come off without jockeying. It is very seldom that an Englishman forgets that he is a man first and an athlete afterwards. Yet admirable as this quality is, it has its defects, at least to the transatlantic mind. Even more, perhaps, than others, Englishmen find a stern joy in eating their hearts at the end of a contest, but they have no taste for the careful preparation that alone enables a man to fight out to a finish to the best advantage. It is no doubt true, as the Duke of Wellington said, that the battle of Waterloo was won on the playing-fields of England; but for any inconsiderable sum I would agree to furnish a similar saying as to why the generals in South Africa ran into ambush after ambush.

In America sportsmanship is almost a religion. Fellows mortify the flesh for months and leave no means untried that may help to bring honor to their college; or, if they don't, public opinion brings swift and sure retribution. It is true that this leads to excesses. Rivalries are so strong that undergraduates have been known to be more than politic in arranging matches with each other. So the graduate steps in to moderate the ardor of emulation—and often ends by keeping alive ancient animosities long after they would have been forgotten in the vanishing generations of undergraduates. The Harvard eleven wants to play the usual football game; but it is not allowed to, because a committee of graduates sees fit to snub Yale; the athletic team wants to accept a challenge from Oxford and Cambridge, but it is not allowed to because Pennsylvania, which is not challenged, has a better team, and it is the policy of the university (which has an eye to its graduate schools) to ingratiate sister institutions. In a word, the undergraduates are left to manage their studies, while the faculty manages their pastimes.

When a contest is finally on, excesses are rampant. Of occasional brutalities too much has perhaps been said; but more serious errors are unreproved. There is a tradition that it is the duty of all non-athletes to inspire the 'varsity teams by cheering the play from the side lines; and from time to time one reads leading articles in the college papers exhorting men to back the teams. The spectator is thus given an important part in every contest, and after a 'varsity match he is praised or blamed, together with the members of the team, according to his deserts. Yale may outplay Harvard, but if Harvard sufficiently outcheers Yale she wins, and to the rooters belongs the praise. In baseball games especially, a season's championship is not infrequently decided by the fact that the partisans of one side are more numerous, or for other reasons make more noise. These are serious excesses, and are worthy of the pen of the robustest reformer; but after all has been said, they are incidents, and in the slow course of time are probably disappearing.

The signal fact is that our young men do what they do with the diligence of enthusiasm, and with the devotion that inspires the highest courage. It is not unknown that, in the bitterness of failure, American athletes have burst into tears. When our English cousins hear of this they are apt to smile, and doubtless the practice is not altogether to be commended; but in the length and breadth of a man's experience there are only two or three things one would wish so humbly as the devotion that makes it possible. Such earnestness is the quintessence of Americanism, and is probably to be traced to the signal fact that in the struggle of life we all start with a fighting chance of coming out on top. Whatever the game, so long as it is treated as a game, nothing could be so wholesome as the spirit that tends to make our young men play it for all it is worth, to do everything that can be done to secure victory with personal honor. In later years, when these men stand for the honor of the larger alma mater, on the field of battle or in the routine of administration, it is not likely that they will altogether forget the virtues of their youth.

The superiority of English sportsmanship arises, not from the spirit of the men, but from the breadth of the development of the sports; and this, climate aside, is the result of the division of the university into colleges. The average college of only a hundred and fifty men maintains two football teams—a Rugby fifteen and an Association eleven—an eight and two torpids, a cricket eleven, and a hockey eleven. Each college has also a set of athletic games yearly. If we add the men who play golf, lawn and court tennis, rackets and fives, who swim, box, wrestle, and who shoot on the ranges of the gun club, the total of men schooled in competition reaches eighty to one hundred. A simple calculation will show that when so many are exercising daily, few are left for spectators. Not a bench is prepared, nor even a plank laid on the spongy English turf, to stand between the hanger-on and pneumonia. A man's place is in the field of strife; to take part in athletic contests is almost as much a matter of course as to bathe. Of late years there has been a tendency in England to believe that the vigor of undergraduates— and of all Englishmen, for the matter of that—is in decadence. As regards their cultivation of sports at least, the reverse is true. Contests are more numerous now than ever, and are probably more earnestly waged. What is called English decadence is in reality the increasing superiority of England's rivals.

Quite aside from the physical and moral benefit to the men engaged, this multiplication of contests has a striking effect in lessening the importance of winning or losing any particular one of them. It is more powerful than any other factor in keeping English sports free from the excesses that have so often characterized our sports. From time to time a voice is raised in America as of a prophet of despair demanding the abolition of inter-university contests. As yet the contests have not been abolished, and do not seem likely to be. Might it not be argued without impertinence that the best means of doing away with the excesses in question is not to have fewer contests, but more of them? If our universities were divided into residential units, corresponding roughly to the English colleges, the excesses in particular contests could scarcely fail to be mitigated; and what is perhaps of still higher importance, the great body of non-athletes would be brought directly under the influence of all those strong and fine traditions of undergraduate life which centre in the spirit of sportsmanship.

On Various Kinds of Thinking [1]

By James Harvey Robinson

We do not think enough about thinking, and much of our confusion is the result of current illusions in regard to it. Let us forget for the moment any impressions we may have derived from the philosophers, and see what seems to happen in ourselves. The first thing that we notice is that our thought moves with such incredible rapidity that it is almost impossible to arrest any specimen of it long enough to have a look at it. When we are offered a penny for our thoughts we always find that we have recently had so many things in mind that we can easily make a selection which will not compromise us too nakedly. On inspection we shall find that even if we are not downright ashamed of a great part of our spontaneous thinking it is far too intimate, personal, ignoble, or trivial to permit us to reveal more than a small part of it. I believe this must be true of every one. We do not, of course, know what goes on in other people's heads. They tell us very little and we tell them very little. The spigot

[1] From *The Mind in the Making*. By permission of Harper and Brothers.

of speech, rarely fully opened, could never emit more than driblets of the ever renewed hogshead of thought—*noch grösser wie's Heidelberger Fass*. We find it hard to believe that other people's thoughts are as silly as our own, but they probably are.

We all appear to ourselves to be thinking all the time during our waking hours, and most of us are aware that we go on thinking while we are asleep, even more foolishly than when awake. When uninterrupted by some practical issue we are engaged in what is now known as a *reverie*. This is our spontaneous and favorite kind of thinking. We allow our ideas to take their own course and this course is determined by our hopes and fears, our spontaneous desires, their fulfillment or frustration; by our likes and dislikes, our loves and hates and resentments. There is nothing else anything like so interesting to ourselves as ourselves. All thought that is not more or less laboriously controlled and directed will inevitably circle about the beloved Ego. It is amusing and pathetic to observe this tendency in ourselves and in others. We learn politely and generously to overlook this truth, but if we dare to think of it, it blazes forth like the noontide sun.

The reverie or "free association of ideas" has of late become the subject of scientific research. While investigators are not yet agreed on the results, or at least on the proper interpretation to be given to them, there can be no doubt that our reveries form the chief index to our fundamental character. They are a reflection of our nature as modified by often hidden and forgotten experiences. We need not go into the matter further here, for it is only necessary to observe that the reverie is at all times a potent and in many cases an omnipotent rival to every other kind of thinking. It doubtless influences all our speculations in its persistent tendency to self-magnification and self-justification, which are its chief preoccupations, but it is the last thing to make directly or indirectly for honest increase of knowledge.[1]

[1] The poet-clergyman, John Donne, who lived in the time of James I, has given a beautifully honest picture of the doings of a saint's mind: "I throw myself down in my chamber and call in and invite God and His angels thither, and when they are there I neglect God and His angels for the noise of a fly, for the rattling of a coach, for the whining

Philosophers usually talk as if such thinking did not exist or were in some way negligible. This is what makes their speculations so unreal and often worthless.

The reverie, as any of us can see for himself, is frequently broken and interrupted by the necessity of a second kind of thinking. We have to make practical decisions. Shall we write a letter or no? Shall we take the subway or a bus? Shall we have dinner at seven or half-past? Shall we buy U. S. Rubber or a Liberty Bond? Decisions are easily distinguishable from the free flow of reverie. Sometimes they demand a good deal of careful pondering and the recollection of pertinent facts; often, however, they are made impulsively. They are a more difficult and laborious thing than the reverie, and we resent having to "make up our mind" when we are tired, or absorbed in a congenial reverie. Weighing a decision, it should be noted, does not necessarily add anything to our knowledge, although we may, of course, seek further information before making it.

A third kind of thinking is stimulated when any one questions our belief and opinions. We sometimes find ourselves changing our minds without any resistance or heavy emotion, but if we are told that we are wrong we resent the imputation and harden our hearts. We are incredibly heedless in the formation of our beliefs, but find ourselves filled with an illicit passion for them when any one proposes to rob us of their companionship. It is obviously not the ideas themselves that are dear to us, but our self-esteem, which is threatened. We are by nature stubbornly pledged to defend our own from attack, whether it be our person, our family, our property, or our opinion. A United States Senator once remarked to a friend of mine that God Almighty could not make him change his mind on our Latin-American

of a door. I talk on in the same posture of praying, eyes lifted up, knees bowed down, as though I prayed to God, and if God or His angels should ask me when I thought last of God in that prayer I cannot tell. Sometimes I find that I had forgot what I was about, but when I began to forget it I cannot tell. A memory of yesterday's pleasures, a fear of to-morrow's dangers, a straw under my knee, a noise in mine ear, a light in mine eye, an anything, a nothing, a fancy, a chimera in my brain troubles me in my prayer."—Quoted by Robert Lynd, *The Art of Letters*, pp. 46-47.

policy. We may surrender, but rarely confess ourselves vanquished. In the intellectual world at least peace is without
victory.

Few of us take the pains to study the origin of our cherished
convictions; indeed, we have a natural repugnance to so doing.
We like to continue to believe what we have been accustomed
to accept as true, and the resentment aroused when doubt is
cast upon any of our assumptions leads us to seek every manner
of excuse for clinging to them. *The result is that most of our
so-called reasoning consists in finding arguments for going on
believing as we already do.*

I remember years ago attending a public dinner to which the
Governor of the state was bidden. The chairman explained that
His Excellency could not be present for certain "good" reasons;
what the "real" reasons were the presiding officer said he would
leave us to conjecture. This distinction between "good" and
"real" reasons is one of the most clarifying and essential in the
whole realm of thought. We can readily give what seem to us
"good" reasons for being a Catholic or a Mason, a Republican
or a Democrat, an adherent or opponent of the League of Nations. But the "real" reasons are usually on quite a different
plane. Of course the importance of this distinction is popularly,
if somewhat obscurely, recognized. The Baptist missionary is
ready enough to see that the Buddhist is not such because his
doctrines would bear careful inspection, but because he happened to be born in a Buddhist family in Tokio. But it would
be treason to his faith to acknowledge that his own partiality for
certain doctrines is due to the fact that his mother was a member of the First Baptist Church of Oak Ridge. A savage can
give all sorts of reasons for his belief that it is dangerous to step
on a man's shadow, and a newspaper editor can advance plenty
of arguments against the Bolsheviki. But neither of them may
realize why he happens to be defending his particular opinion.

The "real" reasons for our beliefs are concealed from ourselves as well as from others. As we grow up we simply adopt
the ideas presented to us in regard to such matters as religion,
family relations, property, business, our country, and the state.

We unconsciously absorb them from our environment. They are persistently whispered in our ear by the group in which we happen to live. Moreover, as Mr. Trotter has pointed out, these judgments, being the product of suggestion and not of reasoning, have the quality of perfect obviousness, so that to question them

. . . is to the believer to carry skepticism to an insane degree, and will be met by contempt, disapproval, or condemnation, according to the nature of the belief in question. When, therefore, we find ourselves entertaining an opinion about the basis of which there is a quality of feeling which tells us that to inquire into it would be absurd, obviously unnecessary, unprofitable, undesirable, bad form, or wicked, we may know that that opinion is a non-rational one, and probably, therefore, founded upon inadequate evidence.[1]

Opinions, on the other hand, which are the result of experience or of honest reasoning do not have this quality of "primary certitude." I remember when as a youth I heard a group of business men discussing the question of the immortality of the soul, I was outraged by the sentiment of doubt expressed by one of the party. As I look back now I see that I had at the time no interest in the matter, and certainly no least argument to urge in favor of the belief in which I had been reared. But neither my personal indifference to the issue, nor the fact that I had previously given it no attention, served to prevent an angry resentment when I heard *my* ideas questioned.

This spontaneous and loyal support of our preconceptions—this process of finding "good" reasons to justify our routine beliefs—is known to modern psychologists as "rationalizing"—clearly only a new name for a very ancient thing. Our "good" reasons ordinarily have no value in promoting honest enlightenment, because, no matter how solemnly they may be marshaled, they are at bottom the result of personal preference or prejudice, and not of an honest desire to seek or accept new knowledge.

In our reveries we are frequently engaged in self-justification, for we cannot bear to think ourselves wrong, and yet have con-

[1] *Instincts of the Herd,* p. 44.

stant illustrations of our weaknesses and mistakes. So we spend much time finding fault with circumstances and the conduct of others, and shifting on to them with great ingenuity the onus of our own failures and disappointments. *Rationalizing is the self-exculpation which occurs when we feel ourselves, or our group, accused of misapprehension or error.*

The little word *my* is the most important one in all human affairs, and properly to reckon with it is the beginning of wisdom. It has the same force whether it is *my* dinner, *my* dog, and *my* house, or *my* faith, *my* country, and *my* God. We not only resent the imputation that our watch is wrong, or our car shabby, but that our conception of the canals of Mars, of the pronunciation of "Epictetus," of the medicinal value of salicine, or the date of Sargon I, are subject to revision.

Philosophers, scholars, and men of science exhibit a common sensitiveness in all decisions in which their *amour propre* is involved. Thousands of argumentative works have been written to vent a grudge. However stately their reasoning, it may be nothing but rationalizing, stimulated by the most commonplace of all motives. A history of philosophy and theology could be written in terms of grouches, wounded pride, and aversions, and it would be far more instructive than the usual treatments of these themes. Sometimes, under Providence, the lowly impulse of resentment leads to great achievements. Milton wrote his treatise on divorce as a result of his troubles with his seventeen-year-old wife, and when he was accused of being the leading spirit in a new sect, the Divorcers, he wrote his noble *Areopagitica* to prove his right to say what he thought fit, and incidentally to establish the advantage of a free press in the promotion of Truth.

All mankind, high and low, thinks in all the ways which have been described. The reverie goes on all the time not only in the mind of the mill hand and the Broadway flapper, but equally in weighty judges and godly bishops. It has gone on in all the philosophers, scientists, poets, and theologians that have ever lived. Aristotle's most abstruse speculations were doubtless tempered by highly irrelevant reflections. He is reported to have had very thin legs and small eyes, for which he doubtless had to find excuses, and he was wont to indulge in very conspicuous dress and rings and was accustomed to arrange his hair carefully.[1] Diogenes the Cynic exhibited the impudence of a touchy soul. His tub was his distinction. Tennyson in beginning his "Maud" could not forget his chagrin over losing his patrimony years before as the result of an unhappy investment in the Patent Decorative Carving Company. These facts are not recalled here as a gratuitous disparagement of the truly great, but to insure a full realization of the tremendous competition which all really exacting thought has to face, even in the minds of the most highly endowed mortals.

And now the astonishing and perturbing suspicion emerges that perhaps almost all that had passed for social science, political economy, politics, and ethics in the past may be brushed aside by future generations as mainly rationalizing. John Dewey has already reached this conclusion in regard to philosophy.[2] Veblen [3] and other writers have revealed the various unperceived presuppositions of the traditional political economy, and now comes an Italian sociologist, Vilfredo Pareto, who, in his huge treatise on general sociology, devotes hundreds of pages to substantiating a similar thesis affecting all the social sciences.[4] This conclusion may be ranked by students of a hundred years hence as one of the several great discoveries of our age. It is by no means fully worked out, and it is so opposed to nature that it will be very slowly accepted by the great mass of those who consider themselves thoughtful. As a historical student I am personally fully reconciled to this newer view. Indeed, it seems to me inevitable that just as the various sciences of nature were,

---

[1] *Diogenes Laertius,* Book V.
[2] *Reconstruction in Philosophy.*
[3] *The Place of Science in Modern Civilization.*
[4] *Traité de Sociologie Générale, passim.* The author's term *"derivations"* seems to be his precise way of expressing what we have called the "good" reasons, and his *"residus"* correspond to the "real" reasons. He well says, *"L'homme éprouve le besoin de raisonner, et en outre d'étendre une voile sur ses instincts et sur ses sentiments"*—hence, rationalization. (P. 788.) His aim is to reduce sociology to the "real" reasons. (P. 791.)

before the opening of the seventeenth century, largely masses of rationalizations to suit the religious sentiments of the period, so the social sciences have continued even to our own day to be rationalizations of uncritically accepted beliefs and customs.

It will become apparent as we proceed that the fact that an idea is ancient and that it has been widely received is no argument in its favor, but should immediately suggest the necessity of carefully testing it as a probable instance of rationalization.

This brings us to another kind of thought which can fairly easily be distinguished from the three kinds described above. It has not the usual qualities of the reverie, for it does not hover about our personal complacencies and humiliations. It is not made up of the homely decisions forced upon us by everyday needs, when we review our little stock of existing information, consult our conventional preferences and obligations, and make a choice of action. It is not the defense of our own cherished beliefs and prejudices just because they are our own—mere plausible excuses for remaining of the same mind. On the contrary, it is that peculiar species of thought which leads us to *change* our mind.

It is this kind of thought that has raised man from his pristine, subsavage ignorance and squalor to the degree of knowledge and comfort which he now possesses. On his capacity to continue and greatly extend this kind of thinking depends his chance of groping his way out of the plight in which the most highly civilized peoples of the world now find themselves. In the past this type of thinking has been called Reason. But so many misapprehensions have grown up around the word that some of us have become very suspicious of it. I suggest, therefore, that we substitute a recent name and speak of "creative thought" rather than of Reason. *For this kind of meditation begets knowledge, and knowledge is really creative inasmuch as it makes things look different from what they seemed before and may indeed work for their reconstruction.*

In certain moods some of us realize that we are observing things or making reflections with a seeming disregard of our personal preoccupations. We are not preening or defending ourselves; we are not faced by the necessity of any practical decision, nor are we apologizing for believing this or that. We are just wondering and looking and mayhap seeing what we never perceived before.

Curiosity is as clear and definite as any of our urges. We wonder what is in a sealed telegram or in a letter in which some one else is absorbed, or what is being said in the telephone booth or in low conversation. This inquisitiveness is vastly stimulated by jealousy, suspicion, or any hint that we ourselves are directly or indirectly involved. But there appears to be a fair amount of personal interest in other people's affairs even when they do not concern us except as a mystery to be unraveled or a tale to be told. The reports of a divorce suit will have "news value" for many weeks. They constitute a story, like a novel or play or moving picture. This is not an example of pure curiosity, however, since we readily identify ourselves with others, and their joys and despair then become our own.

We also take note of, or "observe," as Sherlock Holmes says, things which have nothing to do with our personal interests and make no personal appeal either direct or by way of sympathy. This is what Veblen so well calls "idle curiosity." And it is usually idle enough. Some of us when we face the line of people opposite us in a subway train impulsively consider them in detail and engage in rapid inferences and form theories in regard to them. On entering a room there are those who will perceive at a glance the degree of preciousness of the rugs, the character of the pictures, and the personality revealed by the books. But there are many, it would seem, who are so absorbed in their personal reverie or in some definite purpose that they have no bright-eyed energy for idle curiosity. The tendency to miscellaneous observation we come by honestly enough, for we note it in many of our animal relatives.

Veblen, however, uses the term "idle curiosity" somewhat ironically, as is his wont. It is idle only to those who fail to realize that it may be a very rare and indispensable thing from which almost all distinguished human achievement proceeds, since it may lead to systematic examination and seeking for things hitherto undiscovered. For research is but diligent search which enjoys the high flavor of primitive hunting. Occasionally and fitfully, idle curiosity thus leads to creative thought, which alters and broadens our own views and aspirations and may in turn, under highly favorable circumstances, affect the views and lives of others, even for generations to follow. An example or two will make this unique human process clear.

Galileo was a thoughtful youth and doubtless carried on a rich and varied reverie. He had artistic ability and might have turned out to be a musician or painter. When he had dwelt among the monks at Vallombrosa he had been tempted to lead the life of a religious. As a boy he busied himself with toy machines and he inherited a fondness for mathematics. All these facts are on record. We may safely assume also that, along with many other subjects of contemplation, the Pisan maidens found a vivid place in his thoughts.

One day when seventeen years old he wandered into the cathedral of his native town. In the midst of his reverie he looked up at the lamps hanging by long chains from the high ceiling of the church. Then something very difficult to explain occurred. He found himself no longer thinking of the building, worshipers, or the services; of his artistic or religious interests; of his reluctance to become a physician as his father wished. He forgot the question of a career and even the *graziosissime donne*. As he watched the swinging lamps he was suddenly wondering if mayhap their oscillations, whether long or short, did not occupy the same time. Then he tested this hypothesis by counting his pulse, for that was the only timepiece he had with him.

This observation, however remarkable in itself, was not enough to produce a really creative thought. Others may have noticed the same thing and yet nothing came of it. Most of our observations have no assignable results. Galileo may have seen that the warts on a peasant's face formed a perfect isosceles triangle, or he may have noticed with boyish glee that just as the officiating priest was uttering the solemn words, *Ecce agnus Dei*, a fly lit on the end of his nose. To be really creative, ideas have to be worked up and then "put over," so that they become a part of man's social heritage. The highly accurate pendulum clock was one of the later results of Galileo's discovery. He himself was led to reconsider and successfully to refute the old notions of falling bodies. It remained for Newton to prove that the moon was falling, and presumably all the heavenly bodies. This quite upset all the consecrated views of the heavens as managed by angelic engineers. The universality of the laws of gravitation stimulated the attempt to seek other and equally important natural laws and cast grave doubts on the miracles in which mankind had hitherto believed. In short, those who dared to include in their thought the discoveries of Galileo and his successors found themselves in a new earth surrounded by new heavens.

On the 28th of October, 1831, two hundred and fifty years after Galileo had noticed the isochronous vibrations of the lamps, creative thought and its currency had so far increased that Faraday was wondering what would happen if he mounted a disk of copper between the poles of a horseshoe magnet. As the disk revolved an electric current was produced. This would doubtless have seemed the idlest kind of experiment to the stanch business men of the time, who, it happened, were just then denouncing the child-labor bills in their anxiety to avail themselves to the full of the results of earlier idle curiosity. But should the dynamos and motors which have come into being as the outcome of Faraday's experiment be stopped this evening, the business man of to-day, agitated over labor troubles, might, as he trudged home past lines of "dead" cars, through dark streets to an unlighted house, engage in a little creative thought of his own and perceive that he and his laborers would have no modern factories and mines to quarrel about if it had not been for the strange practical effects of the idle curiosity of scientists, inventors and engineers.

The examples of creative intelligence given above belong to the realm of modern scientific achievement, which furnishes the most striking instances of the effects of scrupulous, objective thinking. But there are, of course, other great realms in which the recording and embodiment of acute observation and insight have wrought themselves into the higher life of man. The great poets and dramatists and our modern story-tellers have found themselves engaged in productive reveries, noting and artistically presenting their discoveries for the delight and instruction of those who have the ability to appreciate them.

The process by which a fresh and original poem or drama comes into being is doubtless analogous to that which originates and elaborates so-called scientific discoveries; but there is clearly a temperamental difference. The genesis and advance of painting, sculpture, and music offer still other problems. We really as yet know shockingly little about these matters, and indeed very few people have the least curiosity about them.[1] Nevertheless, creative intelligence in its various forms is what makes man. Were it not for its slow, painful, and constantly discouraged operations through the ages man would be no more than a species of primate living on seeds, fruit, roots, and uncooked flesh, and wandering naked through the woods and over the plains like a chimpanzee.

The origin and progress and future promotion of civilization are ill understood and misconceived. These should be made the chief theme of education, but much hard work is necessary before we can construct our ideas of man and his capacities and free ourselves from innumerable persistent misapprehensions. There have been obstructionists in all times, not merely the lethargic masses, but the moralists, the rationalizing theologians, and most of the philosophers, all busily if unconsciously engaged in ratifying existing ignorance and mistakes and discouraging creative thought. Naturally, those who reassure us seem worthy of honor and respect. Equally naturally those who puzzle us with disturbing criticisms and invite us to change our ways are objects of suspicion and readily discredited. Our personal discontent

[1] Recently a re-examination of creative thought has begun as a result of new knowledge which discredits many of the notions formerly held about "reason." See, for example, *Creative Intelligence,* by a group of American philosophic thinkers: John Dewey, *Essays in Experimental Logic* (both pretty hard books): and Veblen, *The Place of Science in Modern Civilization.* Easier than these and very stimulating are Dewey, *Reconstruction in Philosophy,* and Woodworth, *Dynamic Psychology.*

does not ordinarily extend to any critical questioning of the general situation in which we find ourselves. In every age the prevailing conditions of civilization have appeared quite natural and inevitable to those who grew up in them. The cow asks no questions as to how it happens to have a dry stall and a supply of hay. The kitten laps its warm milk from a china saucer, without knowing anything about porcelain; the dog nestles in the corner of a divan with no sense of obligation to the inventors of upholstery and the manufacturers of down pillows. So we humans accept our breakfasts, our trains and telephones and orchestras and movies, our national Constitution, our moral code and standards of manners, with the simplicity and innocence of a pet rabbit. We have absolutely inexhaustible capacities for appropriating what others do for us with no thought of a "thank you." We do not feel called upon to make any least contribution to the merry game ourselves. Indeed, we are usually quite unaware that a game is being played at all.

We have now examined the various classes of thinking which we can readily observe in ourselves and which we have plenty of reasons to believe go on, and always have been going on, in our fellow-men. We can sometimes get quite pure and sparkling examples of all four kinds, but commonly they are so confused and intermingled in our reverie as not to be readily distinguishable. The reverie is a reflection of our longings, exultations, and complacencies, our fears, suspicions, and disappointments. We are chiefly engaged in struggling to maintain our self-respect and in asserting that supremacy which we all crave and which seems to us our natural prerogative. It is not strange, but rather quite inevitable, that our beliefs about what is true and false, good and bad, right and wrong, should be mixed up with the reverie and be influenced by the same considerations which determine its character and course. We resent criticisms of our views exactly as we do of anything else connected with ourselves. Our notions of life and its ideals seem to us to be *our own* and as such necessarily true and right, to be defended at all costs.

We very rarely consider, however, the process by which we

gained our convictions. If we did so, we could hardly fail to see that there was usually little ground for our confidence in them. Here and there, in this department of knowledge or that, some one of us might make a fair claim to have taken some trouble to get correct ideas of, let us say, the situation in Russia, the sources of our food supply, the origin of the Constitution, the revision of the tariff, the policy of the Holy Roman Apostolic Church, modern business organization, trade unions, birth control, socialism, the League of Nations, the excess-profits tax, preparedness, advertising in its social bearings; but only a very exceptional person would be entitled to opinions on all of even these few matters. And yet most of us have opinions on all these, and on many other questions of equal importance, of which we may know even less. We feel compelled, as self-respecting persons, to take sides when they come up for discussion. We even surprise ourselves by our omniscience. Without taking thought we see in a flash that it is most righteous and expedient to discourage birth control by legislative enactment, or that one who decries intervention in Mexico is clearly wrong, or that big advertising is essential to big business and that big business is the pride of the land. As godlike beings why should we not rejoice in our omniscience?

It is clear in any case, that our convictions on important matters are not the result of knowledge or critical thought, nor, it may be added, are they often dictated by supposed self-interest. Most of them are *pure prejudices* in the proper sense of that word. We do not form them ourselves. They are the whispering of "the voice of the herd." We have in the last analysis no responsibility for them and need assume none. They are not really our own ideas, but those of others no more well informed or inspired than ourselves, who have got them in the same humiliating manner as we. It should be our pride to revise our ideas and not to adhere to what passes for respectable opinion, for such opinion can frequently be shown to be not respectable at all. We should, in view of the considerations that have been mentioned, resent our supine credulity. As an English writer has remarked:

"If we feared the entertaining of an unverifiable opinion with the warmth with which we fear using the wrong implement at the dinner table, if the thought of holding a prejudice disgusted us as does a foul disease, then the dangers of man's susceptibility would be turned into advantages." [1]

EXERCISES

1. Study the splendid use of transitional words and phrases which unite the paragraphs in Mr. Croly's essay. Emulate Mr. Croly's example in your own work.

2. Use this same form of analysis by enumeration by writing a theme on "John Brown as More than a College Hero" or on "Mr. Smith (Miss Jones) as More than a College Professor." You should find it an excellent model.

3. Write an enumerative analysis on any one of the following subjects:

> The Obscurities of College Catalogues
> The Irritating Prejudices of the Fraternity Man
> The Irritating Prejudices of the Non-Fraternity Man
> The Terrors of Childhood
> Certain Interesting Methods of Advertising
> Alfred E. Smith as a Man of the People

4. Develop by comparison and contrast a theme on any one of the following subjects, being sure to choose some controlling idea as the basis of comparison:

> The Small College and the Large University
> The City and the Country as a Home for Children
> The Fraternity Man and the Barbarian
> The Sorority and the Non-Sorority Woman
> The Relative Advantages of Faculty Government and of Student Self-Government.

5. Write an analysis by classification on one of the following subjects: (Note that here, too, some principle of classification, some controlling purpose, must underlie your work.)

[1] Trotter, *op. cit.*, p. 45. The first part of this little volume is excellent.

March Birds in ———
American Fiction Magazines
College Boarding Places
Tasks for the Self-supporting Student
The Justifiableness of the College "Drive."
Extra-Curricular Activities as Productive of Self-Dependence

6. Use Mr. Robinson's splendid and illuminating essay as a basis for class discussion. No time will be lost if it is used also as a basis for good and honest thought about oneself.

7. Write an analysis by classification on "Typical Class-room Reveries."

8. Read Stuart Chase's article, "My Great-Great-Grandfather and I," in *The Nation* for September 1, 1926, and use it as a model for an analysis of your own on a similar subject.

9. After reading Dr. Eliot's essay on *The Durable Satisfactions of Life,* write an enumerative analysis on "The Durable Satisfactions of College Life." Try treating it satirically, or merely humorously, that is, unless you prefer to be serious.

SUGGESTED READINGS

By Enumeration:

Cabot, Richard, "The Call of the Job," *The Atlantic Monthly,* November 1913.

Eliot, Charles W., *The Durable Satisfactions of Life,* Crowell, New York.

Forster, E. M., "An Englishman's Character," *The Atlantic Monthly,* January 1926.

Lodge, Henry Cabot, "Benjamin Franklin" from *A Frontier Town and Other Essays,* Scribner's, New York.

Roosevelt, Theodore, "The Manly Virtues and Practical Politics" from *American Ideals,* Putnam's.

Santayana, George, "The British Character" from *Soliloquies in England,* Scribner's, New York.

Sweetser, Arthur, "What the League of Nations Has Accomplished," New York. *Times Current History,* September 1922.

By Comparison and Contrast:

Chase, Stuart, "My Great-Great-Grandfather and I," *The Nation,* September 1, 1926.

Galsworthy, John, "American and Briton" from *Another Sheaf,* Scribner's, New York.

Green, John Richard, "The Character of Elizabeth" from *A Short History of the English People,* pp. 370-376, Harper's, New York.

Macaulay, Thomas Babington, "The Country and the City Clergy" from "England in 1685," Chapter III, *The History of England.*

By Classification:

Gayley, Charles Mills, "The Idols of Our Education" from *Idols,* Doubleday, Doran, New York.

Higginson, Thomas Wentworth, "English and American Gentlemen" from *Book and Heart,* Harper's, New York.

Jowett, Benjamin, "Causes of Failure" from *College Sermons,* Macmillan, New York.

Lamb, Charles, "The Two Races of Men" from *Essays of Elia.*

CHAPTER IV

THE HISTORICAL INCIDENT

The writing of historical incidents is to many other forms of composition as an avocation is to a vocation. Here the subject matter lies ready to your hand and for your choice. Having chosen, you have but to consider the materials you have to work with and the best tools with which to work. Your pleasant task is to manipulate, to arrange, and to array the facts before you. Accuracy is not your first aim; you are a would-be artist before you are an historian; and yet you must and can, without impairing your cause in the slightest degree, stay well within the paths of truth.

If you will find Macaulay's essay on Hallam and read the introduction to it, you will discover at once a good watchword and a good recipe for your work. The first lies in a sentence in which Macaulay deplores the fact that the writers of history of his day, exact and accurate though they may be, "present no scene to the imagination." The second, the recipe, is given in the following sentence: "To make the past present, to bring the distant near, to place us in the society of a great man or on the eminence which overlooks the scene of a mighty battle, to invest with the reality of human flesh and blood beings whom we are too much inclined to consider as personified qualities in an allegory, to call up our ancestors before us with all their peculiarities of language, manners and garb, to show us over their homes, to seat us at their tables, to rummage their old-fashioned wardrobes, to explain the uses of their ponderous furniture"—these, he writes, are "parts of the duty which properly belongs to the historian."

And such an historian Macaulay assuredly was. It is to him,

indeed, and to his disciples that one must turn for example as well as for precept.

To present a scene to the imagination must be your motive and aim as a writer of historical incident. You may choose a subject from any age and any circumstances providing there is an incident attached. American History is filled with suggestions. One has but to think of familiar names from Columbus and John Smith to Generals Braddock and Custer, from Ponce de Leon and DeSoto to Lewis and Clark to become convinced of the richness of material within our own borders. English, French, and Medieval History reveal their stores to the well-read mind and imagination; and one has but to page through Gibbon's *Decline and Fall* to realize how full of such wealth is the history of Rome. Nor should contemporary history be neglected. Few incidents of any age are more stirring than the death of Edith Cavell or than the manifold experiences of Lawrence in Arabia.

A study of the models which follow will interpret for you your watchword: *To present a scene to the imagination.* From them you will easily gather the following suggestions for your work:

1. Be sure to adapt your style and your diction to the subject at hand.

This is especially well illustrated by "The Black Hole of Calcutta." Even a careless student must note the rapidity of movement, the brevity of many of the sentences, the quick succession of clauses as the action mounts.

2. Don't neglect vivid detail when it will admirably serve your subject and your purpose. For the value of this read and re-read Froude's account of the marriage of Henry VIII and Anne Boleyn. And yet, on the other hand, you must take care that you do not obscure with detail that which will be most effective without it. For example, Plato's beautiful description of the death of Socrates would be greatly harmed by detail. The incident appeals through the tragic force of its own drama which would be dulled by accessories and additions. Here our minds and our spirits are touched, not our senses.

3. Employ pictorial and suggestive words.

Froude and Parkman will be of greatest help to you here. But again do not, to quote Lamb, "pile honey upon sugar and sugar upon honey to an interminable tedious sweetness." You are, remember, writing an incident. Again you are warned that the mind as well as the senses of your reader must be satisfied.

4. Don't neglect anecdote or incident within incident if it will serve your purpose.

For the value of these read the selection from Francis Parkman.

The Black Hole of Calcutta [1]

By Thomas Babington Macaulay

The great province of Bengal, together with Orissa and Bahar, had long been governed by a viceroy, whom the English called Aliverdy Khan, and who, like the other viceroys of the Mogul, had become virtually independent. He died in 1756, and the sovereignty descended to his grandson, a youth under twenty years of age, who bore the name of Surajah Dowlah. Oriental despots are perhaps the worst class of human beings; and this unhappy boy was one of the worst specimens of his class. His understanding was naturally feeble, and his temper naturally unamiable. His education had been such as would have enervated even a vigorous intellect, and perverted even a generous disposition. He was unreasonable, because nobody ever dared to reason with him, and selfish, because he had never been made to feel himself dependent on the goodwill of others. Early debauchery had unnerved his body and his mind. He indulged immoderately in the use of ardent spirits, which inflamed his weak brain almost to madness. His chosen companions were flatterers sprung from the dregs of the people, and recommended by nothing but buffoonery and servility. It is said that he had arrived at the last stage of human depravity, when cruelty becomes pleasing for its own sake, when the sight of pain as pain, where no advantage is to be gained, no offence punished, no danger averted, is an agreeable excitement. It had early been his

[1] From *Lord Clive.*

amusement to torture beasts and birds; and, when he grew up, he enjoyed with still keener relish the misery of his fellow-creatures. From a child Surajah Dowlah had hated the English. It was his whim to do so; and his whims were never opposed. He had also formed a very exaggerated notion of the wealth which might be obtained by plundering them; and his feeble and uncultivated mind was incapable of perceiving that the riches of Calcutta, had they been even greater than he imagined, would not compensate him for what he must lose, if the European trade, of which Bengal was a chief seat, should be driven by his violence to some other quarter. Pretexts for a quarrel were readily found. The English, in expectation of a war with France, had begun to fortify their settlement without special permission from the Nabob. A rich native, whom he longed to plunder, had taken refuge at Calcutta, and had not been delivered up. On such grounds as these Surajah Dowlah marched with a great army against Fort William.

The servants of the Company at Madras had been forced by Dupleix to become statesmen and soldiers. Those in Bengal were still mere traders, and were terrified and bewildered by the approaching danger. The governor, who had heard much of Surajah Dowlah's cruelty, was frightened out of his wits, jumped into a boat, and took refuge in the nearest ship. The military commandant thought that he could not do better than follow so good an example. The fort was taken after a feeble resistance; and great numbers of the English fell into the hands of the conquerors. The Nabob seated himself with regal pomp in the principal hall of the factory, and ordered Mr. Holwell, the first in rank among the prisoners, to be brought before him. His Highness talked about the insolence of the English, and grumbled at the smallness of the treasure which he had found, but promised to spare their lives, and retired to rest.

Then was committed that great crime, memorable for its singular atrocity, memorable for the tremendous retribution by which it was followed. The English captives were left to the mercy of the guards, and the guards determined to secure them for the night in the prison of the garrison, a chamber known by the fearful name of the Black Hole. Even for a single European malefactor, that dungeon would, in such a climate, have been too close and narrow. The space was only twenty feet square. The air-holes were small and obstructed. It was the summer solstice, the season when the fierce heat of Bengal can scarcely be rendered tolerable to natives of England by lofty halls and by the constant waving of fans. The number of prisoners was one hundred and forty-six. When they were ordered to enter the cell, they imagined that the soldiers were joking; and, being in high spirits on account of the promise of the Nabob to spare their lives, they laughed and jested at the absurdity of the notion. They soon discovered their mistake. They expostulated; they entreated; but in vain. The guards threatened to cut down all who hesitated. The captives were driven into the cell at the point of the sword, and the door was instantly shut and locked upon them.

Nothing in history or fiction, not even the story which Ugolino told in the sea of everlasting ice, after he had wiped his bloody lips on the scalp of his murderer, approaches the horrors which were recounted by the few survivors of that night. They cried for mercy. They strove to burst the door. Holwell, who, even in that extremity, retained some presence of mind, offered large bribes to the gaolers. But the answer was that nothing could be done without the Nabob's orders, that the Nabob was asleep, and that he would be angry if anybody woke him. Then the prisoners went mad with despair. They trampled each other down, fought for the places at the windows, fought for the pittance of water with which the cruel mercy of the murderers mocked their agonies, raved, prayed, blasphemed, implored the guards to fire among them. The gaolers in the meantime held lights to the bars, and shouted with laughter at the frantic struggles of their victims. At length the tumult died away in low gaspings and moanings. The day broke. The Nabob had slept off his debauch, and permitted the door to be opened. But it was some time before the soldiers could make a lane for the survivors by piling up on each side the heaps of corpses on which the burning climate had already begun to do its loathsome work.

When at length a passage was made, twenty-three ghastly figures, such as their own mothers would not have known, staggered one by one out of the charnel-house. A pit was instantly dug. The dead bodies, a hundred and twenty-three in number, were flung into it promiscuously and covered up.

But these things—which, after the lapse of more than eighty years, cannot be told or read without horror—awakened neither remorse nor pity in the bosom of the savage Nabob. He inflicted no punishment on the murderers. He showed no tenderness to the survivors. Some of them, indeed, from whom nothing was to be got, were suffered to depart; but those from whom it was thought that anything could be extorted were treated with execrable cruelty. Holwell, unable to walk, was carried before the tyrant, who reproached him, threatened him, and sent him up the country in irons, together with some other gentlemen who were suspected of knowing more than they chose to tell about the treasures of the Company. These persons, still bowed down by the sufferings of that great agony, were lodged in miserable sheds, and fed only with grain and water, till at length the intercessions of the female relations of the Nabob procured their release. One Englishwoman had survived that night. She was placed in the harem of the Prince at Moorshedabad.

Surajah Dowlah, in the meantime, sent letters to his nominal sovereign at Delhi, describing the late conquest in the most pompous language. He placed a garrison in Fort William, forbade Englishmen to dwell in the neighbourhood, and directed that, in memory of his great actions, Calcutta should thenceforward be called Alinagore, that is to say, the Port of God.

THE MARRIAGE OF HENRY AND ANNE BOLEYN [1]

By James Anthony Froude

On the morning of the 31st of May, the families of the London citizens were stirring early in all houses. From Temple Bar to the Tower, the streets were fresh strewed with gravel, the foot-

[1] From *The History of England*.

paths were railed off along the whole distance, and occupied on one side by the guilds, their workmen, and apprentices, on the other by the city constables and officials in their gaudy uniforms, "with their staves in hand for to cause the people to keep good room and order." Cornhill and Gracechurch-street had dressed their fronts in scarlet and crimson, in arras and tapestry, and the rich carpet-work from Persia and the East. Cheapside, to out-shine her rivals, was draped even more splendidly in cloth of gold, and tissue, and velvet. The sheriffs were pacing up and down on their great Flemish horses, hung with liveries, and all the windows were thronged with ladies crowding to see the pro-cession pass. At length the Tower guns opened, the grim gates rolled back, and under the archway in the bright May sunshine, the long column began slowly to defile. Two states only per-mitted their representatives to grace the scene with their presence —Venice and France. It was, perhaps, to make the most of this isolated countenance, that the French ambassador's train formed the van of the cavalcade. Twelve French knights came riding foremost in surcoats of blue velvet with sleeves of yellow silk, their horses trapped in blue, with white crosses powdered on their hangings. After them followed a troop of English gentle-men, two and two, and then the Knights of the Bath, "in gowns of violet, with hoods purified with miniver like doctors." Next, perhaps at a little interval, the abbots passed on, mitred in their robes; the barons followed in crimson velvet, the bishops then, and then the earls and marquises, the dresses of each order in-creasing in elaborate gorgeousness. All these rode on in pairs. Then came alone Audeley, lord-chancellor, and behind him the Venetian ambassador and the Archbishop of York; the Arch-bishop of Canterbury, and Du Bellay, Bishop of Bayonne and of Paris, not now with bugle and hunting-frock, but solemn with stole and crozier. Next, the lord mayor, with the city mace in hand, and Garter in his coat of arms; and then Lord William Howard—Belted Will Howard, of the Scottish Border, Marshal of England. The officers of the queen's household succeeded the marshal in scarlet and gold, and the van of the procession was closed by the Duke of Suffolk, as high constable, with his silver wand. It is no easy matter to picture to ourselves the blazing trail of splendour which in such a pageant must have drawn along the London streets,—those streets which now we know so black and smoke-grimed, themselves then radiant with masses of colour, gold, and crimson, and violet. Yet there it was, and there the sun could shine upon it, and tens of thousands of eyes were gazing on the scene out of the crowded lattices.

Glorious as the spectacle was, perhaps, however, it passed unheeded. Those eyes were watching all for another object, which now drew near. In an open space behind the constable there was seen approaching "a white chariot," drawn by two palfreys in white damask which swept the ground, a golden canopy borne above it making music with silver bells: and in the chariot sat the observed of all observers, the beautiful occasion of all this glittering homage; fortune's plaything of the hour, the Queen of England—queen at last—borne along upon the waves of this sea of glory, breathing the perfumed incense of greatness which she had risked her fair name, her delicacy, her honour, her self-respect, to win; and she had won it.

There she sate, dressed in white tissue robes, her fair hair flowing loose over her shoulders, and her temples circled with a light coronet of gold and diamonds—most beautiful—loveliest—most favoured perhaps, as she seemed at that hour, of all England's daughters. Alas! "within the hollow round" of that coronet—

> Kept death his court, and there the antick sate,
> Scoffing her state and grinning at her pomp.
> Allowing her a little breath, a little scene
> To monarchize, be feared, and kill with looks,
> Infusing her with self and vain conceit,
> As if the flesh which walled about her life
> Were brass impregnable; and humoured thus,
> Bored through her castle walls; and farewell, Queen.

Fatal gift of greatness! so dangerous ever! so more than dangerous in those tremendous times when the fountains are broken loose of the great deeps of thought; and nations are in the throes of revolution;—when ancient order and law and tradition are

splitting in the social earthquake; and as the opposing forces
wrestle to and fro, those unhappy ones who stand out above the
crowd become the symbols of the struggle, and fall the victims
of its alternating fortunes. And what if into an unsteady heart
and brain, intoxicated with splendour, the outward chaos should
find its way, converting the poor silly soul into an image of the
same confusion,—if conscience should be deposed from her high
place, and the Pandora box be broken loose of passions and
sensualities and follies; and at length there be nothing left of all
which man or woman ought to value, save hope of God's forgiveness.

Three short years have yet to pass, and again, on a summer
morning, Queen Anne Boleyn will leave the Tower of London—
not radiant then with beauty on a gay errand of coronation, but
a poor wandering ghost, on a sad tragic errand, from which she
will never more return, passing away out of an earth where she
may stay no longer, into a Presence where, nevertheless, we know
that all is well—for all of us—and therefore for her.

But let us not cloud her shortlived sunshine with the shadow
of the future. She went on in her loveliness, the peeresses following in their carriages, with the royal guard in their rear. In
Fenchurch-street she was met by the children of the city schools;
and at the corner of Gracechurch-street a masterpiece had been
prepared of the pseudo-classic art, then so fashionable, by the
merchants of the Styll-yard. A Mount Parnassus had been constructed, and a Helicon fountain upon it playing into a basin with
four jets of Rhenish wine. On the top of the mountain sat
Apollo with Calliope at his feet, and on either side the remaining
Muses, holding lutes or harps, and singing each of them some
"posy" or epigram in praise of the queen, which was presented,
after it had been sung, written in letters of gold.

From Gracechurch-street the procession passed to Leadenhall,
where there was a spectacle in better taste, of the old English
catholic kind, quaint perhaps and forced, but truly and even
beautifully emblematic. There was again a "little mountain,"
which was hung with red and white roses; a gold ring was placed
on the summit, on which, as the queen appeared, a white falcon

was made to "descend as out of the sky"—"and then incontinent came down an angel with great melody, and set a close crown of gold upon the falcon's head; and in the same pageant sat Saint Anne with all her issue beneath her; and Mary Cleophas with her four children, of the which children one made a goodly oration to the queen, of the fruitfulness of Saint Anne, trusting that like fruit should come of her."

With such "pretty conceits," at that time the honest tokens of an English welcome, the new queen was received by the citizens of London. These scenes must be multiplied by the number of the streets, where some fresh fancy met her at every turn. To preserve the festivities from flagging, every fountain and conduit within the walls ran all day with wine; the bells of every steeple were ringing; children lay in wait with songs, and ladies with posies, in which all the resources of fantastic extravagance were exhausted; and thus in an unbroken triumph—and to outward appearance received with the warmest affection—she passed under Temple Bar, down the Strand by Charing Cross to Westminster Hall. The king was not with her throughout the day; nor did he intend to be with her in any part of the ceremony. She was to reign without a rival, the undisputed sovereign of the hour.

Saturday being passed in showing herself to the people, she retired for the night to "the king's manour house at Westminster," where she slept. On the following morning, between eight and nine o'clock, she returned to the hall, where the lord mayor, the city council, and the peers were again assembled, and took her place on the high dais at the top of the stairs under the cloth of state; while the bishops, the abbots, and the monks of the abbey formed in the area. A railed way had been laid with carpets across Palace Yard and the Sanctuary to the abbey gates, and when all was ready, preceded by the peers in their robes of parliament, the Knights of the Garter in the dress of the order, she swept out under her canopy, the bishops and the monks "solemnly singing." The train was borne by the old Duchess of Norfolk, her aunt, the Bishops of London and Winchester on either side "bearing up the lappets of her robe." The Earl of Oxford carried the crown on its cushion immediately before her.

She was dressed in purple velvet furred with ermine, her hair escaping loose, as she usually wore it, under a wreath of diamonds.

On entering the abbey, she was led to the coronation chair, where she sat while the train fell into their places, and the preliminaries of the ceremonial were despatched. Then she was conducted up to the high altar, and anointed Queen of England, and she received from the hands of Cranmer, fresh come in haste from Dunstable, with the last words of his sentence upon Catherine scarcely silent upon his lips, the golden sceptre, and St. Edward's crown.

THE DEATH OF SOCRATES [1]

By Plato

Now the hour of sunset was near, for a good deal of time had passed while he was within. When he came out, he sat down with us again after his bath, but not much was said. Soon the jailer, who was the servant of the Eleven, entered and stood by him, saying:—To you, Socrates, whom I know to be the noblest and gentlest and best of all who ever came to this place, I will not impute the angry feelings of other men, who rage and swear at me, when, in obedience to the authorities, I bid them drink the poison—indeed, I am sure that you will not be angry with me; for others, as you are aware, and not I, are to blame. And so fare you well, and try to bear lightly what must needs be—you know my errand. Then bursting into tears he turned away and went out.

Socrates looked at him and said: I return your good wishes, and will do as you bid. Then turning to us, he said, How charming the man is: since I have been in prison he has always been coming to see me, and at times he would talk to me, and was as good to me as could be, and now see how generously he sorrows on my account. We must do as he says, Crito; and therefore let the cup be brought, if the poison is prepared: if not, let the attendant prepare some.

[1] From the translation of the *Phædo* by Benjamin Jowett.

Yet, said Crito, the sun is still upon the hill tops, and I know that many a one has taken the draught late, and after the announcement has been made to him, he has eaten and drunk, and enjoyed the society of his beloved; do not hurry—there is time enough.

Socrates said: Yes, Crito, and they of whom you speak are right in so acting, for they think that they will be gainers by the delay; but I am right in not following their example, for I do not think that I should gain anything by drinking the poison a little later; I should only be ridiculous in my own eyes for sparing and saving a life which is already forfeit. Please then to do as I say, and not to refuse me.

Crito made a sign to the servant, who was standing by; and he went out, and having been absent for some time, returned with the jailer carrying the cup of poison. Socrates said: You, my good friend, who are experienced in these matters, shall give me directions how I am to proceed. The man answered: You have only to walk about until your legs are heavy, and then to lie down, and the poison will act. At the same time he handed the cup to Socrates, who in the easiest and gentlest manner, without the least fear or change of colour or feature, looking at the man with all his eyes, Echecrates, as his manner was, took the cup and said: What do you say about making a libation out of this cup to any god? May I, or not? The man answered: We only prepare, Socrates, just so much as we deem enough. I understand, he said: but I may and must ask the gods to prosper my journey from this to the other world—even so—and so be it according to my prayer. Then raising the cup to his lips, quite readily and cheerfully he drank off the poison. And hitherto most of us had been able to control our sorrow; but now when we saw him drinking, and saw too that he had finished the draught, we could no longer forbear, and in spite of myself my own tears were flowing fast; so that I covered my face and wept, not for him, but at the thought of my own calamity in having to part from such a friend. Nor was I the first; for Crito, when he found himself unable to restrain his tears, had got up, and I followed; and at that moment, Apollodorus, who had been weeping all the time, broke out in a loud and passionate cry which made cowards of us all. Socrates alone retained his calmness: What is this strange outcry? he said. I sent away the women mainly in order that they might not misbehave in this way, for I have been told that a man should die in peace. Be quiet then, and have patience. When we heard his words we were ashamed, and refrained our tears; and he walked about until, as he said, his legs began to fail, and then he lay on his back, according to the directions, and the man who gave him the poison now and then looked at his feet and legs; and after a while he pressed his foot hard, and asked him if he could feel; and he said, No; and then his leg, and so upwards and upwards, and showed us that he was cold and stiff. And then he felt them himself, and said: When the poison reaches the heart, that will be the end. He was beginning to grow cold about the groin, when he uncovered his face, for he had covered himself up, and said—they were his last words—he said: Crito, I owe a cock to Asclepius; will you remember to pay the debt? The debt shall be paid, said Crito; is there anything else? There was no answer to this question; but in a minute or two a movement was heard, and the attendants uncovered him; his eyes were set, and Crito closed his eyes and mouth.

Such was the end, Echecrates, of our friend; concerning whom I may truly say, that of all the men of his time whom I have known, he was the wisest and justest and best.

The Capture of Quebec [1]

By Francis Parkman

Early in June, General Wolfe sailed up the St. Lawrence with a force of eight thousand men, and formed his camp immediately below Quebec, on the island of Orleans. From thence he could discern, at a single glance, how arduous was the task before him. Piles of lofty cliffs rose with sheer ascent on the northern border of the river; and from their summits the boasted citadel of

[1] From *The Conspiracy of Pontiac.*

Canada looked down in proud security, with its churches and convents of stone, its ramparts, bastions, and batteries; while over them all, from the brink of the precipice, towered the massive walls of the Castle of St. Louis. Above, for many a league, the bank was guarded by an unbroken range of steep acclivities. Below, the river St. Charles, flowing into the St. Lawrence, washed the base of the rocky promontory on which the city stood. Lower yet lay an army of fourteen thousand men, under an able and renowned commander, the Marquis of Montcalm. His front was covered by intrenchments and batteries, which lined the bank of the St. Lawrence; his right wing rested on the city and the St. Charles; his left, on the cascade and deep gulf of Montmorenci; and thick forests extended along his rear. Opposite Quebec rose the high promontory of Point Levi; and the St. Lawrence, contracted to less than a mile in width, flowed between, with deep and powerful current. To a chief of less resolute temper, it might well have seemed that art and nature were in league to thwart his enterprise; but a mind like that of Wolfe could only have seen in this majestic combination of forest and cataract, mountain and river, a fitting theatre for the great drama about to be enacted there.

Yet nature did not seem to have formed the young English general for the conduct of a doubtful and almost desperate enterprise. His person was slight, and his features by no means of a martial cast. His feeble constitution had been undermined by years of protracted and painful disease. His kind and genial disposition seemed better fitted for the quiet of domestic life than for the stern duties of military command; but to these gentler traits he joined a high enthusiasm, and an unconquerable spirit of daring and endurance, which made him the idol of his soldiers, and bore his slender frame through every hardship and exposure.

The work before him demanded all his courage. How to invest the city, or even bring the army of Montcalm to action, was a problem which might have vexed a Hannibal. A French fleet lay in the river above, and the precipices along the northern bank were guarded at every accessible point by sentinels and outposts. Wolfe would have crossed the Montmorenci by its upper ford, and attacked the French army on its left and rear; but the plan was thwarted by the nature of the ground and the vigilance of his adversaries. Thus baffled at every other point, he formed the bold design of storming Montcalm's position in front; and on the afternoon of the thirty-first of July, a strong body of troops was embarked in boats, and covered by a furious cannonade from the English ships and batteries, landed on the beach just above the mouth of the Montmorenci. The grenadiers and Royal Americans were the first on shore, and their ill-timed impetuosity proved the ruin of the plan. Without waiting to receive their orders or form their ranks, they ran, pell-mell, across the level ground, and with loud shouts began, each man for himself, to scale the heights which rose in front, crested with intrenchments and bristling with hostile arms. The French at the top threw volley after volley among the hot-headed assailants. The slopes were soon covered with the fallen; and at that instant a storm, which had long been threatening, burst with sudden fury, drenched the combatants on both sides with a deluge of rain, extinguished for a moment the fire of the French, and at the same time made the steeps so slippery that the grenadiers fell repeatedly in their vain attempts to climb. Night was coming on with double darkness. The retreat was sounded, and, as the English re-embarked, troops of Indians came whooping down the heights, and hovered about their rear, to murder the stragglers and the wounded; while exulting cries of *Vive le Roi*, from the crowded summits, proclaimed the triumph of the enemy.

With bitter agony of mind, Wolfe beheld the headlong folly of his men, and saw more than four hundred of the flower of his army fall a useless sacrifice. The anxieties of the siege had told severely upon his slender constitution; and not long after this disaster, he felt the first symptoms of a fever, which soon confined him to his couch. Still his mind never wavered from its purpose, and it was while lying helpless in the chamber of a Canadian house, where he had fixed his headquarters, that he embraced the plan of the enterprise which robbed him of his life, and gave him immortal fame.

The plan had been first proposed during the height of Wolfe's illness, at a council of his subordinate generals, Monckton, Townshend, and Murray. It was resolved to divide the little army; and, while one portion remained before Quebec to alarm the enemy by false attacks, and distract their attention from the scene of actual operation, the other was to pass above the town, land under cover of darkness on the northern shore, climb the guarded heights, gain the plains above, and force Montcalm to quit his vantage-ground, and perhaps to offer battle. The scheme was daring even to rashness; but its audacity was the secret of its success.

Early in September, a crowd of ships and transports, under Admiral Holmes, passed the city under the hot fire of its batteries; while the troops designed for the expedition, amounting to scarcely five thousand, marched upward along the southern bank, beyond reach of the cannonade. All were then embarked; and on the evening of the twelfth, Holmes's fleet, with the troops on board, lay safe at anchor in the river, several leagues above the town. These operations had not failed to awaken the suspicions of Montcalm; and he had detached M. Bougainville to watch the movements of the English, and prevent their landing on the northern shore.

The eventful night of the twelfth was clear and calm, with no light but that of the stars. Within two hours before daybreak, thirty boats, crowded with sixteen hundred soldiers, cast off from the vessels, and floated downward, in perfect order, with the current of the ebb tide. To the boundless joy of the army, Wolfe's malady had abated, and he was able to command in person. His ruined health, the gloomy prospects of the siege, and the disaster at Montmorenci had oppressed him with the deepest melancholy, but never impaired for a moment the promptness of his decisions, or the impetuous energy of his action. He sat in the stern of one of his boats, pale and weak, but borne up to a calm height of resolution. Every order had been given, every arrangement made, and it only remained to face the issue. The ebbing tide sufficed to bear the boats along, and nothing broke the silence of the night but the gurgling of the river, and the low voice of Wolfe, as he repeated to the officers about him the stanzas of Gray's "Elegy in a Country Churchyard," which had recently appeared and which he had just received from England. Perhaps, as he uttered those strangely appropriate words,—

"The paths of glory lead but to the grave,"

the shadows of his own approaching fate stole with mournful prophecy across his mind. "Gentlemen," he said, as he closed his recital, "I would rather have written those lines than take Quebec to-morrow."

As they approached the landing-place, the boats edged closer in toward the northern shore, and the woody precipices rose high on their left, like a wall of undistinguished blackness.

"*Qui vive?*" shouted a French sentinel, from out the impervious gloom.

"*La France!*" answered a captain of Frazer's Highlanders, from the foremost boat.

"*A quel regiment?*" demanded the soldier.

"*De la Reine!*" promptly replied the Highland captain, who chanced to know that the regiment so designated formed part of Bougainville's command. As boats were frequently passing down the river with supplies for the garrison, and as a convoy from Bougainville was expected that very night, the sentinel was deceived, and allowed the English to proceed.

A few moments after, they were challenged again, and this time they could discern the soldier running close down to the water's edge, as if all his suspicions were aroused; but the skilful replies of the Highlander once more saved the party from discovery.

They reached the landing-place in safety—an indentation in the shore, about a league above the city, and now bearing the name of Wolfe's Cove. Here a narrow path led up the face of the heights, and a French guard was posted at the top to defend the pass. By the force of the current, the foremost boats, including that which carried Wolfe himself, were borne a little below the spot. The general was one of the first on shore. He looked upward at the rugged heights which towered above him in the gloom. "You can try it," he coolly observed to an officer near him; "but I don't think you'll get up."

At the point where the Highlanders landed, one of their captains, Donald MacDonald, apparently the same whose presence of mind had just saved the enterprise from ruin, was climbing in advance of his men, when he was challenged by a sentinel. He replied in French, by declaring that he had been sent to relieve the guard, and ordering the soldier to withdraw. Before the latter was undeceived, a crowd of Highlanders were close at hand, while the steeps below were thronged with eager climbers, dragging themselves up by trees, roots, and bushes. The guard turned out, and made a brief though brave resistance. In a moment, they were cut to pieces, dispersed, or made prisoners; while men after men came swarming up the height, and quickly formed upon the plains above. Meanwhile, the vessels had dropped downward with the current, and anchored opposite the landing-place. The remaining troops were disembarked, and, with the dawn of day, the whole were brought in safety to the shore.

The sun rose, and, from the ramparts of Quebec, the astonished people saw the Plains of Abraham glittering with arms, and the dark-red lines of English forming in array of battle. Breathless messengers had borne the evil tidings to Montcalm, and far and near his wide-extended camp resounded with the rolling of alarm drums and the din of startled preparation. He, too, had had his struggles and his sorrows. The civil power had thwarted him; famine, discontent, and disaffection were rife among his soldiers; and no small portion of the Canadian militia had dispersed from sheer starvation. In spite of all, he had trusted to hold out till the winter frosts should drive the invaders from before the town; when, on that disastrous morning, the news of their successful temerity fell like a cannon-shot upon his ear. Still he assumed a tone of confidence. "They have got to the weak side of us at last," he is reported to have said, "and we must crush them with our numbers."

With headlong haste, his troops were pouring over the bridge of the St. Charles, and gathering in heavy masses under the western ramparts of the town. Could numbers give assurance of success, their triumph would have been secure; for five French battalions and the armed colonial peasantry amounted in all to more than seven thousand five hundred men. Full in sight before them stretched the long, thin lines of the British forces,—the half-wild Highlanders, the steady soldiery of England, and the hardy levies of the provinces,—less than five thousand in number, but all inured to battle, and strong in the full assurance of success. Yet, could the chiefs of that gallant army have pierced the secrets of the future, could they have foreseen that the victory which they burned to achieve would have robbed England of her proudest boast, that the conquest of Canada would pave the way for the independence of America, their swords would have dropped from their hands, and the heroic fires have gone out within their hearts.

It was nine o'clock, and the adverse armies stood motionless, each gazing on the other. The clouds hung low, and, at intervals warm light showers descended, besprinkling both alike. The coppice and corn-fields in front of the British troops were filled with sharpshooters, who kept up a distant, spattering fire. Here and there a soldier fell in the ranks, and the gap was filled in silence.

At a little before ten, the British could see that Montcalm was preparing to advance, and, in a few moments, all his troops appeared in rapid motion. They came on in three divisions, shouting after the manner of their nation, and firing heavily as soon as they came within range. In the British ranks, not a trigger was pulled, not a soldier stirred; and their ominous composure seemed to damp the spirits of the assailants. It was not till the French were within forty yards that the fatal word was given, and the British muskets blazed forth at once in one crashing explosion. Like a ship at full career, arrested with sudden ruin on a sunken rock, the ranks of Montcalm staggered, shivered, and broke before the wasting storm of lead. The smoke, rolling along the field, for a moment shut out the view; but when the white wreaths were scattered on the wind, a wretched spectacle was disclosed; men and officers tumbled in heaps, battaliors resolved into a mob, order and obedience gone; and when the British muskets were levelled for a second volley, the masses of the militia were seen to cower and shrink with uncontrollable panic. For a few minutes, the French regulars stood their ground, returning a sharp and not ineffectual fire. But now, echoing cheer on cheer, redoubling volley on volley, trampling the dying and the dead, and driving the fugitives in crowds, the British troops advanced and swept the field before them. The ardor of the men burst all restraint. They broke into a run, and with unsparing slaughter chased the flying multitude to the gates of Quebec. Foremost of all, the light-footed Highlanders dashed along in furious pursuit, hewing down the Frenchmen with their broadswords, and slaying many in the very ditch of the fortifications. Never was victory more quick or more decisive.

In the short action and pursuit, the French lost fifteen hundred men, killed, wounded, and taken. Of the remainder, some escaped within the city, and others fled across the St. Charles to rejoin their comrades who had been left to guard the camp. The pursuers were recalled by the sound of trumpet; the broken ranks were formed afresh, and the English troops withdrawn beyond reach of the cannon of Quebec. Bougainville, with his corps, arrived from the upper country, and, hovering about their rear, threatened an attack; but when he saw what greeting was prepared for him, he abandoned his purpose and withdrew. Townshend and Murray, the only general officers who remained unhurt, passed to the head of every regiment in turn, and thanked the soldiers for the bravery they had shown; yet the triumph of the victors was mingled with sadness, as the tidings went from rank to rank that Wolfe had fallen.

In the heat of the action, as he advanced at the head of the grenadiers of Louisburg, a bullet shattered his wrist; but he wrapped his handkerchief about the wound, and showed no sign of pain. A moment more, and a ball pierced his side. Still he pressed forward, waving his sword and cheering his soldiers to the attack, when a third shot lodged deep within his breast. He paused, reeled, and, staggering to one side, fell to the earth. Brown, a lieutenant of the grenadiers, Henderson, a volunteer, an officer of artillery, and a private soldier, raised him together in their arms, and, bearing him to the rear, laid him softly on the grass. They asked if he would have a surgeon; but he shook his head, and answered that all was over with him. His eyes closed with the torpor of approaching death, and those around sustained his fainting form. Yet they could not withhold their gaze from the wild turmoil before them, and the charging ranks of their companions rushing through fire and smoke. "See how they run," one of the officers exclaimed, as the French fled in confusion before the levelled bayonets. "Who run?" demanded Wolfe, opening his eyes like a man aroused from sleep. "The enemy, sir," was the reply; "they give way everywhere." "Then," said the dying general, "tell Colonel Burton to march Webb's regiment down to Charles River, to cut off their retreat from the bridge. Now, God be praised, I will die in peace," he murmured; and, turning on his side, he calmly breathed his last.

Almost at the same moment fell his great adversary, Montcalm, as he strove, with vain bravery, to rally his shattered ranks. Struck down with a mortal wound, he was placed on a litter and borne to the General Hospital on the banks of the St. Charles. The surgeons told him that he could not recover. "I am glad of it," was his calm reply. He then asked how long he might survive, and was told that he had not many hours remaining. "So much the better," he said; "I am happy that I shall not live to see the surrender of Quebec." Officers from the garrison came to his bedside to ask his orders and instructions. "I will give no more orders," replied the defeated soldier; "I have much business that must be attended to, of greater moment than your ruined garrison and this wretched country. My time is very short; therefore, pray leave me." The officers withdrew, and none remained in the chamber but his confessor and the Bishop of Quebec. To the last, he expressed his contempt for his own mutinous and half-famished troops, and his admiration for the disciplined valor of his opponents. He died before midnight, and was buried at his own desire in a cavity of the earth formed by the bursting of a bombshell.

The victorious army encamped before Quebec, and pushed

their preparations for the siege with zealous energy; but before a single gun was brought to bear, the white flag was hung out, and the garrison surrendered. On the eighteenth of September, 1759, the rock-built citadel of Canada passed forever from the hands of its ancient masters.

EXERCISES

1. From the list of suggested readings select Macaulay's "The Trial of Warren Hastings" and John Richard Green's "The Landing of Augustine." The books which contain these incidents are easily obtainable. Compare them carefully for similarities and differences in (1) the use of color words, (2) picturesque detail, (3) especially dramatic verbs.

2. Read chapters from Lytton Strachey's *Queen Victoria*. In what ways is Strachey a disciple of Macaulay? He differs from him in at least one striking particular. Can you discover it? If you cannot in *Queen Victoria*, perhaps you can in his essay on Cardinal Manning from *Eminent Victorians*. At all events the essay is worth reading.

3. Some people say that Macaulay is pretentious and artificial. Defend or accuse him.

4. You ought while you are studying the historical incident as a type of composition to become acquainted with Philip Guedalla. Read *The Second Empire* or *Palmerston* or both. What does one critic mean by referring somewhat disparagingly to "Mr. Guedalla's fire-works"?

5. As a twenty-minute class-room exercise, write an impromptu 150-word incident on a familiar subject, say, Pocahontas saves John Smith, Washington crosses the Delaware, De Soto is buried in the Mississippi, Joan of Arc is burned at the stake, Charles I loses his head. This may be done without preparation, or the details of a less familiar incident may be prepared by previous reading. Then use the rest of the hour in comparison and criticism of work upon the basis of the suggestions given.

6. Re-read Macaulay's *Lays of Ancient Rome*. In his depiction of such stirring incidents as "Horatius at the Bridge" or "The Battle of Lake Regillus," in what ways does his verse resemble his prose?

7. Suppose Froude had doubled the length of his description of

Henry's and Anne's marriage. What would have been the effect upon you?

8. Consider the dangers in the writing of historical incident. Do they outweigh the possible excellencies?

9. The following sentence is taken from Macaulay's description of the trial of Warren Hastings. What is the effect if you take out one adjective? If you take out two?

> "There were seated round the Queen the fair-haired young daughters of the House of Brunswick."

10. The following sentence from Macaulay's *England in 1685*, the third chapter of his history of England, might be written in twelve carefully chosen words without losing any necessary *facts*. Try it and see what happens.

> "They dressed as if for a gala at Versailles, ate off plate, drank the richest wines, and kept harems on board, while hunger and scurvy raged among the crews, and while corpses were daily flung out of the port-holes."

SUGGESTED READINGS

De Quincey, Thomas, *The Revolt of a Tartar Tribe.*

Gibbon, Edward, "Justinian's Fleet" from *The Decline and Fall of the Roman Empire,* pp. 216-219 Everyman edition, E. P. Dutton, New York.

"The Plague" from the same, pp. 371-374.

Green, John Richard, "The Landing of Augustine" from *A Short History of the English People,* Chapter I, Section 3, Harper's, New York.

"Joan of Arc" from the same, Chapter VI, Section 1.

"The Fall of Wolsey" from the same, Chapter VI, Section 5.

Guedalla, Philip, "The Emperor" from *The Second Empire,* Part III, Putnam's, New York.

Macaulay, Thomas Babington, *The Trial of Warren Hastings* from the essay on Warren Hastings, *Historical Essays,* Scribner's, New York.

The Youth of Frederick the Great from the essay on Frederick the Great, *Historical Essays,* Scribner's.

The Death of Queen Mary, Chapter XX, from *The History of England.*

Parkman, Francis, "Indian Conquerors" from *La Salle and the Discovery of the Great West,* Little, Brown, Boston.

"The Heroine of Verchères," Chapter XIV, from *Frontenac and New France under Louis XIV,* Little, Brown, Boston.

Prescott, William H., "The Marriage of Philip and Mary," Chapter IV, Vol. I, from *The History of Philip II.*

Strachey, Lytton, *Queen Victoria,* pp. 67-70, Harcourt, Brace, New York.

"The End" from the same, Chapter X.

"The End of General Gordon, pp. 344-348, from *Eminent Victorians,* Harcourt, Brace, New York.

CHAPTER V

THE BIOGRAPHY

In the last few years the writing of biography has undergone great changes and, on the whole, changes for the better. Men like Lytton Strachey, Llewelyn Powys, Emil Ludwig, Abbe Dimnet, G. K. Chesterton, and Philip Guedalla, to name but a few, have contributed largely toward forming a new conception of biographical writing. Instead of the meticulous and exhaustive recounting of all available facts, anecdotes, and incidents about a given person, they have sifted and sorted these facts with the idea of seizing the most significant, most lively, and most illuminating. These they have dwelt upon and dealt with in such a way as to make the subjects of their respective biographies live, not only in the minds but also before the eyes of their readers.

Such biography as this is really portraiture on a larger scale and canvas. But whereas portraiture presents Mrs. Battle at her card-table and Eustacia Vye on Egdon Heath, biography of this kind *reveals* and *delineates* the Mrs. Battle suggested by her card-table manners and mannerisms and the Eustacia Vye predicted by her appearance. Revelations such as these afford all kinds of enjoyment and interest from the gathering of material to the consideration of the best method of presentation.

This "best method" will depend largely, of course, upon your subject, the person who intrigues you most. Was his nature many-sided, contradictory, paradoxical? Was he misunderstood by his time, by his contemporaries? Were his actions seemingly dictated by some indomitable trait of character before which all other traits fade into nothingness? Does his life as you unearth its facts make a tale more fascinating to you than any romance or novel? Your answers to such questions as these may well determine your decision as to the kind of biography you will choose to write.

There are three kinds presented here: (1) biography as exposition, (2) biography as interpretation, and (3) biography as fiction. They have one outstanding trait in common: *Each makes no pretense of being exhaustive; rather each selects those details and incidents which will make its subject stand out.* And yet their differences are significant:

1. Expository biography, as its name suggests, exposes in the fullest light possible the man as he was, or is, with his outstanding traits, his foibles and his fancies, his mistakes and his mannerisms. Of the three, it is more full and less concentrated, and is especially adapted for the presentation of a rich and a varied personality.

2. Interpretative biography is likely to seize upon some *one* predominant trait or strain, perhaps hereditary, perhaps not, and to use it as, on the whole, indicative of the person under presentation. It at once explains and discloses the acts and motives of the subject, and it is felt to be so important that events and incidents, unless distinctly related to it, give way before it.

3. Biography as fiction is a delightful way of using one's imagination to present the life of a particularly dramatic figure. Here truth, valuable as it is, may be immensely helped out by tradition and even by fancy. The aim is to interest rather than to instruct the reader, and the finished product, if one has read well and visualized better, is often quite charming. But it must be remembered, the lives and personalities of relatively few characters afford such an opportunity.

These three types of biographical writing are excellently represented by the three models quoted. Thackeray's "Oliver Goldsmith," chatty and old-fashioned as it may seem in spots, is not only purely expository in nature but also singularly complete in its effect. "Lady Hester Stanhope," on the contrary, is interpretative. Note how successfully and yet how briefly Strachey sketches the few facts of her life for which he has time and space. His business is to interpret her strange personality through her nose "of wild ambitions, of pride grown fantastical." And this he does in a memorable way. "The Vagabond Poet of France" is biography as fiction. Who better than François Villon could lend himself so well to such kind of biography? Miss Foster has neglected nothing of great significance in her story of his life, but it is first and foremost as a *story* that she presents it. And what a charming tale it is!

In this matter of writing biography example is far better than precept. And no examples can be better than the following, supplemented by the suggestions on the reading list at the close of the chapter. You cannot read too widely in your preparation for this work, both along general and specific lines. Your success in the end will depend on the breadth and intelligence of your reading, on the perception necessary for the wise selection of material to be used, on the method chosen for presentation, and on the final portrayal of your information.

OLIVER GOLDSMITH [1]

By William Makepeace Thackeray

"Jeté sur cette boule,
Laid, chétif et souffrant;
Étouffé, dans la foule,
Faute d'être assez grand;

"Une plainte touchante
De ma bouche sortit.
Le bon Dieu me dit: Chante,
Chante, pauvre petit.

"Chanter, ou je m'abuse,
Est ma tâche ici-bas.
Tous ceux qu'ainsi j'amuse,
Ne m'aimeront-ils pas?" [2]

[1] From *The English Humorists of the Eighteenth Century.*
[2] Cast upon this earth, plain, insignificant and suffering; stifled in the crowd through not being large enough; I utter a sad complaint. God says to me, Sing, sing, my poor child. To sing or I am mistaken is my work on this earth. Will not all those whom I amuse in this way love me?

In these charming lines of Béranger, one may fancy described the career, the suffering, the genius, the gentle nature of Goldsmith, and the esteem in which we hold him. Who of the millions whom he has amused doesn't love him? To be the most beloved of English writers, what a title that is for a man! A wild youth, wayward, but full of tenderness and affection, quits the country village where his boyhood has been passed in happy musing, in idle shelter, in fond longing to see the great world out of doors, and achieve fame and fortune; and after years of dire struggle and neglect and poverty, his heart turning back as fondly to his native place as it had longed eagerly for change when sheltered there, he writes a book and a poem, full of the recollections and feelings of home; he paints the friends and scenes of his youth, and peoples Auburn and Wakefield with remembrances of Lissoy. Wander he must, but he carries away a home-relic with him, and dies with it on his breast. His nature is truant; in repose it longs for change,—as on the journey it looks back for friends and quiet. He passes to-day in building an air-castle for to-morrow, or in writing yesterday's elegy; and he would fly away this hour, but that a cage and necessity keep him. What is the charm of his verse, of his style and humor?— his sweet regrets, his delicate compassion, his soft smile, his tremulous sympathy, the weakness which he owns? Your love for him is half pity. You come hot and tired from the day's battle, and this sweet minstrel sings to you. Who could harm the kind vagrant harper? Whom did he ever hurt? He carries no weapon save the harp on which he plays to you and with which he delights great and humble, young and old, the captains in the tents or the soldiers round the fire, or the women and children in the villages, at whose porches he stops and sings his simple songs of love and beauty. With that sweet story of "The Vicar of Wakefield" he has found entry into every castle and hamlet in Europe. Not one of us, however busy or hard, but once or twice in our lives has passed an evening with him, and undergone the charm of his delightful music.

Goldsmith's father was no doubt the good Doctor Primrose, whom we all of us know. Swift was yet alive, when the little

Oliver was born at Pallas, or Pallasmore, in the county of Long-
ford, in Ireland. In 1730, two years after the child's birth,
Charles Goldsmith removed his family to Lissoy, in the county
Westmeath, that sweet "Auburn" which every person who hears
me has seen in fancy. Here the kind parson brought up his
eight children; and loving all the world, as his son says, fancied
all the world loved him. He had a crowd of poor dependants
besides those hungry children. He kept an open table, round
which sat flatterers and poor friends, who laughed at the honest
rector's many jokes, and ate the produce of his seventy acres
of farm. Those who have seen an Irish house in the present day
can fancy that one at Lissoy. The old beggar still has his al-
lotted corner by the kitchen turf; the maimed old soldier still
gets his potatoes and buttermilk; the poor cottier still asks his
honor's charity and prays God bless his reverence for the sixpence; the ragged pensioner still takes his place by right of
sufferance. There's still a crowd in the kitchen, and a crowd
round the parlor table; profusion, confusion, kindness, poverty.
If an Irishman comes to London to make his fortune, he has a
half-dozen of Irish dependants who take a percentage of his
earnings. The good Charles Goldsmith left but little provision
for his hungry race when death summoned him; and one of his
daughters being engaged to a Squire of rather superior dignity,
Charles Goldsmith impoverished the rest of his family to provide the girl with a dowry.

The small-pox, which scourged all Europe at that time, and
ravaged the roses off the cheeks of half the world, fell foul of poor
little Oliver's face when the child was eight years old, and left
him scarred and disfigured for his life. An old woman in his
father's village taught him his letters, and pronounced him a
dunce. Paddy Byrne, the hedge-schoolmaster, then took him in
hand; and from Paddy Byrne he was transmitted to a clergyman
at Elphin. When a child was sent to school, in those days, the
classic phrase was that he was placed under Mr. So-and-So's
ferule. Poor little ancestors! it is hard to think how ruthlessly
you were birched, and how much of needless whipping and tears
our small forefathers had to undergo! A relative—kind Uncle

Contarine—took the main charge of little Noll; who went through his school-days righteously doing as little work as he could, robbing orchards, playing at ball, and making his pocket-money fly about whenever fortune sent it to him. Everybody knows the story of that famous "Mistake of a Night," when the young schoolboy, provided with a guinea and a nag, rode up to the "best house" in Ardagh, called for the landlord's company over a bottle of wine at supper, and for a hot cake for breakfast in the morning,—and found, when he asked for the bill, that the best house was Squire Featherstone's, and not the inn for which he mistook it. Who does not know every story about Goldsmith? That is a delightful and fantastic picture of the child dancing and capering about in the kitchen at home, when the old fiddler gibed at him for his ugliness, and called him Æsop; and little Noll made his repartee of:—

> "Heralds proclaim aloud this saying:
> See Æsop dancing and his monkey playing."

One can fancy a queer, pitiful look of humor and appeal upon that little scarred face, the funny little dancing figure, the funny little brogue. In his life and writings, which are the honest expression of it, he is constantly bewailing that homely face and person; anon he surveys them in the glass ruefully, and presently assumes the most comical dignity. He likes to deck out his little person in splendor and fine colors. He presented himself to be examined for ordination in a pair of scarlet breeches, and said honestly that he did not like to go into the Church because he was fond of colored clothes. When he tried to practise as a doctor, he got by hook or by crook a black velvet suit, and looked as big and as grand as he could, and kept his hat over a patch on the old coat. In better days he bloomed out in plum-color, in blue silk, and in new velvet. For some of those splendors the heirs and assignees of Mr. Filby, the tailor, have never been paid to this day; perhaps the kind tailor and his creditor have met and settled their little account in Hades.

They showed until lately a window at Trinity College, Dublin, on which the name of *O. Goldsmith* was engraved with a diamond.

Whose diamond was it? Not the young sizar's, who made but a poor figure in that place of learning. He was idle, penniless, and fond of pleasure; he learned his way early to the pawn-broker's shop. He wrote ballads, they say, for the street-singers, who paid him a crown for his poem; and his pleasure was to steal out at night and hear the verses sung. He was chastised by his tutor for giving a dance in his rooms, and took the box on the ear so much to heart that he packed up his all, pawned his books and little property, and disappeared from college and family. He said he intended to go to America; but when his money was spent, the young prodigal came home ruefully, and the good folks there killed their calf (it was but a lean one) and welcomed him back.

After college he hung about his mother's house, and lived for some years the life of a buckeen,—passed a month with this relation and that, a year with one patron, and a great deal of time at the public-house. Tired of this life, it was resolved that he should go to London, and study at the Temple; but he got no farther on the road to London and the woolsack than Dublin, where he gambled away the fifty pounds given him for his outfit, and whence he returned to the indefatigable forgiveness of home. Then he determined to be a doctor, and Uncle Contarine helped him to a couple of years at Edinburgh. Then from Edinburgh he felt that he ought to hear the famous professors of Leyden and Paris, and wrote most amusing pompous letters to his uncle about the great Farheim, Du Petit, and Duhamel du Monceau, whose lectures he proposed to follow. If Uncle Contarine believed those letters; if Oliver's mother believed that story which the youth related, of his going to Cork with the purpose of embarking for America, of his having paid his passenger money and having sent his kit on board, of the anonymous captain sailing away with Oliver's valuable luggage in a nameless ship, never to return,— if Uncle Contarine and the mother at Ballymahon believed his stories, they must have been a very simple pair, as it was a very simple rogue indeed who cheated them. When the lad, after fail-ing in his clerical examinations, after failing in his plan for study-ing the law, took leave of these projects and of his parents and set out for Edinburgh, he saw mother and uncle, and lazy Bally-mahon, and green native turf and sparkling river for the last time. He was never to look on Old Ireland more, and only in fancy revisit her.

> "But me not destined such delights to share,
>   My prime of life in wandering spent and care,
>   Impelled, with steps unceasing, to pursue
>   Some fleeting good that mocks me with the view
>   That like the circle bounding earth and skies
>   Allures from far, yet, as I follow, flies;
>   My fortune leads to traverse realms alone,
>   And find no spot of all the world my own."

I spoke in a former lecture of that high courage which enabled Fielding, in spite of disease, remorse, and poverty, always to retain a cheerful spirit and to keep his manly benevolence and love of truth intact,—as if these treasures had been confided to him for the public benefit, and he was accountable to posterity for their honorable employ; and a constancy equally happy and admirable I think was shown by Goldsmith, whose sweet and friendly nature bloomed kindly always in the midst of a life's storm and rain and bitter weather. The poor fellow was never so friendless but he could befriend some one; never so pinched and wretched but he could give of his crust, and speak his word of compassion. If he had but his flute left, he could give that, and make the children happy in the dreary London court. He could give the coals in that queer coal-scuttle we read of to his neighbor; he could give away his blankets in college to the poor widow, and warm himself as he best might in the feathers; he could pawn his coat, to save his landlord from jail. When he was a school-usher he spent his earnings in treats for the boys, and the good-natured schoolmaster's wife said justly that she ought to keep Mr. Goldsmith's money as well as the young gentlemen's. When he met his pupils in later life, nothing would satisfy the Doctor but he must treat them still. "Have you seen the print of me after Sir Joshua Reynolds?" he asked of one of his old pupils. "Not seen it! Not bought it! Sure, Jack, if your picture had been published, I'd not have been without it half-an-hour." His purse and his heart were everybody's, and his friend's as much as his own. When he was at the height of his reputation, and the Earl of Northumberland, going as Lord Lieutenant to Ireland, asked if he could be of any service to Doctor Goldsmith, Goldsmith recommended his brother and not himself to the great man. "My patrons," he gallantly said, "are the booksellers, and I want no others." Hard patrons they were, and hard work he did; but he did not complain much. If in his early writings some bitter words escaped him, some allusions to neglect and poverty, he withdrew these expressions when his Works were republished, and better days seemed to open for him; and he did not dare to complain that printer and publisher had overlooked his merit or left him poor. The Court's face was turned from honest Oliver; the Court patronized Beattie. The fashion did not shine on him; fashion adored Sterne; fashion pronounced Kelly to be the great writer of comedy of his day. A little—not ill-humor—but plaintiveness—a little betrayal of wounded pride which he showed renders him not the less amiable. The author of the *Vicar of Wakefield* had a right to protest when Newbery kept back the manuscript for two years; had a right to be a little peevish with Sterne,—a little angry when Colman's actors declined their parts in his delightful comedy, when the manager refused to have a scene painted for it and pronounced its damnation before hearing. He had not the great public with him; but he had the noble Johnson and the admirable Reynolds and the great Gibbon and the great Burke and the great Fox,—friends and admirers illustrious indeed, as famous as those who, fifty years before, sat round Pope's table.

Nobody knows, and I dare say Goldsmith's buoyant temper kept no account of, all the pains which he endured during the early period of his literary career. Should any man of letters in our day have to bear up against such, Heaven grant he may come out of the period of misfortune with such a pure, kind heart as that which Goldsmith obstinately bore in his breast! The insults to which he had to submit were shocking to read of, —slander, contumely, vulgar satire, brutal malignity, perverting his commonest motives and actions. He had his share of these; and one's anger is roused at reading of them, as it is at seeing a woman insulted or a child assaulted, at the notion that a creature so very gentle and weak, and full of love, should have to suffer so. And he had worse than insult to undergo,—to own to fault, and deprecate the anger of ruffians. There is a letter of his extant to one Griffiths, a bookseller, in which poor Goldsmith is forced to confess that certain books sent by Griffiths are in the hands of a friend from whom Goldsmith had been forced to borrow money. "He was wild, sir," Johnson said, speaking of Goldsmith to Boswell, with his great, wise benevolence and noble mercifulness of heart,—"Dr. Goldsmith was wild, sir; but he is no more." Ah! if we pity the good and weak man who suffers undeservedly, let us deal very gently with him from whom misery extorts not only tears but shame; let us think humbly and charitably of the human nature that suffers so sadly and falls so low. Whose turn may it be to-morrow? What weak heart, confident before trial, may not succumb under temptation invincible? Cover the good man who has been vanquished,— cover his face and pass on.

For the last half-dozen years of his life Goldsmith was far removed from the pressure of any ignoble necessity, and in the receipt, indeed, of a pretty large income from the booksellers, his patrons. Had he lived but a few years more, his public fame would have been as great as his private reputation, and he might have enjoyed alive part of that esteem which his country has ever since paid to the vivid and versatile genius who has touched on almost every subject of literature, and touched nothing that he did not adorn. Except in rare instances, a man is known in our profession and esteemed as a skilful workman years before the lucky hit which trebles his usual gains, and stamps him a popular author. In the strength of his age and the dawn of his reputation, having for backers and friends the most illustrious literary men of his time, fame and prosperity might have been in store for Goldsmith had fate so willed it, and at forty-six had not sudden disease taken him off. I say prosperity rather than competence; for it is probable that no sum could

have put order into his affairs, or sufficed for his irreclaimable
habits of dissipation. It must be remembered that he owed
£2000 when he died. "Was ever poet," Johnson asked, "so
trusted before?" As has been the case with many another good
fellow of his nation, his life was tracked and his substance wasted
by crowds of hungry beggars and lazy dependents. If they came
at a lucky time (and be sure they knew his affairs better than
he did himself, and watched his pay-day), he gave them of his
money; if they begged on empty-purse day, he gave them his
promissory bills, or he treated them to a tavern where he had
credit, or he obliged them with an order upon honest Mr. Filby
for coats,—for which he paid as long as he could earn, and until
the shears of Filby were to cut for him no more. Staggering
under a load of debt and labor; tracked by bailiffs and reproach-
ful creditors; running from a hundred poor dependents, whose
appealing looks were perhaps the hardest of all pains for him to
bear; devising fevered plans for the morrow, new histories, new
comedies, all sorts of new literary schemes; flying from all these
into seclusion, and out of seclusion into pleasure,—at last, at
five-and-forty death seized him and closed his career.

*   *   *   *   *   *   *

The younger Colman has left a touching reminiscence of him:
"I was only five years old," he says, "when Goldsmith took me
on his knee one evening whilst he was drinking coffee with my
father, and began to play with me,—which amiable act I returned,
with the ingratitude of a peevish brat, by giving him a very
smart slap on the face: it must have been a tingler, for it left
the marks of my spiteful paw on his cheek. This infantile outrage was followed by summary justice, and I was locked up by
my indignant father in an adjoining room to undergo solitary
imprisonment in the dark. Here I began to howl and scream
most abominably, which was no bad step toward my liberation,
since those who were not inclined to pity me might be likely to
set me free for the purpose of abating a nuisance.

"At length a generous friend appeared to extricate me from
jeopardy; and that generous friend was no other than the man I

had so wantonly molested by assault and battery. It was the tender-hearted Doctor himself, with a lighted candle in his hand and a smile upon his countenance, which was still partially red from the effects of my petulance. I sulked and sobbed as he fondled and soothed, till I began to brighten. Goldsmith seized the propitious moment of returning good-humor, when he put down the candle and began to conjure. He placed three hats, which happened to be in the room, and a shilling under each: the shillings, he told me, were England, France, and Spain. 'Hey, presto cockalorum!' cried the Doctor; and lo, on uncovering the shillings, which had been dispersed each beneath a separate hat, they were all found congregated under one! I was no politician at five years old, and therefore might not have wondered at the sudden revolution which brought England, France, and Spain all under one crown; but as also I was no conjuror, it amazed me beyond measure. . . . From that time, whenever the Doctor came to visit my father, 'I plucked his gown to share the good man's smile;' a game at romps constantly ensued, and we were always cordial friends and merry playfellows. Our unequal companionship varied somewhat as to sports as I grew older; but it did not last long: my senior playmate died in his forty-fifth year, when I had attained my eleventh. . . . In all the numerous accounts of his virtues and foibles, his genius and absurdities, his knowledge of nature and ignorance of the world, his 'compassion for another's woes' was always predominant; and my trivial story of his humoring a forward child weighs but as a feather in the recorded scale of his benevolence."

Think of him reckless, thriftless, vain, if you like,—but merciful, gentle, generous, full of love and pity. He passes out of our life, and goes to render his account beyond it. Think of the poor pensioners weeping at his grave; think of the noble spirits that admired and deplored him; think of the righteous pen that wrote his epitaph, and of the wonderful and unanimous response of affection with which the world has paid back the love he gave it. His humor delighting us still, his song fresh and beautiful as when he first charmed with it, his words in all our mouths, his very weaknesses beloved and familiar,—his benevolent spirit seems still to smile upon us, to do gentle kindnesses, to succor with sweet charity; to soothe, caress, and forgive; to plead with the fortunate for the unhappy and the poor.

LADY HESTER STANHOPE [1]

By Lytton Strachey

The Pitt nose has a curious history. One can watch its transmigrations through three lives. The tremendous hook of old Lord Chatham, under whose curve Empires came to birth, was succeeded by the bleak upward-pointing nose of William Pitt the younger—the rigid symbol of an indomitable *hauteur*. With Lady Hester Stanhope came the final stage. The nose, still with an upward tilt in it, had lost its masculinity; the hard bones of the uncle and the grandfather had disappeared. Lady Hester's was a nose of wild ambitions, of pride grown fantastical, a nose that scorned the earth, shooting off, one fancies, towards some eternally eccentric heaven. It was a nose, in fact, altogether in the air.

Noses, of course, are aristocratic things; and Lady Hester was the child of a great aristocracy. But, in her case, the aristocratic impulse, which had carried her predecessors to glory, had less fortunate results. There has always been a strong strain of extravagance in the governing families of England; from time to time they throw off some peculiarly ill-balanced member, who performs a strange meteoric course. A century earlier, Lady Mary Wortley Montagu was an illustrious example of this tendency: that splendid comet, after filling half the heavens, vanished suddenly into desolation and darkness. Lady Hester Stanhope's spirit was still more uncommon; and she met with a most uncommon fate.

She was born in 1776, the eldest daughter of that extraordinary Earl Stanhope, Jacobin and inventor, who made the first steamboat and the first calculating machine, who defended the French Revolution in the House of Lords and erased the armorial

[1] From *Books and Characters*. By permission of Harcourt, Brace and Company.

bearings—"damned aristocratical nonsense"—from his carriages and his plate. Her mother, Chatham's daughter and the favourite sister of Pitt, died when she was four years old. The second Lady Stanhope, a frigid woman of fashion, left her stepdaughters to the care of futile governesses, while "Citizen Stanhope" ruled the household from his laboratory with the violence of a tyrant. It was not until Lady Hester was twenty-four that she escaped from the slavery of her father's house, by going to live with her grandmother, Lady Chatham. On Lady Chatham's death, three years later, Pitt offered her his protection, and she remained with him until his death in 1806.

Her three years with Pitt, passed in the very centre of splendid power, were brilliant and exciting. She flung herself impetuously into the movement and the passion of that vigorous society; she ruled her uncle's household with high vivacity; she was liked and courted; if not beautiful, she was fascinating—very tall, with a very fair and clear complexion, and dark-blue eyes, and a countenance of wonderful expressiveness. Her talk, full of the trenchant nonchalance of those days, was both amusing and alarming. "My dear Hester, what are you saying?" Pitt would call out to her from across the room. She was devoted to her uncle, who warmly returned her affection. She was devoted, too—but in a more dangerous fashion—to the intoxicating Antinoüs, Lord Granville Leveson Gower. The reckless manner in which she carried on this love-affair was the first indication of something overstrained, something wild and unaccountable, in her temperament. Lord Granville, after flirting with her outrageously, declared that he could never marry her, and went off on an embassy to St. Petersburg. Her distraction was extreme: she hinted that she would follow him to Russia; she threatened, and perhaps attempted, suicide; she went about telling everybody that he had jilted her. She was taken ill, and then there were rumours of an accouchement, which, it was said, she took care to *afficher*, by appearing without rouge and fainting on the slightest provocation. In the midst of these excursions and alarms there was a terrible and unexpected catastrophe. Pitt died. And Lady Hester suddenly found herself a dethroned princess,

living in a small house in Montagu Square on a pension of
£1,200 a year.

She did not abandon society, however, and the tongue of
gossip continued to wag. Her immediate marriage with a former
lover, Mr. Hill, was announced: "il est bien bon," said Lady
Bessborough. Then it was whispered that Canning was "le
regnant"—that he was with her "not only all day, but almost all
night." She quarreled with Canning and became attached to Sir
John Moore. Whether she was actually engaged to marry him
—as she seems to have asserted many years later—is doubtful;
his letters to her, full as they are of respectful tenderness, hardly
warrant the conclusion; but it is certain that he died with her
name on his lips. Her favourite brother, Charles, was killed beside him; and it was natural that under this double blow she
should have retired from London. She buried herself in Wales;
but not for long. In 1810 she set sail for Gibraltar with her
brother James, who was rejoining his regiment in the Peninsula.
She never returned to England.

There can be no doubt that at the time of her departure the
thought of a lifelong exile was far from her mind. It was only
gradually, as she moved further and further eastward, that the
prospect of life in England—at last even in Europe—grew dis-
tasteful to her; as late as 1816 she was talking of a visit to
Provence. Accompanied by two or three English fellow travellers, her English maid, Mrs. Fry, her private physician, Dr.
Meryon, and a host of servants, she progressed, slowly and in a
great state, through Malta and Athens, to Constantinople. She
was conveyed in battleships, and lodged with governors and am-
bassadors. After spending many months in Constantinople, Lady
Hester discovered that she was "dying to see Napoleon with her
own eyes," and attempted accordingly to obtain passports to
France. The project was stopped by Stratford Canning, the
English Minister, upon which she decided to visit Egypt, and,
chartering a Greek vessel, sailed for Alexandria in the winter of
1811. Off the island of Rhodes a violent storm sprang up; the
whole party were forced to abandon the ship, and to take refuge
upon a bare rock, where they remained without food or shelter

for thirty hours. Eventually, after many severe privations, Alexandria was reached in safety; but this disastrous voyage was a turning-point in Lady Hester's career. At Rhodes she was forced to change her torn and dripping raiment for the attire of a Turkish gentleman—a dress which she never afterwards abandoned. It was the first step in her orientalization.

She passed the next two years in a triumphal progress. Her appearance in Cairo caused the greatest sensation, and she was received in state by the Pasha, Mehemet Ali. Her costume on this occasion was gorgeous: she wore a turban of cashmere, a brocaded waistcoat, a priceless pelisse, and a vast pair of purple velvet pantaloons embroidered all over in gold. She was ushered by chamberlains with silver wands through the inner courts of the palace to a pavilion in the harem, where the Pasha, rising to receive her, conversed with her for an hour. From Cairo she turned northwards, visiting Jaffa, Jerusalem, Acre, and Damascus. Her travelling dress was of scarlet cloth trimmed with gold, and, when on horseback, she wore over the whole a white-hooded and tasselled burnous. Her maid, too, was forced, protesting, into trousers, though she absolutely refused to ride astride. Poor Mrs. Fry had gone through various and dreadful sufferings —shipwreck and starvation, rats and blackbeetles unspeakable— but she retained her equanimity. Whatever her Ladyship might think fit to be, she was an Englishwoman to the last, and Philippaki was Philip Parker and Mustapha Mr. Farr.

Outside Damascus, Lady Hester was warned that the town was the most fanatical in Turkey, and that the scandal of a woman entering it in man's clothes, unveiled, would be so great as to be dangerous. She was begged to veil herself, and to make her entry under cover of darkness. "I must take the bull by the horns," she replied, and rode into the city unveiled at midday. The population were thunderstruck; but at last their amazement gave way to enthusiasm, and the incredible lady was hailed everywhere as Queen, crowds followed her, coffee was poured out before her, and the whole bazaar rose as she passed. Yet she was not satisfied with her triumphs; she would do something still more glorious and astonishing; she would plunge into the desert and visit the ruins of Palmyra, which only half-a-dozen of the boldest travellers had ever seen. The Pasha of Damascus offered her a military escort, but she preferred to throw herself upon the hospitality of the Bedouin Arabs, who, overcome by her horsemanship, her powers of sight, and her courage, enrolled her a member of their tribe. After a week's journey in their company, she reached Palmyra, where the inhabitants met her with wild enthusiasm, and under the Corinthian columns of Zenobia's temple crowned her head with flowers. This happened in March, 1813; it was the apogee of Lady Hester's life. Henceforward her fortunes gradually but steadily declined.

The rumour of her exploits had spread through Syria, and from the year 1813 onwards, her reputation was enormous. She was received everywhere as a royal, almost a supernatural personage: she progressed from town to town amid official prostrations and popular rejoicings. But she herself was in a state of hesitation and discontent. Her future was uncertain; she had grown scornful of the West—must she return to it? The East alone was sympathetic, the East alone was tolerable—but could she cut herself off for ever from the past? At Laodicea she was suddenly struck down by the plague, and, after months of illness, it was borne in upon her that all was vanity. She rented an empty monastery on the slopes of Mount Lebanon, not far from Sayda (the ancient Sidon), and took up her abode there. Then her mind took a new surprising turn; she dashed to Ascalon, and, with the permission of the Sultan, began excavations in a ruined temple with the object of discovering a hidden treasure of three million pieces of gold. Having unearthed nothing but an antique statue, which, in order to prove her disinterestedness, she ordered her appalled doctor to break into little bits, she returned to her monastery. Finally, in 1816, she moved to another house, further up Mount Lebanon, and near the village of Djoun; and at Djoun she remained until her death, more than twenty years later.

Thus, almost accidentally as it seems, she came to the end of her wanderings, and the last, long, strange, mythical period of her existence began. Certainly the situation that she had chosen was sublime. Her house, on the top of a high bare hill among great mountains, was a one-storied group of buildings, with many ramifying courts and out-houses, and a garden of several acres surrounded by a rampart wall. The garden, which she herself had planted and tended with the utmost care, commanded a glorious prospect. On every side but one the vast mountains towered, but to the west there was an opening, through which, in the far distance, the deep blue Mediterranean was revealed. From this romantic hermitage, her singular renown spread over the world. European travellers who had been admitted to her presence brought back stories full of Eastern mystery; they told of a peculiar grandeur, a marvellous prestige, an imperial power. The precise nature of Lady Hester's empire was, indeed, dubious; she was in fact merely the tenant of her Djoun establishment, for which she paid a rent of £20 a year. But her dominion was not subject to such limitations. She ruled imaginatively, transcendentally; the solid glory of Chatham had been transmuted into the phantasy of an Arabian Night. No doubt she herself believed that she was something more than a chimerical Empress. When a French traveller was murdered in the desert, she issued orders for the punishment of the offenders; punished they were, and Lady Hester actually received the solemn thanks of the French Chamber. It seems probable, however, that it was the Sultan's orders rather than Lady Hester's which produced the desired effect. In her feud with her terrible neighbour, the Emir Beshyr, she maintained an undaunted front. She kept the tyrant at bay; but perhaps the Emir, who, so far as physical force was concerned, held her in the hollow of his hand, might have proceeded to extremities if he had not received a severe admonishment from Stratford Canning at Constantinople. What is certain is that the ignorant and superstitious populations around her feared and loved her, and that she, reacting to her own mysterious prestige, became at last even as they. She plunged into astrology and divination; she awaited the moment when, in accordance with prophecy, she should enter Jerusalem side by side with the Mahdi, the Messiah; she kept two sacred horses, destined, by sure signs, to carry her and him to their last triumph. The Orient had mastered her utterly. She was no longer an Englishwoman, she declared; she loathed England; she would never go there again; if she went anywhere it would be to Arabia, to "her own people."

Her expenses were immense—not only for herself but for others, for she poured out her hospitality with a noble hand. She ran into debt, and was swindled by the moneylenders; her steward cheated her, her servants pilfered her; her distress was at last acute. She fell into fits of terrible depression, bursting into dreadful tears and savage cries. Her habits grew more and more eccentric. She lay in bed all day, and sat up all night, talking unceasingly for hour upon hour to Dr. Meryon, who alone of her English attendants remained with her, Mrs. Fry having withdrawn to more congenial scenes long since. The doctor was a poor-spirited and muddle-headed man, but he was a good listener; and there he sat while that extraordinary talk flowed on—talk that scaled the heavens and ransacked the earth, talk in which memories of an abolished past—stories of Mr. Pitt and of George III., vituperations against Mr. Canning, mimicries of the Duchess of Devonshire—mingled phantasmagorically with doctrines of Fate and planetary influence, and speculations on the Arabian origin of the Scottish clans, and lamentations over the wickedness of servants; till the unaccountable figure, with its robes and its long pipe, loomed through the tobacco-smoke like some vision of a Sibyl in a dream. She might be robbed and ruined, her house might crumble over her head; but she talked on. She grew ill and desperate; yet still she talked. Did she feel that the time was coming when she should talk no more?

Her melancholy deepened into a settled gloom when the news came of her brother James's death. She had quarrelled with all her English friends, except Lord Hardwiche—with her eldest brother, with her sister, whose kind letters she left unanswered; she was at daggers drawn with the English consul at Alexandria, who worried her about her debts. Ill and harassed, she hardly moved from her bedroom, while her servants rifled her belongings and reduced the house to a condition of indescribable disorder and filth. Three dozen hungry cats ranged through the rooms, filling the courts with frightful noises. Dr. Meryon, in the midst of it all, knew not whether to cry or laugh. At moments the great lady regained her ancient fire; her bells pealed tumultuously for hours together; or she leapt up, and arraigned the whole trembling household before her, with her Arab warmace in her hand. Her finances grew more and more involved —grew at length irremediable. It was in vain that the faithful Lord Hardwiche pressed her to return to England to settle her affairs. Return to England, indeed! To England, that ungrateful, miserable country, where, so far as she could see, they had forgotten the very name of Mr. Pitt! The final blow fell when a letter came from the English authorities threatening to cut off her pension for the payment of her debts. Upon that, after dispatching a series of furious missives to Lord Palmerston, to Queen Victoria, to the Duke of Wellington, she renounced the world. She commanded Dr. Meryon to return to Europe, and he—how could he have done it?—obeyed her. Her health was broken, she was over sixty, and, save for her vile servants, absolutely alone. She lived for nearly a year after he left her— we know no more. She had vowed never again to pass through the gate of her house; but did she sometimes totter to her garden—that beautiful garden which she had created, with its roses and its fountains, its alleys and its bowers—and look westward at the sea? The end came in June, 1839. Her servants immediately possessed themselves of every moveable object in the house. But Lady Hester cared no longer: she was lying back in her bed—inexplicable, grand, preposterous, with her nose in the air.

THE VAGABOND POET OF FRANCE [1]

By Imogen Foster

"Who opens the city gates and lets the wolves in? Let those dogs of peasants stay outside; there's no food in Paris anyway. Wolves howling in the streets! Who ever heard of such times? Merciful Mother, here they come!"

[1] By kind permission of the author and of *The Minnesota Quarterly*.

The women rose from their knees and left the linen they were washing adrift in the margin of the Seine. "Stay back, you little devils!" they screamed to the bare-legged children. "Stay back and watch the linen, or the wolves will eat you!" They were strong-armed women, with swarthy, wrinkled faces; they tore up the pavement stones of the Rue de la Juiverie and flung them toward the four lean wolves that swung into sight around the corner of the Petit Pont.

Even wolves know the meaning of stones; they turned tail, howling.

"Beasts of Hell! Kill them; kill—no, they fly toward the tavern! Let the men kill them! We'll get home; it grows dark."

They gathered up the wet linen, and called to the children, "Here, you little demons, quit splashing water; you'll be wet, and mind, there's no fire at home! Hurry, or the wolves will be back."

At this the ragged children came running; they caught hold of their mothers' skirts, and gave timorous glances back in the direction of the tavern.

What a city it was, to call Paris, and what a decayed, gloomy row of houses to call home! Houses they were, covered with ancient, greenish lichens, and with narrow, sinister windows looking down upon the river, windows from which *anything* might have been lowered into the water, in the dead of night, for "the Seine tells no tales." Houses that might conceal the deadliest band of murderers, in their damp upper stories! But "home" was a shelter from the wolves, and a roof to keep out the cold spring rain; anyway, the poor had nothing to fear from robbers.

"Do the peasants love the wolves, Maman, that they bring them with them when the gates are opened?" asked a child, as they climbed the staircase in one of the ancient houses.

"No, child, no. 'Tis the wolves who love the peasants."

"Why does the Holy Mother let them come to Paris, if they eat us, Maman?"

"Because the filthy English broke the finger of St. Martin in the vestry of Saint-Benoist."

They entered a tiny room on the fourth floor; the woman stuffed a grimy apron into the broken window. "This room gets all the mist, because it is next the river. The room above the street is quite warm, but that villain Marye demands two sous more—the fool! She knows we have not two sous, you and I." The woman shivered and pulled a black crust out from her blouse. "See, François, I found it by the tavern. A nice bit, if it is a little old. Eat, François, and forget you are cold. Summer is coming now and the worst is already past."

Summer was coming indeed. Soon the turnips began to grow in the tiny gardens; war was all over, at last, and Paris began to recover, as Paris does. Music played all night now in the Pomme de Pin down the street, and the sun shone pleasantly in the square of Notre Dame where François used to go to throw stones at the cripples. "The lucky cripples!" François would think. "They need not pound linen in the Seine, or have their ears boxed for stealing chestnuts; people bring their chestnuts to them when they hold out their hands!" Sometimes François would sit down on the steps, too, and cry out that he could not walk; men would give him a small coin in passing, and then swear at him when he jumped up and ran away with the money to the nearest butcher or baker.

François was very sorry to have the summer end. But at last winter came, and the wind blew; the light, bare-shouldered girls in the square crossed themselves and ran, their hair streaming; the barber in the Rue St. Jacques pulled his chair and his brushes into his close little shop for the winter.

Winter was always a terrible time, when one cried a great deal. But this winter something very strange happened; François went to school. He could not pay, but he had learned his "are-avi-atus" so easily as he sat with the priest one day that the good father vowed he would teach him for nothing, if François would promise to stop lying, and not try to eat at noon when the paying students did. Lying? Oh, no; François did not lie. Eat? He could usually manage to steal a sausage from the butcher without being cuffed for it. François was nimble on his legs for a boy of seven.

Learning Latin was even more amusing than stoning beggars, and François worked very hard in the cold school-room. One day as he hugged his book and tried to forget the wind that blew in onto his back, the Abbé Villon came and put his hand on his head.

"Are you cold, François?"

François grinned up at him. "N-non, mon père. I am not cold."

The Abbé lifted his forefinger in warning. "Now, François, you are to tell me no lies!" Then the Abbé smiled and sat down beside him. "François, when you go home to-night, tell your mother to tie your chemises into a bundle for you. Tell her that you are coming to live in the cloister with me, and that some day you shall go to the Sorbonne. Tell her that after to-morrow your name shall be François Villon."

And so François went to live in the Porte Rouge in the cloister. Life here was strange and delightful. One had all the warm soup one could eat, and more books than could be read in a life-time. François said enough *Aves* to last him all the rest of his life; he said all he could, for some time he might need them and not have time to say them. One never lied in the cloister; there was nothing to lie about. Neither did one steal sausages. What would be the good? Probably one would be given a sausage for supper; anyway, there was sure to be a fat yellow cheese on the table, a cheese full of holes and scattered here and there with caraway.

The years went by pleasantly. François loved the Abbé Villon more each day, and each day he learned something new and interesting.

At length it seemed to him that he must know about all the Greek and rhetoric there was to know; he told the Abbé so one day, as they sat on the stone bench throwing barley to the birds. "So much, so much have I learned, mon père!" François spread his arms wide to measure "so much," and the barley fell from his two hands in a wide circle around him.

"So much, have you, my child? Then we shall have to send

for the Abbé Berthé to give you the examination for the Sorbonne. I have thought myself it was time," he added.

And so it was. François was only thirteen years old, but he had become a man over night. Father Villon bought him the strapped sandals and the short vest of the Arts students, and in half an hour François gave fair promise of becoming as big a bully as any of them, for all his slight stature and his cloister breeding.

As a matter of fact, the crowded, ramshackle students' quarters had no terrors for young François. He had not stolen figs and stoned cripples in La Juiverie for nothing. When autumn came, François was carrying a stick half as big as himself, and it would not be strange if he had followed the extreme example of his rough-and-ready colleagues, who carried a broad little dagger stuck in their vests.

Now the students of theology were scamps, and the students of medicine were rogues, but the real ruffians were the students of the Arts. François had strong competition, but he was eventually to become their leader. There was no fellow in Paris more agile at leaping a garden wall and picking out the choicest grapes and melons; when a good fowl was wanted for a roasting, 'twas François who was sent a-foraging down to the Seine, for he always came back wet, breathless, and unscathed, with a fine, plump duck tucked under each arm, and a hair-raising tale of an old dame who pursued him with oaths and a carving knife; and on winter evenings when the fire crackled in the tavern hearth, and the little dice rattled in their cups, no man in Paris was quicker at breaking a chair over his partner's head than was François Villon.

And better than all his *diablerie,* François had a clever pen and an eye for beauty; he rhymed a quatrain as easily as he picked a man's pocket, and men and maids alike surrendered to the wittiest scapegrace the College of Arts had on record.

But even college days have an end. François sat one June day on the bench under the clock of Saint-Benoist le Bien Tourné, resting his head upon Isabelle's shoulder and telling her of the little triumph he had had that morning when he took his

M.A. François and his logic quite often astonished the professors; to-day, he vowed, he had twisted their meanings so that the poor fathers scarce knew themselves what they had asked him! François was quite proud of his last day at the Sorbonne.

Prouder still was he of his last night at the students' public-house. "You'll never guess, my chicken, of what great society I became a member last night," and he pinched Isabelle's plump wrist. "I am a member of those people who send messages by the vultures at night; of those people who spirit each other down off the scaffold under the very eyes of Justice; a member of those dim people who steal through palaces and forests unhurt. Isabelle, you cannot guess! I am a Coquillard! Indeed, indeed, I am one of the Coquillards!" Isabelle drew a long breath of rapture.

"Oh, then you must do something great, François; you with a Master's degree and a cockle-shell badge, François! What shall you do to become great? What?"

"I shall be a poet—or a leader of—think, Petite!—of les Coquillards! Stay, here comes le père Sermoise and le père Mardi." Villon rose quickly and held out his hands for congratulation. "To-day, my good fathers, I have taken my degree!"

Le père Sermoise stepped forward with a black scowl on his brow. "To-day, my young friend, you shall take more than a degree; you shall take a good beating for the quatrain you have circulated about me!"

"The quatrain? Oh-ho, mon Père, do not tell me you're a man to take offense at a neat verse! Why, all Paris whispered tales of you and the pretty Ermène. What harm in praising a discreet love affair when the poet allows for the beauty of the lady—"

"I allow for nothing," cried the enraged priest, and lunged a blow at Villon, quick as a flash. Villon dodged the little, short knife, and picked up a stone. Isabelle screamed and caught the hand of le père Mardi; together they ran away down the street. Behind them, le père Sermoise lay prone on the ground, his ugly little knife still clutched in his hand.

François took to his heels and never stopped running till he was through the city gates and out on the high-road. "A fine way for a young man to begin his life, fleeing the gates of his city! If this is my beginning, I wonder what my end will be?" he thought. Then he thanked his stars that he was a Coquillard now, and had at least a forest camp-fire awaiting him.

François found his fellows in the forest of Fontainebleau; a strange, evil, nomadic lot they were. He wondered how long he should have to stay with them. The summer passed, and he was still wondering. Then the week before Christmas a pickpocket drifted down the road bearing the news of François' pardon. This was joyous! The young poet went singing back through the gates of Paris, thinking of the serenade he should send to his beautiful Katharine de Vaucelles, and of the fine supper he and his friends would have that night—"roast veal, and a goose, and a pie full of plums."

It was good to be back in the Pomme de Pin with Isabelle and Colin Cayeux, the pick-lock. They were as jolly and infamous a company as were to be found in any public-house in France; the conversation took the usual turn; nobody had any money. The question was, where was there any money to be found? Of course, the rich had money, but one was almost sure to be caught and broken on the wheel, if one stole from the rich; true, the poor had money—a little—but only a slave and a traitor would rob the poor. Eventually, Villon's logic won the day. "If we steal from the Church, we steal from all the world, and so really from nobody. A few *Aves*, my friends, will make it all right with God!" And when he added, under his breath, that the Chapel of Saint-Benoist was unguarded and one would be safe as a babe in its crib, it was decided that Villon was right. There was no wrong in stealing from the Church.

The company left their heavy cloaks on the bench under the big clock, and sat Isabelle down to guard them. Then, by the light of the thieves' candle on the altar, they picked the lock of the iron coffer and divided the spoils.

Back in his room, François wrote a little "Testament," bequeathing his undying love to his adored Katharine, the old clippings of his hair to his barber, and some valuable bit of thought or blade of grass to each of his many friends. In the morning he bade a touching farewell to the sympathetic old Abbé Villon (who could not understand why his adopted son should be so anxious to keep away from Paris), and set off toward the high-road and the lonely forest of Fontainebleau. By the time he reached the city gates he had spent all his money, and he astonished his friends the Coquillards by arriving at their camp-fire the day after he said goodby to it, and by announcing that he should remain in their company for at least five years.

The life of the roads was a cruel, threatening life of fear, and folly, and crime. François was a poet, a logician, and a pick-pocket; his companions were swarthy Russians, escaped from prison, ancient seamen from pirate vessels long since under the waves, terrific men from the coast of Barbary, Turks with all the tricks of the curled knife, and now and then an excommunicated priest, or a hag with a past so dark that she cast a shadow on even such foul company.

At times, Villon left the fireside of les Coquillards and wandered off alone, down through the garden-land of France, making love and poetry and stealing cabbages enough to live on. Villon loved Provence, and never wished to leave it. When winter came, he would take refuge from the wolves and the cold with some kind Margot, in her cottage, and when spring came he would wander off over the bright-green wheat-fields, with many a promise to return, and never a thought that he would do so.

One summer day Villon was lying on a stone wall, chewing a wisp of straw and thinking of nothing, when he heard laughter down the road. It occurred to him that it had been a long time since he had laughed with any one. He rolled over on his side and propped his head up with his fist; down the road he saw an old gray horse, three men, and a yellow-haired girl; a group of wandering players, no doubt!

"Miracles or Farces?" Villon called out, merrily.

"Farces, so please your lordship," answered the girl.

"May I join your fair company?"

"Assuredly, if you'll play the Devil!" she called back, wrinkling her nose at him.

"Oh, I *am* the Devil all the time," cried François, jumping down off the wall. "Are we off for Touraine?"

Thereupon the girl set out to teach François a new Spanish dance she had learned while down on the border, and Villon in turn showed off his sleight-of-hand prowess and made rhymes that sent the rough men into shouts of laughter.

Villon spent a most agreeable summer with the strange folk. Touraine had never been so lovely before, not even when he had spent the summer at Blois with the Duke of Orleans, as his highness's rhymester. There was something about sweet green leaves that made them a pleasanter roof than the ceiling of a palace; François dearly loved being a vagabond.

One fair morning he awoke before his comrades in the grove that had sheltered them during the night, to see the dark walls of the quaint old city of Meung rising not far off. "I must see the city of Meung," thought François, and he slipped off, without rousing his companions, through the whispering, fragrant fields of wheat, toward the great gate.

He was just going to enter the gate when some one caught him by the sleeve and held him fast. It was a soldier of the Bishop of Aussignys. Without giving poor François time to inquire what he had done to deserve such treatment, he had tied a rope around his waist and had dropped him into a deep hole in the ground. At first Villon thought it a capital joke, and vowed he would tie his malefactor to the nearest tree when he got out. Then he began crying to Henriette to come and lift him out in a basket; but Henriette was probably miles away. Night came, and he had not so much as a bit of straw to sit on, or a cup of water to drink. The next day some one threw him a crust, and on the following days; (apparently always he had a crust, if somebody did not forget). At first François swore and wrote poetry; then the weather grew cold, his ink gave out, and he did not feel like poetry. At last they lifted him up; the ground was covered with snow, and it was Christmas time.

Nobody took the trouble to tell François why he had been kept in the hole; indeed, he did not stay long to ask. He started on the road to Paris as fast as he could go, which was not very fast, for he was starved and sick, and it was in the dead of winter.

When he reached Paris, only the Abbé Villon and his wrinkled old mother were there to receive him. All the gay crowd that had partaken of that pudding and goose five years before were gone; hanged, or in prison, or exiled to far lands. But as Villon grew stronger he met new members of les Coquillards, and made new friends; there were new suppers in the Cour des Miracles, new outlandish tricks and brawls, and François wrote new poems. His poems were better now. He was past twenty-five years old, and he had suffered.

One night Villon was taken to prison and condemned to death. He sat in his cell in the "House in the Rue Saint-Antoine," and thought about Justice. "Here am I, François Villon, having committed every crime in the calendar six times over, and gone scot-free, now condemned to die for a street brawl that went on while I was asleep in my bed! Peculiar; almost as peculiar as being thrown into a Touraine hole for listening to the skylarks!" Then Villon wrote a few poems and went to sleep. "Ah, well," he thought, as he dozed off on his pile of straw, "better no doubt to be hanged on an honorable scaffold than to be strung to a tree by a drunken gypsy in the forest."

In the morning François wrote a touching petition to the queen, "Sister of the Angels," imploring her to let him visit his friends for a last time to borrow a clean shirt. It hurt his pride, he complained, to be hanged in a soiled chemise. The queen was deeply touched by the tender appellation and the pretty metre, and, of course, she forgave the culprit, without even stopping to inquire whether he was innocent or guilty. However, she admonished him, along with the pieces of gold she gave him, that if he dared show his saucy face in Paris again he need not expect the ceremony of a hanging, but should be run through by the first poignard he met, soiled chemise and all.

So François made good haste out of the Bastille, kissed his

poor old mother goodby, and left her his gold pieces to boot. He vowed he should see her always on her knees beneath the colored window of the Celestines. With that, he filled his ink-horn, plucked a peach-blossom, stuck it in his blowzy hair, hummed a little tune that Katharine de Vaucelles had taught him years before, and tramped out of the gates of Paris toward the fire of the Coquillards that burned somewhere in the forest of Fontaine-bleau.

So perhaps the drunken gypsy strung him up after all, or another bishop had him thrown into a hole and forgot to send down the crusts. Perhaps, just perhaps, he found another Provençal Margot, whose cottage and whose wiles proved too much for his wanderlust. But after all, to ask of his fate is only to repeat his own idle, beautiful question: "Where are the snows of yester-year?"

EXERCISES

1. The biography which you write will probably be considered one of your "long themes." Like the occasion or the situation this theme will require bibliography and footnotes. Your attention is called to the explanation of both on pp. 334-6.

2. Study Thackeray's first sentence. What relation does it bear to his complete sketch?

3. What clear-cut pictures does Thackeray suggest? Could one gifted in drawing actually set forth most of his biographical details by a series of pictures? Is this true of most biography?

4. Note the effect of rapid movement in "Lady Hester Stanhope." Then analyze minutely the causes of that effect.

5. Is there anything of Villon's own attitude toward life in Miss Foster's style? With what adjectives would you characterize her style? Try to find several.

6. If you do not know the Benson family, begin your friendship with it at once by reading A. C. Benson's and E. F. Benson's writings given on the list of suggested readings. *Our Family Affairs* is an excellent start.

7. Dr. Eliot's *John Gilley,* excellent as it is, savors of the old type of biography. Read it and see how you think it could be made more appealing. Your instructor might well read it in class and make its presentation the basis for a class discussion.

8. *Don't fail* to read *The Brontë Sisters* by Abbé Dimnet. It is too good to miss. Why such enthusiasm for *this* biography?

9. Is *The Story of Burnt Njal* a biography, and if it is, why is it not listed under Biography as Fiction? Read and consider.

10. Find in G. K. Chesterton's beautiful presentation of St. Francis the one dominant idea that unifies his interpretation.

11. Suggest to your instructor that he read the class Katherine Mansfield's *Life of Ma Parker*. It might well be the model for many biographies of its sort. *Fair Rosemonde* is also a splendid thing to read aloud on one of those afternoons when the instructor is unprepared or generally bored.

SUGGESTED READINGS

As Exposition:

Benson, Arthur Christopher, *The Life of Edward White Benson, Sometime Archbishop of Canterbury,* Macmillan, New York.
The Leaves of the Tree—Studies in Biography, Smith, Elder, London.
Hugh, Memories of a Brother, Longmans, Green, New York.

Benson, E. F., *Our Family Affairs,* Cassell, London and New York.

Dark, Sidney, *Five Deans,* Harcourt, Brace, New York.

Eliot, Charles W., *John Gilley, Maine Farmer and Fisherman,* Houghton Mifflin.

Meynell, Everard, *The Life of Francis Thompson,* Scribner's, New York.

Neilson, William Allan, *Robert Burns,* Chapter I, Bobbs, Merrill, Indianapolis.

Sagas: *The Story of Grettir the Strong* and *The Story of Burnt Njal,* Everyman edition, E. P. Dutton, New York.

Strachey, Lytton, *Queen Victoria,* Harcourt, Brace, New York.
"Cardinal Manning," "Florence Nightingale," and "Dr. Arnold" from *Eminent Victorians,* Harcourt, Brace, New York.

Tinker, Chauncey Brewster, *Young Boswell,* Little, Brown, Boston.

Vallery-Radot, René, *The Life of Louis Pasteur,* Doubleday, Doran, New York.

As Interpretation:

Chesterton, G. K., *St. Francis of Assisi,* Doubleday, Doran, New
York.

Dimnet, Ernest, *The Brontë Sisters,* Harcourt, Brace, New York.

Drew, Elizabeth, *Jane Welsh and Jane Carlyle,* Harcourt, Brace,
New York.

Ludwig, Emil, *Bismarck,* Little, Brown, Boston.

Paine, Albert Bigelow, *Joan of Arc, Maid of France,* Macmillan,
New York.

Powys, Llewelyn, *Thirteen Worthies,* Harcourt, Brace, New
York.

Sandburg, Carl, *Abraham Lincoln,* Harcourt, Brace, New York.

Strachey, Lytton, "Mr. Creevey" from *Books and Characters,*
Harcourt, Brace, New York.

As Fiction:

Barrie, James Matthew, *Margaret Ogilvy,* Scribner's, New York.

Barrington, E., "Fair Rosemonde," *The Atlantic Monthly,* June,
1921.

The Divine Lady, Dodd, Mead, New York.

The Glorious Apollo, Dodd, Mead, New York.

Barry, Iris, *Lady Mary Wortley Montagu,* Bobbs-Merrill,
Indianapolis.

Cather, Willa, *My Antonia,* Houghton Mifflin, Boston.

Death Comes for the Archbishop, Alfred A. Knopf, New York.

Hewlett, Maurice, *Richard Yea and Nay,* Macmillan, New York.

Mansfield, Katherine, "Life of Ma Parker" from *The Garden
Party,* Alfred A. Knopf, New York.

Maurois, André, *Shelley,* John Lane, London.

Merejkowski, Dmitri, *The Romance of Leonardo da Vinci,* Putnam's, New York.

PART III

THEMES OF THOUGHT AND REFLECTION

The third and last source of theme material, *thought and reflection,* is in reality the natural outgrowth of sources one and two, that is, of *experience* and of *information,* or knowledge. To the thinker it is his own past experience, his own prior knowledge or information which supply him with suggestions to aid in the solution of his intellectual problems. If he has learned to evaluate, to "try out" his own experience in order to separate that which is vital from that which is useless, if, unlike Newman's seafaring men, he has discovered how to relate to the wider knowledge of other men and other ages the information he has stored up from reading and from observation, then the process of thinking for himself should be orderly instead of confused, easy and desirable instead of difficult and unwelcome.

"In the real world," writes Schopenhauer in his fine essay on "Thinking for Oneself," "be it never so fair, favorable, and pleasant, we live subject to the law of gravity, which we have to be constantly overcoming. But in the world of intellect we are disembodied spirits, held in bondage to no such law, and free from penury and distress. Thus it is that there exists no happiness on earth like that which, at the auspicious moment, a fine and fruitful mind finds in itself."

It is in the desire to encourage students to find enjoyment in their own minds, *to have fun with their heads,* that the third part of this book has been planned and executed. An excellent preparation for the study and possible imitation of the selections given here and for those suggested in the reading lists would be the reading not only of Schopenhauer's essay [1] but of those two quoted in Part II, John Dewey's "What is Thought?" and James Harvey Robinson's "On Various Kinds of Thinking." Forget for the moment that they illustrate definition and analysis, and

[1] This essay may be found in the translated works of Schopenhauer in a volume entitled *Chips and Scraps.* It may also be read in *Essays on Current Themes,* edited by C. Alphonso Smith, Ginn and Company, Boston.

read them for their material, for their helpful and revealing presentation of the activities of the human mind.

In the first of these Mr. Dewey in his divisions III and IV distinguishes between the two types of belief, types which differ in degree, not in kind: the first, he says, is the belief or opinion which is accepted before its grounds have been thoroughly considered, although it may rest upon certain evidence or testimony; the second is that which is not accepted before it has been actively, persistently and carefully considered "in the light of the grounds that support it, and the further conclusions to which it tends." Mr. Robinson, working from a slightly different angle, arrives, however, in spite of his difference in terms on precisely the same ground. His "creative thought" as compared with Mr. Dewey's "reflective thought" at its best and highest is a distinction but hardly a difference.

It will be easily seen that the arrangement of the selections which comprise this third part is made in an attempt to carry out the idea and ideal of *constructiveness,* suggested not only in the two essays just cited but also in the title of the book itself. The chapters and models progress through the various types and stages of thought and thinking. All thoughtful, all fundamentally valuable, they yet differ in the degree of their originality, of their creativeness, of the power of their suggestiveness. Editors voice their opinions and the opinions of their publics; critics weigh and appreciate; educators, teachers, and scholars, assured of the validity of their convictions, diagnose and prescribe; those with pet prejudices, *pre-judgments,* air their points of view; and finally those whom reflective and creative thinking has blessed with ideas and perceptions beyond the lot of common men give us nourishment, intellectual and spiritual.

"If a man's thoughts," writes Schopenhauer again, "are to have truth and life in them, they must, after all, be his own fundamental thoughts; for these are the only ones that he can fully and wholly understand." The fundamental thinking of other men which follows is placed here as a suggestion and stimulus for your own; and the various forms in which it is clothed have their mission and purpose also.

CHAPTER I

The Editorial

The term, *editorial,* is not used to designate any particular kind of writing; in point of fact, it may be one of many kinds. It may be, and often is, an analysis, or a definition, or an explanation. It may be a biography. It may even present a place, such as not long ago did one of our leading dailies in its description of Tristan de Cunha, those lonely islands farther from mainland than any other islands in the world. It is not infrequently an appreciation of a person, such as is the editorial on Woodrow Wilson quoted from *The Manchester Guardian Weekly.* It often records such an incident as the discovery of the sarcophagus of King Tutankhamen which is in reality an historical incident. Editors have been known even to write reminiscences on their editorial pages if the application of those reminiscences might conceivably be timely or fruitful.

Not with the form of composition are editorial writers chiefly concerned but rather with (1) the choice of material at hand, (2) the motive or objective in using that material, and (3) the readers they must address. For editors, more perhaps than any other writers, write with a definite purpose, and they must always keep clearly before them the result of that purpose in the minds and in the resultant behavior of their readers. It is not for them to shrug their shoulders with indifference as to how their work is likely to be received. They are giving instruction, forming and directing public opinion, and above all else they are trying to bring about *action,* action based on the convictions or the feelings which they have aroused.

For example, the editor of a college daily, one week before a drive for a new stadium starts, is a busy, and should be a *thoughtful* person. His motive, or objective, is to raise the required sum and more. He knows, or should know, the character of his reading public. Everything depends upon his choice of material and his presentation. The first day he may choose to write as his opening editorial an explanation and description of the proposed stadium. The second day he may devote his space to an analysis by comparison and contrast of the facilities possessed for athletic games by other institutions and the relative distinction gained therefrom. On the third he may well enumerate the ideal qualities of sportsmanship which such a building may better inculcate in all participants in its advantages. On the fourth he concerns himself with a survey of potential subscribers with a tentative and extremely tactful suggestion as to the relative responsibilities of each class or group. On the fifth, his "big" day which he dedicates to his main appeal, he leaves no stone unturned. The fine history of the institution, the inspiration she has given in years past, her great men, living and dead, the love she engenders yearly in her loyal sons, the opportunity now presented for each to prove that love and that loyalty—all these on this day of eloquence he will make use of, for this is the day when feelings must be stirred to concrete action. The sixth he may well give to a note of expectancy and assurance, confidence and trust. Students know their indebtedness and they will not fail!

Now carefully trained in composition as this young man has undoubtedly been, he has not once thought of the forms he has been using. His material, his purpose, his readers have been his concern as they are inevitably the concern of all who write editorials. In addition, he has been careful to write clearly and reasonably, without too great prejudice or bias; he has made sure that he has understood the facts and the principles involved in the subject at hand; and lastly he has taken care that his opinions represent not merely himself but those of enough readers to afford some common ground of agreement. All these, he knows, make up the necessary equipment of one who would learn to write editorials. He knows, too, that greater than any of them and at the root of all are common sense, good judgment, and the ability to think for oneself.

In choosing the models that follow care has been taken to include those illustrative of several forms of composition. "The Coffin of the King," as has been suggested, savors of the historical incident. Here surely a scene is presented to the imagination in all its vividness and richness of detail, no bit of which is dimmed by the accompanying recognition and eulogy of Mr. Howard Carter and his fellow workers. The editorial on Mr. Wilson is in reality an appreciation as well as a portrait. "The Endless Battle" is the analysis of a situation by the enumerative method, and the appeal, on the basis of that situation, toward a better state of affairs. "Advancing Backward" is the definition of the idea of progress as held by the average man and the larger application of that definition to the promises and forebodings of the future.

THE COFFIN OF THE KING [1]

The lid of the sarcophagus of King Tutankhamen has been raised; and Mr. Howard Carter, Mr. Mace, Mr. Burton, and the others assembled in the tomb have looked upon that which no eye had seen for thirty-two centuries—the coffin and the carved face of a monarch who was buried five hundred years before Homer sang, and while the people of Israel were still bond-slaves in Egypt. Beneath the shrouds lay the gigantic gilded coffin, in the form of the King's body; his face of gold, with crystal eyes, a life-like portrait; the signs of kingship on his brow; the flail and the sceptre of kingship in his crossed hands. At the moment it seems but a small matter that the coffin of King Tutankhamen is the most magnificent ever discovered. The capital fact, that which makes every reader of the news glow with something like personal pride, is that the coffin was there. For once success has been dramatic and complete. A splendid

[1] From *The London Times Weekly,* February 21, 1924. Reprinted by the kind permission of the editor.

service has been done to art and history. A great undertaking has been faithfully and wisely carried out with consummate skill. The story is rich in the mysteries of the fitness of exquisite design and marvellously adjusted coincidence. For thirty-two centuries the body of the King lay undisturbed in the darkness, the dryness, the stillness, the sameness, which were the only conditions in which it could be preserved, with all those accessories whose value to knowledge is as great as their beauty, whose beauty is enhanced by their personal appeal. The sun of Egypt blazed down upon the sands, and the heavens wheeled in their course for thousands upon thousands of nights and days. The King and his treasures, "rolled round in earth's diurnal course with rocks and stones and trees," were no more known to the living men about them than their fleeting hours and ephemeral hopes and fears were known to his still, deserted frame. Other tombs were rifled; other bodies were discovered, to become material for science and gazing stocks to far peoples. King Tutankhamen's time was not yet. It was ordained that he should wait for an age that could value and use the discovery better than its forerunners, because it had sufficient knowledge, not only to gauge the importance of its treasure-trove, but to preserve the least fragment that could enrich the learning and the senses of present and future times. With a fitness very rare in mortal concerns, the time, the task, and the men came together; and after nearly sixteen years of labor, of adventure, of towering hopes and sickening disappointments, of luck both magically good and maddeningly bad, of exasperating difficulties and intoxicating successes, the work is done. The King's tomb has yielded up its secret.

Other tombs have been opened, other mummies have been found. But never before have modern eyes looked upon a Royal sarcophagus, a Royal coffin of Egypt, intact since its funeral rites. And that is not all. The body of King Tutankhamen is not, doubtless, the last kingly body of ancient Egypt that research will light upon. Yet two qualities, besides its priority in time, mark off this discovery from others that are possible. We are all by this time so well acquainted with a monarch whose very name was unknown to us less than two years ago that he appeals to us almost as closely as our own King Henry V. or King Charles.

We have seen photographs of his very wine-strainers and his walking-sticks; we may see them for ourselves in Cairo, if art and science can preserve them from falling to pieces in our garish light and air after their long seclusion. We have learned of the love that lived between him and his Queen. We have realized this mighty King, who died and was buried 3,000 years and more ago, as a human being like ourselves; and it is improbable that any other Egyptian monarch will touch us with so intimate a personal appeal. Moreover, it is admitted that history and archæology are great gainers by the accident that the tomb, so nearly missed, so hazardously discovered, was the tomb of Tutankhamen and not of another. His reign fell, as we have read, at an abnormal period of marked transition in the history of his strange and world-old kingdom. He it was who turned from the new ways of an idealistic monotheism back to the old ways of the concrete and dogmatic religion of his country. Other tombs may throw equal light on the still mysterious history of the art that seems to have spread from ancient Egypt to the Mediterranean and thus has poured an influence even into our own civilization. When all the records have been examined, it will be strange if history, and especially the history of religion, which is the history of the human mind, does not learn from the tomb of Tutankhamen something which no other tomb could have revealed.

Be that as it may, the value of the discovery to art and learning may be trusted to grow only the clearer as time strips it of the excitement that naturally gathered about an event so thrilling. For the moment the excitement must hold the field. For once a human effort has made a story which might have been built up by a fine craftsman in story-telling. From the first published groping to the final triumph the tale has kept men, women, and children in many lands agog with interest; and not a man of us but has envied Mr. Howard Carter. To plan a great adventure, to set about it, to rejoice and to suffer in its course, to achieve it definitely, completely, victoriously, before the eyes of the world—that falls to the lot of few. Mr. Howard Carter is not only fortunate. He has suffered in his toil, in difficulties acknowledged and concealed, and in the loss of his friend and patron, who made the adventure possible. And besides his daring and his pertinacity, he exercised two unspectacular qualities, the lack of which might have spoiled his enterprise. The one is reverence: the other is patience. He has entered the resting-place of a King in order that human knowledge may be the richer and the human spirit the more clearly known. And, for his patience, none but they can tell how hard he and his invaluable fellow-workers must have found it again and again to be patient, when the final achievement came within reach, only to float away.

WOODROW WILSON [1]

The death of Ex-President Wilson completes, quietly, as nearly all great tragedy is completed, the most famous personal tragedy of our time. We use the word tragedy in its strict sense of the wreck of something very noble, the breaking of a column really stately and the quenching of a veritable beacon light in dampness and smoke; and all this not wholly by malign accident or the defection of weak friends or the cunning of enemies, but partly, too, through flaws in the fine steel of the victim's own character, faults venial now in any generous eyes but fatal in the time of trial as the indecision that futilised Hamlet or the mystic self-assurance that led Cæsar to extinction. At the time of the Armistice in 1918 President Wilson was the leader of a world which was crying out to be led. By bringing America into the war he had ensured its ultimate result, and he had done wonders of political wisdom in timing her entry so well that virtually the whole of her entered. He seemed slow to many passionate friends of ours like Page, the great ambassador of the United States in London, whose friendship in our time of danger ought to be remembered in England as long as the war.

[1] From *The Manchester Guardian Weekly*, February 8, 1924. Reprinted by the kind permission of the editor.

But probably Wilson knew that the war could not have been a truly national one for Americans if they had joined in it sooner than they did. And then, when the Allied victories of the autumn of 1918 had made Germany's early collapse certain, it was Wilson whose famous Fourteen Points opened to the conquerors and the conquered the prospect of a peace honorable to both and not ruinous to what was left of the civilisation of Europe. The population of Germany believed that the Fourteen Points were an honest offer of terms morally binding on the Allies. In their relief from fear of a peace of savage vengeance they threw off their militarist rulers, conveyed their own will-to-peace to their men in the field, and asked the Allies for an armistice. No words can describe the thrill of enthusiastic delight that passed through our own armies, too, when the Fourteen Points became known to them. Here was peace, it seemed, about to come in the inspiring form at first proclaimed by all as our object and then almost lost to sight during the souring years of indecisive warfare soiled with foul weapons and unknightly spites.

When Wilson came to Europe for the Conference his place in popular imagination and hope throughout Europe was beyond all precedent. If by any miracle he could then have dealt, face to face, with the masses of decent, friendly, and simple people who form the bulk of every nation, a new era of peace and well-being might have opened for the world. But at Versailles he had not peoples to deal with but a few politicians fatally barred by their own past from acceptance of the rule of being just and fearing not. Some had already bound their countries over, by furtive treaties, to carry out bargains that would not square with the Fourteen Points, or indeed with any honorable rules of international conduct. French politicians had, on their country's behalf, gambled so heavily on the wild hope of wringing fantastic sums out of a Germany already half starved that now the alternatives seemed to be French national bankruptcy or the repudiation of the Fourteen Points by which Germany had been persuaded to abridge her resistance. The Prime Minister of England had just won his commission to make the peace by a demagogic appeal to faith in his power of "making Germany pay." In the cool, quiet rooms of Versailles, with all the generous relentments and chivalrous or Christian impulses that were then stirring in Europe safely outside the shut doors, Wilson had to deal alone with that entangled, sophisticated, and materialist diplomatic world which so many Americans believe to be Europe, the whole of Europe, and nothing but Europe. It beat him. But what could he have done? Thrown up his hand and walked out when first the honorable undertakings of the Fourteen Points were repudiated by the others? But that would have been to throw away the last hopes of his dearest project of all, the League of Nations; the others only paid it lip homage; they did not ardently wish or intend its success; still, they might agree to its formal creation as an equivalent to his acquiescence in the wrongs that they specially desired to commit; and then, the League once established, with America a leader in it and infusing her free and uninfected spirit into it, the world might at last be well on the way to a true democracy of free nations. Wilson gave in. To gain, as he hoped, something splendid for the world, he first agreed to let the peace-making go on in the dark. And then in that darkness he accepted, with the same lofty motive, complicity in the ignoble peace of revenge which has given us the Europe that we see to-day.

It was only after the bitter sacrifice had been consummated and Wilson had signed a peace abhorrent to the principles of right for which he had stood up that the smashing blow came. Out of the wreck of his generous leadership among the Allies nothing was left but the Covenant of the League of Nations. Still, in it were boundless possibilities for beneficent American predominance in the world's councils. And then all of Wilsonism that Europe had not destroyed America threw over when the Senate rejected the Covenant. Perhaps the two most tragically closed of modern political careers before Wilson's were Parnell's and Joseph Chamberlain's. Both presented in full measure the essential tragic spectacle of a powerful personality wholly given to a greater object than personal ambition, and wholly wrecked by a casual passion or a faulty calculation. But in no case has the Lucifer-like fall from great power and brilliant distinction to impotence and decay been set off with so many intensifying circumstances as in the tragedy of Wilson. For his stage was not a country, but the world; his opportunity was such as, perhaps, the world never before gave to a man, and the completeness of his collapse was made surpassingly poignant by the circumstance that in his eagerness to achieve at least one half of his ideal he had let himself desert the other half, and then lost all. We do not know enough to try to define here the failings in Wilson's equipment which contributed to his calamity. That he was incompletely endowed for his almost superhuman task seems to be the general opinion of those who knew him. But in a terribly soiled political world he was a most honest and high-minded leader; at a crisis in human civilisation he was the man who told mankind most truly and clearly the right way and the wrong; and already most of those, at any rate in Europe, who pushed him aside can see now that he knew better than they and was a better man.

THE ENDLESS BATTLE [1]

The war to end war, while it did not have the announced result, did have some others. It produced in the United States, as we have so often been told, an era of hysterical repression. Men were sent to jail for holding "dangerous" opinions, however innocent their acts. Professional patriots for the first time found it possible to make a fat living by frightening rich old women as to the activities of alleged "reds." New laws, more invasive of individual liberty than any since the Alien and Sedition Acts of 1798, were put on the statute books. When this hysterical period began, we were told that it was only the result of war emotion, and would soon pass. With the War ten years away, has the repression ended? No organization is better qualified to answer this query than the American Civil Liberties Union, which fights so gallantly and well on behalf of free speech, in every corner of the country. The Union has just issued its

[1] From *The New Republic*, August 15, 1928. Reprinted by the kind permission of the editor.

annual report for 1927, and has produced a document which should be studied by every person who believes it is important that the winds of freedom shall blow.

Active repression, we are told, continues to decrease, as it did in 1926. Yet intolerance is "firmly entrenched," and if repressive measures are taken less often, it is chiefly because there seems no need for them. "There is little to repress. Militancy in the labor movement has declined; the radical political movements do not arouse fear. Insurgency of any sort is at a minimum." If the pendulum should swing the other way, however, "all the instruments of repression remained unchanged," and could quickly be mobilized again. Not only that, but they have been strengthened in the past year by decisions of the U. S. Supreme Court sustaining the state criminal syndicalism laws, some of which, it had been hoped, might be held to be unconstitutional. Thirty-four states still have sedition or criminal syndicalism laws. The Union reminds us, moreover, that the censorship powers of the post office under the Espionage Act are still in force. Injunctions continue to be used in labor disputes. Censorship of books, plays, periodicals and movies is the rule, in almost every part of the country. Two states have anti-evolution laws, and in many others, the same results are achieved by rules of the state or local school authorities. Aliens no longer enjoy the right of political asylum in America; on the contrary, we are more and more inclined to deport people for holding radical views, and to debar immigrants from naturalization if they are suspected of being revolutionaries, or even of being pacifists. The Klan and the Fundamentalists continue their repressive activities; there is no more freedom of thought in the schools and universities than in the past. Mooney and Billings are still in prison, where they were sent on perjured testimony; eight Centralia, Washington, I.W.W.'s continue to serve their long sentences, imposed following the battle which took place when a mob of armed Legionnaires attacked them in their hall. Individual states continue to pass laws making daily reading of the Bible compulsory in the schools, or ordering that children be excused from their class work in order to receive religious instruction in the faith of their fathers. Fifteen hundred persons convicted under the espionage law during the War are still deprived of their citizenship, a matter in which we lag behind all the other chief powers. Particularly outrageous is the treatment of striking miners and textile workers by police, who break up their meetings, refuse to let them picket, and do everything else possible to discourage and harass them.

It is possible that too much attention has been paid to the War as a cause of the invasion of civil liberties in America in recent years. It is true that the conflict ended before the passions aroused by it in this country had had a chance to find outlet along normal channels of activity, and that these passions were all the more intense because they were artificially whipped up. But there are other explanations which need to be invoked for a complete understanding of the characteristic activities of the present day.

The professional patriot, for example, continues his activities primarily because he gets a fat living out of them. His credulous victims pay him handsomely for his tales of red bugaboos; he can lecture at large fees to audiences which would not hear him at any price on any other subject. Much of the work of the Fundamentalists is similarly actuated. Unless "the old-time religion" continues to be the popular brand, Fundamentalist preachers may find their good jobs gone. Most of them, if they could not attack the Modernists, would have nothing to say, and could no longer make the sensational tours of the country of which they are so fond. William Jennings Bryan turned to this sort of witch-hunting partly as a compensation when he ceased to be of any importance in the Democratic party, and when his old-fashioned vein of Chautauqua oratory was running painfully thin.

The motives of the police who violate the civil liberties of the strikers are too plain to need discussion. The police authorities stand in with the wealthy owners of the mills as simply and instinctively as does Mr. Coolidge. They have only the dimmest notion, if any, of the rights of the individual supposed to be inherent in our system of society; but they have a clear and vivid understanding of the sacredness of property. The same psychological scene exists in the case of those states, like California, which punished so ferociously the mere fact of membership, however passive, in any organization preaching "criminal syndicalism." The I.W.W.'s were working men, whose labor was essential on the ranch; but they preached, and sometimes practised, sabotage which cost an individual employer real money. The rage of the dominant element in society came from the pain of a pinched pocketbook nerve.

Since all this is true, it might be asked whether the battle for free speech is not a hopeless one, lost before it starts? What use is there in seeking to go against the current of economic advantage? The answer is that there is every use. In most of the cases cited, those who interfere with liberty are truckling to a real or fancied sentiment in the community. If that sentiment can be changed, the whole background of the problem is altered at once. Though perhaps with more difficulty, people can be induced to make a fetish of individual liberty—this was once true, and still is to a less extent, with the English—as well as of conformity to mass opinion. The forces of propaganda can be mobilized on either side. The recent history of the press in this country serves as an illustration. For many years, critics of American newspapers charged them with unfairness; and while the editors always resisted these accusations, and have never admitted their truth, they have been followed, at least among the more important papers in large cities, by a notable improvement in the handling of controversial matters—labor disputes and news from Russia being two outstanding illustrations.

The officers of the American Civil Liberties Union recognize that changes of this sort can be brought about. Their annual report announces a nation-wide campaign to alter the public mind as to the importance of maintaining the safeguards of individual freedom of thought and speech. Such a process will, of course, be slow at best; and in the event of another war, all the progress made may be expected to be lost overnight. Nevertheless, the effort is worth while, and deserves the support of all who still believe that political democracy is an experiment both possible and desirable.

ADVANCING BACKWARD [1]

It is said that toward the close of the Civil War a patriotic Southern newspaper, anxious to maintain the morale of its readers, published the following dispatch: "Our glorious army is rapidly advancing backward and the enemy is retreating after it." For the truth of this story we do not vouch, but we do give solemn assurance that a metropolitan daily recently headed an article "Rush of Progress Menace to the World, says Rockefeller."

Progress a menace? What then does "progress" mean? It sounds like a meaningless paradox. One would not say that a man was dying from excess of health, but one can, it appears, speak in all seriousness of a civilization which is going backward because it is "progressing" too fast. If there is any word of which the modern world has made a shibboleth, "progress" is the word, and in the language of popular thought it has no definite meaning.

Asked to define it the average man would doubtless give some fairly satisfactory reply; unconsciously he uses it to mean no more than any increase in size, in power, or in speed. Words are but counters, and sometimes it makes little difference what they are taken to mean; but it makes a great deal of difference when an important word happens to mean one thing in theory and another in practice. When progress became the religion of the modern world and came to be identified with things which are not necessarily in themselves good, the present age of confusion began. Gradually men forgot that speed might be uncomfortably hurrying them nowhere and that power might destroy civilization itself. Ceasing to criticize their definition they ceased to criticize their aims, and the result is knowledge and speed and power which are constantly increasing without any

[1] From *The Nation* (New York), December 31, 1924. Reprinted by the kind permission of the editor.

proportionate gain in happiness or virtue. There is wealth enough to make every man comfortable and power enough to relieve him of all except a comfortable minimum of work, but there is no immediate prospect that poverty will disappear or that the majority of men will be released from the necessity of deadly toil; yet the average man never doubts that the world is progressing at an ever-increasing rate. His eyes glitter with enthusiasm when he speaks of the size of his city, which is stifling him with its congestion, he points with pride to accumulated wealth, which is crushing him; he will even regard with complacency the prospect of being blown sky-high with the rest of his family by an aerial bomb because he can rejoice in the "progress" which makes such an event possible.

The present age has little use for logical subtleties; "facts not theories" is its motto. Yet a little dialectic might save civilization. No frequenter of the Platonic Academy would ever have made a word the cornerstone of his faith without first defining it. Plato did not know countless things which we know, but had he known them he would have seen to it that something better came of them than the mad world in which we live. He would have laughed at progress which goes backward and he would have called a halt in the perfection of the machine until he had learned to use it for instead of against himself. We, having already so much power that we are in danger of destroying ourselves, think of nothing except how to make it greater. We can go anywhere we like and faster than we need to go; few realize that it is time to ask where it is most worth while to go.

EXERCISES

1. Outline "The Endless Battle." Of how many distinct parts is it composed? Is its organization superior to that of "The Coffin of the King"? Can you suggest a better plan for the latter? Criticize the development of its second paragraph. There is ground for criticism.

2. Read for one week the editorials in any daily suggested on the reading list. Keep a record of the subjects presented. How many types of composition are exemplified?

3. Choose an editorial from *The New Republic*, and rewrite it so that it would appeal more distinctly to a college public.

4. Compare the editorials in a current issue of *The Manchester Guardian Weekly* with those in *The London Times Weekly*. From the editorials alone try to state the policy or policies of the respective publications.

5. Try from any source to find an editorial distinctly literary in subject matter and in presentation.

6. Study the value of the one literary allusion in "Advancing Backward." Why is Plato the best possible figure of comparison?

7. In "The Coffin of the King" do you note any distinct similarities to the style and diction of a great writer of nineteenth century prose?

8. Write 300-word editorials on two of the following subjects:

The Y.M.C.A. Drive.
Seniors and Automobiles.
The Faculty and the Honor System.
Silence in the Reading-room.
The Freshman Cap.
Conscientious Objectors to Learning.
The Senior Walking-stick.
The Poor Janitor.
The Phi Beta Kappa Mind.
"Go to Church" Sunday.
The All-around Man.
Extra-Curricular Activities.
The Foot-ball Coach Resigns.
The Ownership of Automobiles by Students.
The Election of the Senior President.
Phi Beta Kappa Humor.
The Inevitable Cramming.
Mother's Day.
English 360.
Professor —— Resigns.

SUGGESTED READINGS

The following newspapers and periodicals usually contain the better editorial writing:

American:
The New York Times
The New York Herald-Tribune
The New York World
The Christian Science Monitor
The Boston Transcript
The New Republic
The Nation
The Outlook

English:
The London Times Weekly
The London Times (daily)
The London Observer (Sunday)
The Manchester Guardian Weekly
The London Daily Telegraph
The New Statesman

CHAPTER II

THE CRITICISM

Whenever you attempt honestly and by every means within your power to estimate the worth of something, whether it be an object or an idea, you are a critic. A second reading of that sentence in an endeavor to get not only its statement but its implications will not come amiss. Comments, mere off-hand remarks, are not criticism; neither is the announcement of approval or of dislike. Criticism presupposes an honest attempt by the utilization of every possible means to arrive at an estimate of the intrinsic worth or value of the subject criticised.

Although criticism in its largest and most comprehensive sense may rightly apply to any object or subject from gardening to the drama, from Maine country roads to the underlying principles of Sovietism, we are restricting it in this chapter to literary criticism, that is, to the criticism of a given book, of an author, or of a specific kind or type of literature—a restriction which seems eminently suitable to the study of English.

There are two kinds of literary criticism: (1) the objective or formal kind which attempts to estimate the worth of a book, of an author, of a type of literature on the basis of more or less predetermined standards, and (2) the subjective or informal kind which gives a personal estimate on the basis of the author's own enthusiasm or disapproval. Although no absolutely distinct line can be drawn between the two, although much objective criticism admits easily the personality of the critic and much subjective the more clearly cut standards of the more formal kind, it seems best, at least for the beginner, to look upon the two kinds as distinct and to consider each separately.

473

I. OBJECTIVE AND FORMAL CRITICISM

In choosing the four models of objective criticism which follow an attempt has been made to illustrate different methods of approach and of treatment. A careful analysis of each, together with a listing of the various qualities in the work as they are presented by the critic, will be of the utmost value to one who has yet to write his first book review. For example, a study of Mr. Van Santvoord's survey of Sir Charles Mallet's history of Oxford will reveal the following qualities of Mr. Mallet's work:

1. His thoroughness in giving as far as possible a complete survey.
2. His ability in sifting and co-ordinating huge masses of material.
3. His sense for picturesque and interesting detail.
4. His insistence upon attractiveness in the appearance of his volumes.
5. His distinguished style.
6. His unforgettable portraits.
7. His vivid and full accounts of certain colleges.
8. His relation of certain early educational experiments.
9. His suggestion of the charm of Oxford.

Now, if these be pondered over sufficiently, the following briefer list will result:

1. His thoroughness in dealing with his subject.
2. His ability to select carefully.
3. His sense of the picturesque and the charming.
4. His style, so lucid and terse that he can give much in a brief space.
5. The outward appearance of his work.

Here, then, we have evolved from our study five qualities which any reviewer may well take into consideration: *thoroughness, selection, esthetic appeal, style,* and *outward appearance.* The suggestion is made that before you write a review, you employ this method of study and of listing various points of criticism on several reviews taken from such periodicals as *The Yale Review, The Atlantic Monthly,* or *The Saturday Review of Literature.* Familiarity with the work of reviewers and critics is before all else the way to get ideas for your own approach.

But it is not enough to discover the various conclusions that may conceivably be made about a piece of literature, not enough to know that one may evaluate outward appearance, thoroughness of method, choice of material, style, diction, esthetic appeal, characterization, truth in the light of experience, convincingness in message or thesis, and a dozen other points of attack or of approval. These are only the guide-posts. You must travel the way for yourself by means of your own thinking.

Your task in this thinking may, however, be greatly simplified by asking certain questions of yourself after you have carefully read the novel, play, or poem which you are to criticise or after you have studied a certain type of writing, let us say, detective stories, free verse, or the nonsense rhymes of such men as A. P. Herbert and Arthur Guitermann. These questions were given long ago by one of the most famous of literary critics, Samuel Taylor Coleridge: First, What did the author intend to do? Second, How did he do it? Third, Was his purpose worth striving for?

When you have made up your mind, honestly and sincerely, without confusing your own judgments with those of others, even though those others may know more than you, the next thing you must consider is the expression of your conclusions and your ideas. What method shall you use? Here again you will be best helped by the suggestions as to form to be gained from the reading of reviews in the periodicals already recommended. There are literally hundreds of possible approaches, of possible developments.

The desire to give some commonsense cautions is irresistible:

1. Remember that you must keep your mental eye on what you are judging. Don't be too generous with your own personality. It is your *thinking* that matters.

2. Be sure that what you say means something. Don't indulge in high-sounding, meaningless talk.

3. Be sure that you yourself *know what you mean.*

4. Don't use the stock phrases or words of hundreds of mediocre critics. Avoid such expressions as *interesting, vital, colorful, strong, gripping, true to life.*

There is nothing like objective criticism to snap one's mind out of the mist and fog of vague thinking. It should, and can, kill superficiality; it should, and can, reveal you to yourself, discover your interests, enlarge your conception and appreciation, and immeasurably increase your intelligence.

A History of the University of Oxford [1]

By C. E. Mallet

Reviewed by G. Van Santvoord

These are admirable volumes. The first covers the rise and development of Oxford University during the Middle Ages, and the second carries the story on through the Reformation to the end of the seventeenth century. A third volume, soon to be published, will treat of the eighteenth and nineteenth centuries and complete the work.

Sir Charles Mallet has performed his task with extraordinary skill. He has sifted and co-ordinated here masses of material hitherto scattered in such volumes as the histories of the various colleges and the proceedings of the Oxford Historical Society. Further, he has quietly added most picturesque and interesting details gathered from his researches among college records and other manuscript sources. Footnotes attest the interest and co-operation of Oxford scholars like Mr. Madan, Bodley's Librarian, and Mr. Allen, the editor of Erasmus; and the publishers have done their part to make the book readable by sending it forth in worthy dress, with clear print, and charming illustrations reproduced from Bereblock's quaint sketches and Loggan's engravings.

[1] From *The Yale Review* for April 1926. Reprinted by the kind permission of the editor and of the author.

The style, often reminding one of Froude at his best, gives the work a final touch of distinction. At once lucid and terse, it enables the author to compress into fewer than nine hundred pages the story of Oxford during six eventful centuries, and at the same time to give us by way of historical background admirably clear and comprehensive accounts of the development of English thought as seen in such significant movements as the rise of the schoolmen, the Lollards, humanism, the Reformation, Puritanism, and the stirring of new interest in science at the time of the founding of the Royal Society. Such chapters as these, with their vivid character-sketches, and unforgettable portraits like that of Anthony Wood at the end of the second volume, will be useful to many a student of history, philosophy, or literature.

In the structure of this narrative are set here and there chapters dealing with the more parochial concerns of the collegiate foundations. In each of these, two or three colleges of approximately contemporary origin are treated successively, with epigrammatic accounts of their founders, early statutes, and more important personages and events down to the end of the seventeenth century. This arrangement disposes of much incidental material which might otherwise hinder the flow of the main narrative and makes available for the reader many details of extraordinary interest which are not easy to find elsewhere, for there are accounts of the rare books and MSS. that have been preserved in college libraries, as well as of other college treasures more difficult to authenticate, like the autograph of the devil which Charles the Second inspected during his visit to Queen's College. Many an old Oxford worthy is here restored to life and fame, whether it be the redoubtable Dr. Fell, memorable for much else besides the occurrence of his name in a mere epigram, or the crusty old cavalier dons who in the true Oxford style insisted on calling their opponents not mere Roundheads, but *kuklokephalas*. The lover of romance will delight to be reminded that an Oxford man once sat in the chair of St. Peter as Pope Alexander Fifth, and to read of the stories of Prince Hal's possible sojourn as a student at Queen's College, of Friar

Bacon's mysterious discoveries, and many another fascinating old tale.

Equally picturesque and perhaps more important in these days of educational experiment is the long experience of Oxford in the training and discipline of young men. From the beginning the problem of securing good teachers seems to have been a difficult one, and the medieval students early hit upon an effectual solution in their organization of a "hall," joining in groups to rent a house where they should have their rooms and meals, hiring tutors to supplement the inadequate instruction of the University lecturers, and electing their own master to rule the little society. For needy students there was a University Chest from which funds could be borrowed, until the foundation of the colleges with their scholarships brought still more liberal assistance to poor clerks. Gradually the halls with their democratic student-government gave way before the endowed colleges, where power was vested in the masters and sterner discipline developed regulations about dress and amusements, and finally compulsory attendance at chapel.

In the histories of these ancient foundations, designed to train young men "yearly for ever while the world shall endure," such petty problems seem to be perennial, and one is led to conclude there will always be a ferment over what shall be taught, who shall be admitted to the colleges, and how the University shall maintain its independence against selfish and paralytic forces without and within. Yet the charm of the Book and the Triple Crown seems to enable youth in every generation to triumph over such mundane affairs and to dream of deeper and more mysterious things. It is as Sir Charles Mallet says: "to every boy who grows to manhood in the city where Duns Scotus taught there comes sooner or later the longing to know more of these mysteries, the imperious urge to unravel them if he may. Oxford's inheritance from the Middle Ages is the attempt to think about high things. And so long as youth lasts and inquires and wonders, the voice which the schoolmen vainly tried to answer will call and call not vainly to the hearts and understandings of men."

ISRAFEL: THE LIFE AND TIMES OF EDGAR ALLAN POE [1]

By Hervey Allen

Reviewed by Gamaliel Bradford

Biography seems to be becoming more and more a matter of background. We see eminent men, not so much as errant examples of genius or individuality, but as the product of their surroundings and of their time, influenced, in their strength and in their weakness both, by the numerous and complicated currents of thought and feeling that manifest themselves in the general movement of the age.

It is in this spirit that Mr. Allen has dealt with the life of Poe, and has endeavored to make it clear that not only much of his achievement but much of his limitation and erratic failure was connected with the conditions under which he lived and worked. The early background of Richmond and the complicated relations with the Allans are developed to a point far beyond anything possible hitherto, since Mr. Allen has had access to documents not used by previous biographers. The life at the University, in the army, at West Point, and the confused goings and comings between Baltimore, Philadelphia, and New York, are all elucidated with extraordinary patience and clarity. Poe's varied feminine relations from Frances Allan to Helen Whitman, are all studied and analyzed in their delicate comparative significance, and foremost among them all stand the pathetically contrasted figures of the mother and daughter, Maria Clemm and Virginia Poe, one of whom made the poet's material life possible, if not tolerable, while the other played the chief rôle in his fantastic world of dreams. And everywhere there is the underlying element of dire, insistent, unescapable poverty, the bitter need of snatching bare subsistence from every sort of shift and expedient, which more than anything else drove a sensitive temperament and a high-wrought imagination to the fatal refuges of alcohol and opium.

[1] From *The Atlantic Monthly* for February 1927. Reprinted by the kind permission of the editor and of the author.

The thoroughness and patience of Mr. Allen's research and effort in all this investigation of background cannot be too much commended. Only those who know the enormous difficulty of the subject can appreciate what he has accomplished. Yet, after all this vast research, there is still an almost pathetic incompleteness, which appears in the constant reiteration of "probably" and "we may then imagine." In this close study of the past even plain matter of fact so frequently eludes us. And when it comes to the portrayal of the soul, the complication is far greater. What makes the study of souls the most fascinating in the world is at once its difficulty and its necessity. We can never really know the souls of others, or even our own. Yet no knowledge is so absolutely essential to us, and we must pursue it unfailingly, so long as we think at all. Mr. Allen recognizes this difficulty and complexity to the full, appreciates the subtlety of the general problem, and above all the extreme remoteness and involved intricacy of the soul of Edgar Poe. "All the evidence about Poe is like this, paradoxical, contradictory, and *true*." Mr. Allen applies all his delicate skill of analysis, all the resources of modern psychology, all the sexual conjecture of the Freudians, which I for one could sometimes spare. And still the author of *The Raven* keeps skillfully, elusively, evasively out of reach. The utmost, inner secrets of the spirit are almost beyond our probing. But surely no one has yet supplied, or probably ever will supply, richer material for such research than Mr. Allen furnishes in this biography.

THORNTON WILDER [1]

By Edmund Wilson

Now that Thornton Wilder has become both a best-seller and a Pulitzer prize-winner, he is in an unfortunate situation: on one hand, the literary columnists have accepted him as a Reputation and gossip about him with respect, but without intelligence; and on the other, the literary snobs have been driven by his tre-

[1] From *The New Republic*, August 8, 1928. Reprinted by the kind permission of the editor.

mendous popularity, by the obsequious gossips themselves, into assuming that there must be something meretricious about him. He remains, however, a remarkably interesting writer, with a good deal to be said about him which seems never yet to have been said.

In the first place, Thornton Wilder is the first American novelist who has been profoundly influenced by Proust. In all that I am going to say on this subject, I do not at all mean to imply a lack of originality on Wilder's part: on the contrary, it is quite extraordinary that the first books of so young a man should display such unmistakable originality of style, of form and of point of view. The influence seems simply the influence of a first-rate senior writer on a first-rate junior one. And what Wilder has learned from Proust is not merely Proust's complex impressionism: the side of Proust which Sacheverell Sitwell imitated in "All Summer in a Day" does not figure in Wilder at all. Wilder has listened to Proust's very heart, and his own has been timed to its beat. It is not a formula of style which he has taken, but a formula of emotion, of the criticism of life. And in order to consider Wilder properly, we should try to find out what part of his work represents the poet Wilder himself, from whom quite unProustian things may be expected, and what part is the mere repetition of the lesson of the master.

One of Proust's favorite formulas, then—which we find in almost every situation of *A la Recherche du Temps Perdu*— is that of agonizing, abject and desperate love on the part of a superior person for an inferior person, or at least on the part of a gentle person for a person who treats him cruelly. Thornton Wilder has leaned heavily on this formula. It is less prominent in *The Cabala* than in *The Bridge of San Luis Rey;* but the episode of Alix in the former, which seems to me also the episode which carries the least conviction, is simply a reversal of the Proustian situation, where it is usually a charming man who breaks his heart for an unworthy woman: the part played for Swann by Odette, for Saint Loup by Rachel and for Proust's hero by Albertine, is played by Blair for Alix. But there are other evidences of Proust, in a hundred turns of phrase; Wilder

has even become addicted to a favorite expression of Proust's—
a sort of proverbial phrase in French which I have never seen in
English: he is always talking about somebody or other "making
the fair weather" of somebody else (as Swann made *"la pluie et
le beau temps"* of the Duchesse de Guermantes). And there is
one passage in *The Cabala* where the Proustian note of hypochondriacal melancholy is brought almost to the point of burlesque: a Helen Darrell, a famous beauty, enters suddenly like
one of those unannounced characters in Proust's social scenes.
We are not told precisely what is wrong with her, but, like so
many characters in Proust, she is ill and soon to die; none of her
dearest friends dares to kiss her: they feel that she is blighted
and doomed. "She was like a statue in solitude. She presuffered
her death." Yet the unfortunate Alix envies her: "He would
have loved me," she breathes in the hero's ear, "if I had looked
like that. . . . She is beautiful. She is beautiful," he hears her
mutter. "The world is hers. She will never have to suffer as I
must." The dying beauty asks, before she goes, to be taken to
say goodbye to a saintly old French poet, who is also about to
die. "One wonders what they said to one another as she knelt
beside his chair: as he said later, they loved one another because
they were ill." I have cited this passage at length because it
shows Wilder when he is writing pure Proust—it is one of the only
scenes in Wilder, perhaps, of which this could be said and it is
also one of the only scenes which I feel to be unsuccessful.
Proust's characters are always ill, and Proust thinks that that is
the most pathetic thing on earth—but Proust has the advantage
of *"malade"* and *"maladie,"* words made for him, which he is
able to drop with an irresistible somber mournful cadence—so
that we do not resent his eternal invalids as much as we otherwise might. But "ill" in English has no such beauty: when you
hear in English that somebody is ill, you ask at once what the
doctor is doing for him.

In *The Bridge of San Luis Rey,* the Proustian formula pervades the whole book. The Marquesa de Montemayor distils
marvelous literature out of her insulted love for her daughter,
just as Vinteuil in Proust distils marvelous music out of his in-

sulted love for his. Furthermore, the Marquesa has evidently been transposed from Mme. de Sévigné, who plays herself such an important rôle in Proust. The bad feature here, however, is that Wilder has followed Proust in exaggerating the cruelty of the beloved to the lover. This is sometimes pretty hard to swallow in Proust himself, but then in Proust there is a savage bitterness which seems derived from hard experience; whereas with Wilder we feel that this violence is merely an effective dramatic trick. I cannot quite, for example, believe in the scene where Esteban is dressing Manuel's wound and Manuel repeatedly abuses him in the bitterest terms, and I cannot believe at all in the scene where La Périchole refuses, after twenty years, to allow Uncle Pio to address her by her first name. And it seems to me that there is something very forced about the pining of Captain Alvarados for his dead daughter: it is just one case of hopeless love too many. Also, Wilder slips all too easily into rewriting the death of Bergotte (a natural weakness, certainly: no doubt, like Strachey's death of Queen Victoria, it is destined to be rewritten many times): "We come from a world where we have known incredible standards of excellence, and we dimly remember beauties which we have not seized again, and we go back to that world." ("*Toutes ces obligations qui n'ont pas leur sanction dans la vie présente semblent appartenir à un monde différent, fondé sur la bonté, le scrupule, le sacrifice, un monde entièrement différent de celui-ci, et dont nous sortons pour naître à cette terre, avant peut-être d'y retourner*" . . .)

This is not to say that Proust for Wilder has been anything other than the elder master who supplies every young writer with ideas before his own have fully come to growth. Since I have cited so many passages in which Wilder has filled in with Proust, I must quote at least one in the same key which Proust would never have written, which has a different ring of authenticity: "He regarded love as a sort of cruel malady through which the elect are required to pass in their late youth and from which they emerge, pale and wrung, but ready for the business of living. There were (he believed) a great repertory of errors mercifully impossible to human beings who had recovered from this illness.

Unfortunately there remained to them a host of failings, but at least (from among many illustrations) they never mistook a protracted amiability for the whole conduct of life, they never again regarded any human being, from a prince to a servant, as a mechanical object."

And, in any case, the effect of Wilder is not at all like the effect of Proust, or like the effect of any one we remember. Before we read him, we are likely to think that he is one of those contemporary writers who seem still to date from the nineties— that he is simply another "stylist," another devotee of "beauty" —that we shall, in fact, find him merely a pretty or a precious writer; but Wilder, when we come to read him, turns out to be something quite different. He certainly possesses that quality of "delightfulness" of which Saintsbury has said that Balzac didn't have it, but that Gêrard de Nerval did. But he has a hardness, a sharpness, a precision, quite unlike our Cabells, our Dunsanys, our Van Vechtens and our George Moores. He has an edge which is peculiar to himself and which is never incompatible with a consummate felicity. This felicity, which seems natural to him, which has nothing of the deliberate pose, of the self-conscious effort to "write beautifully," of the professional beautiful writer, pervades his entire work and is felt as much in the conception of the characters and the development of the situations as in the sentences themselves. It is the felicity of a true poet— not merely the "style" of a modern literary man with a yearning for old unhappy fancy far-off things—and it makes possible for him many things which we should not have expected him to bring off. For example, Wilder has never been to Peru, and there are few things ordinarily more deadly than the dream-country of the twentieth-century novelist. But Wilder gives his Peru a solidity, an incandescence and a distinctness of outline, which we should never have thought possible. Take, for example, the Marquesa's pilgrimage to Cluxambuqua: "a tranquil town, slow-moving and slow-smiling; a city of crystal air, cold as the springs that fed its many fountains; a city of bells, soft and musical, and tuned to carry on with one another the happiest quarrels. If anything turned out for disappointment in the town of Cluxambuqua the grief was somehow assimilated by the over-whelming immanence of the Andes and by the weather of quiet joy that flowed in and about the side-streets. No sooner did the Marquesa see from a distance the white walls of this town perched on the knees of the highest peaks than her fingers ceased turning the beads and the busy prayers of her fright were cut short on her lips." Then the church, the hawks, the llama. . . . It is all the city of a fairy-tale, of course; but it is a fairy-tale almost of the same quality as *Kubla Khan*. It has its preciosity; but it is a preciosity at least as sound as *Vathek*.

Wilder has also a form of his own, which is highly individual and which seems to me to promise more than he has hitherto brought it to accomplish. In *The Cabala*, the several heroes of the several episodes seem at first to have in common merely the fact that they are all observed by the American who is telling the story; then, we learn that they are the ancient gods fallen on evil times, and we realize that there is also a significance in their relation to the young American. In *The Bridge of San Luis Rey*, the different characters appear to have in common merely the fact that they were all killed by the fall of the bridge; then, we are finally made to understand that there was a sig-nificance in their having been killed, and that there is a signifi-cance in the relation of the people who fell with the bridge to the people who were left alive. *The Bridge of San Luis Rey* is more ingenious and more completely worked out than *The Cabala;* but I feel that it is incompletely satisfying. God works in too obvious a way: I cannot believe that Mr. Wilder believes in his God. The real higher power at work here is Mr. Wilder's esthetic form, which is struggling to incarnate itself: the God who broke the bridge is only a masquerading prophet. Wilder's real emo-tions and ideas have not yet fully come to the surface—they have not yet fully identified themselves with his peculiar style and form to bring forth his peculiar kind of beauty.

One should say something more about *The Cabala*, which has received less attention than *The Bridge*, but which seems to me, in some ways, more interesting. The circle of clever people in Rome turn out to be the gods grown old: Christianity and modern

society have proved too much for them. The Puritanism of the
young American gives Pan (or Priapus?) such a bad conscience
that he is driven to suicide; and Aphrodite breaks her heart for
an American Adonis who pays no attention to her. A brilliant
peasant Cardinal, who has spent his life as a missionary to China,
robs Artemis—if, as I suppose, Astrée-Luce is an Artemis—of
her religious faith. These are the gods of Europe contending
with the influences of alien races. In the end, the young American goes to call on the Cardinal, whom he finds with *Appearance
and Reality*, Spengler, *The Golden Bough, Ulysses*, Proust and
Freud on the table beside him. In the course of the conversation, the Cardinal shoves them to the ground: "Yes, I could write
a book," he says, "better than this ordure that your age has
offered us. But a Montaigne, a Machiavelli . . . a . . . a . . .
Swift, I will never be." The moment after, just before the
visitor goes, the Cardinal remarks that he would like for his
birthday a small Chinese rug. The young American departs for
the States: "Why was I not more reluctant at leaving Europe?
How could I lie there repeating the Æneid and longing for the
shelf of Manhattan?" The shade of Virgil appears to him.
"Know, importunate barbarian," says the poet, "that I spent my
whole lifetime under a great delusion—that Rome and the house
of Augustus were eternal. Nothing is eternal save Heaven.
Romes existed before Rome and when Rome will be a waste there
will be Romes after her. Seek out some city that is young. The
secret is to make a city, not to rest in it." . . . "The shimmering
ghost faded before the stars, and the engines beneath me pounded
eagerly towards the new world and the last and greatest of all
cities."

Mr. Wilder himself, however, next turns up in Peru. I have
already praised this fairy-tale Peru. I am told that it owes part
of its vividness to its grasp and faithful representation of the
Spanish character. Wilder's feeling for national temperaments
—French, Italian and American—had already, in *The Cabala*,
appeared as one of his most striking gifts. But I wish, for our
sakes at least, and perhaps for his own, that he would now take
Virgil's advice and return for a time to New York. I wish that

he would study the different nations which make up the United States, and give us *their* national portraits. Mr. Wilder already knows Europe, and he also knows the Orient; and we need him at home. I believe that this player on plaintive stops has more than one tune in his flute.

THE FALLACY OF FREE VERSE [1]

By Theodore Maynard

In view of the fact that Miss Harriet Monroe (who seems to be not only editor of *Poetry* but of poetry) has announced that the discussion of free verse is now closed, I feel a little diffident about forcibly reopening it. My apology is that most attacks upon free verse, like most defenses, have been unintelligent; and that mine, I venture with all due modesty to believe, will be intelligent.

The whole controversy, intelligent or not, has become so confused in its issues, so much entangled with personal ambitions and prejudices, that it is difficult as well as dangerous to make any attempt to reduce the matter to orderly arrangement. It can only be done by painfully clearing, at each step, the ground of its cumbering misconceptions.

To be fair to the *vers librists* we should not take the wild eccentricities of the notoriety-seekers among them as typical of the movement. It would, I think, be just to draw unfavorable conclusions from the prevalence of eccentricity among even the staider innovators who, like Miss Amy Lowell, have protested against the "nefarious persons who endeavor to keep themselves before the public by means of a more or less clever charlatanism." But it would not be just to hold Miss Lowell and her co-workers guilty of crimes that, in intention at least, they do not commit. This is an easy, often-used, and discreditable method for bringing free verse into contempt. I disdain to employ it.

Moreover, there is much to be said for the widely diffused

[1] From *The Yale Review*. Reprinted, after slight revision by Professor Maynard, with permission.

notion that free verse is a better mode for expressing the emotions of our age than traditional metrical forms. I think it quite probable myself: so much the worse for the age!

A paradoxical circumstance about modernism, however, is that it is never modernism: it is invariably futurism. And the central doctrine of futurism is that we are all poor fools—which also is a highly tenable proposition. For the modernist is continually making violent efforts to be revolutionary, although he carries in his breast the exasperating knowledge that he must in due course appear a reactionary to his children. He is obliged, in short, to begin as a young freak merely to end up as an old fogy.

Any philosophy behind futurism is a philosophy of negation which doubts, without daring to deny, the validity of reason and the existence of all absolutes. Truth has fallen into the hands of the pragmatists; goodness into the hands of the psychoanalysts; and beauty—well, the natural result of the age's deliquescence is free verse. The one thing certain is that nothing is certain. We have fallen into the abyss of hopeless skepticism. The very title of the most characteristic of Miss Lowell's books *Pictures of the Floating World,* is significant and appropriate.

Mr. Santayana's genius for profound criticism has noted this state of affairs and has drawn from it the correct conclusions. "The interest abroad," he says, to summarize him, "in the condition of flux, in the process of becoming rather than in what has or will result, is the unmistakable mark of the barbarian." In saying so he touches the root of modern æsthetic experimentalism.

The artist is no longer concerned with the impossible but happy task of capturing absolute beauty: he does not believe in an absolute beauty. Consequently, he is thrown back upon himself, and must use as the material of his art not reality but his personal reactions to the unsubstantial phenomena of appearances. He gives up in despair the ancient ambitions of his craft and confines himself to the narrowing circle of his own ego. It is a terrible fate; but one that has, at present, the delusive attraction of novelty. The poet is spurred on by the craving to be "original"; and as he has nothing to reflect in the distorted mirrors of his fantastic art but his reactions, he is compelled to be as idiosyncratic as possible in order to justify himself.

It is frequently asserted that free verse is lacking in form. That is an ignorant contention and one easily demolished by the exponents of modernism. The point at issue is not whether free verse has form but whether it has poetic form; whether it is a satisfactory medium for poetry. Its advocates maintain that they are able to get out of it effects of which other literary modes are incapable. They say, with a great show of reasonableness:

Stick to your traditional forms, if they are adapted to what you are trying to do. Free verse is adapted to what *we* are trying to do. We have not only the right to use it, but—since an artist must work in his medium—no right to use anything else.

It may be so. It would be partially proved to be so if the *vers librists* were able to produce any example of pure poetry that could not have been written in any other way. But one does not feel the inevitability in even "Out of the Cradle Endlessly Rocking" as one feels in it the case of the "Ode to a Nightingale." For free verse is always more or less of a *tour de force*. It has form, but unnatural form.

The mere technic of free verse is a feat. "H. D." achieves it within a small compass; few others do. Most of the so-called free verse poets write either dithyrambic prose, whose cadences they emphasize by a typographical device, or else meters mingled and broken in such a way as to be unrecognized as meters.

Far from traditional poetry concentrating on form, it is free verse that does so. The one mode accepts a convention (not perhaps, as a rule, realizing that it is more than a convention) and is in consequence at liberty to forget form. But not for an instant is free verse able to possess the carelessness of freedom. Its refusal of limitation binds it, of necessity, in the strictest of limits.

Indeed, in the latest developments of technic we have what

is equivalent to an abandonment of the earlier free verse position. Imagism removes the discussion outside of the question of form to that of method; and "polyphonic prose" is nothing more than a synthesis of every conceivable method, ranging from bald statement to frank doggerel—a haggis pie into which innumerable ingredients are thrown at hazard.

Imagism brings together, with an indulgent catholicism, those who use meter with a brilliant exactness, those who use only cadence, and those who use both. But they are to a man sticklers for form. And in the tenets agreed upon among them and published in their first anthology, free verse is fought for merely as a principle of liberty. The sole rule that distinguishes them from other schools is that of the presentation of images. As Miss Lowell, their spokesman, puts it, throwing Aristotle overboard, "Imagism is presentation not representation."

No other of their six rules can be caviled at by the most conservative. Poets have never abandoned the principle of using always the exact and not the nearly exact word, though they have not always been successful in finding it. (Neither are the Imagists.) Poetic diction has practically disappeared as good usage. Every poet of consequence has invented some new rhythms. Most poets have felt free in the choice of subject. Concentration is no new poetic ambition. And poetry that is "clear and hard, never blurred nor indefinite," existed before the Imagist manifesto appeared.

Nevertheless, a restatement of these hoary precepts is to be welcomed. Like all precepts they are frequently forgotten in practice; and to do the Imagists justice they have made an attempt to carry out their rules with meticulous conscientiousness.

Moreover, their central idea—that of rendering particulars exactly without vague generalities—is valuable when not pushed too far. But the Imagists *have* pushed their doctrine too far. They are like that group of painters whose fad it was to paint sand with real sand; hair with real hair. Like them this group of poets is out for "presentation not representation." They will describe sand with words that are as sandy as possible; hair with words that are as hairy as possible. It is onomatopœia ceasing to be a casual trick and stiffening into a habit with the likelihood of freezing into a ritual.

One must, nevertheless, recognize that at the botton of Imagism lies a hunger for actuality, for close contact. This, like the other fine elements in the movement, is not novel. "It is an odd jealousy," said Emerson, "but the poet finds himself not near enough to his object. The pine-tree, the river, the bank of flowers before him, does not seem to be nature. Nature is still elsewhere." The Imagists would accept the first but not the second part of the dictum. Their hands must touch the wood of chairs, the skin of flowers—and reproduce in words the sensations of their curious fingers. So far so good. But their eyes must be pressed against the object of their love—and they will be too close to it to see it. They forget that "Nature is still elsewhere," that beyond the material substance is a mysterious essence—the beauty which should be the object of their search—and the closest scrutiny fails to yield the results that they had expected.

Along with this, as a corollary, goes a desire to strip life to the bare bones, which now and then achieves an austere economy of speech that is, in itself, wholly admirable. But while the Imagists are refining down their material from all alloy, making it ready for use, they generally do not remember that they have to go on and use it. The process is doubtless one that is necessary to poetry. But it is a preliminary process. And the Imagists usually stop there. As Miss Lowell herself states—

> We will scatter little words
> Upon the paper,
> Like seeds about to be planted.

Unfortunately the Imagists omit to plant them.

Wakefulness, for example, is full of the material of poetry carefully prepared for use. The preliminary process is complete. (As a matter of fact all the process should be put into operation simultaneously, and the poet refine, design, and build with the same hand at the same moment. Still, one may be glad of an embryo for purposes of biological data.) A poem and a good poem is ready to be made—but where is the poem?

Jolt of market carts;
Steady drip of horses' hoofs on hard pavement;
A black sky lacquered over with blueness

And the lights of Battersea Bridge
Pricking pale in the dawn.
The beautiful hours are passing
And still you sleep!
Tired heart of my joy,
Incurved upon your dreams,
Will the day come before you have opened to me?

If any one doubts my assertion that this is not a poem, let him read another suggested by it, Wordsworth's sonnet on Westminster Bridge. I am sure that my point will then be clear, and will be accepted by the reader.

The majority of free verse poets, however, do not follow the Imagist example in this matter. I wish they did. Much more common faults are vast prolixity and an utterly unselective dealing with life in raw slabs.

We could not take three more representative examples of the various brands of free verse than that written by Edgar Lee Masters, Carl Sandburg, and Amy Lowell, who among them cover nearly the whole field and will provide more than enough illustrations for our purpose. Their methods differ widely, as do the subject matter and the temperament of each. To classify them roughly, let us say that Masters is a free verse poet by accident; Sandburg by fate; Amy Lowell by choice; Sandburg by natural bent; Amy Lowell by cleverness; Masters by shrewdness helped out by luck.

Edgar Lee Masters, who, oddly, is one of the most famous free verse poets, once told me that he did not call himself a free verse poet at all. It is quite true that the larger part of his work is composed in formal meters. He has an ambition to be known as a poet pure and simple; and he plods along writing bad blank verse and feeble lyrics which would never attract attention were it not for the *éclat* of the *Spoon River Anthology*. Apart from the fine "Silence" (in free verse as it happens) included in *Song and Satires*, none of the other poems in this volume is worth a straw.

The *Domesday Book*, despite its glaring faults, has power. It is in many ways a remarkable performance. But out of its twelve thousand lines hardly twelve possess any distinction.

> An inquisition taken for the people
> Of the State of Illinois here in Le Roy,
> County aforesaid, on the 7th of August,
> Anno Domini, nineteen hundred nineteen,
> Before me, William Merival, coroner.

That passage has no more and no less reason for being written in blank verse than the rest of a volume which may be magnificent but which is not poetry.

Even the *Spoon River Anthology* has no technical subtlety. Mr. Masters, with rare candor, has explained that he picked up his hint from the Greek Anthology. He does not hesitate to go to the length of turning one of Meleager's epigrams into verse before our eyes as an object lesson to explain his own literary method. This is certainly a striking illustration of what typographical arrangement will do:

The holy night and thou, O Lamp, we took as witness of our vows; and before thee we swore, he that he would love me always and I that I would never leave him. We swore, and thou wert witness of our double promise. But now he says that our vows were written on the running waters. And thou, O Lamp, thou seest him in the arms of another.

This becomes:

The holy night and thou,
O Lamp,
We took as witness of our vows;
And before thee we swore,
He that he would love me always
And I that I would never leave him.
We swore,
And thou wert witness of our double promise.

But now he says that our vows were written on the running
waters.
And thou, O Lamp,
Thou seest him in the arms of another.

Reading this Miss Harriet Monroe declares, with a toss of
her head, that Mr. Masters has more of the authentic classic note
than Tennyson, Browning, and Arnold combined! But the indication of where we are to breathe cannot make anything except
prose out of a prose passage. This is still truer of the *Spoon
River Anthology,* for which it served as a model but to which
it did not impart its beauty. We may grant, however, that,
though Mr. Masters defaced his book with a morbid preoccupation with satyriasis and nymphomania, he produced a highly
interesting collection of thumbnail sketches and deserved his
triumph.

To an English reader, and I suppose to many American readers as well, Mr. Carl Sandburg's three volumes, on first acquaintance, must appear to be a chaos of cacophony. The poet
is at no trouble to placate his audience. He throws words as he
might throw bricks at your head.

And yet, amid all this welter of verbiage, a beauty is to be discerned—a beauty often smothered by ugly jargon, but still
beauty. To cite Whitman's superb phrase, one hears "a horn
sounding through the tangle of the forest and the dying echoes."

A great deal of Sandburg's success is, I suspect, due to the
fact that he is supposed to write "American." He does, but not
nearly so often as is generally supposed. He does get, however,
a considerable amount of publicity because of a tendency current in some quarters to connect free verse with "hundred-percent Americanism"—a tendency that can do no good either to
free verse or Americanism. For metrical experiments are by no
means peculiar to America. And Robert Frost and Edwin Arling-
ton Robinson are, to say the least, as rooted in the national soil
and as informed with the national spirit as Carl Sandburg. Chicago is not the world. It is not even the whole of the United
States. And when Mr. Sandburg defends Chicago by bellowing:

"Come and show me another city with head lifted singing so proud to be alive and coarse and strong and cunning!" I feel like saying, with cold contempt, that if Chicago is what he says it is—which I have reason to doubt—then he ought not to be proud of Chicago. He speaks with the brutal violence of the barbarian.

Now, the barbarian, I hasten to add, may possess many splendid qualities which civilized men are inclined, during periods of decay, to neglect. But to exalt the barbarian at the expense of the civilized man is cosmic treason. And Mr. Sandburg, I regret to say, is guilty of that crime. He has many finer elements in him—tenderness, humor, gayety; but to me he is the barbarian.

There are signs, nevertheless, that Mr. Sandburg is mellowing. The crudity of his adolescence is gradually wearing off; and as a consequence his verse is growing more delicate and nearer to the Imagist ideal. In *Smoke and Steel* he is under the disadvantage of being less sure of himself than he was in *Chicago Poems;* but, on the other hand, he was a little too sure of himself in the earlier book. He will acquire poise in time.

Probably the best way of illustrating Carl Sandburg is to set out his poem "Good Night," and let it make its own vivid contrast with a poem bearing a similar title by Walter de la Mare, recently published in the anthology *The Enchanted Years:*

Many ways to spell good night.
Fireworks at a pier on the Fourth of July spell it with red wheels
    and yellow spokes.
They fizz in the air, touch the water and quit.
Rockets make a trajectory of gold and blue and then go out.
Railroad trains at night spell with a smokestack mushrooming
    a white pillar.
Steamboats turn a curve in the Mississippi crying in a baritone
    that crosses lowland cottonfields to a razorback hill.
It is easy to spell good night.
Many ways to spell good night.

Now for Mr. de la Mare's poem, "Goodbye":

    The last of last words spoken is, Goodbye—
    The last dismantled flower in the weed-grown hedge,

The last thin rumor of a feeble bell far ringing,
The last blind rat to spurn the mildewed rye;

A hardening darkness glasses the haunted eye,
Shines into nothing the Watchman's burnt-out candle,
Wreathes into scentless nothing the wasting incense,
The last of last words spoken is, Goodbye.

Love of its muted music breathes no sign,
Thought in her ivory tower gropes in her spinning,
Toss on in vain the whispering trees of Eden,
Last, of all last words spoken, is, Goodbye.

This is one of those few cases in which two poems can be fairly compared. They are equal in theme, in length, and in mood—but how unlike each other they are! Mr. Sandburg has all the originality of detail and of manner; Mr. de la Mare has all the originality of effect.

"Good Night," though characteristic, is not the best of Sandburg's poems. There are other pieces which would supply more vivid examples of single points, and one poem (which, though I cannot quote it here, I must in justice mention), "Flash Crimson" from *Smoke and Steel,* where all of Carl Sandburg's admirable qualities are gathered together, and the ultimate word he has to say—courage.

Miss Amy Lowell is much the most completely equipped and, therefore, the most satisfactory example of a *vers librist* to be found. For Masters writes free verse without finesse, and Sandburg without any clear understanding of his own purpose. Amy Lowell possesses both: she is dexterous and doctrinaire. Moreover, though "H. D." excels all the members of her group in exquisite restraint, Amy Lowell excels "H. D." in power and the width of her sweep. And though no one could accuse of mystical humility the author of a book on American poetry written in order to justify her private poetics, Miss Lowell is at least free of the fantastic egotism of Ezra Pound and the callow pedantry of John Gould Fletcher. In addition there is no "hundred-percent Americanism" nonsense about her—a Lowell does not need it. She is cosmopolitan, complicated, clever, and self-conscious.

All her books have prefatory explanations; and all the poems in them are obviously written to sustain a thesis.

If Miss Lowell were unable to indicate successful instances of regular verse in her later volumes, the early work of *A Dome of Many-Colored Glass* would incline the critic to conclude that she went in for revolution because she was a failure as a conservative.

When, however, *Men, Women and Ghosts* appeared, it became demonstrated beyond question that Miss Lowell is not merely an important free verse poet, but an important poet. Indeed, the finest things in the second book are cast in a strict mold—"Patterns and Pickthorne Manor" being written in odic form, the latter actually in elaborately constructed stanzas; and "The Cremona Violin" in the Chaucerian style affected by Mr. Masefield.

"The Cremona Violin" becomes a literary curiosity by being broken by brief interludes of *vers libre*. They are intended to represent—perhaps I should say "present"—the notes of a violin. If they are read critically they will look more like the notes the poet put down, meaning but omitting to polish in stanzas. This is a thing we come upon frequently, not only in Miss Lowell but in the other poets of her school: the jottings for incomplete poetry or the jottings for incomplete prose allowed to appear before the public as finished articles. How admirably this might have been worked into a descriptive essay:

> Leaves fall,
> Brown leaves,
> Yellow leaves streaked with brown.
> They fall,
> Flutter,
> Fall again.
> The brown leaves,
> And the streaked yellow leaves,
> Loosen on their branches
> And drift slowly downwards.
> One,
> One, two, three,

> One, two, five.
> All Venice is a falling of Autumn leaves—
> Brown,
> And yellow streaked with brown.

Almost invariably the free verse poem that is successful in making its desired effect is very short and suggestive of a translation. Miss Lowell, for her part, has studied to acquire the tang of *hokku*. She will be as delicate, as deliberate, and as limited as the art of Japan—but it is an art remote from us, one alien to the texture of our souls. Whether the *vers librist* translates from the Japanese, like Miss Lowell; or from the Chinese, like Mr. Pound; or from the Greek, like Mr. Aldington, he betrays a natural bent towards translation. And this, I think, is because his original work suggests a flower plucked from the grave of a dead language.

This tendency has made Miss Lowell grow more and more metallic. Whole pages in *Legends* are covered with plates of foil. All her prints might be called, as she calls some of them, *Lacquer Prints*. Her handling of lifeless substances is significant. Where Shakespeare heard the lark singing at heaven's gate, she sees that

> A golden weather-cock flashes smartly,
> His open beak "Cock-a-doodle-dooing"
> Straight at the ear of Heaven.

In the final analysis it will be discovered that what is wrong with the *vers librists* is not so much their technic as their conception of poetry. It would not matter even that they rebelled against one kind of vicious virtuosity to bring in another kind equally vicious, if their fundamental understanding of art were sound.

The Imagist itch to "present" instead of represent, and the "advanced" attitude towards the limitations of meter reveal a false view of the nature of poetry. I have already tried to show that meter is much more than a convention; that though it is not the soul of verse there can be no verse without it—for it is the body which contains the soul. And hence to speak of bad poetry (as I, in this essay, for convenience have done) is a contradiction in terms. Bad poetry is an impossibility: it is either poetry, and therefore good, or nonexistent. Poetry is nothing less than perfect speech—and how rare that is! It is unique among the arts in that it cannot be tolerated unless it attains excellence.

The poet accordingly lays upon himself the most heartbreaking of labors—and the happiest. He is on fire with desire. He is tormented with frustration. Beauty is a constant lure—and forever eludes him. Thrice blest is he who once in a lifetime is able to consummate in himself the marriage of the genius of mortal language with the divine Logos!

The *vers librists,* so far from being daring innovators, are really shirkers of the vocation. They take the safe middle course, in which they will neither fail so badly as those who aspire to the highest nor succeed so well as those who attain the highest. They renounce the hope of perfection.

And yet they have performed an exceedingly useful service to literature—one for which we should be grateful: they have carried out the dead. The vogue of the loose and the sentimental and the decorative is over. The world may learn from the *vers librists'* fantasticality, sometimes, and from their frigidity, always, salutary lessons in technic. They are the schoolmasters —should I not add "and schoolmarms"?—to bring us back to poetry.

II. SUBJECTIVE AND INFORMAL

If even the name of Descartes is at all familiar to you, you will probably recall from that peculiar piece-bag of odd bits of information which hangs in the minds of most of us that he was the philosopher who said, "I *think;* therefore, I am." Descartes' emphasis was entirely upon the word *think;* but years later his misguided followers placed it on the pronoun *I.* It is easy to see the tremendous difference in meaning and significance which the change brings about.

The analogy is not a poor one in an attempt to distinguish between objective and subjective criticism. In both cases the word *think* is important. But in the first the emphasis is thrown upon the verb whereas in the second it is thrown upon the pronoun.

In objective criticism one *thinks;* in subjective, the *individual* thinks.

Subjective criticism is sometimes called *appreciative* criticism, or sometimes simply *appreciation.*[1] Its function is to record in all honesty the appreciation of the person to whom some book or author or type of literature has been filled with meaning, significance, and pleasure. Not for a moment does it imply that such appreciation should be merely ill-bridled and silly enthusiasm. Not for a moment does it do away with standards of judgment. But it does allow wider scope and opportunity for enthusiasm, for personality, for individualism.

The writing of subjective criticism thus allows far greater informality. The writer takes the reader into his confidence, shares with him, if he likes, his own idiosyncrasies, needs not be afraid of an occasional digression. Instead of Coleridge's objective questions he asks other and more subjective ones: First, Wherein lies the appeal of this book to *me?* Second, Why do I personally think it good? Third, What traits of the author live in my imagination?

The three splendid models which follow as well as the wealth of material on the list of suggested readings are better than further precepts. Careful, even minute study of them will prove to you (1) that subjective criticism at its best is not superficial in its individualism and (2) that it allows no room for the merely sentimental and effusive.

A GOSSIP ON ROMANCE [2]
(IN PART)

By Robert Louis Stevenson

In anything fit to be called by the name of reading, the process itself should be absorbing and voluptuous; we should gloat over a book, be rapt clean out of ourselves, and rise from the perusal,

[1] This term may well seem a misnomer to one who may quite rightly wish to write a subjective criticism which shall express his disapproval rather than approval.

[2] From *Memories and Portraits.* By permission of Charles Scribner's Sons, the authorized publishers.

our mind filled with the busiest kaleidoscopic dance of images, incapable of sleep or of continuous thought. The words, if the book be eloquent, should run thenceforward in our ears like the noise of breakers, and the story—if it be a story—repeat itself in a thousand coloured pictures to the eye. It was for this last pleasure that we read so closely, and loved our books so dearly, in the bright, troubled period of boyhood. Eloquence and thought, character and conversation, were but obstacles to brush aside as we dug blithely after a certain sort of incident, like a pig for truffles. For my part, I liked a story to begin with an old wayside inn where, "towards the close of the year 17—," several gentlemen in three-cocked hats were playing bowls. A friend of mine preferred the Malabar coast in a storm, with a ship beating to westward, and a scowling fellow of herculean proportions striding along the beach; he, to be sure, was a pirate. This was further afield than my home-keeping fancy loved to travel, and designed altogether for a larger canvas than the tales that I affected. Give me a highwayman and I was full to the brim; a Jacobite would do, but the highwayman was my favourite dish. I can still hear that merry clatter of the hoofs along the moonlit lane; night and the coming of day are still related in my mind with the doings of John Rann or Jerry Abershaw; and the words "postchaise," the "great North road," "ostler," and "nag," still sound in my ears like poetry. One and all, at least, and each with his particular fancy, we read story-books in childhood, not for eloquence or character or thought, but for some quality of the brute incident. That quality was not mere bloodshed or wonder. Although each of these was welcome in its place, the charm for the sake of which we read depended on something different from either. My elders used to read novels aloud; and I can still remember four different passages which I heard, before I was ten, with the same keen and lasting pleasure. One I discovered long afterwards to be the admirable opening of *What will he Do with It?* It was no wonder that I was pleased with that. The other three still remain unidentified. One is a little vague; it was about a dark, tall house at night, and people groping on the stairs by the light that escaped from the open door of a sickroom. In another, a lover left a ball, and went walking in a cool, dewy park, whence he could watch the lighted windows and the figures of the dancers as they moved. This was the most sentimental impression I think I had yet received, for a child is somewhat deaf to the sentimental. In the last, a poet, who had been tragically wrangling with his wife, walked forth on the sea-beach on a tempestuous night and witnessed the horrors of a wreck. Different as they are, all these early favourites have a common note—they have all a touch of the romantic.

Drama is the poetry of conduct, romance the poetry of circumstance. The pleasure that we take in life is of two sorts—the active and the passive. Now we are conscious of a great command over our destiny; anon we are lifted up by circumstance, as by a breaking wave, and dashed we know not how into the future. Now we are pleased by our conduct, anon merely pleased by our surroundings. It would be hard to say which of these modes of satisfaction is the more effective, but the latter is surely the more constant. Conduct is three parts of life, they say; but I think they put it high. There is a vast deal in life and letters both which is not immoral, but simply a-moral; [1] which either does not regard the human will at all, or deals with it in obvious and healthy relations; where the interest turns, not upon what a man shall choose to do, but on how he manages to do it; not on the passionate slips and hesitations of the conscience, but on the problems of the body and of the practical intelligence, in clean, open-air adventure, the shock of arms or the diplomacy of life. With such material as this it is impossible to build a play, for the serious theatre exists solely on moral grounds, and is a standing proof of the dissemination of the human conscience. But it is possible to build upon this ground the most joyous of verses, and the most lively, beautiful, and buoyant tales.

One thing in life calls for another; there is a fitness in events and places. The sight of a pleasant arbour puts it in our mind to sit there. One place suggests work, another idleness, a third early rising and long rambles in the dew. The effect of night,

[1] Un-moral.

of any flowing water, of lighted cities, of the peep of day, of ships, of the open ocean, calls up in the mind an army of anonymous desires and pleasures. Something, we feel, should happen; we know not what, yet we proceed in quest of it. And many of the happiest hours of life fleet by us in this vain attendance on the genius of the place and moment. It is thus that tracts of young fir, and low rocks that reach into deep soundings, particularly torture and delight me. Something must have happened in such places, and perhaps ages back, to members of my race; and when I was a child I tried in vain to invent appropriate games for them, as I still try, just as vainly, to fit them with the proper story. Some places speak distinctly. Certain dank gardens cry aloud for a murder; certain old houses demand to be haunted; certain coasts are set apart for shipwreck. Other spots again seem to abide their destiny, suggestive and impenetrable, "miching mallecho." The inn at Burford Bridge, with its arbours and green garden and silent, eddying river—though it is known already as the place where Keats wrote some of his *Endymion* and Nelson parted from his Emma—still seems to wait the coming of the appropriate legend. Within these ivied walls, behind these old green shutters, some further business smoulders, waiting for its hour. The old Hawes Inn at the Queen's Ferry makes a similar call upon my fancy. There it stands, apart from the town, beside the pier, in a climate of its own, half inland, half marine—in front, the ferry bubbling with the tide and the guardship swinging to her anchor; behind, the old garden with the trees. Americans seek it already for the sake of Lovel and Oldbuck, who dined there at the beginning of *The Antiquary*. But you need not tell me—that is not all; there is some story, unrecorded or not yet complete, which must express the meaning of that inn more fully. So it is with names and faces; so it is with incidents that are idle and inconclusive in themselves, and yet seem like the beginning of some quaint romance, which the all-careless author leaves untold. How many of these romances have we not seen determined at their birth; how many people have met us with a look of meaning in their eye, and sunk at once into trivial acquaintances; to how many

places have we not drawn near, with express intimations—
"here my destiny awaits me"—and we have but dined there and
passed on! I have lived both at the Hawes and Burford in a
perpetual flutter, on the heels, as it seemed, of some adventure
that should justify the place; but though the feeling had me to
bed at night and called me again at morning in one unbroken
round of pleasure and suspense, nothing befell me in either
worth remark. The man of the hour had not yet come; but
some day, I think, a boat shall put off from the Queen's Ferry,
fraught with a dear cargo, and some frosty night a horseman,
on a tragic errand, rattle with his whip upon the green shutters
of the inn at Burford.

Now this is one of the natural appetites with which any
lively literature has to count. The desire for knowledge, I had
almost added the desire for meat, is not more deeply seated
than this demand for fit and striking incident. The dullest of
clowns tells, or tries to tell, himself a story, as the feeblest of
children uses invention in his play; and even as the imaginative
grown person, joining in the game, at once enriches it with
many delightful circumstances, the great creative writer shows
us the realization and the apotheosis of the day-dreams of common men. His stories may be nourished with the realities of life,
but their true mark is to satisfy the nameless longings of the
reader, and to obey the ideal laws of the day-dream. The right
kind of thing should fall out in the right kind of place; the right
kind of thing should follow; and not only the characters talk
aptly and think naturally, but all the circumstances in a tale
answer one to another like notes in music. The threads of a
story come from time to time together, and make a picture in
the web; the characters fall from time to time into some attitude
to each other or to nature, which stamps the story home like an
illustration. Crusoe recoiling from the footprint, Achilles shouting over against the Trojans, Ulysses bending the great bow,
Christian running with his fingers in his ears,—these are each
culminating moments in the legend, and each has been printed
on the mind's eye forever. Other things we may forget; we may
forget the words, although they are beautiful; we may forget the

author's comment, although perhaps it was ingenious and true; but these epoch-making scenes, which put the last mark of truth upon a story and fill up at one blow our capacity for sympathetic pleasure, we so adopt into the very bosom of our mind that neither time nor tide can efface or weaken the impression. This, then, is the plastic part of literature: to embody character, thought, or emotion in some act or attitude that shall be remarkably striking to the mind's eye. This is the highest and hardest thing to do in words; the thing which, once accomplished, equally delights the schoolboy and the sage, and makes, in its own right, the quality of epics. Compared with this, all other purposes in literature, except the purely lyrical or the purely philosophic, are bastard in nature, facile of execution, and feeble in result. It is one thing to write about the inn at Burford, or to describe scenery with the word-painters; it is quite another to seize on the heart of the suggestion and make a country famous with a legend. It is one thing to remark and to dissect, with the most cutting logic, the complications of life and of the human spirit; it is quite another to give them body and blood in the story of Ajax or of Hamlet. The first is literature, but the second is something besides, for it is likewise art.

*   *   *   *   *   *   *

"THE TEMPEST" [1]

By George Gissing

To-day I have read *The Tempest*. It is perhaps the play that I love best, and, because I seem to myself to know it so well, I commonly pass it over in opening the book. Yet, as always in regard to Shakespeare, having read it once more, I find that my knowledge was less complete than I supposed. So it would be, live as long as one might; so it would ever be, whilst one had the strength to turn the pages and a mind left to read them.

I like to believe that this was the poet's last work, that he

[1] From *The Private Papers of Henry Ryecroft*.

wrote it in his home in Stratford, walking day by day in the fields which had taught his boyhood to love rural England. It is ripe fruit of the supreme imagination, perfect craft of the master hand. For a man whose life business it has been to study the English tongue, what joy can there be to equal that of marking the happy ease wherewith Shakespeare surpasses, in mere command of words, every achievement of these even, who, apart from him, are great? I could fancy that, in *The Tempest,* he wrought with a peculiar consciousness of this power, smiling as the word of inimitable felicity, the phrase of incomparable cadence, was whispered to him by the Ariel that was his genius. He seems to sport with language, to amuse himself with new discovery of its resources. From king to beggar, men of every rank and of every order of mind have spoken with his lips; he has uttered the lore of fairyland; now it pleases him to create a being neither man nor fairy, a something between brute and human nature, and to endow its purposes with words. Those words, how they smack of the warm and spawning earth, of the life of creatures that cannot rise above the soil! We do not think of it enough; we stint our wonder because we fall short in appreciation. A miracle is worked before us, and we scarce give heed; it has become familiar to our minds as any other of nature's marvels, which we rarely pause to reflect upon.

The Tempest contains the noblest meditative passage in all the plays; that which embodies Shakespeare's final view of life, and is the inevitable quotation of all who would sum the teachings of philosophy. It contains his most exquisite lyrics, his tenderest love passages, and one glimpse of fairyland which—I cannot but think—outshines the utmost beauty of *A Midsummer Night's Dream:* Prospero's farewell to the "elves of hills, brooks, standing lakes and groves." Again a miracle; these are things which cannot be staled by repetition. Come to them often as you will, they are ever fresh as though new minted from the brain of the poet. Being perfect, they can never droop under that satiety which arises from the perception of fault; their virtue can never be so entirely savoured as to leave no pungency of gusto for the next approach.

Among the many reasons which make me glad to have been born in England, one of the first is that I read Shakespeare in my mother tongue. If I try to imagine myself as one who cannot know him face to face, who hears him only speaking from afar, and that in accents which only through the laboring intelligence can touch the living soul, there comes upon me a sense of chill discouragement, of dreary deprivation. I am wont to think that I can read Homer, and, assuredly, if any man enjoys him, it is I; but can I for a moment dream that Homer yields me all his music, that his word is to me as to him who walked by the Hellenic shore when Hellas lived? I know that there reaches me across the vast of time no more than a faint and broken echo; I know that it would be fainter still, but for its blending with those memories of youth which are as a glimmer of the world's primeval glory. Let every land have joy of its poet; for the poet is the land itself, all its greatness and its sweetness, all that incommunicable heritage for which men live and die. As I close the book, love and reverence possess me. Whether does my full heart turn to the great Enchanter, or to the Island upon which he has laid his spell? I know not. I cannot think of them apart. In the love and reverence awakened by this voice of voices, Shakespeare and England are but one.

*   *   *   *   *   *   *

17 HERIOT ROW [1]

By Christopher Morley

There is a small black notebook into which I look once or twice a year to refresh my memory of a carnal and spiritual pilgrimage to Edinburgh, made with Mifflin McGill (upon whose head be peace) in the summer of 1911. It is a testament of light-hearted youth, savoury with the unindentured joys of twenty-one and the grand literary passion. Would that one might again steer *Shotover* (dearest of pushbikes) along the Banbury Road,

---

[1] From *Shandygaff*. By permission of the publishers, Doubleday, Doran and Company.

and see Mifflin's lean shanks twirl up the dust on the way to Stratford! Never was more innocent merriment spread upon English landscape. When I die, bury the black notebook with me.

That notebook is memorable also in a statistical way, and perchance may serve future historians as a document proving the moderate cost of wayfaring in those halcyon days. Nothing in Mr. Pepys' diary is more interesting than his meticulous record of what his amusements cost him. Mayhap some future economist will pore upon these guileless confessions. For in the black memorandum book I succeeded, for almost the only time in my life, in keeping an accurate record of the lapse of coin during nine whole days. I shall deposit the document with the Congressional Library in Washington for future annalists; in the meantime I make no excuse for recounting the items of the first sixty hours. Let no one take amiss the frequent entries marked "cider." July, 1911, was a hot month and a dusty, and we were biking fifty miles the day. Please reckon exchange at two cents per penny.

		£	s.	d.
July 16	pint cider			4
	½ pint cider			1½
	lunch at Banbury		2	2
	pint cider at Ettington			3
	supper at Stratford		1	3
	stamp and postcard			2
			4	3½

		£	s.	d.
July 17	Postcards and stamps			9
	pencil			1
	Warwick Castle		2	—
	cider at the *Bear and Baculus* (which Mifflin *would* call the *Bear and Bacillus*)			2½
	Bowling Green Inn, bed and breakfast		3	2
	Puncture		1	—
	Lunch, Kenilworth		1	6
	Kenilworth Castle			6

July 17 Postcards   4
        Lemonade, Coventry...................   4
        Cider 2½
        Supper, Tamworth, *The Castle Hotel*.....   2 1
                                                    ─────────
                                                    16 5½

July 18 Johnson house, Lichfield   3
        cider at *The Three Crowns*..............   4
        postcard and shave.....................   4
        The King's Head, bed and breakfast......   3 7
        cider   2
        tip on road [1].........................   1½
        lunch, Uttoxeter......................   1 3
        cider, Ashbourne, *The Green Man*........   3
        landlord's drink, Ashbourne [2]...........   1
        supper, *Newhaven House,* ....   1 —
        lemonade, Buxton......................   3
                                                    ─────────
                 TOTAL   £1–4–1
                                                    ($5.78)

That is to say, 24 bob for two and a half days. We used to
reckon that ten shillings a day would do us very nicely, barring
luxuries and emergencies. We attained a zealous proficiency in
reckoning shillings and pence, and our fervour in posting our
ledgers would have gladdened a firm of auditors. I remember
lying on the coping of a stone bridge over the water of Teviot
near Hawick, admiring the green-brown tint of the swift stream
bickering over the stones. Mifflin was writing busily in his notebook on the other side of the bridge. I thought to myself,
"Bless the lad, he's jotting down some picturesque notes of something that has struck his romantic eye." And just then he spoke
—"Four and eleven pence half-penny so far to-day!"

Would I could retrogress over the devious and enchanting

[1] As far as I can remember, this was a gratuity to a rather tarnished
subject who directed us at a fork in the road, near a railway crossing.

[2] This was a copper well lavished; for the publican, a ventripotent
person with a liquid and glamorous brown eye, told us excellent gossip
about Dr. Johnson and George Eliot, both heroes in that neighbourhood.
"Yes," we said, "that man Eliot was a great writer," and he agreed.

itinerary. The McGill route from Oxford to Auld Reekie is
417 miles; it was the afternoon of the ninth day when with
thumping hearts we saw Arthur's Seat from a dozen miles away.
Our goal was in sight!

There was a reason for all this pedalling madness. Ever since
the days when we had wandered by Darby Creek, reading R. L. S.
aloud to one another, we had planned this trip to the gray
metropolis of the north. A score of sacred names had beckoned
us, the haunts of the master. We knew them better than any
other syllables in the world. Heriot Row, Princes Street, the
Calton Hill, Duddingston Loch, Antiqua Street, the Water of
Leith, Colinton, Swanston, the Pentland Hills—O my friends, do
those names mean to you what they did to us? Then you are
one of the brotherhood—what was to us then the sweetest
brotherhood in the world!

In a quiet little hotel in Rutland Square we found decent
lodging, in a large chamber which was really the smoking room
of the house. The city was crowded with tourists on account of
an expected visit of the King and Queen; every other room in
the hotel was occupied. Greatly to our satisfaction we were
known as "the smoking-room gentlemen" throughout our stay.
Our windows opened upon ranks of corridor-cars lying on the
Caledonian Railway sidings, and the clink and jar of buffers
and coupling irons were heard all night long. I seem to remember that somewhere in his letters R. L. S. speaks of that
same sound. He knew Rutland Square well, for his boyhood
friend Charles Baxter lived there. Writing from Samoa in later
years he says that one memory stands out above all others of
his youth—Rutland Square. And while that was of course only
the imaginative fervour of the moment, yet we were glad to
know that in that quiet little cul de sac behind the railway
terminal we were on ground well loved by Tusitala.

The first evening, and almost every twilight while we were in
Auld Reekie, we found our way to 17 Heriot Row—famous address, which had long been as familiar to us as our own. I think
we expected to find a tablet on the house commemorating the
beloved occupant; but no; to our surprise it was dark, dusty, and

tenantless. A sign to SELL was prominent. To take the name of the agent was easy. A great thought struck us. Could we not go over the house in the character of prospective purchasers? Mifflin and I went back to our smoking room and concocted a genteel letter to Messrs. Guild and Shepherd, Writers to the Signet.

Promptly came a reply (Scots business men answer at once).

16 Charlotte Square
Edinburgh
26th July, 1911

DEAR SIR,

17 HERIOT ROW

We have received your letter regarding this house. The house can be seen at any time, and if you will let us know when you wish to view it we shall arrange to have it opened.

We are,
Yours faithfully,
GUILD AND SHEPHERD.

Our hearts were uplifted, but now we were mightly embarrassed as to the figure we would cut before the Writers to the Signet. You must remember that we were two young vagabonds in the earliest twenties, travelling with slim knapsacks, and much soiled by a fortnight on the road. I was in knickerbockers and khaki shirt; Mifflin in greasy gray flannels and subfuse Norfolk. Our only claims to gentility were our monocles. Always take a monocle on a vagabond tour: it is a never-failing source of amusement and passport of gentility. No matter how ragged you are, if you can screw a pane in your eye you can awe the yokel or the tradesman.

The private records of the firm of Guild and Shepherd doubtless show that on Friday, July 28, 1911, one of their polite young attachés, appearing as per appointment at 17 Heriot Row, was met by two eccentric young gentlemen, clad in dirty white flannel hats, waterproof capes, each with an impressive monocle. Let it be said to the honour of the attaché in question that he showed no symptoms of surprise or alarm. We explained, I think, that we were scouting for my father, who (it was alleged) greatly desired to settle down in Edinburgh. And we had presence of mind enough to enquire about plumbing, stationary wash-tubs, and the condition of the flues. I wish I could remember what rent was quoted.

He showed us all through the house; and you may imagine that we stepped softly and with beating hearts. Here we were on the very track of the Magician himself: his spirit whispered in the lonely rooms. We imagined R. L. S. as a little child, peering from the windows at dusk to see Leerie light the street-lamps outside—a quaint, thin, elvish face with shining brown eyes; or held up in illness by Cummie to see the gracious dawn heralded by oblongs of light in the windows across the Queen Street gardens. We saw the college lad, tall, with tweed coat and cigarette, returning to Heriot Row with an armful of books, in sad or sparkling mood. The house was dim and dusty: a fine entrance hall, large dining room facing the street—and we imagined Louis and his parents at breakfast. Above this, the drawing room, floored with parquet oak, a spacious and attractive chamber. Above this again, the nursery, and opening off it the little room where faithful Cummie slept. But in vain we looked for some sign or souvenir of the entrancing spirit. The room that echoed to his childish glee, that heard his smothered sobs in the endless nights of childish pain, the room where he scribbled and brooded and burst into gusts of youth's passionate outcry, is now silent and forlorn.

With what subtly mingled feelings we peered from room to room, seeing everything, and yet not daring to give ourselves away to the courteous young agent. And what was it he said?—"This was the house of Lord So-and-so" (I forget the name)—"and incidentally, Robert Louis Stevenson lived here once. His signature occurs once or twice in the deeds."

Incidentally! . . .

Like many houses in Auld Reekie, 17 Heriot Row is built on a steep slant of ground, so that the rear of the house is a storey or more higher than the face. We explored the kitchens, laundries, store-rooms, and other "offices" with care, imagining that little

"Smoutie" may have run here and there in search of tid-bits from the cook. Visions of that childhood, fifty years before, were almost as real as our own. We seemed to hear the young treble of his voice. That house was the home of the Stevensons for thirty years (1857-1887)—surely even the thirty years that have gone by since Thomas Stevenson died cannot have laid all those dear ghosts we conjured up!

We thanked our guide and took leave of him. If the firm of Guild and Shepherd should ever see this, surely they will forgive our innocent deception, for the honour of R. L. S. I wonder if any one has yet put a tablet on the house? If not, Mifflin and I will do so, some day.

In the evenings we used to wander up to Heriot Row in the long Northern dusk, to sit on the front steps of number 17 waiting for Leerie to come and light the famous lamp which still stands on the pavement in front of the dining-room windows:

> For we are very lucky, with a lamp before the door,
> And Leerie stops to light it as he lights so many more;
> And O! before you hurry by with ladder and with light.
> O Leerie, see a little child and nod to him to-night!

But no longer does Leerie "with lantern and with ladder come posting up the street." Nowadays he carries a long pole bearing a flame cunningly sheltered in a brass socket. But the Leerie of 1911 ("Leerie-light-the-lamps" is a generic nickname for all lamplighters in Scotland) was a pleasant fellow even if ladderless, and we used to have a cigar ready for him when he reached 17. We told him of R. L. S., of whom he had vaguely heard, and explained the sanctity of that particular lamp. He in turn talked freely of his craft, and learning that we were Americans he told us of his two sisters "in Pennsylvania, at 21 Thorn Street." He seemed to think Pennsylvania a town, but finally we learned that the Misses Leerie lived in Sewickley where they were doing well, and sending back money to the "kiddies." Good Leerie, I wonder do you still light the lamps on Heriot Row, or have you too seen redder beacons on Flanders fields?

One evening I remember we fell into discussion whether the

lamp-post was still the same one that R. L. S. had known. We were down on hands and knees on the pavement, examining the base of the pillar by match-light in search of possible dates. A very seedy and disreputable-looking man passed, evidently regarding us with apprehension as detectives. Mifflin, never at a loss, remarked loudly "No, I see no footprints here," and as the ragged one passed hastily on with head twisted over his shoulder, we followed him. At the corner of Howe Street he broke into an uneasy shuffle, and Mifflin turned a great laugh into a Scotland Yard sneeze.

Howe Street crosses Heriot Row at right angles, only a few paces from No. 17. It dips sharply downhill toward the Water of Leith, and Mifflin and I used to stand at the corner and wonder just where took place the adventure with the lame boy which R. L. S. once described when setting down some recollections of childhood.

In Howe street, round the corner from our house, I often saw a lame boy of rather a rough and poor appearance. He had one leg much shorter than the other, and wallowed in his walk, in consequence, like a ship in a seaway. I had read more than enough, in tracts and goody story books, of the isolation of the infirm; and after many days of bashfulness and hours of consideration, I finally accosted him, sheepishly enough I daresay, in these words: "Would you like to play with me?" I remember the expression, which sounds exactly like a speech from one of the goody books that had nerved me to the venture. But the answer was not the one I had anticipated, for it was a blast of oaths. I need not say how fast I fled. This incident was the more to my credit as I had, when I was young, a desperate aversion to addressing strangers, though when once we had got into talk I was pretty certain to assume the lead. The last particular may still be recognized. About four years ago I saw my lame lad, and knew him again at once. He was then a man of great strength, rolling along, with an inch of cutty in his mouth and a butcher's basket on his arm. Our meeting had been nothing to him, but it was a great affair to me.

We strolled up the esplanade below the Castle, pausing in Ramsay's Gardens to admire the lighted city from above. In the valley between the Castle and Princes Street the pale blue mist rises at night like an exhalation from the old gray stones. The lamps shining through it blend in a delicate opalescent sheen, shot here and there with brighter flares. As the sky darkens the castle looms in silhouette, with one yellow square below the Half Moon Battery. "There are no stars like the Edinburgh street lamps," says R. L. S. Aye, and the brightest of them all shines on Heriot Row.

The vision of that child face still comes to me, peering down from the dining-room window. R. L. S. may never have gratified his boyish wish to go round with Leerie and light the lamps, but he lit many and more enduring flames even in the hearts of those who never saw him.

EXERCISES

I. OBJECTIVE CRITICISM

1. Note in Mr. Bradford's review the *one* point of approach and of criticism, that of *background*. Does it tend to impress his review more forcibly upon you or does it not?

2. Study the use of the personal pronoun *I* in any ten reviews from any reputable periodicals. What do you think of its use in objective criticism?

3. Outline Mr. Wilson's criticism of Thornton Wilder in no more than five sentences. Study the fine use of transitions between paragraphs in this article.

4. Would you say that Mr. Maynard's criticism of free verse is well-balanced? Why or why not?

5. How does De Quincey's famous *On the Knocking at the Gate in Macbeth* differ from the objective criticisms you have read? Are there good grounds for calling it a subjective criticism?

6. Read in *The Atlantic Monthly* for September 1928 the essay by Robert Lynd called "Why Literature Declines." This is an excellent essay for presentation by one of the members of the class and for subsequent discussion.

II. SUBJECTIVE CRITICISM

1. From the first paragraph of "A Gossip on Romance" list the best adjectives.

2. Find instances in this same paragraph of the adaptation of style to rhythmic effects.

3. What is the best simile in this paragraph? Why?

4. Study the drama in the action of the third paragraph. Is there also drama in style?

5. List the pictorial effects in this selection from Stevenson. Which are clearly expressed and which are implied?

6. Stevenson's essay would seem to appeal almost entirely to the esthetic sense or to the imagination. What ideas are there in it? List them.

7. Discuss George Gissing's appreciation of "The Tempest" as an admirable combination of thought and feeling. If you have not read *The Private Papers of Henry Ryecroft,* from which this is taken, do so *at once.*

8. Use Miss Repplier's title, "Books Which Have Hindered Me," for a theme of your own. Then read her charming essay and see in how many ways she has overwhelmingly beaten you.

9. Suggest to your instructor that he read aloud *A Child's Journey with Dickens.*

10. Is there too much of Morley in *17 Heriot Row?*

11. Read widely from the list. Each entry is too good to be missed.

SUGGESTED READINGS

Objective Criticism:

Brontë, Charlotte, On *Wuthering Heights* from the introduction to *Wuthering Heights,* E. P. Dutton, New York.

Conrad, Joseph, The Preface to *The Nigger of the Narcissus,* Doubleday, Doran, New York.

Cross, Wilbur L., "The Humor of Max Beerbohm," *The Yale Review,* January 1924. "The Mind of H. G. Wells," *The Yale Review,* January 1927.

De Quincey, Thomas, *On the Knocking at the Gate in Macbeth.*

Gosse, Edmund, "Walt Whitman" from *Critical Kit-Kats,* Scribner's, New York.

Guedalla, Philip, "Mandalay" from *A Gallery,* Putnam's, New York.

Lowell, Amy, "Walt Whitman and the New Poetry," *The Yale Review,* April 1927.

Lynd, Robert, "Why Literature Declines," *The Atlantic Monthly,* September 1928. "The Bounds of Decency," *The Atlantic Monthly,* June 1927.

Matthews, Brander, "Theodore Roosevelt as a Man of Letters" from *The Tocsin of Revolt and Other Essays,* Scribner's, New York.

Morris, Lloyd, "Willa Cather," *The North American Review,* May 1924.

Sherman, Stuart Pratt, "The Humanism of George Meredith" from *Our Contemporary Literature,* Macmillan, New York.

Shorey, Paul, "Literature and Modern Life," *The Atlantic Monthly,* May 1928.

Wharton, Edith, "The Great American Novel," *The Yale Review,* July 1927.

Woolf, Virginia, "The Novels of E. M. Forster," *The Atlantic Monthly,* November 1927. "Notes on an Elizabethan Play" from *The Common Reader,* Harcourt, Brace, New York.

Subjective Criticism:

Anonymous, "Honeymoon Books," *The Atlantic Monthly,* October 1927.

Barrie, James Matthew, *George Meredith,* Thomas B. Mosher, Portland, Maine.

Benson, Arthur Christopher, "Books" from *From a College Window,* Putnam's, New York.

Chesterton, G. K., "A Defence of Detective Stories" from *The Defendant,* Dodd, Mead, New York.

Forster, E. M., "Anonymity: An Inquiry," *The Atlantic Monthly,* November 1925.

Hawkins, Ethel Wallace, "Introduced by Mr. Housman," *The Atlantic Monthly,* March 1927.

Hazlitt, William, "On Reading Old Books" from *Table Talk.*

Humphrey, Zephine, "On Re-reading the Bible," *The Saturday Review,* July 4, 1925.

Jowett, Benjamin, "Last Words on Plato" from *Introduction to the Laws of Plato,* Bigelow, Brown, London, New York.

Lang, Andrew, *Adventures Among Books,* Longmans, Green, New York.

Lynn, Margaret, "Concerning Reviewers of Sorts," *The Atlantic Monthly,* August 1926.

Morris, Elisabeth Woodbridge, "Comfortable Books" from *Jonathan Papers,* Houghton Mifflin, Boston.

Morley, Christopher, "A Birthday Letter to Charles Lamb" from *The Romany Stain,* Doubleday, Doran, New York. "Idolatry" from *Pipefuls,* Doubleday, Doran, New York. "Joyce Kilmer" from *Pipefuls.* "Books of the Sea" from *Plumpudding,* Doubleday, Doran, New York.

Pater, Walter, "Charles Lamb" from *Appreciations,* Macmillan, New York.

Pearson, Edmund Lester, "The Cary Girls" from *Books in Black and Red,* Macmillan, New York.

Repplier, Agnes, "American Magazines," *The Yale Review,* January 1927. "Books Which Have Hindered Me" from *Points of View,* Houghton Mifflin, Boston. "English Railway Fiction" from the same. "Three Famous Old Maids" from *Essays in Miniature,* Houghton Mifflin, Boston. "A Short Defence of Villains" from the same. "Words" from *Essays in Idleness,* Houghton Mifflin, Boston.

Santanyana, George, "Dickens" from *Soliloquies in England,* Scribner's, New York.

Smith, Alexander, "A Shelf in My Bookcase" from *Dreamthorp,* Doubleday, Doran, New York.

Tomlinson, H. M., "Bed Books and Night Lights" from *Old Junk,* Alfred A. Knopf, New York.

Whipple, T. K., "Aucassin in the Sierras," *The Yale Review,* July 1927.

Wiggin, Kate Douglas, "A Child's Journey with Dickens" from *My Garden of Memory,* Houghton Mifflin, Boston.

CHAPTER III

Themes On College Life and Problems

THE DISCUSSION THEME

The sub-title of this chapter, "The Discussion Theme," does not mean to imply that certain themes already presented have not been based on the discussion of facts and ideas. It intends merely (1) to bring more forcibly to the mind of the student the fund of theme material based primarily upon the experiences, the information, and the thoughts of his life in college, and (2) to furnish him with various points of view, past and present, in regard to the manifold question of college and university life and education. These points of view, many of them divergent one from the other, are included here in the hope that the reading and study of them may result in an awakened intelligence toward one's own college experience. The essays and selections given here should be widely supplemented by the articles suggested in the reading list at the close of the chapter. Never has there been a time when our press, our magazines, and our books have been so filled with complaints, diagnoses, prescriptions. These range from the behavior of fraternity members at parties to questions of curricula, from religion to the newest "brain-wave" of a professional educator. Surely the student, who is the subject of all this agitation, should himself entertain some honest viewpoints.

To suggest methods for the handling and development of theme subjects is not the object of this chapter, but rather to set in process of action opinions, ideas, points of view, judgments, even "reactions," those most slight and least dependable of mental possessions. Is Newman's definition of a university somewhat ironical in the light (or darkness) of your own experience? Is Mr. Meiklejohn a hopeless idealist? Is Miss Guiney's harmless

519

scholar a ridiculous or a reassuring figure?   Do you think Woodrow Wilson "all off" as to the function of a university?   Can university training even at its best fulfill Newman's high ideal?   Does *your* college "supply true principles to popular enthusiasm"?   Is it possible that a young man of to-day might experience in New York or for that matter in a Middle Western Main Street the same assault of ideas as Marius did in Pisa?   Is Professor Munro prejudiced, even unkind in his judgments, or does he, in your opinion, "hit the nail on the head"?   Have the durable satisfactions of life changed since Dr. Eliot wrote his essay?   Is Miss Carlson in *Harper's Magazine* for March 1928 expressing your own attitude toward religion?

The subjects presented for discussion here in the selections and on the reading list may well lead to others until minds may become more clarified, judgments be stabilized, ideas take root and grow.   Given clear thinking which has resulted in a well-established point of view, the presentation of an opinion, a lament, an ideal, a hope, should not prove an insuperable task.   The possible methods of that presentation are up to you.   Past experiments with other themes, reading and then more reading, and, best of all, clear, unadulterated thinking will help you with suggestions.

WHAT IS A UNIVERSITY? [1]

By John Henry Newman

But I have said more than enough in illustration; I end as I began;—a University is a place of concourse, whither students come from every quarter for every kind of knowledge.   You cannot have the best of every kind everywhere; you must go to some great city or emporium for it.   There you have all the choicest productions of nature and art all together, which you find each in its own separate place elsewhere.   All the riches of the land, and of the earth, are carried up thither; there are the

[1] This is but the closing paragraph of Newman's essay "What is a University?" from his series of lectures called *The Idea of a University*. The student is recommended to read "What is a University?" in full, and other of Newman's lectures if possible.

best markets, and there the best workmen. It is the centre of
trade, the supreme court of fashion, the umpire of rival talents,
and the standard of things rare and precious. It is the place for
seeing galleries of first-rate pictures, and for hearing wonderful
voices and performers of transcendent skill. It is the place for
great preachers, great orators, great nobles, great statesmen. In
the nature of things, greatness and unity go together; excellence
implies a centre. And such, for the third or fourth time, is a
University; I hope I do not weary out the reader by repeating it.
It is the place to which a thousand schools make contributions; in
which the intellect may safely range and speculate, sure to find
its equal in some antagonist activity, and its judge in the tribunal
of truth. It is a place where inquiry is pushed forward, and discoveries verified and perfected, and rashness rendered innocuous,
and error exposed, by the collision of mind with mind, and knowledge with knowledge. It is the place where the professor becomes
eloquent, and is a missionary and a preacher, displaying his
science in its most complete and most winning form, pouring it
forth with the zeal of enthusiasm, and lighting up his own love
of it in the breasts of his hearers. It is the place where the cate-
chist makes good his ground as he goes, treading in the truth
day by day into the ready memory, and wedging and tightening
it into the expanding reason. It is a place which wins the admiration of the young by its celebrity, kindles the affections of
the middle-aged by its beauty, and rivets the fidelity of the old
by its associations. It is a seat of wisdom, a light of the world,
a minister of the faith, an Alma Mater of the rising generation.
It is this and a great deal more, and demands a somewhat better
head and hand than mine to describe it well.

What Does the College Prepare For? [1]

By Alexander Meiklejohn

College education, like all other genuine education, is of course
practical. It is preparation. Its underlying principle is very

[1] From *The Liberal College*. Reprinted by permission of the publishers, Marshall Jones Company.

simple. Young people are to be called upon later to carry on certain activities. The purpose of the preparation is to bring it about that those activities will be better done than they would have been if the preparation had not been given. If in any case it can be shown that a student is not thus made ready for better doing, if it appears that the graduates of a school are not more successful than they would have been had they not attended the school, then study and school are alike condemned and should be discarded. School and college are both to be judged by practical standards.

But what are the activities in which students may be expected to engage, for which they should be prepared? In relation to the goods, the possessions of life, they fall into three groups. If our education prepares properly for each of these then it is socially justified.

The classification suggested above is obvious enough. First, men are making goods, making things which they want. Second, they are distributing these goods, are assigning to each man his share of them. And third, they are using goods, each man the share which falls to his lot.

For example, men take the forces, the stuff of the material world and of human nature, and by processes of cultivation and of manufacture, make out of these books, trees, fruits, sermons, songs, boats, shoes, railways, tennis racquets—all the multitudinous things which taken together become the common stock of human possessions. Again, men build up ways of distributing these possessions, of determining to whom each bit of value shall go to be kept as his own. Thus we have the customs of rent and wages and property and courts and inheritance and taxes and all the rest of our machinery of social justice. And finally each man in his own way uses what he has for such purposes as he thinks best. He reads books, or puts them up for decoration; he listens to sermons, sails a boat, travels in a train, swings a tennis racquet, lies under the shade of a tree, sips the juice of a fruit, in general makes of what he has what he wants in the way of experience.

Now it is these three sets of activities for which our schools

and colleges are making young people ready. We want manufacturing and growing better done; we want distributing better
done; we want using better done. If these ends be accomplished
then our teaching plays its proper part in social and individual
living; if not, it fails to play its part.

As a teacher surveys these three sets of activities with which
his work is concerned, two observations will readily occur to
him—two judgments of comparison. He may ask first as to the
relative importance of the three tasks assigned, and second, as to
their relative difficulty. In both cases he will find, I think, an
ascending scale running from manufacture, through distribution, to use, an ascending scale of importance and of difficulty.

The comparison as to importance is rather hard to put into
a form which will stand the test of criticism. To ask whether
the making or the distributing or the using of wealth is the most
important is dangerously like inquiring whether chickens precede eggs, or eggs chickens. Obviously enough, all three activities are essential. There is not much to be gained by making
things if they are not to be given to any one, nor much gained
by giving them if they are not used. But they cannot be used
unless they are given, nor can they be given unless they are
made. To distinguish relative values in this realm seems like
comparing white and black crows in the dark. And yet there is
a certain sense in which the using of value is more fundamental
than either making or distributing it. In a very real sense, using
is human life itself, it is the human experience for the sake of
which the other activities are carried on. To use what we have
is the very process of living; to that end all other acts are merely
contributory; they are its instruments and machinery.

The differences as to difficulty are much more readily perceived. Relatively, manufacture, the production of goods, is an
easy task for men. It is easy in the sense that we master it with
ease. This does not mean that we are not called by it to stren-
uous endeavors. It does mean that our endeavors are successful.
What we do in this field pays quickly and surely in terms of
results. The last century has seen such a developing control of
the processes of manufacture and growth that our wealth has

increased by leaps and bounds. The technical processes which have been devised by the application of natural science to the accomplishment of human purposes have so enlarged our productive power that as compared with our fathers and grandfathers we roll in wealth and in the assurance of greater wealth in the future. Relatively speaking, we have the processes of the production of wealth in hand.

In the distribution of wealth we are not so successful. The world is torn with conflicting theories as to how this should be done. Men are quarreling as to the possession of goods. Nations quarrel with nations, individuals with individuals, and we do not easily find a basis for the settlement of these quarrels.

In a country driven mad by injustice and tyranny, men have escaped from their bonds and are wildly seeking to formulate and to put into action principles of distribution subversive of all that men in other countries have counted secure and essential. In safer countries where the pressure is not so severe, men are in dread lest it may become so and are forming into parties which view each other with hostile eye and with stealthy suspicion. Here we find the men who believe that whatever has been is right. They hold to the view that to their grandfathers a scheme of social justice was revealed by splendid intuition and that he who would depart from this is a traitor and a thief. To such men the cries of the madmen in the country which has found release are so dreadful that they must stop their ears, nay, must stop the ears of their fellow-countrymen as well. These two groups are the extremists with respect to social justice—the men who would break our present scheme to pieces and start anew and those who hold that scheme so sacred that the suggestion of changing it is not simply false but also vicious and sacrilegious. Between these two are most of us, men who try to have patience and common sense, but who are sadly puzzled and perplexed just now. One thing we know, namely, that the way is not clear, old procedures are not surely right, old answers cannot be accepted without question. The world is seeking wisdom as to social justice in distribution, and that wisdom is hard to get.

But more difficult yet than the distributing of values is the human task of using them. And the most serious aspect of the difficulty is that we do not feel it. We may be baffled by the problems of social justice but at least we are interested in them. In a college community, as well as in a public forum, men can be stirred to eager and desperate activity by the perception that other men are not being fairly treated, that human beings are being robbed of a fair chance at the opportunities of living. We may not know what to do but our impulse is generous and our will resolute to do something, if only the mind would tell us what it is. But in the realm of use, in apprehension of the necessity of taste and insight and appreciation of value, we are hardly conscious of difficulty at all. We have a certain blind faith that if only the opportunities of life are given they will be taken and human lives will be in general what they ought to be. Nothing could be more obvious than the falseness of such a faith as this. Wealth has not very generally brought to those who have it the fineness of taste and the niceness of discrimination which the use of it demands. Quite as often it has brought coarseness of feeling and dulness of appreciation. Our civilization does not very clearly become more fine as it becomes more rich. We are in danger of having the world in our hands and losing it because our fingers slip. What shall we do with the world which is given us? That is, I think, the hardest lesson which the teacher has to learn and teach.

Here then, are the three tasks of the teacher. How do they bear upon the work of the liberal college? In a broad general way it is true that the teaching of the production of value rests with the technical and professional schools. They are engaged in devising ways of making good. And again may we say that relatively speaking their task is an easy one. The liberal schools, on the other hand, are concerned with both the second and the third endeavors. They are expected to inform our people as to how the goods of life should be shared and how they should be used. These are the two fundamental aims of liberal teaching.

In the remainder of this paper I should like to press upon the college the claims of the third of these tasks as against a constant over-emphasis of the second. And may I protest that this is not because one loves the second less but rather because one loves the third more. It would perhaps be truer to say that the second without the third is nothing and that therefore love for it demands that we leave it no longer bereft of its fellow. If only we can show that the notion of social justice is not a complete account of life, that it needs the supplementation of this third conception, then perhaps in homes and churches and schools and colleges we may get a wiser and saner teaching of life than is now given. Let us then condemn and vilify the ideal of social justice in order to bring its adherents to their senses.

The point at issue was brought to clear formulation in a public discussion in which the writer of this paper took part a few years ago. The first of two speakers said, "I would not give a snap of my finger for a scheme of education which does not find its final term of value in Service." To which the second speaker replied, "I would not give a snap of my finger for a scheme of education which does find its final term of value in Service." Such statements as these have all the exaggeration of public controversy, but carefully considered they define an issue which demands the attention of the liberal teacher.

Strictly speaking it seems to me clear that the second of the above statements is right. Service, as such, is not a term of value at all. To give to another is valuable only in a secondary and derivative sense, never in a final one. It is the thing given which is of value. There is nothing gained by giving to another something which is not worth giving. To serve one's fellows is to give to them what they need, what they enjoy, what is worth while. And if one is in search of the final term by which all our activities and all our teachings are to be justified we must find it among those things the having of which is good and the lack of which robs human living of its value. To serve is to give something and service is good only in so far as that something given is good.

At the risk of seeming flippant and unfair I should like to press this point home by a number of statements which though they are only half-truths are yet needed because the other half is so constantly torn away from its fellow and kept before our students as if it were the total and the sufficient truth.

Much of the teaching and preaching which our students hear is far too self-centered in its emphasis upon social justice and upon the duty of service. After all, the essential thing is not that we should make the world right, but that it should be right. One often feels that some of our youthful enthusiasts are haunted by the dreadful fear that there may be no sinners for them to save, no broken lives for them to put together again. As against this, one must protest that in the last analysis the receiving of value does as much for human living as does the giving of it. If for no other reason, this is true because after all no one can give unless there is some one who will take his gift. And if the taking be not good, then the giving, whose final justification lies within it, cannot be good either. Clearly enough, in the grand total of human experience, giving cannot have more value than the taking and using of the thing given. If it be not good to use then it is not good to give the thing used.

And from another point of view, the determination to serve one's fellows needs to be kept clear in mind so that it may be successful. It is well enough for youthful enthusiasts to go out with the determination to make a hundred men happy, to make a hundred lives worth while. But simple arithmetical calculation assures us that such expectations will not be realized. On the average one man cannot make more than one life worth while, for the obvious reason that somebody must have the life which is so practiced upon. If we base our calculation upon "welfares" as the term of measurement, and say that each man would like to make as many welfares as possible, the hard fact remains that on the average we cannot each make more than one of them. A welfare must belong to somebody and if there were actually created more welfares than men, the trouble would be that there would not be enough men to take them. There is no danger of course of such a calamity as this. Human life hardly furnishes us on the whole with half a welfare apiece. But there is danger that our young people misconstrue their task, state it to themselves in exaggerated sentimental terms and so doom themselves to the disappointment and sense of futility which come when idle dreams collapse.

From still another point of view, one is here protesting against the externalism of our social teaching. We teach too much about the machinery of life and far too little about life itself. We tell too much about the things which may be done and too little about what they are done for. As a people we have immense admiration for a man who builds a great library and profound disdain for a man who sits down quietly in the library to read a book. What is he doing there, we ask. Of what use is the reading of the book? What will it enable him to do? And if one answers that he reads because reading a good book is a good human experience and that therefore it may be done not for the sake of something else but for its own sake, practical men think that we have gone mad. But again, let us protest that if reading is not good then the building of the library was not good, and our benefactor is not good and nothing has been accomplished by all that he has given and done. If there are not values in life then doing has no value and the builder and the dreamer go down together in a common crash.

The same principle holds on other sides of our life. We admire men who can write books and men who can paint pictures. Such men seem to us to have succeeded—if some one else tells us that their work is highly regarded. But we as a people are robbing both writers and painters of their proper success because we do not give them readers and seers who can appreciate, who can take the meaning, the beauty which they give. It is true that we pay them money for their efforts, but it is also true that we say "Ah" in the wrong place, that we are thrilled by the vulgar and stupid thing and left cold by the beauty into which the spirit of the artist has poured itself. There is no surer way of killing artists and writers than to be stupid and dull in the presence of what they have created. For such murders a wealthy crass civilization has a heavy burden of guilt to bear.

What then shall the liberal teacher teach as the representation of the learning which seeks to know what life may be? Shall he forbid men to serve their fellows? We have not said that.

To say that in colleges men preach service badly is not to say that in human society we have too much generous friendship. We have far too little of it. By every means in our power we must build it up so that in the sharing of the goods of life men may act toward one another like friends and fellows rather than like competing beasts, each struggling for the plunder which strength and cunning will enable him to take from other men. College students, like other men, must learn how values should be shared and then must pledge themselves to see to it that justice is done, nay rather must be as eager that other men shall have the values which they crave as that the goods they wish should come to them.

But still the point holds good that all such eagerness as this will come to little unless the man who gives and he who takes have taste for life. There is the final test of value. There is the point where all our strivings succeed or fail.

Can college teachers teach that lesson? Perhaps they can if they have learned it. But they will find a hundred other teaching powers outside the college fighting against them. What shall they do? It seems to me that first they should remain apart from the machinery of life, refusing to be busy with it. And second they should with very steady eyes survey the goods which life affords, should try to see what life may be in terms of its experiences, should make a list of books, and trees, and songs, and friends, and games, and arguments, and all the other splendid things that men can use. And third they should be sensitive themselves, discerning what is fine and true and generous and permanent, and cutting it off with sharp, clear-cut avoidance from the vulgar, false, selfish, and transitory things that cheapen life. And finally, having some taste and insight, they should teach them to their pupils, in whatever ways teaching may be done.

There is no one in all our social scheme more ambitious than is the teacher. He is making the mind of his pupil so that it may be fitted to the world in which he lives. Knowledge and skill must be developed for the making of wealth; wisdom and fairness must be established for the distributing and sharing of wealth. But above all, and as the end of all, taste and sensitiveness and fineness and intensity of appreciation must be built up, so that our wealth may be worth giving and worth having.

QUACK-DOCTORING THE COLLEGES [1]

By William Bennett Munro

Many things are wrong with our colleges. I have it on the highest and the lowest authority—that is, on the authority of Nicholas Murray Butler and Upton Sinclair. It has also been intimated to me by athletic coaches and college presidents, who may be said to represent the alpha and the omega of reliability on such matters. As I happen to be both a college professor and a college trustee, I get the bombardment on both flanks. I have positive information that the colleges are no longer educating anybody, and I have equally emphatic assurance that they are educating a lot of youngsters who ought to be left illiterate for the benefit of the unskilled labor market. I hear that the colleges have completely lost the confidence of the business world, and I read in the editorial columns that more business men are sending their sons to college than ever before. I learn from presidents' reports that the colleges have big deficits every year, and from the treasurers' reports that their assets are steadily growing larger. In my spare moments (of which every college professor has an abundance) I have answered no end of questionnaires and participated in at least a dozen educational surveys, each one of which has been able to demonstrate that the methods of instruction used in colleges, although widely diverse in character, are alike in being wrong.

This recalls to mind one of the maxims of equity: to wit, that "there is no wrong without a remedy." In the case of the colleges the remedies far outnumber the wrongs. They are literally uncountable, like the twinklers in the new heavens. Indeed, there is no species of quackery so popular to-day as the educa-

[1] From *Harper's Magazine,* September 1928. Reprinted by permission of the editor and of the author.

tional brand of hocus-pocus. The land is swarming with educational prestidigitators—and no wonder, for to qualify as an educational expert one needs only to be a glib fellow away from home. Every one of these intellectual Æsculapians has his own favorite prescription. He believes it applicable to all institutions, big or little, without discrimination as to age or sex. The college of to-day, unhappily, is like a patient upon whom the allopaths, homeopaths, osteopaths, chiropractors, mental healers, and sun-bath zealots all demand the right to operate simultaneously. It is in a worse position, being beset by medicine-men who are ready to diagnose, prescribe, and cure without license or fee.

Out of this welter let us pick a few of the remedial tonics which are being most assiduously peddled at the present time. Number one may be called the Job-Analysis Serum. It is designed to lower the high fever of those colleges which are excitedly doing a lot of things without knowing what they are doing or why. In the language of the educational technician, the colleges have not "clarified their objectives." It may seem strange that, although some of our older institutions have been on the job for more than two hundred years, they have never thought to stop and "analyze it"; yet such appears to be the case. Of course it is an unpardonable omission. The job-analysis treatment should be applied at once. First, count the patient's pulse—that is to say, begin with a questionnaire. Every survey that aims to be both scientific and sociological (queer combination!) must begin that way. Send the questionnaire to all the professors asking them why they teach. Send it to all the students asking them why they allow themselves to be taught. Send it to the alumni with a demand for information of similar irrelevance. Then, when the replies come in, tabulate the data, find the median and the mode, figure out the coefficient of correlation, and the result will give you a typical conspectus of the pattern of valuation, which is the true collegiate objective reduced to a conventionalized significance. (Not being a psychologist, I cannot be sure of my terminology, but that is the formula as I remember it.)

Having found its true objective, at any rate, the college can then go full-steam ahead. The job analysis will indicate a solution for each and all of its problems—of finance, housing, instruction, athletics, and the social distractions. It will tell you how undergraduate mental vacuity can be transformed into genius as by the touch of a magic wand. There is no other serum like unto this one in its claim to curative accomplishment.

II

Then there is the Orientation Ointment, which has had a brisk sale during the past ten years. Its vendors begin by assuring us that the job-analysts have made a false diagnosis. The colleges know what they are trying to do, but the students don't. Every autumn some thousands of freshmen come thronging through the academic gates and are helplessly whirled into the vortex of an elective curriculum. These young men and women should be promptly "oriented." To that end they should be bidden to arrive for a "freshman week" before the college opens. During this preview performance they can be told, in abbreviated form, all that they would ordinarily learn during the entire four years of a college course.

It is all very simple. They listen to speeches and they stand in line. They are addressed by the president on what they ought to do, and by the dean on what they ought not to do. The chairman of the faculty warns them in the morning that they came to the college to get an education, and in the afternoon the football coach confides to the mass meeting that an education is the last thing any red-blooded young man comes to college for.

The freshman should also be provided with advisers, both from the faculty and from the senior class. These advisers make the most of their opportunities, hence advice is the last thing that any freshman lacks when this curtain-raiser week comes to a close. If he assimilated one-tenth of it—which he does not—he would have enough to last him to the end of his days. It is my observation that among all forms of counsel the kind which is given by the senior student-advisers impresses the average freshman as the most interesting and the most useful. For it is from them that the neophyte finds out what courses in the curriculum are "snap courses," where the college bootlegger resides, how to get bids to the sorority dances, and whether the dean is hard-boiled to the alibi of an alarm clock that did not go off in time for a nine-o'clock class. To the new-comer this information is obviously more utilitarian than the assurance of his faculty mentor "that he must seek adjustment to his highest potential, respond to his creative urge, seek to integrate what he learns into a universal harmony of knowledge, and strive to live the abundant life."

Not all the orientation ointment can be applied during fresh-man week, even with the most vigorous rubbing. Accordingly, this process should have a follow-up in the way of an orientation course given as part of the regular curriculum and counting to-wards a degree. This course should aim to be an outline of every-thing. It should begin with the origin of the cosmos and come down to the election of Al Smith, one lecture a week for ten weeks or thereabouts. To do this, it must cover six centuries per hour, although a little slowing up for the last three or four centuries is permissible in view of the fact that these are somewhat more crowded with happenings. It is said that light travels around the earth in one-seventh of a second; but even at that it is no match for the speed of the orientation lecturer. He flashes through the Eocene, the Miocene, and the Pliocene ages, right down to the Obscene—which is the contemporary era. The great-ness and decline of Rome are master-stroked in seven minutes, the Darwinian theory is elucidated in four, and the industrial revolution gets by while the lecturer pauses for breath.

The title of this course should be both dignified and designa-tory. It may be called, "The Story of Civilization," or "The Universe and Mankind," or perhaps just "Life and Its Prob-lems." But the official title does not much matter, for the under-graduate will soon endow it with a nickname. He calls it "Seeing Civilization," or "The Educational Rubberneck Bus," or, in due tribute to the high spots of the course, he labels it alliteratively as "Drink, Drainage, Divorce, and Democracy."

The orientation course, as given in various institutions which have fallen for this pick-me-up, has developed into a companion-ate miscegenation of history, politics, economics, pietisms, and sex hygiene. It has length and breadth without the third dimension. This means that the instructor must be a sociologist, in other words, some one who has spent his life learning less and less about more and more until he has become intellectually unbuttoned. As a preparation for serious work in college or elsewhere these orientation courses have a value that accountants would express in red ink.

III

Then there is Nostrum Number Three, the abolition of the lecture system and the substitution of active participation by the student in the classroom exercises. The usual academic lecture, we are asked to believe, is a process by which things pass from the notebook of the professor to the notebook of the student without going through the heads of either. So let it be amputated from the curriculum. Anyhow, the lecture is a survival of scholasticism, a medieval hang-over quite out of keeping with the genius of the twentieth-century American youth. In its place let us have creative participation by the student—creative participation, that is the newest phrase, and it has an alluring sound without meaning much.

No more shall some *ex cathedra* dogmatist deliver his pontifical discourses from the rostrum with no opportunity for the benches to hit back; but teacher and pupil will exchange ideas, like Socrates and Plato. Encourage the freshman to assume a "challenging attitude" towards everything which the instructor may say, be it an assertion that the earth is a sphere, or that the poles are colder than the equator, or that the Dutch have captured Amsterdam. Develop his spirit of criticism, his propensity to disagree. If this does not make the undergraduate a more intelligent citizen, it will at least qualify him as a municipal reformer.

Every one who is not himself a teacher likes to scold about the kind of teaching his sons and daughters are getting. It makes them work too hard, or not hard enough. It is too meticulous, or too superficial. It discourages thought by making the subject too simple, or it dampens enthusiasm by making it too complex. It is too old-fashioned, or it exemplifies some transient fad. Pedagogy is like politics in that any one can tell you how to do things better than they are being done. Ideas about teaching, like those concerning government, are all created free and equal.

But teaching is an art, and a true art can never be enslaved to formal rules. Teaching is an intensely personal thing; it cannot be standardized any more than leadership can. To teach is to lead, to inspire, to create disciples. Every good teacher has his own way of doing it. Some subjects lend themselves to the lecture method while others do not. Many poor lectures are delivered in college classrooms, no doubt; but I have a suspicion that poor sermons are also delivered from church pulpits at times. Why not abolish all sermons, therefore, and just leave the text to be discussed for an hour by the more garrulous members of the congregation? That would be "creative participation" in a service of worship—and it would empty the churches.

There is no best method of instruction, whether in the home, the school, or the college. Education does not succeed or fail on the issue of methodology but on the capacity and the personality of the teacher himself. That ought to be commonplace, but it is not. Otherwise we should hardly have these perennial announcements from Rollins or Ripon, from Tucson or Tuscaloosa, that some one has discovered in the two-hour conference, or the pro-seminar, or the socialized recitation, a new educational alchemy which enables the undergraduate to get educated without exertion, no matter what kind of faculty the college employs.

IV

Then there is the Antioch Antidote. It consists of hard work outside the college, given in regular doses to offset the lethargic habits that the student acquires within. The undergraduates attend classes for a stretch; then for an equal interlude they go out and earn their living as best they can. This alternation is continued from entrance to graduation, which covers six years instead of the usual four. The process, in a way, is reminiscent of the Scotch farmer who fed and starved his hogs on alternate days so that the bacon would be of prime quality, a streak of fat and a streak of lean. It aims at the intermingling of the manual and the mental in equal proportions. The hands go to work while the brain lays off; then the intellect is oiled up for another run.

There are some cynics who would argue, of course, that the boy who is both able and willing to do college work ought to spend all his time at it until the job is finished. And as for the boy who needs the spur of alternate months at gainful employment in order to make him appreciate his academic opportunities—well, it is questionable whether he ought to be in college at all, even half the time. Half earning, half studying may be justified in the case of those whose straitened circumstances make it the only way to acquire a college degree. For others, it is a hybrid which sacrifices the highest values of academic training on the one hand and of industrial training on the other by the vain effort to combine them both.

There has been too much deification of the boy who works his way through college. It is natural, in a democracy, that this should be the case. A few fellows derive benefit from the experience of having to earn their way, but the vast majority do nothing of the sort. To them it simply means that these plastic years of young manhood are clouded by financial anxieties which haunt the soul and depress the spirit. It involves a denial of leisure moments at a time when these would be of the highest value. It compels the student to cut corners, to forego many cultural advantages which the college environment provides, and sometimes to undermine his health as well. Many a man does not learn the real cost of working his way through college until he has passed into the fifties. Then he finds that there are prematurely frayed-out nerves to be entered on the debit side of the account. It is my conviction, after having taught more than ten thousand college students during the past quarter of a century, that nine-tenths of those who had to earn their way to a bachelor's degree would have been far better off without any such handicap. A strange doctrine it is, therefore, that young men and women whose parents can afford to educate them should, nevertheless, interrupt their studies for the sake of the "experience." They will get quite enough of it after college days are over.

V

And so one might go on through the long category of reforms which the colleges are being urged to inaugurate. Fraternities should be abolished. The students should not be taught but tutored. They should be separated into sections on the basis of ability. They should study subjects and not merely take courses. They should devote a whole year, indeed, to a single subject like the civilization of ancient Athens, instead of rustling about in a mosaic of Bible, biography, botany, and business—as they do in some colleges. They should read books for themselves and not be content with the professor's version of what is in the books. They should learn a little of everything and one thing well. (The first part of that syllogism, by the way, presents no difficulty in any American college.) They should have required studies for discipline and elective courses for self-expression. They should be objectively rated and psychologically tested. They should have personnel supervision and vocational guidance. The colleges should impose a limitation upon the number of students admitted. As a prophylactic, this has become very popular among the endowed colleges. But the state-supported institutions cannot employ it, so they make use of an emetic instead. They throw out those whom they should never have admitted.

The catalogue of panaceas, indeed, is far too long for insertion here. There is the Johns Hopkins plan for a senior college, the Wisconsin plan for an experimental college, and the Michigan plan for a university college. There is the Swarthmore idea, the Claremont idea, and the Wabash idea. It is a rare thing to have even two or three months pass without the launching of some new scheme of educational rapid transit; some way of getting to the top of Mount Parnassus without climbing there. A few of them have meritorious features, but for the most part they merely reflect the age-old and utterly futile attempt to gain the end without the means, the whole without the parts, the victory without the battle.

There is no substitute and there never can be any substitute for *men* in the process of education—for earnest, enthusiastic, capable men in the faculty and in the student body. Given these, you have a great college; without them, all the newfangled methods will never avail an institution much. Nearly all the problems of collegiate education merge into two fundamental ones— hand-picking the student body and recruiting the faculty. The college that does both these things well is on the high road to ultimate distinction; and the one that relegates them to a secondary place in its program, while it goes philandering after mirages, is inexorably headed to the rear of the procession.

It is men, not methods or measures, that determine whether a college shall be first-rate or second class. Or, to put it more accurately, first find the men and the methods will take care of themselves. I should like to find some college with · the right men and the wrong methods of education. I don't believe there is one. Is it not time to rise and suggest the advisability of less quack-doctoring in the matter of our educational processes, and more earnest concentration upon the vital issue of personnel?

THE TREE OF KNOWLEDGE [1]

By Walter Pater

O mare! O littus! verum secretumque Μουσεῖον,
quam multa invenitis, quam multa dictatis!
—*Pliny's Letters.*

It would hardly have been possible to feel more seriously than did Marius in those grave years of his early life. But the death of his mother turned seriousness of feeling into a matter of the intelligence: it made him a questioner; and, by bringing into full evidence to him the force of his affections and the probable importance of their place in his future, developed in him gen-

[1] From *Marius the Epicurean.*

erally the more human and earthly elements of character. A singularly virile consciousness of the realities of life pronounced itself in him; still however as in the main a poetic apprehension, though united already with something of personal ambition and the instinct of self-assertion. There were days when he could suspect, though it was a suspicion he was careful at first to put from him, that that early, much cherished religion of the villa might come to count with him as but one form of poetic beauty, or of the ideal, in things; as but one voice, in a world where there were many voices it would be a moral weakness not to listen to. And yet this voice, through its forcible preoccupation of his childish conscience, still seemed to make a claim of a quite exclusive character, defining itself as essentially one of but two possible leaders of his spirit, the other proposing to him unlimited self-expansion in a world of various sunshine. The contrast was so pronounced as to make the easy, light-hearted, unsuspecting exercise of himself, among the temptations of the new phase of life which had now begun, seem nothing less than a rival *religion*, a rival *religious* service. The temptations, the various sunshine, were those of the old town of Pisa, where Marius was now a tall schoolboy. Pisa was a place lying just far enough from home to make his rare visits to it in childhood seem like adventures, such as had never failed to supply new and refreshing impulses to the imagination. The partly decayed pensive town, which still had its commerce by sea, and its fashion at the bathing-season, had lent, at one time the vivid memory of its fair streets of marble, at another the solemn outline of the dark hills of Luna on its background, at another the living glances of its men and women, to the thickly gathering crowd of impressions, out of which his notion of the world was then forming. And while he learned that the object, the experience, as it will be known to memory, is really from first to last the chief point for consideration in the conduct of life, these things were feeding also the idealism constitutional with him—his innate and habitual longing for a world altogether fairer than that he saw. The child could find his way in thought along those streets of the old town, expecting duly the shrines at their corners, and their recurrent intervals of garden-courts, or side-views of distant sea. The great temple of the place, as he could remember it, on turning back once for a last look from an angle of his homeward road, counting its tall gray columns between the blue of the bay and the blue fields of blossoming flax beyond; the harbour and its lights; the foreign ships lying there; the sailors' chapel of Venus, and her gilded image, hung with votive gifts; the seamen themselves, their women and children, who had a whole peculiar colour-world of their own—the boy's superficial delight in the broad light and shadow of all that was mingled with the sense of power, of unknown distance, of the danger of storm and possible death.

To this place, then, Marius came down now from *Whitenights*, to live in the house of his guardian or tutor, that he might attend the school of a famous rhetorician, and learn, among other things, Greek. The school, one of many imitations of Plato's Academy in the old Athenian garden, lay in a quiet suburb of Pisa, and had its grove of cypresses, its porticoes, a house for the master, its chapel and images. For the memory of Marius in after-days, a clear morning sunlight seemed to lie perpetually on that severe picture in old gray and green. The lad went to this school daily betimes, in state at first, with a young slave to carry the books, and certainly with no reluctance, for the sight of his fellow-scholars, and their petulant activity, coming upon the sadder sentimental moods of his childhood, awoke at once that instinct of emulation which is but the other side of sympathy; and he was not aware, of course, how completely the difference of his previous training had made him, even in his most enthusiastic participation in the ways of that little world, still essentially but a spectator. While all their heart was in their limited boyish race, and its transitory prizes, he was already entertaining himself, very pleasurably meditative, with the tiny drama in action before him, as but the mimic, preliminary exercise for a larger contest, and already with an implicit epicureanism. Watching all the gallant effects of their small rivalries—a scene in the main of fresh delightful sunshine—he entered at once into the sensations of a rivalry beyond them, into the passion of men, and had already recognised a certain appetite for fame, for distinction among his fellows, as his dominant motive to be.

The fame he conceived for himself at this time was, as the reader will have anticipated, of the intellectual order, that of a poet perhaps. And as, in that gray monastic tranquillity of the villa, inward voices from the reality of unseen things had come abundantly; so here, with the sounds and aspects of the shore, and amid the urbanities, the graceful follies, of a bathing-place, it was the reality, the tyrannous reality, of things visible that was borne in upon him. The real world around—a present humanity not less comely, it might seem, than that of the old heroic days —endowing everything it touched upon, however remotely, down to its little passing tricks of fashion even, with a kind of fleeting beauty, exercised over him just then a great fascination.

That sense had come upon him in all its power one exceptionally fine summer, the summer when, at a somewhat earlier age than was usual, he had formally assumed the dress of manhood, going into the Forum for that purpose, accompanied by his friends in festal array. At night, after the full measure of those cloudless days, he would feel well-nigh wearied out, as if with a long succession of pictures and music. As he wandered through the gay streets or on the sea-shore, the real world seemed indeed boundless, and himself almost absolutely free in it, with a boundless appetite for experience, for adventure, whether physical or of the spirit. His entire rearing hitherto had lent itself to an imaginative exaltation of the past; but now the spectacle actually afforded to his untired and freely open senses, suggested the reflection that the present had, it might be, really advanced beyond the past, and he was ready to boast in the very fact that it was modern. If, in a voluntary archaism, the polite world of that day went back to a choicer generation, as it fancied, for the purpose of a fastidious self-correction, in matters of art, of literature, and even, as we have seen, of religion, at least it improved, by a shade or two of more scrupulous finish, on the old pattern; and the new era, like the *Neuzeit* of the German enthusiasts at the beginning of our own century, might perhaps be discerned, awaiting one just a single step onward—the perfected new manner, in the consummation of time, alike as regards the things of the imagination and the actual conduct of life. Only, while the pursuit of an ideal like this demanded entire liberty of heart and brain, that old, staid, conservative religion of his childhood certainly had its being in a world of somewhat narrow restrictions. But then, the one was absolutely real, with nothing less than the reality of seeing and hearing—the other, how vague, shadowy, problematical! Could its so limited probabilities be worth taking into account in any practical question as to the rejecting or receiving of what was indeed so real, and, on the face of it, so desirable?

And, dating from the time of his first coming to school, a great friendship had grown up for him, in that life of so few attachments—the pure and disinterested friendship of schoolmates. He had seen Flavian for the first time the day on which he had come to Pisa, at the moment when his mind was full of wistful thoughts regarding the new life to begin for him tomorrow, and he gazed curiously at the crowd of bustling scholars as they came from their classes. There was something in Flavian a shade disdainful, as he stood isolated from the others for a moment, explained in part by his stature and the distinction of the low, broad forehead; though there was pleasantness also for the newcomer in the roving blue eyes which seemed somehow to take a fuller hold upon things around than is usual with boys. Marius knew that those proud glances made kindly note of him for a moment, and felt something like friendship at first sight. There was a tone of reserve or gravity there, amid perfectly disciplined health, which, to his fancy, seemed to carry forward the expression of the austere sky and the clear song of the blackbird on that gray March evening. Flavian indeed was a creature who changed much with the changes of the passing light and shade about him, and was brilliant enough under the early sunshine in school next morning. Of all that little world of more or less gifted youth, surely the centre was this lad of servile birth. Prince of the school, he had gained an easy dominion over the old Greek master by the fascination of his parts, and over his fellow-scholars by the figure he bore. He wore already the manly dress; and standing there in class, as he displayed his wonderful quickness in reckoning, or his taste in declaiming Homer, he was like a carved figure in motion, thought Marius, but with that indescribable gleam upon it which the words of Homer actually suggested, as perceptible on the visible forms of the gods—

οἷα θεοὺς ἐπενήνοθεν αἰὲν ἐόντας [1]

A story hung by him, a story which his comrades acutely connected with his habitual air of somewhat peevish pride. Two points were held to be clear amid its general vagueness—a rich stranger paid his schooling, and he was himself very poor, though there was an attractive piquancy in the poverty of Flavian which in a scholar of another figure might have been despised. Over Marius too his dominion was entire. Three years older than he, Flavian was appointed to help the younger boy in his studies, and Marius thus became virtually his servant in many things, taking his humours with a sort of grateful pride in being noticed at all, and, thinking over all this afterwards, found that the fascination experienced by him had been a sentimental one, dependent on the concession to himself of an intimacy, a certain tolerance of his company, granted to none beside.

That was in the earliest days; and then, as their intimacy grew, the genius, the intellectual power of Flavian began its sway over him. The brilliant youth who loved dress, and dainty food, and flowers, and seemed to have a natural alliance with, and claim upon, everything else which was physically select and bright, cultivated also that foppery of words, of choice diction, which was common among the *élite* spirits of that day; and Marius, early an expert and elegant penman, transcribed his verses (the euphuism of which, amid a genuine original power, was then so delightful to him) in beautiful ink, receiving in return the profit of Flavian's really great intellectual capacities, developed and accomplished under the ambitious desire to make his way effectively in life. Among other things he introduced

[1] Such as gleam upon the immortal gods.—From *The Odyssey*, VIII, line 365.

him to the writings of a sprightly wit, then very busy with the pen, one Lucian—writings seeming to overflow with that intellectual light turned upon dim places, which, at least in seasons of mental fair weather, can make people laugh where they have been wont, perhaps, to pray. And, surely, the sunlight which filled those well-remembered early mornings in school, had had more than the usual measure of gold in it! Marius, at least, would lie awake before the time, thinking with delight of the long coming hours of hard work in the presence of Flavian, as other boys dream of a holiday.

It was almost by accident at last, so wayward and capricious was he, that reserve gave way, and Flavian told the story of his father—a freedman, presented late in life, and almost against his will, with the liberty so fondly desired in youth, but on condition of the sacrifice of part of his *peculium*—the slave's diminutive hoard—amassed by many a self-denial, in an existence necessarily hard. The rich man, interested in the promise of the fair child born on his estate, had sent him to school. The meanness and dejection, nevertheless, of that unoccupied old age defined the leading memory of Flavian, revived sometimes, after this first confidence, with a burst of angry tears amid the sunshine. But nature had had her economy in nursing the strength of that one natural affection; for, save his half-selfish care for Marius, it was the single, really generous part, the one piety, in the lad's character. In him Marius saw the spirit of unbelief, achieved as if at one step. The much-admired freedman's son, as with the privilege of a natural aristocracy, believed only in himself, in the brilliant, and mainly sensuous gifts, he had, or meant to acquire.

And then, he had certainly yielded himself, though still with untouched health, in a world where manhood comes early, to the seductions of that luxurious town, and Marius wondered sometimes, in the freer revelation of himself by conversation, at the extent of his early corruption. How often, afterwards, did evil things present themselves in malign association with the memory of that beautiful head, and with a kind of borrowed sanction and charm in its natural grace! To Marius, at a later time, he counted for as it were an epitome of the whole pagan world, the depth of its corruption, and its perfection of form. And still, in his mobility, his animation, in his eager capacity for various life, he was so real an object, after that visionary idealism of the villa. His voice, his glance, were like the breaking in of the solid world upon one, amid the flimsy fictions of a dream. A shadow, handling all things as shadows, had felt a sudden real and poignant heat in them.

Meantime, under his guidance, Marius was learning quickly and abundantly, because with a good will. There was that in the actual effectiveness of his figure which stimulated the younger lad to make the most of opportunity; and he had experience already that education largely increased one's capacity for enjoyment. He was acquiring what it is the chief function of all higher education to impart, the art, namely, of so relieving the ideal or poetic traits, the elements of distinction, in our everyday life—of so exclusively living in them—that the unadorned remainder of it, the mere drift or *débris* of our days, comes to be as though it were not. And the consciousness of this aim came with the reading of one particular book, then fresh in the world, with which he fell in about this time—a book which awakened the poetic or romantic capacity as perhaps some other book might have done, but was peculiar in giving it a direction emphatically sensuous. It made him, in that visionary reception of every-day life, the seer, more especially, of a revelation in colour and form. If our modern education, in its better efforts, really conveys to any of us that kind of idealising power, it does so (though dealing mainly, as its professed instruments, with the most select and ideal remains of ancient literature) oftenest by truant reading; and thus it happened also, long ago, with Marius and his friend.

The Training of Intellect [1]

By Woodrow Wilson

Mr. Toastmaster, Mr. President, and Gentlemen:—I certainly considered it a compliment to myself when Mr. Phelps

[1] From *The Yale Alumni Weekly* for March 25, 1908. Reprinted by the kind permission of the editor.

made the comparison he made a few moments ago, but it was hardly a compliment to Princeton.

I do not feel that in coming to Yale I am coming among strangers. I believe that a man who is accustomed to living among college men finds everywhere the same spirit, the same atmosphere. I feel toward you as a friend of mine felt toward an acquaintance who slapped him on the back familiarly. He looked at the fellow coldly and said, "I do not know your name, but your manners are very familiar." And so I feel with regard to every college gathering that their manners are familiar, but I also feel that there is a quickness of mutual comprehension that is very reassuring to a speaker. And then I feel particularly at ease in appearing before a strange audience because they have not heard my stories, and, moreover, because it is not so difficult to maintain a boast of dignity where you are not known as it is where you are known. When I appear before a Princeton crowd and try to live up to an introduction, I feel like the old woman who went into the side show at the circus and saw a man reading a newspaper through a two-inch board. "Let me out of this place," she exclaimed, "this is no place for me to be with these thin things on." I have an uncomfortable feeling in such circumstances that the disguise is transparent, but perhaps I can maintain a disguise for a little while among you.

I must confess to you that I came here with very serious thoughts this evening, because I have been laboring under the conviction for a long time that the object of a university is to educate, and I have not seen the universities of this country achieving any remarkable or disturbing success in that direction. I have found everywhere the note which I must say I have heard sounded once or twice to-night—that apology for the intellectual side of the university. You hear it at all universities. Learning is on the defensive, is actually on the defensive, among college men, and they are being asked by way of indulgence to bring that also into the circle of their interests. Is it not time we stopped asking indulgence for learning and proclaimed its sovereignty? Is it not time we reminded the college men of this country that they have no right to any distinctive place in any community, unless they can show it by intellectual achievement? that if a university is a place for distinction at all it must be distinguished by the conquests of the mind? I for my part tell you plainly that that is my motto, that I have entered the field to fight for that thesis, and that for that thesis only do I care to fight.

The toastmaster of the evening said, and said truly, that this is the season when, for me, it was most difficult to break away from regular engagements in which I am involved at this time of the year. But when I was invited to the Phi Beta Kappa banquet it had an unusual sound, and I felt that that was the particular kind of invitation which it was my duty and privilege to accept. One of the problems of the American university now is how, among a great many other competing interests, to give places of distinction to men who want places of distinction in the classroom. Why don't we give you men the Y here and the P at Princeton, because after all you have done the particular thing which distinguishes Yale? Not that these other things are not worth doing, but they may be done anywhere. They may be done in athletic clubs where there is no study, but this thing can be done only here. This is the distinctive mark of the place.

A good many years ago, just two weeks before the mid-year examinations, the Faculty of Princeton was foolish enough to permit a very unwise evangelist to come to the place and to upset the town. And while an assisting undergraduate was going from room to room one undergraduate secured his door and put this notice out, "I am a Christian and am studying for examinations." Now I want to say that that is exactly what a Christian undergraduate would be doing at that time of the year. He would not be attending religious meetings no matter how beneficial it would be to him. He would be studying for examinations not merely for the purpose of passing them, but from his sense of duty.

We get a good many men at Princeton from certain secondary schools who say a great deal about their earnest desire to cultivate character among our students, and I hear a great deal about character being the object of education. I take leave to believe that a man who cultivates his character consciously will cultivate nothing except what will make him intolerable to his fellow men. If your object in life is to make a fine fellow of yourself, you will not succeed, and you will not be acceptable to really fine fellows. Character, gentlemen, is a by-product. It comes, whether you will or not, as a consequence of a life devoted to the nearest duty, and the place in which character would be cultivated, if it be a place of study, is a place where study is the object and character the results.

Not long ago a gentleman approached me in great excitement just after the entrance examinations. He said we had made a great mistake in not taking so and so from a certain school which he named. "But," I said, "he did not pass the entrance examinations." And he went over the boy's moral excellencies again. "Pardon me," I said, "you do not understand. He did not pass the entrance examinations. Now," I said, "I want you to understand that if the Angel Gabriel applied for admission to Princeton University and could not pass the entrance examinations, he would not be admitted. He would be wasting his time." It seemed a new idea to him. This boy had come from a school which cultivated character, and he was a nice, lovable fellow with a presentable character. Therefore, he ought to be admitted to any university. I fail to see it from this point of view, for a university is an institution of purpose. We have in some previous years had pity for young gentlemen who were not sufficiently acquainted with the elements of a preparatory course. They have been dropped at the examinations, and I have always felt that we have been guilty of an offense, and have made their parents spend money to no avail and the youngsters spend their time to no avail. And so I think that all university men ought to rouse themselves now and understand what is the object of a university. The object of a university is intellect; as a university its only object is intellect. As a body of young men there ought to be other things, there ought to be diversions to release them from the constant strain of effort, there ought to be things that gladden the heart and moments of leisure, but as a university the only object is intellect.

The reason why I chose the subject that I am permitted to speak upon to-night—the function of scholarship—was that I wanted to point out the function of scholarship not merely in the university but in the nation. In a country constituted as ours is the relation in which education stands is a very important one. Our whole theory has been based upon an enlightened citizenship and therefore the function of scholarship must be for the nation as well as for the university itself. I mean the function of such scholarship as undergraduates get. That is not a violent amount in any case. You cannot make a scholar of a man except by some largeness of Providence in his makeup, by the time he is twenty-one or twenty-two years of age. There have been gentlemen who have made a reputation by twenty-one or twenty-two, but it is generally in some little province of knowledge, so small that a small effort can conquer it. You do not make scholars by that time, you do not often make scholars by seventy that are worth boasting of. The process of scholarship, so far as the real scholar is concerned, is an unending process, and knowledge is pushed forward only a very little by his best efforts. And it is evident, of course, that the most you can contribute to a man in his undergraduate years is not equipment in the exact knowledge which is characteristic of the scholar, but an inspiration of the spirit of scholarship. The most that you can give a youngster is the spirit of the scholar.

Now the spirit of the scholar in a country like ours must be a spirit related to the national life. It cannot, therefore, be a spirit of pedantry. I suppose that this is a sufficient working conception of pedantry to say that it is knowledge divorced from life. It is knowledge so closeted, so desecrated, so stripped of the significances of life itself, that it is a thing apart and not connected with the vital processes in the world about us.

There is a great place in every nation for the spirit of scholarship, and it seems to me that there never was a time when the spirit of scholarship was more needed in affairs than it is in this country at this time.

We are thinking just now with our emotions and not with our minds, we are moved by impulse and not by judgment. We are drawing away from things with blind antipathy. The spirit of knowledge is that you must base your conclusions on adequate grounds. Make sure that you are going to the real sources of knowledge, discovering what the real facts are before you move forward to the next process, which is the process of clear thinking. By clear thinking I do not mean logical thinking. I do not mean that life is based upon any logical system whatever. Life is essentially illogical. The world is governed now by a tumultuous sea of commonalities made up of passions, and we should pray God that the good passions should out-vote the bad passions. But the movement of impulse, of motive, is the stuff of passion, and therefore clear thinking about life is not logical, symmetrical thinking, but it is interpretative thinking, thinking that sees the secret motive of things, thinking that penetrates deepest places where are the pulses of life.

Now scholarship ought to lay these impulses bare just as the physician can lay bare the seat of life in our bodies. That is not scholarship which goes to work upon the mere formal pedantry of logical reasoning, but that *is* scholarship which searches for the heart of man. The spirit of scholarship gives us catholicity of thinking, the readiness to understand that there will constantly swing into our ken new items not dreamed of in our systems of philosophy, not simply to draw our conclusions from the data that we have had, but that all this is under constant mutation, and that therefore new phases of life will come upon us and a new adjustment of our conclusions will be necessary. Our thinking must be detached and disinterested thinking.

The particular objection that I have to the undergraduate forming his course of study on his future profession is this— that from start to finish, from the time he enters the university until he finishes his career, his thought will be centered upon particular interests. He will be immersed in the things that touch his profit and loss, and a man is not free to think inside that territory. If his bread and butter is going to be affected, if he is always thinking in the terms of his own profession, he is not thinking for the nation. He is thinking for himself, and whether he be conscious of it or not, he can never throw these trammels off. He will only think as a doctor, or a lawyer, or a banker. He will not be free in the world of knowledge and in the circle of interests which make up the great citizenship of the country. It is necessary that the spirit of scholarship should be a detached, disinterested spirit, not immersed in a particular interest. That is the function of scholarship in a country like ours, to supply, not heat, but light, to suffuse things with the calm radiance of reason, to see to it that men do not act hastily, but that they act considerately, that they obey the truth whether they know it or not. The fault of our age is the fault of hasty action, of premature judgments, of a preference for ill-considered action over no action at all. Men who insist upon standing still and doing a little thinking before they do any acting are called reactionaries. They want actually to react to a state in which they can be allowed to think. They want for a little while to withdraw from the turmoil of party controversy and see where they stand before they commit themselves and their country to action from which it may not be possible to withdraw.

The whole fault of the modern age is that it applies to everything a false standard of efficiency. Efficiency with us is accomplishment, whether the accomplishment be by just and well-considered means or not; and this standard of achievement it is that is debasing the morals of our age, the intellectual morals of our age. We do not stop to do things thoroughly; we do not stop to know why we do things. We see an error and we hastily correct it by a greater error; and then go on to cry that the age is corrupt.

And so it is, gentlemen, that I try to join the function of the university with the great function of the national life. The life of this country is going to be revolutionized and purified only when the universities of this country wake up to the fact that their only reason for existing is intellect, that the objects that I have set forth, so far as undergraduate life is concerned, are the only legitimate objects. And every man should crave for his university primacy in these things, primacy in other things also if they may be brought in without enmity to it, but the sacrifice of everything that stands in the way of that.

For my part, I do not believe that it is athleticism which stands in the way. Athletics have been associated with the achievements of the mind in many a successful civilization. There is no difficulty in uniting vigor of body with achievement of mind, but there is a good deal of difficulty in uniting the achievement of the mind with a thousand distracting social influences, which take up all our ambitions, which absorb all our thoughts, which lead to all our arrangements of life, and then leave the university authorities the residuum of our attention, after we are through with the things that we are interested in. We absolutely changed the whole course of study at Princeton and revolutionized the methods of instruction without rousing a ripple on the surface of the alumni. They said those things are intellectual, they were our business. But just as soon as we thought to touch the social part of the university, there was not only a ripple, but the whole body was torn to its depths. We had touched the real things. These lay in triumphal competition with the province of the mind, and men's attention was so absolutely absorbed in these things that it was impossible for us to get their interest enlisted on the real undertakings of the university itself.

Now that is true of every university that I know anything about in this country, and if the Faculties in this country want to recapture the ground that they have lost, they must begin pretty soon, and they must go into the battle with their bridges burned behind them so that it will be of no avail to retreat. If I had a voice to which the university men of this country might listen, that is the endeavor to which my ambition would lead me to call.

THE BENEFITS OF UNIVERSITY TRAINING [1]

By John Henry Newman

To-day I have confined myself to saying that that training of the intellect, which is best for the individual himself, best enables him to discharge his duties to society. The Philosopher, indeed, and the man of the world differ in their very notion, but the

---

[1] From *The Idea of a University.*

methods, by which they are respectively formed, are pretty much the same. The Philosopher has the same command of matters of thought, which the true citizen and gentleman has of matters of business and conduct. If then a practical end must be assigned to a University course, I say it is that of training good members of society. Its art is the art of social life, and its end is fitness for the world. It neither confines its views to particular professions on the one hand, nor creates heroes or inspires genius on the other. Works indeed of genius fall under no art; heroic minds come under no rule; a University is not a birthplace of poets or of immortal authors, of founders of schools, leaders of colonies, or conquerors of nations. It does not promise a generation of Aristotles or Newtons, or Napoleons or Washingtons, of Raphaels or Shakespeares, though such miracles of nature it has before now contained within its precincts. Nor is it content on the other hand with forming the critic or the experimentalist, the economist or the engineer, though such too it includes within its scope. But a University training is the great ordinary means to a great but ordinary end; it aims at raising the intellectual tone of society, at cultivating the public mind, at purifying the national taste, at supplying true principles to popular enthusiasm and fixed aims to popular aspiration, at giving enlargement and sobriety to the ideas of the age, at facilitating the exercise of political power, and refining the intercourse of private life. It is the education which gives a man a clear conscious view of his own opinions and judgments, a truth in developing them, an eloquence in expressing them, and a force in urging them. It teaches him to see things as they are, to go right to the point, to disentangle a skein of thought, to detect what is sophistical, and to discard what is irrelevant. It prepares him to fill any post with credit, and to master any subject with facility. It shows him how to accommodate himself to others, how to throw himself into their state of mind, how to bring before them his own, how to influence them, how to come to an understanding with them, how to bear with them. He is at home in any society, he has common ground with every class; he knows when to speak and when to be silent; he is able to converse, he is able to listen; he can ask a question pertinently, and gain a lesson seasonably, when he has nothing to impart himself; he is ever ready, yet never in the way; he is a pleasant companion, and a comrade you can depend upon; he knows when to be serious and when to trifle, and he has a sure tact which enables him to trifle with gracefulness and to be serious with effect. He has the repose of a mind which lives in itself, while it lives in the world, and which has resources for its happiness at home when it cannot go abroad. He has a gift which serves him in public, and supports him in retirement, without which good fortune is but vulgar, and with which failure and disappointment have a charm. The art which tends to make a man all this, is in the object which it pursues as useful as the art of wealth or the art of health, though it is less susceptible of method, and less tangible, less certain, less complete in its result.

The Rabid Versus the Harmless Scholar [1]

By Louise Imogen Guiney

A Philosopher now living, and too deserving for any fate but choice private oblivion, was in Paris, for the first time, a dozen years ago; and having seen and heard there, in the shops, parks, and omnibus stations, much more baby than he found pleasing, he remarked, upon his return, that it was a great pity the French, who are so in love with system, had never seen their way to shutting up everything under ten years of age! Now, that was the remark of an artist in human affairs, and may provoke a number of analogies. What is in the making is not a public spectacle. It ought to be considered criminal, on the death of a painter or a poet, to exhibit those rough first drafts, which he, living, had the acumen to conceal. And if, to an impartial eye, in a foreign city, native innocents should seem too aggressively to the fore, why should not the seclusion desired for them be visited a thousandfold upon the heads, let us say, of students, who are also in a crude transitional state, and undergoing a

[1] From *Patrins*. Reprinted by permission of Miss Grace Guiney.

growth much more distressing to a sensitive observer than the physical? Youth is the most inspiring thing on earth, but not the best to let loose, especially while it carries swaggeringly that most dangerous of all blunderbusses, knowledge at half-cock. There is, indeed, no more melancholy condition than that of healthy boys scowling over books in an eternal protest against their father Adam's fall from a state of relative omniscience. Sir Philip Sidney thought it was "a piece of the Tower of Babylon's curse that a man should be put to school to learn his mother-tongue." The throes of education are as degrading and demoralizing as a hanging, and, when the millennium sets in, will be carefully screened from the laity. Around the master and the pupil will be reared a portly and decorous Chinese wall, which shall pen within their proper precincts the din of *hic, haec, hoc,* and the steam of suppers sacrificed to Pallas.

The more noxious variety of student, however, is not young. He is "in the midway of this our mortal life"; he is fearfully foraging, with intent to found and govern an academy; he runs in squads after Anglo-Saxon or Comparative Mythology; he stops you on 'change to ask if one has not good grounds for believing that there was such a person as Pope Joan. He can never let well enough alone. Heine must be translated and Junius must be identified. The abodes of hereditary scholars are depopulated by the red flag of the *nouveau instruit.* He infests every civilized country: the army-worm is nothing to him. He has either lacked early discipline altogether, or gets tainted, late in life, with the notion that he has never shown sufficiently how intellectual he is. In every contemplative-looking person he sees a worthy victim, and his kindling eye, as he bears down upon you, precludes escape: he can achieve no peace unless he is driving you mad with all which you fondly dreamed you had left behind in old S's accursed lecture-room. You may commend to him, in vain, the reminder which Erasmus left for the big-wigs, that it is the quality of what you know which tells, and never its quantity. It is inconceivable to him that you should shut your impious teeth against First Principles, and fear greatly to displace in yourself the illiteracies you have painfully acquired.

Judge, then, if the learner of this type (and in a bitterer degree, the learneress) could be safely cloistered, how much simpler would become the whole problem of living! How profoundly would it benefit both society and himself could the formationary mind, destined, as like as not, to no ultimate development, be sequestered by legal statute in one imperative limbo, along with babes, lovers, and training athletes! *Quicquid ostendis mihi sic, incredulus odi.*

For the true scholar's sign-manual is not the midnight lamp on a folio. He knows; he is baked through; all superfluous effort and energy are over for him. To converse consumedly upon the weather, and compare notes as to "whether it is likely to hold up for to-morrow,"—this, says Hazlitt, "is the end and privilege of a life of study." Secretly, decently, pleasantly, has he acquired his mental stock; insensibly he diffuses, not always knowledge, but sometimes the more needful scorn of knowledge. Among folk who break their worthy heads indoors over Mr. Browning and Madame Blavatsky, he moves cheerful, incurious, and free, on glorious good terms with arts and crafts for which he has no use, with extraneous languages which he will never pursue, with vague Muses impossible to invite to dinner. He is strictly noneducational.

> "Thou wast not born for death, immortal bird!
> No hungry generations tread thee down."

He loathes information, and the givers and takers thereof. Like Mr. Lang, he laments bitterly that Oxford is now a place where many things are being taught and learned with very great vigor. The main business, to him, is to live gracefully, without mental passion, and to get off alone into a corner for an affectionate view of creation. A mystery serves his turn better than a history. It is to be remembered that had the Reverend Laurence Sterne gone to gaze upon the spandrils of Rouen, we should have lost the *fille de chambre,* the dead ass, and Maria by the brookside. Any one of these is worth more than hieroglyphics; but who is to attain that insight that these are so, except the man of culture, who has the courage to forget at times even his sole science, and fall back with delight upon a choice assortment of ignorances?

The scholar's own research, from his cradle, clothes him in privacy; nor will he ever invade the privacy of others. It is not with a light heart that he contemplates the kindergarten system. He himself, holding his tongue, and fleeing from Junius and Pope Joan, from cubic roots and the boundaries of Hindostan, must be an evil sight to Chautauquans, albeit approved of the angels. By much contact shine divers and sundry; he, not inferior, fears lest it tarnish him. He has little to utter which will sound wise, the full-grown, finished soul! If he had, he would of his own volition seek a cell in that asylum for protoplasms, which we have made bold to recommend.

The truth is, very few can be trusted with an education. In the old days, while this was a faith, boredom and nervous prostration were not common, and social conditions were undeniably dramatic. Then, as now, quiet was the zenith of power: the mellow mind was unexcursive and shy. Then, as now, though the young clerical Masters of Arts went staggering abroad with heads lolling like Sisyphus' stone, the ideal worth and weight grew "lightly as a flower." Sweetly wrote the good Sprat of his famous friend Cowley: "His learning sat exceedingly close and handsomely upon him: it was not embossed on his mind, but enameled." The best to be said of any knowing one among us, is that he does not readily show what deeps are in him; that he is unformidable, and reminds those whom he meets of a distant or deceased uncle. Initiation into noble facts has not ruined him for this world nor the other. It is a beautiful brag which James Howell, on his first going beyond sea, March the first, in the year sixteen hundred and eighteen, makes to his father. He gives thanks for "that most indulgent and costly Care you have been pleased, in so extraordinary a manner, to have had of my Breeding, (tho' but one child of Fifteen) by placing me in a choice Methodical Schoole so far distant from your dwelling, under a Learned (tho' Lashing) Master; and by transplanting me thence to Oxford to be graduated; and soe holding me still up by the chin, until I could swim without Bladders. This patrimony of liberale Education you have been pleased to endow

me withal, I now carry along with me abroad as a sure inseparable Treasure; nor do I feele it any burden or incumbrance unto
me at all!"

There, in the closing phrase, spoke the post-Elizabethan pluck.
Any man does well since, who can describe the aggregated agonies
of his brain as no incumbrance, as less, indeed, than a wife and
posterity! To have come to this is to earn the freedom of cities,
and to sink the schoolmaster as if he had never been.

EXERCISES

1. In the two selections from Newman note the repetition of
sentence beginnings. What elements give to Newman's style the
impression of elevation, of being held evenly in the air? Be specific, not vague in answering this question.

2. Have you found your college or university a place "in which
the intellect may safely range and speculate"?

3. Could Mr. Meiklejohn have improved his essay by allusion,
illustration, and example? Suggest some which he might safely
and profitably have used.

4. Is Professor Munro "smart-alecky" in his style and diction?
Or are both eminently fitted for the job he has undertaken?

5. List Pater's adjectives in "The Tree of Knowledge." Compare them with Stevenson in "A Gossip On Romance." What do
they indicate about the men who selected them?

6. Study the last long sentence in Pater's first paragraph. What
gives it its distinct rhythmic quality. Does the diction help in the
musical effect?

7. Why is *tyrannous reality* an especially fine term?

8. Study Pater's last sentence in the selection, and apply it to
your own experience with books. If your instructor ever allows
you your own choice of a subject, why not use "Truant Reading."

9. Consider in Mr. Wilson's next to last paragraph his comment on social activities. His speech was delivered in 1908. How
pregnant are his remarks in the light of twenty years after?

10. Is Newman's university-trained man an impossible ideal?
Can you think of a quality which he lacks?

11. "A mystery serves his turn better than a history." Consider
this thought, apply it, illustrate it, dwell with it.

12. Would Miss Guiney's "true scholar" fit into a college fra-

ternity or boarding-house? Would he fit ideally into a class-room?

13. Miss Guiney herself should form the material for an oral theme, presented before the class. In preparation of such a theme, read her *Patrins* from which this is taken, and then read her *Life and Letters* by Alice Brown. Hers is one of the great but little known names of our literature. Discover in her own life that which makes this essay so apposite.

14. Why, do you think, no really successful American novel reflecting college life has ever been written? Consider this carefully. Does literature always reflect life or does life perhaps reflect literature? Does the life of young people of college age today in any way reflect the literature of the age? This is an interesting question.

SUGGESTED READINGS

Angell, James Rowland, "The Over-Population of the College," *Harper's Magazine,* October 1927.

Anonymous, "Colleges and Religion," by an Instructor, *Scribner's Magazine,* May 1922.

Bell, Bernard Iddings, "The Church and the Undergraduate," *The Atlantic Monthly,* April 1928. "What Is It All About?" *The Atlantic Monthly,* July 1927.

Benson, Arthur Christopher, *From a College Window,* Putnam's, New York.

Brandon, Frank, "Good Business," *The Atlantic Monthly,* November 1925.

Carlson, Avis D., "Beauty and Religion," *Harper's,* March 1928.

Dewey, John, "American Education and Culture, *The New Republic,* July 1, 1916.

De Voto, Bernard, "The Co-ed: The Hope of Liberal Education," *Harper's Magazine,* September 1927.

Drew, Elizabeth, "Literature in College," *The Atlantic Monthly,* January 1923.

Eliot, Charles W., *The Durable Satisfactions of Life,* Crowell, New York.

Gauss, Christian, "Should Johnny Go to College," *Scribner's Magazine,* October 1927.

Gerould, Gordon Hall, "What is 'English'?," *Scribner's Magazine,* September 1927.

Holmes, Henry W., "Chaos or Cosmos in American Education," *The Atlantic Monthly,* October 1927.

Hudson, Jay William, *The College and New America,* D. Appleton, New York. *The Truths We Live By,* D. Appleton, New York.

James, William, "The Social Value of the College Bred," *McClure's Magazine,* Vol. 30, p. 419. See also *College Readings in English Prose,* Scott and Zeitlin, Macmillan, New York.

Johnson, Gerald, "Should Our Colleges Educate," *Harper's Magazine,* November 1927.

Lowell, A. Lawrence, "The Art of Examination," *The Atlantic Monthly,* January 1926.

Meiklejohn, Alexander, *The Liberal College,* Marshall Jones, Boston.

Pressey, Benfield, "He Asked the Dean," *The Atlantic Monthly,* November 1925.

Rubinow, I. M., "The Revolt of a Middle-Aged Father," *The Atlantic Monthly,* May 1927.

Swisher, Walter Samuel, "Changelings at Our Hearthside," *The Atlantic Monthly,* May 1926.

CHAPTER IV

Points of View and Minor Prejudices

In Hazlitt's fine essay, "On Going a Journey," a part of which is included in the preceding pages, there is a sentence which ably distinguishes the desultory essays which follow from those which deal more weightily with more weighty matters. "I want," he writes, "to see my vague notions float like the down of a thistle before the breeze, and not to have them entangled in the briars and thorns of controversy." In other words, he wants to indulge his pet prejudices and points of view by himself without presenting them for serious discussion or refutation.

Only those few persons in the world who are absolutely without humor are strangers to Hazlitt's mood. Most of us harbor pet prejudices of no great consequence to any one save ourselves. We like to indulge ourselves in them, to storm about them occasionally to sympathetic and longsuffering friends, to laugh at ourselves for now and then becoming disturbed by them. They are hardly stout enough to be termed *beliefs*. We do not care to force them with any degree of seriousness upon others, nor do we in point of fact hold them too seriously ourselves. When we talk or write about them, we do not assume the attitude of the reformer or the preacher. Our manner is less anxious, more random than theirs. As a matter of fact, we enjoy our prejudices, and the last thing we want to do in writing of them is to make our readers uncomfortable.

All this does not for a moment mean that we are not at all serious about these points of view of ours. There is a large grain of sincerity in our respective attitudes; but it is not primarily the sincerity which is motivating our desire to write. Frederick Allen beneath all his humor without doubt entertains

561

his own skepticism about the efficacy of intelligence tests; Walter Prichard Eaton, one feels very sure, hates the early morning smile; Frank Moore Colby is honestly distressed over a deplorable attitude on the part of certain Americans; and I have it straight from Mr. Philip Curtiss that he despises, nay loathes, the game of bridge. And yet, as I said before, the motivation of such essays is not primarily sincerity of attitude or purpose. One is willing to wager that Mr. Allen, Mr. Eaton, Mr. Colby, and Mr. Curtiss all wrote principally because they themselves enjoyed giving vent to their respective prejudices and because they knew perfectly well they could be amusing and entertaining in so doing. The cherishing of the prejudices was one form of self-indulgence and the expressing of them was another. And we are grateful for both!

As a background for such writing as this, you should read, in addition to the four models given, the contributions to "The Lion's Mouth" in several numbers of *Harper's Magazine* and also those in "The Contributors' Club" of *The Atlantic Monthly*. These are the best current sources for the expression of minor prejudices. You should also find especially enjoyable and helpful the essays suggested on the reading list by such authors as Samuel McChord Crothers, Stephen Leacock, and Agnes Repplier.

After reading plentifully from such sources, you should reach the following conclusions:

1. No themes based on points of view and minor prejudices should be overly serious. Addison and Steele, who were never bitter, had a far greater following than the gloomy and disgruntled Swift.

2. The writer should aim always to leave his reader thoughtful, but also amused and tolerant.

3. No such theme needs be thorough or exhaustive in treatment. It is after all a comment, not a conclusion.

4. The author is frankly individual in his point of view, and he can safely talk about himself as much as he pleases.

5. The tone of such themes is unstrained and easy.

6. There needs to be no systematic plan as in the handling of more weighty ideas and judgments. This does not mean that

organization should be lacking, but that the unity of the theme should in the main be gained by tone and feeling rather than by structure.

7. A wealth of anecdote, incident, detail, and allusion is of great value in such work as this.

8. A tone of quiet satire is indispensable; and if one chooses to exaggerate generously for the sake of humor, only the humorless will object.

In Regard to Backgrounds [1]

By F. M. Colby

I have been snubbed so long by cultivated people that I have learned how to snub myself, and I believe I could be almost eloquent in rebuking the sort of vulgarity that I am about to confess. I hate the self-improved, traveled American whom I meet in books and periodicals. I hate him for what seems to me the servility of his spirit in the presence of other people's past. I dare say it may be because I envy him his superior travel and refinement. That is what the cultivated person always implies, and he wonders how any one, in view of the national crudity, can have the heart to find fault with these missionaries of taste from a riper culture who have learned the value of artistic *milieux* and literary backgrounds. After all, he says, what Henry James would call the "European scene" may still be commended to Americans, and surely it is just as well that they should be reminded now and then of what Prof. Barrett Wendell used so admirably to term their "centuries of social inexperience." As he goes on I not only feel that I am coarse, but I like the feeling of it.

I have never been in Poughkeepsie and I have never been in Venice, and so far as direct esthetic personal consequences to myself of golden hours of dalliance in the two places are concerned, I am therefore unable to offer a comparison. But during my life I have met many returned travelers from Venice and from

[1] Reprinted by the kind permission of Mrs. Colby and of *Harper's Magazine*.

Poughkeepsie, and I have read or listened to their narratives with as much attention as they could reasonably demand. Theoretically I accept the opinion of enlightened persons that Venice is superior, in respect to what educators call its "cultural value," to Poughkeepsie. Practically, and judging merely from the effects upon the respective visitors, I am all for Poughkeepsie. I have never met a man who returned from Poughkeepsie talking like the stray pages of a catalogue, of which he had a complete copy before he started. Poughkeepsie never took away part of a man's mind and replaced it with a portion of an encyclopedia. Nobody ever came back from Poughkeepsie damaged as a man and yet inferior as a magazine article. For the careless person I should recommend Venice; for the culture-seeker, Poughkeepsie. Overstrain, that misery of the conscientious self-improving man, with its disagreeable effects upon other people, could be avoided in Poughkeepsie. Out of the essays on Venice that I have read, nine were written by fish out of water who might have swum easily and perhaps with grace in the artistic currents of Poughkeepsie.

A self-improved American delivered an apologetic discourse the other day on the American deficiency in backgrounds. Culture cannot take root, he said; families float; everybody dies in a town he was not born in; art bombinates in a vacuum; literature gathers no moss; manners, when they exist at all, are accidental; history is clean gone out of our heads, while every Englishman is familiar with Bannockburn; poetry cannot be written, and it is foolish to try on account of the dearth of venerable circumstance; no traditions, no memories, no inheritance—in fact, no past at all; not even a present of any consequence, but only a future; and into this future every man, woman, and child in the whole foolish country is moving—though it is not through any fault of theirs; the unfortunate creatures really have no other place to go to.

I bear no grudge against the author of this discourse as an individual, but only as a type. Indeed, I am not sure that he is an individual or that I have reported him correctly, for no sooner does any one begin in this manner than his words run into the words of others, forming a river of sound, and I think not of one man, but of strings of them—all worrying about the lack of backgrounds, like the man who cast no shadow in the sun. I deny that it is any one's voluntary attitude; it is a lockstep that began before I was born, and I have no doubt it will continue indefinitely. Seven centuries after Columbus's injudicious discovery they will still be complaining, with a Baedeker in their hands, of the fatal youth of North America. For they live long, these people, because, as in certain lower orders of animal life, apparently, there is hardly any life worth losing, and the family likeness they bear to one another is astonishing. The very ones that George William Curtis used to satirize as shining in society are still to be found among us at this moment, but they are engaged for the most part in contributing to the magazines. In one respect they seem more the slaves of other people's backgrounds even than Mrs. Potiphar was. Mrs. Potiphar only believed that the right sort of liveries were not produced in this country, whereas they swear that the right sort of literature can never be produced in this country—or at least not till our backgrounds are ever so many centuries thicker than they are now. I am unable, looking back, to see any value whatever in these decades of sheer sterile complaint of sterility, because no ruins can be seen against the sky, because no naiads are dreamed of in the Hudson or mermaids in Cape Cod Bay, and because most people who are born in Indianapolis seem glad to get away from it when they can.

For one sign that we have changed too fast I can produce two signs that we have not changed half fast enough. If there is no moss here on the walls of ancient battlements there is plenty of moss in our heads, and, so far as tenacity of tradition is concerned, I can produce a dozen United States Senators who are fully as picturesque, if only you will regard them internally, as the quaintest peasant in the quaintest part of France. Backgrounds are not lost here just because we move about; backgrounds are simply worn inside, often with the ivy clustering on them. Who has not talked with some expatriated Boston man and found him as reposeful, as redolent of sad, forgotten, far-off things, as any distant prospect of Stoke-Pogis? In fact, it seems as if these pale expositors of backgrounds had merely visited the monuments they praise—*inside some Boston man!*—and that, I confess, is the most irritating thing to me about them. They have never really looked at anything themselves, but only learned from others what they ought to seem to see. And it is absurd to tax us with a lack of memory, when in some of our most exclusive literary circles there is notoriously nothing but a memory to be seen. There is too much Stoke-Pogis in a Boston man, if anything, in proportion to other things. Even the casual foreign visitor has noticed it.

Now I have great respect for the religion of the Quakers, whose name, I understand, comes from the phrase of a founder about quaking and shaking in the fear of the Lord. And if that is the real reason why they quake I believe they are justified not only in their quaking, but in trying to make other people quake. But these Delsartean literary quakers correctly tremulous in the presence of antiquity, these "cultured" minds, not only palsied by their own advantages, but intent on palsying others, bring back no good report to anybody in regard to the good things in the world. Any one had as lief be stung by a gymnotus, as affected as they are by the contemplation of a masterpiece.

I do not know whether a poet, like a sugar beet, requires a soil with peculiar properties; and, in regard to the poet, I do not know what the peculiar properties ought to be. Zoning of verse, comparative literary crop statistics, mean annual density of ideas, ratio of true poetry to square miles and population within a given period, are all outside my limitations. The theory that bone-dust fertilizers are the things for poets does not always seem to work, even when the bone-dust is that of the Crusaders, and I have read lyrics from cathedral towns which, though infinitely more decorous than the brass band of my native village, were equally remote from literature. Still there may be something in it. But I do know, even better than I wish I did, two generations of writers on the theme, who have been saying, with hardly any deviation in their phrases, that this is the land where poets cannot grow; and I know them for the sort of persons who, if by chance a poet should grow in defiance of their theory, could not tell him from a sugar beet. They are unaware of any growing thing which stands before them unaccompanied by bibliography. Unless there were antecedent books about an object they would not know that the object was a poet.

On Being Cheerful Before Breakfast [1]

By Walter Prichard Eaton

I live in a house which admits of less privacy than is desirable and decent before breakfast. As a result, I was recently restrained only with difficulty from committing murder. We had a guest, an otherwise estimable female, who rose cheerful. On the very first morning of her visit she turned on the bath and an aria from "Aïda" at the same moment. I am a reasonable being, and I do not object to cleanliness before coffee, but I am also human, and I do object to cheerfulness. To sing while dressing is a sign either of pathologically good health or a vacant mind. In either case, there is no punishment to fit the crime unless it be to arouse the criminal from the depths of that delicious morning drowse by the loud singing of hymns, and compelling him (or her) to remain awake by listening to a recital from the pages of a "glad" book.

Breakfast itself is an odd meal, and the laxity allowed is an admission of the normal state which precedes it. "Luncheon at one," or "Dinner at seven-thirty," we say. But, "Come down to breakfast any time you feel like it." At luncheon or dinner, too, a guest is expected, and expects, to eat what is placed before him. Not so at breakfast. His individual tastes are carefully consulted, and no two ever concur. One has tea, another coffee. One has cereal, another never touches it. Some quaint appetites demand meat. Now and then comes a kindred spirit who understands the delectable art of dipping doughnuts into a coffee-cup. But, one and all, must, at breakfast, be allowed to get into a rut

[1] Reprinted by the kind permission of the author and of *Harper's Magazine*.

of habit, as if the day could not be started unless that initial track were taken—as, indeed, it probably could not be. Once, when visiting, we ourself ate steak and buckwheat cakes for breakfast, and all that day we moved as in a dream!

Why, indeed, should it not be so? To spring lightly out of bed, wide awake and cheerful, is done only by characters in stories, and the pathologically healthy in real life. Not even in childhood does the normal person spring lightly and happily out of bed. What task is more difficult than getting a small boy up in the morning—unless it be getting him to bed at night? Even he, without a care in the world, with no consciousness of his stomach, is cross and snappy before breakfast, or drugged with the opiate of dreams. As for us adults, when we rise with sleep still heavy upon us, with yesterday's fatigue not quite gone from our muscles, with the insistent morning void in the pit of our modern, hyperacidulous stomachs, with a dull, half-conscious realization that here is another day to put us by so much nearer middle-age, what wonder that we are not cheerful, that we want to be left alone, to drink our coffee in silence, and, by filling the aforementioned void, and slipping thus pleasantly into the chains of habit, to resume at last our wonted way? To eat breakfast is to pick up again the job of living, after a vacation in dreams. It is not lightly to be undertaken.

It is not a lack of hospitality which makes me dread the coming of visitors; it is the fear that some of them may be sincerely, or politely, pleasant before breakfast. What is harder to endure than the guest who comes beaming down the stairs with a cheery, "Well, how are you all this lovely morning?"—unless it be the guest who actually goes out-of-doors before coffee, and comes in to tell us how perfectly heavenly everything is with the dew fresh upon it—as if it were not much fresher at eight o'clock the previous evening! Even the guest who discusses bolshevism at breakfast is preferable to this variety, because nobody is cheerful on the subject of bolshevism, either pro or con. Argument is better than amiability, at any rate.

I have a friend, a plump and pleasing person, a charming and thoughtful hostess, who has had the courage to solve the problem in her country home. Prominently displayed in the upper hall is a neat sign, reading as follows:

GUESTS ARE REQUESTED NOT TO BE CHEERFUL
BEFORE BREAKFAST

It is surprising to some, who have not given the matter thought, to find how many people are almost pathetically grateful for this brave abolition of the social tyranny of politeness before the morning meal. For all of us, in this matter, have been keeping up a painful pretense on all our visits, all our lives. Tell us, at last, that we can be as cross or as glum or as taciturn as we like, and we are almost cheerful at the prospect. This, to be sure, is more especially true of men. When a woman is visiting, she wouldn't feel quite natural if she weren't a bit unnatural.

They will deny this, of course.

THESE INTELLIGENCE TESTS [1]

By Frederick L. Allen

Last October I had to take a literacy test. I had recently moved to New York State, and it appeared that I could not vote in the election unless I either produced a school or college diploma or certificate, or passed a literacy test; and though I searched the house from top to bottom, not a single certificate could I find. I found documents which to my simple mind seemed to bear on the case, such as college class reports with my name in them, and letters which mentioned my being in the publishing business (a fact which ought to establish at least a fair presumption in my favor); yet when I took them to the local schoolhouse and showed them to the State of New York as embodied in the person of its authorized agent, the school-mistress, I was told they wouldn't do. The law said certificates, and these were not certificates. So I laughed a little nervously and sat down in the schoolroom to take the test, in a tiny chair

[1] Reprinted by the kind permission of the author and of *Harper's Magazine*.

before a tiny desk designed for a child of eight, and a little deficient in knee room for a child of thirty-four.

It was a formidable paper which the schoolmistress set before me. First I had to write my name and address, which I did with great care. Then came a series of detailed directions to the effect that I was to read the paragraph of text which followed and write out the answers to some questions bearing on it. The paragraph began somewhat as follows:

Theodore Roosevelt was a great American. His letters to his children have been collected in a book since his death. He was interested in animals and birds. He read many books and magazines. . . .

It ran on in this sprightly and coherent style for some distance. Then came the questions:

1. Who was a great American?
2. What has been done to his letters to his children since his death?
3. What was he interested in?
4. What did he read?

And so forth.

I started to answer the first question when suddenly (as sometimes happens) a thought struck me.

One of the candidates for Governor of New York State in the coming election was named Theodore Roosevelt—and here were humble citizens like myself, of doubtful literacy, being subtly subjected to propaganda on his behalf. Was I to submit to any such nefarious scheme? I was not. I resolved to write:

1. Alfred E. Smith; and still is.

They would throw me out of the schoolhouse for an illiterate fellow, but I would appeal the case. If necessary I would carry it to the Supreme Court, where able counsel would argue brilliantly that *Alfred E. Smith; and still is* was a demonstrably literate reply. There would be a triumphant vindication, and—

But suddenly I cooled. By that time Election Day would be past, and I should have lost my vote. No, there was a better way. So very firmly I seized my pencil and wrote *Theodore Roosevelt*. I received a certificate of literacy, and a few weeks later I went to the polls—and you all know the result.

I had almost forgotten the incident when the other day I picked up a set of the intelligence tests prepared by the learned ones of Columbia University for the selection of young Columbians. As I looked at them I marveled again—as I had marveled that day in the schoolroom—at the abject docility of mind which so many examiners seem to expect of their victims. To them there is only one right answer to any question—the one they had in mind when they framed it—and all others are wrong. If they want you to write *Theodore Roosevelt,* write it you must or flunk.

With most of the Columbia tests I had no quarrel. There were printed alphabets in which you were told to cross out the letter just after A and draw a line under the second letter after K; there were nice little problems in arithmetic, and pictures of rabbits with one ear missing in which you had to point out what was the matter with the rabbit. But soon appeared a lot of questions of a different sort. Each of these questions had several answers appended to it. The miserable examinee was instructed to mark a cross before the "best answer" to each question. No chance for argument; he would be given credit if he picked the right answer and lose credit if he picked the wrong one. For example:

> *When you are out of funds, should you—*
> *get to work and earn*
> *borrow from your friends*
> *write home to your people*
> *steal*

Now what on earth is the "best answer" to that question? I am willing to concede that the worst is *steal*. But as between the other three, it seems to me a toss-up, with the wise selection depending on the circumstances. Presumably *get to work and earn* is the answer favored on Morningside Heights: but to the average subfreshman I should certainly recommend writing home to his people, and to myself I should recommend borrowing, and then evening things up by striking the editor for more cash for my next contribution. Yet apparently there is no chance for the examinee to rise in his wrath and say, "That depends." He must pick the "right answer."

Here is another:

If you are lost in the forest in the daytime, what is the thing to do?

> go straight ahead to a big tree
> hurry to the nearest house you know of
> sit down and cry
> use the sun or compass for a guide

Now here is a very pretty problem, on which whole chapters could be written (and have been). The orthodox Boy Scout would say, *Use the sun or a compass for a guide;* but the only time I ever got lost in a forest the sun was well hidden by clouds and I had no compass—which shows that the kind of answer which will get you into Columbia won't always get you out of the woods. The fellow who would get lost in plain sunshine with a compass in his pocket would be such a nut that he ought to be admitted to a good safe campus and kept there.

There is something to be said for the answer, *Hurry to the nearest house you know of.* I happen to live in a thoroughly wooded suburb, a section so wooded that the real-estate agents sometimes pleasantly refer to it as a forest; and often visitors have told me that they got thoroughly mixed up driving around in the network of roads and succeeded in finding where I lived only by inquiring for me at the nearest house. Ought I to say to them, "Tut, tut, you should have used the sun or a compass for a guide"?

There are occasions when I should recommend going straight ahead to a big tree, climbing it, and getting a good look at the surrounding country, being very careful—and here is a real test of intelligence—not to climb out on the end of a dead branch.

But after all the most delightfully satisfactory answer is *sit down and cry*. There are few enough opportunities for a good long cry in this busy modern life of ours; so if you are all alone and there is nobody to tell you to move on, why not settle right down on a stump and enjoy yourself? Besides, after you have cried for a little while you may have a good idea about what to do next (such as not climbing out on the dead branch), or the sun may come out, or somebody may hear you and come along with a compass, or even point out the moss growing on the north side of a Doctor of Philosophy, thus enabling you to make your triumphal exit according to the best Boy Scout traditions.

In these tests there are also a number of sentences which the victim is to mark T if they could possibly be true and F if they could not; and several of these sentences seem to me equally debatable. For instance, take this one: *Coming down the hill on his bicycle the chain broke, but he rode back again to get it fixed.* I can see the examiners shaking their heads and saying, "Impossible." But who said it was a bicycle chain which broke? In my version of the incident our friend was carrying something heavy by means of a chain (very likely a dangling participle such as the examiner perpetrated in the sentence above) when the chain broke. No damage was done to his bicycle or any part thereof. Will Nicholas Murray Butler raise his right hand and swear to me that our friend could not ride back again (to the English department, let us say) to get the damage repaired?

Here is another: *Fearing that he might waken her patient by his impudent talk, the nurse gave the detested dummy what he wished.* "Impossible!" goes up the cry at Morningside Heights. But what if we were to tell them the whole sordid story? As I recall it, there were four men in the convalescent ward of a hospital, playing bridge. As the game progressed, one of them (who was not taking part in it at the moment) wandered off to the private corridor and, hateful creature that he was, demanded a kiss of a pretty nurse. Whereupon, fearing that he might awaken her patient by his impudent talk, the nurse gave the detested dummy what he wished. I am not quite sure what happened next, though it is my impression that the patient—a former Yale football star—had one eye open all the time and, despite his enfeebled condition, got up and spoiled the dummy for any more bridge that night, subsequently marrying the nurse, much to the regret of several eligible internes. Is it impossible? It is not. Yet if you, ardent bridge player that you are, were taking the examination and marked that sentence as possible, the scoring clerks would set you down as unintelligent.

I have nothing against intelligence tests or literacy tests or any other sort of tests as such. Personally I find them as diverting and twice as ingenious as cross-word puzzles. When I see a question like *a man whose salary is $16 a week spends $10 a week, in how many weeks can he save $300?* I like to see how soon I can get the answer, which is, of course, 50 weeks or more, depending on (a) his private income, and (b) the size of the doctor's bills resulting from his attempt to live on an insufficient diet. But I do wish examiners would try not to be so arbitrary. Young John Keats was a pretty intelligent boy and as Keats, '14, might have been spoken of as one of the more successful members of the Alumni Club of London; but what chance would he have had of picking the "best answer" if he had been up against something like this (which isn't from a Columbia test but might be)?

Mark a cross before the best answer to this question: What can ail thee, knight at arms, alone and palely loitering?
I have mislaid my compass
I have indigestion and my companions have deserted me
I voted for the Republican candidate for Governor of New York.
I met a lady in the meads.

THE BUNCOMBE OF THE BRIDGE TABLE [1]

By Philip Curtiss

Some days ago I took a solemn oath—never to touch a playing card again in my life, except, of course, as I might be called on

[1] Reprinted by the kind permission of the author and of *Harper's Magazine*.

to pick out the ace of spades for some amateur conjuror. Mumbledepeg, skipping the rope, squat tag, and such fine old field sports I shall continue to enjoy, and occasionally in the evening I may relax with a few fast hands of lotto or halma, but anything that depends on the accidental conjunction of a queen and a jack is out of my life for once and forever.

I do not mean to say that I shall actually *snub* card players when I meet them or that when a hostess brings forth the mahogany box of chips I shall put on my hat and walk out in pious dudgeon. I merely mean that when groups of my friends have finished their pleasant coffee and liqueurs and have sat down to snap at one another I shall retire into a corner with *The Life and Letters of Constantine, King of the Greeks,* or from time to time I may stroll and look idly over their shoulders with the amused detachment of one who watches an ant hill.

About such an oath, I realize, there is nothing novel. Coming, we will say, from a broker's clerk, intrusted habitually with large sums of money, it might connote a picture of a white face, a grieving wife, a smoke-filled room, and a forged note at five o'clock in the morning. Coming, however, from an author, whose profession numbers probably the worst card players in the world —unless they can be found among theological students—the oath will tend only to raise a smile. It will imply nothing more than the hint that on Saturday night I must have been rooked even worse than usual.

As a matter of fact, if either of these things were the truth my simple oath would not be worth recording, for the only oath of any possible interest to history is one that has a good chance of being kept, and among the millions of men who have taken this vow I am, I believe, one of the very few who have had a reasonable chance of success. I am not, in brief, swearing off cards because I have been ruined, because family hands are pulling at my coat tails, or because I have devoted to the green table time and thought that should have been devoted to the book of the year. I am swearing off cards simply and solely because I loathe cards, because I have always loathed cards, because I have never entered a game without a feeling of distaste and depression, and because for a quarter of a century the whole stupid business has bored me to tears.

Why, then, have I ever played or, having decided to stop, do I make all this fuss about it? Nice questions to ask in this year of grace 1928! All the social forces that in 1858 would have been brought against a man who *did* play cards are in 1928 brought against a man who *doesn't*. In 1858 if I had refused to play cards books would have been written about me and distributed to school libraries; leading bankers would have offered me junior clerkships, and my wife would have had me photographed with her hand on my shoulder. In 1928, if I do not play cards, I am a prig, a highbrow, a grouch, affected or unsocial, while as for my wife, poor soul, all that I get from her is a dirty look when she sees that I am on the point of refusing. In other words, a man who does not play cards to-day is one step lower than a man who doesn't drink. I, for one, cannot say that he isn't, but what I do object to is the common willingness to credit any reason for my refusal to play except the real one.

The most frequent belief is, of course, that I am a poor player and the most charitable is that I cannot afford it. Strangely I seldom lose much at card games if I really care to "play" them, that is to say, if I deliberately take out of them all elements of play and merely treat them like any other dismal little task I may encounter. In this I find that I am sustained by the highest authority, for the post of minor magistrate has brought me for several years into a humorous intimacy with a professional gambler. This man has never had any occupation in his life but card playing; he has saved money and bought real estate from his winnings, but he has, nevertheless, a widespread reputation for honesty, one of his favorite gestures being to play for an hour or all night without once taking the deal. Occasionally he acts as bondsman for some turbulent townsman, and one day when this errand had caused us both to linger in the empty courtroom, I asked him frankly for the rudiments of successful gambling.

His answer was as prompt and as dull as the rudiments of pawnbroking. "Time and the pickings" it was in effect; never overestimate even a good hand and, if you haven't a good hand, "drop," "pass," or "by."   "Ten dollars here and ten dollars there is the thing that does it.   What man like me is going to risk a night's work in a single throw?"

It was an observation that the dullest amateur could have made if he had given half the common sense to cards which he would give to a cucumber bed; but even so I still had a faint hope that from this master craftsman, this cold-blooded artisan, I might get some secret tip, some professional dodge that would enable me to mop up the tables and crow with triumph the next time I was called on to fill in.   I asked this directly, and my friend the gambler gave me a pitying smile.

"Judge," he replied, "no rule that I could give you would be any use in the crowd that you play with.   There can't be any such thing as real card playing when everybody at the table can afford to lose anything that's likely to be played for.   They may not like to lose it but it doesn't pinch 'em enough so's to teach 'em real play.   Think it over and you'll see what I mean.   One takes a flier, and at least half the table will follow and follow all the way.   *Somebody* will 'see' anything.   In a game like that hands don't have any real value.   All it amounts to is a series of showdowns and they might just as well play them 'cold.'   The man to whom a ten-dollar bill means the least will shoot the most often and so he will probably have the most money at the end of the game.   Set that same bunch to playing for a week's income or a month's income, the way the boys do down at my place, and you'd see some card playing; but over a question of eighteen or twenty dollars an evening no man of that sort is really going to use his brains."

"But how about bridge?" I asked him.   "Did you ever play bridge?"

"Sure, I've played bridge.   You bid in bridge, don't you, where you bet in poker?   What I'm telling you is good for any game where the player makes the running and there isn't any bank.   A damn fool with the cards and the money to back them can beat the best bridge player that ever lived.   The only reason he's a damn fool is that he doesn't always wait until he's got the cards."

So much for cards as a test of the intellect or financial genius, but how about the social element, about cards as a sport? The Mexicans, I believe, have bug races and every now and then in a shop window you will see a chance to win a motor car by guessing the correct number of units in a barrel of beans. For those who might regard it as keen fun to sit on the front steps and count the rain drops, I will admit that cards might be a legitimate sport, but the real tests of a sport are two, which are not as frequently emphasized as they might be.

The first test is this: A true sport must be one in which, at the crucial moment, skill, courage, will power, or wit can change the issue. In other words, it must be one that offers the player a chance to rise above his apparent fate. A blinded and beaten boxer *can* drag himself from the floor and with one last fling of his manhood knock out his unscarred opponent; but when cards come to their final issue no will power, no courage, no deftness, no spirituality, nor even any luck, can vitalize the value of a king and make it beat an ace. I realize all the reservations that can be made to this reasoning but, in strict logic, when the cards have been dealt on the table the possibilities of the game are over and the ultimate has been fixed.

The second test is that a true sport must be one which leaves both winner and loser with something of the same glow. From this aspect tennis is a true sport, and so are charades, if you are not over ten years old. Golf is only half a sport, for although it passes the first test with flying colors, it fails in the second. Baseball, as a rule, seems to pass both tests, and so does rowing; but football, under the second, is doubtful. Fox hunting is a perfect sport, if you don't mind the fox, and so is fishing, except for the fish. And in this connection, it might be noted that Englishmen, the world's truest sportsmen, are notable for sports which pass this second test. Indoors, billiards passes both tests and so, I am sorry to say, does a drinking bout, but card playing is the only pastime I can think of that fails miserably in both. If you believe that the bridge table leaves any glow in the loser and especially in the loser's partner—but why continue with the obvious?

Let us, rather, tell the truth and the whole truth that underlies the practice of modern card playing. Card playing in social gatherings (which is the only place where I am now considering it) is based on the tacit assumption that, out of ten persons asked to a dinner or for an evening, at least four will be individuals so near the line of total idiocy that they cannot be kept awake unless they are given something to do with their fingers. They cannot talk, they cannot banter within the limits of propriety (or, nowadays, outside of it), they cannot enjoy friendly silence in front of a fireplace, and they cannot listen to music. They are given playing cards as babies are given rattles and as prisoners are given hemp.

But why, again, if this is my opinion of cards, don't I just simply stop and say nothing? Why must I borrow the very spirit of cards and swear off with bombast and flourish? Because an imbecile oath of that kind is the only refusal that the card-playing mentality will ever understand. If at a dinner I said that I did not care for creamed onions, that would be the end of it. The lovers of onions would not begin to coax, jeer, threaten, and be offended until I had eaten onions or, at the least, insist that I "cut in" and eat half an onion.

On the other hand, to get rid of cards I cannot say that I do not like cards. I must intimate that I am so lost to cards that only by swearing to the gods in heaven can I keep from making myself a pig over them. My oath will satisfy card players because it will flatter card players. It will make them believe that I was once such as they but that, on one side or the other, I have failed where they have succeeded. The hell-bent, day-and-night players will believe that I was a dub who could not stand their pace and so fell by the wayside. The ordinary, casual players will assume that I was such an arch gambler that only by checking myself on the brink of perdition did I survive for my home and my country.

On the whole, I believe that in the end this will become the general tradition and that, quite by itself, my oath will give me the only amusement I shall ever have had from the card table. Deep questions of bridge and poker will be put to me as one of

the big men of yesterday.   Undoubtedly I shall be called on to
cut, deal, and perform other operations calling for the wisdom of
a spirited neutral.   I shall probably frighten young players when
I stand at their shoulders, and veterans will cast me a humorous
look when some one else plays the jack instead of the joker.   It
may even be that, looking in from the outside only, I shall learn
to like cards, as the Romans liked murder from the grandstand.
Very well.   I have no objection to that.   The only thing I will
not do with cards is play them.

EXERCISES

1. Study the literary and geographical allusions in Mr. Colby's
essay.   Why are they so especially good?

2. Mr. Allen's essay is made particularly delightful by his ability
to draw absurd pictures.   Study these

3. Find instances in these essays of humor attained by a mock-
seriousness of style.

4. Read Agnes Rogers Hyde's "The Modern School" in *Harper's Magazine* for December 1927.   This essay is done almost
entirely by dialogue.   What are the advantages and disadvantages
of this method?   Try to rewrite "In Regard to Backgrounds" in
the dialogue form.

5. Go through the issues of *The Atlantic Monthly* for two years
back and list the titles of the essays in "The Contributors' Club."
Read this list to the class plus fifty more titles which these have
suggested to you.   Do the same with "The Lion's Mouth" of
Harper's.   This is an excellent way to be of invaluable service not
only to the class but to the instructor.

6. Find instances in the essays given of the author's friendliness
toward the reader.   In what ways does he assume the reader's
intelligence?

7. Study Mr. Allen's "On Sleeping Outdoors" suggested on the
reading list.   Are his tactics the same as in "These Intelligence
Tests"?

8. Consider the following as titles for themes having a college
interest:

People Who Long "To Do Good."

The Card Index Expert.

College Intelligentsia.
The Girl Who is Always Late.
Unbuckled Galoshes.
Class-room Courtship.
Infirmary Technique.
The Eager Student.
The Long Paper Enthusiast.
Vocational Guiders.
The Expectant Escort.
Those Who "Hate New Books."
"Coöperative" Book Stores.
The Potential Phi Beta Kappa.
"Heard Melodies are Sweet, but Those Unheard are Sweeter."

SUGGESTED READINGS

Allen, F. L., "On Sleeping Outdoors," *The Century,* November 1913.

Beerbohm, Max, "An Infamous Brigade" from *More,* Dodd, Mead, New York.

Bennett, Charles A., "Winter Sports," *Harper's Magazine,* January 1928.

Conrad, Joseph, "Ocean Travel" from *Last Essays,* Doubleday, Doran, New York.

Contributors' Club, "Answer One to Ten," *The Atlantic Monthly,* November 1927. "Something in the Eye," *The Atlantic Monthly,* August 1927.

Crothers, Samuel McChord, "The Perils of the Literate" from *The Dame School of Experience,* Houghton Mifflin, Boston.

Hunt, Leigh, "Getting up on Cold Mornings," from *Essays.*

Hyde, Agnes Rogers, "The Modern School," *Harper's Magazine,* December 1927.

Leacock, Stephen, "My Friend the Reporter," *Harper's Magazine,* October 1927.

O'Keefe, Pierce, "The Hot Bath," *Harper's Magazine,* January 1928. "The Academy of Foules," *Harper's Magazine,* December 1927.

Repplier, Agnes, "The Customary Correspondent" from *Americans and Others,* Houghton Mifflin, Boston. "Goodness and Gayety" from the same.

Santayana, George, "An Apology for Snobs" from *Soliloquies in England,* Scribner's, New York.

Woodbridge, Elisabeth Morris, "The Tyranny of Facts" from *Days Out,* Houghton Mifflin, Boston.

Woolf, Virginia, "Illness—An Unexploited Mine," *The Forum,* April 1926.

CHAPTER V

THEMES BUILT UPON IDEAS, PERCEPTIONS, REFLECTION, IMAGINATION

A very good way to begin the reading of this chapter and the consideration of any themes which it may conceivably suggest is by an attempt to define, and thus to distinguish among, the words that make its title. What is an idea? From what word is it derived? Is it related to an ideal? How does it differ from an opinion, a belief, a point of view, a conviction, a conclusion? Is a perception the same thing as an impression? What is an intuition? Is it a perception? What is a notion? Did you ever question the term "notion counter"? What is the difference between fancy and imagination? What does the word, reflection, suggest? Nothing could be more interesting than a class discussion over these words, many of which are listed as synonyms, but every one of which unmistakably conveys to the thoughtful reader its own innate personality.

Having defined each to your own satisfaction if not to that of the majority of the class, you may well proceed to the reading of the essays and to any ideas, perceptions, reflections, images, notions, and fancies which they may inculcate, suggest, stimulate, present, nurture, implant, arouse, or inspire. One aim has been uppermost in the choosing of them: *to suggest new subjects for your thought and fancy to play upon*. In this last chapter concern over the material and the construction of your own themes has given way to the more anxious concern that *you* should appreciate to the full the fineness, suggestiveness, and originality of the essays themselves.

If you will turn back to Christopher Morley's essay on Francis Barton Gummere, you may read there how through their association with a great teacher the Haverford boys came to realize "the magical colors and tissues of the human mind, the rich perplexity and many-sided glamour of life." Those magical colors, that rich perplexity are here in abundance from Mr. Dana's delicate understanding of the spirit and soul in words to the wistful reflections and conclusions of Pater's Marius, pensively walking about the environs of Rome.

WORDS THAT LAUGH AND CRY [1]

By Charles Anderson Dana

Did it ever strike you that there was anything queer about the capacity of written words to absorb and convey feelings! Taken separately they are mere symbols with no more feeling to them than so many bricks, but string them along in a row under certain mysterious conditions and you find yourself laughing or crying as your eye runs over them. That words should convey mere ideas is not so remarkable. "The boy is fat," "the cat has nine tails," are statements that seem obviously enough within the power of written language. But it is different with feelings. They are no more visible in the symbols that hold them than electricity is visible on the wire; and yet there they are, always ready to respond when the right test is applied by the right person. That spoken words, charged with human tones and lighted by human eyes, should carry feelings, is not so astonishing. The magnetic sympathy of the orator one understands; he might affect his audience, possibly, if he spoke in a language they did not know. But written words: How can they do it! Suppose, for example, that you possess remarkable facility in grouping language, and that you have strong feelings upon some subject, which finally you determine to commit to paper. Your pen runs along, the words present themselves, or are dragged out, and fall into their places. You are a good deal moved; here you chuckle to yourself, and half a dozen of lines further down a lump comes into your throat, and perhaps you have to wipe

[1] From "Casual Essays of the *Sun*," by permission of the editor of New York *Sun*.

your eyes. You finish, and the copy goes to the printer. When it gets into print a reader sees it. His eye runs along the lines and down the page until it comes to the place where you chuckled as you wrote; then he smiles, and six lines below he has to swallow several times and snuffle and wink to restrain an exhibition of weakness. And then some one else comes along who is not so good a word juggler as you are, or who has no feelings, and swaps the words about a little, and twists the sentences; and behold the spell is gone, and you have left a parcel of written language duly charged with facts, but without a single feeling.

No one can juggle with words with any degree of success without getting a vast respect for their independent ability. They will catch the best idea a man ever had as it flashes through his brain, and hold on to it, to surprise him with it long after, and make him wonder that he was ever man enough to have such an idea. And often they will catch an idea on its way from the brain to the pen point, turn, twist, and improve on it as the eye winks, and in an instant there they are, strung hand in hand across the page and grinning back at the writer: "This is our idea, old man; not yours!"

As for poetry, every word that expects to earn its salt in poetry should have a head and a pair of legs of its own, to go and find its place, carrying another word, if necessary, on its back. The most that should be expected of any competent poet in regular practice is to serve a general summons and notice of action on the language. If the words won't do the rest for him, it indicates that he is out of sympathy with his tools.

But you don't find feelings in written words unless there were feelings in the man who used them. With all their apparent independence they seem to be little vessels that hold in some puzzling fashion exactly what is put into them. You can put tears into them, as though they were so many little buckets; and you can hang smiles along them, like Monday's clothes on the line, or you can starch them with facts and stand them up like a picket fence; but you won't get the tears out unless you first put them in. Art won't put them there. It is like the faculty of getting the quality of interest into pictures. If the quality exists in the artist's mind, he is likely to find means to get it into his pictures, but if it isn't in the man, no technical skill will supply it. So, if the feelings are in the writer and he knows his business, they will get into the words; but they must be in him first. It isn't the way the words are strung together that makes Lincoln's Gettysburg speech immortal, but the feelings that were in the man. But how do such little, plain words manage to keep their grip on such feelings? That is the miracle.

CASTLES IN SPAIN [1]

By John Galsworthy

We of the modern world, what do we dream of? What are our castles in Spain?

The thought came to me in Seville Cathedral, the stone fabric of man's greatest dream in those ages to which we have been accustomed to apply the word "dark." They who, traveling in Spain, consult their guide-books, may read these words: "On the eighth day of July in the year 1401 the Dean and Chapter of Seville assembled in the court of the elms and solemnly resolved: 'Let us build a church so great that those who come after us may think us mad to have attempted it!' . . . The church took one hundred and fifty years to build."

Men dreamed in those "dark" days, and carried out their dreams. In that silent building, incredibly beautiful, in that grove of sixty great trees of stone, whose vast trunks are jeweled by sunlight filtering through the high stained glass, in that stupendous and perfected work of art, raised by five succeeding generations to the glory of themselves and their God, one stood wondering wherein lay the superiority of ourselves, Children of Light, over those Sons of Darkness.

We, too, dream. I have seen some of the results—the Great Dam at Assuan, the Roosevelt Dam in Arizona, the Woolworth Building, the Forth Bridge, the Power Works at Niagara—not

[1] From *Castles in Spain and Other Screeds.* Reprinted by permission of Charles Scribner's Sons, the authorized publishers.

yet the greatest of them all, the Panama Canal (which actually took one-tenth of the time it took the Sons of Darkness to achieve Seville Cathedral). But all these were dreamed and fabricked out for immediate material benefit.

The builders of the giant mosques, the Temples of the Sun, the marvelous old churches, builded for no physical advantage in this life. They carved and wrought and slowly lifted stone on stone, to remote, and, as they thought, spiritual ends.

We moderns mine and forge, and mason up our monuments, to the immediate profit of our bodies. Have we raised anything really great in stone or brick *for a mere idea,* since Christopher Wren built St. Paul's Cathedral?

Now, the Sons of Darkness and the Children of Light, both, I think, have worshipped a half-truth. In the streets of Spain, in the Indian or Egyptian village, to this day you may see the shadow of these ancient great buildings fall as if with dark weight on a miserably poor humanity. The ancients builded for to-morrow in another world; they forgot that all of us have a to-day in this. They spent riches and labor to save the souls of their hierarchy, but they kept their laborers so poor that they had no souls to save. They left astounding testimony to human genius and tenacity, majestic creations which can uplift the spirit of any one who has eyes to see; but with all their dreams in stone to the glory of their gods, they kept simple man a beast of burden. And it never seems to have ruffled their consciousness that they purchased much of that ideal beauty with slavery, misery, and blood.

We moderns have gone another way to work, worshipping our half-truth. In place of those ideals for which the ancients worked—art, and the future life of their princes, politicians, and prelates—we moderns pursue what we call "progress." All our stupendous achievements have this progressive notion at their back. We worship industry and trade. We think that if we make the wheels go round fast enough, mankind is bound to rise on the wings of wealth. Look after the body, we say, and the spirit will look after itself. Whether we save a greater proportion of our bodies than the ancients did of souls, is more than doubtful. But no such trifling doubts shake our belief in "progress."

Our modern castle in Spain is, in a word, "production," and we have no other. It terrifies us, it paralyzes us, it is like a snake in front of a rabbit. It is like that Chinese general at whose name a million trembled. And what was his name? "Wu."

It is machinery, of course, which has divided us from the ancients, given us a new culture and ideal.

Machinery has quietly and gradually shifted the central point of man's philosophy. Before the industrial era set in, men used to make things by hand; they were in some sort artist, with the artist's—or at least the craftsman's—pride in their work. Now they press buttons, they turn wheels; they don't make completed articles, they work with monotony at the section of an article; so many hours of machine-driving per day, the total result of which is never a man's individual achievement. "Intelligent specialism," says an English writer, "is one thing. It consists in one man learning how to do one thing specially well. But the sort of specializing which consists in setting thousands of human beings during their whole working lives to such a soul-destroying job as fixing the bristles into a hair-brush, pasting labels on jam-pots, or nearly any one of the varieties of machine minding, is quite another thing. It is an utter negation of human nature."

A man's real interest in life is now not in his working day, but outside of it. The old artificers drew in their culture, such as it was, from their work; in these days, culture, such as it is, is grafted on to the workman in his leisure, as a sort of antidote to wheel driving. I don't want to exaggerate—hewers, delvers, drawers of water could never have taken much pride in their work, and, on the other hand, we still have many among us to whom their work is of absorbing interest. The modern architect and engineer, for example, have a great deal of the artist in them—they have a passion for the perfection of their job, which they communicate to many of those working under them. But though they may raise in Brooklyn Bridge, or the Woolworth Building, a marvel of efficiency, which in certain lights is also a thing of beauty, Society did not commission them to erect these wonders primarily for the sake of their beauty, or in order that Presidents Wilson and Harding might go to heaven. And, on the whole, I think there has been a great change; pride of quality has given way to pride of quantity. Men used to make things as well as they could for the pride they took in making them (and because they sometimes used the thing themselves). Now it is to their interest to turn out the cheapest, most quickly made, and lowest form of article that the public will take; and we have to rely for quality, not on the maker's pride of work, but on a grafted culture which keeps the public up to demanding a better sort of article. In old days the good thing was naturally supplied, nowadays it is artificially demanded.

Of course there is much truth in the vague modern notion that if you take care of the body the spirit will take care of itself. Only, you must really take care of the body, and not just pretend to. And the trouble about this progress of ours—which is supposed to take care of our bodies, and of which machinery is the mistress—is that it doesn't progress. We used to have the manor-house, with half a dozen hovels in its support. Now we have, say, twenty miles of handsome residences, with a hundred and twenty miles of ugly back streets, reeking with smoke and redolent of dulness, dirt, and discontent. Proportions are unchanged. The purple patches of our great towns are too often as rouge on the cheeks and salve on the lips of a corpse. Real progress would level up and gradually extinguish the disproportion between manor and hovel, residence and back street.

Let us be fantastic for a moment and conceive the civic authorities of London on the eighth day of July in the year 1922, solemnly resolving: "We will remake of London a city so beautiful and sweet to dwell in that those who come after us shall think us mad to have attempted it." It might well take five generations, but it would be real progress. Alas! Our civic authorities have not been brought up to care a button for anything so unpractical as a castle in Spain. And say what you will in favor of democracy, there is always the trouble of getting any farsighted and unbroken policy pursued. If any one can furnish an antidote to the wasting tendency of short immediate policies, inherent in the system of government by bodies elected for short terms, he will be the greatest benefactor of the age. The life of a civic body is, I believe, about four years; we should want a procession of civic bodies who steadily loved castles in Spain, to make of London a stainless city of Portland stone, full of baths and flowers and singing birds—not in cages.

But, seriously, we are very unfortunate in letting our civic life be run in the main by those who were born seeing two inches before their noses, and whose education, instead of increasing, has reduced those inches to one. It seems ungrateful to criticize the practical business man whose faculties and powers, stamina and energy, make the more imaginative person gasp. One owes him, in fact, so much, that one would like to owe him more. But does his vision as a rule extend beyond keeping pace with the present? And without vision the people perish! Why, the age is so practical that the word "visionary" has actually a slighting significance. And yet the really great practical administrators have all his vision—men like Cæsar, Chatham, Lincoln. And great men apart, there are really many naturally both practical and visionary. But in an age of specialism our method of education ever tends to develop one side of our natures at the expense of the other.

If we can't incorporate beauty in our scheme of life to-day, and foster the love of beauty in our children, the life of to-morrow and the children thereof must necessarily be as far from beauty as we are now. Surely it is strange to set men to direct the education, housing, and amusements of their fellow citizens, if they haven't a love of beauty, and some considerable knowledge of art! And is it really going too far to say that the present generation of business men—with, of course, many notable exceptions—have a sort of indulgent contempt for art and beauty? Would they admit that art has been the greatest of all factors in raising mankind from its old savage state? And yet it is the contemplation of beautiful visions, emotions, thoughts, and dreams, expressed beautifully in stone, metal, paint, words, and music, which has slowly, generation by generation, lifted man to his present stature, such as it is, and mollified his savage nature. If it hasn't been that, ask yourselves what it has been! Religion? The uplifting part of religion is the beautiful expression of exalted feeling. The rest of religion is but superstition. Think of the thousand wars fought in the name of superstition; of the cannibal feasts, the human sacrifices; the tortures of the Inquisition; the persecutions, intolerances, and narrow cruelties perpetrated even to this day. The stories and teachings of Buddha, of Christ, of St. Francis d'Assisi, were the beautiful expressions of exalted feeling, simple, and touching the hearts of men, as all true beauty does; and so they have done their ennobling work. They belong to the cult of beauty.

Has trade, perhaps, been the mollifying influence and elevator of mankind? I think, only so far as it has widened the reach of beauty, brought beauty within the range of multitudes, by opening up the lines of communication. In that sense, no doubt, trade has helped. But trade as trade has no real elevating influence—rather the contrary.

No! Only beauty, in the largest sense of the word, the yearning for it, the contemplation of it, has civilized mankind. And yet we don't really take beauty seriously. Immediate profit rules the roost of us all in this age of ours. I leave it to the conscience of the age to decide whether that is good. For every age has a conscience, but it never comes to life till the age is on its death-bed.

The fault of all ages has been this: beauty—the knowledge and the love of it—has been kept as a preserve of the few, as the possession of a caste or clique. No great proportion of us are capable of creating or expressing beauty; but an immensely greater proportion of us are capable of appreciating it than ever have been given a real chance of so doing.

It should be our castle in Spain to clear our age of that defect, and put beauty within the reach of all. Machinery has come to stay, so that we must perforce rely on grafted culture—in other words, on education. We must teach the young now to feel and see the beauties of nature and art. The modern age is not easy to teach. But we have exceptional facilities in these days for teaching what helps to keep life dignified, besides those simple accomplishments, cooking and keeping clean; we could bring an inkling at least of the fine arts, the architecture, literature, and music of the past to children even in the humblest schools. And why should not the children of labor have as much chance to be familiar with beauty as the children of the rich? All economic revolution or evolution is hollow unless it means more demand for beauty—greater dignity of human life. Without that it must be simply retrograde, destroying what beauty and love of it we have, with all to begin over again. What use in B's despoiling A, if B is going to use his spoils no better, probably worse, than A? A mere lap of luxury would only make B fat.

This is all platitude; and a great fuss about beauty, which cannot feed or clothe or warm the body, whatever it may do to that sentimental appanage, the spirit.

I read in a journal not long ago: "One always suspects Mr. Galsworthy of a certain deep-seated sentimentalism." I think the writer must have sold his castles in Spain at a loss. The fact is, one must be sentimental in this life to do anything except make money, and it is really better to have a castle in Spain than a villa at Newport or Cannes.

The precise definitions of beauty are without number or—value, to speak of. I just use the word to mean everything which promotes the real dignity of human life. To illustrate the width of the word beauty as I am using it, I mention what we all understand: good sportsmanship. To be a good "sportsman," a man shuns that which lowers his dignity, that which dims his idea of his own quality; and—his conception of quality derives obscurely from his sense of beauty. The dignity of human life demands in fact not only such desirable embroideries as pleasant sound, fine form, and lovely color, but health, strength, cleanliness, balance, joy in living, just conduct and kind conduct, for there is no beauty in the sight of tortured things. A man who truly loves beauty hates to think that he enjoys it at the expense of starved and stunted human beings or suffering animals. A cruel or pettifogging æstheticism has sometimes smeared the word beauty and given it a bad odor. But that is not the beauty which gleams on the heights in the sunrise. That is not our castle in Spain.

But to put aside for a moment the sentimental, and come to business. Beauty, and the love of it, is surely the best investment modern man can make; for nothing else—most certainly not trade—will keep him from destroying the human species.

Consider what science has become in the hands of engineers and chemists; its destructive powers increase a hundred-fold with each decade; and the reproductive powers and inclinations of the human being do not vary. Recollect that nothing in the world but the love of beauty in its broad sense stands between man and the full and reckless exercise of his competitive greed; and remember the great war—a little war compared to that which, through the development of scientific destruction, we shall be able to wage next time! Remembering all this, we get an inkling of the sheer necessity there is for us to invest in beauty and the love thereof. No other investment will give us interest on our money and our money back. Unbalanced trade, science, industry, will give us a high momentary rate of interest, but only till the crash comes again, and the world goes even more bankrupt than it is at present.

The professor who has invented a rocket which will go to the moon and find out all about it (though whether it is to be boomerang enough to come back with the story, we are not told), that professor would, I venture to think, have done more real good if he had taught a school full of children to see the beauty of—moonshine.

The next war will be fought from the air with explosives and gas, and may very likely be over before war is declared. The war after that will be fought with the germs of disease, distributed by wireless or something choice of that character. The final war necessary for the complete extirpation of mankind will be fought with radium or atomic energy; and we shall have no need to examine the moon, for the earth will be as lifeless.

So much for business! To go back to sentiment, which is really what makes the wheels go round. Not even "big business" rules our instincts, and our passions. Imperialists, chemists, en-

gineers, merchants, militarists—we are all deep-seated senti-
mentalists. The only question for us is: What shall we be sentimental about? Which is the fairer castle in Spain—quantity or
quality?

Consider for a moment the ideals which have been offered us
instead of the pursuit of beauty, or quality, if that be a preferable word.

Take, for instance, the ideal of happiness in a future life. If
there be a future life for the individual, we obviously cannot
reach happiness therein without having longed for and served
quality in this, without having had that kind and free and generous philosophy which belongs to the cult of beauty and alone
gives peace of mind. The pursuit of beauty includes, then, whatever may be true in the ideal—happiness in a future life.

Take the ideal of material comfort in this life. But the cult
of beauty, of quality, includes all that is good in this ideal, for
it surely demands physical health and well-being; sane minds in
sane bodies, which depend of course on a sufficiency of material
comfort. All the rest of the ideal of wealth is mere fat, sagging
beyond the point of balance. As a fact, modern civilization is
offering us a compound between happiness in a future life, and
material comfort in this, lip-serving the first, and stomach-serv-
ing the second. We get the keys of heaven from our banks, and
we don't get them if we haven't a good balance. Modern civilization is, on the whole, camouflaged commercialism, wherein to do
things well, *for the joy of doing them well,* is rarer than we
think. We have even commercialized salvation—for so much
virtue, so much salvation. Always—always—*quid pro quo.*

But let us give the devil its due. Let us admit at once that
in spite of everything this is still the best age on the whole that
man has lived in. It is in its own way very thorough—our modern civilization. It has made advertisement into a fine art,
equipped bedrooms with telephones; it diagnoses maladies with
extreme punctilio. A doctor examined a young lady the other
day, and among his notes were these: "Not afraid of small rooms,
ghosts, or thunderstorms; not made drunk by hearing Wagner;
brown hair, artistic hands; had a craving for chocolate in 1918."

The age is thorough in its way. But there's a kind of deadly practicality about its production: all for to-day, none for to-morrow! The future will never think us mad for attempting what we do attempt; we build no Seville cathedrals. We don't get ahead of time.

We have just let slip, in England, the chance to get our country life going thoroughly once more. At demobilization we might have put hundreds of thousands on the land, which needs them so badly for a dozen reasons. How many have we put? Not so many as the war took away from the land. Admitted that life on the land means hard work, burnt faces, and maybe bowed backs; it also means hearty stock for the next generation. A nation concerned only with its present is like the man who was fishing, and, feeling sleepy, propped his rod up on the bank, with the line in the water. A wag spied him sleeping, took the rod, waded across the river, propped up the rod on the opposite bank, and lay down behind a hedge to watch for the awakening. Such is the awakening in store for nations which enjoy their present and forget there is a future.

The pursuit of beauty as a national ideal, the building of that castle in Spain, is no picnic. Idlers need not apply. Consider the rank growth which must be cut down, the stumps and roots to be burned out and cleared, the swamps to be drained, before even the foundations can be laid. And—after—what long and patient labor and steadfastness of ideal before we begin to see rise a fair edifice of human life upon this earth.

Members of a practical race will say: "Well, what do you want us to do? Cut the flower and come to the fruit?" Alas! All literary men can tell people what they oughtn't to be; that's —literature. But to tell them what they ought to do is—politics, of which no literary man is guilty; for politics and literature afford the only instance known—in virtuous countries—of divorce by mutual consent. The contempt of politicians for literary men is only equalled by the contempt of literary men for politicians. It would be impertinent, then, for a literary man to suggest any-thing practical. Let me, however, make a few affirmations. I do believe that, on the whole, modern man is a little further from being a mere animal than the men of the Dark Ages, however great the castles in Spain those men built and left for us to look upon; but I am sure we are in far greater danger than ever they were, of a swift decline. From that decline I am convinced that only the love and cult of beauty will save us!

By the love and cult of beauty I mean a great deal—*higher and wider conception of the dignity of human life;* the teaching of what beauty is, to all, not merely to the few; the cultivation of good will so that we wish and work and dream that not only ourselves but everybody may be healthy and happy; and, above all, the fostering of the habit of doing things and making things well for the joy of the work and the pleasure of achievement, rather than for the gain they will bring us. With these as the rules, the wheels of an insensate industrialism, whose one idea is to make money and get ahead of other people—careless of direction towards hell or heaven—might conceivably be spoked.

As it seems to me, the great lack of our age is an ideal, expressed with sufficient concreteness to be like a vision, beckoning. To me there is no other ideal worthy of us, or indeed possible to us in these unsuperstitious days, save beauty—or call it, if you will, the dignity of human life. One or two writers of late have urged the need of more *spiritual* beauty in our lives. They mean what I mean, but it is unfortunate to talk of *spiritual* beauty. We must be able to smell, and see, hear, feel, and taste our ideal as well. We must know by plain evidence that it is lifting human life, that it is the heritage of all, not merely of the refined and leisured among us. The body and soul are one for the purpose of all real evolution, and I regret any term which suggests a divorce between them. But nobody, I think, can mistake what is meant by quality, or the dignity of human life. Anything which crosses and offends against that ideal is our Satan. And the only way in which each one can say *"Retro Satana"* is to leave his or her tiny corner of the universe a little more dignified, a little more lovely and lovable than he or she found it.

It may seem absurd to be writing like this in a world whose general mood at the moment is utter disillusionment and gloomy spite. The world is cross-eyed just now; when it weeps out of

one eye, the tear runs down the other cheek. And it is difficult
to be in love with a lady like that. I, for one, find it extremely
hard not to be a cynic. Latest opinion assigns eight or ten thousand years as the outside length of time during which what we
know as civilization has been at work. Still—ten thousand years
is a considerable period of mollification. One had rashly hoped
that mankind was not to be so speedily stampeded; that traditions
of gentleness, fair play, chivalry, had a little more strength among
Western peoples than they have been proved to have had since
1914; that mob feeling might be less, instead of, as it seems,
more potent than it used to be. Only very constant self-remind-
ing that the fault was in one's self, that one was a facile observer,
a dreamer who did not look deeply enough beneath the surface; a
rider before the hounds; only that, and a constant self-remind-
ing of the individual patience, good humor, endurance, and
heroism which goes so queerly hand in hand with stupidity, savagery, greed, and mob violence, can save a man from turning his
back on the world with the words: "Cats and monkeys, monkeys
and cats, all life is there!"

Fear is at the back of nearly all the savagery in the world;
and if there be not present in the individual that potent antidote
—the sense of human dignity, which is but a love of and a belief
in beauty, he must infallibly succumb to fear. There are tremendous difficulties in the way of coherent progress, of all fair
and far ideals under the régime of short-lived elective bodies, a
régime essentially exposed to stampede through popular opinion
and the emotions of the moment. Seeing the violence of which
military autocracy is capable, one is liable to become too blind a
devotee of democracy. But democracy has no greater enemies
than her unthinking friends. Short sight is her danger, short
sight verging on blindness. What will happen if democracy really
goes blind? She must have an ideal, a star on which to fix her
eyes—something distant and magnetic to draw her on, something
to strive towards, beyond the troubled and shifting needs, passions, and prejudices of the moment. Lovers of beauty, those
who wish to raise the dignity of human life, should try to give
her that ideal, to equip her with the only vision which can save

the world from spite and the crazy competition which leads thereto.

We of this still young century may yet leave to those who come after us at least the foundations of a castle in Spain such as the world has not yet seen; leave our successors in mood and heart to continue our work; so that one hundred and fifty years perhaps from now, human life may really be dignified and beautiful, not just a breathless, grudging, visionless scramble from birth to death, of a night with no stars out.

Dreamer—deep-seated sentimentalist—the immortal Don riding his Rosinante on the bare brown uplands of Spain never saw so crazy a vision, so fickle-shining a mirage! Who knows? The world is changing. It *must* change, or perish; the forces of destruction, the inherent futilities of the present order, are too great. And there is in human nature, after all, the instinct of self-preservation, a great saving common-sense.

The past six years have been the result of the past six hundred years. The war was no spasmodic visitation; it was the culmination of age-long competitions. The past six years have devoured many millions of grown men, more millions of little children—prevented their birth, killed them, or withered them for life. If we begin again these crazy competitions, without regard for beauty or the dignity of human life, we shall live to see ten millions perish for every million perished in this war. We shall live to curse the day—this day when, at the end of so great a lesson, we were too sane to take it to heart; too sensible and practical and business-like and unemotional to see visions and dream dreams, and build our castle in Spain.

The Hours of Sleep [1]

By Alice Meynell

There are hours claimed by Sleep, but refused to him. None the less are they his by some state within the mind, which answers rhythmically and punctually to that claim. Awake and at

[1] From *The Spirit of Place*. By permission of Charles Scribner's Sons, the authorized publishers.

work, without drowsiness, without languor, and without gloom, the night mind of man is yet not his day mind; he has night powers of feeling which are at their highest in dreams, but are night's as well as sleep's. The powers of the mind in dream, which are inexplicable, are not altogether baffled because the mind is awake; it is the hour of their return as it is the hour of a tide's, and they do return.

In sleep they have their free way. Night then has nothing to hamper her influence, and she draws the emotion, the senses, and the nerves of the sleeper. She urges him upon those extremities of anger and love, contempt and terror, to which not only can no event of the real day persuade him, but for which, awake, he has perhaps not even the capacity. This increase of capacity, which is the dream's, is punctual to the night, even though sleep and the dream be kept at arm's length.

The child, not asleep, but passing through the hours of sleep and their dominions, knows that the mood of the night will have its hour; he postpones his troubled heart, and will answer it another time, in the other state, by day. "I shall be able to bear this when I am grown up" is not oftener in a young child's mind than "I shall endure to think of it in the daytime." By this he confesses the double habit and double experience, not to be interchanged, and communicating together only by memory and hope.

Perhaps it will be found that to work all by day or all by night is to miss something of the powers of a complex mind. One might imagine the rhythmic experience of a poet, subject, like a child, to the time, and tempering the extremities of either state by messages of remembrance and expectancy.

Never to have had a brilliant dream, and never to have had any delirium, would be to live too much in the day; and hardly less would be the loss of him who had not exercised his waking thought under the influence of the hours claimed by dreams. And as to choosing between day and night, or guessing whether the state of day or dark is the truer and the more natural, he would be rash who should make too sure.

In order to live the life of night, a watcher must not wake

too much. That is, he should not alter so greatly the character of night as to lose the solitude, the visible darkness, or the quietude. The hours of sleep are too much altered when they are filled by lights and crowds; and Nature is cheated so, and evaded, and her rhythm broken, as when larks caged in populous streets make ineffectual springs and sing daybreak songs when the London lamps are lighted. Nature is easily deceived; and the muse, like the lark, may be set all astray as to the hour. You may spend the peculiar hours of sleep amid so much noise and among so many people that you shall not be aware of them; you may thus merely force and prolong the day. But to do so is not to live well both lives; it is not to yield to the daily and nightly rise and fall, cradled in the swing of change.

There surely never was a poet but was now and then rocked in such a cradle of alternate hours. "It cannot be," says Herbert, "that I am he on whom Thy tempests fell all night."

It is in the hours of sleep that the mind, by some divine paradox, has the extremest sense of light. Almost the most shining lines in English poetry—lines that cast sunrise shadows—are those of Blake, written confessedly from the side of night, the side of sorrow and dreams, and those dreams the dreams of little chimney-sweepers; all is as dark as he can make it with the "bags of soot"; but the boy's dream of the green plain and the river is too bright for day. So, indeed, is another brightness of Blake's, which is also in his poem, a child's dream, and was certainly conceived by him in the hours of sleep, in which he woke to write the "Songs of Innocence":—

O what land is the land of dreams?
What are its mountains, and what are its streams?
O father, I saw my mother there,
Among the lilies by waters fair.
Among the lambs clothèd in white,
She walk'd with her Thomas in sweet delight.

To none but the hours claimed and inspired by sleep, held awake by sufferance of sleep, belongs such a vision.

Corot also took the brilliant opportunity of the hours of sleep. In some landscapes of his early manner he has the very light of dreams, and it was surely because he went abroad at the time when sleep and dreams claimed his eyes that he was able to see so spiritual an illumination. Summer is precious for a painter, chiefly because in summer so many of the hours of sleep are also hours of light. He carries the mood of man's night out into the sunshine—Corot did so—and lives the life of night, in all its genius, in the presence of a risen sun. In the only time when the heart can dream of light, in the night of visions, with the rhythmic power of night at its dark noon in his mind, his eyes see the soaring of the actual sun.

He himself has not yet passed at that hour into the life of day. To that life belongs many another kind of work, and a sense of other kinds of beauty; but the summer daybreak was seen by Corot with the extreme perception of the life of night. Here, at last, is the explanation of all the memories of dreams recalled by these visionary paintings, done in earlier years than were those, better known, that are the Corots of all the world. Every man who knows what it is to dream of landscape meets with one of these works of Corot's first manner with a cry, not of welcome only, but of recognition. Here is morning perceived by the spirit of the hours of sleep.

SUNT LACRIMÆ RERUM [1]

By Walter Pater

It was become a habit with Marius—one of his modernisms—developed by his assistance at the Emperor's "conversations with himself," to keep a register of the movements of his own private thoughts and humours; not continuously indeed, yet sometimes for lengthy intervals, during which it was no idle self-indulgence, but a necessity of his intellectual life, to "confess himself," with an intimacy, seemingly rare among the ancients; ancient writers, at all events, having been jealous, for the most part, of affording

[1] From *Marius the Epicurean.*

us so much as a glimpse of that interior self, which in many cases would have actually doubled the interest of their objective informations.

"If a particular tutelary or *genius*," writes Marius, "according to old belief, walks through life beside each one of us, mine is very certainly a capricious creature. He fills one with wayward, unaccountable, yet quite irresistible humours, and seems always to be in collusion with some outward circumstance, often trivial enough in itself—the condition of the weather, forsooth!—the people one meets by chance—the things one happens to overhear them say, veritable ἐνόδιοι σύμβολοι, or omens by the wayside, as the old Greeks fancied—to push on the unreasonable prepossessions of the moment into weighty motives. It was doubtless a quite explicable, physical fatigue that presented me to myself, on awaking this morning, so lack-lustre and trite. But I must needs take my petulance, contrasting it with my accustomed morning hopefulness, as a sign of the ageing of appetite, of a decay in the very capacity of enjoyment. We need some imaginative stimulus, some not impossible ideal such as may shape vague hope, and transform it into effective desire, to carry us year after year, without disgust, through the routine-work which is so large a part of life.

"Then, how if appetite, be it for real or ideal, should itself fail one after awhile? Ah, yes! it is of cold always that men die; and on some of us it creeps very gradually. In truth, I can remember just such a lack-lustre condition of feeling once or twice before. But I note, that it was accompanied then by an odd indifference, as the thought of them occurred to me, in regard to the sufferings of others—a kind of callousness, so unusual with me, as at once to mark the humour it accompanied as a palpably morbid one that could not last. Were those sufferings, great or little, I asked myself then, of more real consequence to them than mine to me, as I remind myself that 'nothing that will end is really long'—long enough to be thought of importance? But to-day, my own sense of fatigue, the pity I conceive for myself, disposed me strongly to a tenderness for others. For a moment the whole world seemed to present itself as a hospital of sick persons; many of them sick in mind; all of whom it would be a brutality not to humour, not to indulge.

"Why, when I went out to walk off my wayward fancies, did I confront the very sort of incident (my unfortunate *genius* had surely beckoned it from afar to vex me) likely to irritate them further? A party of men were coming down the street. They were leading a fine racehorse; a handsome beast, but badly hurt somewhere, in the circus, and useless. They were taking him to slaughter; and I think the animal knew it: he cast such looks, as if of mad appeal, to those who passed him, as he went among the strangers to whom his former owner had committed him, to die, in his beauty and pride, for just that one mischance or fault; although the morning air was still so animating, and pleasant to snuff. I could have fancied a human soul in the creature, swelling against its luck. And I had come across the incident just when it would figure to me as the very symbol of our poor humanity, in its capacities for pain, its wretched accidents, and those imperfect sympathies, which can never quite identify us with one another; the very power of utterance and appeal to others seeming to fail us, in proportion as our sorrows come home to ourselves, are really our own. We are constructed for suffering! What proofs of it does but one day afford, if we care to note them, as we go—a whole long chaplet of sorrowful mysteries! *Sunt lacrimæ rerum et mentem mortalia tangunt.*[1]

"Men's fortunes touch us! The little children of one of those institutions for the support of orphans, now become fashionable among us by way of memorial of eminent persons deceased, are going, in long file, along the street, on their way to a holiday in the country. They halt, and count themselves with an air of triumph, to show that they are all there. Their gay chatter has disturbed a little group of peasants; a young woman and her husband, who have brought the old mother, now past work and witless, to place her in a house provided for such afflicted people. They are fairly affectionate, but anxious how the thing they have to do may go—hope only she may permit them to leave her there behind quietly. And the poor old soul is excited by the noise

[1] "There are tears for fortune, and mortal estate touches the soul."

made by the children, and partly aware of what is going to happen with her. She too begins to count—one, two, three, five—on her trembling fingers, misshapen by a life of toil. 'Yes! yes! and twice five make ten'—they say, to pacify her. It is her last appeal to be taken home again; her proof that all is not yet up with her; that she is, at all events, still as capable as those joyous children.

"At the baths, a party of labourers are at work upon one of the great brick furnaces, in a cloud of black dust. A frail young child has brought food for one of them, and sits apart, waiting till his father comes—watching the labour, but with a sorrowful distaste for the din and dirt. He is regarding wistfully his own place in the world, there before him. His mind, as he watches, is grown up for a moment; and he forsees, as it were, in that moment, all the long tale of days, of early awakings, of his own coming life of drudgery at work like this.

"A man comes along carrying a boy whose rough work has already begun—the only child—whose presence beside him sweetened the father's toil a little. The boy has been badly injured by a fall of brick-work, yet, with an effort, he rides boldly on his father's shoulders. It will be the way of natural affection to keep him alive as long as possible, though with that miserably shattered body—'Ah! with us still, and feeling our care beside him!'—and yet surely not without a heartbreaking sigh of relief, alike from him and them, when the end comes.

"On the alert for incidents like these, yet of necessity passing them by on the other side, I find it hard to get rid of a sense that I, for one, have failed in love. I could yield to the humour till I seemed to have had my share in those great public cruelties, the shocking legal crimes which are on record, like that cold-blooded slaughter, according to law, of the four hundred slaves in the reign of Nero, because one of their number was thought to have murdered his master. The reproach of that, together with the kind of facile apologies those who had no share in the deed may have made for it, as they went about quietly on their own affairs that day, seems to come very close to me, as I think upon it. And to how many of those now actually around me, whose life is a sore one, must I be indifferent, if I ever become aware of their soreness at all? To some, perhaps, the necessary conditions of my own life may cause me to be opposed, in a kind of natural conflict, regarding those interests which actually determine the happiness of theirs. I would that a stronger love might arise in my heart!

"Yet there is plenty of charity in the world. My patron, the Stoic emperor, has made it even fashionable. To celebrate one of his brief returns to Rome lately from the war, over and above a largess of gold pieces to all who would, the public debts were forgiven. He made a nice show of it: for once, the Romans entertained themselves with a good-natured spectacle, and the whole town came to see the great bonfire in the Forum, into which all bonds and evidence of debt were thrown on delivery, by the emperor himself; many private creditors following his example. That was done well enough! But still the feeling returns to me, that no charity of ours can get at a certain natural unkindness which I find in things themselves.

*   *   *   *   *   *   *

"For there is a certain grief in things as they are, in man as he has come to be, as he certainly is, over and above those griefs of circumstance which are in a measure removable—some inexplicable shortcoming, or misadventure, on the part of nature itself—death, and old age as it must needs be, and that watching for their approach, which makes every stage of life like a dying over and over again. Almost all death is painful, and in every thing that comes to an end a touch of death, and therefore of wretched coldness struck home to one, of remorse, of loss and parting, of outraged attachments. Given faultless men and women, given a perfect state of society which should have no need to practise on men's susceptibilities for its own selfish ends, adding one turn more to the wheel of the great rack for its own interest or amusement, there would still be this evil in the world, of a certain necessary sorrow and desolation, felt, just in proportion to the moral, or nervous perfection men have attained to. And what we need in the world, over against that, is a certain

permanent and general power of compassion—humanity's standing force of self-pity—as an elementary ingredient of our social
atmosphere, if we are to live in it at all. I wonder, sometimes,
in what way man has cajoled himself into the bearing of his burden thus far, seeing how every step in the capacity of apprehension his labour has won for him, from age to age, must needs increase his dejection. It is as if the increase of knowledge were
but an increasing revelation of the radical hopelessness of his
position: and I would that there were one even as I, behind this
vain show of things!

"At all events, the actual conditions of our life being as they
are, and the capacity for suffering so large a principle in things
—since the only principle, perhaps, to which we may always safely
trust is a ready sympathy with the pain one actually sees—it
follows that the practical and effective difference between men
will lie in their power of insight into those conditions, their power
of sympathy. The future will be with those who have most of
it; while for the present, as I persuade myself, those who have
much of it, have something to hold by, even in the dissolution
of a world, or in that dissolution of self, which is, for every one,
no less than the dissolution of the world it represents for him.
Nearly all of us, I suppose, have had our moments, in which any
effective sympathy for us on the part of others has seemed impossible; in which our pain has seemed a stupid outrage upon
us, like some overwhelming physical violence, from which we
could take refuge, at best, only in some mere general sense of
goodwill—somewhere in the world perhaps. And then, to one's
surprise, the discovery of that goodwill, if it were only in a not
unfriendly animal, may seem to have explained, to have actually
justified to us, the fact of our pain. There have been occasions,
certainly, when I have felt that if others cared for me as I cared
for them, it would be, not so much a consolation, as an equivalent,
for what one has lost or suffered: a realised profit on the sum-
ming up of one's accounts: a touching of that absolute ground
amid all the changes of phenomena, such as our philosophers have
of late confessed themselves quite unable to discover. In the
mere clinging of human creatures to each other, nay! in one's

own solitary self-pity, amid the effects even of what might appear irredeemable loss, I seem to touch the eternal. Something in that pitiful contact, something new and true, fact or apprehension of fact, is educed, which on a review of all the perplexities of life, satisfies our moral sense, and removes that appearance of unkindness in the soul of things themselves, and assures us that not everything has been in vain.

"And I know not how, but in the thought thus suggested, I seem to take up, and re-knit myself to, a well-remembered hour, when by some gracious accident—it was on a journey—all things about me fell into a more perfect harmony than is their wont. Everything seemed to be, for a moment, after all, almost for the best. Through the train of my thoughts, one against another, it was as if I became aware of the dominant power of another person in controversy, wrestling with me. I seem to be come round to the point at which I left off then. The antagonist has closed with me again. A protest comes, out of the very depths of man's radically hopeless condition in the world, with the energy of one of those suffering yet prevailing deities, of which old poetry tells. Dared one hope that there is a heart, even as ours, in that divine 'Assistant' of one's thoughts—a heart even as mine, behind this vain show of things!"

EXERCISES

1. Why, do you suppose, Mr. Dana preferred not to illustrate his essay by giving specific words with emotional effect? Does the use of the second person help or hinder him? Why does he use so few adjectives?

2. Make a list of words which Mr. Dana might have used as examples of words that laugh and cry.

3. Find in Galsworthy's "Castles in Spain" a fine example of periodic structure; of especially well-chosen adjectives; of sense impressions.

4. Do you agree with Galsworthy's definition of religion? Why, or why not? Is this essay founded upon an *idea,* or a *belief,* or a *perception?*

5. There is one paragraph in Mrs. Meynell's essay which is

unique because it gives the impression of extreme light. How does she obtain this effect? Read the paragraph aloud and see if the sound of your voice helps you to answer the question.

6. Is there any practical, utilitarian value to such an essay as "The Hours of Sleep?"

7. This chapter from *Marius the Epicurean* has been called by a critic "the most appealing piece of English prose." In making this judgment did he, do you suppose, have reference to the subject matter? What other qualities might have earned the right to this criticism?

8. In *Harper's Magazine* for May 1921 there is an essay called "Words with a Tang." Read it and compare its treatment and its tone with Mr. Dana's.

SUGGESTED READINGS

Belloc, Hilaire, "Hills and the Sea," *Scribner's,* New York.

Benson, Arthur Christopher, *From a College Window,* Putnam's, New York. *The Altar Fire,* Putnam's, New York.

Cabell, James Branch, *Beyond Life,* R. M. McBride, New York.

Dodd, Lee Wilson, "One Point of View," *The Yale Review,* July 1928.

Hudson, W. H., "The Plains of Patagonia" from *Idle Days in Patagonia,* E. P. Dutton, New York.

Hunt, Leigh, "Colour" from *Essays and Sketches,* Everyman Edition, E. P. Dutton, New York.

Galsworthy, John, *The Inn of Tranquillity,* Scribner's, New York.

Guiney, Louise Imogen, "The Precept of Peace" from *Patrins.* (The book being long out of print, the reader is advised to see *Modern Essays,* edited by Morley and published by Harcourt, Brace, New York).

Meynell, Alice, *The Rhythm of Life,* Scribner's, New York.

Miles, Herbert D., "The Case for Immortality," *The North American Review,* May 1924.

Pater, Walter, "A Conversation not Imaginary" from *Marius the Epicurean,* Macmillan, New York. *A Child in the House,* Macmillan, New York.

Repplier, Agnes, "The Divineness of Discontent" from *Under Dispute,* Houghton Mifflin, Boston.

Santayana, George, "Ideal Immortality" from *Little Essays,* Scribner's, New York.

Sherwood, Margaret, "Intellectual Death and Spiritual Life," *The Atlantic Monthly*, December 1926.

Smith, Logan Pearsall, *Trivia*, Doubleday, Doran, New York. *More Trivia*.

Stevenson, Robert Louis, "Aes Triplex" from *Virginibus Puerisque*, Scribner's.

Underwood, Sophie Kerr, "Words with a Tang," *Harper's Magazine*, May 1921.

White, Stewart Edward, "On Lying Awake at Night" from *The Forest*, Doubleday, Doran, New York.

Yoxall, Sir James, "The Soul of a Cathedral" from *The Wander Years*, E. P. Dutton, New York.

361 - 363
473 - 476
380 - 394
Index (A, B, C, etc.)

name of author & book etc. in
bibliographic style page of
material

notes

Apr. 6 - Willa Cather